IRELAND

Rick Steves & Pat O'Connor

2017

CONTENTS

▶ **Introduction** 1

**REPUBLIC OF
IRELAND** **16**

▶ **Dublin** 22
  Dun Laoghaire 98
  Howth .103

▶ **Near Dublin** 108
  Valley of the Boyne 108
  Trim 118
  Glendalough and the
    Wicklow Mountains 125
  Irish National Stud 132

▶ **Kilkenny & the
Rock of Cashel** 135
  Kilkenny 135
  Between Kilkenny and
    Waterford 145
  Rock of Cashel 147

▶ **Waterford &
County Wexford** 157
  Waterford 158
  County Wexford 169

▶ **Kinsale & Cobh** 178
  Kinsale .179

Cobh 194
Between Waterford
  and Kinsale 200
Between Kinsale
  and Killarney 202

▶ **Kenmare & the
Ring of Kerry** 205
  Kenmare 205
  Near Kenmare 217
  Ring of Kerry 221
  Skellig Michael 235

▶ **Dingle Peninsula** 238
  Dingle Town 239
  Dingle Peninsula
    Loop Trip 267
  Blasket Islands 277
  Tralee 278

▶ **County Clare &
the Burren** 282
  County Clare 285
  The Burren 300

▶ **Galway** 307

▶ **Aran Islands** 325
  Inishmore 327

Inisheer 337

▶ Connemara &
County Mayo 344

NORTHERN
IRELAND **364**

▶ **Belfast** 372
Bangor. 404

▶ **Portrush & the
Antrim Coast** 410
Portrush 411
Antrim Coast 418

▶ **Derry & County
Donegal** 428
County Donegal 450

▶ **Ireland: Past &
Present** 461

▶ **Practicalities** 498
Tourist Information 498
Travel Tips 499
Money 500
Sightseeing 506
Sleeping 510
Eating 523
Traditional Irish Music 528
Staying Connected 529
Transportation. 535
Resources from Rick Steves .551

▶ **Appendix** 555
Useful Contacts 555
Holidays and Festivals 556
Recommended Books
and Films. 557
Conversions and Climate 561
Packing Checklist. 563

▶ **Index**. 564

▶ **Map Index** 578

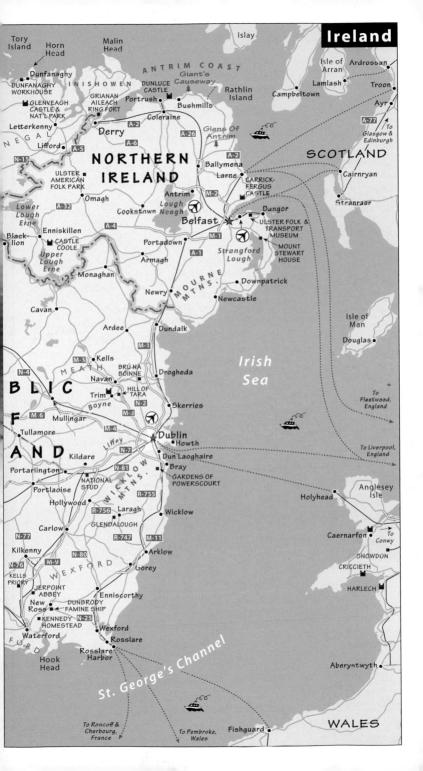

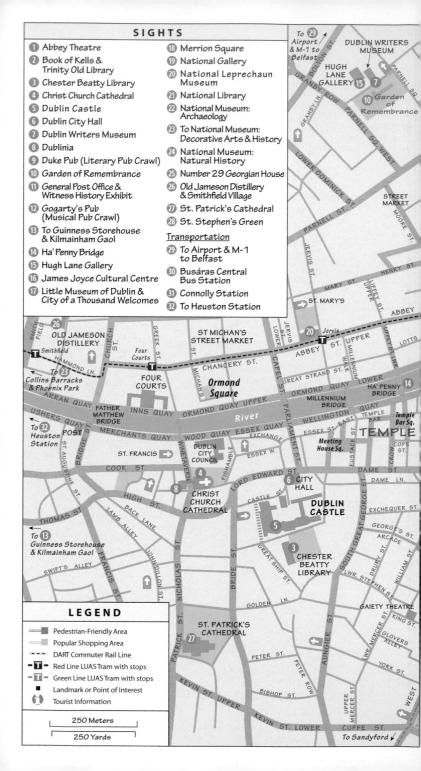

SIGHTS

1. Abbey Theatre
2. Book of Kells & Trinity Old Library
3. Chester Beatty Library
4. Christ Church Cathedral
5. Dublin Castle
6. Dublin City Hall
7. Dublin Writers Museum
8. Dublinia
9. Duke Pub (Literary Pub Crawl)
10. Garden of Remembrance
11. General Post Office & Witness History Exhibit
12. Gogarty's Pub (Musical Pub Crawl)
13. To Guinness Storehouse & Kilmainham Gaol
14. Ha' Penny Bridge
15. Hugh Lane Gallery
16. James Joyce Cultural Centre
17. Little Museum of Dublin & City of a Thousand Welcomes

18. Merrion Square
19. National Gallery
20. National Leprechaun Museum
21. National Library
22. National Museum: Archaeology
23. To National Museum: Decorative Arts & History
24. National Museum: Natural History
25. Number 29 Georgian House
26. Old Jameson Distillery & Smithfield Village
27. St. Patrick's Cathedral
28. St. Stephen's Green

Transportation

29. To Airport & M-1 to Belfast
30. Busáras Central Bus Station
31. Connolly Station
32. To Heuston Station

LEGEND

- Pedestrian-Friendly Area
- Popular Shopping Area
- DART Commuter Rail Line
- **-T-** Red Line LUAS Tram with stops
- **-T-** Green Line LUAS Tram with stops
- Landmark or Point of Interest
- Tourist Information

250 Meters
250 Yards

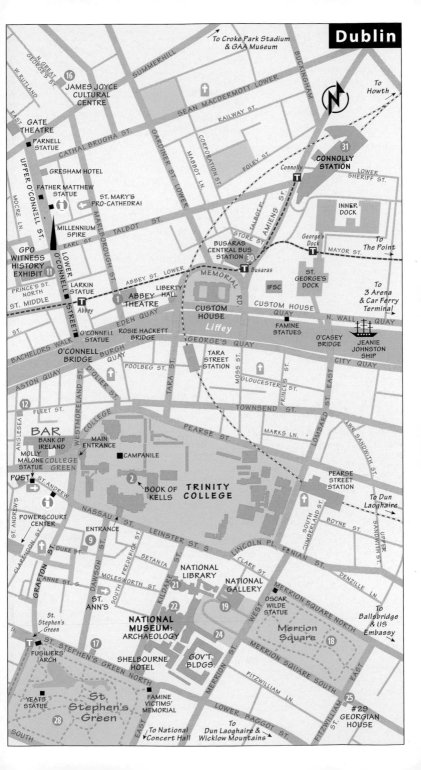

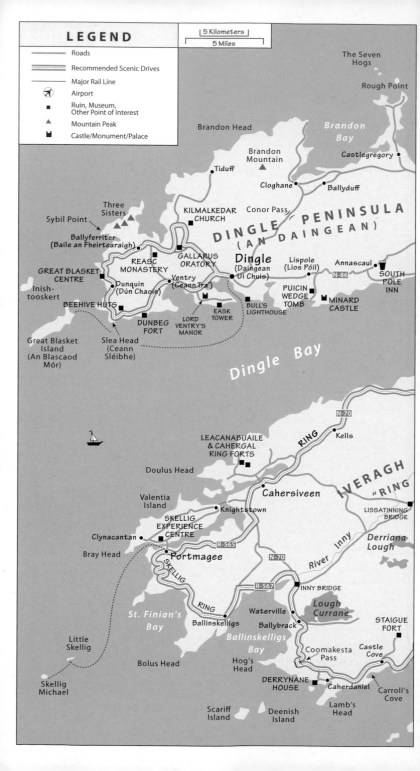

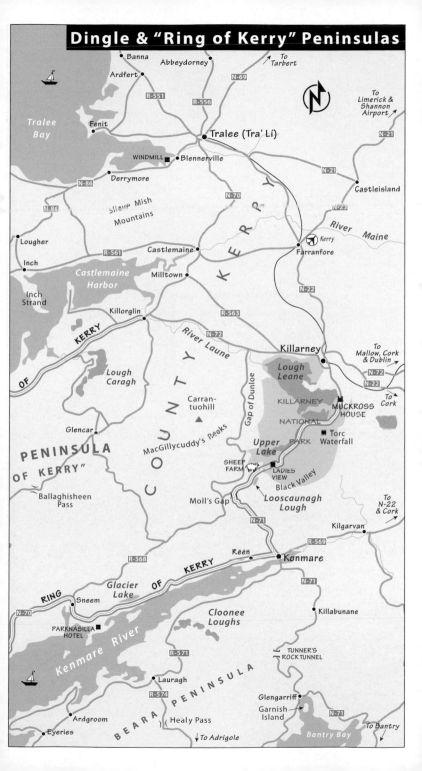

Ireland

You probably won't find the proverbial pot of gold in Ireland, but you will find plenty of treasure, starting with the engaging and feisty Irish people.

Belly up to the bar in a neighborhood pub and engage a local in conversation. Want to really get to know the Irish? Ask for directions. It's almost always a rich experience and a fast way to connect with locals. Nearby friends often chime in with additional tidbits that may or may not be useful, and soon it's a communal chit-chat session.

That legendary Irish "gift of gab" has its roots in the ancient Celtic culture. With no written language (until the arrival of Christianity), the ancient Celts passed their history, laws, and folklore verbally from generation to generation. Even today, most transactions come with an ample side-helping of friendly banter. As an Irishman once joked, "How can I know what I think until I hear what I say?" Contemporary Irish writer Colum McCann described it as, "...maniacal meanderings...kites of language...clouds of logic."

The Irish love their proverbs and revere their past. According to an old Irish adage, "When God made time, he

made a lot of it." Irish history stretches back thousands of years, yet is as close as the mist-shrouded ruins around the next bend of a country road. Ireland is dusted with undisturbed prehistoric stone circles, burial mounds, standing stones, and table-like dolmens...some older than the pyramids, and all speckled with moss. While much of Europe has buried older cultures under new, Ireland still reveals its cultural bedrock, dating back to the time when our ancestors finally stopped hunting and gathering and began to build to last. It's a place to connect with your roots, even if you're not Irish.

Though a relatively small island (about the size of the state of Maine), Ireland has had a disproportionately large impact on the rest of the world. Geographically isolated in the damp

attic of Dark Age Europe, Christian Irish monks tended the flickering flame of literacy, then bravely reintroduced it to the barbaric Continent. Ireland later turned out some of modern literature's greatest authors. In the 1800s, great waves of Irish emigrants fled famine and colonial oppression, seeking new opportunities abroad and making their mark in the US, Canada, New Zealand, and Australia. And although peace now prevails in Northern Ireland, the religious and political conflict there long held the world's attention.

Politically, the Irish people are split between the Republic of Ireland to the south (with 4.8 million people and 80 percent of the land) and Northern Ireland (with 1.8 million people). Northern Ireland is a province of the United Kingdom—like Scotland and Wales—while the Republic is an independent nation with its own seat at the UN...stuck alphabetically between Iraq and Israel. The island is further quartered into four ancient provinces that predate modern borders (Leinster, Munster, Connaught, and Ulster) and 32 counties (26 in the Republic and six in the North), each with its own identity and regional pride.

This 300-mile-long, saucer-shaped island, ringed with some of Europe's most scenic coastal cliffs, is only 150 miles across at its widest point—no matter where you go in Ireland, you're never more than 75 miles from the sea. Despite being as far north as Newfoundland, Ireland has a mild maritime climate, thanks to the Gulf Stream. Snowfall is rare and temporary here. Rainfall, on the other hand, ranges from more than 100 inches a year in soggy, boggy Connemara to about 30 inches a year in Dublin. Any time of year, bring rain gear. As Ireland's own Oscar Wilde once quipped, "There is no bad weather...only inappropriate clothing."

REPUBLIC OF IRELAND

Forget all the clichés you've absorbed from ads for Lucky Charms cereal or Irish Spring soap, and immerse yourself in authentic Ireland.

Passionate, poetic, and pugnacious...the Irish have confounded others throughout time. Queen Elizabet
as tough a British monarch as has ever graced the
once famously hissed in frustration that the Irish
Blarney" as she negotiated with the highly eva
of Blarney Castle. An exasperated Sigmund

Irish are the only race whose insanities cannot be cured by psychoanalysis." And the Irish inspired the English poet G. K. Chesterton to write:

> *The great Gaels of Ireland*
> *The lord hath made them mad*
> *For all their wars are merry*
> *And all their songs are sad.*

The Irish seem born with a love of music. At social gatherings, everyone's ready to sing his or her "party piece." Performances are judged less by skill than by uninhibited sincerity or showmanship. Nearly every Irish household has some kind of musical instrument on a shelf or in a closet. And live music is a weekly (if not nightly) draw at any town pub worth its salt. Pub music ranges from traditional instrumentals (jigs and reels) to ballads (songs of tragic love lost or heroic deeds done) to sing-along strummers. It's worth staying until the wee hours for the magical moment when a rare *sean nos* (Irish for "old style") lament is sung to a hushed and attentive pub crowd.

Part of the fun of traveling in Ireland is getting an ear for how locals express themselves in English (sort of)—from the surprised distant relative who is "gobsmacked" (astounded) by your appearance, to the businessman in the pub who

complains that the economy is utterly "banjaxed" (messed up).

You're most likely to hear the Irish Gaelic language (similar to but different from Scottish Gaelic, and—more distantly—Welsh) spoken in the Gaeltacht, the government-subsidized cultural preserve found mostly in far western coastal regions. But less than 5 percent of the Irish are fluent in Irish, and school kids—who must pass rigorous exams to graduate—agonize over its complex grammar.

The Republic of Ireland tilts toward the US—both culturally and economically. Every Irish family seems to have a brother, niece, cousin, or uncle in America. About 50 million people claim Irish descent in North America alone. Irish immigrants brought with them to the US the first political

organization for the downtrodden: the "green machine" grassroots voting blocks that came to dominate big-city politics in Boston, New York, and Chicago. To cozy

up to these valuable votes, every politician wanted to be seen marching in the parade on St. Patrick's Day. Today, St. Patrick's Day is the most widely celebrated national feast day in the English-speaking world, and a particularly raucous four-day festival in Dublin.

During the "Celtic Tiger" boom years (1995-2007), American corporations saw big tax and labor advantages in locating here, making Ireland an economic beachhead on European turf. Ireland's "Silicon Bog" is the European home to such big names as IBM, Intel, Microsoft, Apple, Facebook, and Google. Ireland's economic success (later tarnished by the 2008 crash and subsequent bank bailouts) was the model that Eastern European nations hoped to emulate when a number of them joined the European Union in 2004. The Irish are also big pharmaceutical producers: More Viagra is made in Ireland than in any other country...though the proudly virile Irish males claim it's all for export.

Other famous exports from the Republic of Ireland include rock and contemporary music (U2, Thin Lizzy, the Corrs, Sinéad O'Connor, Enya), traditional Irish music (the Chieftains, Dubliners, the Clancy Brothers), opera (The Irish Tenors and John McCormack), dance (Riverdance), trivia (*Guinness World Records*—see sidebar on page 76), crystal (Waterford), beer (Guinness—see sidebar on page 526), festivals (Halloween has Celtic roots), British military heroes (the Duke of Wellington), iconic authors (Jonathan Swift, W. B. Yeats, James Joyce, George Bernard Shaw, Samuel

Beckett, Oscar Wilde, and Frank McCourt), and a slew of memorable actors (Geraldine Fitzgerald, Colin Farrell, Jonathan Rhys Meyers, Gabriel Byrne, Richard Harris, Michael Gambon, Barry Fitzgerald, and Maureen O'Hara).

Until recently Ireland was one of the most ethnically homogenous nations on earth, but the Celtic Tiger economy changed all that, attracting thousands of Eastern Europeans (mostly Poles), Africans (mostly Nigerians), and South Americans (mostly Brazilians). The 2011 census found that over 10 percent of Ireland's population had been born elsewhere.

That cultural exchange may have something to do with Ireland's appealing cuisine. At one time known only for its poor imitation of bad British food, today's Irish cuisine has gone global. Expatriate chefs have come home with newly refined tastes, and immigrants have added a world of interesting flavors. Modern Irish cuisine is skillfully prepared with fresh local ingredients. Irish beef, lamb, and dairy products are among the EU's best. And there are streams full of trout and salmon and a rich ocean of fish and shellfish right offshore. While fish and potatoes remain staples, potatoes are often replaced with rice or pasta in many dishes.

Travelers on a budget will invariably encounter the Holy Trinity of pub grub: Irish stew, chicken curry, and fish-and-

chips. Popular beer choices are Guinness (a dark stout), Smithwicks (an amber ale), and Harp (a golden lager). The

most common spirit is triple-distilled Irish whiskey.

Sports in the Republic are dominated by the Gaelic Athletic Association (GAA; see sidebar on page 79), which operates Irish hurling and football (not to be confused with soccer) leagues. Each county fields a team of skilled amateur players—talented athletes who are regular guys during the workweek (teachers, truck drivers, bakers, and the like).

Horse racing and dog racing appeal to those who enjoy a wager. And it's hard to go 25 miles in Ireland without running into a golf course (there are more than 300 on the island). Pro golfer Padraig Harrington made waves by winning three major tournaments in a little over a year (2007 and 2008).

Most Irish claim to be Catholic, and shrines to the Virgin Mary still grace rural roadsides (see sidebar on page 361). The average Catholic Irish family spends €500 on a lavish celebration for the First Holy Communion of each child. But church

attendance has decreased dramatically over the past 40 years, due in part to child-abuse scandals at parochial schools. If not for the influx of newly arriving devout Catholic Poles, attendance would be even lower. Still, the shamrock—used by St. Patrick to explain the concept of the Holy Trinity—remains the most recognizable symbol of Ireland. And the resilient Irish people maintain an unsinkable and optimistic belief in the future.

NORTHERN IRELAND

Northern Ireland is an underrated and often overlooked region that usually surprises visitors with its memorable scenery and friendly people.

An interesting hybrid of Irish and Scottish cultures, Northern Ireland is only 17 miles from Scotland at its closest point. The accents you'll hear in the North are distinctly different from their counterparts south of the border. When a Northern Irishman on a train asks to have a look at your "pepper," he means your "paper" (as in "newspaper").

Northern Ireland is part of the United Kingdom and occupies six of the nine counties of the ancient Irish province of Ulster. With a population just a bit larger than that of Phoenix, it's small enough to have one phone book for the entire province, yet is twice as densely populated as the Republic to the south. Its coast boasts the alligator-skin volcanic geology of the Giant's Causeway and the lush Glens of Antrim, while its interior is dominated by rolling hills of pastoral serenity and Lough Neagh, the UK's biggest lake.

The people of the North generally fall into two categories: those who feel they're British (Unionists) and those who feel they're Irish (Nationalists). Those born in the North can choose which of the two passports they want. The Troubles—the decades-long conflict between Unionists and Nationalists, starting in the 1960s—were always more about nationality than religion. But the ugly ruptures of the past are healing. Both paramilitary camps have set aside their arms, and Northern Ireland is now statistically one of the safer places in the Western world.

The industrious people of Northern Ireland have a legendary work ethic. When they emigrated to the US, they became known as the Scots-Irish and played a crucial role in our nation's founding. They were signers of our Declaration of Independence, a dozen of our presidents, and the ancestors of Davy Crockett and Mark Twain. They have a proclivity for making things that go. They've produced far-reaching inventions like Dunlop's first inflatable tire. The Shorts aircraft factory (in Belfast) built the Wright Brothers' first six aircraft for commercial sale and the world's first vertical takeoff jet. The *Titanic* was the only flop of Northern Ireland's otherwise successful shipbuilding industry. The once-futuristic DeLorean sports car was made in Belfast.

Notable people from Northern Ireland include musicians Van Morrison and James Galway, and actors Liam Neeson, Roma Downey, and Kenneth Branagh. The North also produced Christian intellectual and writer C. S. Lewis, Victorian physicist Lord Kelvin, and soccer-star playboy George Best—who once famously remarked, "I spent most of my money on liquor and women... and the rest I wasted."

The Northern Irish have a good sense of humor and a long memory. Commercial pilots joke to their arriving passengers to set their watches to local time: 1690 (the year of the never-to-be-forgotten Battle of the Boyne).

About half of the people in Northern Ireland attend church weekly—significantly more than in the Republic (30 percent) or the rest of the UK (15 percent). Only in Northern Ireland can a union between a Christian man and woman of the same ethnicity and nationality be considered a "mixed marriage" (Protestant and Catholic).

As in the Republic, sports are big in the North. Ulster-born golfers Rory McIlroy, Graeme McDowell, and Darren

Clarke have won a fistful of majors over the past decade, filling local hearts with pride. With close ties to Scotland, many Northern Irish fans follow the exploits of the soccer teams from Glasgow—but which team you root for betrays which side of the tracks you come from. Those who cheer for Glasgow Celtic are Nationalist and Catholic; those waving banners for the Glasgow Rangers are Unionist and Protestant.

In an effort to maintain peace, some pubs post signs on their doors banning patrons from wearing sports jerseys. Luckily, sports with no sectarian history are now being introduced, such as the Belfast Giants ice hockey team—a hit with both communities.

Northern Ireland has inextricable ties with the Republic. The town of Armagh, in central Northern Ireland, is the seat of both the Protestant and Catholic Archbishops of all Ireland (Republic and North). People from both countries cross the border on a daily basis to shop; there are no crossing restrictions along the 225-mile border. Dublin businessmen from the Republic have invested large sums in the rejuvenation of Belfast's once-derelict Titanic Quarter. And vacationers from the North often head over to the Republic's County Donegal for midsummer holidays. The former president of the Republic, Mary McAleese, was born in Belfast. The fact remains, however, that more citizens of the Republic have been to London than have visited the northern end of their own island.

No matter which side of the border you visit, today's Ireland is cosmopolitan, vibrant, business-savvy, and impressively globalized. The caricatures of muddy-booted bogtrotters and AK-47-armed terrorists have faded. But the

seductive scenery and the culture as old as the stones remain. The Irish people have a worldwide reputation as talkative, athletic, musical, moody romantics with a quick laugh and a ready smile. Come join them.

INTRODUCTION

Flung onto the foggy fringe of the Atlantic pond like a mossy millstone, Ireland drips with mystery, drawing you in for a closer look and then surprising you. An old farmer cuts turf from the bog, while his son staffs the tech helpline for an international software firm. Buy them both a pint in a pub that's whirling with playful conversation and exhilarating traditional music. Pious, earthy, witty, brooding, proud, yet unpretentious, Irish culture is an intoxicating potion to sip or slurp—as the mood strikes you.

This book breaks Ireland into its best big-city, small-town, and rural destinations. It gives you all the information and opinions necessary to wring the maximum value out of your limited time and money in each of these locations. Experiencing Irish culture, people, and natural wonders economically and hassle-free has been my goal for much of my life of traveling, tour guiding, and travel writing. With this new edition, I pass on to you the lessons I've learned, updated for your trip in 2017.

The destinations covered in this book are balanced to include the most exciting big cities and great-to-be-alive-in small towns. Note that this book covers the highlights of the entire island, including Northern Ireland. While you'll find the predictable biggies—such as the Book of Kells, the sacred burial mound of Newgrange (at Brú na Bóinne), and the Cliffs of Moher—I've also mixed in a healthy dose of Back Door intimacy (rope-bridge hikes, holy wells, and pubs with traditional Irish music). This book is selective. On a short trip, visiting both the monastic ruins of Glendalough and Clonmacnoise is redundant; I cover only the best—Glendalough. There are plenty of great manor-house gardens, but I recommend just the top two (one in the Republic and one in Northern Ireland)—the Gardens of Powerscourt and Mount Stewart House.

The best is, of course, only my opinion. But after spending

INTRODUCTION

Map Legend

⅒ Viewpoint	✈ Airport	⫘ Tunnel
♠ Entrance	Ⓣ Taxi Stand	Pedestrian Zone
❶ Tourist Info	Ⓣ Tram Stop	------- Railway
WC Restroom	Ⓑ Bus Stop	.... Ferry/Boat Route
⛫ Castle	⛾ Pub	⊢—⊣ Tram
⛪ Church	Ⓟ Parking	⫽⫽⫽⫽ Stairs
▪ Statue/Point of Interest	)(Mtn. Pass	· · · · · Walk/Tour Route
⊠ Elevator	⬠ Park	------- Trail

Use this legend to help you navigate the maps in this book.

more than half of my adult life exploring and researching Europe, I've developed a sixth sense for what touches the traveler's imagination. The places featured in this book will give anyone the "gift of gab."

ABOUT THIS BOOK

Rick Steves Ireland 2017 is a personal tour guide in your pocket. Better yet, it's actually two tour guides in your pocket: The co-author of this guidebook is Pat O'Connor. Pat has long had a travel passion for the Emerald Isle. He's the Ireland specialist and senior Ireland tour guide at my company, Rick Steves' Europe. Together, Pat and I keep this book up-to-date and accurate (though for simplicity, from this point "we" will shed our respective egos and become "I").

This book is organized by destinations. Each is a mini vacation on its own, filled with exciting sights, strollable lanes, homey and affordable places to stay, and memorable places to eat. For destinations covered in this book, you'll find these sections:

Planning Your Time suggests a schedule for how to best use your limited time.

Orientation has specifics on public transportation, helpful hints, local tour options, easy-to-read maps, and tourist information.

Sights describes the top attractions and includes their cost and hours. Major sights have self-guided tours.

Key to This Book

Updates
This book is updated every year—but things change. For the latest, visit www.ricksteves.com/update.

Abbreviations and Times
I use the following symbols and abbreviations in this book:
Sights are rated:

▲▲▲	Don't miss
▲▲	Try hard to see
▲	Worthwhile if you can make it
No rating	Worth knowing about

Tourist information offices are abbreviated as **TI,** and bathrooms are **WC**s. Accommodations are categorized with a **Sleep Code** (described on page 511); eateries are classified with a **Restaurant Price Code** (page 524). To indicate discounts for my readers, I include **RS%** in the listings.

Like Europe, this book uses the **24-hour clock.** It's the same through 12:00 noon, and then keeps going: 13:00, 14:00, and so on. For anything over 12, subtract 12 and add p.m. (14:00 is 2:00 p.m.).

When giving **opening times,** I include both peak season and off-season hours if they differ. So, if a museum is listed as "May-Oct daily 9:00-16:00," it should be open from 9 a.m. until 4 p.m. from the first day of May until the last day of October (but expect exceptions).

For **transit** or **tour departures,** I first list the frequency, then the duration. So, a train connection listed as "2/hour, 1.5 hours" departs twice each hour, and the journey lasts an hour and a half.

Self-Guided Walks take you through interesting neighborhoods, pointing out sights and fun stops.

Sleeping describes my favorite hotels, from good-value deals to cushy splurges.

Eating serves up a buffet of options, from inexpensive pubs to fancy restaurants.

Connections outlines your options for traveling to destinations by train, bus, and plane, plus route tips for drivers.

The **Ireland: Past & Present** chapter gives you a quick overview of Irish history, a look at contemporary Ireland, a taste of the Irish language, and an Irish-Yankee vocabulary list.

The **Practicalities** chapter is a traveler's tool kit, with my best advice about money, sightseeing, sleeping, eating, staying connected, and transportation (trains, buses, car rentals, driving, and flights).

The **appendix** has the nuts-and-bolts: useful phone numbers

Top Destinations in Ireland

and websites, a list of holidays and festivals, recommended books and films, a climate chart, and a handy packing checklist.

Throughout this book, you'll find money- and time-saving tips for sightseeing, transportation, and more. Some businesses—especially hotels and walking tour companies—offer special discounts to my readers, indicated in their listings.

Browse through this book, choose your favorite destinations, and link them up. Then have a great trip! Traveling like a temporary local, you'll get the absolute most out of every mile, minute, and dollar. And, as you visit places I know and love, I'm happy that you'll be meeting some of my favorite Irish people.

Planning

This section will help you get started planning your trip—with advice on trip costs, when to go, and what you should know before you take off.

TRAVEL SMART

Your trip to Ireland is like a complex play—it's easier to follow and really appreciate on a second viewing. While no one does the same

But Why Don't You Cover...?

This guidebook is selective and opinionated. We are the first to admit that Ireland is full of famous, well-promoted sights that we simply skip over. Here's why: Americans have the shortest vacations in the developed world. And travelers—like guidebook authors—have to make some tough decisions. Rather than overwhelm you with "must-see" places and "to die for" experiences, our goal is to take what we consider the best three weeks or so of sightseeing a country has to offer and cover that well. (If your ancestors or friends came from a certain town, that makes it a worthwhile stop for you—but not necessarily for everyone using this book.) We hope you enjoy visiting our personal picks for the best places in Ireland. For information on the places we choose to omit from this book, you can find plenty of free sources online and through the local TIs.

Happy Travels,
Rick and Pat

trip twice to gain that advantage, reading this book in its entirety before your trip accomplishes much the same thing.

Design an itinerary that enables you to visit sights at the best possible times. Note holidays, specifics on sights, and days when sights are closed or most crowded (all covered in this book). To connect the dots smoothly, read the tips in Practicalities on taking trains and buses, or renting a car and driving. Designing a smart trip is a fun, doable, and worthwhile challenge.

Make your itinerary a mix of intense and relaxed stretches. To maximize rootedness, minimize one-night stands. It's worth considering traveling in the evening to get settled in a town for two nights. Hotels are more likely to give a better price to someone staying more than one night. Every trip—and every traveler—needs slack time (laundry, picnics, people-watching, and so on). Pace yourself. Assume you will return.

Reread this book as you travel, and visit local tourist information offices (abbreviated as TI in this book). Upon arrival in a new town, lay the groundwork for a smooth departure; confirm the train, bus, or road you'll take when you leave.

Even with the best-planned itinerary, you'll need to be flexible. Update your plans as you travel. Get online or call ahead to double-check tourist information, learn the latest on sights (special events, tour schedules, and so on), book tickets and tours, make reservations, reconfirm hotels, and research transportation connections.

Enjoy the friendliness of the Irish people. Connect with the culture. Avert your eyes from exposure to full-frontal tourism. Set up your own quest for the best pub, traditional music, ruined castle,

INTRODUCTION

Ireland at a Glance

These attractions are listed (as in this book) roughly clockwise around the island of Ireland.

Republic of Ireland

▲▲▲**Dublin** Bustling Irish capital, with fascinating tours (historical, musical, and literary), passionate rebel history (Kilmainham Gaol), treasured Dark Age gospels (Book of Kells), intricate Celtic artifacts (National Museum: Archaeology and History), and a rambunctious pub district (Temple Bar).

▲▲**Near Dublin** Great day-trip options: North to the Boyne Valley's ancient pre-Celtic burial mounds of Brú na Bóinne and majestic Norman castle of Trim, west to the green horse-racing pastures of the Irish National Stud, and south to the graceful Gardens of Powerscourt and evocative monastic ruins of Glendalough.

▲▲**Kilkenny and the Rock of Cashel** Best two destinations in Ireland's interior: the town of Kilkenny, with its narrow medieval lanes, cathedrals, and castle; and the Rock of Cashel, with its dramatic hilltop hodgepodge of church ruins overlooking the Plain of Tipperary.

▲**Waterford and County Wexford** Gritty historic port town with famous Waterford Crystal Visitor Centre, and the hinterland of early Norman invasions, with a huge lighthouse and the JFK ancestral farm.

▲▲**Kinsale and Cobh** County Cork's two quaint harbor towns: Gourmet capital Kinsale, guarded by squat Charles Fort, and emigration hub Cobh—the *Titanic*'s last stop.

▲▲**Kenmare and the Ring of Kerry** Colorful, tidy town and ideal base for side-stepping the throngs flocking to drive Ireland's most-famous scenic loop route.

▲▲▲**Dingle Peninsula** My favorite fishing village (a traditional Irish-music pub paradise), which serves as a launchpad for the gorgeous Slea Head loop drive (or bike ride), featuring a wealth of Celtic and early Christian sites.

or ring fort. Slow down and be open to unexpected experiences. Ask questions—most locals are eager to point you in their idea of the right direction. Keep a notepad in your pocket for noting directions, organizing your thoughts, and confirming prices. Wear your money belt, learn the currency, and figure out how to estimate prices in dollars. Those who expect to travel smart, do.

▲▲**County Clare and the Burren** Ireland's rugged western fringe, with the take-your-breath-away Cliffs of Moher, stone landscape of the Burren, cozy trad music crossroads of Doolin, and handy Shannon Airport access from friendly Ennis.

▲**Galway** Energetic university city with thriving pedestrian street scene, great people-watching pubs, and the west coast's best base from which to reach the Burren, Aran Islands, and Connemara.

▲▲▲**Aran Islands** Three windswept, treeless limestone islands in the Atlantic, laced with a maze of angular rock walls, crowned by Iron Age ring forts, and inhabited by sparse villages of hardy fisher-folk.

▲▲**Connemara and County Mayo** Lushly green and hilly Irish outback of cottages, lakes, and holy peaks, dotted with photogenic settlements such as Cong, Kylemore Abbey, and leafy riverside Westport.

Northern Ireland
▲▲**Belfast** No-nonsense industrial revolution metropolis, with stirring sectarian political murals, grandly domed City Hall, sprawling Ulster Folk Park and Transport Museum, and the charming nearby Victorian seaside retreat of Bangor.

▲▲**Portrush and the Antrim Coast** Unpretentious beach resort of arcades and amusement park rides, a stone's throw from the geologic wonderland of the Giant's Causeway, dramatic cliff-edge ruins of Dunluce Castle, and exhilarating Carrick-a-Rede Rope Bridge.

▲**Derry and County Donegal** Seventeenth-century British settlement ringed by stout town walls—infamous as the powder keg that ignited Ireland's tragic modern "Troubles"—with an insightful city history museum and access to the rugged beauty of Donegal.

TRIP COSTS
Five components make up your trip costs: airfare to Europe, transportation in Europe, room and board, sightseeing and entertainment, and shopping and miscellany.

Airfare to Europe: A basic round-trip flight from the US to Dublin can cost, on average, about $1,000-2,000 total, depend-

Ireland's Best Three-Week Trip by Car

Day	Plan	Sleep in
1	Fly into Dublin	Dublin
2	Dublin	Dublin
3	Dublin	Dublin
4	Rent car at Dublin Airport, then drive to Glendalough	Kilkenny
5	Cashel	Waterford
6	Waterford	Waterford
7	Explore County Wexford	Kinsale
8	Charles Fort and Cobh	Kinsale
9	Muckross House and Farms	Kenmare
10	Ring of Kerry	Dingle
11	Dingle Peninsula Loop	Dingle
12	Blasket Island, Dingle town (laundry and rest)	Dingle
13	Cliffs of Moher, the Burren, Dunguaire Castle banquet	Galway
14	Aran Islands	Galway
15	Explore Connemara	Westport
16	Drive to Northern Ireland	Derry
17	Explore Derry	Portrush
18	Explore Antrim Coast	Portrush
19	Belfast	Belfast
20	Drive to Valley of the Boyne sights	Trim
21	Return car and fly home from Dublin	

Spend your first three nights in Dublin, using buses and taxis, then pick up a car for the rest of this itinerary. For three weeks without a car, cut back on the recommended sights with the most frustrating public transportation (Ring of Kerry, the Burren, Valley of the Boyne, Connemara, and County Wexford). You can book day tours by bus for some of these areas at local TIs. For at least two people traveling together, taxis—though expensive—can work in a pinch if bus schedules don't fit your plans (e.g., Cork to Kinsale).

ing on where you fly from and when (cheaper in winter). Smaller budget airlines may provide bargain service from several European capitals to many cities in Ireland. If your trip extends beyond Ireland, consider saving time and money in Europe by flying into one city and out of another; for instance, into Dublin and out of Paris. Overall, Kayak.com is the best place to start searching for flights on a combination of mainstream and budget carriers.

Transportation in Europe: For a three-week whirlwind trip of my recommended destinations by public transportation, allow $350 per person. If you plan to rent a car, allow at least $300 per

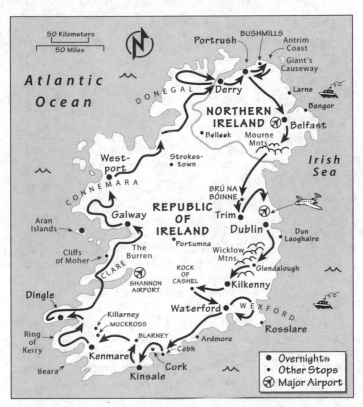

If you have time for only one idyllic peninsula on your trip, I'd suggest the Dingle Peninsula over the Ring of Kerry (for specifics,
see sidebar on page 229). If you're picking up a car at Dublin
Airport, consider a gentler small-town start in Trim, and let Dublin
be the finale, when you're rested and ready to tackle the city.

week, not including tolls, gas, and supplemental insurance. Car
rentals are cheapest if arranged from the US. Because Ireland's
train system has gaps, you'll likely save money by simply buying
train and bus tickets as you go, rather than buying a rail pass. Train
tickets in particular can be as much as 50 percent cheaper if bought
online. Don't hesitate to consider flying—a short flight can be
cheaper than the train (check www.skyscanner.com for intra-European flights). For more on public transportation and car rental,
see "Transportation" in the Practicalities chapter.

   Room and Board: You can thrive in Ireland in 2017 on $135 a

🎧 Rick Steves Audio Europe 🎧

My **Rick Steves Audio Europe app** makes it easy to download audio content to enhance your trip. This includes my audio tours of many of Europe's top destinations, as well as a far-reaching library of insightful travel interviews from my public radio show with experts from around the globe—including many of the places in this book. The app and all of its content are entirely free. (And new content is added about twice a year.) You can download Rick Steves Audio Europe via Apple's App Store, Google Play, or the Amazon Appstore. For more information, see www.ricksteves.com/audioeurope.

day per person for room and board (more in big cities). This allows $20 for lunch, $30 for dinner, $10 for snacks or a Guinness, and $75 for lodging (based on two people splitting a $150 double room that includes breakfast). That's doable, particularly outside Dublin, and it's possible for many travelers to come in under budget. Students and tightwads can enjoy Ireland for as little as $80 a day ($40 for a bed, $40 for meals and snacks).

Lodging rates are best if you book directly with the proprietor using their email address, phone number, or website. If you use an online service such as Booking.com, they'll charge the proprietor 15 percent extra...you'll pay inflated prices and lose any discount you get with this book. Eliminate the middleman or pay more.

Sightseeing and Entertainment: In big cities, figure about $10-15 per major sight (for example, the Book of Kells at Dublin's Trinity College-$12), $5 for minor ones (climbing church towers), $15 for guided walks, $28 for day-trip bus tours, and $55 or more for splurge experiences (such as the Dunguaire Castle medieval banquet or a flight to the Aran Islands).

An overall average of $40 a day works for most people. Don't skimp here. After all, this category is the driving force behind your trip—you came to sightsee, enjoy, and experience Ireland. Two sightseeing passes—the Heritage Card and the Heritage Island Visitor Attraction Guide—can help you economize and simplify your sightseeing (see "Sightseeing Passes," page 508).

Shopping and Miscellany: Figure roughly $2 per postcard, tea, or ice cream cone, and $6 per pint of beer. Shopping can vary in cost from nearly nothing to a small fortune. Good budget travelers find that this category has little to do with assembling a trip full of lifelong memories.

SIGHTSEEING PRIORITIES

So much to see, so little time. How to choose? Depending on the length of your trip, and taking geographic proximity into account, here are my recommended priorities:

3 days:	Dublin
5 days, add:	Dingle Peninsula
8 days, add:	Galway, Aran Islands, slow down
10 days, add:	County Clare/Burren, Kilkenny/Cashel
13 days, add:	Belfast, Antrim Coast
16 days, add:	Kinsale, Kenmare/Ring of Kerry
19 days, add:	Derry, Connemara, Wicklow Mountains/Valley of the Boyne
21 days:	Slow down

This includes nearly everything on the "Ireland's Best Three-Week Trip by Car" map and itinerary on page 8. If you don't have time to see it all, prioritize according to your interests. The "Ireland at a Glance" sidebar can help you decide where to go (page 6).

WHEN TO GO

June and July are my favorite times because of the longer days and the busier schedule of tourist fun. Summer crowds continue to grow in Ireland as they do in much of Europe, especially with the expansion of the cruise ship industry. Cruise crowds hit Dublin, the Cobh/Cork region, and Belfast the hardest. Travel during "shoulder season" (May, early June, Sept, and early Oct) is easier and a bit less expensive. Shoulder-season travelers get smaller crowds, the full range of sights and tourist fun spots, and the ability to book a room with less competition— often at a flexible price.

Winter travelers find absolutely no crowds, soft room prices, shorter sightseeing hours, and colder rain. Some attractions are open only on weekends or are closed entirely in the winter (Nov-Feb). The winter weather can be chilly, blustery, and dreary, and nightfall draws the shades on sightseeing well before dinnertime. In summer, travelers can usually plan on attractions being open from 9:00 to 18:00, while winter travelers are often forced to squeeze everything in between 10:00 and 16:00. Check the hours for each sight of interest to you—many sights stop allowing visitors to enter as much as an hour ahead of closing time. While Ireland's rural charm falls with the leaves, city sightseeing is fine in the winter.

In Ireland, there really isn't a "dry season" that you can plan on, as rainfall is ladled out evenly throughout the year. Plan for rain no matter when you go and consider sunny days a bonus. The weather can change several times in a day, but rarely is it extreme. Just keep traveling and take full advantage of "bright spells." Bring a jacket and dress in layers. Daily averages throughout the year range between 42°F and 70°F. Temperatures below 32°F cause

INTRODUCTION

How Was Your Trip?

Were your travels fun, smooth, and meaningful? You can share tips, concerns, and discoveries at www.ricksteves.com/feedback. To check out readers' hotel and restaurant reviews—or leave one yourself—visit my travel forum at www. ricksteves.com/travel-forum. I value your feedback. Thanks in advance.

headlines, and days that break 80°F—while increasing in recent years—are still rare. For more information, see the climate chart in the appendix.

While sunshine may be rare, summer days are very long. Dublin is as far north as Edmonton, Canada, and Portrush is as far north as Ketchikan on the Alaskan panhandle. The midsummer sun is up from 4:30 until 22:30. It's not uncommon to have a gray day, eat dinner, and enjoy hours of sunshine afterward.

KNOW BEFORE YOU GO

Check this list of things to arrange while you're still at home.

You need a **passport**—but no visa or shots—to travel in Ireland. You may be denied entry into certain European countries if your passport is due to expire within six months of your ticketed date of return. Get it renewed if you'll be cutting it close. It can take up to six weeks to get or renew a passport (for more on passports, see www.travel.state.gov). Pack a photocopy of your passport in your luggage in case the original is lost or stolen.

Book rooms well in advance if you'll be traveling during peak season (mid-June-Aug) or any major holidays, such as St. Patrick's Day (see page 556).

Call your **debit- and credit-card companies** to let them know the countries you'll be visiting, to ask about fees, to request your PIN if you don't already know it, and more. See page 502 for details.

Do your homework if you're considering **travel insurance.** Compare the cost of the insurance to the cost of your potential loss. Also, check whether your existing insurance (health, homeowners, or renters) covers you and your possessions overseas. For more tips, see www.ricksteves.com/insurance.

To guarantee access and minimize your time in lines, especially in peak season, **booking online** in advance is recommended for Dublin's Book of Kells and Kilmainham Gaol, and for Belfast's Titanic Belfast and Gobbins Cliff Path. Garden tours at

Glenveagh Castle and National Park in Donegal are only available with an advance reservation. Purchase tickets well ahead of time if you plan on attending any of September's Gaelic football finals at Croke Park Stadium.

If you plan to hire a **local guide,** reserve ahead by email. Popular guides can get booked up.

If you're bringing a **mobile device,** consider signing up for an international plan for cheaper calls, texts, and data (see page 529). Download any apps you might want to use on the road, such as maps, transit schedules, and **Rick Steves Audio Europe** (see page 10).

Check updates to this book at www.ricksteves.com/update.

Traveling as a Temporary Local

We travel all the way to Ireland to enjoy differences—to become temporary locals. You'll experience frustrations. Certain truths that we find "God-given" or "self-evident," such as cold beer, ice in drinks, bottomless cups of coffee, "the customer is king," and

bigger being better, are suddenly not so true. One of the benefits of travel is the eye-opening realization that there are logical, civil, and even better alternatives. A willingness to go local ensures that you'll enjoy a full dose of Irish hospitality. And with an eagerness to go local, you'll have even more fun.

The Irish generally like Americans. But if there is a negative aspect to the Irish image of Americans, it's that we are loud, wasteful, ethnocentric, too informal (which can seem disrespectful), and a bit naive.

While the Irish look bemusedly at some of our Yankee excesses—and worriedly at others—they nearly always afford us individual travelers all the warmth we deserve. Judging from all the happy feedback I receive from travelers who have used this book, it's safe to assume you'll enjoy a great, affordable vacation—with the finesse of an independent, experienced traveler.

Thanks, and have a grand holiday!

Rick Steves

Back Door Travel Philosophy

From *Rick Steves Europe Through the Back Door*

Travel is intensified living—maximum thrills per minute and one of the last great sources of legal adventure. Travel is freedom. It's recess, and we need it.

Experiencing the real Europe requires catching it by surprise, going casual..."through the Back Door."

Affording travel is a matter of priorities. (Make do with the old car.) You can eat and sleep—simply, safely, and enjoyably—anywhere in Europe for $100 a day plus transportation costs. In many ways, spending more money only builds a thicker wall between you and what you traveled so far to see. Europe is a cultural carnival, and time after time, you'll find that its best acts are free and the best seats are the cheap ones.

A tight budget forces you to travel close to the ground, meeting and communicating with the people. Never sacrifice sleep, nutrition, safety, or cleanliness to save money. Simply enjoy the local-style alternatives to expensive hotels and restaurants.

Connecting with people carbonates your experience. Extroverts have more fun. If your trip is low on magic moments, kick yourself and make things happen. If you don't enjoy a place, maybe you don't know enough about it. Seek the truth. Recognize tourist traps. Give a culture the benefit of your open mind. See things as different, but not better or worse. Any culture has plenty to share. When an opportunity presents itself, make it a habit to say "yes."

Of course, travel, like the world, is a series of hills and valleys. Be fanatically positive and militantly optimistic. If something's not to your liking, change your liking.

Travel can make you a happier American, as well as a citizen of the world. Our Earth is home to seven billion equally precious people. It's humbling to travel and find that other people don't have the "American Dream"—they have their own dreams. Europeans like us, but with all due respect, they wouldn't trade passports.

Thoughtful travel engages us with the world. It reminds us what is truly important. By broadening perspectives, travel teaches new ways to measure quality of life.

Globetrotting destroys ethnocentricity, helping us understand and appreciate other cultures. Rather than fear the diversity on this planet, celebrate it. Among your most prized souvenirs will be the strands of different cultures you choose to knit into your own character. The world is a cultural yarn shop, and Back Door travelers are weaving the ultimate tapestry. Join in!

REPUBLIC OF IRELAND

REPUBLIC OF IRELAND

The modern Irish state has existed since 1922, but its inhabitants proudly claim their nation to be the only contemporary independent state to sprout from purely Celtic roots (sprinkled with a few Vikings and shipwrecked Spanish Armada sailors for good measure). The Romans never bothered to come over and organize the wild Irish. Through the persuasive and culturally enlightened approach of early missionaries such as St. Patrick, Ireland is one of the very few countries to have initially converted to Christianity without much bloodshed. The religious carnage came a thousand years later, with the Reformation. Irish culture absorbed the influences of Viking raiders and Norman soldiers of fortune, eventually enduring the 750-year shadow of English domination.

Just a few decades ago, Ireland was an isolated, agricultural economic backwater that had largely missed out on the Industrial Revolution. Things began to turn around when Ireland joined the European Community (precursor to the EU) in 1973. The Irish government instituted farsighted tax laws, including a corporate tax rate of only 12.5 percent (compared to about 39 percent in the US) to entice foreign corporations to set up shop here. It proved so successful in attracting US business that America has now invested more in Ireland than in Brazil, India, Russia, and China combined.

Today, the Republic of Ireland attracts expatriates returning to their homeland and new foreign investment. As the only officially English-speaking country to have adopted the euro currency (Britain uses the pound), Ireland makes an efficient base from which to access the European marketplace. Nearly 35 percent of the Irish population is under 25 years old, leading many high-tech and pharmaceutical firms to locate here, taking advantage of this young,

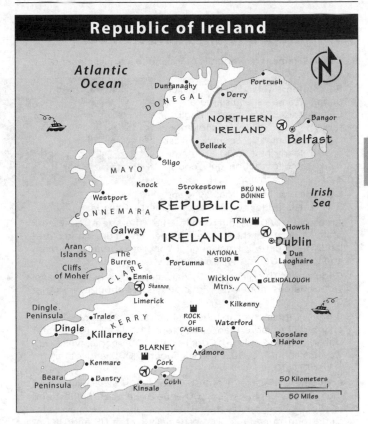

well-educated labor force. And during the Celtic Tiger economic boom, Ireland became a destination for immigrants—mostly from the Third World and the newer EU nations. Eastern Europeans (especially Poles) came in search of higher pay...a reversal from the days when many Irish fled to start new lives abroad.

As time passes, relations between Ireland and her former colonial master Britain are starting to heal. In May 2011, Queen Elizabeth II became the first British monarch to visit the Republic of Ireland since Ireland's 1922 split from the United Kingdom, which occurred during her grandfather's reign. Her four-night visit (to Dublin, Cashel, and Cork) unexpectedly charmed the Irish people and did much to repair old wounds between the two countries, which are now, in the words of the Queen, "equal partners and good neighbors."

Just a couple of days after the Queen's visit, Barack Obama dropped in for a brief 12-hour stop, guided by former American ambassador to Ireland (and Pittsburgh Steelers owner) Dan Rooney. Being one-sixteenth Irish, O'Bama made sure to helicop-

Republic of Ireland Almanac

Official Name: The Republic of Ireland (a.k.a. just "Ireland" or, in Irish, Éire).

Population: Ireland's 4.8 million people (same as Louisiana) are of Celtic stock. They speak English, though Irish Gaelic is spoken in pockets along the country's west coast. Nearly nine in 10 are nominally Catholic, though only one in three attends church.

Latitude and Longitude: 53°N and 8°W. The latitude is equivalent to Alberta, Canada.

Area: With 27,000 square miles—half the size of New York State—it occupies the southern 80 percent of the island of Ireland. The country is small enough that radio broadcasts manage to cover traffic snarls nationwide.

Geography: The isle is mostly flat, ringed by a hilly coastline. The climate is moderate, with cloudy skies about every other day.

Biggest Cities: The capital of Dublin (528,000 people) is the only big city; more than one in four Irish live in the greater Dublin area (1.3 million). Cork has 119,000 people, while Galway has about 76,000, Limerick about 57,000, and Waterford about 47,000.

Economy: The Gross Domestic Product is $225 billion, and the GDP per capita is $54,300—one of Europe's highest and nearly 10 percent more than Britain's. Major moneymakers include tourism and exports (especially to the US and UK) of machines, medicine, Guinness, glassware, crystal ware, and software. Traditional agriculture (potatoes and other root vegetables) is fading fast, but dairy still does well.

Government: The elected president, Michael Higgins, appoints the Taoiseach (TEE-shock) or prime minister (currently Enda Kenny), who is nominated by Parliament. The Parliament consists of the 60-seat Senate, chosen by an electoral college, and the House of Representatives, with 166 seats apportioned after the people vote for a party. Major parties include Fianna Fáil, Fine Gael, and Sinn Fein, the political arm of the (fading) Irish Republican Army. Ireland is divided into 28 administrative counties—including Kerry, Clare, Cork, Limerick, and so on.

Flag: The Republic of Ireland's flag has three vertical bands of green, white, and orange.

The Average Irish: A typical Irish person is 5'7", 36 years old, has two kids, and will live to be 80. An Irish citizen consumes nearly five pounds of tea per year and spends $5 on alcohol each day.

ter into his ancestral home village of Moneygall in County Offaly and have a pint with Henry, his cousin eight times removed, whom he nicknamed "Henry VIII." Later that day, he delivered a speech to a huge crowd packed into Dublin's College Green, drawing cheers when he dusted off his Irish Gaelic and proclaimed, "Is féidir linn." ("Yes we can.")

Don't worry if your Irish Gaelic is rustier than the president's—the vast majority of Irish people speak English, though

you'll still encounter Irish Gaelic (commonly referred to as "Irish") if you venture to the western fringe of the country. The Irish love of conversation shines through wherever you go. All that conversation is helped along by the nebulous concept of Irish time, which never seems to be in short supply. Small shops post their hours as "9:00ish until 5:00ish." The local bus usually makes a stop at "10:30ish." A healthy disdain for being a slave to the clock seems to be part of being Ir-"ish."

And the warm welcome you'll receive has its roots in ancient Celtic laws of hospitality toward stranded strangers. You'll see *"Céad míle fáilte"* in tourism brochures and postcards throughout Ireland—it translates as "a hundred thousand welcomes."

Still, aspects of modern life continue to make inroads in traditional Ireland. In 2003, shops began charging customers for plastic sacks for carrying goods (the surcharge is currently €0.22), which has cut down on litter. In 2004, smoking was banned in all Irish workplaces (including pubs). The Irish were the first nation in the world to enact such a comprehensive law. In the past decade, the Irish Department of Health has reported a 30 percent reduction in strokes and a 25 percent reduction in heart disease. Tourism is up as well. Now other nations are following the Irish lead. Some pubkeepers initially grumbled about lost business, but the air has cleared. Keeping up this progressive trend, in 2015 Ireland became the first country in the world to legalize marriage equality by popular vote (with a resounding 62 percent voting yes).

Time marches on for the Irish government as well. In 2013, the Irish people voted (by a thin 52 percent majority) not to abolish their 90-year-old Senate (Seanad; SHAN-ud), the upper house of the Irish Parliament. The Irish government itself had proposed this revolutionary solution to economic hard times, saying that it would have saved taxpayers €20 million per year. But opponents of the referendum said the Senate was necessary as a watchdog to hold cabinet ministers accountable.

RTE: The Voice of Ireland

Many a long drive or rainy evening has been saved by the engaging programs I've happened upon on RTE: Raidió Teilifís Éireann. What the BBC is to Britain, RTE is to Ireland: This government-owned company and national public broadcaster produces and broadcasts a wide range of programs on television, radio, and online. Look for it as you travel (via RTE's smartphone apps, on the radio in your car, or on TV at your B&B).

First hitting the airwaves on New Year's Eve 1961, today's RTE TV broadcasts are all digital and in the English language on RTE channels 1 and 2. But don't shy away from channel 4 (TG4), with Irish language TV shows subtitled in English—it's a great way to get a feel for the sound of the language. You couldn't find a richer or more accessible introduction to Irish culture.

Got a serious appetite for all things Irish? Online at www.rte.ie/archives, you'll find a treasure trove of fascinating archived RTE programs—everything from coverage of JFK's 1963 visit, to elderly recollections of the 1916 Uprising, to the poetry of Seamus Heaney, to Gaelic sports.

You can't drive too far without running into road construction, as the recently affluent Irish (for a dozen years flush with Celtic Tiger money) try to cope with more cars crowding their streets (three times as many as during my first visit almost 40 years ago). Unlike the old days, Dad isn't the only one with a car; now Mom and the eldest teen are on the road too...just like in the States. New motorways are making travel between bigger cities faster. But the country is still laced with plenty of humble country lanes with diabolically confusing street signs, perfect for getting scenically lost.

At first glance, Ireland's landscape seems unspectacular, with

few mountains higher than 3,000 feet and an interior consisting of grazing pastures and peat bogs. But its seductive beauty slowly grows on you. The gentle rainfall, called "soft weather" by the locals, really does create 40 shades of green—and quite a few rainbows as well. Ancient, moss-covered ring forts crouch in lush valleys, while stone-strewn monastic ruins and lone castle turrets brave the wind on nearby hilltops. Charming fishing villages dot the coast near rugged, wave-battered cliffs. Slow down to contemplate the checkerboard patterns created by the rock walls outlining the many fields. Examine the colorful small-town shop fronts that proudly state the name of the proprietor. Explore the laid-back concept of Irish time...but don't rush into it.

The resilient Irish character was born of dark humor, historical reverence, and a scrappy, "we'll get 'em next time" rebel spirit. The influence of the Catholic Church is less apparent these days, as 30 percent of Irish weddings are now civil ceremonies, and weekly church attendance in Ireland is below the US average. But the Church still plays a part in Irish life. The average Irish family spends almost €500 on celebrations for each of their children's first communions. And the national radio and TV station, RTE, pauses for 30 seconds at noon and at 18:00 to broadcast the chimes of the Angelus bells—signaling the start of Catholic devotional prayers. The Irish say that if you're phoning heaven, it's a long-distance call from the rest of the world, but a local call from Ireland.

DUBLIN

With reminders of its stirring history and rich culture on every corner, Ireland's capital and largest city is a sightseer's delight. Dublin holds its own above its weight class in arts, entertainment, food, and fun. Dublin's fair city will have you humming, "Cockles and mussels, alive, alive-O."

Founded as a Viking trading settlement in the ninth century, Dublin grew to be a center of wealth and commerce, second only to London in the British Empire. Dublin, the seat of English rule in Ireland for 750 years, was the heart of a "civilized" Anglo-Irish area (eastern Ireland) known as "the Pale." Anything "beyond the Pale" was considered uncultured and almost barbaric...purely Irish.

The Golden Age of English Dublin was the 18th century. The British Empire was on a roll, and the city was right there with it. Largely rebuilt during this Georgian era, Dublin—even with its tattered edges—became an elegant and cultured capital.

Those glory days left a lasting imprint on the city. Squares and boulevards built in the Georgian style give the city an air of grandeur ("Georgian" is British for Neoclassical...named for the period when four consecutive King Georges occupied the British throne from 1714 to 1830). The National Museum, the National Gallery, and many government buildings are in the Georgian section of town. Few buildings (notably Christ Church and St. Patrick's cathedrals) survive from before this Georgian period.

But nationalism—and a realization of the importance of human rights—would forever change Dublin. The American and French revolutions inspired Irish intellectuals to buck British rule, and life in Dublin was never quite the same after the Rebellion of 1798. In 1801, the Act of Union with Britain resulted in the loss of Ireland's parliament (no need for two with the dominant one in London). As the Irish members of parliament moved to Westminster, the movers and shakers of the Anglo-Irish aristocracy followed suit, and Dublin slowly began to decay.

Throughout the 19th century, as Ireland endured the Great Potato Famine and saw the beginnings of the modern struggle for independence, Dublin was treated—and felt—more like a British colony than a partner. The tension culminated in the Easter Uprising of 1916, followed by a successful guerilla war of independence against Britain and Ireland's tragic civil war. With many of its grand streets in ruins, Dublin emerged as the capital of the British Empire's only former colony in Europe.

While bullet-pocked buildings and dramatic statues keep memories of Ireland's struggle for independence alive, the city is looking ahead to a brighter future. Dubliners are energetic and helpful, while visitors enjoy a big-town cultural scene wrapped in a small-town smile.

PLANNING YOUR TIME

This bustling city is a must for travelers interested in Celtic/Viking artifacts, Irish literature, or rebel history. If that's not you, head for the charm of smaller towns. For most people, Dublin deserves three nights and two days.

Be aware that some important sights close on Mondays. Consider this ambitious sightseeing plan:

Day 1

10:15   Take the Trinity College guided walk.

11:00   Visit the Book of Kells and Old Trinity Library ahead of midday crowds.

12:00   Browse Grafton Street, have lunch there or picnic on St. Stephen's Green.

13:30   Head to the National Museum: Archaeology branch (closed Mon).

15:00   See Number Twenty-Nine Georgian House (closed Sun-Mon).

17:00   Return to hotel, rest, have dinner—eat well for less during early-bird specials.

19:30   Go for an evening guided pub tour (musical or literary).

22:00   Drop in on Irish music in the Temple Bar area.

Day 2

10:00   Take the Dublin Castle tour.

11:30   Hop on one of the hop-on, hop-off buses, jumping off to see the Guinness Storehouse and Kilmainham

Gaol (bring a sandwich to munch in transit on the open-top bus, or stop off to picnic in one of Dublin's green squares).

15:00   Leave the bus at Parnell Square, visit the Garden of Remembrance, and stroll down to O'Connell Bridge, sightseeing and shopping as you like along the way.

Evening   Catch a play or concert—or try the storytelling dinner at The Brazen Head.

With More Time: Dublin, while relatively small, can keep you busily sightseeing for days without even leaving the center of town. And with all its music, theater, and after-hours tours—not to mention the lively pub scene—evenings are just as fun.

Orientation to Dublin

Greater Dublin sprawls with 1.3 million people—more than a quarter of the country's population. But the center of tourist in-terest is a tight triangle between O'Connell Bridge, St. Stephen's Green, and Christ Church Cathe-dral. Within or near this triangle, you'll find Trinity College (Book of Kells), a cluster of major muse-ums (including the top choice, the National Museum: Archaeology branch), Grafton Street (top pe-destrian shopping zone), Temple  Bar (trendy and touristy nightlife center), Dublin Castle, and the hub of most city tours and buses. The only major sights outside this easy-to-walk triangle are the General Post Office, Kilmain-ham Gaol, the Guinness Storehouse, and the National Museum: Decorative Arts and History branch at Collins Barracks (all west or north of the center).

The River Liffey cuts the town in two. Focus on the southern half, where most of your sightseeing will take place. Dublin's wide main drag, O'Connell Street, starts north of the river at the Parnell Monument and runs south, down to the central O'Connell Bridge. After crossing the bridge, this major city axis changes its name to Westmoreland and continues south, past Trinity College and through pedestrian-only Grafton Street to St. Stephen's Green.

Get used to the fact that many long Dublin streets change their names every few blocks. A prime example of this: the numer-ously named quays (pronounced "keys") that run east-west along the River Liffey.

The suburban port of Dun Laoghaire (dun LEERY) lies south of Dublin, 25 minutes away by DART commuter train. Travelers looking for a mellow town to sleep in outside of urban Dublin can easily home-base here. Another option is the northern suburb of Howth, also 25 minutes away on DART and closer to the airport. Room prices are about one-quarter cheaper in Dun Laoghaire or Howth than in downtown Dublin.

TOURIST INFORMATION

Dublin's **main TI** is a thriving hub, with knowledgeable staffers doling out the lowdown on city offerings and brochures for destinations throughout Ireland (Mon-Sat 9:00-17:30, Sun 10:30-15:00, a block off Grafton Street at 25 Suffolk Street, tel. 01/884-7700, www.visitdublin.com).

A smaller satellite TI, less busy but equally helpful, is halfway down the east side of **O'Connell Street** (Mon-Sat 9:00-17:00, closed Sun). There's another TI at the **airport** (daily 8:00-20:00, Terminal 2).

Note that these are the only branches of Ireland's national tourist service in Dublin, called Fáilte Ireland. These authentic TIs are not allowed to sell anything—watch out for other shops that claim to be TIs, especially on O'Connell Street, aiming to sell you tours and collect commissions.

Dublin Pass: This sightseeing pass is a good deal only if you like to visit lots of sights quickly (€49/1 day, €69/2 days, €79/3 days, €99/5 days, purchase online and collect at TIs, www.dublinpass.ie). It covers 33 museums, churches, literature-related sights, and expensive stops such as the Guinness Storehouse (€20) and the Old Jameson Distillery (€16), plus the Aircoach airport bus (€7)—one-way from the airport to the city only (doesn't cover Airlink buses). For a day at Guinness and Old Jameson connected by the City Sightseeing bus, you would save €6 with this pass—and save a few minutes when you'd otherwise need to wait in line to buy a ticket. The pass doesn't include the famous Book of Kells at Trinity College.

Maps: At any TI, you can pick up *The Guide*, which includes a decent city map (free). Inside is a minimal schedule of happenings in town. The excellent *Collins Illustrated Discovering Dublin Map* (€7.50 at bookstores and newsstands) is the ultimate city map, listing just about everything of interest, along with helpful opinions and tidbits of Dublin history. The best free city map can be found at the Kilkenny Shop at 6 Nassau Street (bordering the south side of the Trinity College campus).

ARRIVAL IN DUBLIN
By Train

Dublin has two train stations. **Heuston Station,** on the west end of town, serves west and southwest Ireland (45-minute walk from O'Connell Bridge; take the LUAS light rail or bus #90—see

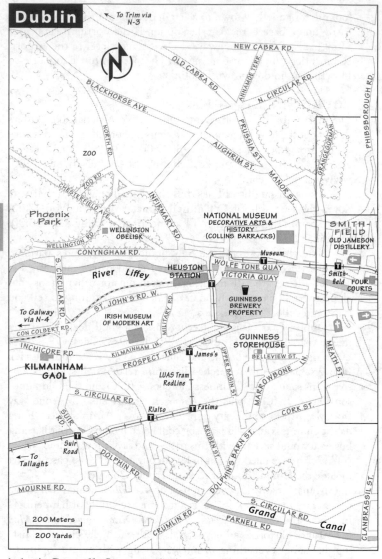

below). **Connolly Station,** which serves the north, northwest, and Rosslare, is closer to the center (15-minute walk from O'Connell Bridge). Each station has ATMs, but no lockers.

The two train stations are connected by the red line of the LUAS light-rail system (see "Getting Around Dublin" on page 31) and by bus. Bus #90 runs along the river, linking the train stations, bus station, and city center (€2, 6/hour).

To reach Heuston Station from the city center, catch bus #90 on the south side of the river; to get to Connolly Station and

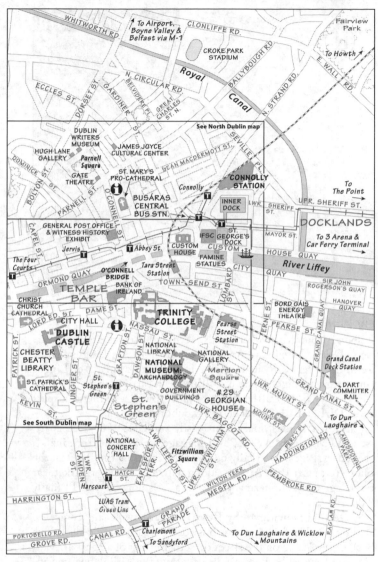

Busáras Central Bus Station from the city center, catch #90 on the north side of the river.

By Bus

Bus Éireann, Ireland's national bus company, uses the **Busáras Central Bus Station** (pronounced bu-SAUR-us...like a dinosaur). Located next to Connolly Station, it's a 10-minute walk or a short ride on bus #90 (described above) to the city center.

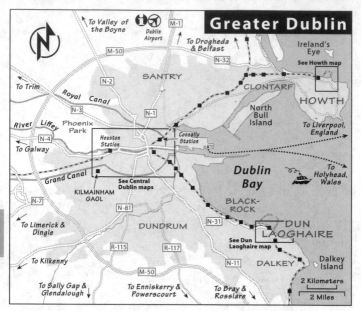

By Plane

Dublin Airport has two terminals. Terminal 2 serves American carriers (Delta, United, and American), plus most Aer Lingus flights. Terminal 1 serves Ryanair, Aer Arann, Air Canada, Aer Lingus (some regional flights), and most European carriers, including British Airways, SAS, Lufthansa, Air France, Swiss, and Iberia (airport code: DUB, tel. 01/814-1111, www.dublinairport.ie).

Both terminals, located an easily walkable 150 yards apart, have ATMs, cafés, Wi-Fi, and luggage storage. At Terminal 1, the left-luggage office (daily 6:00-23:00) is across the street in the Short-Term Car Park Atrium, along with a small supermarket, car rental agency, and pharmacy. Terminal 2 is home to the TI (daily 8:00-20:00).

Getting Downtown by Bus: You have two main choices—Airlink (double-decker green bus) or Aircoach (single-deck blue bus). Both pick up on the street directly in front of airport arrivals, at ground level at both terminals. If taking the Airlink bus, consider getting a Leap Visitor Card, which covers the journey (only the Dublin Pass sightseeing pass covers the Aircoach); for pass info, see page 32. Read the following description first to make sure Airlink is the best choice for your trip.

Airlink: Airlink bus #747 stops at both airport terminals, linking the airport to the city center along a strip a few blocks north and south of the river. This bus generally runs an east-west route that parallels the River Liffey, and includes the Busáras Central

Bus Station, Connolly Station, O'Connell Street, Trinity College, Christ Church, and Heuston Station. Ask the driver which stop is closest to your hotel (€6, pay driver; 3/hour, 35-45 minutes; runs Mon-Sat 5:00-late, Sun from 7:00; tel. 01/873-4222, www.dublinbus.ie).

Aircoach: This bus generally runs a north-south route that follows the O'Connell and Grafton Streets axis. To reach recommended hotels near St. Stephen's Green (south of the city center), the Aircoach bus is best (€7 if paying driver, €6 if booked online, covered by Dublin Pass, 3/hour except fewer late-night, runs 24 hours, tel. 01/844-7118, www.aircoach.ie).

Getting to Dun Laoghaire by Bus: The best way to get to Dun Laoghaire is to take the **Aircoach** bus. See page 99.

Taking a Taxi: Taxis from the airport into Dublin cost about €30; to Dun Laoghaire, about €40; to Howth, about €25 (see "Getting Around Dublin—By Taxi" on page 32).

By Ferry

Coming from the UK, you have two choices. **Irish Ferries** and **Stena Line** both have four sailings per day in summer (possibly less off-season) arriving at Dublin Port at the mouth of the River Liffey, two miles east of the town center. For more information, see "Dublin Connections" on page 95.

By Car

Trust me: You don't want to drive in downtown Dublin. Cars are unnecessary for sightseeing in town, parking is expensive (up to €25/day), and traffic will get your fighting Irish up. Save your car-rental days for cross-country travel between smaller towns and see this energetic city by taxi, bus, or on foot.

If you have a car, sleep out in the suburbs (Dun Laoghaire or Howth), and ask your innkeeper about the best places to park. In central Dublin, a good option is QPark on Werburgh Street behind Jurys Inn Christ Church (€2/hour, €15/day, 01/454-9001).

Drivers renting a car at Dublin Airport but not staying in Dun Laoghaire or Howth can bypass the worst of the big-city traffic by taking the M-50 ring road south or west.

Toll Roads: The M-50 uses an automatic tolling system called eFlow. Your rented car should come with an eFlow tag installed; confirm this when you pick up your car at the airport. The €3.10 toll per trip is automatically debited from the credit card that you used to rent the car (for pass details, see www.eflow.ie).

Your rental car's eFlow tag will work automatically only for the M-50 ring road that circles urban Dublin. On any other Irish toll roads, you'll have to pay with cash (under €3). These roads mostly run outward from Dublin toward Waterford, Cork, Limerick, and

DUBLIN

Galway (roads farther west are free). Toll motorways are usually blue on maps and are shown with the letter "M" followed by the route number (toll info and map: www.tii.ie).

HELPFUL HINTS
Exchange Rate: €1 = about $1.10
Country Calling Code: 353 (see page 530 for dialing instructions)
High Costs: Despite the demise of the Celtic Tiger economic boom (1995-2007—R.I.P.), Ireland is still one of the EU's more expensive countries. Restaurants and lodging—other than hostels—are more expensive the closer you get to the touristy Temple Bar district (see cheaper options under "Sleeping in Dublin" on page 83).
Pickpockets: Irish destinations, especially Dublin, are not immune to this scourge. Wear a money belt or risk spending a couple of days of your cherished vacation in bureaucratic purgatory—on the phone canceling credit cards (see page 504) and at the embassy waiting for a replacement passport. Wasting vacation time this way is like paying to wait in line at the DMV.
Festivals: Book ahead during festivals and for any weekend. St. Patrick's Day is a four-day March extravaganza in Dublin (www.stpatricksday.ie). June 16 is Bloomsday, dedicated to the Irish author James Joyce and featuring the Messenger Bike Rally (www.jamesjoyce.ie). Hotels raise their prices and are packed on rugby weekends (about four per year), during the all-Ireland Gaelic football and hurling finals (Sundays in September), and during summer rock concerts.
Meet a Dubliner: The **City of a Thousand Welcomes** offers a free service that brings together volunteers and first-time visitors for a cup of tea or a pint. Visitors sign up online in advance, pick an available time slot, and meet their Dublin "ambassador" at the Little Museum of Dublin on St. Stephen's Green. You'll head for a nearby tearoom or pub and enjoy a short, informal conversation to get you oriented to the city (free, must be at least 21, 15 St. Stephens Green, tel. 01/661-1000, mobile 087-131-7129, www.cityofathousandwelcomes.com).
Bookstores: The giant granddaddy of them all is **Eason**'s, five minutes north of the O'Connell Bridge (Mon-Sat 8:00-19:00, Sun 12:00-18:00, 40 O'Connell Street Lower, tel. 01/858-3800).
Laundry: Krystal Launderette, a block southwest of Jurys Inn Christ Church on Patrick Street, is full-service only. Allow six hours and about €12 per load (Mon-Sat 8:00-20:00, Sun 12:00-17:00, tel. 01/454-6864). The **All-American Launderette** offers self- and full-service options (€11/load full-ser-

vice, Mon-Sat 8:30-19:00, Sun 10:00-18:00, 40 South Great George's Street, tel. 01/677-2779).

Bike Rental: Phoenix Park Bike Hire offers a stress-free ride option in huge, 1,750-acre Phoenix Park. It's located off Chesterfield Avenue, the main road bisecting the park, at the closest corner of the park to the city center, roughly across the river from Heuston Station (€5/2 hours, €8/4 hours, €10/day, daily 10:00-19:00 "weather depending," mobile 086-265-6258, www.phoenixparkbikehire.com).

Car Rental: Consider renting a car as you leave Dublin for other points in Ireland. It's best to avoid driving in hectic central Dublin—rent your car at the airport instead. Agencies with locations in town and at the airport include **Avis** (35 Old Kilmainham Road, tel. 021/428-1111, airport tel. 01/605-7500, www.avis.ie), **Hertz** (151 South Circular Road, tel. 01/676-7476, airport tel. 01/844-5466, www.hertz.ie), **Budget** (151 Lower Drumcondra Road, tel. 01/837-9611, central reservations tel. 09066/27711, airport tel. 01/844-5150, www.budget.ie), and **Europcar** (2 Haddington Road, tel. 01/614-2888, airport tel. 01/812-0410, www.europcar.ie).

GETTING AROUND DUBLIN

You'll do most of Dublin on foot, though when you need public transportation, you'll find it readily available and easy to use. With a little planning, sightseers can make excellent use of a two-day hop-on, hop-off bus ticket to link the best sights (see page 37).

By Bus: Public buses are cheap and cover the city thoroughly. Most lines start at the four quays, or piers, that are nearest O'Connell Bridge. If you're away from the center, nearly any bus takes you back downtown. Some bus stops are "request only" stops: Be alert to the bus numbers (above the windshield) of approaching buses. When you see your bus coming, hold your arm out from your side with your palm extended into the street to flag it down. Tell the driver where you're going, and he'll ask for €2-3.30 depending on the number of stops. Bring change or lose any excess. Bus #90 connects the bus and train stations (see "Arrival in Dublin—By Train," earlier).

By DART (Train): Speedy commuter trains run along the coast, connecting Dublin with Dun Laoghaire (south of city), Howth's harbor (north of city), and recommended B&Bs. Think of the DART line as a giant "C" that serves coastal suburbs from Bray in the south to Howth in the north (€3.25, €6.15 round-trips valid same day only, Eurail Pass valid if you use a counted flexi-day, tel. 01/703-3504, www.irishrail.ie/home). For more information, see "Getting to Dun Laoghaire" on page 99 and "Getting to Howth" on page 103.

By LUAS (Light Rail): The city's light-rail system has two main lines (red and green) that serve inland suburbs. The more useful line for tourists is the red line, with an east-west section connecting the Heuston and Connolly train stations (a 15-minute ride apart) at opposite edges of the Central 1 Zone. In between, the Busáras Central Bus Station, Smithfield, and Museum stops can be handy (€1.90, buy at machine before boarding, 6/hour, runs 5:30-24:45, tel. 1-800-300-604, www.luas.ie). Check the 15-foot-high pillars at each boarding platform that display the time and destination of the next LUAS train. Make sure you're on the right platform for the direction you want to go.

Transit Cards: The refillable plastic **Leap Card** can be loaded with credit for single transit trips or a bus pass such as the Rambler Pass (see below). Regular Leap Cards are sold at TIs, newsstands, and markets citywide (mostly Centra, Mace, Spar, and Londis)—look for the leaping-frog logo (€5 refundable deposit, www.leapcard.ie).

For those staying in Dun Laoghaire or Howth—or on a long-term stay in Dublin—the special **Leap Visitor Card** may be a better option. It enables unlimited travel on Dublin's buses (including Airlink), DART, commuter rail, and LUAS trams (€10/1 day, €19.50/3 days, €40/7 days, each "day" equals 24 hours from first use, http://about.leapcard.ie/leap-visitor-card). Leap Visitor Cards are available only at the airport's transportation desk and TI, and at a few locations in the city center including the bus office listed below.

The bus office at 59 O'Connell Street Upper has free bus-route maps, and sells the Leap Card and two passes that can be loaded onto the card (Mon 8:30-17:30, Tue-Fri 9:00-17:30, Sat 9:00-14:00, Sun 9:30-14:00, tel. 01/873-4222, www.dublinbus.ie). The **Rambler Pass** (€30.60/5 days) is handiest for a longer stay, and covers the Airlink airport bus (but not Aircoach buses or DART trains). The **Freedom Pass** (€33/3 days) covers city bus, Airlink, and the hop-on, hop-off Dublin Bus Tour (green buses), but not DART trains—the 3-day Leap Visitor Card is usually a better deal. Be sure to confirm what you are purchasing; some passes may change or be unavailable in 2017.

By Taxi: Taxis are everywhere and easy to hail (cheaper for 3-4 people). Cabbies are generally honest, friendly, and good sources of information (€3.60 daytime minimum 8:00-20:00, €4 nighttime minimum 20:00-8:00, €1/each additional adult, figure about €10-12 for most crosstown rides, €40/hour for guided joyride).

Tours in Dublin

While Dublin's physical treasures are lackluster by European standards, the gritty city has a fine story to tell and people with a natural knack for telling it. It's a good town for walking tours, and competition is fierce. Pamphlets touting creative walks are posted all over town. Choices include medieval walks, literary walks, Georgian Dublin walks, and traditional music pub crawls. Taking an evening walk is a great way to meet other travelers. The Dublin TI also offers a variety of free, good-quality "Dublin Discovery Trails" audio tours for travelers with smartphones (download via Apple's App Store or Google Play).

For help finding the departure points of the following recommended tours, see the map on page 46.

DUBLIN

ON FOOT
▲▲Historical Walking Tour
This is your best introductory walk. A group of hardworking history graduates—many of whom claim to have done more than just kiss the Blarney Stone—enliven Dublin's basic historic strip (Trinity College, Old Parliament House, Dublin Castle, and Christ Church Cathedral). You'll get the story of their city, from its Viking origins to the present. Guides speak at length about the roots of Ireland's struggle with Britain. As you listen to your guide, you'll stand in front of buildings that aren't much to look at, but are lots to talk about (May-Sept daily at 11:00 and 15:00, April and Oct daily at 11:00, Nov-March Fri-Sun only at 11:00). All walks last two hours and cost €12 (get the €10 "student" discount rate with this book in 2017, free for kids under 14, departs from front gate of Trinity College, private tours available, mobile 087-688-9412 or 087-830-3523, www.historicalinsights.ie).

▲▲▲Traditional Irish Musical Pub Crawl
This impressive and entertaining tour visits the upstairs rooms of three pubs; there, you'll listen to two musicians talk about, play,  and sing traditional Irish music. While having only two musicians makes the music a bit thin (Irish music aficionados will say you're better off just finding a good session), the evening—though touristy—is not gimmicky. It's an education in traditional Irish music. The musicians clearly enjoy introducing rookies to their art and are very good at it. Humor is their primary educational tool. In the summer, this popular tour frequently sells out. It's easy to reserve ahead online (€13, €1 discount with this book in 2017—use

Dublin at a Glance

▲▲▲Traditional Irish Musical Pub Crawl A fascinating, practical, and enjoyable primer on traditional Irish music. **Hours:** April-Oct daily at 19:30, Nov-March Thu-Sat only. See page 33.

▲▲▲National Museum: Archaeology Interesting collection of Irish treasures from the Stone Age to today. **Hours:** Tue-Sat 10:00-17:00, Sun 14:00-17:00, closed Mon. See page 49.

▲▲▲Kilmainham Gaol Historic jail used by the British as a political prison—today a museum that tells a moving story of the suffering of the Irish people. **Hours:** Daily 9:30-16:30. See page 75.

▲▲Historical Walking Tour Your best introduction to Dublin. **Hours:** May-Sept daily at 11:00 and 15:00, April and Oct daily at 11:00, Nov-March Fri-Sun only at 11:00. See page 33.

▲▲Trinity College Tour Ireland's most famous school, best visited with a 30-minute tour led by one of its students. **Hours:** Departs every 30 minutes May-Sept daily 10:15-15:00, Feb-April and Oct-Nov Sat-Sun only, no tours Dec-Jan; weather permitting. See page 44.

▲▲Book of Kells in the Trinity Old Library An exquisite illuminated manuscript, the most important piece of art from the Dark Ages. **Hours:** Mon-Sat 9:30-17:00, Sun until 16:30, except Sun 12:00-16:30 Oct-April. See page 45.

▲▲Grafton Street The city's liveliest pedestrian shopping mall. **Hours:** Always open. See page 58.

▲▲Dublin Castle The city's historic 700-year-old castle, featuring ornate English state apartments, tourable only with a guide. **Hours:** Mon-Sat 10:00-16:45, Sun 12:00-16:45. See page 59.

▲▲Chester Beatty Library American expatriate's eclectic yet sumptuous collection of literary and religious treasures from Islam, the Orient, and medieval Europe. **Hours:** Mon-Fri 10:00-17:00, Sat 11:00-17:00, Sun 13:00-17:00; closed Mon Oct-April. See page 60.

▲▲Temple Bar Dublin's rowdiest neighborhood, with shops, cafés, theaters, galleries, pubs, and restaurants—a great spot for live traditional music. **Hours:** Always open. See page 65.

▲▲O'Connell Bridge Landmark bridge spanning the River Liffey at the center of Dublin. **Hours:** Always open. See page 39.

▲▲O'Connell Street Dublin's grandest promenade and main drag, packed with history and ideal for a stroll. **Hours:** Always open. See page 39.

▲**Number Twenty-Nine Georgian House** Restored 18th-century house; tours provide an intimate glimpse of middle-class Georgian life. **Hours:** Mid-Feb-mid-Dec Tue-Sat 10:00-17:00, closed Sun-Mon, closed mid-Dec-mid-Feb. See page 58.

▲**National Gallery** Fine collection of top Irish painters and European masters. **Hours:** Mon-Sat 9:30-17:30, Thu until 20:30, Sun 11:00-17:30. See page 56.

▲**Merrion Square** Enjoyable and inviting park with a fun statue of Oscar Wilde. **Hours:** Always open. See page 57.

▲**St. Stephen's Green** Relaxing park surrounded by fine Georgian buildings. **Hours:** Always open. See page 58.

▲**Dublinia** A fun, kid-friendly look at Dublin's Viking and medieval past with a side order of archaeology and a cool town model. **Hours:** Daily March-Sept 10:00-18:00, Oct-Feb until 17:30. See page 64.

▲**Dublin Writers Museum** Modest collection of authorial bric-a-brac. **Hours:** Mon-Sat 10:00-17:00, Sun 11:00-17:00. See page 66.

▲**Hugh Lane Gallery** Modern and contemporary art, starring Monet, Bacon, and Irish artists. **Hours:** Tue-Thu 10:00-18:00, Fri-Sat 10:00-17:00, Sun 11:00-17:00, closed Mon. See page 70.

▲**GPO Witness History Exhibit** Immersive presentation on the 1916 Easter Uprising and its impact on Irish history, situated in the building that served as the rebel headquarters. **Hours:** Daily 9:30-17:00. See page 72.

▲**Guinness Storehouse** The home of Ireland's national beer, with a museum of beer-making, a gallery of clever ads, and Gravity Bar with panoramic city views. **Hours:** Daily 9:30-17:00, July-Aug until 18:00. See page 75.

▲**National Museum: Decorative Arts and History** Shows off Irish dress, furniture, silver, and weaponry with a special focus on the 1916 rebellion, fight for independence, and civil war. **Hours:** Tue-Sat 10:00-17:00, Sun 14:00-17:00, closed Mon. See page 77.

▲**Gaelic Athletic Association Museum** High-tech museum of traditional Gaelic sports such as hurling and Irish football. **Hours:** Mon-Sat 9:30-17:00, Sun 10:30-17:00, June-Aug until 18:00. On game Sundays, it's open to ticket holders only. See page 78.

DUBLIN

code RSIRISH, beer extra, allow 2.5 hours, April-Oct daily at 19:30, Nov-March Thu-Sat only, maximum 50 people, meet upstairs at Gogarty's Pub at the corner of Fleet and Anglesea in the Temple Bar area, tel. 01/475-3313, www.musicalpubcrawl.com).

▲Dublin Literary Pub Crawl

Two actors take 40 or so tourists on a walk, stopping at four pubs. Their clever banter introduces the novice to the high *craic* of James Joyce, Seán O'Casey, and W. B. Yeats. The two-hour tour is punctuated with 20-minute pub breaks (free time). While the beer lubricates the social fun, it dilutes the content of the evening. (If you want straight lit and drama, find a real performance; there are many throughout the summer, such as the lunchtime hour on weekends at 13:00 at the Dublin Writers Museum, described on page 66.) However, the pub crawl is an easygoing excuse to drink beer in busy pubs, hook up with other travelers, and get a dose of Irish witty lit (€13, April-Oct daily at 19:30, Nov-March Thu-Sun only; you can normally just show up, but call ahead in July-Aug when it can fill up; meet upstairs in the Duke Pub—off Grafton on Duke Street, tel. 01/670-5602, mobile 087-263-0270, www.dublinpubcrawl.com). Connoisseurs of Irish pubs will want to buy the excellent *Dublin Literary Pub Crawl* guidebook by pub-crawl founder Colm Quilligan.

1916 Rebellion Walking Tour

This two-hour walk breathes gritty life into the most turbulent year in modern Irish history, when idealistic Irish rebels launched the Easter Uprising—eventually leading to independence from Britain (2016 was the 100th anniversary). Guide Lorcan Collins has written a guidebook called *The Easter Rising*—worth seeking out—and is passionate about his walks (€13, €2 discount with this book in 2017, March-Oct Mon-Sat at 11:30, Sun at 13:00, no tours Nov-Feb, departs from International Bar at 23 Wicklow Street, mobile 086-858-3847, www.1916rising.com).

Pat Liddy's Walking Tours

Pat Liddy is one of Dublin's top historians. He and his guides take groups on enthusiastic and informal two-hour walks of hidden Dublin districts. Unlike most Dublin walks, this one does a good job of covering the often overlooked but historic north side of town. His "Highlights and Hidden Corners" tour starts near the General Post Office building, winds down across the river to City Hall, through Temple Bar, and ends at Trinity College (€12, April-Oct daily at 11:00, fewer off-season, meet in front of Dublin Bus Office at 59 O'Connell Street Upper, tel. 01/832-9406, mobile 087-905-2480, www.walkingtours.ie).

Local Guide

Proud Dubliner Joe Darcy is a friendly and knowledgeable guy with a passion for Irish literature, who enjoys unpeeling the urban layers of his hometown for visitors—when he's not on the road leading Rick Steves tours (mobile 086-218-0357, www.darcysdublinwalks. com, josdarcy@gmail.com).

BY BIKE
Dublin City Bike Tours

You'll "get your *craic* on a saddle" with Dublin City Bike Tours as you pedal across this flat city on innovative urban bikes. Their fun tours visit 20 points of interest north and south of the River Liffey, covering more ground (five miles) than walking tours. Designed for riders of average fitness, they set a casual pace, and rarely let a little rain stop them (€24 includes bike, helmet, snack, and water; €4 discount with this book—show when you pay; cash only, reserve in advance, 2.5 hours; March-Nov daily at 10:00, additional tours Fri and Sat at 14:00; custom tours available for groups of 8 or more; departs Isaac's Hostel a half-block west of Busáras Central Bus Station at 2 Frenchman's Lane, mobile 087-134-1866, www. dublincitybiketours.com).

Lazy Bike Tour Company

For a less strenuous option, you can grab a bright orange electric bike and matching vest, and buzz along on a guided tour that covers sights from Dublin Castle to Kilmainham Gaol. Tours start in Temple Bar and last two hours (€25, daily at 10:00, 12:30, and 15:00; wise to book in advance during the summer; meet at 4 Scarlet Row on Essex Street West in Temple Bar near Christ Church Cathedral, 01/443-3671, www.lazybiketours.com).

BY BUS (ON LAND AND WATER)
▲Hop-on, Hop-off Bus Tours

Three companies (Dublin Bus Tour, City Sightseeing Dublin, and Dublin CityScape) offer hop-on, hop-off bus tours of Dublin. They

all do similar 1.5-hour circuits of up to 30 stops, with buses circling every 10-15 minutes daily from 9:00 to 17:00, and usually later in the summer. Buses are double-deckers (roofless is fun on dry days), with live running commentaries. This type of tour is made-to-order for Dublin, and buses run so frequently that they make your sightseeing super-efficient. Stops include the far-flung Guinness Storehouse and Kilmainham Gaol. Each company's map, free with your ticket, details various discounts that you'll get at Dublin's sights (such as the Guinness Storehouse, Viking Splash tour, Old Jameson Distillery, Dublin Writers Museum, Dublinia, Christ Church Cathedral, and others). To take advantage of the discounts, take a bus tour before you do all your sightseeing.

Dublin Bus Tour (green buses) drivers provide fun and quirky narration, and your ticket includes free entry into the Little Museum of Dublin and a free walking tour from Pat Liddy's Walking Tours (€19/24 hours, €22/48 hours, two kids under 14 ride free with every adult, tel. 01/703-3028, www.dublinsightseeing.ie). **City Sightseeing Dublin** (red buses) has a handy "blue route" that takes you as far as Glasnevin Cemetery and Croke Park, and offers €1 off the Guinness Storehouse and Old Jameson Distillery (€19/24 hours, €22/48 hours, two kids under 12 ride free with every adult, tel. 01/898-0700, https://citysightseeingdublin.ie). **Dublin CityScape** (yellow buses) offers three routes and a €1 discount to the Guinness Storehouse (€10/24 hours, €18/72 hours, two kids under 16 ride free with every adult, tel. 01/465-9972, http://cityscapetours. ie). Look for online discounts.

▲Viking Splash Tours

If you'd like to ride in a WWII amphibious vehicle—driven by a Viking-costumed guide who's as liable to spout history as he is to growl—this is for you. The tour starts with a group roar from the Viking within us all. At first, the guide talks as if he were a Viking ("When we came here in 841..."), but soon the patriot emerges as he tags Irish history onto the sights you pass. Near the end of the 1.25-hour tour (punctuated by occasional group roars at passersby), you don a life jacket for a slow spin up and down a boring canal. The covered boat is breezy—dress appropriately. Kids who expect a Viking splash may feel like they've been trapped in a classroom, while historians will enjoy the talk more than the gimmick (€22, Feb-Nov daily 10:00-17:00, no tours Dec-Jan, departs about hourly from the north side of St. Stephen's Green opposite Dawson Street, buy ticket from driver, tel. 01/707-6000, www.vikingsplash.com).

TOUR PACKAGES FOR STUDENTS

Andy Steves (Rick's son) runs **Weekend Student Adventures** (WSA Europe), offering three-day and 10-day budget travel packages across Europe including accommodations, skip-the-line sightseeing, and unique local experiences. Locally guided and DIY unguided options are available for student and budget travelers in 12 of Europe's most popular cities, including Dublin (guided trips from €199, see www.wsaeurope.com for details).

O'Connell Street Stroll

This self-guided walk, worth ▲▲, follows Dublin's grandest street from O'Connell Bridge through the heart of north Dublin. Since the 1740s, it has been a 45-yard-wide promenade, and ever since the first O'Connell Bridge connected it to the Trinity side of town in 1794, it's been Dublin's main drag. (It was named O'Connell only after independence in 1922.) These days, the city has made the street more pedestrian-friendly, and a new LUAS line extension will eventually run within the median. Though lined with fast-food joints and souvenir shops, O'Connell Street echoes with history.

• *Start your walk on the...*

❶ O'Connell Bridge: This bridge, worth ▲▲, spans the River Liffey, which historically has divided the wealthy, cultivated south side of town from the working-class north side. While there's plenty of culture above the river, even today the suburbs (a couple of miles north of the Liffey) are considered rougher and less safe. Dubliners joke that north-side residents are known as "the accused," while residents on the south side are addressed as "your honor."

From the bridge, look upriver (west) as far upstream as you can. On the left in the distance, the **big concrete building**—nicknamed "the bunker" and considered an eyesore by locals—houses the city planning commission. Ironically, it's in charge of new building permits. It squats on the still-buried precious artifacts of the first Viking settlement, established in Dublin in the ninth century. Archaeologists were given minimal time to study the dig before officials paved paradise and put up a parking lot (actually the Dublin City Council offices).

Across the river from that stands the (still distant) green dome of the **Four Courts**—the Supreme Court building. It was shelled and burned in 1922 during the tragic civil war that followed the controversial treaty establishing the Irish Free State. The national archives office burned, and irreplaceable birth records were lost, making it more difficult today for those with Irish roots to trace their ancestry.

The closest bridge upstream—the elegant iron **Ha' Penny Bridge** (see photo on page 66)—leads into the Temple Bar nightlife district. Just beyond that old-fashioned, 19th-century bridge is Dublin's pedestrian **Millennium Bridge,** inaugurated in 2000. (Note that buses leave from O'Connell Bridge—specifically Aston Quay—for the Guinness Storehouse and Kilmainham Gaol.)

Turn 180 degrees and look east downstream to see the tall **Liberty Hall** union headquarters (16 stories tall, some say in honor of the 1916 Easter Uprising). Modern Dublin is developing downstream. During the Celtic Tiger boom, the Irish (always clever tax

DUBLIN

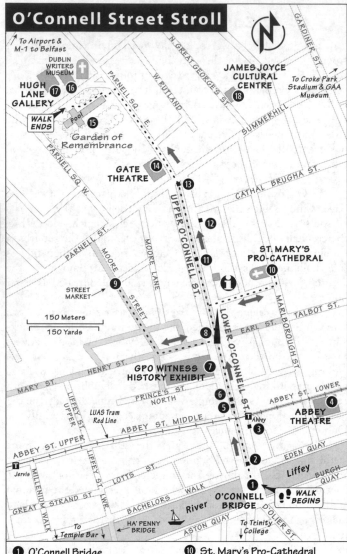

O'Connell Street Stroll

To Airport &
M-1 to Belfast

DUBLIN WRITERS MUSEUM

HUGH LANE GALLERY

WALK ENDS

Pool

Garden of Remembrance

JAMES JOYCE CULTURAL CENTRE

To Croke Park Stadium & GAA Museum

GATE THEATRE

ST. MARY'S PRO-CATHEDRAL

STREET MARKET

150 Meters
150 Yards

GPO WITNESS HISTORY EXHIBIT

LUAS Tram Red Line

ABBEY THEATRE

Abbey

Jervis

Liffey

River

HA'PENNY BRIDGE

To Temple Bar

To Trinity College

O'CONNELL BRIDGE

WALK BEGINS

❶ O'Connell Bridge
❷ Daniel O'Connell Statue
❸ William Smith O'Brien Statue
❹ Abbey Theatre
❺ Sir John Gray Statue
❻ James Larkin Statue
❼ General Post Office & Witness History Exhibit
❽ Millennium Spire
❾ Moore Street Market

❿ St. Mary's Pro-Cathedral
⓫ Father Matthew Statue
⓬ Gresham Hotel
⓭ Charles Stewart Parnell Monument
⓮ Gate Theatre
⓯ Garden of Remembrance
⓰ Dublin Writers Museum
⓱ Hugh Lane Gallery
⓲ James Joyce Cultural Centre

fiddlers) subsidized and revitalized this formerly dreary quarter. A short walk downstream along the north bank leads to a powerful series of gaunt statues memorializing the Great Potato Famine of 1845-1849. Beyond, you'll see the masts of the *Jeanie Johnston,* a replica transport ship (see page 72).

• *Now start north up O'Connell Street, walking on the wide, tree-lined median strip between the lanes of traffic.*

Statues and Monuments: The median is dotted with statues celebrating great figures from Ireland's past—particularly the century (c.1830-1930) when Ireland rediscovered its roots and won its independence. At the base of the street stands the man for whom Dublin's main street is named—❷ **Daniel O'Connell** (1775-1847). He was known as the "Liberator" for founding the Catholic Association and demanding Irish Catholic rights in the British Parliament. He organized thousands of nonviolent protestors into so-called "monster meetings," whose sheer size intimidated the British authorities.

Farther along is ❸ **William Smith O'Brien,** O'Connell's contemporary and leader of the Young Ireland Movement, who was more willing to use force to reach his goals. After a failed uprising in Tipperary, he was imprisoned and exiled to Australia. At Abbey Street, a block detour east leads to the famous ❹ **Abbey Theatre,** where turn-of-the-century nationalists (including the poet-playwright W. B. Yeats) staged Irish-themed plays. The original building suffered a fire and was rebuilt into a nondescript, modern building, but it's still the much-loved home of the Irish National Theatre.

• *Continue up O'Connell Street.*

Look for the statue of ❺ **Sir John Gray,** who, as a newspaperman and politician, was able to help O'Connell's cause. The statue of ❻ **James Larkin,** arms outstretched, honors the founder of the Irish Transport Workers Union.

• *On your left is the...*

❼ **General Post Office (GPO):** This is not just any P.O. It was from here that Patrick Pearse read the Proclamation of Irish Independence in 1916, kicking off the Easter Uprising. The building itself—a kind of Irish Alamo—was the rebel headquarters and scene of a bloody five-day siege that followed the proclamation. The post office was particularly strategic because it housed the telegraph nerve center for the entire country. Its pillars are still pockmarked with bullet holes (open for business and sightseers Mon-Sat 8:00-20:00, closed Sun). The engaging **GPO Witness History Exhibit,** on your right as you enter the GPO, brings the dramatic history of this important building to life (see page 72).

• *Stand at the intersection of O'Connell and Henry streets, at the base of the can't-miss-it...*

❽ **Spire:** There used to be a monument here that didn't wave an Irish flag—a tall column crowned by a statue of the British hero of Trafalgar, Admiral Horatio Nelson. It was blown up in 1966—the IRA's contribution to the local celebration of the Easter Uprising's 50th anniversary. The spot is now occupied by The Spire: 398 feet of stainless steel. While it trumpets rejuvenation on its side of the river, it's a memorial to nothing and has no real meaning. Dubious Dubliners call it the tallest waste of €5 million in all of Europe. Its nickname? Take your pick: the Stiletto in the Ghetto, the Stiffy on the Liffey, the Pole in the Hole, the Poker near the Croker (after nearby Croke Park), or the Spike in the Dike.

• *Detour west (left) down people-filled Henry Street (Dubliners' favorite shopping lane), then wander to the right into the nearby...*

❾ **Moore Street Market:** Many merchants here have staffed the same stalls for decades. Start a conversation. It's a great workaday scene. You'll see lots of mums with strollers—a reminder that Ireland is one of Europe's youngest countries, with more than 35 percent of the population under the age of 25. At the end of the 1916 Easter Uprising, the rebel leaders retreated from the burning post office to the market, where they finally surrendered to British troops (Mon-Sat 8:00-18:00, closed Sun).

• *Return to O'Connell Street. A block east (right) of O'Connell, down Cathedral Street, detour to...*

❿ **St. Mary's Pro-Cathedral:** Although this is Dublin's leading Catholic church, it rather curiously isn't a "cathedral." The pope declared Christ Church to be a cathedral in the 12th century—and later, gave St. Patrick's the same designation. (The Vatican has chosen to stubbornly ignore the fact that Christ Church and St. Patrick's haven't been Catholic for centuries.) Completed in 1821, this Neoclassical church is in the style of a Greek temple.

• *Back on O'Connell Street, head up the street (north) until you find the statue of...*

⓫ **Father Matthew:** A leader of the temperance movement of the 1830s, Father Matthew was responsible, some historians claim, for enough Irish peasants staying sober to enable Daniel O'Connell to organize them into a political force. (Perhaps studying this example, the USSR was careful to keep the price of vodka affordable.)

Nearby, the fancy ⓬ **Gresham Hotel** is a good place for an elegant tea or beer. In an earlier era, the beautiful people alighted

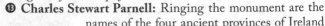

here during visits to Dublin. In the 1960s, Richard Burton and Liz Taylor stayed at the hotel while he was filming *The Spy Who Came in from the Cold*. (In those days, parts of Dublin were drab enough to pass for an Eastern Bloc city.)

• *Standing boldly at the top of O'Connell Street is a monument to...*

⓭ Charles Stewart Parnell: Ringing the monument are the names of the four ancient provinces of Ireland and all 32 Irish counties (including North and South, since this was erected before Irish partition). It's meant to honor Charles Stewart Parnell (1846-1891), the member of Parliament who nearly won Home Rule for Ireland in the late 1800s (and who served time at Kilmainham Gaol). A Cambridge-educated Protestant of landed-gentry stock, Parnell envisioned a modern, free Irish nation of Catholics—but not set up as a religious state. The Irish people, who remembered their grandparents' harsh evictions during the famine, came to love Parnell (despite his privileged birth) for his tireless work to secure fair rents and land tenure. Momentum seemed to be on his side. With the British prime minister of the time, William Gladstone, favoring a similar form of Home Rule, it looked as if Ireland was on its way toward independence as a Commonwealth nation, similar to Canada or Australia. Then a sex scandal broke around Parnell and his mistress, the wife of another Parliament member. The press, egged on by the powerful Catholic bishops (who didn't want a secular, free Irish state), battered away at the scandal until finally Parnell was driven from office. Sadly, after that, Ireland became mired in the Troubles of the 20th century: an awkward independence (1921) featuring a divided island, a bloody civil war, and sectarian violence for decades afterward. Wracked with exhaustion and only in his mid-40s, Parnell is thought to have died of a broken heart.

• *Continue straight up Parnell Square East. At the* **⓮** *Gate Theatre (on the left), actors Orson Welles, Geraldine Fitzgerald, and James Mason had their professional stage debuts. One block up, on the left, is the...*

⓯ Garden of Remembrance: Honoring the victims of the 1916 Uprising, this spot was where the rebel leaders were held before being transferred to Kilmainham Gaol. The park was dedicated in 1966 on the 50th anniversary of the revolt that ultimately led to Irish independence. The bottom of the cross-

DUBLIN

shaped pool is a mosaic of Celtic weapons, symbolic of how the early Irish proclaimed peace by breaking their weapons and throwing them into a lake or river. The Irish flag flies above the park: green for Catholics, orange for Protestants, and white for the hope that they can live together in peace (free, daily 8:30-18:00).

One of modern Ireland's most stirring moments occurred here in May 2011, when Queen Elizabeth II made this the first stop on her historic visit to Ireland. She laid a wreath at the *Children of Lir* sculpture under this flag and bowed her head in silence out of respect for the Irish rebels who had fought and died trying to gain freedom from her United Kingdom. This was a hugely cathartic moment for both nations. Until this visit, no British monarch had set foot in the Irish state since its founding 90 years earlier.

• *Your walk is over. Two excellent museums are nearby, standing side-by-side: the* **16** *Dublin Writers Museum (in a splendidly restored Georgian mansion, see page 66) and the art-filled* **17** *Hugh Lane Gallery (page 70). Here at the north end of town, it's also convenient to visit the* **18** *James Joyce Cultural Centre (a short walk away, see page 68), or the* **Gaelic Athletic Association Museum** *at Croke Park Stadium (described on page 78, a 20-minute walk or short taxi ride away). Otherwise, hop on your skateboard and zip back to the river.*

Sights in Dublin

SOUTH OF THE RIVER LIFFEY
Trinity College

Founded in 1592 by Queen Elizabeth I to establish a Protestant way of thinking about God, Trinity has long been Ireland's most prestigious college. Originally, the student body was limited to rich Protestant men. Women were admitted in 1903, and Catholics—though allowed entrance by the school much earlier—were only given formal permission by the Catholic Church to study at Trinity in the 1970s. Today, half of Trinity's 12,500 students are women, and 70 percent are culturally Catholic (although only about 20 percent of Irish youth are churchgoing).

▲▲Trinity College Tour

Trinity students organize and lead 30-minute **tours** of their campus (look just inside the gate for posted departure times and a ticket seller on a stool). You'll get a rundown of the mostly Georgian architecture; a peek at

student life past and present; and the enjoyable company of your guide, a witty Irish college kid.

Cost and Hours: €6, €13 with entry to see Book of Kells (where the tour leaves you), May-Sept daily 10:15-15:00, Feb-April and Oct-Nov Sat-Sun only, no tours Dec-Jan, departs roughly every 30 minutes, weather permitting.

▲▲Book of Kells in the Trinity Old Library

The Book of Kells—a 1,200-year-old version of the four gospels—was elaborately inked and meticulously illustrated by faithful monks. Combining Christian symbols and pagan styles, it's a snapshot of medieval Ireland in transition. Arguably the finest piece of art from what is generally called the Dark Ages, the Book of Kells shows that monastic life in this far fringe of Europe was far from dark.

Cost and Hours: €11, €13 "fast-track" ticket skips the line—buy in advance online, €13 regular entry with Trinity College tour admission; extra Audi O'Guide commentary-€5; Mon-Sat 9:30-17:00, Sun until 16:30, except Sun 12:00-16:30 Oct-April; tel. 01/896-2320, www.tcd.ie/visitors/book-of-kells.

Crowd-Beating Tips: Lines are longest at midday (roughly 11:00-14:30). Ideally, buy tickets in advance or queue up before the library opens to have the Book of Kells to yourself.

● **Self-Guided Tour:** Your visit has three stages: 1) an exhibit on the making of the Book of Kells, including two brief videos, old manuscripts, and poster-sized reproductions of its pages (your best look at the book's detail); 2) the Treasury, the darkened room containing the Book of Kells itself and other, less-ornate contemporaneous volumes; and 3) the main chamber of the Old Library (called the Long Room), containing historical objects.

Background: The Book of Kells was a labor of love created by dedicated Irish monks cloistered on the remote Scottish island of Iona. They slaughtered 185 calves, soaked the skins in lime, scraped off the hair, and dried the skins into a cream colored writing surface called vellum. Only then could the tonsured monks pick up their swan-quill pens and get to work.

The project may have been underway in 806 when Vikings savagely pillaged and burned Iona, killing 68 monks. The survivors fled to the Abbey of Kells (near Dublin). Scholars debate exactly where the book was produced: It could have been made entirely at Iona or at Kells, or started in Iona and finished at Kells.

For eight centuries, the glorious gospel sat regally atop the high altar of the monastery church at Kells, where the priest would read from it during special Masses. In 1654, as Cromwell's ravaging armies approached, the book was smuggled to Dublin for safety. Here at Trinity College, it was first displayed to the public

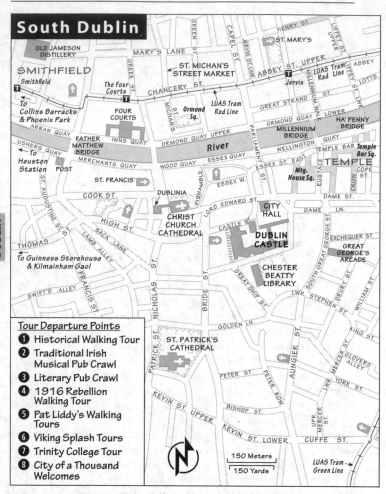

South Dublin

SMITHFIELD

OLD JAMESON DISTILLERY

MARY'S LANE

ST. MICHAN'S STREET MARKET

Smithfield

The Four Courts

To Collins Barracks & Phoenix Park

CHANCERY ST.

ST. MARY'S

ABBEY ST. UPPER

Jervis

LUAS Tram Red Line

ABBEY ST.

LOWER LIFFEY ST. UPPER

HENRY ST.

CAPEL ST.

GREEN ST.

JERVIS ST.

MICHAN ST.

FOUR COURTS

Ormond Sq.

LUAS Tram Red Line

GREAT STRAND ST.

ORMOND QUAY LOWER

HA' PENNY BRIDGE

MILLENNIUM BRIDGE

MILLENNIUM WALK

LIFFEY ST. LWR.

ABBEY ST. LOTTS

ARRAN QUAY

FATHER MATTHEW BRIDGE

INNS QUAY

ORMOND QUAY UPPER

River

WELLINGTON QUAY

PARLIAMENT ST.

TEMPLE BAR

Temple Bar Sq.

TEMPLE

USHERS QUAY

To Heuston Station

MERCHANTS QUAY

POST

WOOD QUAY

ESSEX QUAY

ESSEX ST. EAST

Mtg. House Sq.

EUSTACE ST.

COPE ST.

ST. FRANCIS'

ESSEX W.

FISHAMBLE ST.

CROW ST.

COOK ST.

DUBLINIA

LORD EDWARD ST.

CITY HALL

DAME ST.

DAME LN.

HIGH ST.

THOMAS ST.

To Guinness Storehouse & Kilmainham Gaol

ST. AUGUSTINE ST.

LAMB ALLEY

BACK LANE

CHRIST CHURCH CATHEDRAL

CASTLE ST.

DUBLIN CASTLE

CHESTER BEATTY LIBRARY

SOUTH GREAT GEORGE'S ST.

EXCHEQUER ST.

GREAT GEORGE'S ARCADE

SWIFT'S ALLEY

FRANCIS ST.

NICHOLAS ST.

BRIDE ST.

GREAT SHIP ST.

GOLDEN LN.

LWR. STEPHEN ST.

LWR. MERCER ST.

DRURY ST.

WILLIAM ST.

KING ST.

GLOVERS ALLEY

ST. PATRICK'S CATHEDRAL

PATRICK ST.

PETER ST.

PETER ROW

AUNGIER ST.

KEVIN ST. UPPER

BISHOP ST.

KEVIN ST. LOWER

UPR. MERCER ST.

CUFFE ST.

LWR. YORK ST.

LUAS Tram Green Line

Tour Departure Points

1. Historical Walking Tour
2. Traditional Irish Musical Pub Crawl
3. Literary Pub Crawl
4. 1916 Rebellion Walking Tour
5. Pat Liddy's Walking Tours
6. Viking Splash Tours
7. Trinity College Tour
8. City of a Thousand Welcomes

150 Meters

150 Yards

in the mid-1800s. In 1953, the book got its current covers and was bound into four separate volumes. The 1,200-year journey of the Book of Kells reached its culmination in 2012, when it came out as an iPad app.

The Exhibit: The first-class "Turning Darkness into Light" exhibit, with a one-way route, puts the 680-page illuminated manuscript in its historical and cultural context, preparing you to see the original book and other precious manuscripts in the treasury. Make a point to spend time in the exhibit (before reaching the actual Book of Kells). Especially interesting are the five-minute video clips showing the exacting care that went into transcribing the monk-uscripts and the ancient art of bookbinding. Two small TV screens (on opposite walls of the exhibition room) run continuously, silently demonstrating the monks' work.

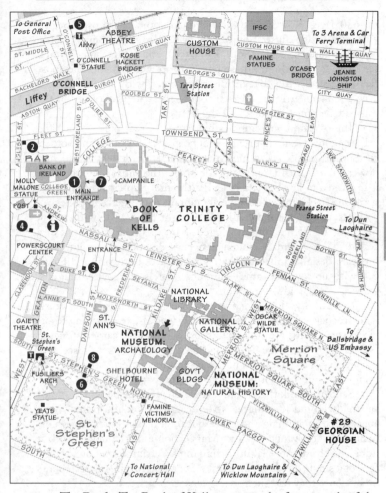

DUBLIN

The Book: The Book of Kells contains the four gospels of the Bible. It's 680 pages long (or 340 "folios," the equivalent of one sheet, front and back). The Latin calligraphy—all in capital letters—follows ruled lines, forming neat horizontal bars across the page. Sentences end with a "period" of three dots. The black-brown ink was made from the galls of oak trees. Scholars have found a number of spelling errors that were never corrected, apparently because the look was more important than accuracy.

The text is elaborately decorated—of

the 680 pages, only two are without decoration. Each gospel begins with a full-page illustration of the Evangelists and their symbols: Matthew (angel), Mark (lion), Luke (ox), and John (eagle)—you'll see these in the exhibit. These portraits are not realistic; the apostles pose stiffly, like Byzantine-style icons, with almond-shaped eyes and symmetrically creased robes. The true beauty lies in the intricate designs that surround the figures.

The colorful book employs blue, purple, red, pink, green, and yellow pigments (all imported)—but no gold leaf. Letters and borders are braided together. On most pages, the initial letters are big and flowery, like in a children's fairytale book. The entire Chi-Rho page is dedicated to just the letters "XP" (the first two letters of Christ's name in Greek), made into an elaborate maze of interlacing lines.

Elsewhere, the playful monks might cross a "t" with a fish, form an "h" from a spindly-legged man, or make an "e" out of a coiled snake. Animals crouch between sentences. It's a jungle of intricate designs, inhabited by tiny creatures both real and fanciful, with no two the same—humans, angels, gargoyles, dragons, wolves, calves, and winged lions.

Stylistically, the monks mixed Christian symbols (the cross, fish, peacock, snake) with pagan motifs (spirals, key patterns, knotwork; some swirls are similar to those seen on the carved stones at Newgrange—see page 112). The designs are also reminiscent of the jewelry of the day, with its ornate filigree patterns studded with knobs (like the Tara Brooch, described on page 52).

Scholars think three main artists created the book: the "goldsmith" (who did the filigree-style designs), the "illustrator" (who specialized in animals and grotesques), and the "portrait painter" (who did the Evangelists and Mary). Some of the detail work is unbelievably minute—akin to drawing a Persian carpet on the tiny face of a single die. Did the monks use a magnifying glass? There's no evidence they had such strong lenses.

The Old Library: The Long Room, the 200-foot-long main chamber of the Old Library (from 1732), is stacked to its towering ceiling with 200,000 books. Among the displays here, you'll find one of a dozen surviving original copies of the **Proclamation of the Irish Republic.** Patrick Pearse read out its words at Dublin's General Post Office on April 24, 1916, starting the Easter Uprising that led to Irish independence. Notice the inclusive opening phrase ("Irishmen and Irishwomen") and the seven signatories (each of whom was executed).

Another national icon is nearby: the oldest surviving Irish **harp,** from the 15th century (sometimes called the Brian Boru harp). The brass pins on its oak and willow frame once held 29 strings. These weren't mellifluous catgut strings, like those on a modern harp, but wire strings that made a twangy sound when plucked. In Celtic days, poets—the equal of kings and druid priests—wandered the land, uniting the people with songs and stories. The harp's inspirational effect on Gaelic culture was so strong that Queen Elizabeth I (1558-1603) ordered Irish harpists to be hung and their instruments smashed. Even today, the love of music is so intense that Ireland is the only country with a musical instrument as its national symbol. You'll see this harp's likeness everywhere, including on the back of Irish euro coins, on government documents, and on every pint of Guinness.

▲▲▲National Museum: Archaeology

Showing off the treasures of Ireland from the Stone Age to modern times, this branch of the National Museum is itself a national treasure. The soggy marshes and peat bogs of Ireland have proven perfect for preserving old objects. You'll see 4,000-year-old gold jewelry, 2,000-year-old bog mummies, Viking swords, and the collection's superstar—the exquisitely wrought Tara Brooch. Visit here to get an introduction to the rest of Ireland's historic attractions: You'll find a reconstructed passage tomb like Newgrange, Celtic art like the Book of Kells, Viking objects from Dublin, a model of the Hill of Tara, and a sacred cross from the Cong Abbey. Hit the highlights of my tour, then browse at will, aided by good posted information. For background information on Irish art, see page 482.

Cost and Hours: Free, Tue-Sat 10:00-17:00, Sun 14:00-17:00, closed Mon, guided tours offered sporadically (€3, mostly weekends, call in morning or check website), €3 audioguide covers only Treasury room, good café, between Trinity College and St. Stephen's Green on Kildare Street, tel. 01/677-7444, www.museum.ie.

➲ Self-Guided Tour

On the ground floor, enter the main hall. In the center (down four steps) are displays of prehistoric gold jewelry. To the left are the bog bodies, to the right is the Treasury, and upstairs is the Viking world. We'll start at Ireland's beginning.

❶ Stone Age Tools: Glass cases hold flint and stone axeheads and arrowheads (7,000 B.C.). Ireland's first inhabitants—hunters and fishers who came from Scotland—used these tools. These early people also left behind standing stones (dolmens) and passage tombs.

❷ Reconstructed Passage Tomb: At the corner of the room, you'll see a typical tomb circa 3,000 B.C.—a mound-shaped, heavy

National Museum: Archaeology

Not to Scale

To
St. Stephen's Green

WC   WC

VIKINGS
VIDEO
(UPSTAIRS)

4 METALWORKING

5 IRELAND'S GOLD

METALWORKING

METALWORKING

8

HEAD

HORN

HOARD

BELT

7

BROOCH

CHALICE

T
R
E
A
S
U
R
Y

KINGSHIP &
SACRIFICE

6

2

1

3

MUSEUM
SHOP

VIKING
ART

BELL   ARM
CONG

CAFE

FADDAN

MORE

ENTER HERE
OFF KILDARE STREET

ENTRANCE

KILDARE STREET

FENCE

Courtyard

To
Trinity College

❶ Stone Age Tools
❷ Reconstructed
   Passage Tomb
❸ Hill of Tara
❹ Metalworking

❺ Ireland's Gold
❻ Bog Bodies
❼ Treasury
❽ Up to First Floor
   (Vikings)

DUBLIN

stone structure, covered with smaller rocks, with a passage leading into a central burial chamber where the deceased's ashes were interred. This is a modest tomb; the vast passage tombs at Newgrange and Knowth (see page 112) are many times bigger.

❸ **The Hill of Tara:** The famous passage-tomb burial site at Tara, known as the Mound of the Hostages, was used for more than 1,500 years as a place to inter human remains. The cases in this side gallery display some of the many exceptional Neolithic and Bronze Age finds uncovered at the site.

Over the millennia, the Mound became the very symbol of Irish heritage. This is where Ireland's kings claimed their power, where St. Patrick preached his deal-clinching sermon, and where, in 1843, Daniel O'Connell rallied Irish patriots to demand their independence from Britain.

❹ The Evolution of Metalworking: Around 2500 B.C., Ireland discovered how to make metal—mining ore, smelting it in furnaces, and casting or hammering it into shapes. The rest is prehistory. You'll travel through the Bronze Age (axeheads from 2000 B.C.) and Iron Age (500 B.C.) as you examine assorted spears, shields, swords, and war horns. The cauldrons made for everyday cooking were also used ceremonially to prepare elaborate ritual feasts for friends and symbolic offerings for the gods. The most impressive metal objects are in the center of the hall.

❺ Ireland's Gold: Ireland had modest gold deposits, mainly gathered by prehistoric people panning for small nuggets and dust in the rivers. But the jewelry they left, some of it more than 4,000 years old, is exquisite. The earliest fashion choice was a broad neck-

lace hammered flat (a *lunula*, so called for its crescent-moon shape). This might be worn with accompanying earrings and sun-disc brooches. The Gleninsheen Collar (c. 700 B.C.) was found by a farmer in a crevice of the exposed bedrock of the Burren. It's thought that this valuable status symbol was hidden there during a time of conflict, then forgotten—if it had been meant as an offering to a pagan god it more likely would have been left in a body of water (the portal to the underworld). Later Bronze Age jewelry was cast from clay molds into bracelets and unique "dress fasteners" that you'd slip into buttonholes to secure a cloak. Some of these gold objects may have been gifts to fertility gods, offered by burying them in marshy bogs.

❻ Bog Bodies: When the Celts arrived in Ireland (c. 500 B.C.-A.D. 500), they brought with them a mysterious practice: They brutally murdered sacrificial slaves or prisoners and buried them in bogs. Several bodies—shriveled and leathery, but remarkably preserved—have been dug up from around the Celtic world (in the British Isles and Northern Europe).

Clonycavan Man is from Ireland. One summer day around 200 B.C., this twentysomething man was hacked to death with an axe and disemboweled. In his time, he stood 5'9" tall and had a Mohawk-style haircut, poofed up with pine-resin hair product imported from France. Today you can still see traces of his hair. Only his upper body survived; the lower part may have been lost in the threshing machine that unearthed him in 2003.

Why were these people killed? It appears to have been a form of ritual human sacrifice of high-status people. Some may have

DUBLIN

been enemy chiefs or political rivals, but regardless, their deaths were offerings to the gods to ensure rich harvests and good luck. Other items (now on display) were buried along with them—gold bracelets, royal cloaks, and finely wrought cauldrons.

❼ Treasury: Irish metalworking is legendary, and this room holds 1,500 years of exquisite objects. Working from one end of the long room to the other, you'll journey from the world of the pagan Celts to the coming of Christianity, explore the stylistic impact of the Viking invasions (9th-12th century), and consider the resurgence of ecclesiastical metalworking (11th-12th century).

Pagan Era Art: A mysterious pagan god greets you, in a **carved stone head** from circa A.D. 100. The god's three faces express the different aspects of his stony personality. This abstract style—typical of Celtic art—would be at home in a modern art museum. A **bronze horn** (first century B.C.) is the kind of curved war trumpet that the Celts blasted to freak out the Roman legions. The fine objects of the **Broighter Hoard** (first century B.C.) include a king's golden collar decorated in textbook Celtic style, with interlaced vines inhabited by stylized faces. The tiny boat was an offering to the sea god. The coconut-shell-shaped bowl symbolized a cauldron. By custom, the cauldron held food as a constant offering to Danu, the Celtic mother goddess, whose mythical palace was at Brú na Bóinne.

Early Christian Objects: Christianity officially entered Ireland in the fifth century (when St. Patrick converted the pagan king), but Celtic legends and art continued well into the Christian era. You'll see various crosses, shrines (portable reliquaries containing holy relics), and chalices decorated with Celtic motifs. The **Belt Shrine**—a circular metal casing that held a saint's leather belt— was thought to have magical properties. When placed around someone's waist, it could heal the wearer or force him or her to tell the truth.

The **Chalice of Ardagh** and the nearby **Silver Paten** were used during Communion to hold blessed wine and bread. Get close to admire the elaborate workmanship. The main bowl of the chalice is gilded bronze, with a contrasting band of intricately patterned gold filigree. It's studded with colorful glass, amber, and enamels. Mirrors below the display case show that even the underside of the chalice was decorated. When the priest grabbed the chalice by its two handles and tipped it to his lips, the base could be admired by God.

Tara Brooch: A rich eighth-century Celtic man fastened his cloak at the shoulder with this elaborate ring-shaped brooch, its seven-inch stick-pin tilted rakishly upward. Made of cast and gilded silver, it's ornamented with fine, exquisitely filigreed gold panels and studded with amber, enamel, and colored glass. The motifs include Celtic spirals, snakes, and stylized faces, but the symbolism is neither overtly pagan nor Christian—it's art for art's sake. Despite its fanciful name, the brooch probably has no actual connection to the Hill of Tara. In display cases nearby, you'll see other similar (but less impressive) brooches from the same period—some iron, some bronze, and one in pure gold.

Viking Art Styles: When Vikings invaded Dublin around A.D. 800, they raped and pillaged. But they also opened Ireland to a vast and cosmopolitan trading empire, from which they imported hoards of silver (see the display case of ingots). Viking influence shows up in the decorative style of reliquaries like the **Lismore Crozier** (in the shape of a bishop's ceremonial shepherd's crook) and the **Shrine of St. Lochter's Arm** (raised in an Irish-power salute). The impressive **Bell of St. Patrick** was supposedly owned by Ireland's patron saint. After his death, it was encased within a beautifully worked shrine (displayed alongside) and kept safe by a single family, who passed it down from generation to generation for 800 years.

DUBLIN

Cross of Cong: "By this cross is covered the cross on which the Creator of the world suffered." Running along the sides of the

cross, this Latin inscription tells us that it once held a sacred relic, a tiny splinter of the True Cross on which Jesus was crucified. That piece of wood (now lost) had been given in 1123 to the Irish high king, who commissioned this reliquary to preserve the splinter (it would have been placed right in the center, visible through the large piece of rock crystal). Every Christmas and Easter, the cross was fitted onto a staff and paraded through the abbey at Cong (see page 346), then placed on the altar for High Mass. The extraordinarily detailed decoration features gold filigree interspersed with colored glass, enamel, and (now missing) precious stones. Though fully Christian, the cross has Celtic-style filigree patterning and Viking-style animal heads (notice how they grip the cross in their jaws).

Before leaving the Treasury and heading upstairs, check out the **Faddan More Psalter**—a (pretty beat-up) manuscript of the Book of Psalms from the same era as the Book of Kells.

❽ Viking Ireland (c. 800-1150, on first floor): Dublin was born as a Viking town. Sometime after 795, Scandinavian warriors rowed their long ships up the River Liffey and made camp on the south bank, around the location of today's Dublin Castle

Modern Ireland's Turbulent Birth: A Timeline

Imagine if our American patriot ancestors had fought both our Revolutionary War and our Civil War over a span of seven chaotic years...and then appreciate the remarkable resilience of the Irish people. Here's a summary of what happened when.

1916: A nationalist militia called the Volunteers (led by **Patrick Pearse**) and the socialist Irish Citizen Army (led by **James Connolly**) join forces in the **Easter Uprising,** but they fail to end 750 years of British rule. The uprising is unpopular with most Irish, who are unhappy with the destruction in Dublin and preoccupied with the "Great War" on the Continent. But when 16 rebel leaders (including Pearse and Connolly) are executed, Irish public opinion reverses as sympathy grows for the martyrs and the cause of Irish Independence.

Two important rebel leaders escape execution. Brooklyn-born **Eamon de Valera** is spared because of his American passport (the British don't want to anger their potential ally in World War I). **Michael Collins,** a low-ranking rebel officer who fought in the uprising at the General Post Office, refines urban guerrilla-warfare strategies in prison, and then blossoms after his release as the rebels' military and intelligence leader in the power vacuum that followed the executions.

1918: World War I ends and a general election is held in Ireland (the first in which women can vote). Outside of Ulster, the nationalist **Sinn Fein** party wins 73 out of 79 seats in Parliament. Only four out of 32 counties vote to maintain the Union with Britain (all four lie in today's Northern Ireland). Rather than take their seats in London, Sinn Fein representatives abstain from participating in a government they see as foreign occupiers.

1919: On January 19, the abstaining Sinn Fein members set

and Christ Church. Over the next two centuries, they built "Dubh linn" ("black pool" in Irish) into an important trading post, slave market, metalworking center, and the first true city in Ireland. (See a model of Dublin showing a recently excavated area near Kilmainham Gaol.)

The state-of-the-art Viking boats ("Viking" means seafarer) worked equally well in the open ocean and shallow rivers, and were perfect for stealth invasions and far-ranging trading. Soon, provincial Dublin was connected with the wider world—Scotland, England, Northern Europe, even Asia. The museum's displays of

up a rebel government in Dublin called Dáil Éireann. On the same day, the first shots of the **Irish War of Independence** are fired as rebels begin ambushing police barracks, which are seen as an extension of British rule. De Valera is elected by the Dáil to lead the rebels, with Collins as his deputy. Collins' web of spies infiltrates British intelligence at Dublin Castle. The Volunteers rename themselves the **Irish Republican Army;** meanwhile the British beef up their military presence in Ireland by sending in tough WWI vets, the Black and Tans. A bloody and very personal war ensues.

1921: Having lived through the slaughter of World War I, the British tire of the extended bloodshed in Ireland and begin negotiations with the rebels. De Valera leads rebel negotiations, but then entrusts them to Collins (a clever politician, de Valera sees that whoever signs a treaty will be blamed for its compromises). Understanding the tricky position he's been placed in, Collins signs the **Anglo-Irish Treaty** in December, lamenting that in doing so he has signed his "own death warrant."

The Dáil narrowly ratifies the treaty (64 to 57), but Collins' followers are unable to convince de Valera's supporters that the compromises are a stepping stone to later full independence. De Valera and his antitreaty disciples resign in protest. **Arthur Griffith,** founder of Sinn Fein, assumes the presidential post.

In June, the antitreaty forces, holed up in the Four Courts building, are fired upon by Collins and his protreaty forces—thus igniting the **Irish Civil War.** The British want the treaty to stand and even supply Collins with cannons, meanwhile threatening to reenter Ireland if the antitreaty forces aren't put down.

1922: In August, Griffith dies of stress-induced illness, and Collins is assassinated 10 days later. Nevertheless, the protreaty forces prevail, as they are backed by popular opinion and better (British-supplied) military equipment.

1923: In April, the remaining IRA forces dump (or stash) their arms, ending the civil war...but many of their bitter vets vow to carry on the fight. De Valera distances himself from the IRA and becomes the dominant Irish political leader for the next 40 years.

swords and spears make it clear that, yes, the Vikings were fierce warriors. But you'll also see that they were respected merchants (standardized weights and coins), herders and craftsmen (leather shoes and bags), fashion-conscious (bone combs and jewelry), fun-loving (board games), and literate (runic alphabet). What you won't see are horned helmets, which, despite the stereotype, were not common. By 1000, the pagan Vikings had intermarried with the locals, become Christian, and were subjects of the Irish king.

The Rest of the Museum: Part of the first floor is dedicated to medieval Ireland—daily life (ploughs, cauldrons), trade (coins, pottery), and religion (crucifixes and saints). Up one more flight, the Egyptian room has coffins, *shabtis*, and canopic jars—but no mummies. Also upstairs, check out the informative video on the Viking influence on Irish culture (25 minutes, in the triangular room in the corner of the building, above the Treasury).

Other National Museums South of Trinity College

Adjacent to the archaeology branch are these other major museums. Also nearby is Leinster House. Once the Duke of Leinster's home, it now hosts the Irish Dáil (parliament) and Seanad (senate), which meet here 90 days each year.

▲National Gallery

While not as extensive as national galleries in London or Paris, the collections here are well worth your time. The museum boasts an impressive range of works by European masters, and also displays the works of top Irish painters, including Jack B. Yeats (the brother of the famous poet).

Cost and Hours: Free, Mon-Sat 9:30-17:30, Thu until 20:30, Sun 11:00-17:30, expect disruptions due to renovations, Merrion Square West, tel. 01/661-5133, www.nationalgallery.ie.

Tours: The museum offers a free audioguide (donations accepted) as well as free 45-minute guided tours (Sat at 12:30; Sun at 12:30 and 13:30).

Visiting the Museum: Study the floor-plan flier and take advantage of the free audioguide. Be sure to walk the series of rooms on the ground floor devoted to Irish painting and get to know artists you may not have heard of before. Visit the National Portrait Gallery on the mezzanine level for an insight into the great personalities of Ireland. You'll find European masterworks on the top floor, including a rare Vermeer (one of only 30-some known works by the Dutch artist), a classic Caravaggio (master of chiaroscuro and dramatic lighting), a Monet riverscape, and an early Cubist Picasso still life.

Try not to miss the wonderfully romantic *Meeting on the Turret Stairs*—Ireland's favorite painting (as voted by readers of the *Irish Times*)—by Frederic Burton. Because this vividly painted watercolor is vulnerable to fading, it's on view for only two hours per week (Mon and Wed 11:30-12:30).

Perhaps the most iconic of all the Irish art in this museum is the melodramatic depiction of the *Marriage of Strongbow and Aiofe* by Daniel Maclise. It captures the chaotic union of Norman and Irish interests that signaled the start of English domination of Ireland 850 years ago. Notice how the defeated Irish writhe and lament in the bright light of the foreground, while the scheming Norman warlords skulk in the dimly lit middle ground. The ruins of conquered Waterford smolder at the back.

National Museum: Natural History

Called "the dead zoo" by Dubliners, this cramped collection of stuffed exotic animals comes across like the locker room on Noah's Ark. But if you're into beaks, bones, bugs, and boars, this Victorian relic is for you. Standing tall above a sea of taxidermy is the regal skeleton of a giant Irish elk from the last Ice Age; it dwarfs a modern moose. The earnest displays need a new home (a collapsed staircase in 2007 closed two upper galleries, but the bottom two floors are open).

Cost and Hours: Free, Tue-Sat 10:00-17:00, Sun 14:00-17:00, closed Mon, Merrion Square West, tel. 01/677-7444, www.museum.ie.

National Library

Literature holds a lofty place in the Irish psyche. To feel the fire-and-ice pulse of Ireland's most influential poet, visit the W. B. Yeats exhibit in the library basement. This space was originally intended to host rotating exhibits, but the display on the life of Yeats proved so popular it became permanent. The artifacts flesh out the very human passions of this poet and playwright, with samples of his handwritten manuscripts and surprisingly interesting mini documentaries of the times he lived in. Upstairs, you can get help making use of library records to trace your genealogy. Take a moment to view the gorgeous baby-blue upstairs reading room under the expansive dome.

Cost and Hours: Free, Mon-Wed 9:30-19:30, Thu-Fri 9:30-16:30, Sat 9:30-12:30, Sun 13:00-16:30 (exhibits only), café, tel. 01/603-0200, 2 Kildare Street, www.nli.ie.

Merrion Square and Nearby
▲Merrion Square

Laid out in 1762, this square is ringed by elegant Georgian houses decorated with fine doors—a Dublin trademark. (If you're inspired by the ornate knobs and knockers, there's a shop by that name on nearby Nassau Street.) The park, once the exclusive domain of the residents, is now a delightful public escape and ideal for a picnic. To learn what "snogging" is, walk through the park on a sunny day, when it's full of smooching lovers. Oscar Wilde, lounging wittily on a boulder on the corner nearest the town center and surrounded by his clever quotes, provides a fun photo op (see photo on page 70).

▲Number Twenty-Nine Georgian House

The carefully restored house at Number 29 Lower Fitzwilliam Street gives an intimate glimpse of middle-class Georgian life (which seems pretty high-class). Before entering, notice how many of the windows in the Georgian building across the street had once been bricked up to cut tax bills (back in the days when glass was a taxable luxury). From the sidewalk, descend the stairs to the basement-level entrance (corner of Lower Fitzwilliam and Lower Mount Streets, opposite southern corner of Merrion Square). Start with an interesting 15-minute video before exploring this 1790 Dublin home. As you climb its five floors, you'll find storyboards in each room explaining the everyday lives lived here.

Cost and Hours: €6, mid-Feb-mid-Dec Tue-Sat 10:00-17:00, closed Sun-Mon, closed mid-Dec-mid-Feb, tours at 15:00, tel. 01/702-6163, www.esb.ie/no29.

Grafton Street and St. Stephen's Green Area
▲▲Grafton Street

Once filled with noisy traffic, today's Grafton Street is Dublin's liveliest pedestrian shopping drag and people-watching paradise. A decade ago, when the Celtic Tiger economy was in mid-roar, this street had the fifth-most expensive retail rents in the world, behind Tokyo, London, New York, and Moscow (rents have since declined). A 10-minute stroll past street musicians takes you from Trinity College to St. Stephen's Green (and makes you wonder why some American merchants are so terrified of a car-free street).

Walking south from Trinity College, you'll pass two venerable department stores: the Irish Brown Thomas and the English Marks & Spencer. Johnson's Court alley leads to the Powerscourt Town-house Shopping Centre, which tastefully fills a converted Georgian mansion. The huge, glass-covered St. Stephen's Green Shopping Centre and the peaceful green itself mark the top of Grafton Street. For fun, gather a pile of coins and walk the street, setting each human statue into action with a donation.

▲St. Stephen's Green

This city park was originally a medieval commons, complete with gory public executions. It was enclosed in 1664 and gradually surrounded with fine Georgian buildings. Today, it provides 22 acres of grassy refuge for Dubliners. At the northwest corner (near the end of Grafton Street) you'll be confronted by a looming marble arch erected to honor British officers killed during the Boer War.

Locals nicknamed it "Traitor's Arch," as most Irish sympathized with the underdog Boers.

During the 1916 Easter Uprising, a group of rebels (who had read about WWI trench warfare in Flanders) dug up the park to hunker down in it, believing they would have a fortified position. Passionate as they were, these rebels were a mishmash of romantic poets, teachers, aristocratic ladies, and slum dwellers. They hadn't figured on veteran British troops easily trumping their move by placing snipers atop the Shelbourne Hotel (with a bird's-eye view into the trenches). During the battle, there were surreal daily truces when both sides held their fire so that the park's keeper could safely feed his flock of ducks. The rebels eventually abandoned their positions in the park for better cover inside the College of Surgeons, at the west end of St. Stephen's Green.

On a sunny afternoon, this open space is a wonderful world apart from the big city. When marveling at the elegance of Georgian Dublin, remember that during the Georgian period, Dublin was the second-most important city in the British Empire. Area big shots knew that any money wrung from the local populace not spent in Dublin would end up in London. Since it was "use it or lose it," they used it—with gusto—to beautify their city.

Little Museum of Dublin

A fun, two-room labor of love just north of St. Stephen's Green, this collection was donated by local Dubliners and focuses on life in the city since 1900. An engaging mix of history and pop culture, this museum also sponsors the City of a Thousand Welcomes Meet a Dubliner program (see page 30). Artifacts range from a first edition of James Joyce's *Ulysses* to memorabilia from JFK's triumphant watershed 1963 visit to Dublin just a few months before his death. Other displays cover local rock band U2 and Muhammad Ali's 1972 fight at Croke Park. History buffs linger at sly Eamon de Valera's five-part memo to his fellow Irish rebel Michael Collins. In part one, he gives Collins complete authority to negotiate with British officials over Irish independence—and then waters down this authority over the next four parts.

Cost and Hours: €7, daily 9:30-17:00, Thu until 20:00, tours hourly on request, 15 St. Stephen's Green, tel. 01/661-1000, www.littlemuseum.ie.

Dublin Castle and Nearby
▲▲Dublin Castle

Built on the spot of the first Viking fortress, this castle was the seat of English rule in Ireland for 700 years. Located where the Poddle and Liffey rivers came together, making a black pool (*dubh linn* in Irish), Dublin Castle was the official residence of the viceroy who implemented the will of the British royalty. In this stirring setting, the Brits handed power over to Michael Collins and the Irish in 1922. Today, it's used for fancy state and charity functions (which may sporadically close it to the public).

Standing in the courtyard, you can imagine the ugliness of the British-Irish situation. Notice the statue of justice above the gate—pointedly without her blindfold and admiring her sword. As Dubliners say, "There she stands, above her station, with her face to the palace and her arse to the nation." The fancy interior is viewable on a 45-minute tour, which offers a fairly boring room-by-room walk through the lavish state apartments of this most English of Irish palaces. (You can also tour on your own using the provided information.) The tour finishes with a look at the foundations of the Norman tower and the best remaining chunk of the 13th-century town wall.

Cost and Hours: €10 for one-hour guided tour, €7 to visit on your own, tickets sold in courtyard under portico opposite clock tower, tours depart hourly, Mon-Sat 10:00-16:45, Sun 12:00-16:45, tel. 01/645-8813, www.dublincastle.ie.

▲▲Chester Beatty Library

This priceless, delightfully displayed collection of constantly rotating artifacts includes rare ancient manuscripts and beautifully illustrated books from around the world, plus a few odd curios. Start on the ground floor with the short film about Beatty (1875-1968), a rich American mining magnate who traveled widely, collected 66,000 objects assiduously, and retired to Ireland. Then head upstairs to see the treasures he bequeathed to his adopted country.

Cost and Hours: Free, Mon-Fri 10:00-17:00, Sat 11:00-17:00, Sun 13:00-17:00, closed Mon Oct-April, coffee shop, tel. 01/407-0750, www.cbl.ie. You'll find the library in the gardens of Dublin Castle (follow the signs).

➲ **Self-Guided Tour:** Start on the second floor. Note that exhibits may rotate, so they may not always be on display in the order outlined here.

Sacred Traditions Gallery: This space is dedicated to sacred texts, illuminated manuscripts, and miniature paintings from around the world. The doors swing open, and you're greeted by a video highlighting a diverse array of religious rites—a Christian wedding, Muslims kneeling for prayer, whirling dervishes, and so on.

• *Tour the floor clockwise, starting with Christian texts on the left side of the room. There you'll find several glass cases containing...*

Ancient Bible Fragments: In the 1930s, Beatty acquired (possibly through the black market) these 1,800-year-old manuscripts, which had recently been unearthed in Egypt. The Indiana Jones-like discovery instantly bumped scholars' knowledge of the early Bible up a notch. There were Old Testament books (Genesis, Deuteronomy), New Testament books (Gospels, Acts, Revelation), and—rarest of all—the Letters of Paul. Written in Greek on papyrus more than a century before previously known documents, these are some of the oldest versions of these texts in existence. Unlike most early Christian texts, the manuscripts were not rolled up in a scroll but bound in a book form called a "codex." On display (the collection changes) you may see pages from a third-century Gospel of Luke or the Gospel of John (c. A.D. 150-200). Jesus died around A.D. 33, and his words weren't recorded until decades later. Most early manuscripts date from the fourth century, so these pages are about as close to the source as you can get.

Letters (Epistles) of Paul: The Beatty has 112 pages of Saint Paul's collected letters (A.D. 180-200). Paul, a Roman citizen (c. A.D. 5-67; see Albrecht Dürer's engraving of the saint), was the apostle most responsible for spreading Christianity beyond Palestine. Originally, Paul reviled Christians. But after a mystical experience, he went on to travel the known world, preaching the Good News in sophisticated Athens and the greatest city in the world, Rome, where he died a martyr to the cause. Along the way, he kept in touch with Christian congregations in cities like Corinth, Ephesus, and Rome with these letters. It's thanks to Paul that we have sayings such as "Money is the root of all evil"; "Love is patient, love is kind"; "Whatever a man sows, so shall he reap"; and "Fight the good fight."

Continuing up the left side of the room, you'll find gloriously illustrated **medieval Bibles** and **prayer books,** including an intricate, colorful, gold-speckled Book of Hours (1408).

• *Turn the corner into the center of the room, to find the sacred texts of...*

Islam: The angel Gabriel visited Muhammad (c. 570-632), instructing him to write down his heavenly visions in a book—the Quran. You'll see Qurans with elaborate calligraphy, such as one made in Baghdad in 1001. Nearby are other sacred Islamic texts, some beautifully illustrated, where you may find the rare illuminated manuscript of the "Life of the Prophet" (c. 1595), produced in Istanbul for an Ottoman sultan.

• *On the right side of the room, you enter the world of...*

East Asian Religions: Statues of Gautama Buddha (c. 563-483 B.C.) and Chinese Buddhist scrolls attest to the pervasive influence of this wise man. Buddha was born in India, but his philosophy spread to China, Japan, and Tibet (see the mandalas). Continuing clockwise, you will reach the writings from India, the land of a million gods—and the cradle of Buddhism, Hinduism, Sikhism, and Jainism.

• *Your visit continues downstairs on the first floor, in the gallery devoted to the...*

Arts of the Book: The focus here is on the many forms a "book" can take—from the earliest clay tablets and papyrus scrolls, to parchment scrolls and bound codexes, to medieval monks' wondrous illustrations, to the advent of printing and bookbinding, to the dawn of the 21st century and the digital age.

• *Tour the floor clockwise. Immediately to the left, find a glass case containing...*

Egyptian and Other Ancient Writings: A hieroglyph-covered papyrus scroll from the Book of the Dead (c. 300 B.C.) depicts a pharaoh on his throne (left) presiding over a soul's judgment in the afterlife. The jackal-headed god Anubis (center-right) holds a scale, weighing the heart of a dead woman to see if it's light enough for her to level up to the next phase of eternity. The Beatty also has a large selection of ancient Egyptian love songs (including, I believe, the number one hit of 1160 B.C., "I Love You, Mummy Dearest"). Nearby (in a freestanding glass case, near the bottom), if you look hard, you could find a few small cuneiform tablets and cylinder seals from as far back as 2,700 B.C. These objects from ancient Sumeria (modern-day Iraq) are older than the pyramids and represent the very birth of writing.

• *Continue up the left side of the room, perusing displays on...*

Printing, Illustrating, and Bookbinding: The printing press with movable type was perfected by Johannes Gutenberg in Germany sometime in the early 1450s. The printed sheets were folded, sewn together, and wrapped in a cover. With the engraving process, beautiful illustrations could also be reproduced on a mass scale. Until the 20th century, it was common for a book buyer to acquire the printed sheets and then select a lavish custom-made cover.

• *Turn the corner to the center of the room.*

Islamic World: These are secular books—science textbooks and poetry—many from the rich Persian culture (modern-day Iran). Some are richly illustrated with elaborate calligraphy. It's often noted that Islam forbids visual art, strictly following the Bible's dictum against "graven" images. But, as you can see, that restriction doesn't apply to nonreligious texts.

• *Continue to the right side of the room.*

Far East: Besides albums and scrolls, you might see eye-catching Japanese woodblock prints, ornate Chinese snuff bottles, rhino-horn cups, and the silk dragon robes of Chinese emperors of the Qing dynasty (1644-1911). The Qianlong Emperor (r. 1736-

1795)—a poet and arts patron—welcomed European Jesuits to his court and commissioned a huge collection of books, including some carved from jade. A graceful Sumatran book, written on tree-bark pages, is bound so that it unfolds like an accordion—yet another example of great ingenuity in presenting the written word.

Dublin City Hall

The first Georgian building in this very Georgian city stands proudly overlooking Dame Street, in front of the gate to Dublin Castle. Built in 1779 as the Royal Exchange, it introduced the Georgian style (then very popular in Britain) to Ireland. Step inside (it's free) to feel the prosperity and confidence of Dublin in her 18th-century glory days. In 1852, this building became the City Hall. Under the grand rotunda, a cycle of heroic paintings tells the city's history. (The mosaics on the floor convey such homilies as "Obedience makes the happiest citizenry.")

Pay your respects to the 18-foot-tall statue of Daniel O'Connell, the great orator and liberator who, in 1829, won emancipation for Catholics in Ireland from the much-despised Protestants over in London. The body of modern Irish rebel leader Michael Collins lay in state here after his assassination in 1922. The greeter sits like the Maytag repairman at the information desk, eager to give you more information. Downstairs is the excellent *Story of the Capital* exhibition, which has storyboards and video clips of Dublin's history.

Cost and Hours: Free, Mon-Sat 10:00-17:15, closed Sun, coffee shop, tel. 01/222-2204.

Dublin's Cathedrals Area

Because of Dublin's English past (particularly Henry VIII's Reformation, which led to the dissolution of the Catholic monasteries in both Ireland and England in 1539), neither of its top two churches is Catholic. Christ Church Cathedral and nearby St. Patrick's Cathedral are both Church of Ireland (Anglican). In the late 19th century, the cathedrals underwent extensive restoration. The rich Guinness brewery family forked out the dough to try to make St. Patrick's Cathedral outshine Christ Church—whose patrons were the equally rich, rival Jameson family of distillery fame. However, in Catholic Ireland, these Anglican sights feel hollow, and they're more famous than visit-worthy.

Christ Church Cathedral

Occupying the same site as the first wooden church built on this spot by King Sitric in late Viking times (c. 1030), the present structure is a mix of periods: Norman and Gothic, but mostly Victorian Neo-Gothic (1870s restoration work). Inside you'll find the reputed tomb of the Norman warlord Strongbow, who led the thin edge of the English military wedge that eventually dominated Ireland for

DUBLIN

centuries. This oldest building in Dublin has an unusually large underground crypt, containing stocks, statues, the cathedral's silver, and an atmospheric café.

Cost and Hours: €6 includes downstairs crypt silver exhibition, €13.25 combo-ticket includes Dublinia (described next); Mon-Sat 9:45-17:00, Sun 12:30-14:30; €4 guided tours Mon-Fri at 11:00, 12:00, 14:00, and 15:00; tel. 01/677-8099, www.christchurchdublin.ie.

Evensong: A 45-minute evensong service is sung Thu at 18:00, Sun at 15:30.

▲Dublinia

This exhibit, which highlights Dublin's Viking and medieval past, is a hit with youngsters. The exhibits are laid out on three floors. The ground floor focuses on Viking Dublin, explaining life aboard a Viking ship and inside a Viking house. Viking traders introduced urban life and commerce to Ireland—but kids will be most interested in gawking at their gory weaponry.

The next floor up reveals Dublin's day-to-day life in medieval times, from chivalrous knights and damsels in town fairs to the brutal ravages of the Plague. Like the rest of Europe at that time (1347-1349), Ireland lost one-third of its population to the Black Death. The huge scale model of medieval Dublin is especially well done. The top floor's "History Hunters" section is devoted to how the puzzles of modern archaeology and science shed light on Dublin's history. From this floor, you can climb a couple of flights of stairs into the tower for so-so views of Dublin, or exit across an enclosed stone bridge to adjacent Christ Church Cathedral.

Cost and Hours: €8.50, €13.25 combo-ticket includes Christ Church Cathedral, daily March-Sept 10:00-18:00, Oct-Feb until 17:30, last entry one hour before closing, top-floor coffee shop open in summer, across from Christ Church Cathedral, tel. 01/679-4611, www.dublinia.ie.

St. Patrick's Cathedral

The first church here was supposedly built on the site where St. Patrick baptized local pagan converts. The core of the Gothic structure you see today was built in the 13th century. After the Reformation, it passed into the hands of the Anglican Church. A century later, Oliver Cromwell's puritanical Calvinist troops—who considered the Anglicans to be little more than Catholics without a pope—stabled their horses here as a sign of disrespect.

Jonathan Swift (author of *Gulliver's Travels*) was dean of the Cathedral for 32 years in the 18th century. His grave is located near the front door (on the right side of the nave), where his cutting, self-penned epitaph reads: "He lies where furious indignation can no longer rend his heart." Check out the large wooden Door of Reconciliation hanging in the north transept, with the rough hole in the middle. This was the Chapter House door through which two feuding, sword-bearing 15th-century nobles shook hands..."chancing their arms" and giving the Irish that expression of trust.

Cost and Hours: €6 donation to church, Mon-Fri 9:30-17:00, Sat 9:00-18:00, Sun 12:30-14:30 & 16:30-18:00, last entry one hour before closing.

Evensong: You'll get chills listening to the local "choir of angels" Mon-Fri at 17:45 and Sun at 15:15.

▲▲Temple Bar

This much-promoted area—with trendy shops, cafés, theaters, galleries, pubs with live music, and restaurants—feels like the heart of the city. It's Dublin's touristy "Left Bank," and as in Paris, it's on the south shore of the river, filling the cobbled streets between Dame Street and the River Liffey.

Three hundred years ago, this was the city waterfront, where tall sailing ships offloaded their goods (a "bar" was a loading dock along the river, and the Temples were a dominant merchant family). Eventually, the city grew eastward, filling in tidal mudflats, to create the docklands of modern Dublin. Once a thriving Georgian center of craftsmen and merchants, this neighborhood fell on hard times in the 20th century. Ensuing low rents attracted students and artists, giving the area a bohemian flair. With government tax incentives and lots of development money, the Temple Bar district has now become a thriving cultural (and beer-drinking) hot spot.

Temple Bar can be an absolute spectacle in the evening, when it bursts with revelers. The noise, pushy crowds, and inflated prices have driven most Dubliners away. But even if you're just gawking, don't miss the opportunity to wander through this human circus. It can be a real zoo on summer weekend nights, holidays, and nights after big sporting events let out. Women in funky hats, part of loud "hen" (bachelorette) parties, promenade down the main drag as drunken dudes shout from pub doorways to get their attention. Be aware that a pint of beer here is at least €1 more than at less glitzy pubs just a couple of blocks away (north of the River Liffey or south of Dame Street).

Temple Bar Square, just off Temple Bar Street (near Ha' Penny Bridge), is the epicenter of activity. It hosts free street theater and a Saturday book market, and has handy ATMs. On busy weekends, people-watching here is a contact sport. You're bound to meet some characters.

Irish music fans find great CDs at humble **Claddagh Records** (Cecilia Street, just around the corner from Luigi Malone's, Mon-Sat 11:00-17:30, closed Sun, tel. 01/677-0262). Unlike big, glitzy chain stores, this is a little hole-in-the-wall shop staffed by informed folks who love turning visitors on to Irish tunes. Grab a couple of CDs for your drive through the Irish countryside. Farther west and somewhat hidden is **Meeting House Square,** with a lively organic-produce market (Sat 10:00-18:00). Bordering the square is the **Irish Film Institute** (main entry on Eustace Street), which shows a variety of art-house flicks. A bohemian crowd relaxes in its bar/café, awaiting the next film (6 Eustace Street, box office daily 13:30-21:00, tel. 01/679-5744, www.irishfilm.ie).

Rather than follow particular pub or restaurant recommendations (mine are listed later, under "Eating in Dublin"), venture down a few side lanes off the main drag to see what looks good. The pedestrian-only **Ha' Penny Bridge,** named for the halfpence toll people used to pay to cross it, leads from Temple Bar over the River Liffey to the opposite bank and more sights. If the rowdy Temple Bar scene gets to be too much, cross over to the north

bank of the River Liffey on the Millennium Pedestrian Bridge (next bridge west of the Ha' Penny Bridge), where you'll find a mellower, more cosmopolitan choice of restaurants with outdoor seating in the Millennium Walk district (see page 81).

NORTH OF THE RIVER LIFFEY
The main attraction north of the river—O'Connell Street—is covered by the self-guided walk on page 39. After you're oriented with the walk, consider the following sights.

▲Dublin Writers Museum
No other country so small has produced such a wealth of literature. As interesting to those who are fans of Irish literature as it is boring to those who aren't, this three-room museum features the lives and works of Dublin's great writers. It's a low-tech museum, where you read informative plaques while perusing display cases with minor memorabilia—a document signed by Jonathan Swift, a photo of Oscar Wilde reclining thoughtfully, an early edition of Bram Stoker's *Dracula,* a George Bernard Shaw playbill, a not-so-famous author's tuxedo, or a newspaper from Easter 1916 announcing "Two More Executions To-day." If unassuming attractions like that stir

your blood—or if you simply want a manageable introduction to Irish lit—it's worth a visit.

Cost and Hours: €7.50, includes helpful audioguide; Mon-Sat 10:00-17:00, Sun 11:00-17:00; coffee shop, 18 Parnell Square North, tel. 01/872-2077, www.writersmuseum.com.

Background: The museum isn't exclusive about "Irish" writers. Born here? Lived here? Wrote about Ireland, wrote in Irish, or were sympathetic to the cause of Irish nationalism? You're in. Some of the writers featured by the museum were born in Ireland, but that's about it—they lived elsewhere, wrote in English, and gained fame for non-Irish works. One trait they all seem to share is a stubborn streak of personal independence, perhaps related to Ireland's national struggle to assert its cultural identity. The museum is housed in a Georgian home, making for an elegant setting to appreciate these pioneering writers who've left a written record of this verbal people. (For an overview of Irish literature, see page 485.)

Visiting the Museum: The collection is chronological. **Room 1** starts with Irish literature's deep roots in the roving, harp-playing **bards** of medieval times. By telling stories in the native language, they helped unify the island's culture. But "literature" came only with the arrival of the English language. **Jonathan Swift** (1667-1745)—Ireland's first great writer—was born in Dublin and served as dean of St. Patrick's Cathedral, though he spent much of his life in London. His stinging satire of societal hypocrisy set the tone of rebellion found in much Irish literature. The **theater** has been another longstanding Irish specialty, starting with the 18th-century playwright Oliver Goldsmith. In the **1890s**, sophisticated Dublin (and Trinity College) was a cradle for great writers who ultimately found their fortunes in England: the playwright/poet/wit Oscar Wilde, Bram Stoker (who married Wilde's girlfriend), and the big-idea playwright George Bernard Shaw. Poet **W. B. Yeats** stayed home, cultivating Irish folklore at soirees (hosted by the literary patron Lady Augusta Gregory) and inspired by his unrequited muse, the feminist Irish revolutionary Maude Gonne (see her portrait).

Room 2 continues with Yeats' **Abbey Theatre,** the scene of premieres by great Irish playwrights (including Yeats, Shaw, and Wilde), and a source of political unrest during the 1916 Easter Uprising. Dublin was also a breeding ground for bold new ideas, producing Modernist writers Samuel *(Waiting for Godot)* Beckett and James Joyce (his Cultural Centre is described next). As the 20th century progressed, playwrights such as Sean O'Casey, Brendan Behan, and Brian Friel kept Dublin at the forefront of modern theater. You can read a long letter by terrorist/bad boy Brendan Behan from Hollywood about schmoozing with Groucho, Harpo, and Sinatra.

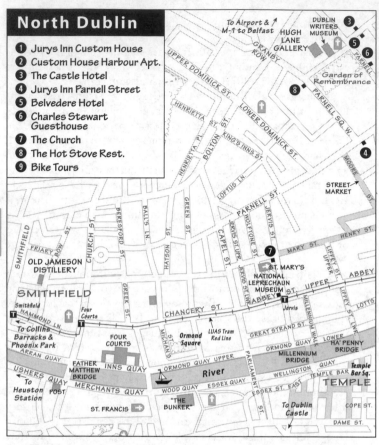

North Dublin

1. Jurys Inn Custom House
2. Custom House Harbour Apt.
3. The Castle Hotel
4. Jurys Inn Parnell Street
5. Belvedere Hotel
6. Charles Stewart Guesthouse
7. The Church
8. The Hot Stove Rest.
9. Bike Tours

Finish your visit by going **upstairs** to see an elegant Georgian library, then peruse the busts and portraits in the Gallery of Writers.

James Joyce Cultural Centre

Aficionados of James Joyce's work (but few others) will want to visit this micromuseum.

Cost and Hours: €5, Mon-Sat 10:00-17:00, Sun 12:00-17:00, closed Mon Oct-March, two blocks east of the Dublin Writers Museum at 35 North Great George's Street, tel. 01/878-8547, www.jamesjoyce.ie.

Background: James Joyce (1882-1941) was born and raised in Dublin, wrote in great detail about his hometown, and mined the local dialect for his pitch-perfect dialogue. His best-known work, *Ulysses,* chronicles one day in the life of the fictional Leopold Bloom (June 16, 1904) as he wanders through the underside of Dublin. In his own life, Joyce left Dublin (on June 17, 1904) to live in Paris. He never took up the cause of Irish nationalism and

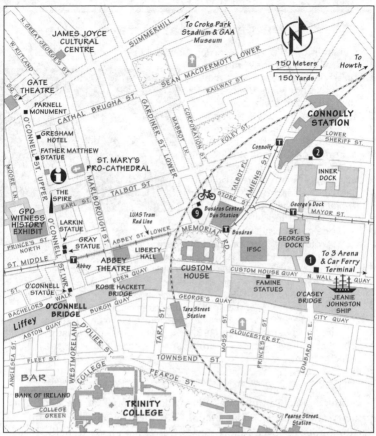

rarely delved into Irish mythology. His focus was the Modernist question of how to find one's place in a post-religious world without traditional guidelines. His stream-of-consciousness writing style (which, truthfully, can be hard to follow and often boring) is meant to mimic the multiple strains of thought running through a person's mind at any one moment. Joyce's frank depictions of sexuality helped employ two generations of censors in Ireland and America.

Visiting the Centre: Your visit begins (top floor) with videos on Joyce's life and his enormous influence on subsequent writers. Next, a touchscreen display traces Bloom's Dublin Odyssey. Photos of Joyce and quotes from his books decorate the walls. A recreation of a messy, cramped study evokes Joyce's struggles through poverty and criticism as he forged his own path. Down one flight, see portraits of Joyce and his wife and muse, Nora Barnacle. (The first time they, um, went on a date was June 16, 1904. Joyce later set the events depicted in his masterpiece *Ulysses,* on that date, which

DUBLIN

Dublin's Literary Life

Dublin in the 1700s, grown rich from a lucrative cloth trade, was one of Europe's most cultured and sophisticated cities. The buildings were decorated in the Georgian style still visible today, and the city's Protestant elite shuttled between here and London, bridging the Anglo-Irish cultural gap. Jonathan Swift (1667-1745) was the era's greatest Anglo-Irish writer—a brilliant satirist and author of *Gulliver's Travels*. He was also dean of St. Patrick's Cathedral (1713-1745) and one of the city's eminent citizens.

Around the turn of the 20th century, Dublin produced some of the world's great modern writers. Bram Stoker (1847-1912) was creator of *Dracula*. Oscar Wilde (1854-1900) penned *The Picture of Dorian Gray* and a clutch of fine plays. George Bernard Shaw (1856-1950) wrote *Pygmalion, Major Barbara, Man and Superman*, and a host of other dramas. William Butler Yeats (1865-1939) was a prolific poet and playwright on Irish themes. And James Joyce (1882-1941) whipped up a masterpiece called *Ulysses*. For more on Irish literature (and to see which of these writers won the Nobel Prize), see page 485.

is commemorated annually as Bloomsday in honor of the book's primary character, Leopold Bloom.) On the ground floor, a film version of one of Joyce's short stories, *The Dead*, plays eternally. In a tiny back courtyard, you can see the original door from 7 Eccles Street, the address of Leopold Bloom.

▲Hugh Lane Gallery

This collection of mostly modern and contemporary art has a sampling of Impressionist masterpieces that come from the gallery's founding collection, once owned by Sir Hugh Lane. Genteel and bite-sized, the museum is particularly worth a visit for a well-known Monet painting, an exhibit on modern artist Francis Bacon, and a few select paintings by Irish artists.

Cost and Hours: Free, Tue-Thu 10:00-18:00, Fri-Sat 10:00-17:00, Sun 11:00-17:00, closed Mon, Parnell Square North, tel. 01/222-5550, www.hughlane.ie.

Visiting the Gallery: Head to **Room 1,** where you'll find **Monet's** *Waterloo Bridge* (1900). On a visit to London, the once-bohemian, now-famous Impressionist Claude Monet checked into Room 618 of the Savoy Hotel and set to work painting Waterloo Bridge at different times of day and in various weather conditions. This painting is the best known of 41 versions of the scene. Monet—the master of capturing hazy, filtered light—loved London for its fog. With the Thames in the foreground, the bridge in the middle, and belching smokestacks in the distance, Monet had three different layers of atmospheric depth to explore.

Also in Room 1 is *Portrait of Hugh Lane* by the American society portraitist John Singer Sargent. In 1905, the dapper Sir Hugh, an art dealer, bought Monet's *Waterloo Bridge* as part of his mission to bring modern art to provincial Dublin (see a Degas painting nearby). Unfortunately, Sir Hugh went down on the *Lusitania* in 1915 and didn't see this gallery open.

Room 3 is devoted to Jack B. Yeats—the famous poet's little brother—who had a long career as a magazine illustrator, novelist, set designer for the Abbey Theatre, painter, and even Ireland's first Olympic medalist (for art). Yeats helped establish the modern movement in Ireland, and he encouraged Hugh Lane to patronize Irish artists. In his own paintings, Yeats turned to the Irish countryside and common laborers for subjects. Over time, his style evolved from realistic rural scenes to thickly painted, swirling works at the edge of abstraction. In **Room 4,** check out the next generation of Irish artists Yeats influenced—abstract and Pop Art of the 1970s and 1980s.

Francis Bacon Studio: Although he spent most of his life in London, Francis Bacon (1909-1992) was born in Dublin and raised in nearby Naas. After his death, his entire London studio was reconstructed here, just as the artist had left it.

After a wandering youth of odd jobs and petty crime, Bacon took up painting in his late thirties. He jumped onto the art stage in 1945 with his bleak canvases of twisted, deformed, screaming-mouthed men caged in barren landscapes—which hauntingly captured the mood of post-WWII Europe. He would become Britain's premier painter, but he continued to live simply. He stayed in his small, cramped flat with an even smaller studio (this one) for his entire life. Here he painted his famous series of "Heads"—portraits of his friends, especially of his life partner, George Dyer.

The place is a mess—empty paint cans, slashed canvases, books, photos, and newspapers everywhere—leaving only enough space for Bacon to set up his canvas in the middle of it all and paint. (If I were caged here, I'd scream.) As trashed as the studio is, it reflects Bacon's belief that "chaos breeds energy."

Spend 10 minutes with the 1985 filmed interview of Bacon, which was conducted in the studio. He speaks articulately about his work and reminisces about his down-and-out days. In nearby rooms are touchscreen terminals, photos of Bacon, a few unfinished works, and display cases of personal items, such as his coffee-table book on Velázquez, the Old Master who inspired Bacon's famous portrait of a screaming pope.

▲GPO Witness History Exhibit

This permanent, new exhibit about Easter Week 1916 is on the right as you enter the working General Post Office (GPO), which served as the rebel headquarters during that fateful time. It features a fairly balanced view of the rebellion, including the less-popular realities (like the lack of widespread support at the beginning of the movement and the civilians who died in the crossfire). The many artifacts are interesting, but don't miss the video screens showing historians from various backgrounds giving their take on how the rebellion affected Irish history.

Cost and Hours: €10, daily 9:30-17:00, last entry one hour before closing, book ahead online to avoid standing around, tel. 01/872-1916, www.gpowitnesshistory.ie.

National Leprechaun Museum

This good-natured, low-tech attraction is fine for kids and light-hearted adults (but too corny for teens). An uninhibited guide leads the group on a 45-minute meander through Irish mythology. You'll visit a wishing well, a giant's living room, and a fairy fort, listening to tales that will enchant your wee ones.

Cost and Hours: €14, daily 10:00-18:30, last entry 45 minutes before closing, a block north of the River Liffey on Abbey Street across from Jervis LUAS stop, tel. 01/873-3899, www.leprechaunmuseum.ie.

Evening Visits: For adults only, a one-hour, interactive "This Dark Land" storytelling performance explores the macabre side of Irish folklore (€16, May-Sept Fri-Sat at 19:30 and 20:30).

Jeanie Johnston Tall Ship and Famine Museum

Docked on the River Liffey, this seagoing sailing ship is a replica of a legendary Irish "famine ship." The original *Jeanie Johnston* embarked on 16 six- to eight-week transatlantic crossings, carrying more than 2,500 Irish emigrants to their new lives in America and Canada in the decade after the Great Potato Famine. While many barely seaworthy hulks were known as "coffin ships," the people who boarded the *Jeanie Johnston* were lucky: With a humanitarian captain and even a doctor on board, not one life was lost. Your tour guide will introduce you to the ship's main characters and help illuminate day-to-day life aboard a cramped tall ship 160 years ago. Because this ship makes goodwill voyages to Atlantic ports, it may be away during your visit.

Cost and Hours: €9.50, visits by 45-minute tour only, tours depart hourly, daily April-Oct 10:00-16:00, Nov-March 11:00-

16:00, on the north bank of the Liffey just east of Sean O'Casey Bridge, tel. 01/473-0111, www.jeaniejohnston.ie.

Dublin's Smithfield Village

This neighborhood is worth a look for the Old Jameson Distillery whiskey tour and Dublin's most authentic traditional-music pub. The two sights are on the long Smithfield Square, two blocks northwest of the Four Courts—the Supreme Court building. The square today still fulfills its original function as a horse market (first Sat morning of the month, great for people-watching). The Fresh Market, near the top of the square, is a handy grocery stop for urban picnic fixings (daily until 22:00).

Old Jameson Distillery

Whiskey fans enjoy visiting the old distillery. You get a 10-minute video, a 20-minute tour, and a free shot in the pub. Unfortunately, the "distillery" feels fake and put together for tourists. The Bushmills tour in Northern Ireland (in a working factory, see page 423) and the Midleton tour near Cork (in the huge original factory, page 201) are better experiences. If you do take this tour, volunteer energetically when offered the chance: This will get you a coveted seat at the whiskey taste-test table at the tour's end.

Cost and Hours: €16, 10 percent discount if booked online, Mon-Sat 9:00-18:00, Sun 10:00-18:00, last tour at 17:15, late tours possible in summer; closed for renovation until March 2017; Bow Street, tel. 01/807-2355, www.jamesonwhiskey.com.

Cobblestone Pub

Hiding in a derelict-looking building at the top of the square, this pub offers Dublin's least glitzy and most rewarding traditional-music venue. The candlelit walls, covered with photos of honored trad musicians, set the tone. Music is revered here, as reflected in the understated sign: "Listening area, please respect musicians."

Cost and Hours: Free, Mon-Sat 16:00-23:45, Sun 13:00-23:00, trad-music sessions Mon-Tue at 21:00, Wed-Sat at 19:00, Sun at 14:00; at north end of square, 100 yards from Old Jameson Distillery's brick chimney tower; tel. 01/872-1799, www.cobblestonepub.ie.

OUTER DUBLIN

The Kilmainham Gaol and the Guinness Storehouse are located west of the old center and can be combined in one visit, linked by a 20-minute walk, a five-minute taxi ride, or public bus #40. (To ride the bus from the jail to the Guinness Storehouse, leave the prison and take three rights—crossing no streets—to reach the bus stop.) Another option is to take a hop-on, hop-off bus (see page 37): City Sightseeing and Dublin Cityscape stop right at Kilmainham

From Famine to Revolution

After the Great Potato Famine (1845-1849), destitute rural Irish moved to the city in droves, seeking work and causing a housing shortage. Unscrupulous landlords came up with a solution: Subdivide the city's once-grand mansions, vacated when gentry moved to London after the 1801 Act of Union. The mansions' tiny rooms could then be crammed with poor renters. Dublin became one of the most densely populated cities in Europe—one of every three Dubliners lived in a slum. On Henrietta Street, once a wealthy Dublin address, these new tenements bulged with humanity (look for the new Museum of Tenement Life, which is planning to open at 14 Henrietta Street in 2017). According to the 1911 census, one district counted 835 people living in 15 houses (many with a single outhouse in back or a communal chamber pot in the room). In cramped, putrid quarters like this, tuberculosis was rampant, and infant mortality skyrocketed.

Those who could get work tenaciously clung to their precious jobs. The terrible working conditions prompted many to join trade unions. A 1913 strike and employer lockout, known as the "Dublin Lockout," lasted for seven months. The picket lines were brutally put down by police in the pocket of rich businessmen, led by newspaper owner and hotel magnate William Murphy. In response, James Larkin and James Connolly formed the Irish Citizen Army, a socialist militia to protect the poor trade unionists.

Murphy eventually broke the unions. Larkin headed for the US to organize workers there. During World War I, he praised the rise of the Soviet Union and later was persecuted during the postwar "Red Scare" (even doing time in Sing Sing prison for advocating "unlawful means" to overthrow the US government). Meanwhile, Connolly stayed in Ireland and brought the Irish Citizen Army into the 1916 Easter Uprising as an integral part of the rebel forces. During the uprising, he slyly had a rebel flag flown over Murphy's prized hotel on O'Connell Street. The uninformed British artillery battalions took the bait and pulverized it.

Connolly was the last of the rebel leaders executed in Dublin in 1916. Unable to stand in front of the firing squad in Kilmainham Gaol (his ankle was shattered by a bullet while he was defending the General Post Office), Connolly was tied to a chair and shot sitting down. Of the 16 rebel executions, his was the one most credited with turning Irish public opinion in favor of the rebel martyrs.

Today you'll find heroic Dublin statues to honor them both. James Larkin, arms outstretched, is in front of the post office on O'Connell Street. James Connolly is on Beresford Place, behind the Customs House.

Gaol, while Dublin Bus Tour stops 200 yards away, in front of the modern art museum in Kilmainham hospital. All three tours stop at the Guinness Storehouse.

▲▲▲Kilmainham Gaol (Jail)

Opened in 1796 as Dublin's county jail and a debtors' prison, Kilmainham was considered a model in its day. In reality, this jail

was frequently used by the British as a political prison. Many of those who fought for Irish independence were held or executed here, including leaders of the rebellions of 1798, 1803, 1848, 1867, and 1916. National heroes Robert Emmett and Charles Stewart Parnell each did time here. The last prisoner to be held in the jail

was Eamon de Valera, who later became president of Ireland. He was released on July 16, 1924, the day Kilmainham was finally shut down. The buildings, virtually in ruins, were restored in the 1960s. Today, it's a shrine to the Nathan Hales of Ireland.

Cost and Hours: €9, €8 if purchased online, daily 9:30-16:30, last entry one hour before closing; book online a few days before your visit during busy season to guarantee a spot on a tour, as walk-up spots can sell out quickly; take bus #69 or #70 from Aston Quay or #13 or #40 from O'Connell Street or College Green—confirm with driver; tel. 01/453-5984, www.kilmainhamgaolmuseum.ie. The humble upstairs café serves sandwiches and coffee.

Visiting the Jail: Start your visit with a one-hour guided **tour** (2/hour, includes 15-minute prison-history slide show in the prison chapel—spend waiting time in museum). It's touching to tour the cells and places of execution—hearing tales of oppressive colonialism and heroic patriotism—alongside Irish schoolkids who know these names well. The museum has an excellent exhibit on Victorian prison life and Ireland's fight for independence. Don't miss the museum's dimly lit Last Words 1916 hall upstairs, which displays

the stirring final letters that patriots sent to loved ones hours before facing the firing squad.

▲Guinness Storehouse

A visit to the Guinness Storehouse is, for many, a devout pilgrimage. But some visitors are surprised to find the vibe to be more like a Disneyland for beer lovers. Don't look for conveyor belts of beer bottles being stamped with bottle caps.

DUBLIN

The Famous Record-Breaking Records Book

Look up "beer" in the *Guinness World Records*, and you'll discover that the strongest brew ever sold had an alcohol volume of 55 percent (a Scottish brew called *The End of History*), and that the record for removing beer bottle caps with one's teeth is 68 in one minute. But aside from listing records for amazing—or amazingly stupid—feats, this famous record book has a more subtle connection with beer.

In 1951, while hunting in Ireland's County Wexford, Sir Hugh Beaver, then the managing director at Guinness Breweries, got into a debate with his companions over which was the fastest game bird in Europe: the golden plover or the red grouse. That night at his estate, after scouring countless reference books, they were disappointed not to find a definitive answer.

Beaver realized that similar questions were likely being debated nightly across pubs in Ireland and Britain. So he hired twins Norris and Ross McWhirter, who ran a fact-finding agency in London, to compile a book of answers to various questions. They set up an office at 107 Fleet Street and began assembling the first edition of the book by contacting experts, such as astrophysicists, etymologists, virologists, and volcanologists. In 1955, the *Guinness Book of Records* (later renamed *Guinness World Records*) was published. By Christmas, it topped the British bestseller list.

In the beginning, entries mostly focused on natural phenomena and animal oddities, but grew to include a wide variety of extreme human achievements. After more than a half-century of noting record-breaking traditions around the globe, the volume continues to answer a multitude of burning trivia questions, such as the wealthiest cat in the world, the largest burrito ever made, and the record time for peeling 50 pounds of onions (an event that likely caused a lot of tears).

The iconic books are now available in more than 100 countries and 26 languages, with more than 3.5 million copies sold annually. As the bestselling copyrighted book of all time, it even earns a record-breaking entry within its own pages.

Instead, you'll find huge crowds, high decibel music, and wall-sized, dreamy TV beer ads.

Arthur Guinness began brewing the renowned stout here in 1759, and by 1868 it was the biggest brewery in the world. Today, the sprawling brewery complex fills several city blocks, but the Storehouse occupies just one of them.

Cost and Hours: €20, includes a €5 pint; €1 off with your hop-on, hop-off bus ticket, up to 20 percent discount when you book online; daily 9:30-17:00, July-Aug until 18:00; enter on Bellevue Street, bus #123 from Dame Street and O'Connell Street; tel. 01/408-4800, www.guinness-storehouse.com.

Visiting the Brewery: Around the world, Guinness brews more than 10 million pints a day. Although the home of Ireland's national beer welcomes visitors with a sprawling modern museum, there are no tours of an actual working brewery here.

The museum fills the old fermentation plant used from 1902 through 1988, which reopened in 2000 as a huge shrine to the tradition. Step into the middle of the ground floor and look up. A tall, beer-glass-shaped glass atrium—14 million pints big—soars upward past four floors of exhibitions and cafés to the skylight. Then look down at Arthur's original 9,000-year lease, enshrined under Plexiglas in the floor...and you realize that at £45 per year, it was quite a bargain. (The brewery eventually purchased the land, so the lease is no longer valid.)

The actual exhibit makes brewing seem more grandiose than it is and presents Arthur as if he were the god of human happiness. His pints contain only 200 calories, but they pack a 4.2 percent alcohol content. Highlights are the cooperage (with 1954 film clips showing the master keg-makers plying their now virtually extinct trade), a display of the brewery's clever ads, and a small exhibit about the beer's connection to the *Guinness World Records* (see sidebar).

The tasting rooms provide a 10-minute detour. In the "white room" you're introduced to using your five senses to appreciate the perfect porter. Then in the "black room" you're told how to taste it from a leprechaun-sized beer glass.

Atop the building, the **Gravity Bar** provides visitors with a commanding 360-degree view of Dublin—with vistas all the way to the sea—and an included beer.

▲National Museum: Decorative Arts and History

This branch of the National Museum, which occupies the huge, 18th-century stone Collins Barracks in west Dublin, displays Irish dress, furniture, weapons, silver, and other domestic baubles from the past 700 years. History buffs will linger longest in the "Soldiers & Chiefs" exhibit, which covers the Irish at war both at home and abroad since 1500 (including the American Civil War). The sober finale is the "Understanding 1916" room, offering Ireland's best coverage of the painful birth of this nation, an event known as the "Terrible Beauty." Guns, personal letters, and death masks help illustrate the 1916 Easter Uprising, War of Independence against Britain, and Ireland's civil war. Croppies Acre, the large park between the museum and the river, was the site of Dublin's largest soup kitchen during the Great Potato Famine in 1845-1849.

Cost and Hours: Free, Tue-Sat 10:00-17:00, Sun 14:00-

17:00, closed Mon, good café; on north side of the River Liffey in Collins Barracks on Benburb Street, roughly across the river from Guinness Storehouse, easy to reach by the LUAS red line—get off at Museum stop; tel. 01/677-7444, www.museum.ie. Call ahead for sporadic tour times.

▲Gaelic Athletic Association Museum

The GAA was founded in 1884 as an expression of an Irish cultural awakening. It was created to foster the development of Gaelic sports, specifically Gaelic football and hurling, and to exclude English sports such as cricket and rugby. The GAA played an important part in the fight for independence. This museum, at 82,000-seat Croke Park Stadium in east Dublin, offers a high-tech, interactive introduction to Ireland's favorite games. Relive the greatest moments in hurling and Irish-football history. Then get involved: Pick up a stick and try hurling, kick a football, and test your speed and balance. A 15-minute film (played on request) gives you a "Sunday at the stadium" experience.

Cost and Hours: €6.50, Mon-Sat 9:30-17:00, Sun 10:30-17:00, July-Aug until 18:00, on game Sundays the museum is open to ticket holders only, café, located under the stands at Croke Park Stadium, a 20-minute walk northeast of Parnell Square—enter from St. Joseph's Avenue off Clonliffe Road, tel. 01/819-2323, www.crokepark.ie/gaa-museum.

Tours: The €13, one-hour museum-plus-stadium-tour option is worth it only for rabid fans who want a glimpse of the huge stadium and yearn to know which locker room is considered the unlucky one. The €20 rooftop tour offers views 17 stories above the field from lofty catwalks (stadium tours daily on the hour, rooftop tours on the half-hour, fewer Oct-April).

Hurling or Gaelic Football at Croke Park Stadium

Actually seeing a match here, surrounded by incredibly spirited Irish fans, is a fun experience. Hurling is like airborne hockey with

no injury time-outs. Gaelic football resembles a rugged form of soccer; you can carry the ball, but must bounce or kick it every three steps. Matches are held most Saturday or Sunday afternoons in summer (May-Aug), culminating in the hugely popular all-Ireland finals on Sunday afternoons in September. Tickets are available at the stadium except during the finals. Choose a county to support, buy their colors to wear or wave, scream yourself hoarse, and you'll be a temporary local.

Ireland's Gaelic Athletic Association

The GAA has long been a powerhouse in Ireland. Ireland's national pastimes of Gaelic football and hurling pack stadiums all over the country. When you consider that 80,000 people—paying at least €20 to €30 each—stuff Dublin's Croke Park Stadium and that all the athletes are strictly amateur, you might wonder, "Where does all the money go?"

Ireland has a long tradition of using the revenue generated by these huge events to promote Gaelic athletics and Gaelic cultural events throughout the country in a grassroots and neighborhood way. So, while the players (many of whom are schoolteachers whose jobs allow for evenings and summers free) participate only for the glory of their various counties, the money generated is funding children's leagues, school coaches, small-town athletic facilities, and traditional arts, music, and dance—as well as the building and maintenance of giant stadiums such as Croke Park (which claims to be the third-largest stadium in Europe).

In America, sports are usually considered to be a form of entertainment. But in Ireland, sports have a deeper emotional connection. Gaelic sports are a heartfelt expression of Irish identity. There was a time when the Irish were not allowed to be members of the GAA if they also belonged to a cricket club (a British game).

In 1921, during the War of Independence, Michael Collins (leader of the early IRA, the man who practically invented urban guerrilla warfare) orchestrated the simultaneous assassination of a dozen British intelligence agents around Dublin in a single morning. The same day, the Black and Tans retaliated. These grizzled British WWI veterans, clad in black police coats and tan surplus army pants, had been sent to Ireland to stamp out the rebels. Knowing Croke Park would be full of Irish Nationalists, they entered the packed stadium during a Gaelic football match and fired into the stands, killing 13 spectators as well as a Tipperary player. It was Ireland's first Bloody Sunday, a tragedy that would be repeated 51 years later in Derry.

Today Croke Park's "Hill 16" grandstands are built on rubble dumped here after the 1916 Uprising; it's literally sacred ground. And the Hogan stands are named after the murdered player from Tipperary. Queen Elizabeth II visited the stadium during her historic visit in 2011. Her warm interest in the stadium and in the institution of the GAA did much to heal old wounds.

Cost and Hours: €20-55, box office open Mon-Fri 9:30-13:00 & 14:15-17:30, purchase tickets for September finals well in advance, www.gaa.ie.

Glasnevin Cemetery and Museum

This is the final resting place for Ireland's most passionate patriots, writers, politicians, and assorted personalities. What Père Lachaise is to Paris, Glasnevin is to Dublin. Here you'll find the graves of Michael Collins, Charles Stewart Parnell, and teenage rebel/martyr Kevin Barry (of patriot song fame), surrounding a replica round tower atop the crypt of Daniel O'Connell. Among other notables interred here are tragically short-lived writers Brendan Behan and Christy Brown (the subject of the film *My Left Foot*). The cemetery's 120 leafy acres are surrounded by a tall wall and a half-dozen watchtowers (one of which was once moveable) used to deter grave robbers. Guided tours of the cemetery are fascinating to those who love Irish culture and history. A wall of memorials was added in 2016 to commemorate all who were lost during the struggle for Irish independence a hundred years ago, including civilians and British soldiers. The adjacent museum offers more detail—you'll dig the graveyard superstitions (free to enter cemetery, €6 for museum only, €12 includes tour; open daily 9:00-18:00, 1.5-hour tours at 11:30 and 14:30, more in summer; tel. 01/882-6550, www.glasnevintrust.ie). It's two miles north of the city center (get here on the hop-on, hop-off bus, or take buses #40 or #140 from O'Connell Street).

Shopping in Dublin

Shops are open roughly Monday-Saturday 9:00-18:00 and until 20:00 on Thursday. Hours are shorter on Sunday (if shops are open at all). Good shopping areas include:

• **Grafton Street,** with its neighboring streets and arcades (such as the fun Great George's Arcade between Great George's and Drury Streets), and nearby shopping centers (Powerscourt Townhouse and St. Stephen's Green). Francis Street creaks with antiques.

• **Henry Street,** home to Dublin's top department stores (pedestrian-only, off O'Connell Street).

• **Nassau Street,** lining Trinity College, with the popular Kilkenny department store, the Irish Music store, and lots of touristy shops.

• **Temple Bar,** worth a browse any day for its art, jewelry, New Age paraphernalia, books, music (try Claddagh Records—see page 66), and gift shops. On Saturdays at Temple Bar's Meeting

House Square, it's food in the morning (from 9:00) and books in the afternoon (until 18:00).

• **Millennium Walk,** a trendy lane stretching two blocks north from the River Liffey to Abbey Street. It's filled with hip restaurants, shops, and coffee bars. It's easy to miss—look for the south entry at the pedestrian Millennium Bridge, or the north entry at Jervis Street LUAS stop.

• **Street markets,** such as Moore Street (produce, noise, and lots of local color, Mon-Sat 8:00-18:00, closed Sun, near General Post Office), and St. Michan Street (fish, Tue-Sat 7:00-15:00, closed Sun-Mon, behind Four Courts building).

Entertainment in Dublin

Ireland has produced some of the finest writers in the English and Irish languages, and Dublin houses some of Europe's best theaters. Though the city was the site of the first performance of Handel's *Messiah* (1742), these days Dublin is famous for its rock bands: U2, Thin Lizzy, Sinéad O'Connor, and Live Aid founder Bob Geldof's band the Boomtown Rats all started here.

Theater

Abbey Theatre is Ireland's national theater, founded by W. B. Yeats in 1904 to preserve Irish culture during British rule (€15-40, generally nightly at 20:00, Sat matinees at 14:30, 26 Lower Abbey Street, tel. 01/878-7222, www.abbeytheatre.ie). **Gate Theatre** does foreign plays as well as Irish classics (Cavendish Row, tel. 01/874-4045, www.gatetheatre.ie). The **Gaiety Theatre** offers a wide range of quality productions (King Street South, toll tel. 0818-719-388, www.gaietytheatre.ie). The **Bord Gáis Energy Theatre** is the newest and spiffiest venue (Grand Canal Square, tel. 01/677-7999, www.bordgaisenergytheatre.ie). Street theater takes the stage in Temple Bar on summer evenings. Browse the listings and fliers at the TI.

Concerts

The **3 Arena,** once a railway terminus (easy LUAS access), is now sponsored by a hip phone company. Residents call it by its geographic nickname: The Point. It's considered one of the country's top live-music venues (East Link Bridge, toll tel. 01/819-8888, http://3arena.ie).

At the **National Concert Hall,** the National Symphony Orchestra performs most Friday evenings (€15-40, off St. Stephen's Green at Earlsfort Terrace, tel. 01/417-0077, www.nch.ie).

Pub Action

Folk music fills Dublin's pubs, and street entertainers ply their trade in the midst of the party people in Temple Bar and among shoppers on Grafton Street. The Temple Bar area in particular thrives with music—traditional, jazz, and pop. Although it's pricier than the rest of Dublin, it really is the best place for tourists and locals (who come here to watch the tourists). For locations, see the "Dublin Restaurants" map on page 92.

Gogarty's Pub has foot-tapping sessions downstairs daily at 13:00 and upstairs nightly from 21:00 (at corner of Fleet and Anglesea, tel. 01/671-1822). Use this pub as a kickoff for your Temple Bar evening. It's also where the Traditional Irish Musical Pub Crawl starts (see page 33).

A 10-minute hike up the river west of Temple Bar takes you to a twosome with a local and less-touristy ambience. **The Brazen Head,** which lays claim to being the oldest pub in Dublin, is a hit for an early dinner and late live music (nightly from 21:30), with atmospheric rooms and a courtyard perfect for balmy evenings. They also host great "Food, Folk, and Fairies" storytelling dinner evenings (see page 90). **O'Shea's Merchant Pub,** just across the street, is encrusted in memories of County Kerry football heroes. It's filled with locals taking a break from the grind. There's live traditional music nightly at 21:30 (the front half is a restaurant, the magic is in the back half—enter on Bridge Street, tel. 01/679-3797, www.themerchanttemplebar.com).

The **Palace Bar** is a well-preserved gin joint, with almost 135 years of history. It attracted Dublin's literary greats from the start, and contrasts sharply (and refreshingly) with the prefab offerings down the street in the Temple Bar mayhem (east end of Temple Bar, where Fleet Street hits Westmoreland Street at 21 Fleet Street, tel. 01/671-7388, www.thepalacebardublin.com).

Porterhouse has an inviting and varied menu, Dublin's best selection of microbrews, and live music. You won't find Guinness here, just tasty homebrews. Try one of their fun sampler trays. You can check their music schedule online (corner of Essex Street East and Parliament Street, tel. 01/671-5715, www.theporterhouse.ie).

For guided **pub crawls** (focusing on either Irish literature or music), see page 33.

Sleep Code

Hotels are classified based on the average price of a typical en suite double room with breakfast in high season.

$$$$	**Splurge:** Most rooms over €170
$$$	**Pricier:** €130-170
$$	**Moderate:** €90-130
$	**Budget:** €50-90
¢	**Backpacker:** Under €50
RS%	**Rick Steves discount**

Unless otherwise noted, credit cards are accepted and free Wi-Fi is available. Comparison-shop by checking prices at several hotels (on each hotel's own website, on a booking site, or by email). For the best deal, *book directly with the hotel*. Ask for a discount if paying in cash; if the listing includes **RS%**, request a Rick Steves discount.

Sleeping in Dublin

Dublin is popular, loud, and expensive. Rooms can be tight. Book ahead for weekends any time of year, particularly in summer and during rugby weekends. In summer, occasional big rock concerts can make rooms hard to find. On Sundays in September, fans converge on Dublin from all over the country for the all-Ireland finals in Gaelic football and hurling. Prices are often discounted on weeknights (Mon-Thu) and from November through February. Many Dublin hotels use dynamic pricing (adjusting rates upward or downward with demand); check for the latest prices and specials on hotel websites. Book directly with the hotel for the best deals.

Big and practical places (both cheap and moderate) are most central near Christ Church Cathedral, on the edge of Temple Bar. For classy, older Dublin accommodations, you'll stay a bit farther out (southeast of St. Stephen's Green). If you're a light sleeper or on a tight budget, get a room in quiet Dun Laoghaire (page 101) or small-town Howth (page 106), where rooms are cheaper. Both spots are an easy 25-minute DART train ride into the city.

SOUTH OF THE RIVER LIFFEY
Near Christ Church Cathedral

These lodging options cluster near Christ Church Cathedral, a five-minute walk from the rowdy and noisy evening scene (at Temple Bar), and 10 minutes from the sightseeing center (Trinity College and Grafton Street). The cheap hostels in this neighborhood have some double rooms. Full Irish breakfasts, which cost €8-10 at the hotels, are cheaper at the many small cafés nearby; try the **Queen**

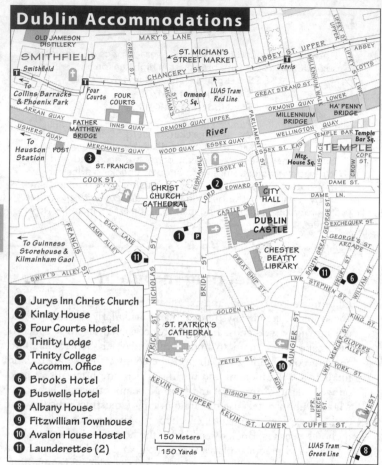

Dublin Accommodations

1. Jurys Inn Christ Church
2. Kinlay House
3. Four Courts Hostel
4. Trinity Lodge
5. Trinity College Accomm. Office
6. Brooks Hotel
7. Buswells Hotel
8. Albany House
9. Fitzwilliam Townhouse
10. Avalon House Hostel
11. Launderettes (2)

of Tarts or Chorus Café (see listings under "Eating in Dublin," later).

$$$ Jurys Inn Christ Church, one of three Jurys Inns in downtown Dublin, is central and offers business-class comfort in 182 identical rooms. This no-nonsense, American-style hotel chain has a winning keep-it-simple-and-affordable formula. If "ye olde" is getting old—and you don't mind big tour groups—this is a good option. Request a room far from the noisy elevator (breakfast extra, book long in advance for weekends, pay parking, Christ Church Place, tel. 01/454-0000, US tel. 800-423-6953, www.jurysinns. com, jurysinnchristchurch@jurysinns.com). The other Jurys Inns, described later, are near Connolly Station and Parnell Square.

¢ Kinlay House is the backpackers' choice—definitely the place to go for cheap beds, a central location, and an all-ages-welcome atmosphere. This huge, red-brick, 19th-century Victo-

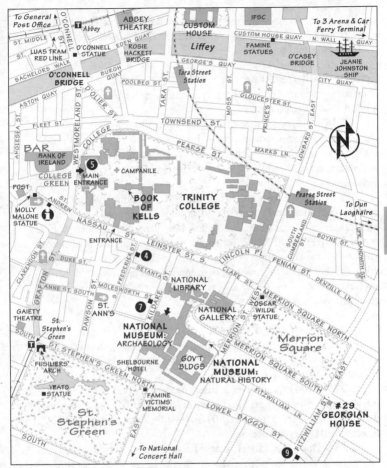

rian building has 200 metal, prison-style beds in spartan rooms. There are singles, doubles, and four- to six-bed coed dorms (good for families), as well as a few giant dorms. It fills up most days; call well in advance, especially for singles, doubles, and summer weekends (private rooms available, includes continental breakfast, travel desk, TV lounge, lots of stairs, Christ Church, 2 Lord Edward Street, tel. 01/679-6644, www.kinlaydublin.ie, info@kinlaydublin.ie).

¢ **Four Courts Hostel** is a 234-bed hostel beautifully located immediately across the river from the Four Courts. It's within a five-minute walk of Christ Church Cathedral and Temple Bar. Bare and institutional (as hostels typically are), it's also spacious and well-run, with a focus on security and efficiency (private rooms available, elevator, game room, some pay parking, 15 Merchant's Quay, from Connolly Station or Busáras Central Bus Station take LUAS to Four Courts stop and cross river via Father Matthew Bridge, tel. 01/672-5839, www.fourcourtshostel.com, info@fourcourtshostel.com).

Trinity College Area

You can't get more central than Trinity College; these listings offer a good value for the money.

$$$$ Trinity Lodge offers fine, quiet lodging in 26 rooms split between two Georgian townhouses on either side of Frederick Street South, just south of Trinity College (12 South Frederick Street, tel. 01/617-0900, www.trinitylodge.com, trinitylodge@eircom.net).

$$ Trinity College turns its 800 student-housing dorm rooms on campus into no-frills, affordable accommodations in the city center each summer. Look for the Accommodations Office (open Mon-Fri 8:00-18:00) through the door on the right before you come into the courtyard (late-May-early-Sept, cheaper rooms with shared bath, includes continental breakfast, cooked breakfast extra, tel. 01/896-1177, www.tcd.ie/accommodation/visitors, reservations@tcd.ie).

Near St. Stephen's Green

Dublin is filled with worn-yet-comfy townhouses. Albany House and Fitzwilliam Townhouse are dependable, basic lodgings, while Brooks and Buswells are cushier.

$$$$ Brooks Hotel is a fine choice for great service, tending 98 plush rooms in an ideal central location. This splurge rarely disappoints (Drury Street, tel. 01/670-4000, www.brookshotel.ie, reservations@brookshotel.ie).

$$$$ Buswells Hotel, one of the city's oldest, is a pleasant Georgian-style haven with 67 rooms in the heart of the city (breakfast extra, between Trinity College and St. Stephen's Green at 23 Molesworth Street, tel. 01/614-6500, www.buswells.ie, info@buswells.ie).

$$$ Albany House's 50 restful rooms come with high ceilings, Georgian ambience, and some stairs (just one block south of St. Stephen's Green at 84 Harcourt Street, tel. 01/475-1092, www.albanyhousedublin.com, info@albanyhousedublin.com).

$$$ Fitzwilliam Townhouse rents 14 basic rooms in a Georgian townhouse near St. Stephen's Green (family rooms, breakfast extra, 41 Upper Fitzwilliam Street, tel. 01/662-5155, www.fitzwilliamtownhouse.com, info@fitzwilliamtownhouse.com).

¢ Avalon House Hostel, near Grafton Street, rents 282 simple, clean backpacker beds (private rooms available, includes continental breakfast, elevator, a few minutes off Grafton Street at

SE Dublin Hotels

1 Number 31
2 The Schoolhouse Hotel
3 Mespil Hotel
4 Roxford Lodge Hotel
5 Waterloo House

55 Aungier Street, tel. 01/475-0001, www.avalon-house.ie, info@avalon-house.ie).

Away from the Center, Southeast of St. Stephen's Green

The listings that follow are unique places (except for the business-class Mespil Hotel), and they charge accordingly. If you're going to break the bank, do it here. See map above for locations.

$$$$ Number 31 is a hidden gem reached via gritty little Leeson Close (a lane off Lower Leeson Street). Ask Noel about the VIPs who attended dinner parties here 50 years ago. Its understated elegance is top-notch, with six rooms in a former coach house and 15 rooms in an adjacent Georgian house; the two buildings are connected by a quiet little garden. Guests appreciate the special touches (such as a sunken living room with occasional peat fires) and tasty breakfasts served in a classy glass atrium (family rooms, free parking, 31 Leeson Close, tel. 01/676-5011, www.number31.ie, info@number31.ie).

$$$ The Schoolhouse Hotel taught as many as 300 students in its heyday (1861-1969) and was in the middle of the street-fight that was the 1916 Easter Uprising. Now it's a serene hideout with 31 pristine rooms and a fine restaurant (breakfast extra, book early,

2 Northumberland Road, tel. 01/667-5014, www.schoolhousehotel. com, reservations@schoolhousehotel.com).

$$$ Mespil Hotel is a huge, modern, business-class hotel renting 254 identical three-star rooms (most with a double and single bed, phone, TV) at a good price with all the comforts. This place is a cut above Jurys Inn (breakfast extra, elevator; small first-come, first-served free parking; 10-minute walk southeast of St. Stephen's Green or take bus #37, #38, #39, or #46A; 50 Mespil Road, tel. 01/488-4600, www.mespilhotel.com, mespil@leehotels. com).

$$ Roxford Lodge Hotel is well-managed and a great value. In a quiet residential neighborhood a 20-minute walk from Trinity College, it has 24 tastefully decorated rooms awash with Jacuzzis and saunas. The executive suite is honeymoon-worthy (family rooms, breakfast extra, elevator, parking, 46 Northumberland Road, tel. 01/668-8572, www.roxfordlodge.ie, reservations@ roxfordlodge.ie).

$$ Waterloo House sits proudly Georgian on a quiet residential street with 19 comfortable and relaxing rooms and a pleasant back garden (family rooms, parking, 8 Waterloo Road, tel. 01/660-1888, www.waterloohouse.ie, info@waterloohouse.ie).

NORTH OF THE RIVER LIFFEY
Near Connolly Station

This once-tattered neighborhood (like much of the north side) is gradually being rejuvenated. To locate these hotels, see the map on page 68.

$$$ Jurys Inn Custom House, on Custom House Quay, offers the same value as the other Jurys Inns in Dublin, but it's less central. Its 239 rooms border the financial district, a 10-minute riverside hike from O'Connell Bridge. Of the three Jurys Inns in the city center, this one is most likely to have rooms available (breakfast extra, pay parking, tel. 01/854-1500, US tel. 800-423-6953, www. jurysinns.com, jurysinncustomhouse@jurysinns.com).

Near Parnell Square

A swanky neighborhood 250 years ago, this is now workaday Dublin with a steady urban hum. To locate these hotels, see the map on page 68.

$$$ The Castle Hotel is a formerly grand but still comfortable Georgian establishment embedded in the urban canyons of North Dublin. A half-block east of the Garden of Remembrance, it's a good value with pleasant rooms and the friendly Castle Vaults pub with live music in its basement (Great Denmark Street, tel. 01/874-6949, www.castle-hotel.ie, info@castle-hotel.ie).

$$$ Jurys Inn Parnell Street has 253 predictably soulless but good-value rooms. It's a block from the north end of O'Connell Street and the cluster of museums on Parnell Square (breakfast extra, tel. 01/878-4900, www.jurysinns.com, jurysinnparnellst@ jurysinns.com).

$$$ Belvedere Hotel has 92 plain-vanilla rooms that are short on character but long on dependable, modern comforts (Great Denmark Street, tel. 01/873-7700, www.belvederehotel.ie, reservations@belvederehotel.ie).

$$ Charles Stewart Guesthouse, big and basic, offers 60 forgettable rooms. But it's in a good location for a fair price (family rooms, breakfast extra, ask for a quieter room in the back, just beyond top end of O'Connell Street at 5 Parnell Square East, tel. 01/878-0350, www.charlesstewart.ie, info@charlesstewart.ie).

APARTMENTS

For general advice on short-term rentals in Ireland, see page 519.

$$ For a great self-catering option north of the river, try a bright, cheery one-bedroom apartment with a full kitchen and pull-out sofa tucked quietly in the **Custom House Harbour apartments,** only a minute's walk from Connolly Station (sleeps 3-4, washer/dryer, UK tel. 44-28-7126-9691, saddlershouse@ btinternet.com). See map on page 68 for location.

Eating in Dublin

It's easy to find fine, creative eateries all over town. While you can get decent pub grub for €15 on just about any corner, consider saving that for the countryside. There's just no pressing reason to eat Irish in cosmopolitan Dublin. In fact, going local these days is the same as going ethnic. The city's good restaurants are packed from 20:00 on, especially on weekends. Eating early (17:30-19:00) saves time and money, as many better places offer an early-bird special. Many restaurants serve free jugs of ice water with a smile.

AFTERNOON TEA

$$$$ The **Shelbourne Hotel** has been a Dublin landmark since 1824, built to attract genteel patrons and Dublin's upper-crust socialites (not to mention British Army snipers during the 1916 Easter Uprising). But schlubs like us can dip our toes in the aristocratic fantasy by enjoying the tradition of afternoon tea (no shorts, tank tops, or Molly Hatchet T-shirts). The menu is a swirl of finger sandwiches, buttermilk scones, clotted cream, strawberry jam, ginger loaf, and fine coffee...as well as 22 varieties of tea. You'll find it in the ground floor Lord Mayor's Lounge (€45, €57 with champagne; seatings Mon-Thu at 1:00, 15:15, and 17:30; Fri-Sun

Restaurant Price Code

I've assigned each eatery a price category, based on the average cost of a typical main course. Drinks, desserts, and splurge items (steak and seafood) can raise the price considerably.

$$$$	**Splurge:** Most main courses over €25
$$$	**Pricier:** €20-25
$$	**Moderate:** €15-20
$	**Budget:** Under €15

In the Republic of Ireland, carryout fish-and-chips and other takeout food is **$**; a basic pub or sit-down eatery is **$$**; a gastropub or casual but more upscale restaurant is **$$$**; and a swanky splurge is **$$$$**.

at 11:45, 14:00, 16:15, and 18:30; reservations smart, especially on weekends; 27 St. Stephen's Green, tel. 01/663-4500).

DINNER WITH ENTERTAINMENT

$$$$ The Brazen Head hosts "Food, Folk and Fairies" evenings, which are more culturally highbrow than the title might suggest, while still remaining fun. Even at €46, the evening is a great value and gives your mind as much to chew on as your mouth. You get a hearty, four-course meal that's punctuated between courses by soulful Irish history and fascinating Irish mythology, delivered by an engaging local folklorist (March-Dec daily 19:00-22:00, Jan-Feb Thu and Sat only; reservations smart; by south end of Father Matthew Bridge, 2 blocks west of Christ Church Cathedral at 20 Bridge Street; pub tel. 01/677-9549, show tel. 01/218-8555, www. irishfolktours.com).

Further down the intellectual food chain is the **$$$$ Parliament Hotel,** which hosts "Celtic Nights," featuring dinner shows with Irish music and dance. You'll be entertained by an Irish Rovers-type band singing ballads and a dance troupe scuffing up the floorboards to the delight of tour groups (€34, shows nightly at 20:00, dinner reservations required, south of the river at the corner of Lord Edward Street and Exchange Street Upper, roughly opposite City Hall, tel. 01/670-8777, www.parliament.ie).

QUICK AND EASY NEAR GRAFTON STREET

$$ Cornucopia is a small, earth-mama-with-class, proudly vegetarian, self-serve place two blocks off Grafton. It's friendly and youthful, with hearty lunches and dinner specials (Mon-Tue 8:30-21:00, Wed-Sat 8:30-22:00, Sun 12:00-21:00, 19 Wicklow Street, tel. 01/677-7583).

$$$ The Farm, Dublin's healthiest dining option, shuns processed food and features fresh, organic, and free-range fare that's affordable and pretty darn tasty (daily 11:00-22:00, a half-block south of Trinity College at 3 Dawson Street, tel. 01/671-8654).

$$ The Hairy Lemon has a weird name (like a lot of Dublin pubs do), but its friendly staff, central location, and above-average menu keep me coming back. Hearty eaters will love their famous stew-like Dublin Coddle (daily 11:30-22:00, 41 Lower Stephen Street, tel. 01/671-8949).

$$ O'Neill's Pub is a venerable, dark, and tangled retreat offering good grub, including dependable €12-15 carvery lunches. It's very central, located near the main TI (daily 12:00-22:30, Suffolk Street, tel. 01/679-3656).

$$ Avoca Café is a good-value eatery on two levels. The upstairs, on the second floor above the Avoca department store, has simple yet satisfying meals (Mon-Sat 9:30-17:30, Sun 11:00-17:30, close to the TI at 11-13 Suffolk Street, tel. 01/672-6019). The **$ Avoca Sandwich Counter** is a cramped basement dweller brightened by whitewashed walls. It whips up portable sandwiches that you can enjoy on the run (daily generally 10:00-17:00).

$$ Two pubs on Duke Street—**The Duke** and **Davy Burns**— serve reliable pub lunches. (The nearby Cathach Rare Books shop, at 10 Duke Street, displays a rare edition of *Ulysses* inscribed by James Joyce, among other treasures, in its window.)

$ Wagamama, like its popular sisters in Britain, is a pan-Asian slurp-a-thon with great and healthy noodle and rice dishes served at long communal tables by energetic waiters (daily 12:00-22:00, often a line but it moves quickly, South King Street underneath St. Stephen's Green Shopping Centre, tel. 01/417-1878).

$$ Yamamori is a plain, mellow, and modern Japanese place serving seas of sushi and noodles (daily 12:00-22:30, 71 South Great George's Street, tel. 01/475-5001).

Supermarkets: Dunnes, on South Great George's Street, is your one-stop shop for assembling a picnic meal (Mon-Sat 8:30-19:00, Thu-Fri until 20:00, Sun 11:00-19:00, across from Yamamori). They have another outlet in the basement of St. Stephen's Green Shopping Centre. **Marks & Spencer** department store has a fancy grocery store in the basement, with fine takeaway sandwiches and salads (Mon-Sat 8:00-20:00, Thu until 21:00, Sun 10:00-19:00, Grafton Street).

HIP AND FUN IN NORTH DUBLIN

The Church is a trendy café/bar/restaurant/nightclub/beer garden housed in the former St. Mary's Church. In its former life as a church, it hosted the baptism of Irish rebel Wolfe Tone and the marriage of brewing legend Arthur Guinness. The **$$$ choir balcony** has a huge pipe organ and a refined menu; the ground floor **$$ nave** is dominated by a long bar and pub grub; and a disco

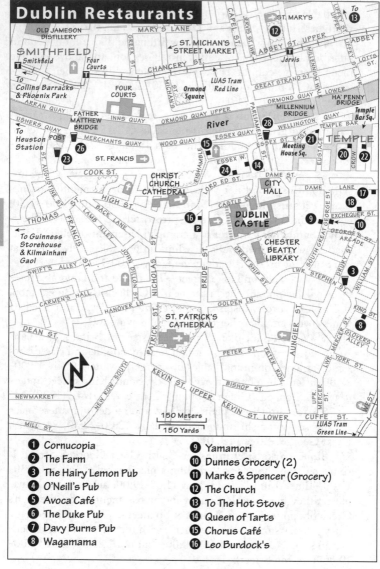

Dublin Restaurants

OLD JAMESON DISTILLERY

MARY'S LANE

ST. MARY'S

CAPEL ST.

JERVIS ST. LWR.

ABBEY ST. UPPER

LIFFEY ST. UPPER

ABBEY ST.

LOTTS ST.

To ⑬

SMITHFIELD

Smithfield

Four Courts

ST. MICHAN'S STREET MARKET

GREEK ST.

CHANCERY ST.

Jervis

MILLENNIUM WK.

LOWER LIFFEY ST.

To Collins Barracks & Phoenix Park

ARRAN QUAY

FOUR COURTS

MICHAN'S

Ormond Square

LUAS Tram Red Line

GREAT STRAND ST.

ORMOND QUAY UPPER

MILLENNIUM BRIDGE

HA' PENNY BRIDGE

Temple Bar Sq.

USHERS QUAY

FATHER MATTHEW BRIDGE

INNS QUAY

ORMOND QUAY UPPER

River

ORMOND QUAY

WELLINGTON QUAY

TEMPLE BAR

TEMPLE

To Heuston Station

POST

MERCHANTS QUAY

WOOD QUAY

ESSEX QUAY

ESSEX ST. EAST

Meeting House Sq.

EUSTACE ST.

CROW

ST. AUGUSTINE ST.

㉖

ST. FRANCIS

COOK ST.

FISHAMBLE

ESSEX W.

LORD ED. ST.

DAME ST.

DAME ST.

DAME LANE

㉓

HIGH ST.

BACK LANE

CHRIST CHURCH CATHEDRAL

CASTLE ST.

CITY HALL

DUBLIN CASTLE

THOMAS ST.

FRANCIS ST.

LAMB ALLEY

JOHN DILLON ST.

NICHOLAS ST.

BRIDE ST.

GREAT SHIP ST.

CHESTER BEATTY LIBRARY

EXCHEQUER ST.

GEORGE'S ST. ARCADE

DRURY ST.

STEPHEN ST.

WILLIAM ST.

To Guinness Storehouse & Kilmainham Gaol

SWIFT'S ALLEY

CARMEN'S HALL

HANOVER LN.

ST. PATRICK'S CATHEDRAL

GOLDEN LN.

ANGIER ST.

KING ST.

GLOVERS ALLEY

DEAN ST.

NEW ROW SOUTH

PATRICK ST.

PETER ST.

PETER ROW

BISHOP ST.

LWR. MERCER ST.

NEWMARKET

MILL ST.

KEVIN ST. UPPER

KEVIN ST. LOWER

CUFFE ST.

LWR. YORK ST.

UPR. MERCER ST.

WEST

LUAS Tram Green Line

N

150 Meters

150 Yards

① Cornucopia
② The Farm
③ The Hairy Lemon Pub
④ O'Neill's Pub
⑤ Avoca Café
⑥ The Duke Pub
⑦ Davy Burns Pub
⑧ Wagamama

⑨ Yamamori
⑩ Dunnes Grocery (2)
⑪ Marks & Spencer (Grocery)
⑫ The Church
⑬ To The Hot Stove
⑭ Queen of Tarts
⑮ Chorus Café
⑯ Leo Burdock's

thumps like hell in the bunker-like basement. On warm summer nights, the outdoor terrace is packed. Eating here is as much about the scene as the cuisine (pub grub daily 12:00-21:00, balcony restaurant open daily 17:00-22:30, reservations smart Fri and Sat nights, corner of St. Mary's and Jervis Streets, tel. 01/828-0102, www.thechurch.ie).

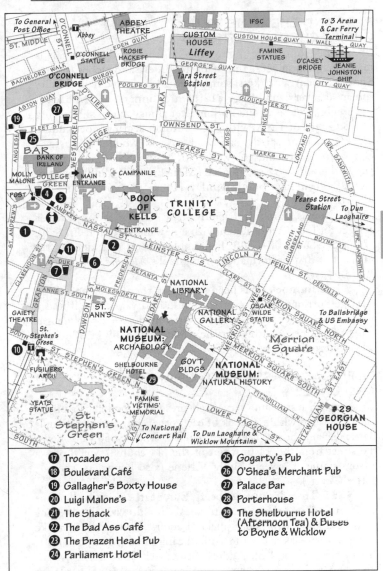

DUBLIN

⑰ Trocadero	㉕ Gogarty's Pub
⑱ Boulevard Café	㉖ O'Shea's Merchant Pub
⑲ Gallagher's Boxty House	㉗ Palace Bar
⑳ Luigi Malone's	㉘ Porterhouse
㉑ The Shack	㉙ The Shelbourne Hotel
㉒ The Bad Ass Café	(Afternoon Tea) & Buses
㉓ The Brazen Head Pub	to Boyne & Wicklow
㉔ Parliament Hotel	

$$$ **The Hot Stove** is an elegant and serene little basement operation serving locally sourced dishes created by chef Joy Beattie (Tue-Fri 12:00-14:30 & 17:30-21:30, Sat 17:30-22:00, closed Sun-Mon; behind the Garden of Remembrance at 38 Parnell Square West, see map on page 68, tel. 01/874-7778, www. thehotstove.ie).

FAST AND CHEAP NEAR CHRIST CHURCH CATHEDRAL

Many of Dublin's late-night grocery stores sell cheap salads, microwaved meat pies, and made-to-order sandwiches (such as **Spar** and **Centra** markets, some open 24 hours a day in the city, spread all over Dublin). A €12 picnic dinner brought back to the hotel might be a good option after a busy day of sightseeing.

$ Queen of Tarts, with some outdoor seating, does yummy breakfasts, fruit salads, sandwiches, and wonderful pastries. Get yours to go, and enjoy a picnic with a Georgian view in one of Dublin's grassy squares (Mon-Fri 8:00-19:00, Sat-Sun 9:00-19:00, hidden beside Kinlay House on Cow's Lane, tel. 01/670-7499).

$ Chorus Café is a friendly little hole-in-the-wall diner, perfect for breakfast or lunch with a newspaper (Mon-Fri 8:30-17:00, Sat-Sun 9:00-17:00, Fishamble Street, next door to the site of the first performance of Handel's *Messiah*, tel. 01/616-7088).

$ Leo Burdock's has been serving authentic fish and chips, in large portions, for more than a hundred years. You'll find it around the corner from Jurys Inn on your left—just follow the line of Dubliners waiting for their haddock (daily 12:00-23:30, 2 Werburgh Street, tel. 01/454-0306).

DINING AT CLASSY RESTAURANTS AND CAFÉS

These stylish restaurants serve well-presented food at fair prices. They're located within a block of each other, just south of Temple Bar and Dame Street, near the main TI. And just 50 yards down the street from the TI (in front of the old church), you'll pass a buxom statue of "sweet" Molly Malone (also known as "the tart with the cart").

$$$$ Trocadero serves beefy European cuisine to Dubliners interested in a slow, romantic meal. The dressy, red-velvet interior is draped with photos of local actors. Come early or make a reservation—it's a favorite with theatergoers (Mon-Sat 17:00-24:00, closed Sun, 4 St. Andrew Street, tel. 01/677-5545, www.trocadero.ie). The three-course pre-theater special is a fine value at €27 (17:00-19:00, leave by 19:45).

$$$ Boulevard Café is mod, trendy, and likeable, dishing up Mediterranean cuisine that's heavy on the Italian. It's smart to reserve for dinner (Mon-Sat 12:00-22:00, Sun 12:30-20:00, 27 Exchequer Street, tel. 01/679-2131, www.boulevardcafe.ie).

IN TEMPLE BAR

$$ Gallagher's Boxty House is touristy and traditional—a good, basic value with creaky floorboards and old Dublin ambience. Its specialty is the boxty, the generally bland-tasting Irish potato pancake filled and rolled with various meats, veggies, and sauces. The "Gaelic Boxty" is the liveliest (Mon-Fri 12:00-22:00, Sat-Sun 11:00-22:00, also serves stews and corned beef, reservations wise, 20 Temple Bar, tel. 01/677-2762, www.boxtyhouse.ie).

$$ Luigi Malone's, with its fun atmosphere and varied menu of pizza, ribs, pasta, sandwiches, and fajitas, is just the place to take your high-school date (Mon-Sat 12:00-22:00, Sun 13:00-21:30, corner of Cecilia and Fownes streets, tel. 01/679-2723).

$$$ The Shack, while a bit touristy, has a reputation for good quality. It serves traditional Irish, chicken, seafood, and steak dishes (open daily 12:00-22:00, in the center of Temple Bar, 24 East Essex Street, tel. 01/679-0043).

$$ The Bad Ass Café, where Sinéad O'Connor once waitressed, has been spiffed up since her tenure. The fare is uncomplicated pizza, pasta, burgers, and salads that are cheap by Temple Bar standards. There's even a fun kids' menu (daily 12:00-22:00, 9 Crown Alley, tel. 01/675-3005, live music or comedy most Fri and Sat evenings).

Dublin Connections

Note that trains and buses generally run less frequently on Sundays. Irish Rail train info: Toll tel. 1850-366-222, www.irishrail.ie.

By Train from Dublin's Heuston Station to: Tralee (every two hours, 6/day on Sun, most change in Mallow but one direct evening train, 4 hours), **Ennis** (10/day, 3.5-4 hours, change in Limerick, Limerick Junction, or Athenry), **Galway** (8/day, 3 hours).

By Train from Dublin's Connolly Station to: Rosslare (3-4/day, 3 hours), **Portrush** (7/day, 2/day Sun, 5 hours, transfer in Belfast or Coleraine). The **Dublin-Belfast train** connects the two Irish capitals in two hours at 90 mph on one continuous, welded rail (8/day Mon-Sat, 5/day Sun, about €40 for "day return" ticket). Northern Ireland train info: Tel. 048/9089-9400, www.translink.co.uk.

To Dun Laoghaire: See "Getting to Dun Laoghaire" on page 99.

By Bus to: Belfast (hourly, most via Dublin Airport, 3 hours), **Trim** (almost hourly, 1 hour), **Ennis** (almost hourly, 4-5.5 hours), **Galway** (hourly, 3.5 hours; faster on CityLink—hourly, 2.5 hours, tel. 091/564-164, www.citylink.ie), **Limerick** (hourly, 3-3.5 hours), **Tralee** (7/day, 6 hours), **Dingle** (4/day, 8-9 hours, transfer at Limerick and Tralee). Bus info: Toll tel. 1850-836-611, www.buseireann.ie.

Dublin Airport: The airport is well-connected to the city center seven miles away; for transportation options into the city, see "Arrival in Dublin" on page 25 (airport code: DUB, tel. 01/814-1111, www.dublinairport.ie). To sleep at Dublin Airport, a safe bet is the **$$$ Radisson Blu Dublin Airport** (book online direct for best prices, tel. 01/844-6000, www.radissonblu.ie).

CONNECTING IRELAND AND BRITAIN

Spend a few minutes online researching your transportation options across the Irish Sea. Most airline and ferry companies routinely offer discounts for tickets purchased from their websites. If you must buy a ferry ticket in person or by phone, you'll be hit with an additional €3 fee. Before sorting out rail/ferry prices with individual companies, try www.arrivatrainswales.co.uk/sailrail, which deals with several companies and has fares low enough to compete with cheap airlines.

Flights

If you're going directly to London, flying is your best bet. There's no need to waste a valuable day going by slower surface transportation.

Ryanair dominates the discount airline market, but note that its London-bound flights often land at Luton or Stansted—airports some distance from the city center (1.5 hours, Irish toll tel. 1520/444-004, www.ryanair.com). Options to Heathrow include **British Airways** (Irish tel. 1-890-626-747, US tel. 800-247-9297, www.ba.com) and **Aer Lingus** (tel. 1-890-800-600, www.aerlingus.com). To get the lowest fares, ask about round-trip ticket prices and book months in advance (though Ryanair offers nearly constant deals).

Ferries

Discount airlines have cut into ferry business in a big way. But there are still eight daily crossings from Dublin Port (two miles

east of O'Connell Bridge) that connect to Holyhead, Wales. It's slightly more for a fast, two-hour crossing (€44) than for the slower 3.5-hour sailing (€39). You must board at least 30 minutes before the scheduled sailing time or risk being denied boarding. Since these boats can fill up in advance on summer weekends, try to book at least a week ahead during this peak period.

Irish Ferries sails between Dublin Port and Holyhead four times daily, departing at 8:05, 8:45, 14:30, and 20:55 (Dublin tel. 0818-300-400, UK tel. 08705-329-129, www.irishferries.com). **Stena Line** sails between Dublin Port and Holyhead four times daily, departing at 2:15, 8:20, 15:10 and 20:40 (Dublin tel. 01/204-7777, UK tel. 08447-707-070, www.stenaline.ie).

FERRIES TO FRANCE

It makes little sense to waste your valuable time on a 20-hour ferry ride when you can fly to France cheaply in three hours. But if the nostalgia of a long, slow ferry ride and the risk of rough seas appeal to you, check **Irish Ferries,** which connects Ireland (Rosslare) with France (Cherbourg and Roscoff) a few days per month from May through September. Cherbourg has the quickest train connection to Paris, but your overall time between Ireland and Paris is about the same regardless of which port is used (20-hour ferry ride plus 2-hour train trip). One-way fares (€64-84) are cheapest if booked online. In both directions, departures are generally between 18:00 and 21:30 and arrive the next afternoon.

While passengers can nearly always get on, reservations are wise in summer and easy online. You can reserve a seat for free; cabins (2 beds) go for €59-99. The cafeteria serves bad food at reasonable prices. Upon arrival in France, buses and taxis connect you to Paris-bound trains (Irish Ferries: Dublin tel. 0818-300-400, www.irishferries.com).

Dublin Bay

Dangling from opposite ends of Dublin Bay's crescent-shaped shoreline, Dun Laoghaire (dun LEERY) and Howth (rhymes with "growth") are two peas in a pod. They offer quiet, cheap lodging alternatives to Dublin. Both have easy DART light-rail access to the city center, just a 25-minute ride away. Each houses its only worthwhile sightseeing options in pillbox martello (masonry) towers. And they were each once home to a famous Irish writer: James Joyce in Dun Laoghaire and W. B. Yeats in Howth. Dun Laoghaire is bigger and has more going on while Howth has a sleepier vibe and a fishing fleet.

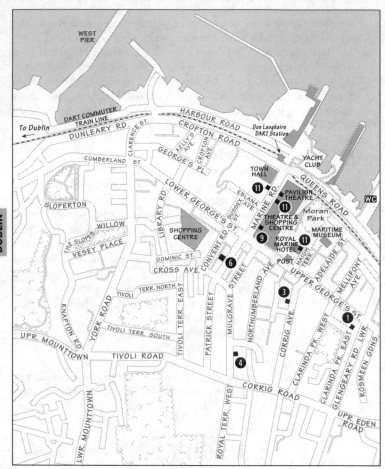

Dun Laoghaire

Dun Laoghaire is seven miles south of Dublin. This snoozy suburb, with easy connections to downtown Dublin, is a convenient small-town base for exploring the big city.

The Dun Laoghaire harbor was strategic enough to merit a line of martello towers, built to defend against an expected Napoleonic invasion (one tower now houses the James Joyce Museum). By the mid-19th century,

its massive breakwaters were completed, protecting a huge harbor.

Dun Laoghaire

1. Ferry House B&B
2. Windsor Lodge
3. Ophira B&B
4. Lynden B&B
5. Fallon & Byrnes
6. Bits and Pizza Restaurant
7. Toscana Restaurant
8. Fish Shack Café
9. Centra Markets (2)
10. Laundry
11. Aircoach Stop to/from Airport (3)

DUBLIN

Ships sailed regularly from here to Wales (75 miles away), and the first train line in Ireland connected the terminal with Dublin. Since the ferries left, Dun Laoghaire has gotten quieter, and it no longer has a TI.

GETTING TO DUN LAOGHAIRE

Buses run between Dublin and Dun Laoghaire, but the **DART** commuter train is much faster and not subject to Dublin traffic delays (4/hour, 25 minutes, runs Mon-Sat about 6:00-23:30, Sun from 9:00, €3.25 one-way, €6.15 round-trips are good same day only, 3-day pass on Leap Visitor Card—€19.50, Eurail Pass valid if you use a counted flexi-day, tel. 01/703-3504, www.irishrail. ie). If you're coming from Dublin, catch a DART train marked *Bray* or *Greystones* and get off at the Sandycove/Glasthule or Dun Laoghaire stop, depending on which B&B you choose. If you're leaving Dun Laoghaire, catch a train marked *Howth* to get to Dublin. Get off at the central Tara Street Station to sightsee in Dublin, or, for train connections north, ride one stop farther to Connolly Station.

The **Aircoach bus** makes it easy to connect Dublin Airport and Dun Laoghaire. The bus leaves from both Terminal 1 and Terminal 2 at the airport. In Dun Laoghaire, catch it by the Pavilion Theatre on Marine Road or at the front steps of the Royal Marine Hotel (€8, runs hourly, 50 minutes, tel. 01/844-7118, www.aircoach.ie).

A **taxi** from Dun Laoghaire to central Dublin costs about €30; to the airport, about €40. With the DART and Aircoach options listed above, taking a taxi is like throwing money away. But if you really need one, try ABC Taxi service (tel. 01/285-5444).

With DART access into Dublin, and cheap or sometimes free parking, Dun Laoghaire is ideal for those with **cars** (which can cost up to €25/day to park in Dublin).

Orientation to Dun Laoghaire

Once a busy transportation hub, Dun Laoghaire has a coastline defined by its nearly mile-long breakwaters—reaching like two muscular arms into the Irish Sea. The breakwaters are popular for strollers, bikers, bird-watchers, and fishermen.

HELPFUL HINTS

Post Office: It's on Lower George's Street (Mon-Fri 9:00-18:00, Sat until 13:00, closed Sun).

Laundry: Try **Jeeves,** located in the village of Glasthule, a five-minute downhill walk from Sandycove/Glasthule DART station (€20/load, Mon-Sat 8:30 or 9:00-18:00, closed Sun, full-service only, 34 Glasthule Road, tel. 01/230-1120).

Parking: If you don't have free parking at your B&B, try the pay-and-display street-parking system. Buy a ticket at machines spaced along the street, and display it on your dashboard (enforced Mon-Sat 8:00-19:00, €1.50/hour, 3-hour maximum, free Sun).

Best Views: Hike out to the lighthouse, at the end of the East Pier; or climb the tight stairs to the top of the James Joyce Tower and Museum.

Sights in Dun Laoghaire

James Joyce Tower and Museum

This squat martello tower at Sandycove was originally built to repel a Napoleonic invasion, but it became famous chiefly because of its association with James Joyce. The great author lived here briefly and made it the setting for the opening of his novel *Ulysses*. Unfortunately, the museum, which is run by volunteers, has a history of temporary closures due to funding problems; visitors should call ahead to check its current status. If open, the museum's round exhibition space is filled with literary memorabilia, including photographs and rare first editions. For a fine view, climb the claustrophobic, two-story spiral stairwell sealed inside the thick wall to reach the rooftop gun mount.

Cost and Hours: Free, daily 10:00-18:00, Nov-Feb until 16:00, tel. 01/280-9265, www.joycetower.ie.

National Maritime Museum of Ireland

Maritime exhibits fill a former church with model steamships, brass fittings, accounts of heroic rescue attempts, and a huge lighthouse optic (lamp lens, installed where the altar once stood). As earnest as it is, landlubbers may find it underwhelming.

Cost and Hours: €5, daily 11:00-17:00, Haigh Terrace, tel. 01/280-0969, www.mariner.ie.

Plays and Concerts

The Pavilion Theatre offers performances in the center of town (€15-25, box office open Mon-Sat 12:00-17:00, open 2 hours before Sun performances, Marine Road, tel. 01/231-2929, www.paviliontheatre.ie).

Swimming

Kids of all ages enjoy swimming at the safe, sandy little cove bordered by rounded rocks beside the martello tower.

Sleeping in Dun Laoghaire

The first two places are near the Sandycove/Glasthule DART Station; the last two places are near the Dun Laoghaire DART Station.

$ Ferry House B&B, with four high-ceilinged rooms, is a family-friendly place on a dead-end street (family room, 15 Clarinda Park North just off Clarinda Park West, tel. 01/280-8301, mobile 087-267-0511, www.ferryhousedublin.com, ferry_house@hotmail.com, Eamon and Pauline Teehan).

$ Windsor Lodge rents four fresh, inviting rooms on a quiet street a block off the harbor and a block from the DART station (cash only, 3 Islington Avenue, tel. 01/284-6952, mobile 086-844-

6646, www.windsorlodge.ie, windsorlodgedublin@gmail.com, Mary O'Farrell).

$ Ophira B&B is a historic house with four comfortably creaky rooms run by active diver-hiker-biker John O'Connor and his wife, Cathy (family room, parking, 10 Corrig Avenue, tel. 01/280-0997, www.ophira.ie, johnandcathy@ophira.ie).

$ Lynden B&B, with a classy 150-year-old interior hiding behind a somber front, rents four big rooms (cheaper rooms with shared bath, go past Mulgrave Street to 2 Mulgrave Terrace, tel. 01/280-6404, www.lyndenbandb.com, lynden@iol.ie, Maria Gavin).

Eating in Dun Laoghaire

If staying in Dun Laoghaire, I'd definitely eat here rather than in Dublin. George's Street—Dun Laoghaire's main drag, three blocks inland—has plenty of eateries and pubs, many with live music.

$$ Fallon & Byrnes is your best bet for fine wine and good food in a lovely glassed-in space beside the pleasant People's Park (daily 12:00-21:00, Summerhill Road, tel. 01/230-3300).

$$ Bits and Pizza is kid-friendly and a good bet for families (daily 12:00-22:00, off George's Street at 15 Patrick Street, tel. 01/284-2411).

$$ Toscana, on the seafront, is a popular little cubbyhole, serving hearty Italian dishes and pizza. Its location makes it easy to incorporate into your evening stroll. Reserve for dinner (€22 three-course early-bird specials before 18:30, daily 12:00-22:00, 5 Windsor Terrace, tel. 01/230-0890, http://toscana.ie).

$$ Fish Shack Café, also on the stroll-worthy waterfront, serves fresh fish dishes to beachcombers (daily 12:00-22:00, take-out available, 1 Martello Terrace, tel. 01/284-4555).

Centra Market is centrally located for picnic shopping right on Marine Road (Mon-Sat 7:00-22:00, Sun 8:30-22:00).

Glasthule (called simply "the village" locally, just down the street from the Sandycove/Glasthule DART station) has an array of fun, hardworking little restaurants. Another **Centra Market** is right next door and has your picnic makings (daily 7:00-22:00, Glasthule Road).

Howth

Eight miles north of Dublin, Howth rests on a teardrop-shaped peninsula that pokes the Irish Sea. Its active harbor teems with

fishing boats bringing in the daily catch, and seals trolling for scraps. Weary Dubliners come here for refreshing coastal cliff walks near the city. Located at the north terminus of the DART light-rail line, Howth makes a good place for travelers to settle in, with easy connections to Dublin for sightseeing. But there are only a couple centrally located and worthwhile lodging options.

Howth was once an important gateway to Dublin. Near the neck of the peninsula is the suburb of Clontarf, where Irish High King Brian Boru defeated the last concerted Viking attack in 1014. Eight hundred years later, a squat martello tower was built on a bluff above Howth's harbor to defend it from a Napoleonic invasion that never came. The harbor then grew as a port for shipping from Liverpool and Wales. It was eventually eclipsed by Dun Laoghaire, which was first to gain rail access. Irish rebels smuggled German-supplied guns into Ireland via Howth in 1914, making the 1916 Easter Uprising possible. These days, this is a pleasant, sleepy hamlet.

GETTING TO HOWTH

The **DART** light-rail system zaps travelers between Howth and the city twice as fast as the bus and sans traffic (4/hour, 25 minutes, Mon-Sat about 6:00-23:30, Sun from 9:00, €3.25 one-way, €6.15 round-trips good same day only, 3-day pass on Leap Visitor Card—€19.50, Eurail Pass valid if you use a counted flexi-day, tel. 01/703-3504, www.irishrail.ie). If you're coming from Dublin, catch a DART train marked "Howth" (not *Howth Junction, Malahide,* or *Drogheda*) and ride it to the end of the line—passing through Howth Junction en route. All trains departing Howth head straight to Dublin's Connolly Station, and then continue on to Tara and Pearse stations.

A **taxi** from the airport takes about 20 minutes and costs about €25. Try Executive Cabs (tel. 01/839-6020). With easy DART access into Dublin and plentiful parking, Howth is a good option for those with **cars.**

DUBLIN

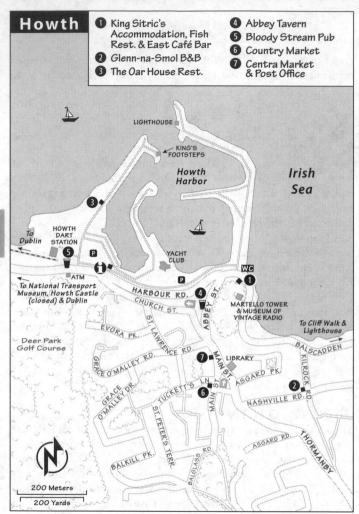

Howth

1 King Sitric's Accommodation, Fish Rest. & East Café Bar
2 Glenn-na-Smol B&B
3 The Oar House Rest.
4 Abbey Tavern
5 Bloody Stream Pub
6 Country Market
7 Centra Market & Post Office

DUBLIN

Orientation to Howth

Howth perches on the north shore of the peninsula, clustered along a quarter-mile harborfront promenade that stretches from the DART station (in the west) to the martello tower on the bluff (in the east). Its two stony piers clutch like crab claws at the Irish Sea.

The West Pier has the fishing action and helpful **TI**, located on Harbour Road, across from Howth's old courthouse (daily 9:30-17:00, may have shorter hours off-season, tel. 085/858-1695, www. howthismagic.com). If the TI is closed, another good info source is your innkeeper.

The East Pier extends to a stubby 200-year-old lighthouse and views of a rugged nearby island, Ireland's Eye. Abbey Street extends south, uphill from the harbor near the base of the martello tower bluff, becoming Main Street with most of the shops and pubs. Along the street, you'll find the **post office** in the back of the Centra Market (Mon-Fri 9:00-17:30, Sat until 13:00, closed Sun). Ulster Bank has the only **ATM** in town, across the street from the DART station and to the left of the Gem Market.

Sights in Howth

Other than coastal walks, sightseeing here pales in comparison to Dublin. Nearby Howth Castle is privately owned and cannot be toured.

Museum of Vintage Radio

The three-story martello tower on the bluff overlooking the East Pier is the only sight in Howth worth a glance. Curator Pat Herbert has spent decades acquiring his collection of lovingly preserved radios, phonographs, and even a hurdy-gurdy (a crank-action musical oddity)—all of which still work. Check out the radio disguised as a picture frame, which was used by the resistance in occupied France during World War II.

Before leaving the compact bluff, catch the views of the harbor and the nearby island of Ireland's Eye. Spot the distant martello tower on the island's west end and the white guano coating its eastern side, courtesy of a colony of gannets.

Cost and Hours: €5, daily 11:00-16:00, Sat-Sun only Nov-April, entry up driveway off Abbey Street, mobile 086-815-4189.

National Transport Museum

Housed in a large shed on the castle grounds, this is a dusty waste of time unless you find rapture in old trams and buses (€3.50, Sat-Sun only 14:00-17:00, tel. 01/848-0831, www. nationaltransportmuseum.org).

St. Mary's Abbey

Looming above Abbey Street, the current ruins date from the early 1400s. Before that, a church built by Norse King Sitric in 1042 stood at this site. The entrance to the ruins is on Church Street, above the abbey grounds.

East and West Piers

The piers make for mellow strolls after a meal. Poke your head into the various fishmonger shops along the West Pier to see the day's catch. At the end of the pier (on the leeward side), you'll find the footsteps of King George IV carved into the stone after his 1821 visit. The East Pier is a quiet jetty barbed with a squat lighthouse and the closest views of Ireland's Eye. If you want to get even closer to the island, book a boat excursion (€15 round-trip, daily in summer on demand 10:30-18:00, call for off-season trips, mobile 086-845-9154, www.islandferries.net).

Hiking Trails

Trails above the eastern cliffs of the peninsula offer enjoyable, breezy exercise. For a scenic three-hour round-trip, walk past the East Pier and martello tower, following Balscadden Road uphill. You'll soon pass Balscadden House, where writer W. B. Yeats spent part of his youth (watch for plaque on left). Where the road dead-ends, you'll find the well-marked trailhead. The trail is easy to follow, and soon you'll be walking south around the craggy coastline to grand views of the Bailey Lighthouse on the southeast rim of the peninsula. The gate to the lighthouse grounds is always locked, so enjoy the view from afar before retracing your steps back to Howth.

Sleeping in Howth

$$$ **King Sitric's Accommodation** is Howth's best lodging option and has a fine harborfront seafood restaurant (described later). It fills the old harbormaster's house with eight well-kept rooms and a friendly staff (discounts for 2-night stay with dinner, East Pier below martello tower, tel. 01/832-5235, www.kingsitric.ie, info@kingsitric.ie, Aidan and Joan MacManus).

$ **Glenn-na-Smol B&B** is a homey house with six unpretentious rooms in a quiet setting, a 15-minute walk uphill along the coast behind the martello tower (family room, cash only, parking, corner of Nashville Road & Kilrock Road, tel. 01/832-2936, mobile 085-758-1083, rickards@indigo.ie, Sean and Margaret Rickard).

Eating in Howth

$$$$ **King Sitric's Fish Restaurant,** one of the area's most famous seafood experiences, serves Irish versions of French classics in a dining room (upstairs) with harbor views. Chef Aidan MacManus rises early each morning to select the best of the day's catch on the pier, to be enjoyed that evening by happy customers (Wed-Sat 18:00-21:30, Sun 13:00-17:00, closed Mon-Tue, reservations a good idea, tel. 01/832-5235, www.kingsitric.ie). They also operate

the more economical **$$ East Café Bar,** on the ground floor with extra seating out front. Their soups, salads, steak sandwiches, and fish dishes are a good value (daily 10:00-22:00).

$$$ The Oar House sits halfway down the West Pier, serving a variety of great fish dishes in a bustling atmosphere (daily 12:00-"the cows come home," 8 West Pier, tel. 01/839-4568).

For pub grub, try the **$$ Abbey Tavern** up the hill on Abbey Street (occasional trad music and dance, call for schedule, tel. 01/839-0307). Another good choice is the **$$ Bloody Stream Pub** in front of the DART station (tel. 01/839-5076). The **Country Market** sells picnic supplies, and its cheap and friendly upstairs tearoom offers lunch (Mon-Sat 7:00-19:00, Sun 7:00-18:00, Main Street). The **Centra Market** is a block closer to the waterfront (Mon-Fri 6:30-22:00, Sat-Sun 7:00-22:00, Main Street).

DUBLIN

NEAR DUBLIN

Valley of the Boyne • Trim • Glendalough • Wicklow
Mountains • Irish National Stud

Not far from urban Dublin, the stony skeletons of evocative ruins sprout from the lush Irish countryside. The story of Irish history is told by ancient burial mounds, early Christian monastic settlements, huge Norman castles, and pampered estate gardens. In gentler inland terrain, the Irish love of equestrian sport is nurtured in grassy pastures ruled by spirited thoroughbreds. These sights are separated into three regions: north of Dublin (the Valley of the Boyne, including Brú na Bóinne and the town of Trim), south of Dublin (Powerscourt Gardens, Glendalough, and the Wicklow Mountains), and west of Dublin (the Irish National Stud).

Valley of the Boyne

The peaceful, green Valley of the Boyne, just 30 miles north of Dublin, has an impressive concentration of historical and spiritual sights: The enigmatic burial mounds at Brú na Bóinne are older than the Egyptian pyramids. At the Hill of Tara (seat of the high kings of Celtic Ireland), St. Patrick preached his most persuasive sermon. The valley also contains the first monastery in Ireland built in the style used on the Continent, and several of the country's finest high crosses. You'll see Trim's 13th-century castle—Ireland's biggest—built by Norman invaders, and you can wander the site of the historic Battle of the Boyne (1690), which cemented Protestant British domination over Catholic Ireland until the 20th century.

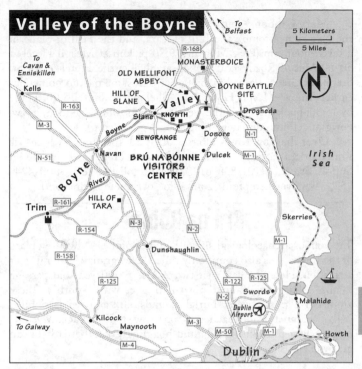

PLANNING YOUR TIME

Of these sights, only Brú na Bóinne is worth ▲▲▲ (and deserves a good three hours). The others, while relatively meager physically, are powerfully evocative to anyone interested in Irish history and culture. Without a car, I'd try to visit only Brú na Bóinne, taking a tour from Dublin.

The region is a joy by car, because all of the described sights are within a 30-minute drive of one another. If you eat your Weet-abix and get an early start, you could see the entire region in a day. Though the sights are on tiny roads, they're well-marked with brown, tourist-friendly road signs. You'll navigate best using an Ordnance Survey atlas.

As you plan your Ireland itinerary, if you're flying into or out of Dublin but want to avoid the intensity and expense of that big city, consider using Trim as an overnight base (45-minute drive from airport; accommodations listed on page 122) and tour these sights from there.

TOURS OF THE VALLEY OF THE BOYNE

If you lack a car and like tours, consider a round-trip excursion from Dublin.

Mary Gibbons' tours visit Brú na Bóinne (including inside the Newgrange tomb), the Hill of Tara, and the Hill of Slane in a seven-hour trip (€35, Mon-Fri, 9:30 pickup at Mespil Hotel at 50-60 Mespil Road, 9:50 pickup at Shelbourne Hotel at 27 St. Stephen's Green, home by 16:30; Sat-Sun same pickup points but earlier times—Mespil Hotel 7:40, Shelbourne Hotel 8:00, home by 15:30; book direct via the website, mobile 086-355-1355, www.newgrangetours.com, newgrangetours@gmail.com).

Over the Top Tours offers a "Celtic Experience," which has similar prices and times (pickup at Gresham Hotel or central TI on Suffolk Street, tel. 01/838-6128, Ireland toll-free tel. 1-800-424-252, www.overthetoptours.com, info@overthetoptours.com).

Brú na Bóinne

The famous archaeological site of Brú na Bóinne—"dwelling place of the Boyne"—is also commonly called "Newgrange," after its star attraction. Here you can visit two ▲▲▲, 5,000-year-old passage tombs—**Newgrange** and **Knowth** (rhymes with "south"). These are massive grass-covered burial mounds built atop separate hills, with a chamber inside reached by a narrow stone passage. Mysterious, thought-provoking, and mind-bogglingly old, these tombs can give you chills.

PLANNING YOUR VISIT

There are three sights to see at Brú na Bóinne: Newgrange, Knowth, and the state-of-the-art visitors center with its excellent museum. You start at the visitors center—no one is allowed to visit the tombs on their own. From here, you buy your ticket and catch the next available shuttle bus to the tomb sites, where a guide gives a 30-minute tour.

Each tomb site takes about 1.5 hours to visit (30-minute round-trip bus ride plus 30-minute guided tour plus 30 minutes of free time). The museum at the visitors center is well worth an additional 30-60 minutes. If you add in waiting time for the next available shuttle bus, you're looking at a minimum of 2.5 hours to do one of the tombs (along with the museum), or 4 hours to do both tombs (and museum).

Which tomb is best? If you can't see both, I'd pick Newgrange because it's more famous and allows you inside. (On the other hand, wait times for the Newgrange shuttle bus can be longer.) Knowth is bigger and flanked by small mounds, but you can't access its narrow passages. Each site is different enough and worthwhile, but for many, seeing just one is adequate. You might pick your tomb according to whichever shuttle bus is leaving next.

ORIENTATION TO BRÚ NA BÓINNE

Cost: Newgrange—€7, Knowth—€6, both—€12, museum only—€4, the museum is included in tomb prices.

Hours: June-mid-Sept daily 9:00-19:00, slightly shorter hours off-season, last entry to visitors center 45 minutes before closing. Newgrange is open year-round, while Knowth is open May-Oct only.

Crowd-Beating Tips: Arrive early—ideally before 10:00 in peak season—to avoid the big midday bus-tour crowds from Dublin. Visits are limited, and on busy summer days those arriving in the afternoon may not get a spot on a shuttle bus. No reservations are possible, and the last bus to the tombs leaves 1.75 hours before closing.

Getting There: By **car,** drive 45 minutes north from Dublin on N-1 to Drogheda, where signs direct you to the visitors center. If you're using a GPS, input "Brú na Bóinne" rather than "Newgrange" to get to the visitors center, where you must check in.

Without a car, you could take a tour with a private company, which includes entry to the passage tombs (see "Tours of the Valley of the Boyne," earlier).

Information: Tel. 041/988-0300, www.heritageireland.ie.

BRÚ NA BÓINNE VISITORS CENTER AND MUSEUM

Buy your ticket (to one or both tombs), find out when the next shuttle bus leaves, then spend your waiting time in the excellent museum, grabbing lunch in the cheery downstairs cafeteria, and using the WCs (there are no WCs at the tomb sites).

The museum introduces you to the Boyne River Valley and its tombs. No one knows who built the 40 burial mounds found in the surrounding hills. Exhibits re-create what these pre-Celtic people might have been like—simple farmers and hunters living in huts, fishing in the Boyne, equipped with crude tools of stone, bone, or wood.

Then around 3200 B.C., someone had a bold idea. They constructed a chamber of large stones, with a long stone-lined passage leading up to it. They covered it with a huge mound of dirt and rocks in successive layers. Sailing down the Boyne to the sea, they beached at Clogherhead (12.5 miles from here), where they found hundreds of five-ton stones, weathered smooth by the tides. Somehow they transported them back up the Boyne, possibly by tying a raft to the top of the stone so it was lifted free by a high tide. They then hauled these stones up the hill by rolling them atop logs and up dirt ramps, and laid them around the perimeter of the burial mound to hold everything in place. It would have taken anywhere from five years to a generation to construct a single large tomb.

Why build these vast structures? Partially, it was to bury VIPs. A dead king might be carried up the hill to be cremated on a pyre. Then they'd bring his ashes into the tomb, parading by torchlight down the passage to the central chamber. The remains were placed in a ceremonial basin, mingled with those of his illustrious ancestors.

To help bring the history to life, the museum displays replicas of tools and objects found at the sites, including the ceremonial basin stone and a head made out of flint, which may have been carried atop a pole during the funeral procession. Marvel at the craftsmanship of the perfectly spherical stones (and the phallic one), and wonder at their purpose.

The tombs also have served an astronomical purpose; they're precisely aligned to the movements of the sun, as displays and a video illustrate. You can request a short tour and winter solstice light-show demo at a full-size replica of the Newgrange passage and interior chamber.

Since the tombs are aligned with the heavens, it begs the question: Were these structures sacred places where primal Homo sapiens gathered to ponder the deepest mysteries of existence?

NEWGRANGE

This grassy mound atop a hill is 250 feet across and 40 feet high. Dating from 3200 B.C., it's 500 years older than the pyramids at Giza. The base of the mound is ringed by dozens of "kerbstones," each about nine feet long and weighing five tons.

The entrance facade is a mosaic of white quartz and dark granite. This is a reconstruction done in the 1970s, and not every archaeologist agrees it originally looked like this. Above the doorway is a square window called the roofbox, which played a key role (as we'll see). In front of the doorway lies the most famous of the kerbstones, the 10- by 4-foot entrance stone. Its left half is carved with three mysterious spirals, which have become a kind of poster child for prehistoric art.

Most of Newgrange's kerbstones have designs carved into them. This was done with super-hard flint tools; the Neolithic ("New Stone Age") people had not mastered metal. The stones feature common Neolithic motifs: not people or animals, but geometric shapes—spirals, crosshatches, bull's-eyes, and chevrons. (For more information on prehistoric art, see page 482.)

Entering the tomb, you walk down a narrow 60-foot passage lined with big boulders. Occasionally you have to duck or turn sideways to squeeze through. The passage opens up into a central room—a cross-shaped central chamber with three alcoves, topped by a 20-foot-high igloo-type stone dome. Bones and ashes were placed here in a ceremonial stone basin, under 200,000 tons of stone and dirt.

While we know nothing of Newgrange's builders, it most certainly was a sacred spot—for a cult of the dead, a cult of the sun, or both. The tomb is aligned precisely east-west. As the sun rises around the shortest day of the year (winter solstice—usually on Dec 21—and two days before and after), a ray of light enters through the roofbox and creeps slowly down the passageway. For 17 minutes, it lights the center of the sacred chamber (your guide will demonstrate this). Perhaps this was the moment when the souls of the dead were transported to the afterlife, via that ray of life-giving and life-taking light. Then the light passes on, and, for the next 361 days, the tomb sits again in total darkness.

KNOWTH

This site is an impressive necropolis, with one grand hill-topping mound (similar to Newgrange) surrounded by several smaller satellite tombs. The central mound is 220 feet wide, 40 feet high, and covers 1.5 acres.

You'll see plenty of mysteriously carved kerbstones and new-feeling grassy mounds that you can look down on from atop the grand tomb.

Knowth's big tomb has two passages: one entering from the east, and one from the west. Like Newgrange, it's likely aligned so the rising and setting sun shone down the passageways to light the two interior chambers, but these are aligned to the equinox rather than the solstice. Neither passage is open to the public, but you can visit a room carved into the mound by archaeologists, where a cutaway lets you see the layers of dirt and rock used to build the mound. You also get a glimpse down one of the passages.

The Knowth site thrived from 3000 to 2000 B.C. The central tomb dates from about 2000 B.C. It was likely used for burial rituals and sun-tracking ceremonies to please the gods and ensure the regular progression of seasons for crops. The site then evolved into the domain of fairies and myths for the next 2,000 years, and became an Iron Age fortress in the early centuries after Christ. Around A.D. 1000, it was an all-Ireland political center, and later, a Norman fortress was built atop the mound. Now, 4,000 years after prehistoric people built these strange tombs, you can stand atop the hill at Knowth, look out over the surrounding countryside, and contemplate.

More Sights in the Valley of the Boyne

▲▲Battle of the Boyne Site

One of Europe's lesser-known battlegrounds (but huge in Irish and British history), this is the pastoral riverside site of the pivotal battle in which the Protestant British decisively broke Catholic resistance, establishing Protestant rule over all Ireland and Britain.

Cost and Hours: €5, daily May-Sept 10:00-17:00, March-April 9:30-16:30, Oct-Feb 9:00-16:00, last admission one hour before closing, tearoom/cafeteria, tel. 041/980-9950, www.battleoftheboyne.ie.

"Living History" demonstrations: The Sunday afternoon "Living History" demonstrations (June-Aug) are a treat for history buffs and photographers, with guides clad in 17th-century garb. You'll get a bang out of the musket loading and firing demo (at 11:00, 13:00, 15:00, and 16:45), see cavalry combat in full gallop (at 12:00, 14:00, and 16:00), and learn that to be an Irish watermelon is to fear the sword.

Background: It was here in 1690 that Protestant King William III, with his English/Irish/Dutch/Danish/French Huguenot army, defeated his father-in-law—who was also his uncle—Catholic King James II and his Irish/French army. At stake was who would sit on the British throne, who would hold religious power in Ireland, and whether or not French dominance of Europe would continue.

King William's forces, on the north side of the Boyne, managed to fight their way across the river, and by the end of the day, King James was fleeing south in full retreat. He soon left Ireland, but his forces fought on until their final defeat a year later. James the Second (called "James da Turd" by those who scorn his lack of courage and leadership) never returned, and he died a bitter ex-monarch in France. His "Jacobite" claim to the English throne lived on among Catholics for decades, and was finally extinguished in 1745, when his grandson, Bonnie Prince Charlie, was defeated at the Battle of Culloden in Scotland.

King William of Orange's victory, on the other hand, is still celebrated in Northern Ireland every July 12, with controversial marches by Unionist "Orangemen." The battle actually took place on July 1, but was officially shifted 11 days later when the Gregorian calendar was adopted in 1752. (Even the calendar has been affected by religious strife: Protestant nations were reluctant to use a calendar developed by a Catholic—Pope Gregory in 1582. So England delayed adoption of Gregory's calendar for 170 years.)

The 50,000 soldiers who fought here made this the largest battle ever to take place in the British Isles. Yet it was only a side skirmish in an even larger continental confrontation pitting France's King Louis XIV against the "Grand Alliance" of nations threatened by France's mighty military and frequent incursions into neighboring lands.

Louis ruled by divine right, answerable only to God—and James modeled himself after Louis. Even the pope (who could control neither Louis nor James and was equally disturbed by Catholic France's aggressions) backed Protestant King William against Catholic King James—just one example of the pretzel logic that was the European mindset at the time.

The site of the Battle of the Boyne was bought in 1997 by the Irish Office of Public Works, part of the Republic's governmental efforts to respect a place sacred to Unionists in Northern Ireland—despite the fact that the battle's outcome ensured Catholic subordination to the Protestant minority for the next 230 years.

Visiting the Site: The **Visitors Centre** is housed in a mansion built on the battlefield 50 years after the conflict. The exhibits do a good job illustrating the international nature of the battle and its place in the wider context of European political power struggles. The highlight is a huge battleground model with laser lights that move troops around the terrain, showing the battle's ebb and flow on that bloody day. A separate 15-minute film (shown in the former stable house) runs continuously and does a fine job of fleshing out the battle.

As you exit the site to the north (on the L-16014 access road that connects to the main N-51 road), you'll cross the River Boyne on a **metal bridge.** This spot, called "old bridge," is where the most frantic action took place on that bloody day.

Pull over and gaze down at the river. Picture crack Dutch troops (from King William's homeland) marching south in formation. They were the first to cross the river here, while their comrades behind on the north bank covered their exposed position with constant protective fire. Low tides (the sea is only 7 miles downstream) allowed these soldiers to cross the river in water up to their waist. Between the gun smoke, weapon fire, and shouts filling the air, it was tough to tell friend from foe in the close, chaotic combat. Neither force had standard uniforms, so King William's troops wore sprigs of green while the troops of King James pinned white pieces of paper to their coats. Both sides bled red.

▲Hill of Tara

This site was the most important center of political and religious power in pre-Christian Ireland. While aerial views show plenty of mystifying circles and lines, wandering with the sheep among the well-worn ditches and hills leaves you with more to feel than to see. Visits are made meaningful by an excellent 20-minute video presentation and the caring 20-minute guided walk that follows (available upon request and entirely worthwhile). Wear good walking shoes—the ground is uneven and often wet.

Cost and Hours: €5, includes video and guided walk, tickets sold in old church near the trees above parking lot; open mid-May-mid-Sept daily 10:00-18:00, last tour at 17:00; during off-season access is free but visitors center is closed; WCs in café next to parking lot, tel. 046/902-5903.

Visiting the Site: You'll see the Mound of Hostages (a Bronze Age passage grave, c. 2500 B.C.), a couple of ancient sacred stones, a war memorial, and vast views over the Emerald Isle. While ancient Ireland was a pig pile of minor chieftain-kings scrambling for power, the high king of Tara was king of the mountain. It was at this ancient stockade that St. Patrick directly challenged the king's authority. When confronted by the high king, Patrick convincingly explained the Holy Trinity using a shamrock: three petals with one stem. He won the right to preach Christianity throughout Ireland, and the country had a new national symbol.

This now-desolate hill was also the scene of great modern events. In 1798, passionate young Irish rebels chose Tara for its defensible position, but were routed by better organized (and more sober) British troops. (The cunning British commander had sent three cartloads of whiskey along the nearby road earlier in the day, knowing the rebels would intercept it.) In 1843, the great orator and champion of Irish liberty Daniel O'Connell gathered 500,000 Irish peasants on this hill for his greatest "monster meeting"—a peaceful show of force demanding the repeal of the Act of Union with Britain (kind of the Woodstock of its day). In a bizarre final twist, a small group of British Israelites—who believed they were one of the lost tribes of Israel, who had ended up in Britain—spent 1899 to 1901 recklessly digging up parts of the hill in a misguided search for the Ark of the Covenant.

Stand on the Hill of Tara. Think of the history it's seen, and survey Ireland. It's understandable why this "meeting place of heroes" continues to hold a powerful place in the Irish psyche.

Old Mellifont Abbey

This Cistercian abbey (the first in Ireland) was established by French monks who came to the country in 1142 to bring the Irish monks more in line with Rome. (Even the abbey's architecture was unusual, marking the first time in Ireland that a formal, European-style monastic layout was used.) Cistercians lived isolated rural lives; lay monks worked the land, allowing the more educated monks to devote all their energy to prayer. After Henry VIII dissolved the abbey in 1539, centuries of locals used it as a handy quarry. Consequently, little survives beyond the octagonal lavabo, where the monks would ceremonially wash their hands before entering the refectory to eat. The lavabo gives a sense of the abbey's former grandeur.

The excellent 45-minute tours, available upon request and included in your admission (late May to early Sept only), give meaning to what you're seeing. To get a better idea of the extent of the site, be sure to check out the model of the monastery in its heyday, located at the back of the small museum next to the ticket desk.

Cost and Hours: €5, late May-Aug daily 10:00-18:00, last tour at 17:30, last entry 45 minutes before closing, no tours Sept-late May—when the site is free and you can explore on your own, tel. 041/988-0300, www.heritageireland.ie.

Monasterboice

This ruined monastery is visit-worthy for its round tower and its ornately carved high crosses—two of the best such crosses in Ireland. In the Dark Ages, these crosses, illustrated from top to bottom with Bible stories, gave monks a teaching tool as they preached to the illiterate masses. Imagine the crosses in their prime, when they were brightly painted (before years of wind and rain weathered the paint away). Today, Monasterboice is basically an old graveyard.

Cost and Hours: Free and always open.

Visiting the Site: The 18-foot-tall **Cross of Murdock** (Muiredach's Cross, c. 923, named after an abbot) is considered the best high cross in Ireland. The circle—which characterizes the Irish high cross—could represent the perfection of God. Or, to help ease pagans into Christianity, it may represent the sun, which was worshipped in pre-Christian Celtic society. Whatever its symbolic

purpose, its practical function was to support the weight of the crossbeam.

Face the cross (with the round tower in the background) and study the carved sandstone. The center panel shows the Last Judgment, with Christ under a dove, symbolizing the Holy Spirit. Those going to heaven are on Christ's right, and the damned are being ushered away by a pitchfork-wielding devil on his left. Working down, you'll see the Archangel Michael weighing souls, as the Devil tugs demonically at the scales; the adoration of the three—or four—Magi; Moses striking the rock to bring forth water; scenes from the life of David; and, finally, Adam, Eve, and the apple next to Cain slaying Abel. Imagine these carvings with their original, colorful paint jobs. Check out the plaque at the base of the nearby tree, which further explains the carvings on the cross.

Find the even taller cross nearest the tower. It seems the top section was broken off and buried for a period, which protected it from weathering. The bottom part remained standing, enduring the erosive effect of Irish weather, which smeared the once-crisp features.

The door to the round tower was originally 15-20 feet above the ground (accessible by ladder). After centuries of burials, the ground level has risen.

Trim

The sleepy, workaday town of Trim, straddling the River Boyne, is marked by the towering ruins of Trim Castle. Trim feels littered with mighty ruins that seem to say, "This little town was big-time...800 years ago." The tall Yellow Steeple (over the river from the castle) is all that remains of the 14th-century Augustinian Abbey of St. Mary. Not far away, the Sheep's Gate is a humble remnant of the once-grand medieval town walls. Near the town center, the modest, 30-foot-tall Wellington Column honors native son Arthur Wellesley, the First Duke of Wellington (1769-1852), who spent his childhood in Trim, defeated Napoleon at Waterloo, and twice became prime minister.

Trim makes a great landing pad into—or launching pad out of—Ireland. If you're flying into or out of Dublin Airport and don't want to deal with big-city Dublin, this is a perfect alternative— an easy 45-minute, 30-mile drive away. You can rent a car at the airport and make Trim your first overnight base (getting used to driving on the other side of the road in easier country traffic). Or spend your last night here before returning your car at the airport. Weather permitting, my evening stroll (described later) makes for a fine first or last night in the Emerald Isle.

Orientation to Trim

Trim's main square is a traffic roundabout, and everything's within a block or two. Most of the shops and eateries are on or near Market Street, along with banks and a supermarket.

TOURIST INFORMATION
The TI is right next to the castle entrance and includes a handy coffee shop. Drop in to pick up a free map (June-Aug Mon-Fri 9:30-17:30, Sat-Sun 12:00-17:00, shorter hours Sept-May, Castle Street, tel. 046/943-7227). Outside, 100 feet to the right of the TI door, you'll find a plaque with photos showing the castle dolled up for the filming of *Braveheart*.

HELPFUL HINTS
Post Office: It's tucked in the back of the **Spar Market** (Mon-Fri 9:00-17:30, Sat 9:00-13:00, closed Sun, Emmett Street).

Laundry: The launderette is located close to Market Street (€12/load, Mon-Sat 9:00-13:00 & 13:30-17:30, closed Sun, Watergate Street, tel. 046/943-7176).

Parking: To park on the street or in a public lot, use the pay-and-display parking system. Buy a ticket at one of the machines spaced along the street, and display it on your dashboard (€1/hour, 2-hour maximum, Mon-Sat 9:00-18:00, free Sun).

Taxi: Donie Quinn can give you a lift to nearby Boyne sites (tel. 046/943-6009).

Tours in Trim

Walking Tours
The TI organizes sporadic one-hour **Trim Living History Tours,** led by Paddy the town fireman—who dresses in medieval gear (€5, tours depart from TI, call ahead to reserve, tel. 046/943-7227, www.trimtown.ie).

Medieval Trim Tours are led by Cynthia Simonet (€2.50, 45 minutes, tours depart from castle parking lot in front of Franzini's restaurant, call ahead to reserve, mobile 086-370-7522).

Tours Beyond Trim
Boyne Valley Activities offers kayaking, rafting, high-rope walks, and archery excursions...luckily not simultaneously (€20 for archery; €40 for rafting, kayaking, and high-rope walks; call ahead to reserve, mobile 086-734-2585, www.boynevalleyactivities.ie).

Marc O'Regan leads backcountry trout and pike fishing tours, making a splash with anglers who want to experience Ireland's bountiful lakes and rivers (tel. 046/943-1635, www.crannmor.com). O'Regan and his wife also run the recommended Crannmór Guest House.

Sights in Trim

▲▲Trim Castle

This is the biggest Norman castle in Ireland. Set in a grassy riverside park at the edge of this sleepy town, its mighty keep towers above a very ruined outer wall. It replaced a wooden fortification that was destroyed in 1173 by Irish High King Rory O'Connor, who led a raid against the invading Normans. The current castle was completed in the 1220s and served as a powerful Norman statement to the restless Irish natives. It remained a sharp barb at the fringe of "the Pale" (English-controlled territory), when English rule shrank to just the area around Dublin in the 1400s. By that time, any lands farther west were "beyond the Pale."

Cost and Hours: €5 for entrance to keep and required tour, €2 for gardens only; mid-March-Oct daily 10:00-18:00; Nov-mid-March Sat-Sun 10:00-17:00, closed Mon-Fri; last entry one hour before closing, 45-minute tours run 2/hour but spots are limited and can fill up—so arrive early in peak season, tel. 046/943-8619, www.heritageireland.ie.

Visiting the Castle: Today the castle remains an impressive sight—so impressive that it was used in the 1994 filming of *Braveheart* (which was actually about Scotland's—not Ireland's—fight for freedom from the English). The best-preserved walls ring the castle's southern perimeter and sport a barbican gate that contained two drawbridges.

At the base of the castle walls, notice the cleverly angled "batter" wall—used by defenders who hurled down stones that banked off at great velocity into the attacking army. Notice also that the castle is built directly on bedrock, visible along the base of the walls. During sieges, while defenders of other castles feared that attackers would tunnel underground to weaken the defensive walls, that was not an issue here.

The massive 70-foot-high central keep, which is mostly a hollow shell, has 20 sides. This experimental design was not implemented elsewhere because it increased the number of defenders needed to cover all the angles. You can go inside the keep only with the included tour, where you'll start by checking out the cool ground-floor models showing the evolution of the castle. Then you'll climb a series of tightly winding original staircases and modern, high catwalks, learn about life in the castle, and end at the top with great views of the walls and the countryside.

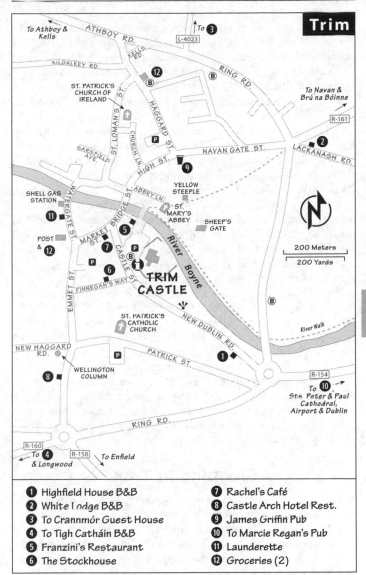

Trim

1 Highfield House B&B
2 White Lodge B&B
3 To Crannmór Guest House
4 To Tigh Catháin B&B
5 Franzini's Restaurant
6 The Stockhouse
7 Rachel's Café
8 Castle Arch Hotel Rest.
9 James Griffin Pub
10 To Marcie Regan's Pub
11 Launderette
12 Groceries (2)

Make time to take a 15-minute walk outside, circling the castle walls and stopping at the informative plaques that show the castle from each viewpoint during its gory glory days. Night strollers are treated to views of the castle hauntingly lit in blue-green hues.

Trim Evening Stroll

Given good weather, here's my blueprint for a fine night in Trim. Start the evening by taking the pleasant **River Walk** stroll along the River Boyne from Trim Castle. Cross the wooden footbridge over the River Boyne behind the castle and turn right (east). The paved, level trail eventually leads under a modern bridge/overpass and extends a mile along fields that serfs farmed 750 years ago. During the filming of *Braveheart*, Mel Gibson's character met the French princess in her tent in these fields, with the castle looming in the background.

The trail ends in the medieval ruins of **Newtown.** This was indeed once the "new town" (mid-1200s) that sprouted as a religious satellite community to support the political power housed in the castle. Wander the sprawling, ragtag ruins of **Saints Peter and Paul Cathedral** (1206), once the largest Gothic church in Ireland.

Just beyond the ruins, cross the old Norman bridge to the 13th-century scraps of the **Hospital of St. John the Baptist.** Medieval medicine couldn't have been fun, but this hospital was the best you could hope for back when life was nasty, brutish, and short. Many a knight was spent here.

Cross back over the bridge and stop for a pint at tiny, atmospheric **Marcie Regan's,** one of the oldest pubs in Ireland (an exterior sign calls it "Regan's," but most locals call it "Marcie's"). It's set beside one of the oldest bridges in Ireland (the one you just crossed). Drink a toast to Rock Hudson, who filmed a pivotal scene from *Captain Lightfoot* (1955) on the bridge.

Then walk back along the river the way you came and have dinner at the recommended **Franzini's** restaurant beside the castle. After dinner, assist your digestion by walking a lap around the castle (beautifully lit up at night). End the evening a few blocks away with a pint at the **James Griffin** pub (described later). A fine night 'tis...or 'twas.

Sleeping in Trim

Because Trim is a popular spot for weddings, book as early as possible if you are visiting on a summer weekend.

$ Highfield House B&B, across the street from the castle and a five-minute walk from town, is a stately 190-year-old former maternity hospital, with hardwood floors and ten spacious, high-ceilinged rooms (family rooms; above the roundabout where Dublin Road hits Trim, just before castle at Castle Street; tel. 046/943-6386, mobile 086-857-7115, www.highfieldguesthouse.com, info@highfieldguesthouse.com, Geraldine and Edward Duignan).

$ White Lodge B&B, a 10-minute walk northeast of the castle, has six comfortably unpretentious rooms with an oak-and-granite lounge (RS% for active-duty members of the US and Canadian armed forces, family room, parking, New Road, tel. 046/943-6549, www.whitelodge.ie, info@whitelodge.ie, Todd O'Loughlin).

Sleep Code

Hotels are classified based on the average price of a typical en suite double room with breakfast in high season.

$$$$	**Splurge:** Most rooms over €170
$$$	**Pricier:** €130-170
$$	**Moderate:** €90-130
$	**Budget:** €50-90
¢	**Backpacker:** Under €50
RS%	**Rick Steves discount**

Unless otherwise noted, credit cards are accepted and free Wi-Fi is available. Comparison-shop by checking prices at several hotels (on each hotel's own website, on a booking site, or by email). For the best deal, *book directly with the hotel.* Ask for a discount if paying in cash; if the listing includes **RS%,** request a Rick Steves discount.

They also offer a family-friendly self-catering house next door. A handy 300-yard trail leads from across the street to the castle (enter next to the modern sculptures).

Countryside B&Bs: These two B&Bs are in the quiet countryside about a mile outside Trim (phone ahead for driving directions).

$ At ivy-draped **Crannmór Guest House,** Anne O'Regan decorates five rooms with cheery color schemes (family room, north of the Ring Road on Dunderry Road L-4023, tel. 046/943-1635, mobile 087-288-7390, www.crannmor.com, cranmor@circom.net). Anne's professional-guide husband Marc knows all the best fishing holes (see "Tours in Trim," earlier).

$ Marie Keane's **Tigh Catháin B&B,** southwest of town, has four large, bright, lacy rooms with a comfy, rural feel and organically grown produce at breakfast (cash only, on R-160/Longwood Road, tel. 046/943-1996, mobile 086-257-7313, www.tighcathain-bnb.com, tighcathain.bnb@gmail.com).

Eating in Trim

A country-market town, Trim offers basic meat-and-potatoes lunch and dinner options. Don't waste time searching here for gourmet food. The restaurants and cafés along Market Street are friendly, wholesome, and unassuming.

$$$ Franzini's is the only place in town with a fun dinner menu and enough business to make it work. They serve pasta, steak, fish, and good salads in a modern, candlelit ambience. Nothing's Irish except the waiters (Mon-Sat 17:00-21:00, Sun 14:00-20:00, on French's Lane across from the castle parking lot, tel. 046/943-1002).

Restaurant Price Code

I've assigned each eatery a price category, based on the average cost of a typical main course. Drinks, desserts, and splurge items (steak and seafood) can raise the price considerably.

$$$$	**Splurge:**	Most main courses over €25
$$$	**Pricier:**	€20-25
$$	**Moderate:**	€15-20
$	**Budget:**	Under €15

In the Republic of Ireland, carryout fish-and-chips and other takeout food is **$**; a basic pub or sit-down eatery is **$$**; a gastropub or casual but more upscale restaurant is **$$$**; and a swanky splurge is **$$$$**.

$$$ The Stockhouse serves hearty steaks and poultry, plus creative desserts. Sit upstairs and take in the history of Trim from the walls while you wait (Mon-Thu 17:00-21:00, Fri-Sat 16:30-22:00, Sun 13:00-20:30, Finnegan's Way, tel. 046/943-7388).

$$ Rachel's Café is a good bet along Market Street for salads, sandwiches, and meat pies (Mon-Sat 8:30-17:30, Sun until 17:00, tel. 046/943-1636).

$$ The Castle Arch Hotel, popular with locals, serves hearty pub grub at reasonable prices in its bistro (daily 12:30-21:00, tel. 046/943-1516).

Pubs: For a fun pub experience, check out Trim's two best watering holes. The **James Griffin** (on High Street) is full of local characters with traditional Irish music sessions on Monday, Wednesday, and Thursday nights. Tiny, low-ceilinged **Marcie Regan's** is a fun, unpretentious pub next to the old Norman bridge over the River Boyne. You'll find it at the north end of the bridge, a half-mile stroll outside of town next to the ruins of Newtown.

Supermarkets: Spar Market has everything you need to create a picnic (Mon-Sat 7:30-20:00, Sun 8:30-19:00, Emmett Street). The same goes for **Super Valu,** a larger store on Haggard Street that's a bit farther from the town center (daily 8:00-22:00).

Trim Connections

Trim has no train station; the nearest is in Drogheda, 25 miles away on the coast. Buses from Trim to **Dublin** (almost hourly, 1 hour) pick you up at the bus shelter next to the TI and castle entrance on Castle Street. For details, see www.buseireann.ie.

Glendalough and the Wicklow Mountains

The Wicklow Mountains, while only 15 miles south of Dublin, feel remote—enough so to have provided a handy refuge for opponents to English rule. Rebels who took part in the 1798 Irish uprising hid out here for years. The area only became more accessible in 1800, when the frustrated British built a military road to help flush out the rebels. Today, this same road—now R 115—takes you through the Wicklow area to Glendalough at its south end. While the valley is the darling of the Dublin day-trip tour organizers, for the most part it doesn't live up to the hype. But two blockbuster sights—Glendalough and the Gardens of Powerscourt—make a visit worth considering.

GETTING AROUND

By car or tour, it's easy. If you lack wheels, take a tour. It's not worth the trouble on public transport.

By Car: It's a delight. Take N-11 south from Dublin toward Bray, then R-117 to Enniskerry, the gateway to the Wicklow Mountains. Signs direct you to the gardens and on to Glendalough. From Glendalough, if you're heading west, you can leave the valley (and pick up the highway to the west) over the famous but dull mountain pass called the Wicklow Gap.

By Tour from Dublin: Wild Wicklow Tours covers the region with an entertaining guide who packs every minute with information and *craic* (interesting, fun conversation). With a gang of 40 packed into tight but comfortable, mountain-gripping buses, the guide kicks into gear from the first pickup in Dublin. Tours cover Dublin's embassy row, Dun Laoghaire, the Bay of Dublin (with the mansions of Ireland's rich and famous), the windy military road over scenic Sally Gap, and the Glendalough monasteries (€28, €25 for students and readers with this book in 2017, daily year-round, 8:50 pickup at Shelbourne Hotel at 27 St. Stephen's Green—northern edge, 9:20 pickup at Gresham Hotel at 23 Upper O'Connell Street, stop for lunch at a pub—cost not included, return to Dublin by 17:30, advance booking required, tel. 01/280-1899, www.wildwicklow.ie).

Over the Top Tours bypasses mansions and gardens to focus on Wicklow rural scenery. Stops include Glendalough, Sally Gap, the Glenmacnass waterfall, and Blessington lakes (€28, 9:20 pickup at Gresham Hotel at 23 Upper O'Connell Street, 9:45 pickup at Dublin TI on Suffolk Street, return by 17:30, 14-seat minibus, reservations required, hold seat by leaving credit-card number, Ireland

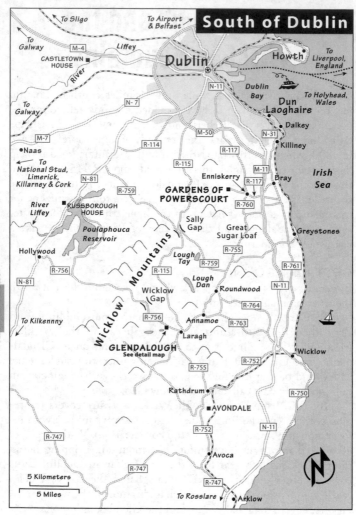

South of Dublin

toll-free tel. 1-800-424-252, Dublin tel. 01/860-0404, mobile 087-259-3467, www.overthetoptours.com, info@overthetoptours.com).

Sights in the Wicklow Area

▲▲Gardens of Powerscourt

A mile above the village of Enniskerry, the Gardens of Powerscourt cover 47 acres within the 700-acre estate. The dreamy driveway alone is a mile long. While the mansion's interior, only partially restored after a 1974 fire, isn't much, its meticulously kept aristo-cratic gardens are Ireland's best. The house was commissioned in the 1730s by Richard Wingfield, first viscount of Powerscourt. The

gardens you see today were created during the Victorian era (1858-1875).

Upon entry, you'll get a flier laying out 40-minute and one-hour walks. The "one-hour" walk takes 30 minutes at a relaxed amble. With the impressive summit of the Great Sugar Loaf Mountain as a backdrop, and a fine Japanese garden, Italian garden, and goofy pet cemetery along the way, this attraction provides the scenic greenery I hoped to find in the rest of the Wicklow area. Parts of the lush movies *Barry Lyndon* and *The Count of Monte Cristo* were filmed in this well-watered aristocratic fantasy.

Spend five minutes checking out the easy-to-miss "To Have and To Hold" room, which provides a history of the estate and a model of Powerscourt House before the fire.

Cost and Hours: €9.50, daily March-Oct 9:30-17:30, Nov-Feb 9:30-dusk, last entry at 16:30, great cafeteria, tel. 01/204-6000, www.powerscourt.ie, info@powerscourt.net.

Nearby: Kids may enjoy a peek at the antique dollhouses of the upstairs Museum of Childhood (€5, proceeds go to children's charities, Mon-Sat 10:00-17:00, Sun 12:00-17:00). Skip the Powerscourt Waterfall (4 miles/6.5 km away).

▲Military Road over Sally Gap

This trip is only for those with a car. From the Gardens of Powerscourt and Enniskerry, go to Glencree, where you drive the tiny military road over Sally Gap and through the best scenery of the Wicklow Mountains (on Sundays, watch for dozens of bicycle racers). Look for the German military cemetery, built for U-boat sailors who washed ashore in World War II. Near Sally Gap, notice the peat bogs and the freshly cut peat bricks drying in the wind. Many locals are nostalgic for the "good old days," when homes were always peat-fire heated. At the Sally Gap junction, turn left, where a road winds through the vast Guinness estate. Look down on the glacial lake (Lough Tay) nicknamed "Guinness Lake," as the water looks like Ireland's favorite dark-brown stout, and the sand of the beach actually looks like the head of a Guinness beer. The nearby (out of sight) mansion on the Guinness estate was the scene of jet-set parties a few decades ago. The History Channel series *Vikings* was primarily filmed on a temporary set built on the shores of the lake. From here, the road meanders scenically down into the village of Roundwood and on to Glendalough.

▲▲Glendalough

The steep wooded slopes of Glendalough (GLEN-da-lock, "Valley of the Two Lakes"), at the south end of Wicklow's military road,

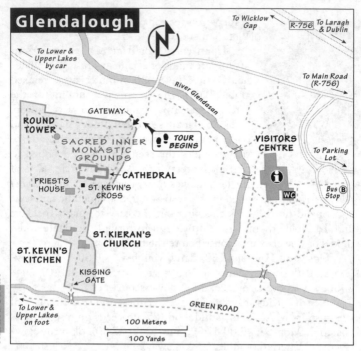

hide Ireland's most impressive monastic settlement. Founded by St. Kevin in the sixth century, the monastery flourished (despite repeated Viking raids) throughout the Age of Saints and Scholars until the English destroyed it in 1398. A few hardy holy men continued to live here until it was finally abandoned during the Dissolution of the Monasteries in 1539. But pilgrims kept coming, especially on St. Kevin's Day, June 3. (This might have something to do with the fact that a pope said seven visits to Glendalough had the same indulgence—or forgiveness from sins—value as one visit to Rome.) While much restoration was done in the 1870s, most of the buildings date from the 10th to 12th century.

In an Ireland without cities, these monastic communities were mainstays of civilization. They were remote outposts where ascetics (with a taste for scenic settings, but abstaining from worldly pleasures) gathered to commune with God. In the 12th century, with the arrival of grander monastic orders such as the Cistercians, Benedictines, Augustinians, Franciscans, and Dominicans, and with the growth of cities, these monastic communities were eclipsed. Today, Ireland is dotted with the reminders of this age: illuminated manuscripts, simple churches, carved crosses, and about 100 round towers.

The valley sights are split between the two lakes. The smaller, lower lake is just beyond the visitors center and nearer the best remaining ruins. The upper lake has scant ruins and feels like a state park, with a grassy lakeside picnic area and school groups. Walkers and hikers will enjoy a choice of nine different trails of varying lengths through the lush Wicklow countryside (longest loop takes four hours, hiking-trail maps available at visitors center).

Planning Your Time: Summer tour-bus crowds are terrible all day on weekends and 11:00-14:00 on weekdays. If you're there at midday, your best bet is to take the once-daily, 45-minute tour of the site (June-Aug only at 13:30, departs from visitors center). Otherwise, ask if you can tag along with a prebooked tour group's tour. If you're on your own, find the markers that give short descriptions of the ruined buildings.

Here's a good day-plan: Park for free at the visitors center. Visit the center; take the guided tour if possible; wander the ruins surrounding the round tower on your own (free); or walk the traffic-free Green Road a half-mile to the upper lake, and then walk back to the visitors center and your car along the trail that parallels the public road (an easy, roughly one-mile loop). Or you can drive to the upper lake. If you're rushed, skip the upper lake.

Cost and Hours: Free to enter site, €5 for visitors center, €4 to park at upper lake; open daily 9:30-18:00, mid-Oct-mid-March until 17:00; last entry 45 minutes before closing, tel. 0404/45352.

Visiting Glendalough: Start out at the **Glendalough Visitors Centre,** where a 20-minute video provides a good thumbnail background on monastic society in medieval Ireland. While the video is more general than specific to Glendalough, the adjacent museum room does feature this particular monastic settlement. The model in the center of the room re-creates the fortified village of the year 1050. A browse through the interactive exhibits shows the contribution these monks made to intellectual life in Dark Age Europe (such as illuminated manuscripts and Irish minuscule, a more compact alphabet developed in the seventh century).

When you're ready to visit the site, head out behind the visitors center, cross the bridge over the brook, and follow the lane 100 yards to the original stone **gateway.** From here you enter the sacred inner-monastic grounds that provided sanctuary for anyone under threat. Look for the cross carved into the sanctuary stone in the gateway (at knee level). A refugee had 90 days to live safely within the walls. But on the 91st day, he would be tossed out to the waiting authorities...

unless he became a monk (in which case he could live there indefinitely, no matter what his crime).

The graceful **round tower** rises from an evocative tangle of tombstones. Easily the best ruins of Glendalough gather within 100 yards of this famous 110-foot-tall tower. Towers like this (usually 60-110 feet tall with windows facing the four cardinal compass points) were standard features in such monastic settlements. They functioned as bell towers, storage lofts, beacons for pilgrims, and last-resort refuges during Viking raids. (But given enough warning, monks were safer hiding in the surrounding forest.) The towers had a high door with a pull-up ladder—both for safety and because a door at ground level would have weakened the tower's foundation. Several ruined churches (10th-12th century) lurk nearby... seek them out.

The **cathedral** is the largest and most central of all the ruins. It evolved over time with various expansions and through the reuse of stones from previous structures. The larger nave came first, and the chancel (up the couple of stairs where the altar later stood) was an addition. The east window faces toward Jerusalem and the rising sun, symbolic of Christ rising from the dead. Under the southern window is a small wall cupboard with a built-in basin. The holy vessels used during Mass were rinsed here so that the holy sacramental water would drain directly into the ground, avoiding any contamination (look for the tiny drain in the center).

Nearby is **St. Kevin's Cross.** At 10 feet tall and carved from a single block of granite, this cross was a statement of utter devotion. (Most other famous Irish high crosses were carved of sandstone— which is softer than granite—allowing their carvers to create more ornate depictions of biblical stories than you'll see here.) According to legend, if you hug this cross and can reach your hands around to touch your fingers on the other side, you'll have your wish granted (and your jealous friends labeling you a knuckle dragger). St. Kevin: the patron saint of dislocated shoulders.

Heading downhill, you'll pass the tiny **priests' house,** which was completely reconstructed (using the original stones) from a 1779 sketch. It might have originally acted as a kind of treasury, housing the relics of St. Kevin.

Farther down, you'll come to perhaps the prettiest structure surviving on the site: **St. Kevin's "kitchen"** (actually a church). Its short round tower appeared to earlier visitors to be a chimney, but its function was always as a belfry. The steeply stacked stone roof conceals a croft (upper story) perhaps used as a scriptorium for copying holy manuscripts. Nearby is the less-impressive stone footprint of **St. Kieran's Church,** possibly dedicated to the saint and contemporary of St. Kevin who founded Clonmacnoise Monastery (another scenic sanctuary, on the banks of the River Shannon south of the town of Athlone).

From here, pass through the kissing gate and cross the bridge over the brook. On the other side, if you're short of time, turn left to go back to the visitors center and parking lot. With more time, turn right and explore the lovely tree-shrouded **Green Road,** which leads past the **lower lake** for a half-mile to the **upper lake** as part of a pleasant one-mile loop.

The oldest ruins—scant and hard to find—lie near the upper lake. **St. Kevin's bed** is a cave where the holy hermit-founder of the monastery took shelter. It lies above the left (southern) shore and is visible and reachable only by boat. The story goes that St. Kevin's devotion was so strong that he would strip off his clothes and jump into thorn bushes rather than submit to the pleasures of the flesh. Another tale has him standing in pious stillness with arms outstretched while a bird builds its nest in his hand. If you want a scenic Wicklow walk, begin here.

Avondale House

Located in south County Wicklow (known as the Garden County), this mansion is the birthplace and lifelong home of Charles Stewart Parnell, the Nationalist politician and dynamo often called the "uncrowned King of Ireland" (see page 43).

Upon entering the opulent Georgian "big house" (built in 1777), you'll first view an informative 20-minute video on Parnell's life. Then you're set free to roam with a handout outlining each room's highlights. A fine portrait of Parnell graces the grand, high ceilinged entry hall, and a painting of his American grandfather, who manned the USS *Constitution* in the War of 1812, hangs in one room. The dining room is all class, with fine plasterwork and hardwood floors. Original furniture, such as Parnell's sturdy canopied bed, graces the remaining rooms, many of which come with cozy fireplaces and views. The lush surrounding estate of over 500 acres, laced with pleasant walking trails, was used by the Irish Forestry Service (Coillte) to try out forestry methods.

Cost and Hours: €7, parking-€5; Easter-Oct Thu-Sun 11:00-17:00, closed Mon-Wed and Nov-Easter; café, tel. 0404/46111, www.heritageireland.com.

Getting There: It's best to visit by car, as Avondale House is too far for the Dublin day-tour buses (45 miles south of Dublin). In good weather, avoid the parking fee by parking along the road (R-752) just outside the estate gate and walking 200 yards to the house. Trains depart Dublin's Connolly station (4/day, 1.5 hours) to Rathdrum; Avondale is a short taxi ride away (1.5 miles south of town). Try Aughrim Cabs (mobile 086-852-5553).

Irish National Stud

Ireland's famed County Kildare—just west of Dublin—has long been known to offer the perfect conditions for breeding horses. Its reputation dates all the way back to the 1300s, when Norman war horses were bred here. Kildare's grasslands lie on a bedrock table of limestone, infusing the soil with just the right mix of nutrients for grazing horses. And the nearby River Tully sparkles with high levels of calcium carbonate, essential for building strong bones in the expensive thoroughbreds (some owned by Arab sheikhs) raised and raced here.

In 1900, Colonel William Hall-Walker (Scottish heir to the Johnny Walker distilling fortune) bought a farm on the River Tully and began breeding a line of champion thoroughbreds. His amazing successes and bizarre methods were the talk of the sport. In 1916, the colonel donated his land and horse farm to the British government, which continued breeding horses here. The farm was eventually handed over to the Irish government, which in 1945 created the Irish National Stud Company to promote the thoroughbred industry.

Today, a tour of the grounds at the Irish National Stud gives you a fuller appreciation for the amazing horses that call this place home. Animal lovers and horse-racing fans driving between Dublin and Galway can enjoy a couple of hours here, combining the tour with lunch (inside the decent cafeteria or at a picnic table by the parking lot) and a stroll through the gardens.

ORIENTATION TO THE IRISH NATIONAL STUD

Cost: €12.50 includes guided tour of the Irish National Stud, plus entry to Japanese Gardens, St. Fiachra's Garden, and Horse Museum.

Hours: Daily Feb-Oct 9:30-18:00, Nov 9:30-17:00, closed Dec-Jan, last entry one hour before closing, 30-minute tours run 4/day at 10:30, 12:00, 14:30, and 16:00, tel. 045/521-617, www.irishnationalstud.ie.

Getting There: From M-7, **drivers** take exit #13 and follow the signs five minutes south (don't take exit #12 for the Curragh Racecourse). **Trains** departing Dublin's Heuston Station stop at Kildare town (1-3/hour, 45 minutes, www.irishrail.ie). A shuttle bus runs from Kildare's train station to the National Stud (2/hour), or you can take a taxi (about €12-15). One **bus** departs Dublin's Busáras Station Monday through Saturday at 9:30 and returns from the National Stud at 15:45. On Sunday, two buses run, departing Busáras at 10:00 and 12:00, with

When Irish Horses Are Running

Every Irish town seems to have a betting shop for passionate locals who love to closely follow (and wager on) their favorite horses. A quick glance at the weekend sports sections of any Irish newspaper gives you an idea of this sport's high profile. Towns from Galway to Dingle host annual horse races that draw rabid fans from all over. Interestingly, Irish horse races run the track clockwise (the opposite direction from races in the US).

The five most prestigious Irish races take place at the **Curragh Racecourse,** just south of Kildare town (March-Oct, 1 hour west of Dublin, 10 minutes from the National Stud, www.curragh.ie). Horses have been raced here since 1741. The broad, open fields nearby are where the battle scenes in *Braveheart* were filmed (the neighboring Irish army base provided the blue-face-painted extras).

returns at 15:00 and 17:30. Confirm this schedule at the bus station in Dublin.

VISITING THE IRISH NATIONAL STUD

The guided tour begins in the **Sun Chariot Yard** (named for the winner of the 1942 Fillies Triple Crown), surrounded by stables housing pregnant mares. A 15-minute film of a foal's birth runs continuously in a stall in the corner of the yard.

The adjacent **Foaling Unit** is where births take place, usually from February through May. The gestation period for horses is 11 months, with 90 percent of foals born at night. (In the wild, a mare and her foal born during the day would have been vulnerable to predators as the herd moved on. Instead, horses have adapted so that foals are born at night—and are able to keep up with the herd within a few hours.) Eccentric Colonel Hall-Walker noted the position of the moon and stars at the time of each foal's birth, and sold those born under inauspicious astrological signs (regardless of their parents' stellar racing records).

From here, you'll pass a working saddle-making shop and a forge where horseshoes are still hammered out on an anvil.

At the **Stallion Boxes,** you'll learn how stargazing Colonel Hall-Walker installed skylights in the stables—allowing the heavens maximum influence over the destiny of his prized animals. A brass plaque on the door of each stall proudly states the horse's name and its racing credentials. One stall bears the simple word,

"Teaser." The unlucky occupant's job is to identify mares in heat... but rarely is the frustrated stallion given the opportunity to breed. Bummer.

After the tour, meander down the pleasant tree-lined **Tully Walk,** with paddocks on each side. You'll see mares and foals running free, with the occasional cow thrown in for good measure (cattle have a calming effect on rowdy horses). To ensure you come home with all your fingers, take full note of the *Horses Bite and Kick* signs. These superstar animals are bred for high spirits—and are far too feisty to pet.

Other Sights: Visitors with extra time can explore three more attractions (all included in your entry ticket). The tranquil and photogenic **Japanese Gardens** were created by the colonel to depict the trials of life (beware the Tunnel of Ignorance). A wander through the more extensive and natural **St. Fiachra's Garden** (the patron saint of gardening) demands more time. Equestrian buffs may want to linger among the memorabilia in the small **Horse Museum,** where you can get a grip on how many hands it takes to measure a horse.

KILKENNY & THE ROCK OF CASHEL

If you're driving from Dublin (on Ireland's east coast) to Dingle (on Ireland's west coast), the best two stops to break the long journey across the Irish interior are Kilkenny, Ireland's finest medieval town; and the Rock of Cashel, a thought-provoking early Christian site crowning the Plain of Tipperary.

Counties Kilkenny and Tipperary ("Tipp" to locals) are blood rivals on the hurling field, with the lion's share of the GAA national championships split between them. Watch for sporting kids carrying their hurlies (ash-wood sticks with broad, flat ends) to or from school. These two counties also boast some of the finest agricultural land on this rocky and boggy island. Farm tractors rumble the back roads where it's not a long way to Tipperary.

With a few extra days, consider additional worthwhile destinations along the southeast coast, such as Waterford and County Wexford (described in the next chapter). Folks with more time can continue on the scenic southern coastal route west via Cobh, Kinsale, Kenmare, and the Ring of Kerry (all covered in later chapters).

Kilkenny

Ireland's loveliest inland city—winner of Ireland's "Tidy Town" award in 2014—Kilkenny gives you a feel for salt-of-the-earth Ireland. Its castle and cathedral stand like historic bookends on a higgledy-piggledy High Street of colorful shops and medieval facades. It's nicknamed the "Marble City" for its nearby quarry (actually black limestone, not marble), and you can see white seashells fossil-

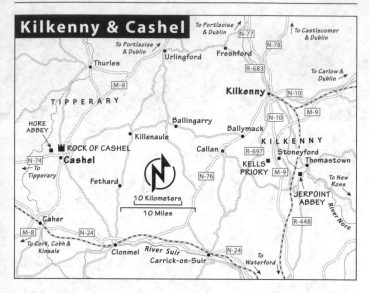

Kilkenny & Cashel

ized within the black stone steps around town. While a small town today (around 25,000 residents), Kilkenny has a big history. It was even the capital of Ireland for a short spell in the turbulent 1640s. And actor George Clooney traces his roots to Kilkenny.

Kilkenny is a good overnight for drivers wanting to break the journey from Dublin to Dingle (necessary if you want to spend time at Powerscourt and Glendalough on the way to the Rock of Cashel). A night in Kilkenny comes with plenty of traditional folk music in its pubs.

Orientation to Kilkenny

TOURIST INFORMATION

The TI is a block off the bridge in the 16th-century Shee Alms poorhouse (Mon-Sat 9:00-17:30, Sun 11:00-17:00, shorter hours and closed Sun off-season; Rose Inn Street, tel. 056/775-1500).

ARRIVAL IN KILKENNY

The train/bus station is four blocks from John's Bridge, which marks the center of town.

If you're arriving by car, the Market Yard Car Park behind Kyteler's Inn is handy for a few hours (€1.30/hour, daily 8:00-18:00, entry off Bateman's Quay). The multistory parking garage on Ormonde Street is the best long-term bet (€1.50/hour, or get the 3-day pass for €10 if staying overnight—it allows you to come and go; open 7:00-23:00, Fri-Sat until 24:00). If parking overnight, wait until you depart to pay since some hotels will validate parking. Otherwise, you can use the pay-and-display meters on the street (€1.50/hour, enforced Mon-Sat 8:00-19:00).

HELPFUL HINTS

Exchange Rate: €1 = about $1.10

Country Calling Code: 353 (see page 530 for dialing instructions)

Market: The square in front of Kilkenny Castle hosts a friendly produce, cheese, and crafts market on Thursdays (8:00-14:30).

Post Office: It's on High Street (Mon-Fri 9:00-17:30, Sat 9:00-13:00, closed Sun).

Laundry: The Laundry Basket trumpets its existence in vivid red at 21 Patrick Street at the south end of town (Mon-Fri 9:00-18:00, Sat 10:00-15:00, closed Sun, tel. 056/777-0355).

Bookstore: The Book Centre, with a cheap and cheery café upstairs, is a great place to hang out on a rainy day (Mon-Sat 9:00-18:00, Sun 13:00-17:00, 10 High Street, tel. 056/776-2177).

Bike Rentals: Kilkenny Cycling rents bikes for €15 a day (with a €50 refundable deposit). They provide safety gear, deliver bikes to your hotel on request (€1.50 charge), and have route maps for exploring the pastoral charms of County Kilkenny (office in courtyard through the arches behind the Kilkenny Design Centre, mobile 086-895-4961, www.kilkennycyclingtours.com).

Tours In Kilkenny

Walking Tours

Local guide **Pat Tynan** and his staff offer hour-long town walks that depart from the TI (€8; mid-March-Oct Mon-Sat at 10:30, 12:15, and 15:00, Sun at 11:15 and 12:30; Nov-mid-March by prior arrangement only; mobile 087-265-1745).

Amanda Pitcairn runs tours focusing on the history of medieval Kilkenny and the daily life of its inhabitants—witchcraft and skullduggery included (€8; check at TI for times or contact Amanda, mobile 087-277-6107, pitcaira@tcd.ie).

Bike Tours

At **Kilkenny Cycling,** Jason Morrissey is the man with the plan for a two-hour "easy-paced" guided tour (€20), which takes in a half-dozen of the town's best sights, including Kilkenny Castle, Rothe House, and St. Canice's Cathedral (usually departs at 10:00 and 14:00, also at 19:00 May-Sept). His €20, four-hour unguided "bike-and-hike" tour includes a seven-mile ride to Bennettsbridge (leave bikes there), followed by a pretty hike back along the river. He also offers a €15 medieval mile cycling treasure hunt for history

KILKENNY & CASHEL

buffs (10 percent discount with 2017 edition of this book, cash only, can arrange for tour to leave from your hotel, see "Bike Rentals," above, for contact info).

Sights in Kilkenny

▲▲Kilkenny Castle

Dominating the town, this castle is a stony reminder that the Anglo-Norman Butler family controlled Kilkenny for 500 years. The castle once had four sides, but Oliver Cromwell's army knocked down one wall when it took the castle, leaving it as the roughly "U" shape we see today.

Cost and Hours: €8, daily June-Aug 9:00-17:30, slightly shorter hours off-season, tel. 056/770-4100, www.kilkennycastle. ie.

Visiting the Castle: Enter the castle gate, turn right in the courtyard, and head into the base of the turret. Here you'll find the continuously running 12-minute video explaining how the wooden fort built here by Strongbow in 1172 evolved into a 17th-century château. Then go into the main castle entrance, diagonally across the courtyard from the turret, to buy your entry ticket. You'll be free to walk through the castle. A pamphlet explains the exhibits, and you can also talk to stewards in the important rooms.

Now restored to its Victorian splendor, the castle's highlight is the beautiful family-portrait gallery, which puts you face-to-face with the wealthy Butler family ghosts.

Nearby: The **Kilkenny Design Centre,** across the street from the castle in some grand old stables, is full of local crafts and offers handy cafeteria-style lunches in the food hall (shops open Mon-Sat 10:00-19:00, Sun 10:00-18:00; food hall open daily 8:30-18:30; tel. 056/772-2118, www.kilkennydesign.com).

▲Rothe House

This is the crown jewel of Kilkenny's medieval architecture: a well-preserved merchant's house that expanded around interior courtyards as the prosperous Rothe family grew in the early 1600s.

Cost and Hours: €5.50; April-Oct Mon-Sat 10:30-17:00, Sun 12:00-17:00; Nov-March closes at 16:30 and all day Sun; Parliament Street, tel. 056/772-2893, http://rothehouse.com.

Visiting the Rothe House: Check out the graceful top-floor timberwork supporting the roof, which uses wooden dowels (pegs)

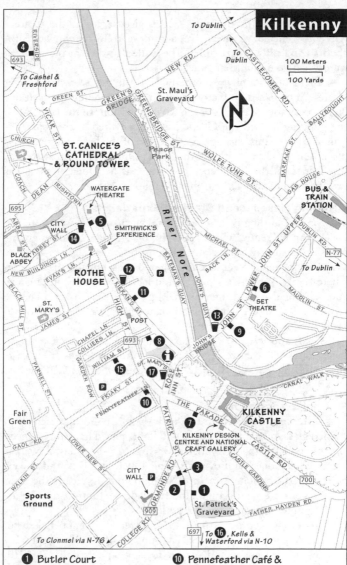

Kilkenny

To Dublin
To Dublin
RIVERSIDE
693
To Cashel & Freshford
GREEN ST.
GREEN'S BRIDGE
GREENSBRIDGE ST.
NEW RD.
CASTLECOMER RD.
BALLYBOUGHT ST.
St. Maul's Graveyard
VICAR ST.
CHURCH ST.
ST. CANICE'S CATHEDRAL & ROUND TOWER
Peace Park
WOLFE TUNE ST.
BARRACK ST.
GAS HOUSE
COACH RD.
DEAN ST.
IRISHTOWN
695
ABBEY ST.
CITY WALL
WATERGATE THEATRE
SMITHWICK'S EXPERIENCE
River Nore
MICHAEL ST.
BUS & TRAIN STATION
N-77
To Dublin
BLACK ABBEY
NEW BUILDINGS LN.
EVAN'S LN.
ROTHE HOUSE
BATEMAN'S QUAY
BACK LN.
JOHN ST. UPPER
JOHN ST. LOWER
DUBLIN RD.
MAUDLIN ST.
BLACK MILL ST.
ST. MARY'S ST.
HIGH ST.
ST. KIERAN'S ST.
JOHN'S QUAY
JOHN ST.
SET THEATRE
JAMES ST.
CHAPEL LN.
COLLIERS LN.
POST
693
JOHN'S BRIDGE
PARNELL ST.
WILLIAM ST.
GARDEN ROW
ST. MARY'S LN.
ROSE INN ST.
CANAL WALK
FRIARY ST.
EUSKARY ST.
PENNEFEATHER LN.
PATRICK ST.
THE PARADE
KILKENNY CASTLE
Fair Green
GAOL RD.
LOWER NEW ST.
CITY WALL
CASTLE RD.
KILKENNY DESIGN CENTRE AND NATIONAL CRAFT GALLERY
CASTLE GARDENS
WALKIN ST.
ORMONDE RD.
909
700
Sports Ground
St. Patrick's Graveyard
FATHER HAYDEN RD.
To Clonmel via N-76
COLLEGE RD.
697
To Kells & Waterford via N-10

100 Meters
100 Yards

KILKENNY & CASHEL

① Butler Court
② Club House Hotel
③ Zuni Townhouse & Rest.
④ Pinecrest B&B
⑤ Kilkenny Tourist Hostel
⑥ Langton's Restaurant
⑦ Ristorante Rinuccini
⑧ Ripley's Steak House
⑨ Ristorante Di Giacomo
⑩ Pennefeather Café & The Book Centre
⑪ Kyteler's Inn & Dunnes Store
⑫ Bollard's Pub
⑬ Matt the Miller's Pub
⑭ O'Riada's Pub
⑮ The Hole in the Wall Tavern
⑯ To Laundry & Lawcus Farm Guest House
⑰ Legends Hurling Bar (The Kilkenny Way Starting Point)

instead of nails. The museum, which also serves as the County Kilkenny genealogy center, gives a glimpse of life here in late Elizabethan and early Stuart times. The walled gardens at the far back were a real luxury in their time.

The Rothe family eventually lost the house when Oliver Cromwell banished all Catholic landowners, sending them to live on less desirable land west of the River Shannon. In the late 1800s, the building housed the Gaelic League, devoted to the rejuvenation of Irish culture through preservation of the Irish language and promotion of native Irish sports (such as hurling). One of the future leaders of the 1916 rebellion—Thomas McDonagh, who was executed at Dublin's Kilmainham Gaol—taught here.

▲Hurling Museum and Stadium Experience

The sport of hurling is historically and culturally important to the Irish. And Kilkenny, which hosts more all-Ireland hurling championships than any other county, is a hurling mecca. The Kilkenny Way tour includes a visit to a hurling pub/museum and the stadium where the Kilkenny Cats play. You'll learn about the long history and rules of this lightning-fast field game, and also get a chance to play as you figure out how to balance your *sliotar*—and how to pronounce it.

Cost and Hours: €25 for two-hour tour, includes pub meal; daily at 13:45, reserve ahead in summer; leaves from Legends Hurling Bar, 28 Rose Inn Street, tel. 056/772-1718, www.thekilkennyway.com.

St. Canice's Cathedral

This 13th-century cathedral is early-English Gothic, rich with stained glass, medieval carvings, and floors paved in history. Check out the model of the old walled town in its 1641 heyday, as well as a couple of modest audiovisuals. The 100-foot-tall **round tower,** built as part of a long-gone pre-Norman church, recalls the need for a watchtower and refuge. The fun ladder-climb to the top affords a grand view of the countryside.

Cost and Hours: Cathedral-€4, tower-€3, combo-ticket-€6; June-Aug Mon-Sat 9:00-18:00, Sun 14:00-18:00; Sept-May slightly shorter hours and closed for lunch; tel. 056/776-1910, www.cashel.anglican.org.

Smithwick's Experience Kilkenny

Smithwick's (pronounced SMITH-icks) reddish ale was born in Kilkenny...and has been my favorite Irish beer since my first visit to Ireland. Older than Guinness (but now owned by the same parent company), Smithwick's marked its tercentennial (300th anniversary) in 2010. After a corporate shake-up in 2013, the brewery consolidated its operations in Dublin and opened an "Experience" visitors center here on the former brewery grounds.

Tours focus on the historic origins of the tasty ale, first brewed by the monks of St. Francis Abbey (the 14th-century ruins of the abbey lie adjacent to the site). In the days of the monks, beer was a safer and healthier alternative to local water sources that were often contaminated. I'll drink to that.

Note that—like the Guinness Storehouse in Dublin—this is not a tour of a working brewery. It's a corporate-sponsored homage to the history of the brewery that once operated here.

Cost and Hours: €13, 10 percent discount if booked online, entry includes a pint at the tour's end, daily March-Oct 10:00-18:00, Nov-Feb 11:00-16:00, one-hour tours run hourly, last tour at 17:00, tel. 056/778-6377, www.smithwicksexperience.com.

Nightlife in Kilkenny

Pubs and Traditional Music Sessions

Kilkenny has its fair share of atmospheric pubs. Visitors seeking fun trad music sessions may want to try the first three places listed here. Those seeking friendly conversation in utterly unvarnished Irish splendor should seek out the memorable duo at the end of these listings. A fun pub crawl could link all five of these places with less than 20 minutes of walking (30 minutes crawling).

Bollard's Pub, an unpretentious landmark at the north end of St. Kieran's Street, is a good bet for lively traditional music sessions (Tue and Thu-Fri at 21:00) and good pub grub. Or sit out front under the awning and enjoy a pint as Kilkenny's humanity flows past you. Just down the same street is **Kyteler's Inn,** with a stony facade and medieval cellar (music almost nightly in summer at 18:30, 27 St. Kieran's Street). You can saunter over John's Bridge to check out the tunes at **Matt the Miller's Pub,** with its multilevel, dark-wood interior (around 21:00 most nights, next to bridge on John Street across the river from the castle).

Lacking music but high on character, **O'Riada's** is an endangered species—a wonderful, old-fashioned place that your Irish grandfather would recognize and linger in (across from the Watergate Theatre at 25 Parliament Street). Meanwhile, **The Hole in the Wall** is a tiny, restored Elizabethan tavern (1592) hidden down an alley. Owner Michael Conway, a cardiologist by day and a historian/playwright/actor/barman by night, presides over the speakeasy-like space as a labor of love. His music sessions can be an uninhibited go-for-broke thump-a-thon (he plays bass drum). He also writes and occasionally performs eclectic, history-based "singspiel" shows. Both take place in the larger, but equally ancient, timber-beamed upstairs hall (sporadic hours but always Fri-

Sat from 20:00 and sometimes weeknights, call ahead, look for the alley beside Bourkes shop at 17 High Street, tel. 087/807-5650, www.holeinthewall.ie).

Theater

The **Watergate Theatre** houses live plays and other performances in its 300-seat space (€12-25, Parliament Street, tel. 056/776-1674, www.watergatetheatre.com).

The **Set Theatre,** adjacent to sprawling Langton's Restaurant, is a fine, modern, 250-seat music venue attracting top-notch Irish acts in an intimate setting (€10-25, John Street, tel. 056/772-1728, www.set.ie).

Sleeping in Kilkenny

The first three listings are more central, clustered within a block of each other along Lower Patrick Street. The last two are at the north end of town, but still just a short walk from the action.

$$ Butler Court is Kilkenny's best lodging value. Ever-helpful Yvonne and John offer 10 modern, spacious rooms behind the beige, flag-draped archway. Bo the dog quietly patrols the courtyard (wheelchair-accessible, continental breakfast in room, will validate parking in nearby multistory garage on Ormonde Street for length of your stay, 14 Lower Patrick Street, tel. 056/776-1178, www.butlercourt.com, info@butlercourt.com).

$$ Club House Hotel, originally a gentlemen's sporting club, comes with fading Georgian elegance; a musty, creaking ambience; a palatial, well-antlered breakfast room; and 35 comfy bedrooms (secure parking, Lower Patrick Street, tel. 056/772-1994, www. clubhousehotel.com, info@clubhousehotel.com).

$$ Zuni Townhouse, above a fashionable restaurant, has 13 boutique-chic rooms sporting colorfully angular furnishings. Ask about two-night weekend breaks and midweek specials that include a four-course dinner (parking in back, 26 Lower Patrick Street, tel. 056/772-3999, www.zuni.ie, info@zuni.ie).

$ Pinecrest B&B has four nice rooms in a modern house on a quiet homey street, just a 10-minute walk from the center of town (cash only, parking, Bishop Meadows, just off Freshford Road about 100 yards north of the roundabout to the Green's Bridge, tel. 056/776-3567, mobile 087-934-4579, pinecrestbnb@eircom.net, friendly Helen Heffernan).

¢ Kilkenny Tourist Hostel, filling a fine Georgian townhouse with ramshackle fellowship in the town center, offers 60 cheap beds, a friendly family room, a well-equipped members' kitchen, and a wealth of local information (private rooms available, cash

---

Sleep Code

Hotels are classified based on the average price of a typical en suite double room with breakfast in high season.

$$$$	**Splurge:** Most rooms over €170
$$$	**Pricier:** €130-170
$$	**Moderate:** €90-130
$	**Budget:** €50-90
¢	**Backpacker:** Under €50
RS%	**Rick Steves discount**

Unless otherwise noted, credit cards are accepted and free Wi-Fi is available. Comparison-shop by checking prices at several hotels (on each hotel's own website, on a booking site, or by email). For the best deal, *book directly with the hotel*. Ask for a discount if paying in cash; if the listing includes **RS%**, request a Rick Steves discount.

---

only, 2 blocks from cathedral at 35 Parliament Street, tel. 056/776-3541, www.kilkennyhostel.ie, info@kilkennyhostel.ie).

NEAR KILKENNY

$$ Lawcus Farm Guest House is a quirky, seductive confection of rural comfort 10 miles south of Kilkenny between Kells Priory and the village of Stoneyford. Hosts Mark and Ann Marie have crafted a tasteful vibe from a passion for recycled materials and environmental sensitivity. Mark, an inventive craftsman, built the house from scratch. A menagerie of friendly pets and farm animals shares the 20-acre property straddling the Kings River. Ask about the tiny secluded tree house (family rooms, cash only, parking, mobile 086-603-1667 or 087-291-1056, www.lawcusfarmguesthouse.com, lawcusfarm@hotmail.com). To reach the farm, go south out of Kilkenny on N-10, which becomes R-713 after crossing over the M-9 motorway. Just as you enter the village of Stoneyford, turn right onto L-1023. Go 500 yards down that lane and watch for a brown sign directing you to turn right into a 100-yard-long gravel driveway.

Eating in Kilkenny

$$$ Langton's is every local's first choice, serving high-quality Irish dishes under a labyrinthine, multichambered, Tiffany-skylight expanse (daily 12:00-22:00, 69 John Street, tel. 056/776-5133).

$$$$ Ristorante Rinuccini serves classy, romantic, candlelit Italian meals (daily 12:00-14:30 & 17:00-22:00, reservations smart, 1 The Parade, tel. 056/776-1575, www.rinuccini.com).

Restaurant Price Code

I've assigned each eatery a price category, based on the average cost of a typical main course. Drinks, desserts, and splurge items (steak and seafood) can raise the price considerably.

$$$$	**Splurge:** Most main courses over €25
$$$	**Pricier:** €20-25
$$	**Moderate:** €15-20
$	**Budget:** Under €15

In the Republic of Ireland, carryout fish-and-chips and other takeout food is **$**; a basic pub or sit-down eatery is **$$**; a gastropub or casual but more upscale restaurant is **$$$**; and a swanky splurge is **$$$$**.

$$$ Ripley's Steak House delights carnivores (believe it or not) with choice cuts of locally raised beef. Try the flaky-crusted, veggie-stuffed steak hot pot (daily 13:00-21:00, Oct-May closed Mon-Tue, hidden down Butterslip Lane, tel. 056/777-0699).

$$ Ristorante Di Giacomo is the friendly, informal Italian option in town, presided over by charming Giacomo (daily 12:00-22:30, 84 John Street, tel. 056/777-0907).

$$$$ Zuni is a stylish splurge, offering international cuisine (daily 12:30-17:00 & 18:00-20:45, weekend reservations a good idea, 26 Lower Patrick Street, tel. 056/772-3999, http://zuni.ie).

$ Pennefeather Café, above the Kilkenny Book Centre, is good for a quick, cheap, light lunch (Mon-Sat 9:00-17:30, closed Sun, 10 High Street, tel. 056/776-4063).

$$$ Kyteler's Inn serves decent pub grub in a timber-and-stone atmosphere with a heated and covered beer garden out back. Visit their fun 14th-century cellar and ask about their witch. Watch your head or risk leaving some of your DNA embedded in the low stone arches (Mon-Sat 12:00-21:00, Sun until 20:00, 27 St. Kieran's Street, tel. 056/772-1064).

Grocery: Dunnes Stores has an ample selection of supplies for a grassy picnic (a few doors down from Kyteler's Inn on St. Kieran's Street, Mon-Sat 8:00-22:00, Sun 10:00-20:00).

Kilkenny Connections

From Kilkenny by Train to: Dublin (6/day, 1.5 hours), **Waterford** (6/day, 45 minutes). For details, see www.irishrail.ie.

By Bus to: Dublin (8/day, 2.5 hours), **Waterford** (2/day, 1 hour), **Tralee** (3/day, 5.5 hours, change in Cork), **Galway** (3/day, 5 hours). For details, see www.buseireann.ie.

Between Kilkenny and Waterford

The M-9 motorway links Kilkenny and Waterford with an hour's drive. But drivers in no rush can savor the journey by spending a couple of enjoyable backroad hours taking in two pastoral sights: Jerpoint Abbey and Kells Priory. (You can also stitch these places into a more leisurely itinerary for an easy, triangular day trip beginning and ending in Kilkenny—about 28 miles/45 km total.) The rural roads come with old stone bridges spanning placid rivers that weave among tiny villages and abandoned mills. Bring an Ordnance Survey atlas (available at most bookstores) to navigate. It's easier to visit Jerpoint Abbey first. There are no guided tours at Kells Priory; ask at the abbey for directions and pointers.

▲▲Jerpoint Abbey

Evocative abbey ruins dot the Irish landscape, but few are as well-presented as Jerpoint (founded in 1180). Its claim to fame is fine stone carvings on the sides of tombs and on the columns of the cloister arcade. If you visit only one abbey in Ireland, make sure it's this one.

Without the excellent guided tours, the site is a cold, rigid ruin. But once in the hands of the unusually well-versed hosts, the place truly comes alive with insights into the monastic culture that imprinted Ireland 850 years ago.

Cost and Hours: €5; March-Oct daily 9:00-17:30; off-season Mon-Fri 9:30-16:00, closed Sat-Sun except in Nov; tel. 056/772-4623.

Getting There: It's located about 11 miles (17 km) south of Kilkenny or 2 miles (3 km) south of Thomastown, beside R-700.

Visiting the Abbey: The Cistercian monks, who came to Ireland from France in the 12th century, were devoted reformers bent on following the strict rules of St. Benedict. Their holy mission was to bring the wild Irish Christian church (which had evolved, unsupervised, for centuries on the European fringe) back in line with Rome. With an uncompromising my-way-or-the-hell-way attitude, they steamrolled their belief system across the island and stamped the landscape with a network of identical, sprawling monasteries. The preexisting form of Celtic Christianity that had thrived in the Dark Ages was no match for the organization and determination of the Cistercians.

For the next 350 years, these new monasteries held the moral high ground and were the dominant local religious authority. Monks got closer to God by immersing themselves in the hardships of manual field work, building water mills, tending kilns, and advancing the craft of metallurgy. The wealth created by this turbo-charged industriousness caused communities to form around these magnetic monastic cores.

What eventually did them in? King Henry VIII's marriage problems, his subsequent creation of the (Protestant) Church of England, and his eventual dissolution of the (Catholic) monasteries. Walls were knocked down and roofs were torn off monasteries such as Jerpoint to make them uninhabitable. Their lands were forfeited to the king, who sold them off and enriched his treasury. It's good to be king.

Kells Priory

Locals claim that the massive religious complex of Kells Priory (more than 3 acres) is the largest monastic site in Europe. It's an isolated, deserted ruin that begs a curious wander, a nimble shutter finger on your camera, and alert side-stepping of sheep droppings.

Don't confuse this Kells with the identically named town farther north in County Meath. This place did not spawn the famous Book of Kells (housed in Trinity College Library in Dublin).

Cost and Hours: Free, no set hours.

Getting There: You'll find Kells Priory about 9 miles (15 km) south of Kilkenny or 6 miles (10 km) west of Jerpoint Abbey, just off the R-697 road. From Jerpoint Abbey, turn left, then take your first right through the village of Stoneyford. At the end of the village, turn left (at the sign for Kells Priory), then continue straight.

Visiting the Site: The main parking lot lies on a slope above the south side of the ruins. But I like to park at the pretty mill beside the Kings River on the north side of the ruins. The 100-yard stroll from the mill along the river makes for a photogenic approach to the complex. Watch where you walk and explore at your leisure. Consider bringing a picnic to enjoy. But please respect the site and leave no trash.

Founded in 1193 by Norman soldiers of fortune with Augustinian monks in tow, this priory grew into the intimidating structure that locals call "the seven castles" today. These "castles," however, were actually Norman tower houses connected by a wall that enclosed the religious functions within. Inside the walls, the site is divided into two main areas: one is a huge interior courtyard (larger than a football field) dominated by the encircling tower houses; the other is a tangled medieval maze of rock walls (remnants of a cloister, a church, cellars, a medieval dormitory, and a graveyard).

The most dramatic 75-year period of the site's history took place between 1252 and 1327, when it was attacked and burned three times (once by Edward the Bruce's army of Scots). It was set to be the location of the famous Kilkenny witch trial of Alice Kyteler in 1324. But she had the money to engineer a secret escape while leaving her maid to take the heat...literally.

Rock of Cashel

Rising high above the fertile Plain of Tipperary, the ▲▲▲ Rock of Cashel is one of Ireland's most historic and evocative sights. Seat of the ancient kings of Munster (c. A.D. 300-1100), this is where St. Patrick baptized King Aengus in about A.D. 450. Strategically located and perfect for fortification, the Rock was fought over by local clans for hundreds of years. Finally, in 1101, clever Murtagh O'Brien gave the Rock to the Church. His seemingly benevolent donation increased his influence with the Church, while preventing his rivals, the powerful McCarthy clan, from regaining possession of the Rock. As Cashel evolved into an ecclesiastical center, Iron Age ring forts and thatch dwellings gave way to the majestic stone church buildings enjoyed by visitors today. Queen Elizabeth II's history-making, four-day visit to Ireland in 2011 included a visit to the Rock.

Note that an extensive and essential restoration project should be finished by the time of your visit.

ORIENTATION TO THE ROCK OF CASHEL

Cost and Hours: €8, families—€20, daily 9:00-19:00, mid-March-early June and mid-Sept-mid-Oct until 17:00, mid-Oct-mid-March until 16:30, last entry 45 minutes before closing; tel. 062/61437, www.heritageireland.ie.

Crowd-Beating Tips: Summer crowds flock to the Rock (worst June-Aug 11:00-15:00). Try to plan your visit for early or late in the day. If you're here at a peak time, tour the Rock first and save the movie, museum, and Hall of the Vicars Choral for the end of your visit, when the tourist tide has receded. Otherwise, see the movie and museum first.

Dress Warmly: Bring a coat—deceptively sheltered conditions in the parking lot may not reflect those on the high, windy, exposed Rock. If you wear a hat, hold on to it.

Tours: Call ahead for the tour schedule (included in entry price, 45

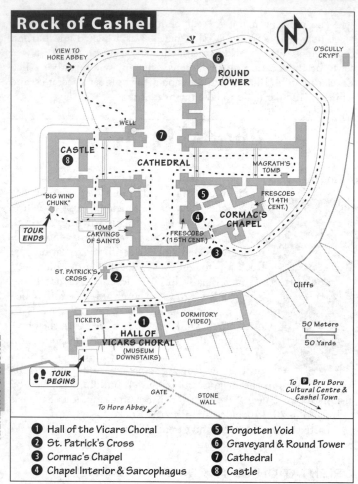

Rock of Cashel

1 Hall of the Vicars Choral
2 St. Patrick's Cross
3 Cormac's Chapel
4 Chapel Interior & Sarcophagus
5 Forgotten Void
6 Graveyard & Round Tower
7 Cathedral
8 Castle

KILKENNY & CASHEL

minutes, tel. 062/61437). Otherwise, set your own pace with my self-guided tour.

Parking: Pay the €4.50 fee at the machine (under the Plexiglas shelter to the left of the exit) before returning to your car.

WCs: Use the basic ones at the base of the Rock next to the parking lot or the nicer ones in the Bru Boru Centre below the parking lot (there are none up on the Rock).

OVERVIEW

If you have time, start by visiting the Sounds of History Museum under the Bru Boru Cultural Centre (at the base of the Rock; see page 155) to learn more about the Rock before you ascend. From there, it's a steep 100-yard walk up to the Rock itself. On this 200-foot-high outcrop of limestone, the first building you'll encounter is the 15th-century Hall of the Vicars Choral, housing the ticket desk, a tiny museum (with an original 12th-century high cross dedicated to St. Patrick and a few replica artifacts), and a 20-minute video (2/hour, shown in the hall's former dormitory). You'll also find a round tower, an early Christian cross, a delightful Romanesque chapel, and a ruined Gothic cathedral, all surrounded by my favorite Celtic-cross graveyard.

⊙ SELF-GUIDED TOUR

In a sense, architecture is the marriage of art (what can be imagined) and science (what's possible). When this union is blended to serve God, it's a potent mix. Nowhere else in Ireland can you better see the evolution of Irish devotion expressed in stone. This large lump of rock is a pedestal supporting a compact tangle of three dramatic architectural styles: early Christian (round tower and St. Patrick's high cross), Romanesque (Cormac's Chapel), and Gothic (the main cathedral).

• *Follow this tour counterclockwise around the Rock. To start the tour, climb the indoor stairs opposite the ticket desk.*

❶ Hall of the Vicars Choral

This is the youngest building on the Rock (early 1400s). It housed the minor clerics appointed to sing during cathedral services. These vicars—who were granted nearby lands by the archbishop—lived comfortably here, with a large fireplace and white, lime-washed walls (to reflect light and act as a natural disinfectant that discouraged bugs as well). Window seats gave the blessedly literate vicars the best light to read by. The furniture is original, but the oak timber roof is a reconstruction, built to medieval specifications using wooden dowels instead of nails. The large wall tapestry, showing King Solomon with the Queen of Sheba, contains intentional errors—to remind viewers that only God can create perfection.

The vicars, who formed a sort of corporate body to assist the bishop with local administration, used a special seal to authorize documents such as land leases. You can see an enlarged wooden copy of the seal (hanging above the fireplace), depicting eight vicars surrounding a seated organist. It was a good system—until some of the greedier vicars duplicated the seal for their own purposes, forcing the archbishop to curtail its use.

• *Go outside the hall into the grassy space 50 feet away and find...*

❷ St. Patrick's Cross

St. Patrick baptized King Aengus at the Rock of Cashel in about A.D. 450. Legend has it that St. Patrick, intensely preoccupied with the holy ceremony, accidentally speared the foot of the king with his crosier staff while administering the baptismal sacrament. But the pagan king stoically held his tongue until the end of the ceremony, thinking this was part of the painful process of becoming a Christian. Probably not that many other converts stepped forward that day.

This 12th-century cross, a stub of its former glory, was carved to celebrate the handing over of the Rock to the Church 650 years after St. Patrick's visit. Typical Irish high crosses use a ring around the cross' head to support its arms and to symbolize the sun (making Christianity more appealing to the sun-worshipping Celts). But instead, this cross uses the Latin design: The weight of the arms is supported by two vertical beams on each side of the main shaft, representing the two criminals who were crucified beside Christ (today only one of these supports remains).

On my first visit, more than 30 years ago, the original cross still stood here, outside. But centuries of wind and rain were slowly eroding away important detail, so the cross was moved into the adjacent museum (opposite the ticket desk) and replaced by this replica.

• *Turn your back on St. Patrick's Cross, and walk about 100 feet slightly uphill along the gravel path beside the cathedral. Roughly opposite the far end of the Hall of the Vicars Choral is the entry to...*

❸ Cormac's Chapel

As the wild Celtic Christian church was reined in and reorganized by Rome 850 years ago, new architectural influences from continental Europe began to emerge on the remote Irish landscape. This small chapel—Ireland's first and finest Romanesque church, constructed in 1134 by King Cormac MacCarthy—reflects this evolu-

tion. Travel in your imagination back to the 12th century, when this chapel and the tall round tower were the only stone structures on the Rock.

The "new" Romanesque style reflected the ancient Roman basilica floor plan. Its columns and rounded arches created an overall effect of massiveness and strength. Romanesque churches were like dark fortresses, with thick walls, squat towers, few windows, and minimal decoration. Irish stone churches of this period (like the one at Glendalough in the Wicklow Mountains) were simple rectangular buildings with few ornate stone carvings.

Legend says that the chapel's easy-to-cut sandstone was quarried 12 miles away, and the blocks were passed from hand to hand back to the Rock. (It's unlikely that they had the manpower to form a conga line that long—they probably used oxen-pulled carts.) The two square towers resemble those in Regensburg, Germany, further suggesting that well-traveled medieval Irish monks brought back new ideas from the Continent.

• *The modern, dark-glass chapel door (always unlocked) is a recent addition to keep out nesting birds. Enter the chapel (remembering to close the door behind you) and let your eyes adjust to the low light.*

❹ Chapel Interior

Just inside the chapel, on your left, is an empty stone **sarcophagus.** Nobody knows for sure whose body once lay here (possibly the brother of King Cormac MacCarthy). The damaged front relief is carved in the Scandinavian Urnes style. Vikings raided Ireland, intermarried with the Irish, and were melting into Irish society by the time this chapel was built. Some scholars interpret the relief design (a tangle of snakes and beasts) as a figure-eight lying on its side, looping back and forth forever, symbolizing the eternity of the afterlife.

With your back to the sarcophagus, let your eyes wander around the chapel interior. You're standing in the **nave,** lit by the three windows (partially blocked by the later cathedral, which is outside to the left) in the wall behind you. Overhead is a round vaulted ceiling with support ribs. The strong round arches support not only the heavy stone roof, but also the (unseen) second-story scriptorium chamber, where chilly monks, warmed only by candlelight, once carefully copied manuscripts.

The **chancel arch,** studded with fist-size heads, framed the altar (now gone). The lower heads are more grotesque, while those nearing the top become serene as they climb closer to God. The arch is off-center in relation to the nave, symbolic of Christ's head drooping to the side as he died on the cross.

Walk into the chancel and look up at the ceiling, examining the faint **frescoes,** a labor of love from 850 years ago. Frescoes are rare in Ireland because of the perpetually moist climate. (Mixing pigments into wet plaster worked better in dry climates like Italy's.) Once vividly colorful, then fading over time, these frescoes were further damaged during the Reformation. Such ornamentation was considered vain by Protestants, who piously whitewashed over them. These surviving frescoes were discovered under multiple layers of whitewash during painstaking modern restoration. The rich blue color came from lapis lazuli, an expensive gemstone imported from Asia.

• *Walk through the other modern, dark-glass doorway (don't let the birds in), opposite the door you used to enter the chapel. You'll find yourself in a...*

❺ Forgotten Void

This enclosed space (roughly 30 feet square) was created when the newer cathedral was wedged between the older chapel and the round tower. Once the main entrance into the chapel, this forgotten doorway is crowned by a finely carved tympanum that decorates the arch above it. It's perfectly preserved because the huge cathedral shielded it from the wind and rain. The large lion (symbol of St. Mark's gospel) is being hunted by a centaur (half-man, half-horse) archer wearing a Norman helmet (essential conehead attire in the late Middle Ages).

As you exit the chapel (turning left), take a look at the more exposed and weathered tympanum outside, above the south entrance. The carved, bloated "hippo" is actually an ox, representing Gospel author St. Luke.

• *Tiptoe through the tombstones around the east end of the cathedral to the base of the round tower.*

❻ Graveyard and Round Tower

This graveyard still takes permanent guests—but only those put on a waiting list by their ancestors in 1930. A handful of these chosen few are still alive, and once they're gone, the graveyard will be considered full. The 20-foot-tall stone shaft at the edge of the graveyard, marking the O'Scully family crypt, was once crowned by an elaborately carved Irish high cross—destroyed during a lightning storm in 1976.

Look out over the **Plain of Tipperary.** Called the "Golden Vale," its rich soil makes it Ireland's most prosperous farmland. In St. Patrick's time, it was covered with oak forests (Ireland is now the most deforested nation in the EU). A path leads to the ruined 13th-century **Hore Abbey** in the fields below (free, always open and peaceful). The abbey is named for the Cistercian monks who wore simple gray robes, roughly the same color as hoarfrost (the ice crystals that form on morning grass).

Gaze up at the **round tower,** the first stone structure built on the Rock after the Church took over in 1101. The shape of these towers is unique to Ireland. Though you might think towers like this were chiefly intended as a place to hide in case of invasion, they were instead used primarily as bell towers and lookout posts. (Enemies could smoke out anyone inside the tower, and with enough warning, monks were better off concealing themselves in the countryside.) The tower stands 92 feet tall, with walls more than three feet thick. The doorway, which once had a rope ladder, was built high up not only for security, but also because having it at ground level would have weakened the foundation of the top-heavy structure. The interior once contained wooden floors connected by ladders, and served as safe storage for the monks' precious sacramental treasures. The tower's stability is impressive when you consider its age, the winds it has endured, and the shallowness of its foundation (only five feet below present ground level).

Continue walking around the cathedral's north transept, noticing the square "put-log" holes in the exterior walls. During construction, wooden scaffolding was anchored into these holes. After the structure was completed, the builders simply sawed off the scaffolding, leaving small blocks of wood embedded in the walls. With time, the blocks rotted away, and the holes became favorite spots for birds to build their nests.

On your way to the cathedral entrance, in the corner where the north transept joins the nave, you'll pass a small, easy-to-miss **well.** Without this essential water source, the Rock could never have withstood a siege and would not have been as valuable to clans and clergy. In 1848, a chalice was dredged from the well, likely thrown there by fleeing medieval monks intending to survive a raid. They didn't make it. (If they had, they would have retrieved the chalice.) • *Now enter the...*

❼ Cathedral

Traditionally, the choir of a church (where the clergy celebrate Mass) faces east, while the nave stretches off to the west. Because this cathedral was squeezed between the preexisting chapel, round tower, and drinking well, the builders were forced to improvise—giving it an extra-long choir and a cramped nave.

Built between 1230 and 1290, the church's pointed arches and high, narrow windows proclaim the Gothic style of the period (and let in more light than earlier Romanesque churches). Walk under the central bell tower and look up at the rib-vaulted **ceiling.** The hole in the middle was for a rope used to ring the church bells. The wooden roof is long gone. When the Protestant Lord Inchiquin (who became one of Oliver Cromwell's generals) attacked the Catholic town of Cashel in 1647, hundreds of townsfolk fled to the sanctuary of this cathedral. Inchiquin packed turf around the exterior and burned the cathedral down, massacring those inside.

Ascend the terraces at the choir end of the cathedral, where the main altar once stood. Stand on the gravestones (of the 16th-century rich and famous) with your back to the east wall (where the narrow windows have crumbled away) and look back down toward the nave. The right wall of the choir is filled with graceful Gothic windows, while the solid left wall hides Cormac's Chapel (which would have blocked any sunlight). The line of stone supports on the left wall once held the long, wooden balcony where the vicars sang. Closer to the altar, high on the same wall, is a small, rectangular window called the "leper's squint"—which allowed unsightly lepers to view the altar during Mass without offending the congregation.

The grand **wall tomb** on the left contains the remains of archbishop Miler Magrath, the "scoundrel of Cashel," who lived to be 100. From 1570 to 1622, Magrath was the Protestant archbishop of Cashel who simultaneously profited from his previous position as Catholic bishop of Down. He married twice, had lots of kids, confiscated the ornate tomb lid here from another bishop's grave, and converted back to Catholicism on his deathbed.

• *Walk back down the nave and turn left into the south transept.*

Take a peek into the modern-roofed wooden structure against the wall on your left. It's protecting 15th-century **frescoes** of the Crucifixion of Christ that were rediscovered during renovations in 2005. They're as patchy and hard to make out (and just as rare for Ireland) as the century-older frescoes in the ceiling of Cormac's Chapel. On the opposite side of this transept, in alcoves built into the wall, wonderful **carvings** of early Christian saints line the outside walls of tombs (look down at shin level).

• *Return to the nave and continue down to the far end. Exit the cathedral on the left, through the porch entrance.*

❽ Castle

Back outside, stand beside the huge chunk of wall debris and try to picture where it might have fit in the ruins above. This end of the cathedral was converted into an archbishop's castle in the 1400s (shortening the nave even more). Looking high into the castle's damaged top floors, you can see the bishop's residence chamber and the secret passageways that were once hidden in the thick walls. Lord Inchiquin's cannons weakened the structure during the 1647 massacre, and in 1848, a massive storm (known as "Night of the Big Wind" in Irish lore) flung the huge chunk next to you from the ruins above.

In the mid-1700s, the Anglican Church transferred cathedral status to St. John's in town, and the archbishop abandoned the drafty Rock for a more comfortable residence, leaving the ruins that you see today.

NEAR THE ROCK: BRU BORU CULTURAL CENTRE

Nestled below the Rock of Cashel parking lot, below the statue of the three blissed-out dancers, this center adds to your understanding of the Rock in its wider historical and cultural context. The highlight of the **Sounds of History Museum** downstairs is the exhibit showing the Rock's gradual evolution from ancient ring fort to grand church ruins—projected down onto a large disc that visitors gather around.

Those interested in Ireland's traditional music scene will enjoy the surprisingly good 15-minute film introduction to Irish trad music in the small museum theater.

Cost and Hours: Cultural Centre-free, Sounds of History Museum-€5; June-Aug Mon-Sat 9:00-18:00, closed Sun; Sept-May Mon-Fri 9:00-17:00, closed Sat-Sun; cafeteria, tel. 062/61122, www.bruboru.ie.

Performances: If you stay overnight in Cashel in summer, consider taking in a performance of the Bru Boru musical dance troupe in the center's large theater (€20, €50 with dinner, July-Aug Tue-Sat, dinner at 18:30, performance at 21:00).

TOWN OF CASHEL

The huggable town at the base of the Rock affords a good break on the long drive from Dublin to Dingle (**TI** open daily 9:30-17:30, Nov-mid-March closed Sat-Sun, tel. 062/61333). The Heritage Centre, next door to the TI, presents a modest six-minute audio explanation of Cashel's history around a walled town model. Parking requires a pay-and-display ticket (€1, enforced Mon-Sat 9:00-18:00, free Sun).

Sleeping: If you spend the night in Cashel, you'll be treated to beautifully illuminated views of the ruins. The first listing is a classy hotel in the center of town (15-minute walk from the Rock). The rest are cozy, old-fashioned, and closer to the Rock.

$$ Bailey's Hotel is Cashel's best boutique hotel, housed in a fine Georgian townhouse (1709). Its 19 refurbished rooms are large, inviting, and well-appointed, perched above a great cellar-pub restaurant (parking, 42 Main Street, tel. 062/61937, www.baileyshotelcashel.com, info@baileyshotelcashel.com).

$ Joy's Rockside House B&B is closest to the Rock, resting on its lower slopes. With four large, fresh rooms (three with views of the Rock), it's the best value in Cashel (family room, cash only, Rock Villas Street, parking, tel. 062/63813, mobile 087-222-1676, www.joyrockside.com, joyrocksidehouse@eircom.net, Joan and Rem Joy).

$ Cashel Lodge is a well-kept rural oasis housed in an old stone grain warehouse, a 10-minute walk from the Rock near the Hore Abbey ruins. Its seven comfortable rooms combine unpretentious practicality with Irish country charm (camping spots, parking, Dundrum Road R-505, tel. 062/61003, www.cashel-lodge.com, info@cashel-lodge.com, Tom and Brid O'Brien).

$ Rockville House, 100 yards from the Rock, is a traditional place run by gentleman owner Patrick Hayes. The house itself has six fine rooms, and its old stablehouse, lovingly converted by Patrick, has five more (family room, cash only, 10 Dominic Street, tel. 062/61760, rockvillehse@eircom.net).

$ Wattie's B&B has three rooms that feel lived-in and comfy (cash only, parking, 14 Dominic Street, tel. 062/61923, www.wattiesbandb.ie, wattiesbandb@eircom.net, Maria Dunne).

Eating: The following places are good lunch options near the Rock. **$ Granny's Kitchen** is a tiny, violet-colored place with basic soup-and-sandwich lunches (next to the parking lot at the base of the Rock, daily 11:00-16:00). Popular **$$ Chez Hans Café,** with the best lunch selection and biggest crowds, is 75 yards down the road from the parking lot (Tue-Sat 12:00-17:30, closed Sun-Mon). And 50 yards farther down that same road, you'll find the **$ Rock House,** an enthusiastically hosted cafeteria-style restaurant that's upstairs above O'Dwyer's pharmacy (daily 9:30-16:00, mobile 086-252-4268).

For a splurge dinner, look for the old stone church housing **$$$$ Chez Hans,** the classy cousin of Chez Hans Café, listed above (Tue-Sat 18:00-21:30, closed Sun-Mon, in an old church a block below the Rock, tel. 062/61177, www.chezhans.net).

In town, you'll find several options. Next door to the TI, **$ Feehan's Bar** is a convenient stop for a pub grub lunch (daily 12:00-16:00, tel. 062/61929). A couple of blocks farther into town, the **$$ Cellar Pub** hides beneath Bailey's Hotel and serves satisfying dishes (daily 12:00-21:30, tel. 062/61937). **Super Valu** is the town's supermarket (Mon-Sat 7:00-22:00, Sun 8:00-21:00, 30 Main Street).

Cashel Connections: Cashel has no train station; the closest one is 13 miles away in the town of Thurles. Buses run from Cashel to **Dublin** (4/day, 3 hours), **Kilkenny** (3/day, 2.5 hours), and **Waterford** (6/day, 2 hours). Bus info: www.buseireann.ie.

WATERFORD &
COUNTY WEXFORD

If you need an overnight stop in southeast Ireland, the historic Viking port and Norman beachhead town of Waterford is your best choice. From here, you can explore the varied sights of County Wexford (including a 12th-century lighthouse, the Kennedy homestead—now a museum—the re-creation of a famine ship, and more). But humble Waterford town is of most interest to crystal devotees and Irish history enthusiasts. If that's not you, then give it a miss. Instead, consider staying in Kilkenny (covered in the previous chapter) and using that as a home base to see this area via day trips.

This region has a pastoral serenity and a strong history of trading from its sheltered ports facing England. The Vikings built the ports and developed the trade routes. Their cousins, the Normans, came along 200 years later and carefully fortified the ports. In 1170, King Henry II visited his new Irish realm with a huge fleet, calling Waterford the "Gateway to Ireland." With more efficient farming techniques and advanced military technology, the Normans cranked up their dominant culture and shoved the locals aside.

But the Irish made them fight to hang on to it. Like medieval Fort Apaches, Norman-fortified tower-house castles dot the landscape in this area more so than in most other parts of Ireland. And throughout your travels here, you'll see evidence of the region's Norman (French) roots in its high concentration of family names with old Norman prefixes: De

Berg, De Lacy, Devereux, Fitzgilbert, Fitzsimmons, Fitzgerald, and so on.

And how about this: Zorro was from Wexford. Or so say some historians, who claim that the inspiration for the colorful fictitious character was locally born, multilingual, 17th-century Catholic adventurer William Lamport. Lamport ran afoul of the English, fled to Spain, became a pirate, then joined a Spanish regiment fighting Swedes in the Thirty Years War. He was sent to Mexico as a spy (El Zorro means "the fox") but was executed for sympathizing with native slaves against the Mexican Inquisition.

Waterford

The oldest city in Ireland, Waterford was once more important than Dublin, and its three fine museums reflect this history. But today, while tourists associate the town's name with its famous crystal, locals are quick to remind you that the crystal is named after the town, not vice versa (come for the crystal, stay for the history). That said, Waterford is a plain, gray, workaday town of 45,000. Pubs outnumber cafés, and freighters offload cargo at the dock. It's a dose of gritty Ireland, with fewer leprechauns per capita than other Irish destinations. Wandering the back streets, you're reminded that until three generations ago, Ireland was one of the poorest countries in Western Europe.

PLANNING YOUR TIME

A day is enough time for Waterford's compact historic core. Visit the Waterford Crystal Visitor Centre early or late to avoid the big bus-tour crowds at midday. Beyond that, your best activity is the historic walk (at 11:45 or 13:45 in peak season), followed by a visit to the branch of the Waterford Museum of Treasures housed in Reginald's Tower. History buffs may want to dig deeper with visits to the other two nearby branches of this three-museum complex: Chorister's Hall (medieval life) and Bishop's Palace (Georgian to modern age). To feel the pulse of contemporary Waterford, hang out on Barronstrand Street—the town's pedestrian artery—and stroll through its big, modern shopping mall. All of these sights (and the TI) are within a four-block area nicknamed the "Viking Triangle." The three museums, the Waterford Crystal Visitor Centre, and the Theatre Royal are clustered behind Reginald's Tower, facing a street called The Mall.

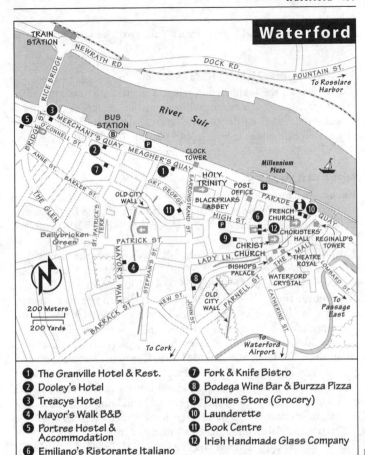

1. The Granville Hotel & Rest.
2. Dooley's Hotel
3. Treacys Hotel
4. Mayor's Walk B&B
5. Portree Hostel & Accommodation
6. Emiliano's Ristorante Italiano
7. Fork & Knife Bistro
8. Bodega Wine Bar & Burzza Pizza
9. Dunnes Store (Grocery)
10. Launderette
11. Book Centre
12. Irish Handmade Glass Company

WATERFORD & COUNTY WEXFORD

Orientation to Waterford

Waterford's main drag runs along its ugly harbor, where you'll find the bus station and easy parking lots (€1.80/hour, best overnight lot—entry next to bus station—costs €5 for a stay from 17:00-11:00). Some of the harborfront lots, including the overnight lot, have automated pay stations where you pay before exiting (check the payment/exit procedures as you walk out of the lot; you may need exact change in coins).

All recommended accommodations and sights are within a 10-minute walk of the harbor. The TI and Reginald's Tower are opposite Millennium Plaza, at the far eastern end of the harborfront from Rice Bridge. The stubby three-story Victorian clock tower marks the middle of the harbor. It's also the start of the pedestrian Barronstrand Street, which runs two blocks inland to the town square.

TOURIST INFORMATION

The TI sits on the harborfront, where Greyfriars Street meets Parade Quay, facing a modern, white, tent-like structure covering a raised stage called Millennium Plaza (Mon-Sat 9:00-17:00, usually closed Sun, shorter hours Nov-March; 120 Parade Quay, tel. 051/875-823, www.discoverireland.ie/waterford).

HELPFUL HINTS

Exchange Rate: €1 = about $1.10

Country Calling Code: 353 (see page 530 for dialing instructions)

Post Office: It's on Parade Quay (Mon-Fri 9:00-17:30, Sat 9:00-13:00, closed Sun).

Laundry: A-Class Cleaners does full-service loads the same day if you drop off early (Mon-Fri 9:00-18:00, Sat 9:30-17:30, closed Sun, 129 Parade Quay, tel. 051/844-100).

Bookstore: The multilevel **Book Centre,** right off the main square, is a fun browse and has a cozy soup and sandwich café on an upstairs balcony (Mon-Sat 9:00-18:00, Fri until 21:00, Sun 13:00-17:00, 25 John Roberts Square, tel. 051/873-823).

Shopping: The **Irish Handmade Glass Company** features artisans trained at the old Waterford Crystal factory, who work right in front of you fashioning unique crystal creations (Mon-Fri 9:00-17:00, Sat 10:00-17:00, closed Sun, behind the Kite Design Studio storefront, 11 Henrietta Street, tel. 051/858-914, www.theirishhandmadeglasscompany.com).

Taxis: Try **Premiere Taxi Service** (tel. 051/373-373) or **Rapid Cabs** (tel. 051/858-585). **Rapid Express** offers coaches to Dublin's airport (tel. 051/872-149).

Historic Walking Tour: Jack Burtchaell and his partners lead entertaining, informative, hour-long, historical town walks (worth ▲▲) that go from the TI to the Waterford Crystal Visitor Centre, giving you a good handle on the story of Waterford. They meet at the TI every day at 11:45 and 13:45—or join the tour as it swings by the Granville Hotel at 12:00 and 14:00 (just show up, pay €7 at the end, mid-March-mid-Oct only, tel. 051/873-711, www.jackswalkingtours.com).

Theater: Waterford's small but lively **Theatre Royal** claims a 225-year tradition. Given the dearth of other nighttime options in Waterford beyond pubs, it's worth checking out their schedule of plays, concerts, and light opera (€15-30 tickets, located on The Mall across from the Waterford Crystal Visitor Centre, tel. 051/874-402, www.theatreroyal.ie).

Waterford's History

Arriving in 819, Vikings first established Waterford as their base for piracy. Waterford was a perfect spot for launching their ships, since it's located at the gateway to one of the most extensive river networks in Ireland. From here, raiders could sail 50 miles into Ireland, an island with no towns, just scattered monastic settlements, and small gatherings of clans—perfect for the Vikings' plan of rape, pillage, and plunder.

Later, the Vikings decided to "go legit." They turned to profiteering, setting up shop in an established trading base

they named Vandrafjord, or "safe harbor." Ireland's first permanent town eventually became known as Waterford. It was from this base that the Norsemen invaded northern England.

In the 12th century, a deposed Irish king named Diarmuid Mac-Murrough opened the Irish version of Pandora's box by inviting the Normans over from England, hoping to use their advanced military technology to regain his land from a rival clan. The great warrior knight Strongbow came...and never left, beginning Ireland's long and troublesome relationship with the English. In 1170, Strongbow married the Irish princess Aoife in the Gothic church that once stood where Waterford's Christ Church Cathedral stands today. One of Ireland's most famous paintings (hanging in the National Gallery in Dublin) depicts this event, and a copy of it covers a wall in Chorister's Hall Medieval Museum. With this marriage, Strongbow was next in line for the title of King of Leinster, which he was named after the death of his father-in-law, MacMurrough, a year later.

Strongbow's success was so rapid that King Henry II got worried about a rival kingdom blossoming on his flank. He quickly gathered his navy and sailed over from England to make sure Strongbow knew who was boss—and to intimidate Irish clan leaders into swearing loyalty to the Crown. England's first roots in Ireland had been planted.

For the English, Waterford has often proved to be a tough nut to crack. During Oliver Cromwell's brutal scorched-earth campaign of 1649-1650, he destroyed any town still loyal to King Charles I, whom he had beheaded (see "The Curse of Cromwell" sidebar, later). His forces decimated Ireland. But Waterford was the only Irish city to withstand his siege.

Sights in Waterford

▲▲Waterford Crystal Visitor Centre

With a tradition dating back to 1783, Waterford was, until recently, the largest and most respected glassworks in the world. The economic downturn of 2008 shattered the market for luxury items like crystal, forcing the huge Waterford Crystal factory outside town to close. The company was bought by American investors who opened a new, scaled-down factory in the town center (and later sold it to a Finnish company for a handsome profit). While 70 percent of Waterford Crystal is now manufactured by cheaper labor in Poland, Slovenia, and the Czech Republic, the finest glass craftsmen still reside here, where they create "prestige pieces" for special-order customers. The one-hour tour of this hardworking little factory is a joy. It's more intimate than the old, larger factory, and you're encouraged to interact with the craftsmen.

Cost and Hours: Tours cost €13.50 and depart every 30 minutes; April-Oct Mon-Sat 9:00-17:00 (last tour at 16:30), Sun from 9:30, shorter hours off-season, call to confirm, shop open longer hours; on The Mall, one block south of Reginald's Tower; tel. 051/317-000, www.waterfordvisitorcentre.com.

Visiting the Factory: The tour begins with a bit of history and a look at an impressive six-foot-tall crystal grandfather clock. It then loses momentum as you're ushered into a glitzy and pointless five-minute fireworks film montage set to a techno beat. But things pick up again as your guide takes you into the factory to meet the craftsmen in their element. Glassblowers magically spin glowing blobs of molten crystal into exquisite and recognizable shapes in minutes. If you get dizzy blowing up balloons for a kid's party, consider the lung stamina that these craftsmen display (hot crystal is a lot heavier to heave with a breath than thin rubber balloons). Watch closely as the glassblower puts his thumb over the opening between breaths to keep the heat and pressure inside the blob constant.

Heavy molten crystal has an intentionally high lead content (it's what distinguishes fine crystal from common glassware). A cooling-off stage allows the crystal to set. Then glasscutters deftly cradle the fragile creations against diamond-edged cutting wheels, applying exactly enough pressure to ensure that the grooves are replicated with surgical skill. The glasscutters will be glad to demonstrate if you ask.

Watch the skilled cutters muscle rough unfinished pieces—weighing as much as bowling balls—and cut intricate patterns. The crystal vases and bowls may look light and delicate, but hold an unfinished piece (with its lead-enhanced heft) and you'll gain a new appreciation for the strength, touch, and hand-eye coordination of the glasscutters.

Afterward, visit the glittering salesroom, surrounded by hard-to-pack but easy-to-ship temptations. Take a look at the copies of famous sports trophies (they make backups of their most important commissions, just in case). Be sure to ask about getting a VAT refund (see page 505).

MUSEUM OF TREASURES COMPLEX

Waterford presents its impressive history in a three-museum complex called the Museum of Treasures, with the locations just a damsel's handkerchief-drop from each other. This "Viking Triangle" rests on the original triangular-shaped Viking fort section of town. Each branch is connected to the other by a two-minute walk (the museum's tagline is "Vikings to Victorians: 1,000 years of history in 1,000 paces"). To see the branches in historical sequence, first visit Reginald's Tower on the harborfront to understand the Viking roots of the city. Then stroll up The Mall to find Chorister's Hall Medieval Museum, a modern structure tucked behind the Theatre Royal. This branch shows Norman and Tudor artifacts above an original 13th-century vaulted wine cellar. Finally, right next door, you can visit the imposing Bishop's Palace, a fine mansion full of everything Waterford from 1700 to the present. Few Irish towns can claim a meatier bite of Irish history than Waterford.

Note: Entry to Reginald's Tower is covered by the Heritage Card (see "Sightseeing Passes," page 508). The Chorister's Hall and Bishop's Palace are not, but they do offer a combo-ticket for entry into both.

▲Reginald's Tower

This oldest part of the oldest town in Ireland is named after Regnall, the first (Norwegian) Viking leader of Waterford, who built

a fortified oaken tower here in A.D. 914 and later invaded Jorvik (York, England). Dating from the late 1100s, the stone Norman tower you see today replaced the wooden one and was once the most important corner of the town wall. The tower is Ireland's oldest intact building and the first made with mortar. Today, its four floors creak with Viking artifacts.

Cost and Hours: €5; includes guided tour upon request—ask for the one-hour version, which adds a historical walk around the

Thomas Francis Meagher (1823-1867)

Waterford's favorite son had a short but amazing life. The son of the town's mayor, Meagher joined Daniel O'Connell's nonviolent movement to repeal the Act of Union with Britain. Impatient with the slow-moving political process of constant compromise, Meagher joined the radical Young Irelander movement that advocated separation from Britain by force of arms. He became an inspiring and fiery speaker nicknamed "Meagher of the Sword." He went to France in 1848 and returned with the first Irish tricolor flag—a gift from the French that represented the Catholics (green), the Protestants (orange), and peaceful coexistence between the two (white).

Involved in a failed uprising, Meagher was sentenced to hang, but his sentence was commuted to life in prison in Tasmania. In 1852, Meagher escaped Tasmania via an American whaling ship and sailed to New York, where he eventually became a lawyer and started an Irish newspaper. After a trip to Nicaragua (to study the feasibility of building a canal or railway across the isthmus), he returned to New York to fight in the American Civil War. Meagher was made a Union general, raised a regiment of Irish immigrants, and famously led them into battle at Antietam and Fredericksburg. After the war, he became the first governor of the Montana territory. At age 44, Thomas Francis Meagher fell off a riverboat one night and drowned in the Missouri River. Sheer accident, foul play, or careless drunkenness? Nobody knows—but his body was never found.

block to French Church; daily 9:30-17:30, Jan-Feb until 17:00, tel. 051/304-220, www.waterfordtreasures.com.

Visiting the Museum: Before you enter, look for the **cannonball** embedded high above the entrance, courtesy of Cromwell's siege cannons.

Once inside, you'll find an interesting Viking town **model** opposite the ticket counter. Upstairs, a display of early coins explains how the Vikings introduced the concept of coinage to the Irish after they eventually settled down and set up trade posts. Look for the tiny **Kite Brooch** that delicately blends both Scandinavian and Irish styles. In their day, brooches were considered badges of status, and this one's owner must have been at the top of the heap. As you climb the narrow stone stairways, watch your head (people were shorter 800 years ago). And be sure to go all the way to the top floor, where an informative 10-minute animated **video** traces the evolution of the town from muddy fort to modern city.

The **statue** outside (in the middle of the street) is of Thomas Francis Meagher (see sidebar), whose short, hell-bent-for-leather life took him on precarious adventures from Waterford to Tasmania to Nicaragua to Montana and, finally, to an unknown watery grave.

Chorister's Hall Medieval Museum

This middle branch of the museum triumvirate uses its three floors to focus on life in Waterford from the Norman invasion of the late 1100s to the Williamite English triumph of the late 1600s. Your visit is enhanced by an excellent free audioguide that plays automatically as you move from room to room (don't miss the changing images it displays).

Cost and Hours: €7, €10 combo-ticket with Bishop's Palace; June-Aug Mon-Sat 9:15-18:00, Sun 11:00-18:00; Sept-May Mon-Sat 10:00-17:00, Sun 11:00-17:00; last entry one hour before closing, tel. 051/304-500, www.waterfordtreasures.com.

Visiting the Museum: Begin by descending under the modern building and into an original wine-vault cellar from the 1200s (long on atmosphere but otherwise empty).

Ride the elevator to the top floor to see a grand collection of well-described Anglo-Norman artifacts. The Great Charter Roll of 1372 was compiled to reinforce Waterford's claim to a monopoly of the lucrative wine-import trade. Check out the wall-size copy of the famous painting depicting the pivotal marriage of Norman leader Strongbow to Irish princess Aoife, then bring it to life on your audioguide. Detailed town models and an informative 10-minute audiovisual presentation complete the history here.

Down one floor, you'll learn how religion played out on Waterford's historic stage. Watch this floor's audiovisual presentation first to understand the broader context of this town's role in Irish history. Then feast your eyes on "Heaven's Embroidered Cloths," a collection of priestly vestments produced in Medici Florence, decorated in affluent Bruges, and shipped to conflicted Waterford. Hidden under a flagstone in the floor of Christ Church Cathedral during a siege, they were rediscovered 123 years later during renovation.

▲Bishop's Palace

Housed in the former mansion (built 1743) of the local Protestant bishop (with his Christ Church Cathedral looming right behind it), this museum presents a grand sweep through the history of Waterford since 1700. The refined interior hints of the privileged lifestyle of the holy resident and contains the world's largest collection of old Waterford glass. The bishop would meet you at the top of the grand stairway if you were an upper-class visitor, greet you at his office doorway if you were a middle-class merchant, and not budge from the chair behind his desk if you were lower-class. Under no circumstances would he come downstairs to greet anyone.

Cost and Hours: €7, €10-combo ticket with Chorister's Hall, same hours and contact info as Chorister's Hall.

Tours: Entertaining 45-minute free tours are led by actors in period dress, who inhabit the palace as servants of the bishop (tours runs hourly June-Aug 9:30-18:00, Sept-May 10:00-16:00).

Visiting the Palace: You'll work your way through three floors spiced with characters like Waterford-born action hero Thomas Francis Meagher (see sidebar). You'll learn why the province of Newfoundland in Canada owes over 50 percent of its population to immigrants from Waterford. And if you've ever wondered what bull baiting is, you'll be filled in on this equally cruel (and long outlawed) Irish version of a bullfight.

OTHER SIGHTS IN WATERFORD
Cathedral of the Holy Trinity
In 1793, the English king granted Ireland the Irish Relief Act, which, among other things, allowed the Irish to build Catholic churches and worship publicly. With Catholic France (30 million) threatening Protestant Britain (8 million) on one side, and Catholic Ireland (6 million) stirring things up on the other, the king needed to take action to lessen Irish resentment. Allowed new freedom, the Irish built this interesting cathedral in 1796. It's Ireland's first Catholic post-Reformation church and its only Baroque church. The building was funded by wealthy Irish wine merchants who were flourishing in Cádiz, Spain. Among its treasures are 10 Waterford Crystal chandeliers.

Cost and Hours: Free, daily 8:00-19:00.

Nearby: The cathedral faces **Barronstrand Street,** which leads from the clock tower on the harborfront through the pedestrian-friendly **town square** to Patrick Street. The street separates the medieval town (on your left when the river is behind you) from the 18th-century city (on your right). A river once flowed here—part of the town's natural defenses just outside the old wall. The huge **shopping center** that dominates the old town was built right on top of the Viking town. In fact, the center is built over a church dating from 1150, which you can see at the bottom of the escalator (behind the glass, next to the kiddie rides).

Christ Church Cathedral
The Protestant cathedral, with 18th-century Georgian architecture, is the fourth church to stand here. Look for the exposed Gothic column six feet below today's floor level, a remnant from an earlier church where the Norman conqueror Strongbow was married (see sidebar on page 161).

Sleep Code

Hotels are classified based on the average price of a typical en suite double room with breakfast in high season.

$$$$	**Splurge:** Most rooms over €170
$$$	**Pricier:** €130-170
$$	**Moderate:** €90-130
$	**Budget:** €50-90
¢	**Backpacker:** Under €50
RS%	**Rick Steves discount**

Unless otherwise noted, credit cards are accepted and free Wi-Fi is available. Comparison-shop by checking prices at several hotels (on each hotel's own website, on a booking site, or by email). For the best deal, *book directly with the hotel*. Ask for a discount if paying in cash; if the listing includes **RS%**, request a Rick Steves discount.

Wander over to the macabre tomb of 15th-century mayor James Rice, which bears a famous epitaph: "I am what you will be, I was what you arc, pray for me." To emphasize the point, he requested that his body be dug up one year after his death (1482) and his partially decomposed remains be used to model his likeness, now seen on the tomb's lid...complete with worms and frogs.

Cost and Hours: Free, €2 donation requested, Mon-Fri 10:00-17:00, Sat 10:00-16:00, closed Sun except for services, tours available on request.

Sleeping in Waterford

Waterford is a working-class city. Cheap accommodations are fairly rough; fancy accommodations are venerable old places that face the water. I recommend one historic option, two modern options, and two budget options (little else in town splits the difference). Many find sleepy Ardmore, an hour southwest down the coast, a smaller and more scenic home base (see page 200).

$$$ The Granville Hotel is Waterford's best and most historic hotel, grandly overlooking the center of the harborfront. The place is plush, from its Old World lounges to its 98 well-tended rooms (super breakfasts, Meagher's Quay, tel. 051/305-555, www. granville-hotel.ie, stay@granville-hotel.ie).

$$$ Dooley's Hotel, a more modern, family-run place on the harbor with 113 big rooms, can be less expensive than the Granville but is still high quality (Merchant's Quay, tel. 051/873-531, www.dooleys-hotel.ie, hotel@dooleys-hotel.ie).

$$ Treacys Hotel is another family-run, modern hotel on the waterfront, close to the Rice Bridge and with 163 pleasant, earth-toned rooms (1 Merchants Quay, tel. 051/877-222, www. treacyshotelwaterford.com, res@thwaterford.com).

$ Mayor's Walk B&B is a well-worn, grandmotherly place that takes you right back to the 1950s. Bob and Jane Hovenden rent four humble, economical rooms with sincere hospitality (rooms with shared bath, cash only, 12 Mayor's Walk, no B&B sign—look for the number on the door; tel. 051/855-427, www.mayorswalk. com, mayorswalkbandb@eircom.net).

¢ Portree Hostel & Accommodation, just across the bridge from the train station, combines 24 basic budget rooms upstairs with 15 dorm beds in its basement hostel (private rooms available, breakfast extra, guest kitchen in hostel section, parking, 10 Mary Street, tel. 051/874-574, www.portreehostel.ie, info@ portreeguesthouse.ie).

Eating in Waterford

For something livelier than tired pub grub, consider these good restaurants found on less-frequented back streets. They're small and popular with locals.

$$$ Emiliano's Ristorante Italiano is the most romantic place in town, hidden on a tiny lane behind Reginald's Tower. They serve a great selection of tasty pasta dishes and fine wines (Tue-Sun 12:30-14:30 & 17:00-22:00, closed Mon, 21 High Street, tel. 051/820-333).

$$ Fork & Knife Bistro is a friendly Polish place with a B.Y.O.B. liquor policy. It serves hearty Eastern European fare, including potato pancakes stuffed with pork goulash and topped with sour cream (Tue-Sun 10:00-21:00, closed Mon, 11a O'Connell Street, tel. 087/171-8688).

The relaxed **$$ Bodega** is my favorite wine bar, run by laid-back Cormac in a warm-glow Mediterranean atmosphere. Their lamb sliders get raves (Mon-Sat 12:00-22:00, closed Sun, 54 John Street, tel. 051/844-177).

$ Burzza Pizza, right next door and under the same ownership, serves not only pizza but also "proper" hamburgers (Mon-Sat 12:00-22:00, closed Sun, 53 John Street, tel. 051/844-969).

On the Harborfront: $ The Granville Hotel's carvery is your best budget lunch option in a central waterfront location (daily 12:30-14:30, otherwise good bar food daily 10:30-21:30, Meagher's Quay).

Pub Grub and Music: Waterford's staple food seems to be pub grub. Several typical pubs serve dinner in the city center. For your musical entertainment, hum a medley of your favorite show tunes. For some reason, not much live music exists in town. Ask at your hotel, or just wander around, read the notices, and follow

Restaurant Price Code

I've assigned each eatery a price category, based on the average cost of a typical main course. Drinks, desserts, and splurge
items (steak and seafood) can raise the price considerably.

$$$$	**Splurge:** Most main courses over €25
$$$	**Pricier:** €20-25
$$	**Moderate:** €15-20
$	**Budget:** Under €15

In the Republic of Ireland, carryout fish-and-chips and other
takeout food is **$**; a basic pub or sit-down eatery is **$$**; a gas-
tropub or casual but more upscale restaurant is **$$$**; and a
swanky splurge is **$$$$**.

your ears. Anything with a pulse will be found on George Street,
Barronstrand Street, and Broad Street.

Supermarket: Dunnes Store in the shopping center is your
best grocery option (Mon-Sat 9:00-19:00, Thu-Fri until 21:00, Sun
12:00-18:00).

Waterford Connections

From Waterford by Train to: Dublin (8/day, 2.5 hours), **Kilkenny**
(6/day, 45 minutes). For details, see www.irishrail.ie.

By Bus to: Cork (almost hourly, 2.25 hours), **Kilkenny** (2/
day, 1 hour), **Rosslare** (4/day, 1.5-2.5 hours), **Wexford** (5/day, 1
hour). Waterford bus station info: Tel. 051/879-000. For details,
see www.buseireann.ie.

County Wexford

The southeast corner of Ireland, peppered with pretty views and
historic sites, is easily accessible to drivers as a day trip from
Kilkenny or Waterford. While most of the sights are mediocre, five
worth considering are within an hour's drive of Waterford and can
also be done as a day loop from Kilkenny (if you get an early start).

The dramatic Hook Head Lighthouse—capping an intriguing
and remote peninsula—comes with lots of history and a great tour.
The Kennedy Homestead is a pilgrimage site for Kennedy fans.
These two stops involve more back-roads navigation, but they feel
more intimate (study your map south of the town of New Ross).

The *Dunbrody* Famine Ship in New Ross gives a sense of what
50 days on a "coffin ship" with dreams of "Americay" must have
been like. The Irish National Heritage Park near Wexford is like a

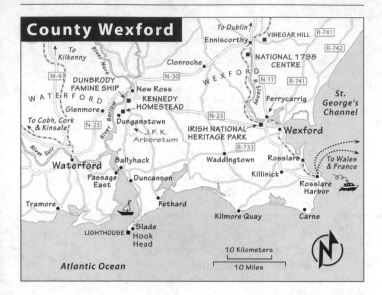

Knott's Berry Farm...circa the Stone Age. And the National 1798 Centre in Enniscorthy explains the roots of the Irish struggle for liberty. These three stops, which are no strangers to tour buses, form an easy driving triangle whose legs are N-25, N-11, and N-30.

If you're driving from Waterford to Kilkenny, consider a visit to the ruins at Jerpoint Abbey and Kells Priory on the way (see the "Between Kilkenny and Waterford" section in the previous chapter.)

PLANNING YOUR TIME

New Ross, Enniscorthy, and Wexford are each less than 30 minutes apart, connected by fast roads. The Kennedy Homestead is a 15-minute drive south of New Ross, and the lighthouse is a one-hour trip from Waterford to the end of the Hook Peninsula. All are well-signposted and easy to find...except for Hook Head Lighthouse (see details later).

Connecting Dublin with Waterford, you could visit several of these sights in a best-of-County Wexford day en route. On a quick trip, the sights are not worth the trouble by public transit. If you'll be spending the night, blue-collar Enniscorthy (with decent hotels and B&Bs) provides a good glimpse of workaday Ireland.

If connecting Waterford to Hook Head, use the car-ferry shortcut from Passage East to Ballyhack. Book a roundtrip and carefully save the tiny receipt for the return journey...the scrap of paper seems determined to ride the next breeze out to sea (€12 round-trip, €8 one-way, 5-minute crossing; runs continuously April-Sept Mon-Sat 7:00-22:00, Sun 9:30-22:00; Oct-March daily until 20:00). To reach the ferry from Waterford, take Lombard Street (near Reginald's Tower) south, and follow it all the way to Passage East (it becomes R-683).

Sights in County Wexford

▲Hook Head Lighthouse

This claims to be the oldest operating lighthouse in Europe. According to legend, St. Dubhan arrived in the fifth century and discovered the bodies of shipwrecked sailors. Dismayed, he and his followers began tending a fire on the headland to warn future mariners. What you see today is essentially a structure from the 12th century, built by the Normans, who first landed five miles up the east coast (at Baginbun Head, in 1169). They established Waterford Harbor—a commercial beachhead for the rich Irish countryside they intended to conquer. This beacon assured them safe access.

Today's lighthouse is 110 feet tall and looks modern on the outside. (It was automated in 1996, and its light can be seen for 23 miles out to sea.) But it's actually 800 years old, built following a plan inspired by the lighthouse of Alexandria in Egypt—one of the seven wonders of the ancient world. Since it's a working lighthouse, it can be toured only with a guide.

Cost and Hours: Fine 45-minute tours cost €9 and depart every half-hour July-Aug, every hour off-season, last tour usually at 16:00; daily July-Aug 9:30-18:00, May and Sept until 17:30, Oct-April until 17:00; tel. 051/397-055, www.hookheritage.ie.

Getting There: The lighthouse can be a bit tricky to find. But if you follow the brown *Hook Scenic Route* signs south of Ballyhack and remind yourself that you're on a narrow peninsula with the lighthouse at the southern tip, you'll be funneled straight there (more or less).

Visiting the Lighthouse: As you view the black-stained, ribbed, vaulted ceilings and stout, 10-foot-thick walls, you can

almost feel the presence of the Cistercian monks who tended this coal-burning beacon for the Normans. Climbing 115 steps through four levels rewards you with a breezy, salt-air view from the top.

Oliver Cromwell passed through here to secure the English claim to this area (see "The Curse of Cromwell" sidebar, later). He considered his two options and declared he'd take strategic Waterford "by Hook or by Crooke." Hook is the long peninsula

JFK in Ireland

JFK arrived in Ireland for a three-day visit in late June 1963, straight from the Berlin Wall and his inspiring "Ich bin ein Berliner" speech. The Irish gave him a deliriously warm welcome in those Cold War days. Bursting with pride in his presidency (he was the first Catholic to hold the office), the Irish saw what was possible at a time when the state of the Irish economy was dire and emigration was high. Kennedy's every move was televised. Only 10 percent of Irish households had a TV at that time, so people crowded into pubs with TVs to watch. Kennedy's whirlwind itinerary included stops in Dublin, Galway, Limerick, Cork, and County Wexford, where he visited the farm of his Irish ancestors near Dunganstown.

As the third-born son, JFK's great-grandfather Patrick Joseph Kennedy had little hope of inheriting the family farm. He had learned the trade of coopering (barrel making) at a brewery in nearby New Ross and decided to emigrate to Boston in 1848 near the end of the Great Potato Famine. There he clawed out a new start from desperate poverty and started a family. But he succumbed to cholera in 1858...105 years to the day (November 22) before his great-grandson would be assassinated.

JFK's death came only five months after his triumphant Irish visit, at perhaps the peak of his popularity. After the assassination, Kennedy staffer and later New York senator Daniel Patrick Moynihan was quoted as saying, "To be Irish is to know that in the end the world will break your heart."

An old Irish superstition holds that it's bad luck to take a stone away from a "fairy fort" (the Iron Age ring forts that dot the landscape). Some say that the reason the Kennedy clan has suffered so many tragedies over the years is that an ancestor may have taken a stone from a fort, way back when.

with the lighthouse. Crooke is a little village on the other side, just south of Passage East.

There's a decent cafeteria and a shop with fliers explaining other sights on the peninsula. Kids-at-heart can't resist climbing out on the rugged rocky tip of the windy Hook Head.

▲Kennedy Homestead

Patrick Joseph Kennedy, President John F. Kennedy's great-grandfather, left Ireland in 1858. Distant relatives have turned the family homestead into a little museum/shrine for Kennedy pilgrims. Physically, it's not much: A barn and a wing of the modern house survive from 1858. JFK and his entourage visited here in June 1963, a few months before he was assassinated. While it's now just a private home, anyone interested in the Kennedys will find it worth driving the long narrow lane to see.

Cost and Hours: €7.50; daily 9:30-17:30, tel. 051/388-264, www.kennedyhomestead.ie.

Getting There: It's four miles (6 km) south of New Ross near Dunganstown (from R-733 follow brown signs with JFK's face in profile, down a long one-lane road). Don't confuse the Kennedy Homestead with the nearby JFK Arboretum—a huge park with 4,500 species of trees. It's nice if you like trees and plants, but there's no Kennedy history there.

Visiting the Homestead: Park behind the modern visitors center. Inside is a fascinating exhibition on Kennedy's Irish heritage, his brief visit here, and the aftermath of his tragic death. A little barnyard houses one long shed with knick-knacks and photos of his visit. Look for the old bench-style car seat (with furniture legs added by Kennedy's second cousin). This was the nicest seat in the homestead's modest home, where the eminent visitor sat to take tea. There are a couple of short videos: JFK chatting with his distant relatives, and then being whisked away by helicopter to continue his triumphant tour of the country. JFK's assassin denied him the opportunity of a promised return visit. But his widow, Jackie, made sure that his Irish relatives here got some of his precious memorabilia.

▲▲*Dunbrody* Famine Ship

Permanently moored on a river in the tiny port of New Ross, this ship was built as a re-creation of similar vessels that sailed to America full of countless hungry Irish emigrants. The *Dunbrody* is a full-scale reconstruction of a 19th-century three-masted bark built in Quebec in 1845. It's typical of the trading vessels that originally sailed, empty, to America to pick up goods; during the famine, ship owners found that they could make a little money on the westward voyage. On board, extended families camped out for 50 days on bunk beds no bigger than a king-size mattress. Commonly, boats like this would arrive in America with

only 80 percent of their original human cargo (in the worst cases, only 50 percent). Those who succumbed to "famine fever" (often typhus or cholera) were dumped overboard, and the ships gained their morbid moniker: "coffin ships."

Cost and Hours: €10, daily April-Sept 9:00-18:00, Oct-March

The Curse of Cromwell

The scariest bogeyman in all of Irish history was Oliver Cromwell. In 1649, he led Parliamentary forces to victory in the English Civil War and had King Charles I beheaded. Assuming the title of Lord Protector, he created a commonwealth (instead of a kingdom) and initiated one of the longest periods in the past 1,000 years during which England functioned without a monarch. Cromwell then turned his attention to Ireland, determined to root out the last royalists loyal to the English monarchy and to punish the Irish for the 1641 massacre of Protestant settlers.

Driven by his Puritan Calvinist beliefs, Cromwell claimed a divine right to carry out God's work as he saw it. To him, all Catholics were complicit in the Protestant deaths by virtue of their misguided faith. He saw priests as little more than witch doctors. Even Protestant Anglicans (the faith founded by Henry VIII a century before) were looked on with suspicion as "Catholics without a pope." Cromwell's self-righteous army of 12,000 soldiers had God on their side and Ireland in their musket-sights.

Cromwell and his tough New Model Army landed in Dublin on August 15, 1649, and marched north to the town of Drogheda. In a bloody siege lasting three days, his soldiers massacred almost all of the town's 3,000 inhabitants. A handful of lucky survi-

10:00-17:00, 45-minute tours go 2/hour, last tour starts one hour before closing, upstairs café handy for lunch with nice views of the ship, tel. 051/425-239, www.dunbrody.com.

Getting There: The *Dunbrody* is in New Ross, near the Kennedy Homestead. During work hours, you'll need to feed the parking meters in the lot (€1/hour, free on Sun).

Visiting the Ship: Your visit starts with an audiovisual presentation on the life Irish emigrants were leaving behind, followed by coverage about the building of the vessel. Then you'll follow an excellent guide on board the ship, encountering a couple of grumpy passengers who tell vivid tales about life onboard. At the end, you'll get a glimpse of the new life Irish immigrants would encounter in New York. Most arrived filthy (try skipping a shower for six weeks), illiterate, and often penniless.

Roots-seekers are welcome to peruse the computerized file of the names of the million immigrants who sailed on these ships from 1846 through 1865. Before you leave, check out the Irish America Hall of Fame, commemorating the contributions Irish

vors silently slipped into the River Boyne and played dead, floating downstream out of harm's way. Cromwell then turned south to Wexford, where his army again massacred 3,000-some civilians and Irish troops. Few garrison towns resisted after that. Cromwell's merciless efficiency brought almost the entire island under English control in less than a year.

Catholic landowners were forced to give up their land or face execution...a deal with the devil known as "to hell or to Connaught." About 11 million acres of productive land was taken from Catholic landowners and handed over to Cromwell's soldiers as payment for service. In "exchange," these Catholics got unfertile ground west of the River Shannon. This forced mass migration essentially destroyed Ireland's Catholic landowning class. (In 1641, Catholics owned 59 percent of Ireland—by 1714 they owned 7 percent.) Some Catholics were allowed to stay on as tenants, providing labor for their new English masters.

Upon Cromwell's death in 1658, his less-dynamic son took over, and the English began to miss their monarchy. In 1660, Charles I's son, Charles II, was invited back from exile in France and the monarchy was restored. Soon after, Cromwell's body was dug up, hung, and beheaded—his head was stuck on a pike and displayed in front of London's Parliament for 20 years (curiously, a heroic statue of him stands there today). But most of Ireland's Catholics never regained their land, and for the next 250 years Ireland continued its slow downward cultural spiral at the hands of the English government.

men and women have made to US history (with short videos on Henry Ford and JFK, whose roots lie in this part of Ireland).

Ros Tapestry

Before you leave New Ross, consider a short visit to see the Ros Tapestry. Outlining the colorful Norman history of the region, it's a bit like a recently woven version of the ancient Bayeux Tapestry in Normandy. Consisting of 15 large embroidered panels, not all of which are complete yet, this is a labor of love that local women have been working on for more than 20 years. Visitors are invited upstairs to do one stitch themselves to take part in its creation.

Cost and Hours: €7, includes audioguide, daily 10:00-17:00, tel. 051/445-396, www.rostapestry.com. It's housed on the ground floor of an old six-story stone warehouse about 100 yards north of the *Dunbrody* Famine Ship, across the street; leave your car in the *Dunbrody* parking lot.

▲Irish National Heritage Park

This 35-acre wooded park, which contains an 1857 tower com-memorating local boys killed in the Crimean War, features replicas of buildings from each era of Irish history. Since Ireland's countless ancient sights are generally unrecognizable ruins—hard to re-create in your mind—this park is intended to help out. You'll find buildings and settlements illustrating life in Ireland from the Stone Age through the 12th-century Norman Age. As a bonus, you'll see animal-skin-clad characters doing their prehistoric thing—gnawing on meat, weaving, making arrowheads, and so on.

Cost and Hours: €9.50, daily 9:30-18:30, winter until 17:30, last entry 1.5 hours before closing, audioguide-€2, tel. 053/912-0733, www.inhp.com.

Getting There: It's clearly signposted on the west end of Wexford—you'll hit it before entering town on the N-11 Enniscorthy road.

Visiting the Park: Your visit begins with a 15-minute video. Then you have the choice of using a self-paced audioguide or following a live guide on an hour-long tour (hourly 10:00-16:00). Along 16 stops, the guide explains various stages of Irish civilization. The highlight is a monastic settlement from the age when Europe was dark, and Ireland was "the island of saints and scholars." While you can wander around on your own, there's hardly anything actually old here and the visit is only worthwhile if you take the included tour.

National 1798 Centre

Located in Enniscorthy, this museum creatively tells the story of the rise of revolutionary thinking in Ireland, which led to the ill-fated rebellion of 1798 (Ireland's deadliest). Enniscorthy was the crucial Irish battleground of a populist revolution (inspired by the American and French revolutions). The town witnessed the bloodiest days of the doomed uprising. The material is compelling for anyone intrigued by the struggles for liberty, but there's little more here than video clips of reenactments and storyboards on the walls.

Cost and Hours: €7; April-Sept Mon-Fri 9:30-17:00, Sat 12:00-17:00, closed Sun; shorter hours off-season; last entry one hour before closing, tel. 053/923-7596, www.1798centre.ie.

Getting There: Enniscorthy is 12 miles (19 km) north of

Wexford town. The National 1798 Centre is the town's major sight and is well-signposted (follow the brown *Aras 98 Centre* signs).

Nearby: Leaving the center, look east across the River Slaney, which divides Enniscorthy, and you'll see a hill with a stumpy tower on it. This is **Vinegar Hill.** The tower is the old windmill that once flew the green rebel flag. Drive to the top for the views that the rebels had of the surrounding British forces. The doomed rebels tried desperately to hold the high ground, with no shelter from the merciless British artillery fire.

KINSALE & COBH

County Cork, on Ireland's south coast, is fringed with historic port towns and scenic peninsulas. The typical tour-bus route here includes Blarney Castle and Killarney—places where most tourists wear nametags. But rather than kissing the spit-slathered Blarney Stone, spend your time in County Cork enjoying the bustling, historic maritime towns of Kinsale and Cobh. Although Cobh is a growing cruise ship port, most cruise travelers are booked on day excursions that clog iconic stops like Blarney Castle, and blessedly spare Kinsale and Cobh all but the briefest of drive-by glimpses.

Kinsale makes a great home base for a visit to the coast of County Cork. From Kinsale, you can wade through the salty his-

tory of Cobh. Travelers approaching this region from Waterford can easily visit Ardmore and the Old Midleton Whiskey Distillery en route. Blarney Castle and Macroom make convenient stops when connecting to the Ring of Kerry or Dingle.

Avoid the mistake many travelers make—allowing destinations into their itineraries simply because they're famous from a song or as part of a relative's big-bus-tour memory. If you have the misfortune to spend the night in Killarney town (next door in County Kerry), you'll understand what I mean. The town is a sprawling line of green Holiday Inns and outlet malls littered with pushy shoppers looking for plastic shamrocks.

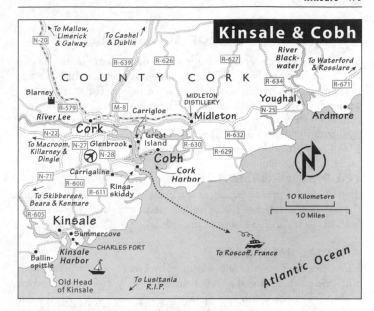

Kinsale

While nearby Cork is the biggest town in southern Ireland, Kinsale (15 miles south) is actually more historic and certainly cuter. It's delightful to visit. Thanks to the naturally sheltered bay barbed by a massive 17th-century star fort, you can submerge yourself in maritime history, from the Spanish Armada to the sailor who inspired Daniel Defoe's *Robinson Crusoe* to the *Lusitania* (2015 marked the 100th anniversary of its sinking). Apart from all the history, Kinsale has a laid-back feel with a touch of wine-sipping class. Or, as a local told me with a wry smile, "Welcome to Happy Valley" (Eli Lilly manufactures much of its Prozac just outside town).

PLANNING YOUR TIME

Kinsale is worth two nights and a day. Spend the morning checking out one or two of the town's sights, and make sure to take Don and Barry's excellent Kinsale walking tour (at 11:15; some days also at 9:15). After lunch at the Blue Haven Café, head out to Charles Fort for great bay views and insights into British military life in colonial Ireland. On the way back, stop for a pint at the Bulman Bar. Finish the day with a good dinner at Fishy Fishy Café and live music in a pub. Those on the blitz tour can give Kinsale four hours—see the fort, wander the town, and have a nice lunch—before driving on.

Orientation to Kinsale

Kinsale has a great natural harbor and is older than Cobh (the city of Cork's harbor town). While the town is prettier than the actual harbor, the harbor was its reason for being. Today, Kinsale is a vibrant bustle of 2,500 residents. The town's long and skinny old center is part modern marina (attracting wealthy yachters) and part pedestrian-friendly medieval town (attracting scalawags like us). It's an easy 20-minute stroll from end to end.

TOURIST INFORMATION

The TI is as central as can be, at the head of the harbor across from the bus stop (Mon-Sat 9:00-17:00, closed Sun, shorter hours Dec-Feb; tel. 021/477-2234, www.kinsale.ie).

ARRIVAL IN KINSALE

Kinsale doesn't have a train station. The **bus** stop is on Pier Road, 100 yards behind the TI, just before the gray swooping modern sculptures at the south end of town. Drivers should park the **car** and enjoy the town on foot. While Kinsale's windy medieval lanes are narrow and congested, parking is fairly easy. The most central lot is at the head of the harbor behind the TI (€1.50/hour, 2-hour maximum, use pay-and-display machine, exact coins required, enforced Mon-Sat 10:30-18:00, free on Sun). There's a big, safe, free parking lot across the street from St. Multose Church at the top of town, a five-minute walk from most recommended hotels and restaurants. An even larger free lot is farther away, a 10-minute walk east of town by the fire station. Parking on the street is pay-and-display (€1.50/hour, 2-hour maximum, enforced Mon-Sat 10:30-18:00, free on Sun). Outlying streets, a 10-minute stroll from the action, have wide-open parking.

HELPFUL HINTS

Exchange Rate: €1 = about $1.10

Country Calling Code: 353 (see page 530 for dialing instructions)

Crowds: The Kinsale Rugby Sevens Tournament draws dozens of teams and hundreds of loud and proud rowdy rugby fans on the first weekend in May (with its associated Bank Holiday Monday). If you're not up for the scrum, then scram.

Market: Check out the lively open-air market on Wednesdays from June through September (9:00-14:00) in the town square on Market Quay, in front of the recommended Jim Edward's Steak & Seafood restaurant.

Money: The two banks in town are **Allied Irish Bank** on Pearse Street and **Bank of Ireland** on Emmett Street (both open Mon 10:00-17:00, Tue-Fri 10:00-16:00, closed Sat-Sun).

Post Office: It's on Pearse Street (Mon-Fri 9:00-13:00 & 14:00-17:30, Sat 9:00-13:00, closed Sun).

Bookshop: You'll find the radioactive-yellow walls of friendly **Kinsale Bookshop** proudly pinching traffic on Main Street (daily 10:00-18:00 except Sun from 12:00, 8 Main Street, tel. 021/477-4244).

Laundry: Take your dirty duds to **Elite Laundry.** They'll do an average-sized load for about €12 (Mon-Fri 9:00-17:30, Sat 10:00-17:00, closed Sun, The Glen, tel. 021/477-7345).

Bike Rental: Mylie Murphy's rents bikes from a handy spot near the Centra Market (€15/day, includes lock and helmet; Mon-Sat 9:30-18:00 year-round, Sun 11:00-17:00 May-Aug only, shorter hours in winter; arrangements can be made for pickup or drop-off, tel. 021/477-2703). They can recommend paths good for biking or walking that stretch around the harbor.

For a good short-and-scenic route, bike south on the Pier Road, past the marina a couple miles, and turn left across the first bridge. Turn left again at the far end of the bridge to reach the dead end of the road marked by the Dock pub. Jump off your bike and explore the great views from the grassy ruins of James Fort, uphill behind the pub (2 miles each way).

Taxi: Tom Canty can drive you where you need to go, including Cork Airport for €25 or Cork city for €30 (mobile 087-237-1022).

Tours in Kinsale

▲▲Don & Barry's Kinsale Historic Stroll

To understand the important role Kinsale played in Irish, English, and Spanish history, join gentlemen Don Herlihy or Barry Moloney on a fascinat-ing 1.5-hour walking tour (€7, daily April-mid-Oct at 11:15, additional early-bird tour May-Sept Mon-Sat at 9:15, no reservation necessary, meet outside the TI, private tours possible, tel. 021/477-2873, www.historicstrollkinsale.com). Both guides are a

joy, creatively bringing to life Kinsale's past, placing its story in the wider sweep of history, and making the stony sights more than just buildings. They collect payment at the end, giving anyone disappointed in the talk an easy escape midway through. Don't get hijacked by imitation tours that pretend to be recommended by me

KINSALE & COBH

on my blog—ask for Don or Barry. This walk is Kinsale's single best attraction.

Ghost Walk Tour

This is not just any ghost tour; it's more Monty Python-style slapstick comedy than horror. Two actors (Brian and David) weave funny stunts and stories into a loose history of the town, offering an entertaining 1.25 hours of fun on Kinsale's after-dark streets (€10, April-Oct Sun-Fri at 21:00, no tours Sat, leaves from Tap Tavern, call ahead to confirm, mobile 087-948-0910). You'll spend the first 15 minutes in the back of the Tap Tavern—time to finish your drink and get to know some of the group. This tour doesn't overlap with the more serious historic town walk described earlier.

Kinsale Harbour Cruise

Enjoy a 45-minute voyage around the historic harbor aboard the nimble little 50-passenger *Spirit of Kinsale*. The voyage offers sea-level views of both Charles and James forts, as well as seal and seafowl sightings with informative commentary from captain/historian/naturalist Jerome (€12.50, July-Aug daily at 11:00, 12:00, 14:00, and 15:00; June and Sept at 14:00 and 15:00, one sailing per day April-May and Oct, check schedule online; departs from Pier Road in front of Acton's Hotel roughly 200 yards south of the TI, not necessary to book ahead but be at dock 30 minutes before departure, mobile 086-250-5456, www.kinsaleharbourcruises.com).

Sights in Kinsale

Kinsale's top sight is the town walking tour with Don and Barry (listed earlier, under "Tours in Kinsale"). But with extra time, there's much more to explore.

Kinsale Town Wander

Stroll the old part of town. The medieval walled town's economy was fueled by the harbor, where ships came to be stocked. The old walls defined the original town and created a small fortified zone that made taxation of goods coming in or going out easier. The wall followed what is now O'Connell Street and Main Street.

The subtle curves of Main Street trace the original coastline. Walking this street, you'll see tiny lanes leading to today's harbor. These originated as piers—just wide enough to roll a barrel down to an awaiting ship. The wall detoured inland to protect St. Multose Church, which dates from Norman times. In these days, worshippers sharpened their swords on the doorway of the church. Just like today, there were more right-handers than left-handers—check it out.

A block downhill from the church (across from today's Tap

Tavern) was the town pound: a small enclosure where goods and livestock would be impounded until the owner could pay the associated tax. After the James and Charles forts were built in the 1600s, the wall became obsolete—and also boxed in the town, preventing further expansion. The townspeople later disassembled the wall and used its ready-cut stones to build out the piers in the harbor.

What seems like part of the old center was actually built later on land reclaimed from the harbor. The town sits on the floor of a natural quarry, with easy-to-cut shale hills ideal for a ready supply of fill. Notice the mudflats in the harbor at low tide. Clear-cutting of the once-plentiful oak forest upriver (for shipbuilding and barrel-making) hastened erosion and silted up the harbor. By the early 1800s—when British ships needed lots of restocking for the Napoleonic Wars—Kinsale's port was slowly dying, and nearby Cobh's deepwater port took over the lion's share of shipping.

▲▲Charles Fort

Kinsale is protected by what was Britain's biggest star-shaped fort—a state-of-the-art defense when artillery made the tradition-al castle obsolete (low, thick walls were tougher for cannons to breach than the tall, thin, curtain walls of a castle). The British occupied it until Irish independence in 1922. Its interior buildings were torched in 1923 by antitreaty IRA forces to keep it from being used by  Free State troops during the Irish Civil War. Guided 45-minute tours (which depart on the hour—confirm at entry) engross you in the harsh daily life of 18th-century British soldiers and the few "lucky" wives allowed to live in the fort and earn their keep doing laundry for an army.

Before or after your tour, peruse the exhibits and audiovisuals in the barracks stores building. Spend a moment checking out the model of the fort. Great views await those who walk the walls.

Cost and Hours: €5, daily 10:00-18:00, Nov-mid-March until 17:00, last entry one hour before closing, a half-mile south of town in Summercove, tel. 021/477-2263. A little coffee-and-pastry café stands inside the walls, downhill across from the ticket office (daily May-Sept 10:00-18:00).

After Your Visit: For a beer or meal nearby, try the recommended Bulman Bar in Summercove, where the road runs low near the water on the way back to town (with small parking lot). And to see how easily the forts could bottle up this key harbor, pull over at

Kinsale

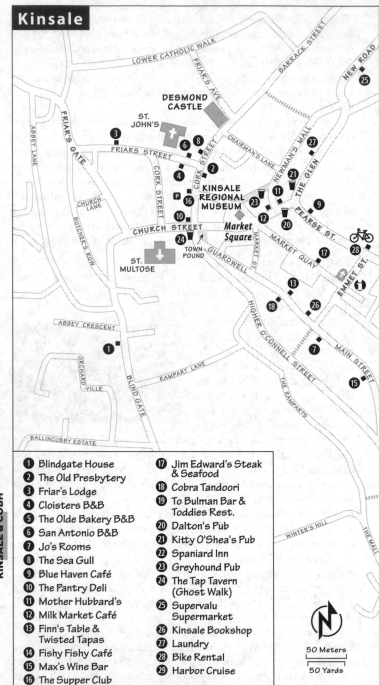

1. Blindgate House
2. The Old Presbytery
3. Friar's Lodge
4. Cloisters B&B
5. The Olde Bakery B&B
6. San Antonio B&B
7. Jo's Rooms
8. The Sea Gull
9. Blue Haven Café
10. The Pantry Deli
11. Mother Hubbard's
12. Milk Market Café
13. Finn's Table & Twisted Tapas
14. Fishy Fishy Café
15. Max's Wine Bar
16. The Supper Club
17. Jim Edward's Steak & Seafood
18. Cobra Tandoori
19. To Bulman Bar & Toddies Rest.
20. Dalton's Pub
21. Kitty O'Shea's Pub
22. Spaniard Inn
23. Greyhound Pub
24. The Tap Tavern (Ghost Walk)
25. Supervalu Supermarket
26. Kinsale Bookshop
27. Laundry
28. Bike Rental
29. Harbor Cruise

50 Meters
50 Yards

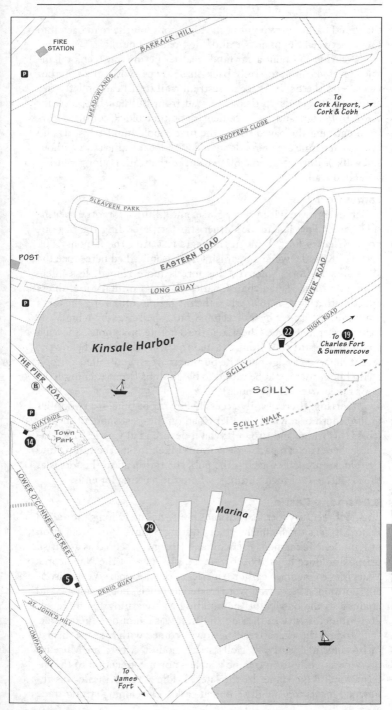

FIRE STATION

BARRACK HILL

P

To Cork Airport, Cork & Cobh

MEADOWLANDS

TROOPERS CLOSE

SLEAVEEN PARK

EASTERN ROAD

POST

LONG QUAY

P

Kinsale Harbor

RIVER ROAD

22

HIGH ROAD

To 19, Charles Fort & Summercove

SCILLY

SCILLY

THE PIER ROAD

B

P

QUAYSIDE

14

Town Park

SCILLY WALK

Marina

LOWER O'CONNELL STREET

29

5

DENIS QUAY

ST. JOHN'S HILL

COMPASS HILL

To James Fort

KINSALE & COBH

the grand harbor viewpoint at the high point on the road back into town (between Summercove and The Spaniard pub).

Nearby: Without a car (and weather permitting), enjoy Kinsale's best 45-minute stroll back into town—with great harbor views—on the Scilly Walk pedestrian trail (trailhead on left after climbing 200 yards up the steep road from Bulman Bar; look for *Scilly Walk* sign and large cement slabs that block confused cars from entering the paved trail). The first couple hundred yards and last quarter-mile are on roads shared with local traffic (and without sidewalks). But the middle 80 percent of the walk is along a lushly vegetated trail.

James Fort

Older, overgrown with yellow gorse, and filling a forgotten peninsula, James Fort is Kinsale's other star fort, guarding the bay opposite Charles Fort. Built in the years just after the famous 1601 battle of Kinsale (when a Spanish force disembarked here—see the "Kinsale's History" sidebar), this fort is more ruined, less interesting, and less visited than Charles Fort. Its military usefulness ended with a bang in 1690 when the magazine containing the fort's ammunition was hit by a direct and fatal shell fired by King William's besieging army. Check out the satellite blockhouse (down a straight, 75-yard trail from the main walls), which sits below the fort at the water's edge opposite Summercove. It controlled a strong chain boom that could be raised to block ships from reaching Kinsale's docks (free, always open).

Getting There: Easily accessible by car or bike, it's two miles (3 km) south of town along Pier Road on the west shore of the bay (cross the bridge and turn left; you'll dead-end at Castle Park Marina, where you can park or leave your bike). It's up the hill behind the Dock pub. When facing the pub, the trailhead to the fort is at the far left end of the buildings, where the parking lot ends.

▲Desmond Castle

This 15th-century fortified customs house has had a long and varied history. It was the Spanish armory during Spain's 1601 occupation of Kinsale. Nicknamed "Frenchman's Prison," it served as a British prison and once housed 600 cramped prisoners of the Napoleonic Wars (not to mention earlier American Revolutionary War prisoners captured at sea—who were treated as rebels, not prisoners, and chained to the outside of the building as a warning to any rebellion-minded Irish). In the late 1840s, it was a famine-relief center.

Today, the evocative little tower comes with a scant display of its colorful history, as well as the modest two-room Museum of Wine, highlighting Ireland's little-known connection to the international wine trade. In the late Middle Ages, Kinsale was renowned for its top-quality wooden casks. Developing strong trade links with Bordeaux and Jerez, local merchants traded their dependable empty casks for casks full of wine. Later, Kinsale became a "designated wine port" for tax-collection purposes.

Cost and Hours: €5, daily 10:00-18:00, closed Oct-Easter, last entry at 17:15; tours generally at 10:15, 12:00, 14:15, and 16:00; Cork Street, tel. 021/477-4855.

▲Kinsale Regional Museum

In the center of the old town, traffic circles the market, which later became a courthouse and is now the Regional Museum. Its Dutch architecture reflects the influence of Dutch-born King William of Orange at the end of the 1600s. Drop by at least to read the fun 1788 tax code for all Kinsale commercial transactions (outside at the front door).

Cost and Hours: Free, Tue-Sat 10:30-14:00, closed Sun-Mon, staffed by volunteers—hours can be erratic, Market Square, tel. 021/477-7930.

Visiting the Museum: The modest museum is worth a quick visit for its fun mishmash of domestic and maritime bygones. It also gives a good perspective on the controversial *Lusitania* tragedy. Kinsale had maritime jurisdiction over the waters 12 miles offshore, where the luxury liner was torpedoed in 1915. Hearings were held upstairs here in the courthouse shortly afterward to investigate the causes of the disaster—which helped propel America into World War I—and to paint the German Hun as a bloodthirsty villain. Claims by Germany that the *Lusitania* was illegally carrying munitions (and using innocent passengers as human shields) may have been inspired by the huge explosion and rapid sinking of the vessel. As the wreck slowly succumbs to a century of gravity and rust, it's collapsing on itself and the truth of its cargo may forever be lost in the ocean floor muck.

The museum displays are sparse, but include *Lusitania* flotsam such as a wicker deck chair and a US mail bag. A flickering black-and-white film shows the last happy glory days of the vessel in port. Apart from the *Lusitania* footage, you'll find a gritty little model of medieval Kinsale surrounded by its once-proud walls. Perhaps even more memorable, in the side room is the boot of the 8-foot-3-inch Kinsale giant, who lived here in the late 1700s.

Nightlife in Kinsale

Kinsale's pubs are packed with atmosphere and live music (though not always traditional Irish). Rather than target a certain place, simply walk the area between Guardwell, Pearse Street, and the Market Square. Pop into each pub that has live music, and then

KINSALE & COBH

Kinsale's History

Kinsale's remarkable harbor has made this an important port since prehistoric times. The bay's 10-foot tide provided a natural shuttle service for Stone Age hunter-gatherers: They could ride it, at two miles per hour twice a day, for the eight miles up and down the River Bandon. In the Bronze Age, when people discovered that it takes tin and copper to make bronze, tin came from Cornwall (in southwest England) and copper came from this part of Ireland. From 500 B.C. to A.D. 500, Kinsale was a rich trading center. The result: Lots of Stonehenge-type monuments are nearby. The best is Drombeg Stone Circle (a one-hour drive west, just off R-597/Glandore Road).

Kinsale's importance peaked during the 16th, 17th, and 18th centuries, when sailing ships ruled the waves, turning maritime countries into global powers. Kinsale was Ireland's most perfect natural harbor and the gateway to both Spain and France—potentially providing a base for either of these two powers in cutting off English shipping. Because of this, two pivotal battles were fought here in the 17th century: in 1601 against the Spanish, and in 1690 against the French. Two great forts were built to combat these threats from the Continent. England couldn't rule the waves without ruling Kinsale.

To understand the small town of Kinsale, you need to understand the big picture: In about 1500, the pope divided newly discovered lands outside Europe between Spain and Portugal. With the Reformation breaking Rome's lock on Europe, maritime powers such as England were ignoring the pope's grant. This was important because trade with the New World and Asia brought huge wealth in spices (necessary for curing meat), gold, and silver. England threatened Spain's New World piñata, and Ireland was Catholic. Spain had an economic and a religious reason to defend the pope and Catholicism. The showdown between Spain and England for mastery of the seas (and control of all that trade) was in Ireland. The excuse: to rescue the dear Catholics of Ireland from the terrible treachery of Protestant England.

So the Irish disaster unfolded. The powerful Ulster chieftains Hugh O'Neill and Red Hugh O'Donnell and their clans had been on a roll in their guerilla battles against the English on their home turf up in Ulster. With Spanish aid, they figured they could actually drive the English out of Ireland. In 1601, a Spanish fleet dropped off 3,000 soldiers, who established a beachhead in Kinsale. After the ships left, the Spaniards were pinned down in Kinsale by the English commander (who, breaking with martial etiquette, actually fought in the winter). In harsh winter conditions, virtually the entire Irish-clan fighting force left the north and marched to the south coast, thinking they could liberate their Spanish allies and win freedom from England.

The numbers seemed reasonable (8,000 Englishmen versus 3,000 Spaniards with 7,000 Irish clansmen approaching). The Irish attacked on Christmas Eve in 1601. But, holding the high ground around fortified and Spanish-occupied Kinsale, a relatively small English force kept the Spaniards hemmed in, leaving the bulk of the English troops to rout the fighting Irish, who were adept at ambushes but not at open-field warfare. (Today's visitors will be reminded of this crucial battle as they wander past pubs with names like "The 1601" and "The Spaniard"—see pub sign on opposite page.)

The Irish resistance was broken, and its leaders fled to Europe (the "flight of the Earls"). England made peace with Spain and began the "plantation" of mostly Scottish Protestants in Ireland (the seeds of today's Troubles in Ulster). England ruled the waves, and it ruled Ireland. The lesson: Kinsale is key. England eventually built two huge, star-shaped fortresses to ensure control of the narrow waterway, a strategy it would further develop in later fortifications built at Gibraltar and Singapore.

Kinsale's maritime history continued. Daniel Defoe used the real-life experience of Scottish privateer Alexander Selkirk, who departed from Kinsale in 1703 and was later marooned alone on a desert island, as the basis for his book *Robinson Crusoe*. (Selkirk was lucky to have been marooned when he was—his ship and all aboard later perished in a hurricane off Costa Rica.)

It was just 10 miles offshore from Old Kinsale Head that the

passenger liner *Lusitania* was torpedoed by a German submarine in 1915. At the time, the liner was the fastest vessel on the seas (with a top speed of 25 knots). The primitive U boats of the day were much slower (8 knots), giving Lusitania's crew a false sense of security. Because World War I was the first conflict to employ submarine warfare, evasion tactics were largely untested. As the *Lusitania* sank, nearly 1,200 people were killed, sparking America's eventual entry into the war.

KINSALE & COBH

settle in to your favorite. **Dalton's** and **Kitty O'Shea's** are good bets.

Irish music purists will be rewarded if they take the five-minute taxi ride (€8 one-way) out to the **$$ Bulman Bar** near the base of Charles Fort. This is one of Kinsale's two most famous pubs for traditional Irish music sessions and the only pub listed here to consider as a dinner option (Thu-Sat at 21:30, Sun at 17:00, get there early to ensure a seat, see listing in "Eating in Kinsale," tel. 021/477-2131). Otherwise, get your trad fix at the charmingly claustrophobic **Spaniard Inn,** a 10-minute walk out to the Scilly peninsula across the harbor from town. It fills the center of a hairpin turn on the crest of the peninsula. The darkly atmospheric interior is about the size of a rail car, with the long bar taking up half the space, so only about 10 seats get an actual view of the musicians (most nights at 21:30, you'll stand all night unless you arrive before 20:30, tel. 021/477-2436).

For conversation or an introspective pint with a newspaper, I like the **Greyhound** (off Newman's Mall, behind the Milk Market Café)—no live music, just a scruffy, multichambered throwback with no pretenses. Another joint filled with characters who haven't changed in decades is the **Tap Tavern** (corner of Church Street and Guardwell). It's presided over by Mary O'Neill, the unofficial godmother of Kinsale, and her slyly humorous son Brian, who runs the town's recommended Ghost Tours. Check out the ancient holy well that came to light when they built their appealing back patio.

Sleeping in Kinsale

Kinsale is a popular place in summer for yachters and golfers (who don't flinch at paying $250 for 18 holes out on the exotic Old Head of Kinsale Golf Course). It's wise to book your room in advance. These places are all within a 10-minute walk of the town center.

$$$ Blindgate House, high up on the fringe of town behind St. Multose Church, offers 11 pristine rooms in fine modern comfort (tel. 021/477-7858, mobile 087-237-6676, www.blindgatehouse.com, info@blindgatehouse.com, Maeve Coakley).

$$ The Old Presbytery is a fine, quiet house a block outside the commercial district, with a meandering floor plan, plush lounge, and 10 pleasant rooms. Listed in most guidebooks, it has lots of American guests. The breakfasts are a delight, the rooms are stocking-feet cozy, and Noreen McEvoy runs the place with a passion for excellence. Join the other guests for a complimentary wine-and-cheese happy hour every afternoon (RS%, 10 percent discount with cash, family rooms, private parking, 43 Cork Street, tel. 021/477-2027, www.oldpres.com, info@oldpres.com).

$$ Friar's Lodge is a slate-shingled hotel, perched up the hill

```
┌─────────────────────────────────────────────────────┐
│                    Sleep Code                        │
│                                                      │
│  Hotels are classified based on the average price    │
│  of a typical en suite double room with breakfast    │
│  in high season.                                     │
│    $$$$   Splurge: Most rooms over €170              │
│    $$$    Pricier: €130-170                          │
│    $$     Moderate: €90-130                          │
│    $      Budget: €50-90                             │
│    ¢      Backpacker: Under €50                      │
│    RS%    Rick Steves discount                       │
│                                                      │
│  Unless otherwise noted, credit cards are accepted   │
│  and free Wi-Fi is available. Comparison-shop by     │
│  checking prices at several hotels (on each hotel's  │
│  own website, on a booking site, or by email). For   │
│  the best deal, book directly with the hotel.        │
│  Ask for a discount if paying in cash; if the        │
│  listing includes RS%, request a Rick Steves         │
│  discount.                                           │
└─────────────────────────────────────────────────────┘
```

past St. John's Catholic Church. What its 18 spacious rooms lack in Old World character, they make up for in dependable quality. Three pleasant, self-catering cottages located up the slope behind their parking lot are great for families wanting their own space (family rooms, private parking, Friar Street, tel. 021/477-7384, www.friars-lodge.com, mtierney@indigo.ie).

$$ Cloisters B&B has four snug but bright and inviting rooms with a friendly atmosphere fostered by Orla Kenneally and Aileen Healy (2 Friars Street, tel. 021/470-0680, www.cloisterskinsale.com, info@cloisterskinsale.com).

$ The Olde Bakery B&B makes you feel at home, with six quilt-bedded rooms, Lilly the loveable mute mutt, and a jovial breakfast at the kitchen table cooked up by charmingly chatty Chrissie and beekeeper Tom Quigley (cash only, laundry service, 56 Lower O'Connell Street, tel. 021/477-3012, www.theoldebakerykinsale.com, oldebakery@gmail.com).

$ San Antonio B&B is a 200-year-old house with five rooms and a funky budget feel, lovingly looked after by gentleman Jimmie Conron (cash only, 1 Friar Street, tel. 021/477-2341, mobile 086-878-9800, jimmiesan@yahoo.ie).

$ Jo's Rooms is a good value, offering five fresh, practical rooms in the center of town (breakfast extra, cash only, small rooms with smaller double beds, 55 Main Street, mobile 087-948-1026, www.joskinsale.com, joskinsale@gmail.com).

$ The Sea Gull, perched up the hill right next to Desmond Castle, offers six retro-homey rooms. It's run by Mary O'Neill, who also runs the Tap Tavern down the hill (RS%, cash only, Cork Street, tel. 021/477-2240, mobile 087-241-6592, marytap@iol.ie).

Eating in Kinsale

Back in the 1990s, when Ireland was just getting its cuisine act together, Kinsale was the island's self-proclaimed gourmet capital.

 While good restaurants are commonplace in Irish towns today, Kinsale still has an edge at mealtime. Local competition is fierce, and restaurants offer creative and tempting menus. Seafood is king. With so many options in the ever-changing scene, it's worth a short stroll to assess your options. Reservations are smart, especially if eating late or on a weekend. Restaurant connoisseurs can check the menu details of Kinsale's most famous restaurants at www.kinsalerestaurants.com.

LUNCH

The following places are good for lunch, but only the Blue Haven also does dinner.

Inviting cafés are **$$ Blue Haven Café** (daily, at Blue Haven Hotel on Pearse Street, nice salads and mellow atmosphere) and **$$ The Pantry** (Tue-Sat 9:00-18:00, Sun 9:00-14:00, closed Mon, across street from St. Multose Church, your chance to try spiced lamb burger, tel. 021/477-4453).

Cheap and Cheery Lunches: Tiny **$ Mother Hubbard's**, packed with happy locals near Market Square, serves sandwiches or salads with coffee (daily 8:30-14:30). The **$ Milk Market Café**—right next door—offers burgers, pizza, and fish-and-chips. Or, gather picnic supplies at the **SuperValu** supermarket (daily 8:00-21:00, New Road, tel. 021/477-2843).

GOOD DINNERS IN THE OLD CENTER

Colorfully fronted **$$$$ Finn's Table** offers a refined vibe and a scrumptious menu ranging from lamb to lobster (Mon-Sat 18:00-22:00, closed Sun year-round; also closed Wed Dec-May and all of Nov; 6 Main Street, tel. 021/470-9636, www.finnstable.com).

$$ Fishy Fishy Café has spacious seating (indoor, balcony, and terrace) and a wonderful fish menu. It's a good lunch or early dinner option. Look at the lobsters on death row in the tank and ponder this: Several years ago, a soft-hearted, deep-pocketed Buddhist tourist bought up the tank's entire supply of live lobsters and set them free in the bay (with stories to tell their crustacean cousins about how they'd been abducted by aliens). They've refilled the tank since. Owner Martin Shanahan's cooking prowess has led him to host a weekly cooking show on Irish TV (daily 12:00-21:00, reservations recommended, Pier Road, tel. 021/470-0415, www.fishyfishy.ie).

KINSALE & COBH

Restaurant Price Code

I've assigned each eatery a price category, based on the average cost of a typical main course. Drinks, desserts, and splurge items (steak and seafood) can raise the price considerably.

$$$$	**Splurge:** Most main courses over €25
$$$	**Pricier:** €20-25
$$	**Moderate:** €15-20
$	**Budget:** Under €15

In the Republic of Ireland, carryout fish-and-chips and other takeout food is **$;** a basic pub or sit-down eatery is **$$;** a gastropub or casual but more upscale restaurant is **$$$;** and a swanky splurge is **$$$$.**

Several atmospheric wine-bar restaurants vie for your attention along the gently curving Main Street. **$$$ Max's Wine Bar** leads the pack, with subdued lighting and a menu that's big on quality seafood (daily 18:00-21:30 except closed Sun in Oct-April, 48 Main Street, tel. 021/477-2443).

$$$ The Supper Club is a linen-and-leather upmarket joint with a meat smoker, strong cocktails, and creative desserts (Tue-Sat 18:30-22:00, closed Sun-Mon, 3 Cork Street, tel. 021/477-2847).

Jim Edward's Steak & Seafood keeps eaters happy. Choose between the **$$$ restaurant's** maritime setting or simpler food in the no-nonsense **$$ bar.** Arrive early or wait. While cheaper and less gourmet than other Kinsale eateries, it's a high-energy place that's clearly a local family favorite for its decent steaks, seafood, and vegetables (bar daily 12:30-22:00, restaurant daily 18:00-22:00, Market Quay, tel. 021/477-2541).

Ethnic Food: Walk around the old-town block for an array of inviting international eateries. **$$ Twisted** is hip and youthful, serving Spanish tapas and lighter fare "with a twist" (5 Main Street, tel. 021/477-4218). **$$ Cobra Tandoori** is good for tasty Punjabi/Indian cuisine (daily 16:00-23:00, 69 Main Street, tel. 021/477-7911).

NEAR CHARLES FORT

$$$ Bulman Bar and Toddies Restaurant serves seafood with seasonal produce. The mussels are especially tasty; on a balmy day or evening, diners take a bucket and a beer out to the seawall. This is the only way to eat on the water in Kinsale. The **$$ pub,** strewn with fun decor and sporting a big fireplace, is also good for a coffee or beer after your visit to the fort (daily 12:30-21:00, 200 yards toward Kinsale from Charles Fort in hamlet of Summercove, tel. 021/477-2131).

Kinsale Connections

Like many worthwhile corners of Ireland, Kinsale is not accessible by train. The closest train station is in Cork, 15 miles north. But buses run frequently between Kinsale (stop is on Pier Road, 100 yards behind TI, at south end of town) and Cork's bus station (14/day Mon-Sat, fewer on Sun, 50 minutes, www.buseireann.ie).

In **Cork,** the bus station and train station are a 10-minute walk apart. The bus station (corner of Merchant's Quay and Parnell Place) is on the south bank of the River Lee, just over the nearest bridge from the train station (north of the river on Lower Glanmire Road).

From Cork by Train to: Dublin (hourly, 3 hours, www.irishrail.ie).

From Cork by Bus to: Dublin (every 2 hours, 3.5 hours), **Galway** (hourly, 4.5 hours), **Tralee** (hourly, 2.5 hours), **Kilkenny** (4-5/day, 2 direct, 3.5 hours). Bus info: Tel. 021/450-8188 or www.buseireann.ie.

Cobh

If your ancestry is Irish, there's a good chance that this was the last Irish soil your ancestors had under their feet. Cobh (pronounced

"cove") was the major port of Irish emigration in the 19th century. Of the six million Irish who have emigrated to America, Canada, and Australia since 1815, nearly half left from Cobh.

The first steam-powered ship to make a transatlantic crossing departed from Cobh in 1838—cutting the journey time from 50 days to 18. When Queen Victoria came to Ireland for the first time in 1849, Cobh was the first Irish ground she set foot on. Giddy, the town renamed itself "Queenstown" in her honor. It was still going by that name in 1912, when the *Titanic* made its final fateful stop here before heading out on its maiden (and only) voyage...just over 100 years ago. To celebrate their new independence from British royalty in 1922, locals changed the town's name back to its original Irish moniker. Today the town's deep harbor attracts 60 cruise ships per year (with their large packs of eager visitors).

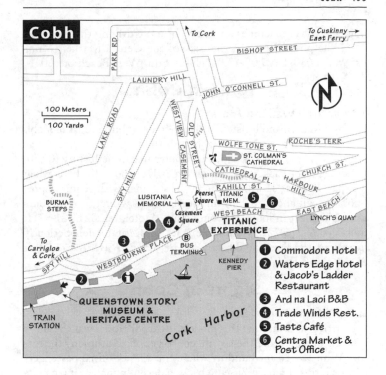

Map of Cobh

Cobh

To Cork →
To Cuskinny → East Ferry →

BISHOP STREET
LAUNDRY HILL
JOHN O'CONNELL ST.
PARK RD.
WEST VIEW STREET
CASEMENT
OLD STREET
LAKE ROAD
SPY HILL
WOLFE TONE ST.
ROCHE'S TERR.
ST. COLMAN'S CATHEDRAL
CATHEDRAL PL.
CHURCH ST.
HARBOUR HILL
RAHILLY ST.
BURMA STEPS
LUSITANIA MEMORIAL
Pearse Square
TITANIC MEM.
WEST BEACH
EAST BEACH
LYNCH'S QUAY
Casement Square
TITANIC EXPERIENCE
To Carrigloe & Cork
SPY HILL
WESTBOURNE PLACE
BUS TERMINUS
KENNEDY PIER
TRAIN STATION
QUEENSTOWN STORY MUSEUM & HERITAGE CENTRE
Cork Harbor

100 Meters
100 Yards

N

❶ Commodore Hotel
❷ Waters Edge Hotel & Jacob's Ladder Restaurant
❸ Ard na Laoi B&B
❹ Trade Winds Rest.
❺ Taste Café
❻ Centra Market & Post Office

Orientation to Cobh

Cobh sits on a large island in Cork Harbor, connected to the mainland by a short bridge (on the north shore) or a handy drive-on ferry (on the west shore). The town's inviting waterfront is colorful yet salty, with a playful promenade. The butcher's advertisement reads, "Always pleased to meet you and always with meat to please you." Stroll past the shops along the water. Ponder the large and dramatic *Lusitania* memorial on Casement Square and the modest *Titanic* memorial nearby on Pearse Square.

A hike up the hill to the towering Neo-Gothic St. Colman's Cathedral rewards you with a fine view of the port. To get to the cathedral, walk behind the *Lusitania* memorial, go under the stone arch, and strut up steep Westview Street, passing the photogenic row of colorful houses on your right (nicknamed the "deck of cards" by locals). After panting your way to the top, turn right—you can't miss the cathedral steeple.

Tourist Information: The TI is in the Old Yacht Club on the harbor (Mon-Fri 9:00-17:30, Sat-Sun 10:30-16:30, tel. 021/481-3301, www.cobhharbourchamber.ie).

Helpful Hints: If you're driving into Cobh, there's a two-hour **parking** maximum anywhere in town (first hour-free, second hour—€1, pay at machines on street; for more driving tips, see page 199). The **post office** is at the back of the Centra Market (Mon-Fri 9:00-17:30, Sat 9:00-13:00, closed Sun, West Beach Street).

Tours in Cobh

Titanic Trail Walking Tours

Michael Martin and his staff lead one-hour walking tours of Cobh that give you unexpected insights into the tragic *Titanic* and *Lusitania* voyages, Spike Island, and Cobh's maritime history (€9.50, €1 discount for Rick Steves readers in 2017—show this book when you pay, daily at 11:00, also 14:00 in summer with required pre-booking, call ahead to confirm tour times in winter, private tours available, meet in lobby of Commodore Hotel, tel. 021/481-5211, mobile 087-276-7218, www.titanic.ie, info@titanic.ie). Seriously interested travelers should look for his book, *RMS Lusitania: It Wasn't and It Didn't.*

Sights in Cobh

▲The Titanic Experience

It's stirring to think that this modest little port town was the ship's final anchorage—and the last chance to get off. Occupying the former White Star Line building where the *Titanic*'s final passengers boarded, this compact museum packs a decent punch as it recounts the story of the ship and its final moments.

Cost and Hours: €9.50, daily 9:00-18:00, Oct-April until 17:30, last entry 45 minutes before closing, Casement Square, tel. 021/481-4412, www.titanicexperiencecobh.ie.

Visiting the Museum: As you look off the back balcony into the harbor, note the decayed pilings in front of you. These once supported the old pier and represent the passengers' last chance to turn back. One lucky surviving crewman with a premonition did.

Inside the museum, you travel room to room with your host, the ship's fourth mate, in audiovisual form. He meets you at the boarding dock, full of pride in the new vessel. He joins you in replicas of a posh first-class cabin and a no-frills third-class cabin before his commentary is interrupted by the sound of ice tearing at the hull. You then enter a small theater to view an animation that silently depicts the ship sinking in its steel-twisting, slow-motion ballet to the bottom (settling as two crunched hulls 600 yards apart and 12,000 feet deep).

The last stop is a room highlighting the luxurious ship's innovative firsts. It was one of the first equipped with a wireless "Marconi room" to send messages from sea to shore—or to other ships. *Titanic* was the first ever to issue an SOS message by Morse code.

Another wall explains in grim detail the effects of hypothermia on the human body.

Before you leave, check out the list of 123 passengers who boarded the *Titanic* in Cobh. Your entry ticket has one of these passenger's names on it. See if you survived (you've got a 30 percent chance). A passenger with the same name as one of this book's co-authors is listed among the third-class passengers lost.

▲The Queenstown Story

Filling a harborside Victorian train station, this museum is an earnest attempt to make the city's history come to life. The topics—the famine, Irish emigration, Australia-bound prison ships, the sinking of the *Lusitania,* and the ill-fated voyage of the *Titanic*—are interesting enough to make it a worthwhile stop.

Cost and Hours: €9.50; Mon-Sat 9:30-18:00, Sun 11:00-18:00; Nov-April until 17:00; last entry one hour before closing, Cobh Heritage Centre, handy café, tel. 021/481-3591, www.cobhheritage.com, info@cobhheritage.com.

Visiting the Museum: Coverage of the *Titanic* and the *Lusitania* was beefed up for the centennials of these famous ships' sinking (2012 and 2015, respectively). You'll learn about one priest who got off the *Titanic* at Cobh. His photos of the early legs of the voyage are a priceless historical reference. But in general, the museum itself, while kid-friendly and engaging, is weak on actual historical artifacts. It reminds me of a big, interesting history picture book with the pages expanded and tacked on the wall.

Before departing, walk over to the Annie Moore statue next to the water, 25 yards from the front door. She emigrated from Cobh and was the first person to be processed through Ellis Island when it opened on January 1, 1892.

Nearby: Those with Irish roots to trace can use the Heritage Centre's **genealogy search service,** located right across from the Queenstown Story ticket booth. Since Cobh was the primary Irish emigration port, this can be a great place to start your search (€30 consultation and research assistance by appointment only, email ahead to book—genealogy@cobhheritage.com). See the sidebar for more tips on researching your Irish heritage.

Sleeping in Cobh

These hotels are all centrally located near the harbor, less than a five-minute walk from the Queenstown Story.

$$ Commodore Hotel is a grand 165-year-old historic landmark with 40 rooms. This place was once owned by the Humbert family, wealthy Germans who opened it up to *Lusitania* refugees after the 1915 sinking. Its high-ceilinged rooms creak with Vic-

KINSALE & COBH

Irish Genealogy

Lots of travelers come to the Emerald Isle intent on tracing their Irish ancestry. But too few give it enough thought before they set foot on the old sod, and instead head straight to what they think might be the right town or region to start "asking around." While this approach may bear fruit (or at least give you an opportunity to meet nice Irish people), a bit of preparation can save time and increase your chances of making a real connection to your Celtic bloodlines.

First, a common false assumption: Many novice root-searchers think their Irish ancestors were from County Cork, because Cobh is listed as their emigration departure port. But Cobh was the primary departure port for the vast majority of Irish emigrants—regardless of where they had resided in Ireland. An even earlier wave of Irish emigrants (mostly Scots-Irish from Ulster) sailed from the port of Derry (the second busiest emigration port).

If you have an idea of what town your ancestors hailed from, search for its location (www.google.com/maps is a good starting point). Correct spelling is essential: Ballyalloly is up north in County Down while Ballyally is down south in County Cork (close enough only counts in horseshoes and hand grenades). Just as there's a Springfield in almost every state in the Union, the same goes for some common Irish town names: There's a town named Kells in four different Irish counties.

Fáilte Ireland, the official government-sponsored Irish tourist board, is a safe bet for reputable genealogy sources (www. discoverireland.ie). Some fertile websites to consider browsing are www.irishgenealogy.ie or www.ancestry.com. The recently

torian character (Westbourne Place, tel. 021/481-1277, www. commodorehotel.ie, commodorehotel@eircom.net).

$$ Waters Edge Hotel, located 50 yards from the Queenstown Story, has 19 bright, modern rooms and a pleasant harbor-view restaurant (Yacht Club Quay, tel. 021/481-5566, www. watersedgehotel.ie, info@watersedgehotel.ie).

$ Ard na Laoi B&B is a friendly place with five fresh rooms in a great central location (cash only, 15 Westbourne Place, tel. 021/481-2742, www.ardnalaoi.ie, info@ardnalaoi.ie, Michael O'Shea).

Eating in Cobh

The nicest place in town is **Trade Winds,** with both a **$$$ pub** (downstairs) and **$$$$ restaurant** (upstairs). It's near the Commodore Hotel, facing the waterfront at 16 Casement Square. I also like the **$$$ Jacob's Ladder** restaurant in the Waters Edge Hotel.

enabled online access to both the 1901 and 1911 Irish censuses has been a boon (www.census.nationalarchives.ie). However, it's not a perfect science: Many precious birth records (some dating back to the 1200s) went up in smoke when offices in the Four Courts building in Dublin burned in 1922 during the Irish Civil War.

Before you get to Ireland, make contact with the Genealogy Advisory Service at the National Library in Dublin (tel. 01/603-0213, www.nli.ie, genealogy@nli.ie). Others to contact in advance of your trip include the helpful genealogy search service in Cobh (tel. 021/481-3591, www.cobhheritage.com/genealogy, genealogy@cobhheritage.com), or, if you think your heritage might be Scots-Irish, the Mellon Centre for Migration Studies, near Omagh in Northern Ireland (tel. 028/8225-6315, www.qub.ac.uk/cms, mcms@librariesni.org.uk).

Another option is to hire a qualified expert to assist you in drilling deeper and navigating obstacles; Fáilte Ireland may be able to give you a recommendation. This kind of help doesn't come cheap, but if you're willing to invest in an experienced researcher, you may get better results. One worth considering is Sean Quinn of My Ireland Heritage (tel. 01/689-0213, www.myirelandheritage.com, sean@myirelandheritage.com, based near Dublin in Trim, County Meath, but able to work across Ireland). Top-end services like Sean's can then drive you to the locations where your ancestors lived.

With a few emails, phone calls, and Internet searches, you may just end up having a pint with some Irish guy who looks a lot like you. (For tips on dialing Irish phone numbers from North America, see page 530.)

$ **Taste** is a hip little sandwich joint, a couple of doors down from the *Titanic* memorial. For picnic fixings, there's the **Centra Market** (daily 9:00-22:00, facing the water on West Beach Street).

Cobh Connections

By Car: Driving to Cobh from Cork or Waterford, leave N-25 about eight miles (13 km) east of Cork, following little R-624 over a bridge, onto the Great Island, and directly into Cobh.

Kinsale to Cobh is 25 miles (40 km), takes an hour, and involves catching a small ferry. Leave Kinsale north on R-600 toward Cork. Just south of Cork and its airport, go east on R-613. You'll follow little *car-ferry* signs, but they ultimately take you to the wrong ferry (Ringaskiddy—to France). Instead, after you hit N-28, take R-610 to Monkstown and then Glenbrook, where a (poorly signposted) shuttle ferry takes you to Carrigloe on the Great Island (€5 one-way, €7 round-trip, 5 minutes, daily 7:00-22:00). Once on the island, turn right and drive two miles (3 km) into Cobh. In Cobh, follow the *Heritage Centre* signs to The Queenstown Story, where you'll find easy parking at the museum (first hour free, second hour—€1, 2-hour maximum).

By Train: Cork's **Kent Station** has frequent short-hop service to both Cobh and Midleton, which are on separate lines (€5 one-way, €8.50 round-trip, 25 minutes, usually depart on the hour, return on the half-hour, www.irishrail.ie).

By Plane: Cork Airport is a handy entry point into (or exit point from) Ireland. Some travelers (with limited time and no interest in urban Dublin) choose to start their trip to Ireland here, in order to focus on the island's scenic south and west. Located four miles south of Cork city (on N-27/R-600 to Kinsale, a 30-minute drive away), it offers connecting flights from London Heathrow and Edinburgh on Aer Lingus, as well as from London's Stansted and Gatwick on Ryanair. More distant connections can be made from Munich, Amsterdam, Paris, Pisa, Prague, Warsaw, and Málaga (tel. 021/431-3131, airport code: ORK, www.corkairport.com). Citylink airport buses run to Kinsale (hourly Mon-Sat, fewer on Sunday) and less frequently to other destinations, including Galway (6/day, 4 hours).

To sleep near Cork Airport, consider **$$$ Cork Airport Hotel** (book directly on their website for best prices, tel. 021/494-7500, www.corkairporthotel.com, reservations@corkairporthotel.com).

Between Waterford and Kinsale

If you're driving from Waterford (see previous chapter) to Cobh and Kinsale, you can easily visit these sights just off N-25 (listed roughly from east to west).

Ardmore

This funky little beach resort, with a famous ruined church and round tower, is a handy stop (just east of Youghal, 3 miles/5 km south of N-25 between Waterford and Cobh). A couple of buses run daily from Ardmore to Cork and to Waterford.

This humble little port town is just a line of pastel houses that appear frightened by the sea. Its beach claims (very modestly) to be "the most swimmable in Ireland."

The town's historic claim to fame: Christianity came to Ireland here first (thanks to St. Declan, who arrived in A.D. 416—15 years before St. Patrick...but with a weaker public-relations team). As if to proclaim that feat with an 800-year-old exclamation mark, one of Ireland's finest examples of a round tower stands perfectly intact, 97 feet above an evocative graveyard and a ruined church (noted for the faint remains of some early Christian carvings on its west facade). You can't get into the tower—the entrance is 14 feet off the ground.

An easy, scenic coastal loop hike (3 miles, 1 hour) leads from the parking lot of the ritzy Cliff House Hotel along the coast, eventually cutting inland and back into town (simple to follow, ask for free rudimentary map in newsstand at end of Main Street).

Sleeping in Ardmore: $$$$ Cliff House Hotel is a died-and-gone-to-heaven splurge with 39 impeccably modern rooms, all with ocean views (tel. 024/87800, www.thecliffhousehotel.com, info@thecliffhousehotel.com).

$ Duncrone B&B, run by Jeanette Dunne, has four vividly colorful rooms (half-mile outside town, up past the round tower, tel. 024/94860, www.duncronebandb.com, info@duncronebandb.com).

Eating in Ardmore: The local favorite is **$$ White Horses Restaurant** (Tue-Sun 11:00-22:00, closed Mon, Main Street, tel. 024/94040). For a fine lunch or dinner with cliff-perch views, check out the restaurant in the luxurious **$$$$ Cliff House Hotel** (turn right at the coastal end of Main Street and drive up narrow lane to dead end, tel. 024/87800). **An Tobar,** the only pub in town, is down near the water (but does not serve food).

▲Old Midleton Distillery

Sometime during your Ireland trip, even if you're a teetotaler, you'll want to tour a whiskey distillery. Of the three major distillery tours

(this one, Jameson in Dublin, and Bushmills in Northern Ireland), the Midleton experience is the most interesting. After a 10-minute video, you'll walk with a guide through a great old 18th-century plant on a 45-minute tour; see waterwheel-powered crankshafts and a 31,000-gallon copper still—the largest of its kind in the world; and learn the story of whiskey. Predictably, you finish in a tasting room and enjoy a free, not-so-wee glass. The finale is a Scotch vs. Irish whiskey taste test. Your guide will take two volunteers for this. Don't be shy—raise your hand like an eager little student and enjoy an opportunity to taste the different brands.

Cost and Hours: Tour-€16, discount if booked online, open daily 10:00-18:00, tours run regularly 10:00-16:30 in summer—3/day in winter, cafeteria, tel. 021/461-3594, www.jamesonwhiskey.com.

KINSALE & COBH

Getting There: It's 12 miles (19 km) east of Cork in Midleton, about a mile off N-25, the main Cork-Waterford road. There's easy parking—just drive right into the distillery lot.

Between Kinsale and Killarney

If you're driving between Kinsale and the Ring of Kerry (see next chapter), you can easily visit these sights (listed from east to west).

Blarney Stone and Castle

The town of Blarney is of no importance, and the 15th-century Blarney Castle is an empty hulk (with little effort put forth to make it meaningful or interesting). It's only famous  as the place of tourist pilgrimage, where busloads line up to kiss a stone on its top rampart and get "the gift of gab." The stone's origin is shrouded in myth (perhaps brought back from the Holy Land by crusaders). The best thing about this lame sight is the opportunity to watch a cranky man lower lemming tourists over the edge, belly up and head back, to kiss the stone while an automated camera snaps a photo—which will be available for purchase back by the parking lot. After a day of tour groups mindlessly climbing up here to perform this ritual, the stone can be literally slathered with spit and lipstick.

The tradition goes back to the late 16th century, when Queen Elizabeth I was trying to plant loyal English settlers in Ireland to tighten her grip on the rebellious island. She demanded that the Irish clan chiefs recognize the Crown, rather than the clan chiefs, as the legitimate titleholder of all lands. One of those chiefs was Cormac MacCarthy, Lord of Blarney Castle (who was supposedly loyal to the queen). He was smart enough never to disagree with the

queen—instead, he would cleverly avoid acquiescing to her demands by sending a never-ending stream of lengthy and deceptive excuses, disguised with liberal doses of flattery (while subtly maintaining his native Gaelic loyalties). In her frustration, the queen declared his endless words nothing but "blarney."

While the castle is a shell, the surrounding grounds are beautiful and well kept. There are even some hints of Ireland's pre-Christian past on the grounds; you can see dolmens beside the trail in the forested Rock Close.

Cost and Hours: €13, Mon-Sat 9:00-18:30, Sun 9:00-18:00, later in peak season, shorter hours in winter, free parking lot, helpful TI, tel. 021/438-5252, www.blarneycastle.ie.

Getting There: It's five miles (8 km) northwest of Cork, the major city in south Ireland. Looking for shopping galore? Adjacent Blarney Woolen Mills has it all (right next to the castle parking lot).

Beal na Blath: Michael Collins Ambush Site

Irish history fans may want to make a brief detour en route from Kinsale to Macroom to visit nearby Beal na Blath (BALE-nuh-BLAH), where dynamic Irish rebel leader Michael Collins was assassinated on August 22, 1922, during the Irish Civil War. The site is not much more than a bend in a country road, with an Irish high cross on a raised platform to mark the spot. But it's Ireland's equivalent of Dallas' infamous "grassy knoll."

Take a moment to step out of the car and climb the steps onto the fenced platform. Next to the high cross, a plaque with a photo shows the road as it appeared in 1922, with arrows approximating the position of the Collins convoy and the spots from which the ambushers fired.

Dusk was falling as the convoy carrying Collins to Cork came under attack. Collins could have ordered his driver to speed off, but chose instead to stand and fight. The identity of the antitreaty IRA guerilla who fired the fatal shot (thought to have been an errant ricochet) remains in dispute. Following his death, Collins' body lay in state for three days at Dublin City Hall, drawing massive crowds. Although his protreaty Free State army later won the civil war, it's likely that modern Irish history would have been much different had Collins lived.

Getting There: Beal na Blath is just off N-22, the road that runs west from Cork to Macroom, and is easiest to find if you have a detailed Ordnance Survey atlas (it covers all tiny rural lanes). About halfway between Cork and Macroom, take R-585 south off N-22 through the tiny village of Crookstown. From Crookstown, follow *Beal na Blath* signs south for about a mile to the ambush site (well-marked, but be alert in case foliage on leafy rural lanes obscures a sign at a crossroads).

Macroom

This colorful, inviting market town makes a handy coffee or lunch stop between Cork and Killarney. The romanticized gateway where its ruined castle once stood was owned by the father of William Penn (who founded Pennsylvania). It overlooks an entertaining main square, where you'll find limited parking. The Next Door Café, in the Castle Hotel, serves a good, fast lunch. The 2006 Irish Civil War saga *The Wind That Shakes the Barley* was filmed in this area.

KENMARE &
THE RING OF KERRY

It's no wonder that, since Victorian times, visitors have been attracted to this dramatic chunk of Ireland. Mysterious ancient ring forts stand sentinel on mossy hillsides. A beloved Irish statesman maintained his ancestral estate here, far from 19th-century power politics. And early Christian hermit-monks left a lonely imprint of their devotion, in the form of simple stone dwellings atop an isolated rock crag far from shore...a holy retreat on the edge of the then-known world.

Today, it seems like every tour bus in Ireland makes the ritual loop around the scenic Ring of Kerry, using the bustling and famous tourist town of Killarney as a springboard. Killarney National Park is gorgeous and well worth driving through. But I prefer to skip Killarney town (useful only for its transportation connections). Instead, make the tidy town of Kenmare your home base, and use my suggestions to cleverly circle the much-loved peninsula—entirely missing the convoy of tour buses.

Kenmare

Cradled in a lush valley, this charming little town (known as Neidín, or "little nest," in Irish) hooks you right away with its rows of vividly colored shop fronts and go-for-a-stroll atmosphere. The nearby finger of the gentle sea feels more like a large lake (called the Kenmare River, just to confuse things). Far from the assembly-line tourism of Killarney town, Kenmare (rhymes with "been there") also makes a great launchpad for enjoying the sights along the road around the Iveragh (eev-er-AH) Peninsula—known to shamrock lovers everywhere as the Ring of Kerry.

PLANNING YOUR TIME

All you need in compact Kenmare is one night and a couple of hours to wander the town. Check out the Heritage Centre (in the back rooms of the TI) to get an overview of the region's history. Visit the Kenmare Lace and Design Centre (above TI, entry next door) to get a close look at its famously delicate lace. A five-minute walk from the TI gives you hands-on access to an ancient stone circle at the edge of town. Finish up by taking a peek inside Holy Cross Church to see the fine ceiling woodwork. Don't stay out too late in the pubs if you'd like to get an early start on the Ring of Kerry in the morning.

Orientation to Kenmare

Carefully planned Kenmare is shaped like an "X," forming two triangles. The upper (northern) triangle contains the town square

(colorful market Wed in summer), the adjacent TI and Heritage Centre, and a cozy park. The lower (southern) triangle contains three one-way streets busy with shops, lodgings, and restaurants. Use the tall Holy Cross Church spire to get your bearings (next to the northeast parking lot). Public WCs across the street are vile...if possible, wait to use one wherever you settle for lunch.

Tourist Information: The helpful TI is on the town square (Mon-Sat 9:30-13:30 & 14:00-17:15, closed Thu in spring and fall, Sun year-round, and all of Nov-March; tel. 064/664-1233).

HELPFUL HINTS

Exchange Rate: €1 = about $1.10

Country Calling Code: 353 (see page 530 for dialing instructions)

Money: Bank of Ireland faces the town square, and **Allied Irish Bank** takes up the corner of Henry and Main streets (both open Mon-Fri 10:00-16:00, Mon until 17:00, closed Sat-Sun).

Post Office: It's located on Henry Street, at the intersection with Shelbourne Street (Mon-Fri 9:00-17:30, Sat 9:00-13:00, closed Sun).

Laundry: O'Shea's Cleaners and Launderette is across from the Lansdowne Arms Hotel, hidden in the back recesses of

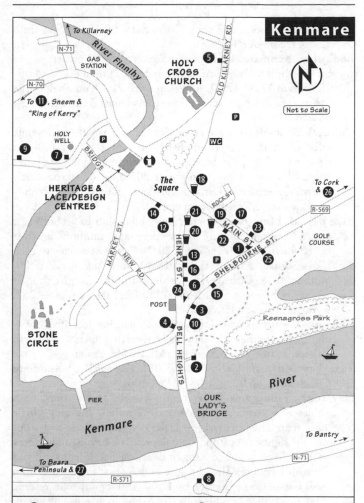

1. Lansdowne Arms Hotel/Bar
2. Sallyport House
3. Hawthorn House
4. Whispering Pines B&B
5. Willow Lodge
6. Virginia's Guesthouse
7. Limestone Lodge
8. Watersedge B&B
9. Rockcrest House
10. Kenmare Fáilte Hostel
11. To Parknasilla Hotel & Ring of Kerry Golf
12. Jam Deli
13. The Purple Heather
14. Café Mocha
15. The Lime Tree Rest.
16. Packies Restaurant
17. Mulcahy's Restaurant
18. Horse Shoe Pub & Rest.
19. P. F. McCarthy's Pub & Rest.
20. Crowley's Pub
21. Foley's Pub
22. Supermarket
23. Launderette
24. Bike Rental
25. Kenmare Bookshop
26. To River Valley Riding Stables
27. To Star Sailing (Boat Rental)

O'Shea's photography shop (Mon-Sat 9:00-18:00, Sun from 12:00, tel. 064/664-0808).

Bookstore: Kenmare Bookshop is a cozy one-room cottage run by friendly John O'Connor (Mon-Sat 10:00-13:00 & 14:00-17:30, Sun 12:00-17:30, July-Aug until 21:00, on Shelbourne Street at roundabout across from Lansdowne Arms Hotel, tel. 064/664-1578).

Cultural Events: Carnegie Arts Center is a small-town venue offering a mixed bag of quality local concerts in its 140-seat theater (€5-20), art exhibitions, and films. In summer (June-Aug), Thursday is movie night at 20:00 for €7 (across Shelbourne Street from Lansdowne Arms Hotel, tel. 064/664-8701, www.carnegieartskenmare.ie).

Bike Rental: Finnegan's Corner rents bikes and has route maps and advice on maximizing scenery and minimizing traffic (standard bike-€15/day, €20/24 hours, beefed-up road bike-€30/day; Mon-Sat 9:30-18:30, July-Aug until 19:00; Sun 12:00-18:00; leave ID for deposit, office in gift shop at 37 Henry Street, across from post office, tel. 064/664-1083, www.finneganscycles.com).

Parking: The town's two largest public parking lots (free overnight) cling to the two main roads departing town to the north (otherwise free street parking is allowed for 2 hours).

Taxi: Try **Murnane Cabs** (mobile 087-236-4353) or **Kenmare Coach and Cab** (mobile 087-248-0800).

Day Tours: Finnegan's Tours runs a variety of day tours, with guides who give a fun, anecdotal narration. The tour—little more than a scenic joyride—generally makes three rest stops and one sightseeing stop (route depends on day: Ring of Kerry on Mon, Wed, and Fri; Ring of Beara on Tue; Glengarriff and Garnish Island on Thu). In July and August tours leave from the TI at 10:00 and return by 17:00 (€30 for any tour, reserve a day in advance by phone or three days in advance by email; for Sept-June, call to arrange tours; can book private tours for small groups with enough notice; tel. 064/664-1491, mobile 087-248-0800, www.kenmarecoachandcab.com, info@kenmarecoachandcab.com).

Sights in Kenmare

Heritage Centre

This museum, in the back rooms of the TI, consists of a series of storyboards and a model of the planned town. A 20-minute visit here explains the nearby ancient stone circle, the history of Kenmare's lacemaking fame, and the story of a feisty, troublemaking nun (see the sidebar on Kenmare's history).

Cost and Hours: Free, May-Oct Mon-Sat 9:00-18:00, Sun 10:00-18:00, closed Nov-April, tel. 064/664-1233.

Kenmare Lace and Design Centre

A single large room (above the TI) displays the delicate lacework that put Kenmare on the modern map. From the 1860s until World

War I, the Poor Clare convent at Kenmare was the center of excellence for Irish lacemaking. Inspired by antique Venetian lace, but creating their own unique designs, nuns taught needlepoint lacemaking as a trade to girls in a region struggling to get back on its feet in the wake of the catastrophic famine. Queen Victoria commissioned five pieces of lace in 1885, and by the end of the century tourists began visiting Kenmare on their way to Killarney just for a peek at the lace. Nora Finnegan, who runs the center, usually has a work in progress to demonstrate the complexity of fine lacemaking to visitors.

Cost and Hours: Free, Mon-Sat 10:00-13:00 & 14:15-17:30, closed mid-Oct-Easter and Sun year-round, tel. 064/664-2978, mobile 087-234-6998, www.kenmarelace.ie.

Ancient Stone Circle

Of the 100 stone circles that dot southwest Ireland (Counties Cork and Kerry), this is one of the most accessible. More than 3,000 years old, it may have been used both as a primitive calendar and as a focal point for rituals. The circle has a diameter of 50 feet and consists of 15 stones ringing a large center boulder (possibly a burial monument). Experts think this stone circle (like most) functioned as a celestial calendar—it tracked the position of the setting sun to determine the two solstices (in June and December), which mark the longest and shortest days of the year.

Cost and Hours: €2, drop coins into honor box in hut by entry when attendant is away, always open.

Getting There: It's a five-minute walk from the TI. From the city center, face the TI, turn left, and walk 200 yards down Market Street, passing a row of cute 18th-century houses on your right. Beyond the row of houses, veer right through an unmarked modern gate mounted in stone columns, and continue 50 yards down the paved road. You'll pass the entry hut on your right. The stone circle is behind the adjacent hedge.

Holy Cross Church

Finished in 1864, this is Kenmare's grand Catholic church. It's worth visiting to see the ornate wooden ceiling with 10 larger-

Kenmare's History:
Axes, Xs, Nuns, and Lace

Bronze Age people (2000 B.C.), attracted to this valley for its abundant game and fish, stashed their prized ax heads and daggers in hidden hoards. Almost 4,000 years later (in 1930), a local farmer from the O'Sullivan clan pried a bothersome boulder from one of his fields and discovered it to be a lid for a collection of rare artifacts that are now on display in the National Museum in Dublin (the "Killaha hoard"). The O'Sullivans (Irish for "descendants of the one-eyed") were for generations the dominant local clan, and you'll still see their name on many Kenmare shop fronts.

Oliver Cromwell's bloody Irish campaign (1649), which subdued most of Ireland, never reached Kenmare. However, Cromwell's chief surveyor, William Petty, knew good land when he saw it and took a quarter of what is now County Kerry as payment for his valuable services, marking the "lands down" on maps. His heirs, the Lansdownes, created Kenmare as a model 18th-century estate town and developed its distinctive "X" street plan. William Petty-Fitzmaurice, the first Marquis of Lansdowne and landlord of Kenmare, became the British prime minister who negotiated the peace that ended the American War of Independence in 1783.

Sister Margaret Cusack, a.k.a. Sister Mary Francis Clare, lived in the town from 1862 to 1881, becoming the famous Nun of Kenmare. Her controversial religious life began when she decided to become an Anglican nun after her fiancé's sudden death. Failing to be accepted as one of Florence Nightingale's nurses during the Crimean War, she converted to Catholicism, joined the Poor Clare order as Sister Mary Francis Clare, and moved with the order to Kenmare. She became an outspoken writer who favored women's rights and lambasted the tyranny of the landlords during the Great Potato Famine (1845-1849). She eventually took church funds and attempted to set herself up as abbess of a convent in Knock. Her renegade behavior led to her leaving the Catholic faith, converting back to Protestantism, writing an autobiography, and lecturing about the "sinister influence of the Roman Church."

After the devastation of the famine, an industrial school was founded in Kenmare to teach trades to destitute youngsters. The school, run by the Poor Clare sisters, excelled in teaching young girls the art of lacemaking. Inspired by lace created earlier in Italy, Kenmare lace caught the eye of Queen Victoria and became much coveted by Victorian society. Examples of it are now on display in the Victoria and Albert Museum (London), the Irish National Museum (Dublin), and the US National Gallery (Washington, DC).

than-life angels (carved in Germany's Black Forest), which support the roof beams.

Horseback Riding

River Valley Riding Stables offers day treks for all levels of experience through beautiful hill scenery in the Roughty River Valley (adult-€20/hour, child-€15/hour, discounts for groups, long hours; located about 7 miles east of Kenmare off R-569 near Kilgarvan, mobile 087-958-5895, rivervalleystables@hotmail.com).

Boating and Hiking

Star Sailing rents boats, gives sailing lessons, and organizes hill walks. Hop on a small two-person sailboat (€45/1 hour, €35/each additional hour) or a six-person boat (€60/1 hour, €50/each additional hour). Or kick around in a kayak (single-€20/hour, double-€36/hour). Phone ahead to reserve boats (daily 10:00-17:00, located 5 miles southwest of Kenmare on R-571 on Beara Peninsula, courtesy shuttle can pick you up in Kenmare, tel. 064/664-1222, www.staroutdoors.ie; adjacent Con's Restaurant is open daily 12:00-20:00).

Golfing

Another way to experience Ireland's 40 shades of green is to splurge on a scenic day on the links. The Kenmare Golf Club is right on the edge of town (€40 greens fee June-Aug, €30 Sept-May, on R-569 toward Cork, tel. 064/664-1291, www.kenmaregolfclub.com). Or try the Ring of Kerry Golf and Country Club (weekdays-€55 greens fee, weekends €65, 4 miles west of town on N-70, prebook on weekends, tel. 064/664-2000, www.ringofkerrygolf.com).

Nightlife in Kenmare

Wander the compact Kenmare town triangle and stick your head in wherever you hear something you like. Music usually starts at 21:30 (although some pubs have early 18:30 sessions—ask at the TI) and ranges from Irish traditional sessions to sing-along strummers. **Crowley's** is an atmospheric little shoebox of a pub with an unpretentious clientele. **Foley's** jug-stacked window invites you in for a folksy songfest. The recommended Lansdowne Arms Hotel sponsors live traditional sessions in their **Bold Thady Quill Bar.**

Sleeping in Kenmare

$$$ **Lansdowne Arms Hotel** is the town's venerable grand hotel, with generous public spaces. This centrally located, 200-year-old historic landmark rents 25 large, crisp rooms (music in pub until late on Fri-Sat, parking, corner of Main and Shelbourne Streets, tel.

Beara: The Other Peninsula

This sleepy yet scenic wedge of land (just south of Kenmare) deserves honorable mention as a distant third choice after the Dingle and Ring of Kerry peninsulas. But locals rave about it like we would our home sports team. If you have the luxury of two nights in Kenmare, Beara is worth considering. If you don't have a full day to spare to drive the length of it, you can spend a memorable half-day enjoying Garnish Island and Healy Pass, skipping the western half of the peninsula.

Garnish Island is a rocky island refuge, cloaked by a lush garden, plopped down in the corner of Bantry Bay. Crowned by a martello tower (a stout bunker built to repel feared Napoleonic invasions, free to climb for views), the gardens were the creation of a rich landlord, who turned the barren 37 acres into a lushly vegetated fantasy in the early 1900s. You'll meander past Italian reflecting pools, a Grecian temple  framing views of a placid bay, and a walled garden nursery clad in roses. Pine-forested trails, punctuated with rhododendrons, connect it all. Boats depart from the well-marked pier in Glengarriff, about 18 miles (30 km) south of Kenmare, for the scenic 15-minute cruise past seals sunning on rocks to the island (boat-€12 round-trip, 2/hour; gardens-€5, June-Aug Mon-Sat 9:30-18:00, Sun from 11:00, shorter hours off-season and closed Nov-March; tearoom, snacks, and WCs at island's pier; tel. 027/63116, www.harbourqueenferry.com).

A narrow, eight-mile mountain road (R-574) feels like a toboggan run as it squiggles over the peninsula's lumpy spine at **Healy Pass.** The road linked the north coast (County Kerry) to the south coast (County Cork) to facilitate food-relief deliveries 170

064/664-1368, www.lansdownearms.com, info@lansdownearms. com).

$$$ Sallyport House, an elegant, quiet house with five rooms filled with antique furniture, has been in Helen Arthur's family for generations. Ask her to point out the foot-worn doorstep that was salvaged from the local workhouse and built into her stone chimney (cash only, no kids, parking, closed Nov-mid-March, 5-minute walk south of town before crossing Our Lady's Bridge, tel. 064/664-2066, www.sallyporthouse.com, port@iol.ie).

$$ Hawthorn House is a fine, modern, freestanding house with a lounge, a warm and friendly hostess, and 10 comfy rooms sporting fine woodwork courtesy of Mr. O'Brien, who's also a car-

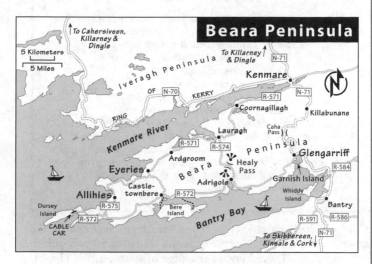

Beara Peninsula

5 Kilometers
5 Miles

To Cahersiveen,
Killarney &
Dingle

To Killarney
& Dingle

Iveragh Peninsula

Kenmare

N-71

OF

N-70

KERRY

R-571

Coornagillagh

Killabunane

RING

Kenmare River

Lauragh

Caha
Pass

R-571

R-574

Peninsula

Glengarriff

Eyeries

Ardgroom

Beara

Healy
Pass

R-584

Adrigole

Garnish Island

Castle-
townbere

R-572

Whiddy
Island

Bantry

Allihies

Dursey
Island

R-575

Bere
Island

R-572

Bantry Bay

R-591

R-586

CABLE
CAR

To Skibbereen,
Kinsale & Cork

N-71

years ago. The views from the 1,000-foot summit make you marvel at the road-building skills of the famine-era workmen. The barren, rocky landscape makes it easy to spot approaching cars (remember to look up on hairpin turns). Be cooperative by pulling over at wide spots to allow safe passage, and honk to alert other cars as you approach blind, rocky curves.

The rest of the peninsula is pastoral in the middle and edged with scenic cliffs near the tip. Ireland's only cable car connects the headland with mellow Dursey Island. Cattle can be transported on it (one at a time). The floor is slatted so water can be sloshed over the boards to wash out the dung. Castletownbere (on the south coast) is a fishing port with plenty of pubs for lunch. Allihies and Eyeries (on the north coast) are two of the most colorfully painted towns in Ireland, splattered with pastels and vivid hues.

penter. Its quiet residential location is just a block from all the pub and restaurant action (family rooms, parking, Shelbourne Street, tel. 064/664-1035, www.hawthornhousekenmare.com, port@iol. ie, Mary and Noel O'Brien). Their modern, self-catering apartment next door works well for those wanting to linger (weekly rentals).

$$ Willow Lodge, on the main road at the edge of town, feels American-suburban, with friendly hosts and seven comfortable rooms (cash only, family rooms, parking, 100 yards beyond Holy Cross Church, tel. 064/664-2301, www.willowlodgekenmare.com, willowlodgekenmare@yahoo.com, jovial Paul and talkative Gretta Gleeson-O'Byrne).

$ Whispering Pines B&B offers five rooms with sincere,

Sleep Code

Hotels are classified based on the average price of a typical en suite double room with breakfast in high season.

$$$$	**Splurge:** Most rooms over €170
$$$	**Pricier:** €130-170
$$	**Moderate:** €90-130
$	**Budget:** €50-90
¢	**Backpacker:** Under €50
RS%	**Rick Steves discount**

Unless otherwise noted, credit cards are accepted and free Wi-Fi is available. Comparison-shop by checking prices at several hotels (on each hotel's own website, on a booking site, or by email). For the best deal, *book directly with the hotel*. Ask for a discount if paying in cash; if the listing includes **RS%,** request a Rick Steves discount.

traditional Irish hospitality in a spacious house warmed by the presence of hostesses Mary Fitzgerald and daughter Kathleen (cash only, closed Oct-May, at the edge of town on Bell Height, tel. 064/664-1194, www.whisperingpineskenmare.com, wpines@eircom.net).

$ Virginia's Guesthouse, ideally located near the best restaurants, is well kept by Neil and Noreen. Its nine rooms are fresh, roomy, and appealing (breakfast extra, 36 Henry Street, mobile 086-306-5291, www.virginias-kenmare.com, virginias.guesthouse@gmail.com).

$ Limestone Lodge stands rock-solid beside a holy well, with five comfy rooms in a quiet location. Friendly hosts Sinead and Siobhan Thomas are experts on Kenmare's famous lace, and Casey, their wiggly Jack Russell terrier, is an expert at being cute (cash only, family rooms, parking, tel. 064/664-2231, mobile 087-757-4411, www.limestonelodgekenmare.com, info@limestonelodgekenmare.com).

$ Watersedge B&B is a mile south of town, serenely isolated on a forested hillside and overlooking the estuary. The modern house has four clean, colorful rooms and a kid-pleasing backyard (cash only, parking, tel. 064/664-1707, mobile 087-413-4235, www.watersedgekenmare.com, watersedgekenmare@gmail.com, Noreen and Vincent O'Shea). To get here, drive south over Our Lady's Bridge, bear left, immediately look for the B&B sign, and take the first right onto the road heading uphill. Go 100 yards up the paved road, then—at the end of the white cinder-block wall (on left)—turn right onto the gravel lane and drive 50 yards to the dead-end. It's worth it.

$ Rockcrest House is secluded down a quiet, leafy lane, with six large rooms and a fine front-porch view (cash only; as you pass the TI heading north out of town, take the first left after crossing the bridge; tel. 064/664-1248, mobile 087-904-3788, www.visit-kenmare.com, info@visit-kenmare.com, Marian and David O'Dwyer). Ask about their two self-catering cottage rentals.

¢ **Kenmare Fáilte Hostel** (fawl-chuh) maintains 34 budget beds in a well-kept, centrally located building with more charm than most hostels (private rooms available, closed mid-Oct-April, Shelbourne Street, tel. 064/664-2333, mobile 087-711-6092, run by Finnegan's Corner bike rental folks directly across street, www.kenmarehostel.com, info@kenmarehostel.com).

SLEEPING IN LUXURY ON THE RING OF KERRY

$$$$ **Parknasilla Hotel** is a 19th-century luxury hotel (82 rooms) lost in 500 plush acres of a subtropical park overlooking the wild Atlantic Ocean. The tranquility, combined with old-fashioned service and Victorian elegance, makes this a good stop for anyone interested in luxuriating on the Ring of Kerry. Originally an old railroad hotel for Romantic Age tourists, in recent decades it has been a ritual splurge for Irish families and wedding groups (highest rates July-Aug, 19th-century diversions, park walks, tel. 064/667-5600, www.parknasillahotel.ie, info@parknasillahotel.ie).

Eating in Kenmare

This friendly little town offers plenty of quality options. If dining, make a reservation or get a table early, as many finer places book up later in the evening during the summer. Pub dinners are a good value and easier on the budget, but pub kitchens close earlier than restaurants.

LUNCH

Soup-and-sandwich lunch options abound. **$ Jam** is a handy deli that can make sandwiches or wraps to go for picnics (Mon-Sat 8:00-17:00, Sun 10:00-17:00 except closed Sun off-season, Henry Street, tel. 064/664-1591). **$$ The Purple Heather** has great salads and omelets (Mon-Sat 11:00-17:45, closed Sun, Henry Street, tel. 064/664-1016). **$ Café Mocha** is a basic sandwich shop (Mon-Fri 9:00-17:30, Sat-Sun 10:00-17:00, on the town square, tel. 064/664-2133). **Murphy's Daybreak** supermarket is a good place to stock up for a Ring of Kerry picnic (Mon-Sat 8:00-22:00, Sun 9:00-21:00, Main Street).

DINNER

$$$ **The Lime Tree Restaurant** occupies the former Lansdowne Estate office, which gave more than 4,000 people free passage to

Restaurant Price Code

I've assigned each eatery a price category, based on the average cost of a typical main course. Drinks, desserts, and splurge items (steak and seafood) can raise the price considerably.

$$$$	**Splurge:** Most main courses over €25
$$$	**Pricier:** €20-25
$$	**Moderate:** €15-20
$	**Budget:** Under €15

In the Republic of Ireland, carryout fish-and-chips and other takeout food is **$**; a basic pub or sit-down eatery is **$$**; a gastropub or casual but more upscale restaurant is **$$$**; and a swanky splurge is **$$$$**.

America in the 1840s. These days, it serves delicious, locally caught seafood dishes in a modern yet cozy dining hall. It's wise to reserve ahead (daily 18:30-21:30, closed Nov-March, Shelbourne Street, tel. 064/664-1225, www.limetreerestaurant.com).

$$$$ Packies is a popular bistro that has a leafy, low-light interior and cottage ambience, and serves traditional cuisine with French influence. Their seafood gets rave reviews (Mon-Sat 18:00-22:00, closed Sun, reservations wise, Henry Street, tel. 064/664-1508).

$$$$ Mulcahy's Restaurant has a jazz-mellowed, elegant ambience and creatively presented gourmet dishes. Given the Indian, Japanese, and American influences, there's always a good vegetarian entrée (Thu-Tue 17:00-22:00, closed Wed, reservations smart, Main Street, tel. 064/664-2383).

$$$ Horse Shoe Pub and Restaurant, specializing in steak and spareribs, somehow turns rustic farm-tool decor into a romantic candlelit sanctuary (daily 17:00-22:00, Main Street, tel. 064/664-1553).

$$ P. F. McCarthy's Pub and Restaurant feels like a sloppy saloon, serving reasonable salad or sandwich lunches and filling dinner fare (Mon-Sat 10:30-21:00, closed Sun, 14 Main Street, tel. 064/664-1516).

Kenmare Connections

Kenmare has no train station (the nearest is in Killarney, 20 miles away) and only a few bus connections (www.buseireann.ie). Most buses transfer in Killarney.

From Kenmare by Bus to: Killarney (4/day, 45 minutes), **Tralee** (3/day, 2 hours), **Dingle** (3/day, 3 hours, change in Killarney), **Kinsale** (3/day, 4 hours, 2 changes), **Dublin** (4/day, 7.5 hours, change in Killarney and Limerick).

Near Kenmare

These attractions are near Kenmare, at the eastern (inland) end of the Ring of Kerry. If you're approaching the region from Kinsale and Cobh, drive through Killarney and hop on the Ring to visit Muckross House and Muckross Traditional Farms (near the lakes), Killarney National Park, and Kissane Sheep Farm (in the mountains) en route to Kenmare. By taking a bite out of the Ring the day before you sleep in Kenmare, you'll be better situated to drive most of the remainder of the Ring of Kerry loop the next day. Get an early start from Kenmare and you should be able to avoid the worst of the bus traffic on the Ring.

KILLARNEY

Killarney is a household word among American tourists, and it seems to be on every big-bus tour itinerary. Springing from the bus and train station of this thriving regional center are a few colorful streets lined with tourist-friendly shops and restaurants. Killarney's suburbs sprawl with vast hotels that, except for the weather, feel more like Nebraska than Ireland. Killarney's elegant Neo-Gothic church stands tall, as if to say the town existed and mattered long before tourism. But then you realize it dates from 1880...just about when Romantic Age tourism here peaked. For nonshoppers, Killarney's value is its location at the doorstep of the lush Killarney National Park. And for most tour organizers, it's the logical jumping-off point for excursions around the famous Ring of Kerry peninsula.

If you're traveling in the region without a car, you'll have to stop here. The Killarney bus and train stations flank the big, modern Killarney Outlet Centre mall. (In some touristy parts of Ireland, like this one, every other shopping center is called an "outlet"—implying factory-direct values.) If you have a layover between connections, walk five minutes straight out from the front of the mall, and check out Killarney's shop-lined High Street and New Street. The **TI** is a 15-minute walk from the train station, on Beech Street.

Killarney Connections

From Killarney Around the Ring of Kerry: Bus Éireann drives the loop around the Ring of Kerry from Killarney—suitable for a quick peek. While it generally stops only long enough to pick up and drop off travelers en route, there is a 50-minute stop in Sneem (€23, daily July-mid-Sept, departs the Killarney bus station at 12:45 and returns to Killarney at 17:45, no reservation needed, www.buseireann.ie). You can catch this same bus from Tralee at 11:50, returning to Tralee by 18:45 (€25).

By Bus to: **Kenmare** (3/day, 45 minutes), **Tralee** (hourly, 40 minutes), **Dingle** (2/day direct, 1.5 hours, 2/day with change in Tralee, 2.5 hours), **Shannon Airport** (6/day, 3.5 hours), **Dublin** (every 2 hours, 6 hours, change in Limerick). The bus station has a left-luggage desk. For bus schedules: Toll tel. 1850-836-611, www.buseireann.ie.

By Train to: **Tralee** (8/day, 35 minutes), **Cork** (every 2 hours, 2 hours, most with change in Mallow), **Waterford** (5/day, 4-6 hours), **Dublin** (every 2 hours, fewer on Sun, 3.5 hours, 1 direct in morning, rest with change in Mallow). For train schedules, call 01/836-6222 or visit www.irishrail.ie.

To Muckross House: There's no bus service. You can hike 30 minutes (get directions from TI), rent a bike, hire a horse buggy, or catch a cab (€12).

SIGHTS NEAR KILLARNEY
Muckross House and Farms

Perhaps the best stately Victorian home you'll see in the Republic of Ireland, Muckross House (built in 1843 and worth ▲▲) is

magnificently set at the edge of Killarney National Park. It's adjacent to Muckross Farms, a fascinating open-air farm museum that shows rural life in the 1930s (worth ▲). Besides the mansion and farms, this regular stop on the tour-bus circuit also includes a fine garden idyllically set on a lake and an information center for the national park. The poignant juxtaposition of the magnificent mansion and the humble farmhouses illustrates in a thought-provoking way the vast gap that once separated rich and poor in Ireland.

Cost and Hours: House-€9, farms-€9, €15 combo-ticket includes both (Heritage Cards not accepted for farms). House open daily 9:00-17:30, July-Aug until 19:00, last entry one hour before closing. Farms open daily June-Aug 10:00-18:00, May and Sept daily 13:00-18:00, March-April and Oct Sat-Sun only 13:00-18:00, closed Nov-Feb, tel. 064/667-0144, www.muckross-house.ie, info@muckross-house.ie.

Tours: The only way to see the interior of the house is with the 45-minute guided tour, which gives meaning to your visit (included with admission, offered frequently throughout the day). Book your tour as soon as you arrive (they can fill up). Then enjoy a walk in the gardens or lunch in their better-than-average cafeteria until your tour begins.

Getting There: Muckross House is conveniently located for a break on the long ride from Kinsale or Cashel to Dingle or Kenmare. From Killarney, follow signs to Kenmare, where you'll find Muckross House three miles (5 km) south of town. As you approach from Killarney, you'll see a small parking lot two miles before the actual parking lot. This is used by horse-and-buggy bandits to hoodwink tourists into thinking they have to pay to clip-clop to the house. Giddy-up on by to find a big, safe, and free parking lot right at the mansion.

Visiting the House and Farms: A visit to **Muckross House** takes you back to the Victorian period—the 19th century boom time when the sun never set on the British Empire and the Industrial Revolution (born in England) was chugging the world into the modern age. Of course, Ireland was a colony back then, with big-shot English landlords. During the Great Potato Famine of 1845-1849, most English gentry lived very well—profiting off the export of their handsome crops to lands with greater buying power—while a third of Ireland's population starved.

Muckross House feels lived-in (and it was, until 1933). Its fine Victorian furniture is arranged around the fireplace under Waterford crystal chandeliers and lots of antlers. You'll see Queen Victoria's bedroom (ground floor, since she was afraid of house fires). The owners of the house spent a couple of years preparing for the royal visit in 1861, eager to gain coveted titles and nearly bankrupting themselves in the process. The queen stayed only three nights and her beloved Prince Albert died soon after the visit. The depressed queen never granted the titles that the grand house's owners had so hoped for.

The house exit takes you through an **information center** for Killarney National Park, with a relaxing 15-minute video on "Ireland's premier national park," featuring lots of geology, flora, and fauna (free, shown on request).

The **garden** is a hit for those with a green thumb, and a €1.50 booklet makes the nature trails interesting. A bright, modern cafeteria (with indoor/outdoor seating) faces the garden. The adjacent crafts shop shows weaving and pottery-making in action.

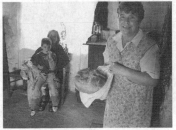

The **Muckross Traditional Farms** consists of six different vintage farmhouses. The farms are strung along a mile-long road, with an old bus shuttling those who don't want to hike (free, 4/hour).

For those interested in Irish farm life from the 1920s until electricity arrived in 1955, this is a great experience—but only if you engage the attendants in conversation. Each farm is staffed by a Kerry local who enjoys telling tales of life on the farm in the old days. When they first got electricity in 1955, they'd pull on their rubber Wellington boots for safety and nervously "switch it on." Poor farmers could afford electricity only with the help of money from relatives in America. They'd have one bulb hanging from the ceiling and, later, one plug for a hot pot. Every table had a Sacred Heart of Jesus shrine above it. The plug went directly below it. No one dreamed of actually heating the house with electricity. Children slept six to a bed, "three up and three down... feet in your face." You'll learn what happened when you had the only radio in the area, and how one flagstone on the mud floor was enough for the fiddler and dancer to set the beat. Probe with your questions...get personal.

Killarney National Park

As you drive from Killarney to Kenmare, heading south on N-71, you'll sweep through scenic Killarney National Park (just south of Killarney town) on the most mountainous stretch of the Ring of Kerry. This 25,000-acre park (Ireland's oldest) was established when Muckross Estate was donated to the nation in 1932. Glacially sculpted rock ridges cradle three large lakes teeming with trout and salmon, which lure sport fishermen.

Hikers enjoy an easy 10-minute stroll along a mossy trail from the roadside up to **Torc Waterfall** (look for small parking lot beside N-71, 2 miles—3 km—south of Muckross House), then lace up their boots to take on more strenuous trails beyond. If you go early or late in the day, keep an eye out for Ireland's only native herd of red deer. The park's old-growth oak, yew, and alder groves are the best preserved in Ireland, and rhododendrons explode beside the road in late May and June.

Take a quiet moment to contemplate your lush surroundings. This is what the majority of Ireland looked like 8,000 years ago, before Neolithic man settled and began rudimentary slash-and-burn farming. Later English colonial harvesting of timber exacerbated the deforestation process. Today, Ireland has the smallest proportion of forested land—10.5 percent—of any EU nation.

Enjoy expansive lake views from **Ladies View,** right beside the N-71 road, half a mile (1 km) from the park's southern exit. Just south of the park exit, you'll pass long, thin Looscaunagh Lough (beside the road on the left). A few hundred yards farther, the Black Valley opens up beneath you on the right. This remote valley was the last chunk of Ireland to get electricity—in 1978. The highest bump on the distant ridge across the Black Valley to the west is Carrauntoohil, Ireland's tallest mountain at 3,400 feet.

▲▲Kissane Sheep Farm

Animal lovers will enjoy an hour's visit to this hardworking 2,500-acre Irish farm, perched on a scenic slope above the Black Valley. John Kissane, whose family has raised sheep here for five generations, gives hands-on demonstrations of sheep shearing. John (or his brother Noel) explains the process and invites you to touch the pile of fresh wool afterward. You can feel the lanolin, which acts as natural waterproofing for the sheep and is extracted from the wool to sell to pharmaceutical firms (synthetic manufacturing has driven the price of wool so low, it's not worth selling otherwise). But the highlight of any visit is the demonstration of sheepherding by the highly alert family dogs (border collies trained here since puppyhood). John commands the dogs from afar using an array of verbal calls and hand signals.

Note that this is a working farm—demonstration times fluctuate depending on necessary farm work. Call ahead for times (usually in the afternoon), or check the current schedule on their website.

Cost and Hours: €7, most afternoons April-Sept by appointment only (minimum 15 people), closed Oct-March, on N-71 between Ladies View and Moll's Gap, tel. 064/663-4791, mobile 087-260-0410, www.kissanesheepfarm.com, noel@kissanesheepfarm.com.

From Kissane Sheep Farm to Kenmare: Continue driving south on N-71. Going over Moll's Gap (WCs and Avoca Café beside parking lot), you'll descend into Kenmare. The rugged, bare rock on either side of the road was rounded and smoothed by the grinding action of glaciers over thousands of years. In the distance to the north (on your right) you can see the Gap of Dunloe, a perfect example of a U-shaped glacial valley notch.

Ring of Kerry

The Ring of Kerry (the Iveragh Peninsula) has been the perennial breadwinner of Irish tourism for decades now. Lassoed by a winding coastal road (the Ring), this mountainous, lake-splattered region comes with breathtaking scenery and the highest peak in Ireland. While a veritable fleet of big, tourist-laden buses circles it each day, they generally stay together and seem to stop at the same handful of attractions. Therefore, if you avoid those places at rush hour, the Ring feels remarkably unspoiled and dramatically isolated. Clever motorists, armed with a good map and a reliable alarm clock, can sidestep the crowds and enjoy one of the most rewarding days in Ireland.

PLANNING YOUR TIME

More than twice the size of the Dingle Peninsula (see next chapter) and backed by a muscular tourism budget that promotes every sight as a "must-see," the Iveragh Peninsula can seem overwhelming. Be selective, and don't let them pull the turf over your eyes.

By Car: You can explore the Ring (primarily on N-70) in one satisfying day. Travelers linking overnights in Kinsale and Dingle can insert a night between them in Kenmare (a good base for enjoying the best of the Ring of Kerry). If visiting Muckross House and Kissane Sheep Farm (on the mountainous section of the Ring of Kerry), do so in the afternoon on your way to Kenmare to save all of the following day for the rest of the Ring.

Tackling the Kinsale-to-Dingle drive plus the Ring of Kerry all in the same day is doable with an early start (no later than 8:30)—but you add about two hours of driving just to reach the actual Ring, meaning you have little time to stop and enjoy what you came here to see. You also run the risk of meeting the big-bus convoy head on (see "Driving the Ring of Kerry").

If you're considering a boat trip out to the desperately remote and evocative island of Skellig Michael, you'll need to add another day to allow for an overnight in the Portmagee area...and hope for good weather.

By Public Transportation: You have three options for seeing the Ring of Kerry without a car, none of which is as enjoyable as driving the loop yourself: minibus tour from Kenmare (see page 208); big-bus tour from Killarney (TI tel. 064/663-1633); or public bus from Killarney (see page 217).

DRIVING THE RING OF KERRY (MADE LESS SCARY)

The entire Ring of Kerry loop is 135 miles and takes 4.5 hours to drive without making any stops. Be sure to factor in time to stop and see the sights. On a one-day visit to the Ring, I'd leave Kenmare by 8:30 and head clockwise (against the prevailing tour-bus traffic you'll encounter later in the middle of the loop). Allow time for stops at Staigue Ring Fort (45 minutes) and Derrynane House (1 hour), and get

to Waterville before noon. To entirely miss the chain of tour buses, which slithers (like a python swallowing a pig) counterclockwise around the Ring, get to Waterville by 11:00; shortly after that, leave the main drag for the Skellig Ring (with a road that's too narrow for big buses). Plan to have lunch out on the Skellig Ring, either as a picnic on the lovely beach at St. Finian's Bay, or in Portmagee. By the time you rejoin the main route, the python has slunk by. On the last half of the route, there are two more hour-long stops: the Skellig Experience Centre (near Portmagee) and two additional big ring forts (near Cahersiveen).

For me, the two most photogenic coastal stretches are out near the tip of the peninsula: between Caherdaniel and Waterville (on the Ring of Kerry) and from Ballinskelligs to Portmagee (on the Skellig Ring). For a stop-by-stop description of this route, follow my "Ring of Kerry Driving Tour."

The only downside of going against all the bus traffic is that, on the narrow parts of the Ring road, buses always have the right-of-way. It's up to you to back up to the nearest wide spot in the road to let a less-nimble bus get through a tight curve. But every year I notice that the road has been improved and bottlenecks widened. There are also lots of scenic-view pullouts. With an early start, you can avoid these hassles: On my last circuit, I got to Waterville by 11:30, from where I slipped happily into the bus-free Skellig Ring...and didn't have to pass a single bus all day.

Smart drivers equip themselves with a good map before driving the Ring of Kerry loop. If you don't have one already, pick up the *Complete Road Atlas of Ireland* by Ordnance Survey (€10-13, sold in most TIs and bookstores in Ireland). The *Fir Tree Aerial* series provides a useful map that covers both the Iveragh (Ring of Kerry) and Dingle peninsulas, giving you a bird's-eye feel for the terrain (€9, sold in many TIs and bookstores in County Kerry).

The flat, inland, northeastern section of the Ring, from Killorglin to Killarney on N-72, is entirely skippable. Tank up before leaving, as gas in Kenmare is cheaper than out on the Ring.

Ring of Kerry Driving Tour

Here's a self-guided sightseeing tip sheet for my preferred clockwise route, kilometer by kilometer. If you do any exploring, you'll likely get hopelessly off pace, but the kilometer references still help—just do the arithmetic to figure out how far various stops are from each other. Several of these stops are explained in far greater detail later in this chapter, in the same order in which they're listed here. To understand your options, read the rest of this chapter before you start on your tour.

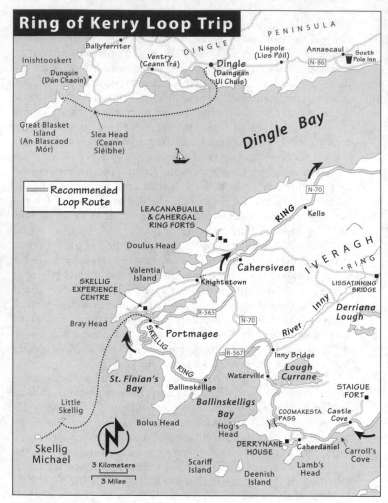

Ring of Kerry Loop Trip

PENINSULA

Ballyferriter

DINGLE

Lispole
(Lios Póil)

Annascaul

N-86

South
Pole Inn

Inishtooskert

Ventry
(Ceann Trá)

Dingle
(Daingean
Uí Chúis)

Dunquin
(Dún Chaoin)

Great Blasket
Island
(An Blascaod
Mór)

Slea Head
(Ceann
Sléibhe)

Dingle Bay

Recommended
Loop Route

LEACANABUAILE
& CAHERGAL
RING FORTS

RING

N-70

Kells

IVERAGH

Doulus Head

Cahersiveen

"RING"

Valentia
Island

Knightstown

LISSATINNING
BRIDGE

SKELLIG
EXPERIENCE
CENTRE

R-565

N-70

Inny

Derriana
Lough

Bray Head

SKELLIG

Portmagee

River

St. Finian's
Bay

RING

R-567

Inny Bridge

Lough
Currane

Waterville

STAIGUE
FORT

Little
Skellig

Ballinskelligs

Ballinskelligs
Bay

COOMAKESTA
PASS

Castle
Cove

Bolus Head

Hog's
Head

DERRYNANE
HOUSE

Caherdaniel

Carroll's
Cove

Skellig
Michael

3 Kilometers

3 Miles

Scariff
Island

Lamb's
Head

Deenish
Island

0 km: Leave Kenmare.

17.6 km: On the right is Glacier Lake, with a long, smooth limestone "banister" carved by a glacier 10,000 years ago.

22.8 km: The recommended Parknasilla Hotel—a posh 19th-century hotel—is a great stop for tea and scones.

26 km: Visit the town of Sneem.

40.4 km: Turn off for the Staigue Ring Fort.

41.5 km: On the left, enjoy great views of the Beara Peninsula beyond a ruined hospital with IRA ties (it was funded about 1910 by a local Englishwoman sympathetic to the Irish Republican cause). No one wants to touch these ruins today, out of fear of "kicking up a beehive."

43.5 km: Carroll's Cove has a fine beach with some of the

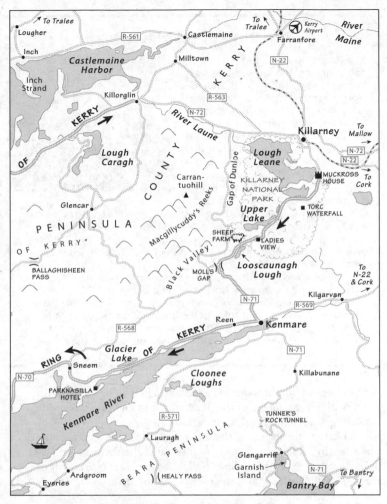

warmest water in Ireland, grand views of Kenmare Bay, a local trailer park, and "Ireland's only beachside bar."

46.4 km: Take the turnoff for Derrynane House (home of Daniel O'Connell).

50.4 km: Enjoy brilliant views for the next two kilometers to Coomakesta Pass.

52.4 km: The Coomakesta Pass lookout point (700-foot altitude) offers grand vistas in both directions.

54.5 km: Watch for fine views of the Skellig Islands.

56.4 km: Notice the ruins of famine villages on both sides of the road.

59.6 km: In the town of Waterville, you'll see a sculpture of Charlie Chaplin on the left. Waterville is also home to the Butler

The Ring Forts of Kerry

The Ring of Kerry comes with three awe-inspiring prehistoric ring forts—among the largest and best preserved in all of Ireland. Staigue Fort (near the beginning of my recommended clockwise Ring route) is most impressive and in a desolate setting. The two others—Cahergal and Leacanabuaile, side by side just north of Cahersiveen (closer to the end of the Ring, after Valentia Island)—are easier to visit and plenty evocative. Each ring fort is about a

2.5-mile (4-km) side-trip off the main drag. If you're trying to beat the tour-bus convoy, Staigue Fort is problematic because it eats up morning time before the buses have passed you. The Cahersiveen ring forts are your last stop in the Ring of Kerry, when bus traffic is of no concern.

All of these ring forts have the same basic features. The circular drystone walls were built sometime between 500 B.C. and A.D. 300 without the aid of mortar or cement. About 80 feet across, with walls 12 feet thick at the base and up to 25 feet high, these brutish structures would have taken 100 men six months to complete. Expert opinion is divided on the reason they were

Arms Hotel—a fine stop for tea and scones in its Charlie Chaplin room (with lots of photos of the silent-film icon and his young wife frolicking as they lived well in Ireland).

65 km: After rejoining the main road, cross the small bridge that's locally famous for salmon fly-fishing. Take the first left (R-567) for the Skellig Ring loop (follow brown *Skellig Ring* signs through Ballinskelligs, and then scenically to Portmagee). At this point, you've left the big-bus route.

75 km: St. Finian's Bay lies about halfway around, with a pleasant little picnic-friendly beach that's recently been discovered by surfers (no WCs). Just before the bay is the small, modern Skelligs Chocolate Factory, with free, tasty samples as well as a café for coffee and muffins (Mon-Fri 10:00-17:00—but longer hours in summer, Sat-Sun 12:00-17:00, especially fun for kids, tel. 066/947-9119, www.skelligschocolate.com).

80 km: Photographers and walkers will want to turn left into the driveway that advertises "Best View in County Kerry." Park and pay the €4 fee at the B&B reception. Then walk 10 minutes straight up the gravel road, where you'll be confronted by a dramatic coastal cliff that opens up onto what may indeed be the best

built, but most believe that the people who built them would have retreated here at times of tribal war. Civilization was morphing from nomadic hunter-gatherers to settled farmers, so herders used these forts to gather their valuable cattle inside and protect them from ancient rustlers. Other experts see the round design  as a kind of amphitheater, where local clan chieftains would have gathered for important meetings or rituals. However, the ditch surrounding the outer walls of Staigue Fort suggests a defensive, rather than ceremonial, function. Without written records, we can only imagine the part these magnificent piles of finely stacked stones played in ancient dramas.

Because this region had copper mines, southwest Ireland has a wealth of prehistoric sights. The Bronze Age wouldn't have been the Bronze Age without copper, which was melted together with tin to make bronze for better weapons and tools (2000 to 500 B.C.). The many ring forts and stone circles reflect the affluence that the abundance of copper brought to the region.

view in County Kerry. The beehive huts nearby are replicas but true to the originals.

83 km: You reach Portmagee, a small port town and jumping-off point for boats to the Skellig Islands.

83.2 km: Cross the bridge to the Skellig Experience Centre. You're now on Valentia Island, its name hinting at medieval trading connections with nearby Spain—which lies due south. Dinosaur hunters may want to detour and follow the signs to the modest but ancient tetrapod tracks, frozen in stone, on the north side of the island.

91.2 km: At the church in Knightstown, turn left for the Knightstown Heritage Museum.

93 km: Return to the main road and go through Knightstown to the tiny ferry (€7/car, runs constantly 8:00-21:00, 1-km trip).

95 km: Leaving the ferry, rejoin N-70 (the main Ring of Kerry route), turning left for the town of Cahersiveen. From here, you can detour a few kilometers to two impressive stone ring forts, Cahergal and Leacanabuaile.

100 km: Return to N-70 at Cahersiveen and follow signs for *Glenbeigh* and *Killorglin*. Enjoy views of the Dingle Peninsula across Dingle Bay to your left (you can see the harbor and Ersk Tower) and Inch Beach.

The rest of the loop is less scenic. At Killorglin, you've seen all there is to see. From here, go either to Dingle (left) or to Kenmare/Killarney/Kinsale (right).

Sights on the Ring of Kerry

FROM KENMARE TO PORTMAGEE
Sneem

Sneem is inundated by tour buses daily from 14:00 to 16:00. The rest of the day, Sneem is peaceful and laid-back. This humble town has two entertaining squares. The Irish joke, "Since we're in Kerry, the square on the east side is called South Square and the one on the west is called North Square." On the first (South) square, you'll see a statue of Steve "Crusher" Casey, the local boy who reigned as world champion heavyweight wrestler (1938-1947). A sweet little peat-toned rapid gurgles under the one-lane bridge connecting the two Sneem squares. The North Square features a memorial to former French president Charles de Gaulle's visit (Irish on his mother's side, de Gaulle came here for two weeks of R&R after his final retirement from office in 1969). Locals call it "da gallstone."

▲Staigue Fort

This ring fort is worth a stop on your way around the Ring (always open, drop €1 in the little gray donation box beside the gate). While viewing the imposing pile of stone, read "The Ring Forts of Kerry" sidebar, on previous page.

Getting There: The fort is 2.5 miles (4 km) off the main N-70 road up a narrow rural access lane (look for signs just after the hamlet of Castle Cove). Honk on blind corners to warn oncoming traffic as you drive up the hedge-lined lane.

▲Derrynane House

This is the home of Daniel O'Connell, Ireland's most influential 19th-century politician, whose tireless nonviolent agitation gained equality for Catholics 185 years ago. The coastal lands of the O'Connell estate that surround Derrynane (rhymes with Mary-Ann) House are now a national historic park. A visit here is a window into the life of a man who not only liberated Ireland from the last oppressive anti-Catholic penal laws, but also first developed the idea of a grassroots movement—organizing on a massive scale to achieve political ends without bloodshed (see sidebar).

Cost and Hours: €5; May-Sept daily 10:30-18:00; mid-March-April and Oct Wed-Sun 10:30-17:00, closed Mon-Tue; open weekends only in Nov, closed Dec-mid-March; last entry 45 minutes before closing, tel. 066/947-5113.

The Ring of Kerry vs. the Dingle Peninsula

If I had to choose one spot to enjoy the small-town charm of traditional Ireland, it would be Dingle and its history-laden scenic peninsula. But the Ring of Kerry—a much bigger, more famous, and more touristed peninsula just to its south—is also great to visit. If you go to Ireland and don't see the famous Ring of Kerry, your uncle Pat will never forgive you. Here's a comparison to help with your itinerary planning.

Both peninsulas come with a scenic loop drive. Dingle's is 30 miles. The Ring of Kerry is 120 miles. Both loops come

with lots of megalithic wonder. Dingle's prehistory is more intimate, with numerous little evocative stony structures. The Ring of Kerry's prehistory shows itself in three massive ring forts—far bigger than anything on Dingle.

Dingle town is the perfect little Irish burg—alive with traditional music pubs, an active fishing harbor, and the sturdy cultural atmosphere of an Irish-speaking Gaeltacht region. You can easily spend three fun nights here. In comparison, Kenmare (the best base for the Ring of Kerry loop) is pleasant but forgettable. Those spending a night on the west end of the Ring of Kerry find a rustic atmosphere in Portmagee (the base for a cruise to magical Skellig Michael).

Near Dingle, the heather-and moss-covered Great Blasket Island and the excellent Great Blasket Centre offer insights into the storytelling traditions and simple lives of hardy fisherfolk who—until 60 years ago—lived just off the tip of the Dingle Peninsula. Skellig Michael is a brutally rugged and remote chunk of rock in the Atlantic off the tip of the Ring of Kerry, with evocative medieval stone ruins of its long-gone hermit-monks. It's a world-class sight, but the Skellig Experience Centre near Portmagee on the mainland is less impressive than Dingle's Great Blasket Centre.

Muckross House, with its fascinating open-air farmhouse museum and beautiful lake views of Killarney National Park, is on the eastern side of the Ring of Kerry. It's also an efficient and natural stop for those driving between Kinsale and Dingle—so you can see it regardless of which scenic peninsula drive you take.

Both regions are beyond the reach of the Irish train system and require a car or spotty bus service to access. Both offer memorable scenery, great restaurants, warm B&B hospitality, and similar prices. The bottom line: With limited time, choose Dingle. If you have a day or two to spare, the Ring of Kerry is also a delight.

Getting There: Just outside the town of Derrynane, pick up a handy free map of the area from the little private TI inside the brown Wave Crest market (TI open daily May-Sept 9:00-18:00, closed Oct-April, tel. 066/947-5188; market is a great place to buy picnic food). One mile after the market, take a left and follow the signs into Derrynane National Historic Park.

Visiting the House: The house has a quirky floor plan. Ask about the next scheduled 20-minute audiovisual show, which fleshes out the highlights of O'Connell's turbulent life and makes the contents of the house more interesting. Self-guided info sheets are available in the main rooms (in both English and Irish).

Downstairs in the study, look for the glass case containing the pistols used in O'Connell's famous duel. Beside them are his black gloves, one of which he always wore on his right hand when he went to Mass (out of remorse for the part it played in taking a man's life). The dining room is lined with family portraits. Upstairs in the drawing room, you'll find his ornately carved chair with tiny harp strings and wolfhound collars made of gold. In a drawer in an upstairs bedroom is a copy of O'Connell's celebrated speech imploring the Irish not to riot when he was arrested. And in another upstairs room is his deathbed, brought back from Genoa.

The coach house (out back) shows off the enormous grand chariot that carried O'Connell through throngs of joyous Dubliners after his release from prison in 1844. He added the small chapel wing to the house in gratitude to God for his prison release. O'Connell's summer retreat, a small tower down the path behind the coach house, should be open by the time you visit.

Portmagee

Just a short row of snoozy buildings lining the bay, Portmagee is the best harbor for boat excursions out to the Skellig Islands (see "Getting There" on page 235). It's a quiet village with a handful of B&Bs, two pubs, a bakery, a market, and no ATMs—the closest ATM is 6 miles (10 km) east in Cahersiveen. On the rough harborfront, a slate memorial to sailors lost at sea from here reads, "In the nets of God may we be gathered."

A 100-yard-long bridge connects Portmagee to gentle Valentia Island, where you'll find the Skellig Experience Centre (on the left at the Valentia end of the bridge). A public parking lot is at the Portmagee end of the bridge, with award-winning WCs (no kidding: look for the proudly displayed "Irish Toilet of the Year 2002 runner-up" plaque). The first permanent transatlantic cable (for telegraph communication) was laid from Valentia Island in 1866. The tiny post office hides inside O'Connell's Market (both open Mon-Fri 9:00-17:30, Sat 9:00-13:00, closed Sun).

Daniel O'Connell (1775-1847)

Born in Cahersiveen and elected from Ennis as the first Catholic member of the British Parliament, O'Connell was the hero of

Catholic emancipation in Ireland. Educated in France at a time when punitive anti-Catholic laws limited schooling for Irish Catholics at home, he witnessed the carnage of the French Revolution. Upon his return to Ireland, he saw more bloodshed during the futile Rebellion of 1798. He chose law as his profession and reluctantly killed a man who challenged him to a duel.

Abhorring all this violence, O'Connell dedicated himself to peacefully gaining equal rights for Catholics in an Ireland dominated by a wealthy Protestant minority. He formed the Catholic Association with a one-penny-per-month membership fee and quickly gained a huge following (especially among the poor) with his persuasive speaking skills. Although Catholics weren't allowed to hold office, he ran for election to Parliament anyway and won a seat in 1828. His unwillingness to take the anti-Catholic Oath of Supremacy initially kept him out of Westminster, but the moral force of his victory caused the government to give in and concede Catholic emancipation the following year.

Known as "the Liberator," O'Connell was working toward his next goal—repealing the Act of Union with Britain—when he was imprisoned in 1844 for what the British considered seditious conspiracy. His massive "monster meeting" rallies attracted thousands of peaceful poor, and his popularity spooked the British authorities, who threw him in jail on trumped-up charges. When the Great Potato Famine hit in 1845, some in the Irish ranks advocated for more violent action against the British, something O'Connell had long opposed. He died two years later in Genoa on his way to Rome, but his ideals lived on: His Catholic Association was the model of grassroots organization for the Irish, who later emigrated and rose within American big-city political "green machines."

Sleeping in Portmagee: The first two listings are in town. The last listing is south of Portmagee, on St. Finian's Bay.

$$$ Moorings Guesthouse feels like a small hotel, with 17 rooms, a pub and a fine restaurant downstairs, and the most convenient location in town, 50 yards from the end of the pier (family rooms, tel. 066/947-7108, www.moorings.ie, moorings@iol.ie, Gerard and Patricia Kennedy).

$$$ Portmagee Heights B&B is a modern, solid slate home up above town, renting eight fine rooms (cash only, family rooms, on the road into town, tel. 066/947-7251, www.portmageeheights.

com, portmageeheights@gmail.com, hostess Monica Hussey can arrange Skellig boat trips).

$$ Beach Cove B&B offers three comfortable, fresh, and lovingly decorated rooms in splendid isolation four miles south of Portmagee, over lofty Coomanaspic ridge, beside the pretty beach at St. Finian's Bay (100 yards from the Skelligs Chocolate Factory). Charming Bridie O'Connor will arrange a boat trip out to the Skelligs for you. Her adjacent cottage out back has two double rooms, making it ideal for families (two-story family cottage out back sleeps four but no breakfast, tel. 066/947-9301, mobile 087-139-0224, www.stayatbeachcove.com, beachcove@eircom.net). Bridie's husband, Jack, was the head coach of the Kerry football team until he retired in 2012...making him a very important person in this part of Ireland (Kerry has won more football titles than any other Irish county, three of them with Jack at the helm).

Eating in Portmagee: These options all line the waterfront (between the pier and the bridge to Valentia Island). **$$$ The Moorings** is a nice restaurant with great seafood caught literally just outside its front door (March-Oct Tue-Sun 18:00-22:00, closed Mon and in winter, reservations a good idea, tel. 066/947-7108, www.moorings.ie). The **$$ Bridge Bar,** next door, does traditional pub grub. Call ahead to check on their traditional music and dance schedule (daily 12:00-22:00, live music Fri and Sun nights, tel. 066/947-7108). The **$$ Fisherman's Bar** is less flashy, with more locals and cheaper prices (daily 10:00-21:00, tel. 066/947-7103).

For picnic supplies, **O'Connell's Market** is the only grocery (Mon-Sat 9:00-19:00, Sun 9:30-12:30). **Skellig Mist Bakery** can make basic lunch sandwiches to take on Skellig boat excursions (daily 9:00-17:30, tel. 066/947-7250).

VALENTIA ISLAND

These two sights are on Valentia Island, across the bridge from Portmagee.

Skellig Experience Centre

Whether or not you're actually sailing to Skellig Michael (described later), this little center (with basic exhibits and a fine 15-minute film) explains it well—both the story of the monks and the natural environment.

Cost and Hours: €5, daily July-Aug 10:00-19:00, May-June and Sept until 18:00, March-April and Oct-Nov until 17:00, closed Dec-Feb, last entry one hour before closing, call ahead outside of peak season as hours may vary, on Valentia Island beside bridge linking it to Portmagee, tel. 066/947-6306, www. skelligexperience.com.

Evolution in Ireland: Tetrapods to Marconi

Evolution, literacy, communication—Ireland has played a starring role in all three.

Many Irish paleontologists believe that the fossilized tetrapod tracks preserved on Valentia Island are the oldest in Europe. It was here  that some of the first fish slithered out of the water on four stubby legs 385 million years ago, onto what would become the Isle of Saints and Scholars. Over time, those tetrapods evolved into the ancestors of today's amphibians, reptiles, birds, mammals...and humans, with the desire to record their thoughts and history, and communicate with others across the miles.

Irish scribes—living in remote outposts like the Skellig Islands, just off this coast—kept literate life alive in Europe through the darkest depths of the so-called Dark Ages. In fact, in about the year 800, Charlemagne imported monks from this part of Ireland to be his scribes.

Just more than a thousand years later, in the mid-19th century, Paul Julius Reuter—who provided a financial news service in Europe—knew his pigeons couldn't fly across the Atlantic. So he relied on ships coming from America to drop a news capsule overboard as they rounded this southwest corner of Ireland. His boys would wait in their little boats with nets to "get the scoop." They say Europe learned of Lincoln's assassination (1865) from a capsule tossed out of a boat here.

The first permanent telegraph cables were laid across the Atlantic from here to Newfoundland, giving the two hemispheres instantaneous electronic communication. Queen Victoria was the first to send a message—greeting American president James Buchanan in 1858. The cable broke more than once, but it was finally permanently secured in 1866. Radio inventor Guglielmo Marconi, who was half-Irish, achieved the first wireless transatlantic communication from this corner of Ireland to America in 1901.

Today, driving under the 21st-century mobile-phone and satellite tower that crowns a hilltop above Valentia Island, while gazing out at the Skellig Islands, a traveler has to marvel at humanity's progress—and the part this remote corner of Ireland played in it.

Boat Trips: The Skellig Experience Centre arranges two-hour boat trips, circling both Skellig Michael and Little Skellig (without actually bringing people ashore)—ideal for those who want a close look without the stair climb and vertigo that go with a visit to the island (€30, sailing daily about 14:45 and returning by 17:00, weather permitting, depart from Valentia Island pier 50 yards below the Skellig Experience Centre).

Valentia Heritage Museum

The humble Knightstown schoolhouse, built in 1861, houses an equally humble but interesting little museum highlighting the quirky things of historic interest on Valentia Island. Coming from Portmagee, take a hairpin left as you enter the village (at the lighthouse sign) and find it on your right past the church. You'll see a 19th-century schoolroom and learn about tetrapods (those first fish to climb onto land—which locals claim happened here). You'll also follow the long story of the expensive, frustrating, and heroic battle to lay telegraph cable across the Atlantic, which—after some false starts—finally succeeded in 1866, when the largest ship in the world connected this tiny island of Valentia with Newfoundland. This project was the initiative of the Atlantic Telegraph Company, which later became Western Union. These stories and more are told with intimate black-and-white photos and typewritten pages.

Cost and Hours: €3.50, daily 10:30-17:00, closed Oct-March, tel. 066/947-6985, www.valentiaisland.ie.

Nearby: If you're interested in those tetrapods, the actual "first footprints" are a 15-minute drive from the museum, on a rugged bit of rocky shoreline, a 10-minute hike below a parking lot (free, always viewable, get details locally).

CAHERGAL AND LEACANABUAILE RING FORTS

Crowning bluffs in farm country, 2.5 miles (4 km) off the main road at Cahersiveen, these two windy and desolate forts are each different and worth a look. Just beyond the Cahersiveen town church at the tourist office, turn left, cross the narrow bridge, turn left again, and follow signs to the ancient forts—you'll see the huge stone structures in the distance. You'll hike 10 minutes from the tiny parking lot (free, always open, no museum). Both forts are roughly 100 yards off the road (uphill on the right) and are 200 yards from each other. For details, see "The Ring Forts of Kerry" sidebar, earlier.

Skellig Michael

A trip to this jagged, isolated pyramid—the Holy Grail of Irish monastic island settlements—rates as a truly memorable ▲▲▲ experience. After visiting Skellig Michael a hundred years ago, Nobel Prize-winning Irish playwright George Bernard Shaw called it "the most fantastic and impossible rock in the world."

Rising seven miles offshore, the Skelligs (Irish for "splinter") are two gigantic slate-and-sandstone rocks crouched aggressively on the ocean horizon. The larger of the two, Skellig Michael, is more than 700 feet tall and a mile around, with a tiny cluster of abandoned beehive huts clinging near its summit like stubborn barnacles. The smaller island, Little Skellig, is home to a huge colony of gannet birds (like large, graceful seagulls with six-foot wingspans), protected by law from visitors setting foot onshore.

Skellig Michael (dedicated to the archangel) was first inhabited by sixth-century Christian monks. Inspired by earlier hermit-monks in the Egyptian desert, they sought the purity of isolation to get closer to God. Neither Viking raids nor winter storms could dislodge them, as they patiently built a half-dozen small, stone, igloo-like dwellings and a couple of tiny oratories. Their remote cliff-terrace perch is still connected to the sea 600 feet below by an amazing series of rock stairs. Viking Olav Trygvasson, who later became king of Norway and introduced Christianity to his country, was baptized here in 956.

Chiseling the most rudimentary life from solid rock, the monks lived a harsh, lonely, disciplined existence here, their colony surviving for more than 500 years. They collected rainwater in cisterns and lived off fish and birds. To supplement their meager existence, they traded bird eggs and feathers with passing boats for cereals, candles, and animal hides (used for clothing and for copying scripture). They finally moved their holy community ashore to Ballinskelligs in the early 1100s. But Christian pilgrims continued to visit Skellig Michael for centuries as penance...edging out onto a ledge to kiss a stone cross that has since toppled into the ocean.

GETTING THERE

Boat trips cost €60 and officially run to Skellig Michael daily from mid-May to September, but the schedule is heavily dependent on weather conditions. If the seas are too choppy, the boats cannot safely drop people at the concrete island pier (it's a bit like jumping off a trampoline onto an ice rink). Experienced boat captains say they are able to bring visitors ashore roughly five days out of seven in an average summer week.

Boat trips normally depart Portmagee at 10:00 (depending on tides), sail for an hour, leave you on the island from roughly 11:00 until 13:30, and get you back into Portmagee by 14:30 (with plenty of time to drive on to Dingle). Fifteen small boats (from Portmagee, Ballinskelligs, Waterville, and Valentia Island) have permits to land on Skellig Michael. Each boat can carry a dozen passengers. This limits the number of daily visitors and minimizes the impact on the sensitive island ecosystem.

To book a trip, contact **Patrick Murphy** (tel. 066/947-7156, mobile 087-234-2168, www.esatclear.ie/~skelligsrock, murphyseacruise@esatclear.ie), **Joe Roddy** (mobile 087-284-4460), or **Brendan Casey** (tel. 066/947-2437, mobile 087-228-7519). For a list of everyone that runs trips to the island, see www.skelligexperience.com/other-sea-tours.

Bring your camera, a sandwich lunch (easy to buy at the recommended Skellig Mist Bakery in Portmagee), water, sunscreen, rain gear, hiking shoes, and your sense of wonder.

Planning Tips: Your best bet is to reserve a room near Portmagee or St. Finian's Bay—whichever best fits your itinerary. (It's possible to sleep in Kenmare and get up early to drive two hours straight to Portmagee—but you'll be frustrated by not having time to enjoy the Ring's attractions along the way.) Then call a few days in advance to make a boat reservation. Keep your fingers crossed for good weather. Contact the boat operator on the morning of departure to get the final word. If the seas are too rough, he can tell from Portmagee and will make a decision that morning whether to go (rather than taking passengers halfway out, then aborting).

VISITING SKELLIG MICHAEL

Since you'll have only 2.5 hours to explore the island, begin by climbing the seemingly unending series of stone stairs to the monastic ruins (600 vertical feet of uneven steps with no handrails). Save most of your photographing for the way down. Photo-bugs who linger too long below risk missing the enlightening 20-minute free talk among the beehive huts, given by guides who camp on the island from April through October. Afterward, poke your head into some of the huts and try to imagine the dark, damp, and devoted life of a monk

here more than 1,000 years ago. After rambling through the ruins, you can give in to the puffin-spotting photo frenzy as you wander back down the stairs.

The two lighthouses on the far side of the island are now automated, and access to them has been blocked off. There are no WCs or modern shelters of any kind on Skellig Michael.

If you visit between May and early August, you'll be surrounded by fearless rainbow-beaked puffins, which nest here in underground burrows. Their bizarre swallowed cooing sounds like a distant chainsaw. These portly little birds live off fish, and divers have reported seeing them 20 feet underwater in pursuit of their prey.

Your return boat journey usually includes a pass near Little Skellig, which looms like an iceberg with a white coat of guano—courtesy of the 20,000 gannets that circle overhead like feathered confetti. These large birds suddenly morph into sleek darts when pursuing a fish, piercing the water from more than 100 feet above. You're also likely to get a glimpse of gray seals lazing on rocks near the water's edge.

In summer of 2014, the ruggedly exotic Skellig Michael was used as a filming location for the final scenes of *Star Wars: The Force Awakens*. To keep the filming top-secret, the Irish Navy was called in to enforce a two-mile exclusionary zone around the island. But controversy soon arose: UNESCO voiced concerns about the impact on the island's fragile ecosystem, especially native seabirds who are sensitive to disturbances in the Force and might be spooked into seeking other nesting grounds. Disney scrapped the plans for filming the next installment, *Star Wars VIII*, on the island. Instead it built its own version of the location at Sibéal Head on the Dingle Peninsula. Expect a steady stream of *Star Wars* tourists at both filming locations. *Go mbeidh an Fórsa leat!* (May the Force be with you!)

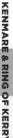

DINGLE PENINSULA

*Dingle Town • Dingle Peninsula Loop Trip •
Blasket Islands • Tralee*

The Dingle Peninsula, the westernmost tip of Ireland (and Europe, for that matter), offers just the right mix of far-and-away beauty, isolated walks and bike rides, and ancient archaeological wonders—all within convenient reach of its main town. Dingle town is just large enough to have all the necessary tourist services and a steady nocturnal beat of Irish traditional music.

Although Dingle is crowded in summer, it still feels like the fish and the farm really matter. A half-dozen fishing boats sail from here, tractors leave tracks down the main drag, and a faint whiff of peat fills the nighttime streets.

For over 35 years, my Irish dreams have been set here on this sparse but lush peninsula, where locals are fond of saying, "The next parish over is Boston." There's a feeling of closeness to the land in Dingle. When I asked a local if he was born here, he thought for a second and said, "No, it was about six miles down the road." When I told him where I was from, a faraway smile filled his eyes, and he looked out to sea and sighed, "Ah, the shores of Americay." I asked his friend if he'd lived here all his life. He said, "Not yet."

Dingle feels so traditionally Irish because it's part of the Gaeltacht, a region where the government subsidizes the survival of the Irish language and culture. While English is always there, the signs, chitchat, and songs come in Irish Gaelic. Children carry Gaelic footballs to class, and the local preschool brags "ALL Gaelic."

Dingle Town

Of the peninsula's 10,000 residents, 1,500 live in Dingle town (Daingean Ui Chuis). Its few streets, lined with ramshackle but gaily painted shops and pubs, run up from a rain-stung harbor always busy with fishing boats and leisure sailboats. Traditionally, the buildings were drab gray or whitewashed, but Ireland's "Tidy Town" competition a few decades back prompted everyone to paint their buildings in playful pastels.

It's a peaceful town. The courthouse (1832) is open one hour a month. The judge does his best to wrap up business within a half hour. During the day, you'll see teenagers—already working on ruddy, beer-glow cheeks—roll kegs up the streets and into the pubs in preparation for another night of music and *craic* (fun conversation and atmosphere).

PLANNING YOUR TIME

For the shortest visit, give Dingle two nights and a day. By car, it takes five hours to get here from Dublin, four hours from Galway, and three hours from Cork. By spending two nights, you'll feel more like a local on your second evening in the pubs. You'll need the better part of a day to explore the 30-mile loop around the peninsula by bike or car (following my "Dingle Peninsula Loop Trip" in this chapter). To do any serious walking or relaxing, you'll need three nights and two days. It's not uncommon to find Americans slowing way, way down in Dingle.

Dingle's activity level peaks in July and August and really dies off-season.

Dingle Area

1 Kilometer
1 Mile
(Approx. Scale)

To Tralee via
Conor Pass

R-569

To
Gallarus
Oratory

R-559

OCEAN-
WORLD

Dingle
Town
(Daingean
Ui Chuis)

N-86

To Ventry (Ceann
Trá) & Slea Head
(Ceann Sléibhe)

R-559

LORD
VENTRY'S
MANOR

*Dingle
Harbor*

To Inch &
Killarney

FOLLY

LIGHTHOUSE

EASK
TOWER

FUNGIE

To Great
Blasket Island

Dingle ⚓ *Bay*

If you're traveling during the summer months, it's wise to reserve your B&B in advance. I've generally listed hours for the tourist

DINGLE PENINSULA

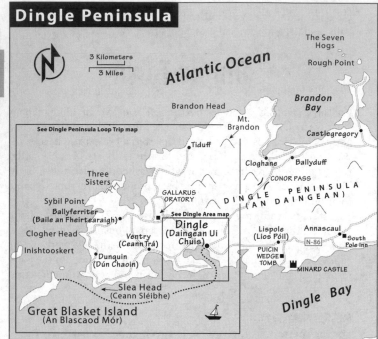

Dingle Peninsula

3 Kilometers
3 Miles

Atlantic Ocean

The Seven Hogs

Rough Point

Brandon Head

Mt. Brandon

Brandon Bay

Castlegregory

See Dingle Peninsula Loop Trip map

Tiduff

Cloghane Ballyduff

CONOR PASS

Three Sisters

GALLARUS ORATORY

DINGLE PENINSULA (AN DAINGEAN)

Sybil Point
Ballyferriter
(Baile an Fheirtéaraigh)

See Dingle Area map

Clogher Head

Ventry (Ceann Trá)

Dingle (Daingean Uí Chúis)

Lispole (Lios Póil)

Annascaul

N-86 South Pole Inn

Inishtooskert

Dunquin (Dún Chaoin)

PUICIN WEDGE TOMB

MINARD CASTLE

Slea Head (Ceann Sléibhe)

Great Blasket Island (An Blascaod Mór)

Dingle Bay

season (April-Sept). Hours may be longer in July and August, and many places cut back or shut down entirely from October to March.

Orientation to Dingle

Dingle—extremely comfortable on foot—hangs on a medieval grid of streets between the harborfront (where the bus to Tralee, with the nearest train station, stops) and Main Street (three blocks inland). Nothing in town is more than a 15-minute walk away. Street numbers are used only when more than one place is run by a family of the same name. Most locals know most locals, and people on the street are fine sources of information. Remember, locals love their soda bread, and tourism provides the butter. You'll find a warm and sincere welcome.

TOURIST INFORMATION

The TI has a great town map (free) and a staff who know the town, but less about the rest of the peninsula (Mon-Sat 9:00-13:00 & 13:30-17:00, generally closed Sun, shorter hours off-season, on Strand Street by the water, tel. 066/915-1188). For additional advice on outdoor activities, drop by the Mountain

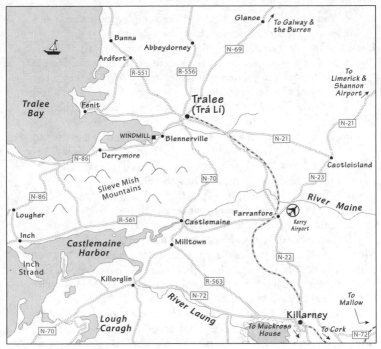

Man shop on Strand Street (see "Helpful Hints," below), or talk to your B&B host.

ARRIVAL IN DINGLE

By Bus: Dingle has no bus station and only one bus stop, on the waterfront behind the SuperValu supermarket (look for the bus shelter with the roof made from an overturned black *currach* boat).

By Car: Drivers choose two roads into town: the easy southern route on N-86 or the much more dramatic, scenic, and treacherous Conor Pass on R-569 (see "Route Tips for Drivers" at the end of this chapter). It's 30 miles (48 km) from Tralee either way. If you're not staying overnight (i.e., parking at your B&B), use the waterfront parking lot extending west from the TI (€1/hour, pay-and-display, daily 8:00-18:00).

By Plane: Kerry Airport, halfway between Tralee and Killarney, is a one-hour drive from Dingle. Short puddle-jumper flights connect the region to Dublin and make a visit to Dingle possible even for travelers with limited time. For more on Kerry Airport, see the end of this chapter.

HELPFUL HINTS

Exchange Rate: €1 = about $1.10
Country Calling Code: 353 (see page 530 for dialing instructions)

Before You Go: Check the local website for a list of festivals and events (www.dingle-peninsula.ie).

Crowds: Crowds trample Dingle's charm throughout July and August. The absolute craziest times here are during the Dingle Races (early Aug), Dingle Regatta (early to mid-Aug), the Blessing of the Boats (end of Aug or beginning of Sept), and the Dingle Food Festival (first weekend in October). The first Mondays in May, June, and August are Bank Holidays, giving Ireland's workers three-day weekends—and ample time to fill up Dingle. The town's metabolism (prices, schedules, activities) rises and falls with the tourist crowds, so late October through March is sleepy, windy, and chilly.

Farmers Market: From mid-April to mid-October on Fridays from 9:00 to 15:00, farmers gather to sell their fresh produce, homemade marmalade, and homespun crafts (across the street from SuperValu grocery store in a small parking lot).

Money: Two banks in town face each other across Main Street (Mon-Fri 10:00-16:00, closed Sat-Sun) and have ATMs. Expect to use cash (rather than credit cards) to pay for most peninsula activities.

Post Office: It's off Main Street, down the lane behind the Centra grocery (Mon-Fri 9:00-17:30, Sat 9:00-13:00, closed Sun).

Bookstore: An Café Liteartha is a perfect rainy-day hideout, with stacks of books and a backroom café. It lurks across the lane from Paddy's Bike Hire (daily 10:00-18:00 except closed Sun in Oct-May, Dykegate Street, tel. 066/915-2204).

Laundry: Dingle Cleaners is convenient (€14/load, Mon-Sat 9:00-18:00, closed Sun, beside Moran's Market and gas station, tel. 066/915-0680, run by Ciarán—pronounced key-a-RAWN). There is no self-service laundry in Dingle.

Bike Rental: Try **Paddy's Bike Hire,** with the only reliably maintained 21-speed hybrids in town (€15/day, includes helmet and lock, daily 9:00-19:00, directly across Dykegate from An Café Liteartha, tel. 066/915-2311). Plan on leaving a driver's license or passport as a security deposit. If you're biking the peninsula, get a bike with skinny street tires, not slow and fat mountain-bike tires. Before you leave, take a lap around the block to be sure your seat remains stable.

Taxi: Try **Diarmuid Begley** (mobile 087-250-4767), Sean with **S.O.L. Cabs** in Dingle (mobile 087-660-2323), or **Tom Kearney** out in Dunquin (mobile 087-933-2264).

Travel Agency: Maurice O'Connor at **Galvin's Travel Agency** can book plane tickets, as well as ferry rides to Britain (Mon-Fri 9:30-18:00, Sat 10:00-14:00, closed Sun, John Street, tel. 066/915-1409).

Activities: The **Mountain Man,** a hiking shop run by local guide

Adrian Curran, is a clearinghouse for information on hiking, horseback riding, sea kayaking, climbing, and peninsula tours. Call a few days ahead to see which guided, scenic, mountain day-hikes are scheduled (daily 9:00-18:00, June-mid-Sept until 21:00, just off harbor at Strand Street, tel. 066/915-2400, www.themountainmanshop.com).

The **Dingle Hillwalking Club** is an informal, visitor-friendly hiking group and a great way to connect with fun, active locals. But you must have serious footwear for the rugged terrain (free, every other Sun at 10:00, meets in front of SuperValu, www.dinglehillwalkingclub.com).

Tours in Dingle

Minibus Tours

Sciuird (SCEW-erd, Irish for "excursion") **Archaeology Tours,** worth ▲▲▲, are offered by a father-son team with Dingle his-

tory—and a knack for sharing it—in their blood. Gentleman Tim Collins, the retired Dingle police chief, and son Michael give serious 2.5-hour minibus tours (€25, departing at 10:30 and 14:00, depending upon demand). Because of the popularity of these tours, it's best to book as soon as you know your dates. Contact Tim via email at his wife's recommended Eileen Collins Kirrary B&B (collinskirrary@ eircom.net, tel. 066/915-1606). Off-season (Oct-April), you may have to call back to see if a minimum of five people have signed up to make a 14-seat bus worth taking out. Skipping the folk legends, your guide will show you the highlights while driving down tiny farm roads (the Irish word for road literally means "cow path"), over hedges, and up ridges to hidden Celtic forts, mysterious stone tombs, and forgotten castles with sweeping seaside views. The running commentary gives an intimate peek into the history of Dingle, and their sound system allows you to hear clearly, no matter where you sit. Dress for the weather. In a gale storm with slashing winds, Tim kept telling me, "You'll survive it."

Boat Tours

From April to September, **Dingle Bay Charters** is the one-stop clearinghouse for everything afloat in Dingle. Their **Harbour Cruises** (€10, 1 hour, daily at 12:30, 14:30, and 16:00) are an easy introduction to the gentle bay and may well include a sighting of

Dingle, An Daingean, or Daingean Ui Chuis?

Linguistic politics have stirred up a controversy over the name of this town and peninsula. As a Gaeltacht, the entire region gets subsidies from the government (which supports the survival of the traditional Irish culture and language). A precondition of this financial support is that towns use their Irish Gaelic name. In 2005, well-meaning government officials in Dublin dictated that Dingle convert its name to the Irish Gaelic "An Daingean" ("on DANG-un"). But as it turns out, four separate Irish towns are named Daingean ("fortress"), so in 2012 Dingle's name was changed again—to Daingean Ui Chuis ("Fortress of the Husseys," a Norman founding family back in the late Middle Ages).

The town has resisted these dictates from Dublin. Dingle has become so wealthy from the tourist trade that it sees its famous name as a trademark, and doesn't want to become "the cute tourist town with the unpronounceable name, formerly known as Dingle." Until recently, official road signs identified the town only as *Daingean Ui Chuis;* however, so many were modified by stubborn locals, who stenciled in a crude *DINGLE,* the government eventually gave up and changed the signs back to *Dingle.* In town, most businesses, all tourist information, and nearly all people—locals and tourists alike—refer to it as Dingle.

For the sake of clarity, in this book I follow the predominant convention: Dingle instead of An Daingean or Daingean Ui Chuis, Great Blasket Island instead of An Blascaod Mór, and so on. But for ease of navigation, I've also included the place's Irish name in parentheses. For a list of these bilingual place names, see the sidebar on page 265.

Fungie the dolphin. The **Blasket Island** ferry (€40, see page 277) gets hikers ashore to explore the island. The popular five-hour **Eco Tour** circles the Great Blasket Island, highlighting the birds and sea life of the peninsula with the option of a couple-hour stop on the island itself (€60, daily at 12:00, weather permitting). **Sea Fishing Excursions** include all the fishing gear you'll need and vary in length (€30/2 hours, €50/4 hours). For an additional €10, you can take your catch to John Benny Moriarty's Pub (on the waterfront; see page 264) where they'll cook it for you to eat that evening. **Boat rentals** seating 10 (€100/hour, €180/2 hours) round out their guerilla flotilla (office around corner from TI, tel. 066/915-1344, mobile 087-672-6100, www.dinglebaycharters.com).

Dingle Town Walk

This quick, self-guided, 10-stop circle through town, worth ▲, gives you a once-over-lightly historical overview and good orientation. To trace the route of this walk, see the map on page 261.

Start at the **"old roundabout"** (next to O'Flaherty's pub, not the "new roundabout" by the hospital), which replaced the big bridge over the town river in the 1980s. Step out to the tiny pedestrian bridge (toward the bay) with the black wrought-iron railing. This was the original train line coming into Dingle (the westernmost train station in all of Europe from 1891 to 1953). The train once picked up fish here; its operators boasted that the cargo would be in London markets within 24 hours. The narrow-gauge tracks ran right along the harborfront. All the land beyond the old buildings you see today has been reclaimed from the sea. Look inland and find the building on the left with the slate siding (the back wall of O'Flaherty's pub) facing the worst storms coming in from the sea. This was the typical design for 19th-century weatherproofing. The radio tower marks the salmon-pink police station.

Cross the roundabout and walk 20 yards along the river up "The Mall" to the two stubby red-brick **pillars** that mark the entry to the police station. These pillars are all that remain of the 19th-century British Constabulary, which afforded a kind of Green Zone for British troops when they tried to subdue the local insurgents here. It was burned down in 1922, during the Civil War; the present building dates from 1938.

The big white **crucifix** across the street and 50 yards up The Mall is a memorial to heroes who died in the 1916 Uprising. Note that it says in the people's language, "For honor and glory of Ireland, 1916 to 19__." The date is unfinished until Ireland is united and free. The names listed are of patriots executed by the English, and one who died while on a hunger strike.

At the *Russels B&B* sign, take 15 paces up the driveway to see an old stone etched with a cross sitting atop the fence (on the right). This marks the site of a former **Celtic holy well,** a sacred spot for people here 2,000 years ago. Back across the street, check out the gurgling stream straddled by a couple of houses.

A few yards up is another much-honored spot: the distribution center for **Guinness.** From this warehouse, pubs throughout the peninsula are stocked with beer. The wooden kegs have been replaced by what locals fondly call "iron lungs."

Farther up and across the street is the 19th-century **courthouse.** Once a symbol of British oppression, today it's a laid-back place where, on the last Friday of each month, the roving County Kerry judge drops by to adjudicate cases (mostly domestic disputes

Dingle at a Glance

▲▲▲**Dingle Peninsula Loop Trip** Scenic 30-mile loop (easy by car, demanding four hours by bike) featuring the Gallarus Oratory (impressive early-Christian church), Iron Age stone huts and "fairy forts," Norman ruins, and spectacular coastal views. See page 267.

▲▲▲**Sciuird Archaeology Tours** Fascinating 2.5-hour mini-bus tours helmed by a father-son team who offer an up-close look into the peninsula's ancient history. **Hours:** Tours generally depart at 10:30 and 14:00 in peak season. See page 243.

▲▲**Harry Clark Windows of Díseart** Imaginative stained-glass Bible scenes inside a lovely Neo-Gothic chapel in the middle of Dingle town. **Hours:** Mon-Fri 9:00-17:00, Sat 10:00-15:00, closed Sun, shorter hours off-season. See page 249.

▲▲**Traditional Music** Best enjoyed at one of Dingle's many pubs; early birds can take in early-evening folk concerts at St. James' Church or the Siopa Ceoil music shop. See page 255.

▲▲**Great Blasket Island** Until quite recently home to one of Ireland's most traditional communities; best appreciated after visit to the excellent Great Blasket Centre in Dunquin on the mainland. **Hours:** Great Blasket Centre open Mon-Sat 10:00-18:00, Sun 11:00-18:00, closed Nov-Easter. See page 277.

▲**Fungie** Dingle Harbor's resident dolphin (and town mascot), who makes regular appearances in the bay (hop a boat tour for a chance at a personal encounter). **Hours:** Boats depart 11:00-17:00; frequency depends on demand. See page 249.

▲**Oceanworld** Aquarium with penguin exhibit, petting pools, and no shortage of Fungie lore. **Hours:** Daily 10:00-17:00, shorter hours off-season. See page 250.

▲**Short Hikes** Bike-ride-plus-hike to nearby Eask Tower for great town and peninsula views, or mellow waterside stroll out to the town's lighthouse. See page 250.

and drunken disorderliness). Next door, with the blue walls, is the popular and recommended **Court House Pub.**

The next intersection is the "Small Bridge" (a little stream runs under the road). Continuing straight would take you up the road a few miles to the ruggedly scenic Conor Pass. Instead, turn left into the commercial heart of the town, up **Main Street.** The old stagecoach from Tralee ended at Dingle's first hotel, the recommended Benners (halfway up on the left), with its Georgian facade and door surviving.

Across the street, up a short gravel alley, is St. James' Church. Since the 13th century, a church has stood here (just inside the medieval wall). Today, it's Anglican on Sundays and filled with great traditional music several nights a week (schedule on gate; also see "Nightlife in Dingle," later). In 2003, a midwinter concert series sprang up at the church, featuring internationally known artists seeking an intimate venue. It became known as the "Other Voices" series and grew to become an annual event. Perhaps the best-known performance was by the late Amy Winehouse, whose "One Shining Moment" TV concert was filmed here in 2006.

Continue uphill and poke your head into two of Dingle's most unapologetically traditional drinking holes, which face each other across Main Street: **Ó Curráin's** (on the right) and **Foxy John's** (on the left, both recommended). Like many Irish pubs, these two throwbacks were originally shops by day and pubs by night. Decades ago, small-town pubs often also served as the town morgue (because they had the only large refrigerated space in town)—where you could literally drink until you dropped.

At the first intersection, take a left onto Green Street. The brownish-red building on your right (as you turn the corner) was once intended to be the residence-in-exile for Marie-Antoinette. Her escape from execution in Paris had been arranged by an Irish officer who owned this house and was employed by the Habsburgs. But Marie-Antoinette refused to leave her husband and children (see the plaque near the front door).

Down the street on the right, pop into the beautiful, modern St. Mary's Church. The convent behind it shows off its delightful **Díseart windows** (described later, under "Sights in Dingle"). Wander in the backyard to check out the tranquil nuns' cemetery, with its white-painted iron crosses huddling peacefully together under a big copper beech tree. Across from St. Mary's is the rec-  ommended **Dick Mack's Pub,** another traditional pub well worth a peek, even for nondrinkers.

Green Street leads past lots of inviting boutiques, estate agents (showing the current price of houses here), and the library. The **library,** a gift from the Carnegie Foundation, has a shelf of tourist-information books and a small exhibit (in the foyer and upstairs) about local patriot Thomas Ashe and the Blasket Island writers.

Dingle's History

The wet sod of Dingle is soaked with medieval history. In the dimmest depths of the Dark Ages, peace-loving, book-ish monks fled the chaos of the Continent and its barbarian raids. They sailed to the drizzly fringe of the known world—to places like Dingle. These monks kept literacy alive in Europe, and later provided scribes to Charlemagne, who ruled much of central Europe in the year 800.

It was from this peninsula that the semi-mythical explor-er-monk St. Brendan is said to have set sail in the sixth century in search of a legendary western paradise. Some think he beat Columbus to North America by almost a thousand years (see sidebar on page 290).

Dingle was a busy seaport in the late Middle Ages. Dingle and Tralee (covered later in this chapter) were the only walled towns in Kerry. Castles stood at the low and high ends of Din-gle's Main Street, protecting the Normans from the angry and dispossessed Irish outside. Dingle was a gateway to northern Spain—a three-day sail due south. Many 14th- and 15th-centu-ry pilgrims left from Dingle for the revered Spanish church in Santiago de Compostela, thought to house the bones of St. James.

In Dingle's medieval heyday, locals traded cowhides for wine. When Dingle's position as a trading center waned, the town faded in importance. In the 19th century, it was a linen-weaving center. Through most of the 20th century, fishing dominated, and the only visitors were scholars and students of old Irish ways. Then, in 1970, the movie *Ryan's Daughter* introduced the world to Dingle. The trickle of Dingle fans has grown to a flood as word of its musical, historical, gastronomi-cal, and scenic charms—not to mention its friendly dolphin—has spread.

The best historic photos you'll find in town decorate the library's walls with images of 19th-century Dingle. Green Street continues to the Strand, where a right turn takes you to the harbor.

The **harbor** was built on land reclaimed (with imported Dutch expertise) in 1992. The string of old stone shops facing the harbor was the loading station for the railway that hauled the fish from Dingle until 1953. Walk out to the end of the breakwater—recently paved and illuminated at night. The Eask Tower, on the distant hill, helped ships locate Dingle's hidden harbor in preradar days (though it was built primarily as a famine-era make-work project). The fancy manor house (now a school) across the harbor was built in the 18th century by Lord Ventry, a big-shot landlord. Near the dolphin statue, you'll find an office where you can get information about the various boat excursions.

Sights in Dingle

▲▲Harry Clark Windows of Díseart

Just behind Dingle's St. Mary's Church stands St. Joseph's Convent and Díseart (dee-SHIRT, rhymes with "T-shirt"), containing

a beautiful Neo-Gothic chapel built in 1884. The sisters of this order, who came to Dingle in 1829 to educate local girls, worked heroically during the famine. During Mass in the chapel, the Mother Superior would sit in the covered stall in the rear, while the sisters—filling the carved stalls—chanted in response.

The chapel was graced in 1922 with 12 windows—the work of Ireland's top stained-glass man, Harry Clark. Long appreciated only by the sisters, these special windows—showing six scenes from the life of Christ—are now open to the public. The convent has become a center for sharing Christian Celtic culture and spirituality.

Cost and Hours: €3, Mon-Fri 9:00-17:00, Sat 10:00-15:00, closed Sun, shorter hours off-season, tel. 066/915-2476, www.diseart.ie.

Visiting the Chapel: Enjoy a quick orientation by the attendant, followed by a 15-minute recorded narration explaining the chapel and its windows. The scenes (clockwise from the back entrance) are the visit of the Magi, the Baptism of Jesus, "Let the little children come to me," the Sermon on the Mount, the Agony in the Garden, and Jesus appearing to Mary Magdalene. Each face is lively and animated in the imaginative, devout, medieval, and fun-loving style of Harry Clark, whom locals talk about as if he's the kid next door.

▲Fungie

In 1983, a dolphin moved into Dingle Harbor and became a local celebrity. Fungie (FOON-ghee, with a hard *g*) is now the darling of

the town's tourist trade and one reason you'll find so many tour buses parked along the harbor. A recent study theorizes that he may be one of a half-dozen dolphins that were released from "Dolphinariums" (under pressure from animal rights activists) on the southern coast of Britain. This would account for

Fungie's loner ways, comfort around humans, and British accent.

Hardy little tour boats thrive by baiting passengers with the chance of an up-close Fungie encounter, then motoring out to the mouth of the harbor, where they troll around looking for him. You're virtually assured of seeing the dolphin, but you don't pay unless you do (€16, kids-€8, one-hour trips depart 11:00-17:00 depending on demand, behind TI at Dolphin Trips office, tel. 066/915-2626, www.dingledolphin.com).

To actually swim with Fungie, rent wetsuits at Brosnan's B&B (Cooleen Street, tel. 066/915-1146 or mobile 087-273-4970) and catch the early morning 8:00-10:00 trip (€25 for the boat trip, €20 for the wetsuit—unless you've packed your own, minimum 6 people or they won't go).

As Fungie is getting on in years, locals admit that he doesn't come up as often as he used to. But regardless, Fungie is a fun guy.

▲Oceanworld

This aquarium offers a little peninsula history, 300 different species of fish in thoughtfully described tanks, and the easiest way to see Fungie the dolphin: on video. Walk through the tunnel while fish swim overhead. You'll see local fish as well as a colorful Amazon collection. The penguin exhibit has a dozen of the little tuxedo torpedoes darting underwater and splashing up onto their fake Arctic ice block. The aquarium's mission is to teach, and you're welcome to ask questions. The petting pool is fun. Splashing attracts the rays, which are unplugged.

Cost and Hours: €13.50, families with children (4-6 people)-€38-44, daily 10:00-17:00, shorter hours off-season, cafeteria, just past harbor on west edge of town, tel. 066/915-2111, www. dingle-oceanworld.ie.

WALKS, RIDES, AND GOLF
▲Short Harbor Walk from Dingle

This easy stroll along the harbor out of town gives you a chance to see Fungie and takes about 1.5 hours round-trip. Head east from the old roundabout (just past O'Flaherty's pub) and walk uphill past the Esso station. Just after Bambury's B&B, take a right, then immediately bear left (toward the cell-phone tower). You'll head downhill and soon spot a tiny Irish Coast Guard station beside the bay. Turn left at the station, climbing the steps over the low wall and following the seashore path to the mouth of Dingle Harbor (passing Hussey's folly, an empty two-story shell of a tower built by a 19th-century fat cat). Ten minutes beyond that is a two-story (white with red trim) lighthouse. This is Fungie's neighborhood. If you see tourist boats out, you're likely to see the dolphin. The trail continues another half-mile to dramatic cliff views and an intimate little beach.

▲Bike and Hike to Eask Tower

Here's a good compromise for those wanting more exercise than the mellow harbor walk to the lighthouse, but less sweat than biking the entire 30-mile Slea Head Loop (described on page 267). Lazybones can skip the bike portion of the following excursion and just drive to the trailhead.

Rent a bike in town and pedal west past the aquarium, going left at the roundabout that takes you over the bridge onto R-559 toward Slea Head. After about 3 km, turn left at the brown sign to *Holden's Leather Workshop*. A narrow leafy lane leads another 3 km to a hut on the right marked *Eask Tower* (the tower looms on the bare hill above). Pay the €2 trail fee at the hut (if unattended, feed the honor box) and hike straight up the hill. Pace yourself on this steep trail. You'll zigzag around sheep and tiptoe over their droppings. You'll also need to navigate through (possibly climb) a couple of waist-high, metal-rung gates. After 45 minutes, you'll have huffed and puffed up to the stone signal tower on the crown of the hill. Enjoy fantastic views of Dingle town (to the north) and Dingle Bay with the Iveragh Peninsula (home of the Ring of Kerry to the south). Try to spot the two jagged Skellig Islands off the distant tip of the Iveragh Peninsula. The right-hand island (farthest from the mainland) was home to the monastic Skellig hermitage for five centuries (see previous chapter). Those islands were once the edge of the known world.

Horseback Riding

Dingle Horse Riding takes out beginners (€45/hour for a trail ride) and experienced riders on two-hour (€75), half-day (€125),

and full-day (€175) excursions (call ahead to book, follow Main Street out of Dingle, turn right at sign, tel. 066/915-2199, www.dinglehorseriding.com). **Long's Horseriding Centre** is farther out on the peninsula just past Ventry (look for sign on right)—an easy stop for bikers or drivers doing the Slea Head Loop (€35/one-hour beach ride, €60/two-hour beach and mountain trail ride, short rides often depart at 10:00, call to book, tel. 066/915-9034, mobile 087-225-0286, www.longsriding.com). In either case, mountain rides are only for advanced riders, and all horses come with English-style saddles (no horns to hang on to).

Dingle Pitch & Putt

This course's humble 18 holes (ranging from 30 to 70 yards in length) offer a relaxing diversion for average duffers on a green headland overlooking the harbor.

Cost and Hours: €7, includes gear, daily 10:00-19:00, closed Nov-March, 20-minute walk out of town—over bridge take first left and then your first right, curling behind Milltown House, tel. 066/915-2020.

Golf

Located out west, near the wildly scenic tip of the Dingle Peninsula and the town of Ballyferriter, Ceann Sibéal/Dingle Links offers a round of golf in a hard-to-beat setting.

Cost and Hours: €60-70 green fees April-Sept, €30-55 Oct-March, open daily till dusk, Baile an Fheirtearaigh, 9 miles west of Dingle town, tel. 066/915-6255, www.dinglelinks.com.

EAST OF DINGLE TOWN
▲Minard Castle

Three miles southwest of the town of Annascaul (Abhainn an Scáil), off the Lispole (Lios Póil) Road, is the largest fortress on the peninsula. Built by the

Knights of Kerry in 1551, Minard Castle was destroyed by Cromwell's troops in about 1650. With its corners undermined by Cromwellian explosives, it looks ready to split—it's no longer safe to enter this teetering ruin.

From the outside, look for the faint scallop in the doorway, the symbol of St. James. Medieval pilgrims would stop here before making a seafaring pilgrimage from Dingle to St. James' tomb at Santiago de Compostela in northern Spain. Imagine the floor plan of the castle: ground floor for animals and storage, main-floor living room with fireplace, then a floor with sleeping quarters; and, on top, the defensive level.

The setting is dramatic, with the Ring of Kerry across the way and Storm Beach below. The beach is notable for its sandstone boulders that fell from the nearby cliffs. Grinding against each other in the wave and tidal action, the boulders eroded into cigar-shaped rocks. Pre-Christian Celts would carry them off and carve them into ogham stones to mark clan boundaries (for more on ogham stones, see page 276).

Next to the fortress, look for the "fairy fort," an Iron Age fort from about 500 B.C. Locals thought it unlucky to pluck stones from these ring forts, so they remain undisturbed, overgrown with greenery, all across Ireland.

Puicin Wedge Tomb

While pretty obscure, this is worth the trouble for its evocative setting. Above the hamlet of Lispole (Lios Póil) in Doonties, park your car and hike 10 minutes up a ridge. At the summit is a pile of rocks made into a little room with one of the finest views on the peninsula. Beyond the Ring of Kerry you may just make out the jagged Skellig Michael, noted for its sixth-century monastic settlement (see previous chapter).

South Pole Inn

This pub, once owned by modest-yet-heroic Antarctic explorer Tom Crean, is still open for business. You'll see it as you pass through Annascaul on N-86 (at the bottom of a hill, on the left if you're heading east). Consider dropping in to have a pint and peruse the walls of lovingly maintained photos devoted to Crean's incredible adventures (see sidebar).

Inch Strand

This four-mile sandy beach was made famous by the movie *Ryan's Daughter*. It's rated a "Blue Flag" beach for its clean water and safe swimming (usually has a lifeguard in summer).

Shopping in Dingle

Dingle is a petri dish of capitalism, with boutiques and charming shops popping up all the time to meet the rising demand of all the tourists. Shoppers enjoy plenty of options.

Crafts

Many fine Dingle shops show off work by local artisans. **Dingle Crystal,** on Green Street with a cozy little café, features Sean Daly and his Waterford-trained crystal-cutting skills. Sean prides himself on his deeper, sharper design cuts (Mon-Sat 10:00-18:00, Sun 11:00-16:00, shorter hours off-season; ask about crystal-cutting demonstrations in their workshop just outside town; tel. 066/915-1550, www.dinglecrystal.ie). **Lisbeth Mulcahy Weaver,** filled with traditional but stylish woven wear, is also the Dingle sales outlet of the well-known potter from out on Slea Head (Mon-Sat 10:00-18:00, Sun 12:00-16:00, slightly longer hours June-Sept, Green Street, tel. 066/915-1688). **John Weldon Jewellers** features fine, handcrafted workmanship of Celtic designs by the local Dingle goldsmith (Mon-Sat 9:30-18:00, Sun 12:00-17:00, Green Street, tel. 066/915-2522, www.johnweldonjewellers.com).

Tom Crean, Unsung Antarctic Explorer

Kerrymen are known as a hardy lot, and probably none more so than Antarctic explorer and Annascaul native Thomas Crean. As a 15-year-old lad looking for steady employment and a chance to see the world, Crean left these shores in 1893 to join the British Royal Navy, and in 1901 volunteered to join the crew of the RSS *Discovery*. Onboard were Captain Robert Falcon Scott and other soon-to-be famous explorers, including Ernest Shackleton. Their mission: to be the first men to reach the South Pole.

It was the world's first serious attempt to reach the pole, an effort that required pulling sleds laden with tons of supplies across miles and miles of ice in extreme conditions. One of the team's most able man-haulers, Crean quickly gained his mates' trust and respect for his hard work, calm presence, and cheerful (if tuneless) singing. The *Discovery* Expedition pushed the boundaries of Antarctic exploration, but didn't reach the pole (Britain's second attempt, in 1909 under Shackleton, got much closer before also turning back).

Determined to try again, Scott chose Crean among the first of his handpicked crew for the *Terra Nova* Expedition (1910-1913). Early on, Crean saved some expedition members stranded on a drifting ice floe—encircled by orcas (who can tip ice to make vulnerable seals slide off)—by leaping between floating chunks of ice, then scaling an ice wall, to get help. Later, Crean and two others were the last support team ordered to turn back as Scott made the final push to the pole (having come so close, the unshakable Crean wept at the news). Near the end of the 730-mile

Music Shops

Danlann Gallery sells musical instruments and woodcrafts (Mon-Fri 10:00-18:00 in summer, "flexible hours" on weekends, shorter hours off-season, owner makes violins, Dykegate Street). **Siopa Ceoil** is a grand little music shop worth seeking out. It's enthusiastically run by Michael Herlihy, who plays a mean accordion and offers free quick-and-dirty *bodhrán* (traditional drum) lessons. Michael, his son Dara, and omni-pleasant Caitriona are virtual encyclopedias of Irish music knowledge. The shop hosts "unplugged" traditional music concerts several nights a week, and sells advance tickets for concerts at St. James' Church (see "Folk Concerts," later; open Mon-Sat 9:30-20:00, Sun 14:00-19:00, shorter hours off-season, near the waterfront and the recommended Mountain Man

return trip, Crean's two mates, sick and freezing, could go no farther. Exhausted and provisioned with only three cookies and two sticks of chocolate, Crean made a nonstop, solo, 35-mile march through a blizzard to reach help, saving his mates' lives. (Though Scott's party did reach the pole, a Norwegian team led by Roald Amundsen beat them to it—by a month; Scott and his men didn't survive the trip back.)

Crean's most famous act of heroism took place on his third and final polar expedition (1914-1917), led by Shackleton. Their ship, the *Endurance*, was crushed by ice, marooning the crew on Elephant Island. Hoping to find help at a whaling station, Shackleton, Crean, and four others sailed a modified open lifeboat 800 miles in 17 days to South Georgia Island. There they were forced to hike across the rugged, unexplored interior to reach the station on the other side. A ship was sent to rescue the exhausted and malnourished crew, all of whom had miraculously survived the 18-month ordeal.

Crean never did reach the South Pole himself, turning down Shackleton's request to join him on his next (and last) trek. But Crean distinguished himself as a hero among explorers—who named both a mountain and a glacier after him in Antarctica—and was honored by King George V. In 1920, he retired from the navy, returned to County Kerry, and stashed his medals away, never again speaking of his experiences—partly out of modesty, and partly because his service in the (British) navy could have made him a target for Irish nationalists. An uneducated farmer's son, Crean left few records of his exploits and didn't achieve the fame of his lauded (and more well-to-do) contemporaries. Crean married, bought a pub (South Pole Inn—see "East of Dingle Town"), and raised three daughters. After bravely escaping many near-deaths in the Antarctic, he finally died in 1938 of a burst appendix.

shop on a short dead-end lane called The Colony, tel. 066/915-2618, mobile 087-914-5826).

Nightlife in Dingle

▲▲▲Music in Dingle Pubs

Traditional pub music is Dingle town's best experience. Even if you're not into pubs, take a nap and then give these a whirl. Dingle is renowned among traditional musicians as a good place to get work ("€40 a day, tax-free, plus drink"). The town has piles of pubs that feature music most nights, and with nary a cover charge. The scene is a decent mix of locals, Americans, and Germans. Music normally starts at 21:30-ish, and the last call for drinks is at "half eleven" (23:30), sometimes later on weekends. For a seat near the music, arrive early. If the place is chockablock with people, power in and find breathing room in the back. By midnight, the door is usually closed and the chairs are stacked. For some background, see "Traditional Irish Music" on page 528. For locations of the following pubs, see the map on page 263.

While two pubs, the **Small Bridge Bar** (An Droichead Beag) and **O'Flaherty's,** are the most famous for their atmosphere and devotion to traditional Irish music, make a point to wander the town and follow your ear. Smaller pubs may feel a bit foreboding to a tourist, but rest assured that people—locals as well as travelers—are out for the *craic.* Irish culture is very accessible in the pubs; they're like highly interactive museums waiting to be explored. If you sit at  a table, you'll be left alone. But stand or sit at the bar and you'll be engulfed in conversation with new friends. Have a glass in an empty, no-name pub and chat up the publican. Pubs are no longer smoky, but can be stuffy and hot, so leave your coat at home. I know it's going to be a great trad music session when my eyeglasses steam up as I enter.

Pub Crawl: The best place to start a pub crawl is at **O'Flaherty's,** the first music pub in Dingle, located on Holyground street. Quietly intense owner Fergus O'Flaherty, a fixture since my first visit to Dingle, can belt out a song as he joins a varying lineup of loyal local musicians. Talented Fergus sings and plays a half-dozen different instruments during almost nightly traditional-music sessions. His domain has a high ceiling and is dripping in old-time photos and town memorabilia—it's unpretentious, cluttered fun.

Moving up Strand Street, find **John Benny Moriarty's.** Its dependably good traditional-music sessions come with John himself joining in on accordion when he's not pouring pints.

Then head up Green Street. **Dick Mack,** across from the church, is nicknamed "the last pew." This was once a tiny leather shop that expanded into a pub at night. Today, Dick Mack keeps the old leather-shop ambience but sells only drinks, with several rooms, a fine snug (private booth, originally designed to allow women to drink discreetly), ample beer choices, and a fascinating ambience. Notice the Hollywood-type stars on the sidewalk outside, recalling famous visitors. The pub was established in 1899 by Dick Mack (master of the westernmost train station in Europe), whose mission was to provide "liquid replenishment" to travelers. The grandson of the original Dick Mack runs the place today. A painting in the window shows Dick Mack II with the local gang.

Green Street climbs to Main Street, where two more Dick

Mack-type places are filled with locals deep in conversation (but no music): **Foxy John's** (a hardware shop by day) and **Ó Curráin's** (across the street, a small clothing shop by day).

A bit higher up Main Street is **McCarthy's Bar,** a smoke-stained relic. It's less touristy and has occasional traditional-music sessions on its little stage. Wander down Main Street. The **Dingle Pub** is well established as *the* place for folk-ballad singing rather than the churning traditional beat of an Irish folk session. At the bottom of Main Street, **Small Bridge Bar** offers live music nightly. These days, its dimly lit confines are popular with a younger, late-night crowd.

And the **Court House Pub** (on The Mall, next to the old gray courthouse) is a steamy little hideaway with low ceilings and high-caliber musicians. Owner Tommy O'Sullivan is a guitar-strum-ming fixture on the trad music scene.

Off-Season: From October through April, the music hiber-nates for the most part. But on weekends, your best bets are the Small Bridge Bar, O'Flaherty's, the Court House Pub, and John Benny Moriarty's.

▲▲Folk Concerts

If you're not a night owl, these are your best opportunities to hear Irish traditional music in a more controlled, early evening environ-ment. Keep in mind that in these settings, many of the musicians find flash photography to be an irritating distraction.

Top local musicians offer a quality evening of live, acoustic, traditional Irish music in the fine little **St. James' Church** (100 seats), just off Main Street. If you prefer not to be packed into a pub with the distractions of conversation, these concerts are a good option. They are organized by local piper Eoin Duignan, whose command of the melodic *uileann* bagpipes is a highlight most nights. Surprisingly, this humble church is the home venue of the acclaimed "Other Voices" winter concert TV series that has drawn the likes of Amy Winehouse, Sinéad O'Connor, and Donovan, among others (€13 in advance, €15 at the door; Mon, Wed, and Fri at 19:30, May-Oct only; mobile 087-284-9656; see sign on church gate or, for more details or to book a ticket, drop by the Whole Food Vegetarian Café, Paul Geaneys Pub, Leac a Ré craft shop, or Siopa Ceoil music shop).

The **Siopa Ceoil** music shop hosts intimate "unplugged" tra-ditional Irish music sessions in its cozily cramped, 35-seat venue (€15, includes a tasty Irish coffee during break between sets; May-Sept Tue, Thu, and Sat at 19:30; 2 The Colony, tel. 066/915-2618, mobile 087-914-5826, www.siopaceoil.ie).

Cinema

Dingle's great little theater is The Phoenix on Dykegate. Its film club (50-60 locals) meets here Tuesdays year-round at 20:45 for coffee and cookies, followed by a film at 21:00 (€8 for film, anyone is welcome). The leader runs it almost like a religion, with a sermon on the film before he rolls it. The regular film schedule for the week is posted on the door.

Sleeping in Dingle

Prices vary with the season, with winter cheap, and July and August tops.

IN OR NEAR THE TOWN CENTER

$$ **Greenmount House** sits among chilly palm trees in the countryside at the top of town. A five-minute hike up from the town center, this guesthouse commands a fine view of the bay and mountains. Gary Curran runs one of Ireland's best B&Bs, with two fine rooms, three superb rooms, and seven sprawling suites in a modern building with lavish public areas and breakfast in a solarium (reserve in advance, most rooms at ground level, parking, top of John Street, tel. 066/915-1414, www.greenmounthouse.ie, info@greenmounthouse.ie). Seek out the hot tub in their back-garden cabin.

$$ **Bambury's Guesthouse,** hosted by cheerful Bernie Bambury, is big and modern with views of grazing sheep and the harbor. The 12 rooms are airy and comfy (coming in from Tralee it's on your left on Mail Road, 2 blocks before Esso station; tel. 066/915-1244, www.bamburysguesthouse.com, info@bamburysguesthouse.com).

$$$ **Benners Hotel** was the only hotel in town a hundred years ago. It stands bewildered by the modern world on Main Street, with sprawling public spaces and 52 abundant, overpriced rooms (tel. 066/915-1638, www.dinglebenners.com, info@dinglebenners.com).

$$ **Alpine Guesthouse** looks like a Monopoly hotel, and is fittingly comfortable and efficient. Its 14 bright and fresh rooms come with pastoral views, a cozy lounge, and friendly owner Paul O'Shea (RS%, family rooms, easy parking, Mail Road, tel. 066/915-1250, www.alpineguesthouse.com, alpinedingle@gmail.com). Driving into town from Tralee, this will be the first lodging on your right, next to the sports field and a block uphill from the Dingle Esso station.

$ **Eileen Collins Kirrary B&B,** which takes up a quiet corner in the town center, is run by the same Collins family that does archaeological tours of the peninsula (see page 243). They offer five fine rooms, great prices, a large garden, and a homey friendli-

Sleep Code

Hotels are classified based on the average price of a typical en suite double room with breakfast in high season.

$$$$	**Splurge:** Most rooms over €170
$$$	**Pricier:** €130-170
$$	**Moderate:** €90-130
$	**Budget:** €50-90
¢	**Backpacker:** Under €50
RS%	**Rick Steves discount**

Unless otherwise noted, credit cards are accepted and free Wi-Fi is available. Comparison-shop by checking prices at several hotels (on each hotel's own website, on a booking site, or by email). For the best deal, *book directly with the hotel*. Ask for a discount if paying in cash; if the listing includes **RS%**, request a Rick Steves discount.

ness (cash only, tel. 066/915-1606 or mobile 087-150-0017, Kirrary House, just off The Mall on Avondale at Dykegate and Grey's Lane, www.collinskirrary.com, collinskirrary@eircom.net, Eileen Collins). They also rent a cozy, family-friendly, self-catering cottage that sleeps five people (minimum 3-night stay). A couple of hundred yards high up behind town, it has Dingle's best views.

$ Sraíd Eoin House offers five pleasant, top-floor rooms above Galvin's Travel Agency (RS%, family rooms, John Street, tel. 066/915-1409, www.sraideoinbnb.com, sraideoinhouse@hotmail.com, friendly Kathleen and Maurice O'Connor).

$$ Barr Na Sráide Inn, central and hotel-like, has 29 basic rooms (family deals, self-service laundry, bar, parking, past McCarthy's pub on Upper Main Street, tel. 066/915-1331, www.barrnasraide.com, info@barrnasraide.ie).

$ O'Neill's B&B is homey and friendly, with six decent rooms on a quiet street at the top of town (cash only, parking, John Street, tel. 066/915-1639, www.oneillsbedandbreakfast.com, info@oneillsbedandbreakfast.com, Mary and Stephen O'Neill).

BEYOND THE PIER

These accommodations are a 10-15-minute walk from Dingle's town center. They tend to be quieter, since they are farther from the late-night pub scene.

$$ Heaton's Guesthouse, big, peaceful, and comfortable, is on the water just west of town at the end of Dingle Bay—a five-minute walk past Oceanworld on The Wood. The 16 thoughtfully appointed rooms come with all the amenities (creative breakfasts, parking, The Wood, tel. 066/915-2288, www.heatonsdingle.com, info@heatonsdingle.com, David Heaton).

DINGLE PENINSULA

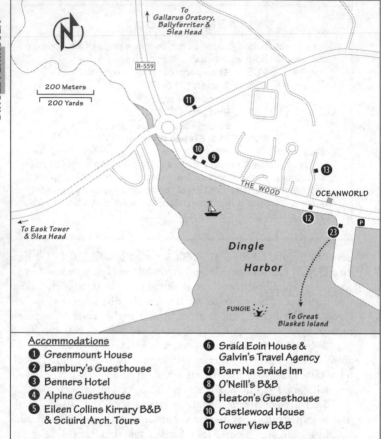

To Gallarus Oratory,
Ballyferriter &
Slea Head

R-559

200 Meters
200 Yards

To Eask Tower
& Slea Head

THE WOOD

OCEANWORLD

Dingle

Harbor

FUNGIE

To Great
Blasket Island

Accommodations

1. Greenmount House
2. Bambury's Guesthouse
3. Benners Hotel
4. Alpine Guesthouse
5. Eileen Collins Kirrary B&B
   & Sciuird Arch. Tours
6. Sraíd Eoin House &
   Galvin's Travel Agency
7. Barr Na Sráide Inn
8. O'Neill's B&B
9. Heaton's Guesthouse
10. Castlewood House
11. Tower View B&B

\$\$\$ Castlewood House is a palatial refuge with 12 tasteful rooms, classy furnishings, and delicious breakfasts. The breakfast room and patio have a wonderful view of Dingle Harbor (parking, The Wood, tel. 066/915-2788, www.castlewooddingle.com, info@castlewooddingle.com, Brian and Helen Heaton).

\$ Tower View B&B is a big, bright-yellow modern home just outside of town on a lovely wooded lot. This kid-friendly mini-farm, with pettable animals, rents eight fine rooms (cash only, family rooms, just past the roundabout on the west side of town on High Road, tel. 066/915-2990, www.towerviewdingle.com, info@towerviewdingle.com, Mary and Robbie Griffin).

\$ Harbour Nights B&B weaves together a line of old row houses to create a 14-room guesthouse facing the harbor (just past the aquarium on The Wood, parking, tel. 066/915-2499, mobile 087-686-8190, www.harbournightsguesthouse.com, info@dinglebandb.com, Seán and Kathleen Lynch).

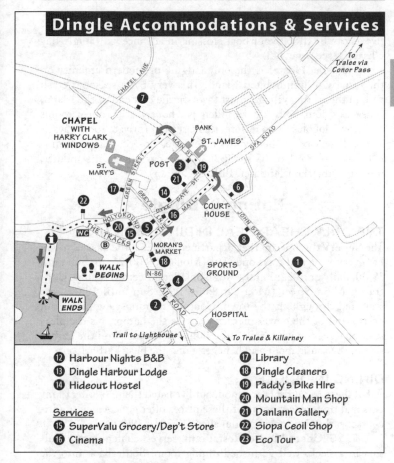

Dingle Accommodations & Services

- ⑫ Harbour Nights B&B
- ⑬ Dingle Harbour Lodge
- ⑭ Hideout Hostel

Services
- ⑮ SuperValu Grocery/Dep't Store
- ⑯ Cinema

- ⑰ Library
- ⑱ Dingle Cleaners
- ⑲ Paddy's Bike Hire
- ⑳ Mountain Man Shop
- ㉑ Danlann Gallery
- ㉒ Siopa Ceoil Shop
- ㉓ Eco Tour

HOSTELS AND DORMS

$$ Dingle Harbour Lodge is a hostel-hotel hybrid with 29 rooms on the edge of town. You have the feeling of being a guest in a comfy hotel without the fancy prices (family rooms, up a long driveway off The Wood past the aquarium, tel. 066/915-1577, www.dingleharbourlodge.com, info@dingleharbourlodge.com).

¢ Hideout Hostel has 36 beds and is friendly and central, just across the lane from the movie theater. Michael (ME-hall) grew up on this street and manages a relaxed, fun atmosphere (private rooms available, Dykegate Street, tel. 066/915-0559, www. thehideouthostel.com, info@thehideouthostel.com).

On Great Blasket Island

You can really get away from it all on Great Blasket Island, a couple of miles off the tip of the peninsula. No phone, no lights, no cars.

Not a single luxury. Like Robinson Crusoe (or Gilligan), it's primitive as can be. Book your boat crossing in advance via Dingle Bay Charters (see page 243).

¢ **Blasket Hostel** is the only lodging or modern amenity on the otherwise uninhabited island. This very basic seasonal crash pad, in the fishing village ghost town on the east end of the island, consists of four houses (two toilets per house), with dorm rooms and a few doubles in an unforgettable setting (private rooms available, self-service kitchen, views no charge, closed off-season, mobile 087-264-8531 or 086-057-2626, www.greatblasketisland.net, info@greatblasketisland.net, Billy O'Connor).

Eating in Dingle

THE ONLY CHEAP MEAL IN DINGLE: PICNIC

The **SuperValu** supermarket/department store, at the base of town, has everything and stays open late (Mon-Sat 8:00-21:00, Sun until 19:00, daily until 22:00 July-Aug). Smaller groceries, such as **Centra** on Main Street (Mon-Sat 8:00-21:00, Sun until 18:00), are scattered throughout the town. Consider a grand-view picnic out on the end of the newer pier (as you face the harbor, it's the pleasure-boat pier on your right). You'll find picnic tables on the harbor side of the roundabout and benches along the busy harborfront.

DINING IN DINGLE

All of these restaurants are good, but I've listed them in order of my personal preference. Some of these places offer good-value, multi-course, early-bird specials from about 17:30 to 19:00.

$$$$ Chart House Restaurant serves contemporary cuisine in a sleek, well-varnished dining room. Settle back into the shipshape, lantern-lit, harborside ambience. The menu is shaped by what's fresh and seasonal. The chef, who has a Tuscan connection and a passion for South African wines, is committed to always offering a good vegetarian entrée (daily 18:00-22:00 except closed Mon Oct-May, at roundabout at base of town, reservations wise, tel. 066/915-2255, www.thecharthousedingle.com, Jim McCarthy).

$$$$ Out of the Blue Seafood-Only Restaurant is the locals' choice for just plain great fresh fish. The interior is bright and elegantly simple. The menu—not printed, but on a chalkboard—is dictated by what the fishermen caught that morning. If they're closed, you know there's been a storm and the fishermen couldn't go out. Dinners are artfully presented, with a touch of nouvelle cuisine and certainly no chips (Mon-Sat 17:00-21:30, Sun 12:30-15:00, closed after a storm, some outdoor picnic-table seating, reservations smart, just past the TI, facing the harbor on The Waterside, tel. 066/915-0811, www.outoftheblue.ie).

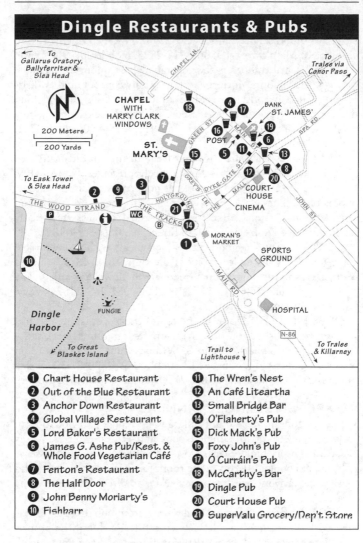

Dingle Restaurants & Pubs

To Gallarus Oratory, Ballyferriter & Slea Head

To Tralee via Conor Pass

CHAPEL WITH HARRY CLARK WINDOWS

ST. MARY'S

BANK
ST. JAMES'

POST

To Eask Tower & Slea Head

THE WOOD STRAND

HOLYGROUND

THE TRACKS

COURT-HOUSE

CINEMA

MORAN'S MARKET

SPORTS GROUND

Dingle Harbor

FUNGIE

HOSPITAL

To Great Blasket Island

Trail to Lighthouse

To Tralee & Killarney

200 Meters
200 Yards

❶	Chart House Restaurant	⓫	The Wren's Nest
❷	Out of the Blue Restaurant	⓬	An Café Liteartha
❸	Anchor Down Restaurant	⓭	Small Bridge Bar
❹	Global Village Restaurant	⓮	O'Flaherty's Pub
❺	Lord Baker's Restaurant	⓯	Dick Mack's Pub
❻	James G. Ashe Pub/Rest. & Whole Food Vegetarian Café	⓰	Foxy John's Pub
❼	Fenton's Restaurant	⓱	Ó Curráin's Pub
❽	The Half Door	⓲	McCarthy's Bar
❾	John Benny Moriarty's	⓳	Dingle Pub
❿	Fishbarr	⓴	Court House Pub
		㉑	SuperValu Grocery/Dep't. Store

$$ **Anchor Down** is another fresh fish option that is much easier on the wallet. The Sheehy family, who are local fishermen, supply their simple little cottage up the lane with a variety of fresh fish—and chips if you want them (daily 11:30-21:30, closed Dec-Feb, up the lane behind Out of the Blue, 3 The Colony, tel. 066/915-1545).

At the $$$$ **Global Village Restaurant,** Nuala Cassidy and Martin Bealin—with inspiration gleaned from his world travels—concoct their favorite dishes. Martin has a passion for making things from scratch and giving dishes a creative twist. No chips, no deep-fat-fried anything. It's an eclectic, healthy, fresh seafood-eaters' place (good salads; daily 17:30-22:00, Nov-Feb open Fri-Sun only; top of Main Street, tel. 066/915-2325, mobile 087-917-5920).

$$$$ Lord Baker's is the venerable elder among fine Dingle dining options. John Moriarty and his family concoct quality dishes served in a friendly yet refined atmosphere. The seafood soup is a memorable specialty (Fri-Wed 18:00-21:30, closed Thu, reservations smart, Main Street, tel. 066/915-1277 or 066/915-1141, www.lordbakers.ie).

$$$ James G. Ashe Pub and Restaurant, an old-fashioned joint, is popular with locals for its nicely presented, top-quality, traditional Irish food and seafood at good prices. Check out the photos of Gregory Peck, who was related to the Ashe family and visited the pub often. I like their beef-and-Guinness stew (daily 12:00-15:00 & 17:30-21:30, Main Street, tel. 066/915-0989).

$$$$ Fenton's is good for seafood meals with a memorable apple-and-berry-crumble dessert (Tue-Sun 18:00-21:30, closed Mon, reservations smart, on Green Street down the hill below the church, tel. 066/915-2172, mobile 087-248-2487, www. fentonsrestaurantdingle.com).

$$$$ The Half Door, at the top of the town, is one of Dingle's long-established top-notch restaurants (on John Street), satisfying diners with hearty portions. While elegant, the dining room feels a bit congested (Mon-Sat 12:30-14:00 & 18:00-21:30, closed Sun, reservations smart, tel. 066/915-1600, www.iol.ie/~halfdoor).

INEXPENSIVE DINGLE DINNERS

While the top-end restaurants charge on average €20-30, you can eat well for €15-19 in Dingle's pubs and ethnic eateries. Many cheap and cheery lunch places close at 18:00. Most pubs stop serving food at about 21:00 (to make room for their beer drinkers and musicians). Anyone will serve tap water for free. Here are some ideas:

$$ John Benny Moriarty's is a waterfront pub dishing up traditional Irish fare with a relatively cozy interior. John, the proprietor, hopes people will come here for dinner, and stay for a drink and to enjoy his nightly live music (food daily 12:30-21:30, music after 21:30, The Pier).

$$ Whole Food Vegetarian Café is a peaceful little place serving healthy soups, salads, pancakes, fruit smoothies, and home-baked cakes. Its serene back garden is perfect for enjoying a light lunch (Mon-Sat 12:00-17:00, closed Sun except in July-Aug, Lower Main Street, mobile 087-741-6947).

$ Fishbarr has all the cinder-block charm you'd expect in a great fish-and-chips lunch joint. It's off the beaten path at the end of the modern yacht pier, with outdoor tables to track the boating

DINGLE PENINSULA

All Roads Lead to Daingean Ui Chuis

The western half of the Dingle Peninsula is part of the Gaeltacht, where locals speak the Irish Gaelic language. In an effort

to ward off English-language encroachment, all place names on road signs were controversially changed to Irish-only in the past decade, though some are now back in English (see "Dingle, An Daingean, or Daingean Ui Chuis?" sidebar on page 244). As you travel along Slea Head Drive (known as Ceann Sléibhe in Irish), refer to this cheat sheet of the most useful destination names. A complete translation of all Irish place names is included in the Gazetteer section at the back of the *Complete Road Atlas of Ireland* by Ordnance Survey.

English Name	Irish Gaelic Name
Dingle	*Daingean Ui Chuis* (DANG-un e koosh)
Ventry	*Ceann Trá* (k'yown—rhymes with "crown"—traw)
Slea Head	*Ceann Sléibhe* (k'yown SHLAY-veh)
Dunquin	*Dún Chaoin* (doon qween)
Blasket Islands	*Na Blascaodaí* (nuh BLAS-kud-ee)
Great Blasket Island	*An Blascaod Mór* (on BLAS-kade moor)
Ballyferriter	*Baile an Fheirtearaigh* (BALL-yuh on ERR-ter-ee)
Reasc Monastery	*Mainistir Riaisc* (MON-ish-ter REE-isk)
Gallarus	*Gallaras* (GAHL-russ)
Kilmalkedar	*Cill Mhaoil-cheadair* (kill moyle-KAY-dir)
Annascaul	*Abhainn an Scáil* (ow'en on skahl)
Lispole	*Lios Póil* (leesh pohl)
Tralee	*Trá Lí* (tra-LEE)

DINGLE PENINSULA

action in the bay (daily 11:00-15:00, closed Oct-April, cash only, mobile 086-378-8584).

$ The Wren's Nest is a mellow coffeehouse, reflecting musician-owner John Ryan's philosophical demeanor. This lunch-only refuge, with an ultra-appealing back garden, serves wholesome omelets, sandwiches, cakes, and tea. A small corner stage hosts occasional open-mic acoustic music gigs; you can also check out the schedule of *bodhrán* and music lessons (daily 11:00-17:00, Dykegate Street, mobile 086-177-3119).

$ An Café Liteartha, a simple refuge hidden behind a wonderfully cluttered bookstore, serves soup and sandwiches to a good-natured crowd of Irish speakers (daily 10:00-18:00, Oct-April until 17:00 and closed Sun, Dykegate Street, tel. 066/915-2204).

MEALS ON SLEA HEAD LOOP

$$ The Stone House is an appealing lunch or dinner option about seven miles (12 km) west of Dingle on the Slea Head Loop road. Serving local specialties, from scones to fresh seafood and steak dishes, David and Michelle Foran nurture a cozy atmosphere. Their front porch outdoor tables are popular seaview perches on warm summer evenings. You gotta try the fresh Dingle Bay crab salad (daily 10:00-18:00, June-Aug until 20:00, reservations smart, tel. 066/915-9970, www.stonehouseventry.com).

Dingle Connections

Tralee (Trá Lí), 30 miles from Dingle, is the region's transportation hub (with the nearest train station to Dingle). Most bus trips make connections in Tralee.

From Dingle by Bus to: Galway (5/day, 6.5 hours), **Dublin** (4/day, 8-9 hours, transfer in Tralee and Limerick), **Rosslare** (1/day, 9 hours), **Tralee** (5/day, fewer off-season and Sun, 1.5 hours). Most bus trips out of Dingle require at least one or two (easy) transfers. Remember, buses stop on the waterfront behind the Super-Valu (bus info toll tel. 1850-836-611, www.buseireann.ie, or Tralee station at 066/712-3566; Tralee train info tel. 066/712-3522). For more information, see "Tralee Connections" at the end of this chapter.

Dingle Peninsula Loop Trip

DINGLE PENINSULA

A sight worth ▲▲▲, the Dingle Peninsula loop trip is about 30 miles (47 km) long and must be driven in a clockwise direction. It's easy by car, or it's a demanding four hours by bike—if you don't stop to catch your breath. Cyclists should plan on an early start (preferably by 9:00) to allow for enough sightseeing and lunch/rest time.

While you can take a great guided tour of the peninsula (see "Tours in Dingle" on page 243), the self-guided tour that follows allows you to do it on your own. I've provided distances to help locate points of interest. I've given distances in kilometers so you can follow along with your rental-car odometer.

If you're driving, check your odometer at Oceanworld, as you leave Dingle (ideally, reset your odometer to zero). Even if you get off track or are biking, you can subtract the kilometers listed below to figure out distances between points. To get the most out of your trip, read through this entire section before departing. Then go step-by-step (staying on R-559 the entire way and following the brown *Ceann Sléibhe/Slea Head Drive* signs most of the way—through kilometer 37.7). Roads are very congested mid-July to late August.

The Dingle Peninsula is 10 miles wide and runs 40 miles from Tralee to Slea Head. The top of its mountainous spine is Mount Brandon—at 3,130 feet, it's the second-tallest mountain in Ireland (after a nearby peak above Killarney that's almost 500 feet higher). While only a few tiny villages lie west of Dingle town, the peninsula is home to 50,000 sheep.

Dingle Driving/Biking Tour

For this self-guided tour, leave Dingle town west along the waterfront (0.0 km at Oceanworld). Driving out of town, on the left you'll see a row of humble "two up and two down" flats from a 1908 affordable-housing government initiative. Today, even these little places cost more than €200,000.

0.5 km: There's an eight-foot tide here. The seaweed was used to make formerly worthless land arable. (Seaweed is a natural source of potash—it's organic farming, before it was trendy.) Across the River Milltown estuary, the white **Milltown House** was Robert Mitchum's home for a year during the filming of *Ryan's Daughter*. (Behind that is a scruffy pitch-and-putt range—described on

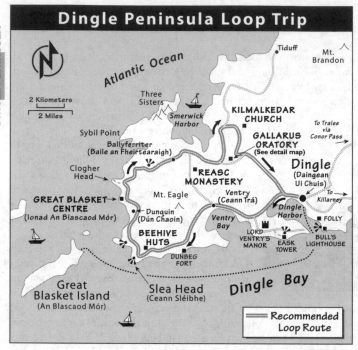

Dingle Peninsula Loop Trip

Atlantic Ocean

• Tiduff   人 Mt. Brandon

Three Sisters

Smerwick Harbor

KILMALKEDAR CHURCH

To Tralee via Conor Pass

Sybil Point

Ballyferriter (Baile an Fheirtearaigh)

GALLARUS ORATORY (See detail map)

Dingle (Daingean Uí Chúis)

Clogher Head

REASC MONASTERY

To Killarney

GREAT BLASKET CENTRE (Ionad An Blascaod Mór)

Mt. Eagle

Ventry (Ceann Trá)

Dingle Harbor

• FOLLY

Dunquin (Dún Chaoin)

Ventry Bay

BEEHIVE HUTS

LORD VENTRY'S MANOR

EASK TOWER

BULL'S LIGHTHOUSE

DUNBEG FORT

Great Blasket Island (An Blascaod Mór)

Slea Head (Ceann Sléibhe)

Dingle Bay

━━━ Recommended Loop Route

2 Kilometers
2 Miles

---

page 252.) Look for the narrow mouth of this blind harbor (in the distance at the opposite end of the bay, where Fungie the dolphin frolics) and the Ring of Kerry beyond that. Dingle Bay is so hidden that ships needed the Eask Tower to find its mouth.

0.7 km: At the roundabout, turn left over the bridge. On the far side, the blue building on the right was the site of a corn-grinding mill in the 18th century (you'll get a glimpse of the huge black waterwheel snug behind it). Today it's a modern warehouse that shelters the **Dingle Distillery.** Not far beyond that, you'll go by the junction (on the right) where you'll complete this loop trip later. The gas station on your left is a handy spot to top up your tank (there aren't many gas options beyond this point).

1.3 km: The Milestone B&B is named for the stone **pillar** (*gallaun* in Irish) in its front yard. This pillar may have been a pre-historic grave or a boundary marker between two tribes. Half of the stone's length is buried underground. This peninsula, literally an open-air museum, is dotted with more than 2,000 such monuments dating from the Neolithic Age (4000 B.C.) through early Christian times. Another stone pillar stands in the field across the street (100 yards away, on the left), in the direction of the distant yellow manor house of Lord Ventry. The pillar's function today: cow scratcher.

Lord Ventry, whose family came to Dingle as post-Cromwellian War landlords in 1666, built this mansion in about 1750. Today it houses an all-Irish-language boarding school for 140 high school girls.

As you drive past the **Ventry estate,** you'll pass palms, magnolias, and exotic flora, which were introduced to Dingle by Lord Ventry. The Gulf Stream is the source of the mild climate (it rarely snows here), which supports subtropical plants. Consequently, fuchsias—imported from Chile and spreading like weeds—line the roads all over the peninsula and redden the countryside from June through September. More than 100 inches of rain a year gives this area its "40 shades of green."

The old red-sandstone and slate-roof cottages along the roadside housed Ventry estate workers in the 1840s.

3 km: A brown sign reading *Holden's Leather Workshop* leads up a road to the left. This is the narrow lane that eventually leads to the trailhead up to **Eask Tower** (see page 251 for details on this active hiking/biking option).

4.6 km: Stay off the "soft margin" as you enjoy views of Ventry Bay, its four-mile-long beach (to your right as you face the water), and distant Skellig Michael, which you'll see all along this part of the route. **Skellig Michael**—an island jutting up like France's Mont St. Michel—contains the rocky remains of a sixth-century monastic settlement (described in previous chapter). Next to it is a smaller island, Little Skellig—a breeding ground for gannets (seagull-like birds with six-foot wingspans). In 1866, the first transatlantic cable was laid from nearby Valentia Island to Canada's Newfoundland (see sidebar on page 233). It was in use until 1965. Mount Eagle (1,660 feet), rising across the bay, marks the end of Ireland.

In the town of **Ventry**—a.k.a. Ceann Trá (translated roughly as "beach head")—Irish is the first language. Ventry is little more than a bungalow holiday village today. Urban Irish families love to come here in the summer to immerse their kids in the traditional culture and wild nature. A large hall at the edge of the village is used as a classroom where big-city students come on field trips to learn the Irish language.

Just past the town, a lane leads left to a fine beach and mobile-home vacation community. An information board explains the history, geology, and bird life of this bay. The humble trailer park has no running water or electricity. Locals like it for its economy and proximity to the beach. From here, a lane also leads inland to **Long's Horseriding Centre** (described earlier, under "Sights in Dingle").

During World War II, a German U-boat churned into this bay and put 28 Greek sailors ashore on this beach (and therefore onto neutral Irish soil). They were survivors from a merchant ship that the sub had sunk...not the kind of humanitarian gesture that German U-boat captains were known for making.

5.2 km: The bamboo-like **rushes** on either side of the road are the kind used to make the local thatched roofs. Thatching, which nearly died out because of the fire danger, is more popular now that antiflame treatments are available. It's not the cheapest roofing alternative, however, as it's expensive to pay the few qualified craftsman thatchers who remain in Ireland. Black-and-white magpies fly overhead.

8.6 km: The Irish football (GAA) star Páidí Ó Sé (Paddy O'Shea) was a household name in Ireland. He won eight all-Ireland football titles for Kerry as a player. He then trained the Kerry team for many years, and then ran the pub on the left. A heroic **statue** stands outside today (also notice the tiny grocery on the right; easy beach access from here).

9.2 km: The plain blue **cottage** hiding in the trees 100 yards off the road on the left (view through the white gate, harder to see in summer when foliage is thickest) was kept cozy by Tom Cruise and Nicole Kidman during the filming of *Far and Away*. Just beyond are fine views of the harbor and Dingle's stone tower.

10.7 km: *Taisteal go Mall* means "go slowly"; there's a red-colored, two-room **schoolhouse** on the right (20 students, two teachers). In summer it's used for Irish Gaelic courses for kids from the big cities. On the left is the small Celtic and Prehistoric Museum, a quirky private collection of prehistoric artifacts, including arrowheads and ancient jewelry, collected by a retired busker (musician) named Harris (€5, daily 10:00-17:00).

11.1 km: The circular mound (which looks like an elevated hedge) on the right is a late-Stone Age **ring fort.** In 500 B.C., it was a petty Celtic chieftain's headquarters—a stone-and-earth stockade filled with little thatched dwellings. These "Raths" survived untouched through the centuries because of superstitious beliefs that they were "fairy forts." While this site is unexcavated, archaeologists have found evidence that people have lived on this peninsula since well before 4000 B.C.

11.7 km: Look ahead up Mount Eagle at the patchwork of stone-fenced fields.

12.5 km: Dunbeg Fort (50 yards downhill on the left) is made up of a series of defensive ramparts and ditches around a central *clochan* (€3, May-Sept 9:00-18:00, July-Aug until 19:00, includes video at nearby Stone House). A chunk of the fort was lost in February 2014, when waves from fierce winter storms caused a quarter of it to fall into the sea. Forts like this are the most important relics left from Ireland's Iron Age (500 B.C.-A.D. 500).

The modern stone-roofed dwelling across the street was built to blend in with the landscape and the region's ancient rock-slab architecture (A.D. 2000). It's the **Stone House,** a recommended and friendly restaurant with an adjacent visitors center, where you can check out a 10-minute video that gives a bigger picture of the prehistory of the peninsula (included with Dunberg Fort ticket). A traditional *currach* boat is permanently dry-docked in the parking lot.

12.6 km: Roughly 50 yards up the hill is a thatched **cottage** abandoned by a family named Kavanaugh 165 years ago, during the famine. With a few rusty and chipped old artifacts and good descriptions, it offers an evocative peek into the simple lifestyles of the area in the 19th century (€3, family-€10, daily 10:00-18:00, closed Nov-April, tel. 066/915-6241, mobile 087-762-2617). The owner, Gabriel, also runs working sheep dog demonstrations (in Irish for the dogs, English for tourists; €5/person, must book ahead at the mobile number above, www.dinglesheepdogs.com).

13.4 km: A group of **beehive huts** *(clochans)* is a short walk uphill (€3, daily 9:00-19:00, WC). These mysterious stone igloos, which cluster together within a circular wall, are a better sight than the similar group of beehive huts a mile down the road. Look over the water for more Skellig views.

Farther on, you'll ford a stream. There's never been a bridge here; this bit of road—nicknamed the "upside-down bridge"—was designed as a ford.

14.9 km: Pull off to the left at this second group of beehive huts. Look downhill at the rocky field—in the movie *Far and Away,* that's where Lord Ventry evicted (read: torched) peasants from their cottages. Even without Hollywood, this is a bleak and godforsaken land. Look above, at the patches of land slowly made into **farmland** by the inhabitants of this westernmost piece of Europe. Rocks were cleared and piled into fences. Sand and seaweed were laid on the clay, and in time it was good for grass. The created land, if at all tillable, was generally used for growing potatoes; otherwise, it was only good for grazing. Much of it has fallen out of use now. Look across the bay at the Ring of Kerry in the distance and ahead at the Blasket Islands (Na Blascaodaí).

16.1 km: At **Slea Head** (Ceann Sléibhe)—marked by a crucifix, a pullout, and great views of the Blasket Islands (described later)—you turn the corner on this tour. On stormy days, the waves are "racing in like white horses."

16.9 km: Pull into the little parking lot (at *Dún Chaoin* sign) for **views** of the Blasket Islands and Dunmore Head (the westernmost point in Europe) and to review the roadside map (which traces your route) posted in the parking lot. The scattered village of Dunquin (Dún Chaoin) has many ruined rock homes abandoned during the famine. Some are fixed up, as this is a popular place these days for summer homes. You can see more good examples of land reclamation, patch by patch, climbing up the hillside. Mount Eagle was the first bit of land that Charles Lindbergh saw after crossing the Atlantic on his way to Paris in 1927. Villagers here were as excited as he was—they had never seen anything so big in the air. About a kilometer down a road on the left, a plaque celebrates the 30th anniversary of the filming of *Ryan's Daughter*. From here, a trail leads down to a wild beach.

19.3 km: The Blasket Islands' residents had no church or cemetery on the island. This was their **cemetery.** The famous Blascaod

storyteller Peig Sayers (1873-1958) is buried in the center. At the next intersection, drive down the little lane that leads left (100 yards) to a small stone marker (hiding in the grass on the left) commemorating the 1588 shipwreck of the *Santa María de la Rosa* of the Spanish Armada. Below that is the often-tempestuous Dunquin Harbor. Island farmers—who on a calm day could row across in 30 minutes—would dock here and hike 12 miles into Dingle to sell their produce.

19.4 km: Back on the main road, follow signs to the *Ionad An Blascaod Mór* (Great Blasket Centre). You'll pass a village school from 1914 (its two teachers still teach 18 students, grades one through six).

22.3 km: Leave the Slea Head Road, turning left for the **Great Blasket Centre** (provides a worthwhile introduction to Blasket Islands—see page 278; also has a good cafeteria).

23.1 km: Back at the turnoff, head left (sign to *Louis Mulcahy Pottery*).

23.2 km: *Ryan's Daughter* film buffs will take a left turn here (a gravel lane) to visit the **schoolhouse** built for crucial scenes in

Building a Rock Fence

The Emerald Isle is as rocky as it is green. When the English took the best land, they told the Irish to "go to hell or go to Connaught" (the rugged western part of Ireland where the soil was particularly poor and rocky). Every spring, farmers "harvest" rocks driven up by the winter frost in order to plant more edible fare. Over generations, Irish farmers stacked these rocks into fences, which still divide so much of the land.

The fences generally have no visible gates. But upon closer look, you'll see a "V" built into the wall by larger rocks, which are then filled in with smaller rocks. When a farmer needs to move some cattle, he slowly unstacks the smaller rocks, moves the cattle through, and then restacks them. Flying low over western Ireland, the fields—alligatored by these rock fences—seem to stretch forever. And nearly all have these labor-intensive V-shaped gates built in.

that movie. Drive down the lane a hundred yards and park at the dead end. Walk the trail another hundred yards (through a couple of kissing gates), and you'll see the schoolhouse below, ringed by a low stone wall. Never intended to be a permanent structure, it's the only building still standing from that outdoor movie set of more than 40 years ago—and it's falling apart, too. But the lonely setting is memorable.

24.5 km: Passing land that was never reclaimed, think of the work it took to pick out the stones, pile them into fences, and bring up sand and seaweed to nourish the clay and make soil for growing potatoes. Look over the water to the island aptly named the **"Sleeping Giant"**—see his hand resting happily on his beer belly.

24.9 km: Grab the **scenic pullout.** The view is spectacular. Ahead, on the right, study the top fields, untouched since the planting of 1845, when the potatoes didn't grow, but rotted in the ground. The faint vertical ridges of the potato beds can still be seen—a reminder of the famine (easier to see a bit later). Before the famine, 40,000 people lived on this peninsula. After the famine, the population was so small that there was never again a need to farm so high up. Today, only 10,000 live on the peninsula.

The lousy farmland on both sides of the straight stretch of road was stripped of seven feet of peat (turf) in the 19th century. The land may have provided a lot of warmth back then...but it provides no food today.

A breezy 15-minute walk leads out to **Clogher Head.** The dirt road stretches off to the left and peters out after 200 yards. But it's all open ground and easy to navigate. Just step carefully over bog puddles and head uphill through the rocky heather to the lumpy summit. There you'll be rewarded with postcard-worthy panoramic views.

30 km: The town of **Ballyferriter** (Baile an Fheirtearaigh), established by a Norman family in the 12th century, is the largest on this side of Dingle. The pubs serve grub, and the old schoolhouse is a museum. Its modest exhibits provide the best coverage of this very historic peninsula (€2.50, hours vary but usually daily 10:00-17:00, closed Oct-May, tel. 066/915-6333, www.westkerrymuseum.com). The early Christian slab cross in front of the schoolhouse looks real. Tap it...it's fiberglass—a prop from the *Ryan's Daughter* bus-stop scenes.

31.9 km: At the T-junction, signs direct you left to *Daingean Ui Chuis* (Dingle, 11 km). Go left, via *Galros* (and still following *Ceann Sléibhe/Slea Head Drive* signs). Take a right over the barely noticeable yellow bridge, following signs to *Galros* (or *Gallarus*).

32 km: A few yards beyond the bridge, you'll pass the Tigh Bhric pub on the right. Fifty yards up on the right is the easy-to-miss sign to *Mainistir Riaisc* (Reasc Monastery), detour right up the lane. After 0.3 km (up the unsigned turnout on your right), you'll find the scant remains of the walled **Reasc Monastery** (dating from the 6th to 12th centuries, free, always open). The inner wall divided the community into sections for prayer and business (cottage industries helped support the monastery). In 1975, only the stone pillar was visible, as the entire site was buried. The layer of black tar paper (near the base of the walls) marks where the original rocks stop and the excavators' reconstruction begins. The stone pillar is Celtic (c. 500 B.C.).

When the Christians arrived in the fifth century, they didn't throw out the Celtic society. Instead, they carved a Maltese-type cross over the Celtic scrollwork. The square building was an oratory (church—you'll see an intact oratory at the next stop). The round buildings would have been *clochan*s—those stone igloo-type dwellings. One of the cottage industries operated by the monastery was a double-duty kiln. Just outside the wall (opposite the oratory, past the duplex *clochan*, at the bottom end), find a stone hole with a passage facing the southwest wind. This was the kiln—fanned by the wind, it was used for cooking and drying grain. Locals would bring their grain to be dried and ground, and the monks would keep a 10 percent tithe. With the arrival of the Normans in the 12th century, these small religious communities were replaced by relatively big-time state and church governments.

32.8 km: Return to the main road, and continue to the right.

34.6 km: At the big hotel (Smerwick Harbor), turn left following the sign to *Gallarus/Galros* (Gallarus Oratory; rhymes with walrus).

35.6 km: At the big building (with the *camping* sign), make a

Gallarus Oratory Area

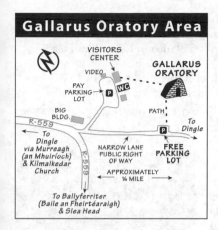

hard right up the long lane bordered by hedges. To park for free near the **Gallarus Oratory,** continue along this lane (between the dashed lines) for a quarter-mile, to a five-car parking lot—which occasionally fills up (be prepared to cooperate with other drivers exiting this small lot). From the free parking lot, a sign points you up the fuchsia-hedge-lined path leading you to the oratory (about 100 yards away).

If, however, you don't mind paying €3 to park, veer left just at the start of the hedge-lined lane into a large paved parking area. Nearby is a small visitors center with a coffee shop, WC, and video theater. I prefer to park for free in the small lot (especially since it's closer to the oratory). But many will appreciate the large lot, handy WC, and informative 17-minute video overview of the Dingle Peninsula's historic sights (daily 9:00-21:00, Oct-April until 19:00, tel. 066/915-5333). This visitors center is the business initiative of a man who simply owns the adjacent land—not the oratory. If you park in his lot, you'll have to pay the fee, even if you skip the facilities and walk up the public right-of-way lane.

The Gallarus Oratory, built about 1,300 years ago, is one of Ireland's best-preserved early Christian churches. Shaped like an upturned boat, its finely fitted drystone walls are still waterproof. Lower your head (notice how thick the walls are), walk inside, and give your eyes a moment to adjust to the low light. A simple, small arched window offers scant daylight to the opposite wall, where the

altar would have stood. Picture the interior lit by candles during medieval monastic services. It would have been tough to fit more than about a dozen monks inside (especially if they decided to do jumping jacks). Notice the holes once used to secure covering at the door, and the fine alternating stonework on the corners.

From the oratory, return to the main road and continue, following the brown *Ceann Sléibhe/Slea Head Drive* signs. If instead you continue up the narrow lane from the free parking lot, you'll end up on R-559 (a shortcut to Dingle that misses the Kilmalkedar Church ruins).

37.7 km: Bear right at the fork and immediately take a right at the next fork. Here you leave the Slea Head Drive and head for Dingle (10 km away) by staying on R-559 (**do not** follow Slea Head Drive from this point onward).

39.5 km: The **ruined church of Kilmalkedar** (Cill Mhaoil-cheadair, on the left) was the Norman center of worship for this end of the peninsula. It was built when England replaced the old monastic settlements in an attempt to centralize their rule. The 12th-century Irish Romanesque church is surrounded by a densely populated graveyard (which has risen noticeably above the surrounding fields over the centuries). In front of the church, you'll find the old-

est medieval tombs, a stately early Christian cross (substantially buried by the rising graveyard and therefore oddly proportioned), and a much older ogham stone. This stone, which had already stood here 900 years when the church was built, is notched with the mysterious Morse code-type ogham script used from the third to seventh centuries. It marked a grave, indicating this was a pre-Christian holy spot. The hole was drilled through the top of the stone centuries ago as a place where people would come to seal a deal—standing on the graves of their ancestors and in front of the house of God, they'd "swear to God" by touching thumbs through this stone. You can still use this to renew your marriage vows (free, B.Y.O. spouse). The church fell into ruin during the Reformation.

40.2 km: Continue uphill, overlooking the water. You'll pass another **"fairy fort"** (Ciher Dorgan) on the right dating back to 1000 B.C. (free, go through the rusty kissing gate). The bay stretched out below you is Smerwick Harbor. In 1580 a force of 600 Italian and Spanish troops (sent by the pope to aid a rebellion against the Protestant English) surrendered at this bay to the English. All 600 were massacred by the English forces, which included Sir Walter Raleigh.

41.7 km: At the crest of the hill, enjoy a three-mile-long coast back into Dingle town (sighting, as old-time mariners did, on the Eask Tower).

46.3 km: *Tog Bog É* means "take it easy." At the T-junction, turn left. Then turn right at the roundabout.

47.5 km: You're back in Dingle town. Well done.

Blasket Islands

This rugged group of six islands (Na Blascaodaí) off the tip of Dingle Peninsula seems particularly close to the soul of Ireland. The population of Great Blasket Island (An Blascaod Mór), once home to as many as 160 people, dwindled until the government moved the last handful of residents to the mainland in 1953. Life here was hard, but the sea provided for all, and no one went hungry. Each family had a cow, a few sheep, and a plot of potatoes. They cut their peat from the high ridge and harvested fish from the sea. To these folk, World War I provided a bonus, as occasional valuable cargo washed ashore from merchant ships sunk by U-boats. There was no priest, pub, or doctor. Because they were not entirely dependent upon the potato, island inhabitants survived the famine relatively unscathed. These people formed the most traditional Irish community of the 20th century—the symbol of ancient Gaelic culture.

A special closeness to an island—combined with a knack for vivid storytelling—is inspirational. From this simple but proud fishing/farming community came three writers of international repute whose Gaelic works—basically tales of life on Great Blasket Island—have been translated into many languages. You'll find *Peig* (by Peig Sayers) and *The Islandman* (Thomas O'Crohan) in shops everywhere. But the most readable and upbeat is *Twenty Years A-Growing* (Maurice O'Sullivan), a somewhat-true, Huck Finn-esque account of the author's childhood and adolescence and of island life as it was a hundred years ago.

The island's café closed down some time ago, but the simple hostel reopened several years ago on a seasonal basis (see page 262). Today Great Blasket is little more than a ghost town overrun with rabbits on a peaceful, grassy, three-mile-long poem.

Getting There: In summer, various boats run between Dingle town and the Blasket Islands. The ride (which may include a quick look at Fungie the dolphin) traces the spectacular coastline all the way to Slea Head. The boats offer similar services from Dingle town and operate when there's enough demand. These boats also do three-hour eco-tours for those interested in puffins, dolphins, and seals. The tricky landing at Great Blasket Island's primitive and slippery little boat ramp makes getting off a challenge and landing virtually impossible in wet weather (€40 same-day round-trip; generally departs from the marina pier in Dingle at 11:00 and returns from Great Blasket at 15:00, includes 45-minute ride each way with 3 hours to explore the island, call to confirm sailing times—or for more details on the €60 eco-tours—at tel. 066/915-1344 or mobile 087-672-6100).

▲▲Great Blasket Centre (Ionad An Blascaod Mór)

Note that this sight isn't on the Blasket Islands, but on the mainland facing the islands. It's an essential stop before visiting the islands—or a good place to learn about them without making the crossing (fits neatly with my recommended "Dingle Peninsula Loop Trip," earlier).

This state-of-the-art Blascaod and Gaelic heritage center gives visitors the best look possible at the language, literature, and way of life of Blasket Islanders. The building's award-winning design mixes interpretation and the surrounding countryside. Its spine, a sloping village lane, leads to an almost sacred view of the actual island. Don't miss the exceptional 20-minute video (shows on the half-hour), then hear the sounds, read the poems, browse through old photos, and gaze out the big windows at those rugged islands... and imagine. Even if you never got past limericks, the poetry of these people—so pure and close to each other and nature—will have you dipping your pen into the cry of the birds.

Cost and Hours: €5, Mon-Sat 10:00-18:00, Sun 11:00-18:00, closed Nov-Easter, fine cafeteria run by friendly Christy (who was featured as a little "Celtic warrior child" in the June 1981 edition of *National Geographic*), well-signposted on the Slea Head Drive near Dunquin/Dún Chaoin, tel. 066/915-6444.

Tralee

While Killarney is the tour-bus capital of County Kerry, Tralee (Trá Lí in Irish, both pronounced Tra-LEE) is its workaday market and transit hub. For drivers zipping between Dingle and Galway, this amiable town near the base of the Dingle Peninsula is worth an hour's stop.

The town comes alive for the famous Rose of Tralee International Festival, usually held in mid-August. It's a celebration of arts and music, culminating in the election of the Rose of Tralee—the most beautiful woman at the festival (no matter which country she was born in, as long as she has Irish heritage).

Sights in Tralee

▲Kerry County Museum

Easily the best place to learn about life in Kerry, this museum (located in Ashe Memorial Hall in the center of town) has three parts: Kerry slide show, museum, and medieval-town walk.

Cost and Hours: €5; daily 9:30-17:30, Oct-May until 17:00 and closed Sun-Mon; tel. 066/712-7777, www.kerrymuseum.ie.

Visiting the Museum: Get in the mood by relaxing for 10 minutes through the Enya-style continuous slide show of Kerry's spectacular scenery. Then wander through 7,000 years of Kerry history in the museum (well-described, no need for free headphones). The Irish joke that when a particularly stupid guy moved from Cork to Kerry, he raised the average IQ in both counties—but this museum is pretty well done. It starts with good background info on the archaeological sites of Dingle, progresses through Viking artifacts found in the area, and goes right up to a video showing highlights of the Kerry football team (a fun look at Irish football, which is more like rugby than soccer). Good coverage is given to adventurous Kerryman Tom Crean, who survived three Antarctic expeditions with Scott and Shackleton (see sidebar on page 254). The lame finale is a stroll back in time on a re-creation of Tralee's circa-1450 Main Street. Before leaving, horticulture enthusiasts will want to ramble through the rose garden in the adjacent park.

Blennerville Windmill

On the western edge of Tralee, just off the N-86 Dingle road, spins a restored mill originally built in 1780. Its eight-minute video tells the story of the windmill, which ground grain to feed Britain as

that country steamed into the Industrial Age. In the 19th century, Blennerville was a major port for America-bound emigrants. It was also the home port where the *Jeanie Johnston* was built. This modern-day replica of a 19th-century ship occasionally tours Atlantic ports, explaining the Irish emigrant experience. Most of the time, it's docked and available to tour in Dublin, on the north shore of the River Liffey (see page 72).

Cost and Hours: €5 gets you a one-room emigration exhibit, the video, and a peek at the spartan interior of the working windmill; daily June-Aug 9:00-18:00, April-May and Sept-Oct 9:30-17:30, closed Nov-March, last entry 45 minutes before closing, tel. 066/712-1064.

Tralee Connections

Travelers headed for Dingle using public transportation will likely find themselves passing through Tralee.

From Tralee by Train to: Dublin (every 2 hours, 6/day on Sun, 1 direct in morning, otherwise change in mellow Mallow, 4 hours), **Killarney** (8/day, 35 minutes). Train info: Tel. 066/712-3522, www.irishrail.ie.

By Bus to: Dingle (5/day, fewer off-season and on Sun, 1.5 hours), **Galway** (8/day, 4.5 hours), **Limerick** (7/day, 2 hours), **Doolin/Cliffs of Moher** (2/day, 5 hours), **Ennis** (6/day, 3.5 hours, change in Limerick), **Rosslare** (2/day, 7.5 hours), **Shannon** (7/day, 3 hours), **Dublin** (7/day, 6 hours). Tralee's bus station is across the parking lot from the train station. Bus info: Tel. 066/716-4700, www.buseireann.ie.

By Plane: Kerry Airport is a 20-minute drive from Tralee and a one-hour drive from Dingle (airport code: KIR, tel. 066/  976-4644, www.kerryairport. ie). It's just off the main N-22 road, halfway between Killarney and Tralee. It has a half-dozen handy rental-car outlets and an ATM. Dingle Shuttle Bus is your best connection to Dingle town, but you must reserve in advance (€20/person one-way, minimum 3 passengers, mobile 087-250-4767, www. dingleshuttlebus.com). You can also connect to the airport via taxi (€25 from Tralee, €75 from Dingle) or bus (3/day to Dingle via Tralee). The Kerry Airport offers connecting flights from **Dublin** on Aer Lingus (2/day, www.aerlingus.com). International destinations served from this tiny airport include London's Stanstead and Luton airports as well as Frankfurt Hahn airport.

Route Tips for Drivers: If you're **driving to Dingle,** you have two choices as you enter the neck of the Dingle Peninsula: the narrow, but very exciting, Conor Pass road; or the faster, easier, N-86 through Lougher and Annascaul (Abhainn an Scáil). On a clear day, Conor Pass comes with incredible views over Tralee Bay and Brandon Bay. On the north slope approaching the pass, pull out at the waterfall. From here, there's a fun five-minute scramble to a dramatic little glacier-created lake. Pause also at the summit viewpoint to look down on Dingle town and harbor.

If you're **driving from Dingle,** heading north straight to Galway, the inland Limerick route is fastest and cheapest (roughly €2 in tolls). But if you're going to the Cliffs of Moher and the Burren, the 20-minute Killimer-Tarbert ferry connection allows you to avoid the 80-mile detour around the River Shannon and is more scenic (€18/carload, departs hourly, June-Sept every 30 minutes; generally departs :30 past the hour going north and on the hour going south—check timetables online; no need to reserve, tel. 065/905-3124, www.shannonferries.com).

COUNTY CLARE & THE BURREN

Ennis • Cliffs of Moher • Doolin • Lisdoonvarna • The Burren • Ballyvaughan • Kinvarra • Irish Workhouse Centre

Those connecting Dingle in the south with Galway up the coast to the north can entertain themselves along the way by joyriding through the fascinating landscape and tidy villages of County Clare. Ennis, the county's major city, is a workaday Irish place with a medieval history and a market bustle—ideal for anyone tired of the tourist crowds. Overlooking the Atlantic, the dramatic Cliffs of Moher offer tenderfeet a thrilling hike. The Burren is a unique, windblown limestone moonscape that hides an abundance of flora, fauna, caves, and history. Contemplate the country's economic and social struggles at the Irish Workhouse Centre in Portumna. For your evening entertainment, you can join a tour-bus group in a castle for a medieval banquet in Kinvarra or meet up with traditional Irish music enthusiasts from around Europe for tin-whistling in Doolin.

PLANNING YOUR TIME

By Car: A car is the best way to experience County Clare and the Burren. The region can be an enjoyable daylong drive-through or a destination in itself. None of the sights has to take much time. But do get out and walk a bit.

If you're driving from Dingle to Galway, I'd recommend the following day plan. Rather than taking the main N-21 road via Limerick, drive north from Tralee on the N-69 via Listowel to catch the Tarbert-Killimer car ferry (avoiding Limerick's rush-hour traffic; even though the ferry is slower and more expensive, it's more direct to the Burren; see "Route Tips for Drivers" at the end of the previous chapter). From Killimer, drive north on N-67 via Kilkee and Milltown Malbay. The little surfer-and-golfer village

County Clare & the Burren

of Lahinch makes a good lunch stop. Then drive the coastal route to the Cliffs of Moher for an hour-long break. (You could wait to eat at the cafeteria at the cliffs, but big-bus tour groups can clog it at midday in summer.) The scenic drive from the cliffs through the Burren, with a couple of stops, takes about two hours. Consider partaking in the 17:30 medieval banquet at Dunguaire Castle, near Kinvarra (just 30 minutes south of Galway).

By Train or Bus: Using public transportation, your gateways to this region are Ennis from the south and Galway from the north; Limerick (via Ennis) and Galway are connected by rail—a big plus for those staying in Ennis without a car. Linking the smaller sights within County Clare and the Burren by bus is difficult: Book a tour instead (see "Tours in the Burren").

Tips: Visit an **ATM** in Ennis, Galway, or Lahinch before you enter this region (there are no ATMs in Doolin, Lisdoonvarna, Kilfenora, or Ballyvaughan). Skip the **Bunratty Castle and Folk Park**—I'd leave this most commercial and least lively of all European open-air folk museums to the jet-lagged, big-bus American tour groups (it's located just a potty stop from the Shannon Airport, past Limerick on the road to Ennis).

COUNTY CLARE & THE BURREN

Tours in the Burren

WALKING TOURS

Most travelers zip through the seemingly barren Burren without stopping, grateful for the soft soil they garden back home. But healthy hikers and armchair naturalists may want to slow down and take a closer look. Be sure to wear comfortable shoes for the wet, uneven, rocky bedrock. These guides can bring the harsh landscape to life.

From Oughtmama, Bellharbour (between Ballyvaughan and Kinvarra): **Burren Wild Tours**' motto, "Don't be nuts, get off the bus," distinguishes its active hiking focus from other, more sedate tour outfits. They offer a two-hour walk and a more rugged 2.5-hour hike (walk-€20/person, daily at 10:00; hike-€30/person, 12:15 by appointment only, call ahead for meeting place directions, mobile 087-877-9565, www.burrenwalks.com).

From Ballyvaughan (at the northern entrance to the Burren): **Shane Connolly** leads in-depth, three-hour guided walking tours, explaining the region's history, geology, and diverse flora, and the role humans have played in shaping this landscape. This proud farmer really knows his stuff (€15, daily at 10:00 and 15:00, call to book and confirm meeting place in Ballyvaughan, tel. 065/707-7168, http://homepage.eircom.net/~burrenhillwalks).

From Kilfenora (at the southern entrance to the Burren): **Tony Kirby** leads regularly scheduled two-hour "Heart of Burren Walks" during the summer, and the rest of the year by appointment. His expertise peels back the rocky surface to reveal the surprisingly fascinating natural and human history that has created this unique region (€20, June-Aug Tue-Thu at 10:30, Fri-Sun at 14:15, meet at the Burren Centre in Kilfenora, tel. 065/682-7707, mobile 087-292-5487, www.heartofburrenwalks.com, info@heartofburrenwalks.com).

BUS TOURS

From Galway: Three Galway-based companies—**Lally Tours, Healy Tours,** and **Galway Tour Company**—run standard all-day bus tours of nearby regions (€20-25, up to 25 percent discount if you book online). Their similar tours of the Burren do a loop south of Galway, covering Kinvarra, Aillwee Cave, Poulnabrone Dolmen, and the Cliffs of Moher (on a 2-hour lunch stop). Galway Tour Company also offers a €45 all-day tour connecting the Cliffs of Moher, Doolin (lunch stop), and the island of Inisheer—a handy way to get a quick taste of an Aran Island and the cliffs in one day.

Tours depart at 9:45 (except Galway Tour Company's Moher/Doolin/Inisheer tour, which leaves at 9:00) and get you back by about 17:30 (departing from Galway's private coach station on Fairgreen Road—across from TI; call to confirm exact itinerary: Lally Tours tel. 091/562-905, www.lallytours.com; Healy Tours tel. 091/770-066, mobile 087-259-0160, www.healytours.ie; Galway Tour Company tel. 091/566-566, www.galwaytourcompany.com, info@galwaytourcompany.com). All three companies also offer all-day tours of Connemara, with discounts if you book two separate tours. Drivers take cash only; to pay with a credit card, book in advance.

From Ennis: Barratt Tours runs tours of the Burren and Cliffs of Moher (see page 288).

County Clare

Ennis

This bustling market town (pop. 24,000), the main town of County Clare, provides those relying on public transit with a handy transportation hub (good rail connections to Limerick, Dublin, and Galway). Ennis is 15 miles from Shannon Airport and makes a good first- or last-night base in Ireland for travelers not locked into Dublin flights. It also offers a chance to wander around an Irish town that is not reliant upon the tourist dollar (though not shunning it either). Muhammad Ali visited the town in 2008 after discovering that one of his great-grandfathers had been born in Ennis. Locals credit his success to his fightin' Irish side.

The center of Ennis is a tangle of contorted streets (often one-way). Use the steeple of Saints Peter and Paul Cathedral and the Daniel O'Connell monument column (at either end of the main shopping drag, O'Connell Street) as landmarks.

Orientation to Ennis

TOURIST INFORMATION
The TI is just off O'Connell Street Square (Mon-Sat 9:30-17:30, closed Sun year-round and Mon Oct-May; some lunchtime closures, tel. 065/682-8366).

COUNTY CLARE & THE BURREN

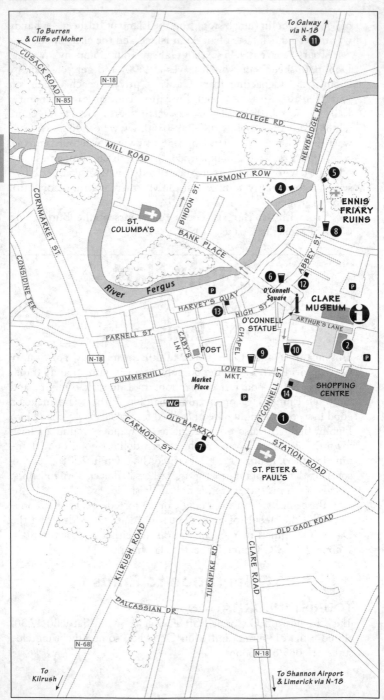

Ennis

1. Old Ground Hotel & Poet's Corner Pub
2. Temple Gate Hotel
3. Grey Gables B&B
4. Rowan Tree Hostel
5. The Cloisters Rest.
6. Knox's Pub & Bistro
7. Numero Uno Pizzeria
8. Cruise's Pub
9. Quinn's Pub
10. Brogan's Pub
11. To Cois na hAbhna Show
12. Ennis Bookshop
13. Launderette
14. Dunnes Stores (Grocery)

COUNTY CLARE & THE BURREN

NEW ROAD

River Fergus

CUSACK PARK STADIUM

FRANCIS STREET

ENNIS SHOPPING CENTRE

CLON ROAD

To Galway

GLÓR IRISH MUSIC CENTRE

PARKING GARAGE

→ One-way streets

FRIARS WALK

PARK AVE.

CLON ROAD

100 Meters

100 Yards

N

3

CLON ROADMOR

To Craggaunowen Open-Air Folk Museum

R-469

TRAIN & BUS STATION

To Limerick

ARRIVAL IN ENNIS

By Car: If you're not spending the night (i.e., stowing your car at your B&B), parking is best in one of several pay-and-display lots (€1.30/hour, enforced Mon-Sat 9:30-17:30, free on Sun, pay at meter in lot and display ticket on dashboard, usually 3-hour maximum). The centrally located multistory lot on Market Place Square charges €5 per day (Mon-Sat 7:30-19:30, closed Sun).

By Train or Bus: The train and bus station is located southeast of town, a 15-minute walk from the town center. To reach town, exit the station parking lot and turn left on Station Road, passing through a roundabout and past the recommended Grey Gables B&B. Turn right after the recommended Old Ground Hotel onto O'Connell Street.

By Plane: Shannon Airport is about 15 miles south of Ennis. For information, see "Shannon Airport" on page 293.

HELPFUL HINTS

Exchange Rate: €1 = about $1.10

Country Calling Code: 353 (see page 530 for dialing instructions)

Festivals: Two festivals (*fleadh,* pronounced "flah") may make it difficult to find accommodations: Fleadh Nua at the end of May and Fleadh Cheoil in mid-August. Check online for details: www.fleadhnua.com and www.fleadhcheoil.ie.

Post Office: It's on Bank Place (Mon-Fri 9:00-13:00 & 14:00-17:30, Sat 9:00-13:00, closed Sun).

Bookstore: The **Ennis Bookshop** has a good selection (Mon-Fri 9:30-18:30, Sat until 18:00, closed Sun, 13 Abbey Street, tel. 065/682-9000).

Laundry: Fergus launderette is opposite the Parnell Street parking lot (Mon-Sat 8:30-18:00, closed Sun, tel. 065/682-3122).

Supermarket: Dunnes Stores has a location in the shopping center on O'Connell Street (daily 8:00-22:00, Sun until 21:00).

Taxi: A good local bet is **Burren Taxis** (tel. 065/682-3456).

Walking Tours: Jane O'Brien leads 1.5-hour walking tours of Ennis departing from the TI (€10, mid-May-mid-Sept Mon-Tue and Thu-Sat at 11:00; no tours Wed, Sun, or off-season; mobile 087-648-3714, www.enniswalkingtours.com).

Bus Tours: Barratt Tours runs bus tours of the Cliffs of Moher and the Burren (€27, April-Oct daily, Nov-March Sat only, departs from the TI at 10:30 and returns by 17:30, call to confirm schedule, tel. 061/333-100, mobile 087-237-5986, www.4tours.biz).

Sights in Ennis

Clare Museum

This small but worthwhile museum, housed in the large TI building, has eclectic displays about ancient ax heads, submarine development, and local boys who made good—from 10th-century High King Brian Boru to 20th-century statesman Eamon de Valera. Coverage includes the Battle of Dysert O'Dea in 1318. One of the few Irish victories over the invading Normans, it delayed English domination of most of County Clare for another 200 years.

Cost and Hours: Free, Mon-Sat 9:30-12:30 & 14:00-17:00, closed Sun year-round and Mon Oct-May, tel. 065/682-1616, www.clarelibrary.ie.

Ennis Friary

The Franciscan monks arrived here in the 13th century, and the town grew up around their friary (which is like a monastery). Today, it's still worth a look for its 15th-century limestone carvings (now protected by a modern roof to keep their details from further deterioration).

Cost and Hours: €5, sometimes includes tour—depends on staffing, April-Sept daily 10:00-17:30, Oct until 17:00, closed Nov-March, tel. 065/682-9100.

Visiting the Friary: If more than one guide is on duty, ask for a brief introduction to the five carvings taken from the McMahon family tomb. The last one, of Christ rising on the third day, has a banner with a tiny swastika. But look closely: it's rotating as the rising sun would (the opposite of the infamous symbol of Nazism). Despite the swastika's detestable WWII association, it's actually a centuries-old symbol of good luck (the word "swastika" comes from Sanskrit and means "good"). Postwar visitors, unaware of the symbol's older meaning, misunderstood it and tried to rub it out of the carving, thus its very faint presence today.

The guides can also fully explain the crucifixion symbolism in the 15th-century *Ecce Homo* carving on a nearby pillar. Every item surrounding Christ on the cross has its own purposeful meaning (nothing on this carving is done just for the sake of decoration). It's a fascinating glimpse into how illiterate worshippers 600 years ago could understand icons even though they couldn't read.

NEAR ENNIS
▲Craggaunowen

This open-air folk museum nestles in a pretty forest, an easy 20-minute drive east of Ennis. All the structures are replicas, except for the small 16th-century castle (tower house), which the park was built around. A friendly weaver, spinning her wool on the castle's ground floor, is glad to tell you the tricks of her fuzzy

The Voyage of St. Brendan

It has long been part of Irish lore that St. Brendan the Navigator (A.D. 484-577) and 12 followers sailed from the southwest of Ireland to the "Land of Promise" (what is now North America) in a *currach*—a wood-frame boat covered with ox hide and tar. According to a 10th-century monk who poetically wrote of the journey, St. Brendan and his crew encountered a paradise of birds, were attacked by a whale, and suffered the smoke of a smelly island in the north before finally reaching their Land of Promise.

The legend and its precisely described locations still fascinate modern readers. Parts of the tale hold up: The smelly island could well be the sulfuric volcanoes of Iceland. Other parts seem like devoted delirium: The holy monks claimed to have come upon Judas, chained to a rock in the middle of the ocean for all eternity.

A British scholar of navigation, Tim Severin, re-created the entire journey in 1976-1977. He and his crew set out from Brendan Creek in County Kerry in a *currach*. The prevailing winds blew them to the Hebrides, the Faeroe Islands, Iceland, and finally to Newfoundland. While this didn't successfully prove that St. Brendan sailed to North America, it did prove that he could have. (You can visit Tim Severin's boat at the Craggaunowen open-air folk museum.)

According to his 10th-century biographer, "St. Brendan sailed from the Land of Promise home to Ireland. And from that time on, Brendan acted as if he did not belong to this world at all. His mind and his joy were in the delight of heaven."

trade. A highlight is the Crannog, a fortified Iron Age thatch-roofed dwelling built on a small man-made island, which gives you a grubby idea of how clans lived 2,000 years ago. A modern surprise hides in a corner of the park under a large glass teepee: the *Brendan*, the original humble boat that scholar Tim Severin sailed from Ireland to North America in 1976 (via frosty stepping stones like Iceland and Greenland). He built this boat out of tanned hides, sewn together using primitive methods, to prove that Ireland's St. Brendan may indeed have been the first to discover America on his legendary voyage, 900 years before Columbus and 500 years before the Vikings.

Cost and Hours: €9, Easter-Sept daily 10:00-17:00, shorter hours off-season, last entry one hour before closing, tel. 061/360-788, www.shannonheritage.com.

Getting There: The park is well-signposted nine miles (15 km) east of Ennis off R-469, which leads out of town past the train station.

Nightlife in Ennis

Glór Irish Music Centre

The town's modern theater center (*glór* is Irish for "sound") connects you with Irish culture. It's worth considering for traditional
music, dance, or storytelling performances.

Cost and Hours: €10-25, year-round usually at 20:00, 5-min-
ute walk behind TI, Friar's Walk, ticket office open Mon-Sat
10:00-17:00, closed Sun, tel. 065/684-3103, www.glor.ie.

Cois na hAbhna

This original stage show, housed in the local Cois na hAbhna Hall,
is a fine way to spend an evening. Sponsored by Comhaltas, a non-
profit focused on Irish traditional music, it's a celebration of Irish
performing arts presented in two parts. The first features great
Irish music, song, and dance. After the break, you're invited to kick
up your heels and take the floor as the dancers teach some famous
Irish set dances. Phone ahead to see if a *ceilidh* is scheduled on off
nights.

Cost and Hours: €10-15, sporadically May-Sept Wed and Fri
at 20:30, call ahead to confirm, at edge of town on N-18 Galway
road, tel. 065/682-4276, www.coisnahabhna.ie.

Traditional Music

Live music begins in the pubs at about 21:30. The best is **Cruise's**
on Abbey Street, with music nightly year-round and good food (bar
is cheaper than restaurant, tel. 065/682-8963). Other pubs offering
weekly traditional music nights (generally on weekends, but schedules vary) are **Quinn's** on Lower Market Street (tel. 065/682-8148)
and **Brogan's** on O'Connell Street (tel. 065/682-9480). The **Old
Ground Hotel** hosts live music year-round in its pub (Tue-Sun,
open to anyone); although tour groups stay at the hotel, the pub is
low-key and feels real, not staged.

Sleeping in Ennis

With central locations in mind, I've listed two fancy hotels that
you'll share with tour groups, a B&B, and a hostel. Book directly
with the hotel to get the best rates.

$$$ Old Ground Hotel is a stately, ivy-covered 18th-century
manse with 105 rooms and a family feel. Pan Am clipper pilots
stayed here during the early days of transatlantic seaplane flights
(2-night weekend stays include a dinner, a few blocks from station
at intersection of Station Road and O'Connell Street, tel. 065/682-
8127, www.flynnhotels.com, reservations@oldgroundhotel.ie).

$$ Temple Gate Hotel's 70 rooms are more modern and less
personal (breakfast extra, just off O'Connell Street, in courtyard

Sleep Code

Hotels are classified based on the average price of a typical en suite double room with breakfast in high season.

$$$$	**Splurge:** Most rooms over €170
$$$	**Pricier:** €130-170
$$	**Moderate:** €90-130
$	**Budget:** €50-90
¢	**Backpacker:** Under €50
RS%	Rick Steves discount

Unless otherwise noted, credit cards are accepted and free Wi-Fi is available. Comparison-shop by checking prices at several hotels (on each hotel's own website, on a booking site, or by email). For the best deal, *book directly with the hotel*. Ask for a discount if paying in cash; if the listing includes **RS%,** request a Rick Steves discount.

with TI, tel. 065/682-3300, www.templegatehotel.com, info@ templegatehotel.com).

$ Grey Gables B&B has 12 tastefully decorated rooms (cash only, wheelchair access, family rooms, parking, on Station Road 5 minutes from train station toward town center, tel. 065/682-4487, marykeane.ennis@eircom.net, Mary Keane).

¢ Rowan Tree Hostel is a well-run budget option, centrally located beside the gurgling River Fergus. It incorporates a grand old gentleman's club into its modern additions with better-than-expected private rooms and tidy dorm rooms. A pleasant café/bar rounds out the complex (on Harmony Row next to the bridge, tel. 065/686-8687, www.rowantreehostel.ie, info@rowantreehostel.ie).

Eating in Ennis

The Cloisters, next door to Ennis Friary, inhabits equally historic 800-year-old walls. Its steak, lamb, and fish dishes are the best in town and are served in a tasteful atmosphere (upstairs **$$$$ restaurant** Tue-Sun 17:30-21:00, downstairs **$$$ pub** Tue-Sun 12:00-17:30, both sections closed Mon, Abbey Street, tel. 065/686-8198).

The Old Ground Hotel serves up hearty meals in its **$$$ Poet's Corner pub** (Mon-Sat 12:00-21:00, Sun 16:00-21:00).

For better than average pub grub, I like **$ Knox's Pub & Bistro** on Abbey Street (daily 12:00-21:00, tel. 065/682-287). Or try one of the places mentioned under "Nightlife in Ennis," earlier.

The simple **$ Numero Uno Pizzeria** is good for an easy pub-free dinner (Mon-Sat 12:00-23:00, Sun from 15:00, on Old Barrack Street off Market Place, tel. 065/684-1740).

Restaurant Price Code

I've assigned each eatery a price category, based on the average cost of a typical main course. Drinks, desserts, and splurge items (steak and seafood) can raise the price considerably.

$$$$	**Splurge:** Most main courses over €25
$$$	**Pricier:** €20-25
$$	**Moderate:** €15-20
$	**Budget:** Under €15

In the Republic of Ireland, carryout fish-and-chips and other takeout food is **$;** a basic pub or sit-down eatery is **$$;** a gastropub or casual but more upscale restaurant is **$$$;** and a swanky splurge is **$$$$.**

Ennis Connections

From Ennis by Train to: Galway (5/day, 1.5 hours), **Limerick** (9/day, 40 minutes), **Dublin** (7/day, 3.5-4 hours, change in Limerick, Limerick Junction, or Athenry). Train info: Tel. 065/684-0444, www.irishrail.ie.

By Bus to: Galway (hourly, 1.5 hours), **Dublin** (almost hourly, 4-5.5 hours), **Rosslare** (2/day, 6.5 hours), **Limerick** (hourly, 1 hour), **Lisdoonvarna** (5/day, 1.5-3 hours), **Ballyvaughan** (1/day, 2-3 hours), **Tralee** (6/day, 3.5 hours, change in Limerick), **Doolin** (5/day, 1.5-2.5 hours). Bus info: Tel. 065/682-4177, www.buseireann.ie.

SHANNON AIRPORT

The major airport in western Ireland comes with far less stress than its overcrowded counterpart in Dublin (airport code: SNN, airport tel. 061/712-000, www.shannonairport.ie). It has a TI (daily 6:30-19:30, Oct-May until 17:30, tel. 061/471-664), ATMs, Wi-Fi, a change bureau, and a baggage storage desk. Direct flights link to New York, Boston, London, Edinburgh, and various destinations on the European continent.

From Shannon Airport by Bus to: Ennis (bus #51 runs between the airport and the Ennis train station hourly, 20 minutes after the hour starting at 8:20, 30 minutes), **Galway** (hourly, 1.75 hours), **Limerick** (hourly, 30-50 minutes, can continue to Tralee—2 hours more, and Dingle—4/day, another 2 hours; bus tel. 061/313-333, www.buseireann.ie).

Sleeping near Shannon Airport: Consider **$$ Park Inn by Radisson Shannon Airport** (tel. 061/471-122, www.parkinn.com).

Cliffs of Moher

A visit to the Cliffs of Moher (pro-nounced "MO-hur"...because who would visit the Cliffs of Less?)—a ▲▲▲ sight—is one of Ireland's great natural thrills. For five miles, the dramatic cliffs soar as high as 650 feet above the At-lantic.

GETTING THERE

The Cliffs of Moher are located on R-478, south of Doolin. The parking lot across the road from the visitors center is for the general public; pay the attendant as you drive in. The lot next to the visitors center is for tour buses and visitors with dis-abilities. If you're without wheels, you can get here by bus from Galway (8/day in summer, some with change in Ennis, 2 hours, €15.80 round-trip, www.buseireann.ie). Or—to see (but not visit) the cliffs—you can take a boat from Doolin (described later).

ORIENTATION TO THE CLIFFS OF MOHER

Cost: €6/person, includes parking and admission to the visitors center and its Atlantic Edge exhibit (buy tickets online for a 10 percent discount). It costs €2 to climb O'Brien's Tower (probably not worth it).

Hours: Daily May-Sept 9:00-19:30, gradually later closing times toward midsummer—as late as 21:00 July-Aug; Oct-April 9:00-17:00.

Information: You'll find a TI and ATM in the visitors center—the Tolkienesque building tucked under the grassy hill-side—flanked by six hobbit garages housing gift shops (across the street from the parking lot). Tel. 065/708-6141, www.cliffsofmoher.ie.

Eating: Long Dock restaurant, upstairs in the visitors center, serves coffee and substantial cafeteria-style meals until 19:00. There's also a small café downstairs.

VISITING THE CLIFFS OF MOHER

Start in the **visitors center,** built in a concentric-circle layout with local stone. Upstairs you'll find a photo diorama showing aerial views of the cliffs and underwater photos of local marine life. Also upstairs are the WCs, where you can enjoy a huge panoramic photo of the cliffs on the stall doors as you wait in line.

The **Atlantic Edge exhibit,** downstairs, focuses mainly on natural and geological history, native bird and marine life, and vir-

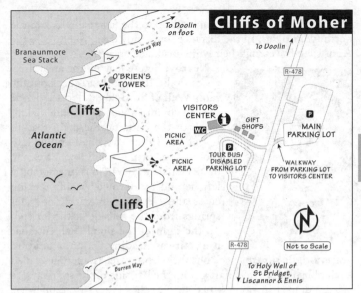

tual interactive exhibits aimed at children. You may even learn why the cliffs are always windy. A small theater with an IMAX-style screen shows *The Ledge,* a film following a gannet who's a Jonathan Livingston Seagull wannabe, as he flies along the cliffs and then dives underwater, encountering puffins, seals, and even a humpback whale along the way.

After leaving the visitors center, walk 200 yards to the **cliff** edge and along the wall of the local Liscannor slate. Notice the squiggles made by worms, eels, and snails long ago when the slate was still mud on the seafloor.

For years, the Irish didn't believe in safety fences, just natural selection. Anyone could walk right up to the cliffs, until numerous fatal accidents prompted the hiring of "rangers"—ostensibly there to answer questions and lead guided tours, but mainly there to keep you from getting too close to the edge (wind gusts can be sudden, strong, and deadly).

As you gaze down at the waves crashing far, far below you, consider this: Surfing in wet suits is popular in Ireland. Most sane Irish surfers stick to the predictable waves at Lahinch (5 miles south of here). But the monster waves that rear up beneath the Cliffs of Moher on stormy days are coveted by extreme surfers, who work in tandem with tow/rescue helpers skimming the waves on Jet Skis. Don't strain your eyes looking for them...there aren't too many surfers crazy enough to attempt this.

O'Brien's Tower, built in 1835, marks the highest point of the cliffs (but isn't worth the fee to climb...30 feet up doesn't improve the views much). Hike five minutes up to the tower and look to the north (your right). In the distance, on windy days, you can see the Aran Islands wearing their white necklace of surf.

Nearby: Before leaving the area, drivers can take 10 minutes to check out the **Holy Well of St. Bridget,** located beside the tall column about a half-mile (1 km) south of the cliffs on the main road to Liscannor. In the short hall leading into the hillside spring, you'll find a treasure of personal and religious memorabilia left behind by devoted visitors seeking cures and blessings. A trickle of water springs from the hillside at the far end. To the right of the simple hall entrance is a stairway heading up into a peaceful graveyard. Be sure to check out the wishing tree (sometimes called a fairy bush or rag tree) halfway up the left side of the stairway. It's usually draped in ribbons tied to branches. These were offerings to saints as part of a healing ritual. The simple gray column outside was a folly erected over 150 years ago by a local landlord with money and ego to burn.

CRUISIN' FROM DOOLIN

To get a different perspective of the cliffs (looking up instead of down), take a boat cruise along their base. Try for an afternoon cruise, when the sun is coming from the west, illuminating the detail on the dramatic cliffs. Two companies—**Doolin2Aran Ferries** (tel. 065/707-5949, mobile 087-245-3239, www.doolin2aranferries. com) and **O'Brien Line** (tel. 065/707-5618, www.obrienline. com)—offer almost identical cruises. Both make the one-hour voyage past sea stacks and crag-perching birds. Boats depart from the pier in Doolin (same dock as Aran Islands boat, €20, cheaper if booked online, runs daily April-Oct, 3/day, weather and tides permitting, call or go online for sailing schedule and to reserve). They also operate day-trip cruises from Doolin to Inisheer (the closest Aran Island—described in the Aran Islands chapter), then along the base of the Cliffs of Moher and back to Doolin (for details, see page 341).

Doolin

This town was once a strange phenomenon: It had long been a mecca for Irish musicians, who came together here to play before a few lucky aficionados. Many music lovers would come here directly from Paris or Munich, as the town was on the tourist map for its traditional music. But now crowds and the foreigners have overwhelmed the musicians, and the quality of music is not as reliable—I prefer Dingle's richer music scene. Still, as Irish and European fans crowd the pubs, the *bodhrán* beat goes on.

Doolin has plenty of accommodations and a Greek-island-without-the-sun ambience. The "town" is just a few homes and shops strung out along a valley road from the tiny harbor. Residents generally divide the town into an Upper Village and Lower Village. The Lower Village is the closest thing to a commercial center (meaning it has a couple of pubs and a couple of music shops). The Upper Village has a TI at Hotel Doolin that generally exists to book lodging and Aran Islands boat trips (mid-March-Oct daily 8:30-19:00, tel. 065/707-5642). You'll find a similar boat-booking outfit in the Lower Village; Doolin is without an official and un-biased TI.

The **Lodge Doolin** offers a handy grab bag of services, including recommended accommodations and a launderette (drop-off only, pick up clothes in 6 hours, daily 8:00-21:00). The staff can also recommend local horseback riding, hiking, and fishing options.

Activities in Doolin

Traditional Music

Doolin is famous for three pubs, all featuring Irish folk music: Nearest the harbor, in the Lower Village, is **Gus O'Connor's Pub** (tel. 065/707-4168). A mile farther up the road, the Upper Village—straddling a bridge—is home to two other destination pubs: **McGann's** (tel. 065/707-4133) and **McDermott's** (tel. 065/707-4328). Music starts in the pubs between 21:30 and 22:00, finishing at about midnight. Get there before 21:00 if you want a place to sit, or pop in later and plan on standing. The *craic* is fine regardless. Pubs serve decent dinners before the music starts. (**Alamo Cabs** is handy for folks without wheels wanting to link a night of fun in Doolin with a bed in Lisdoonvarna; mobile 086-235-3100.)

Hike or Cruise to the Cliffs of Moher

From Doolin, you can hike up the Burren Way along the coast for three miles to the Cliffs of Moher. Local guide and farmer Pat Sweeny operates **Doolin Cliff Walk,** leading walking tours that depart daily at 10:00 from O'Connor's Pub. The five-mile walk to the cliffs takes three hours and is not safe for kids under age 10; you catch the 13:30 bus back to Doolin (€5, May-Sept, mobile 086-822-9913, www.doolincliffwalk.com, phone ahead to reserve and check weather/trail conditions). Doolin also offers boat cruises along the Cliffs of Moher (see facing page).

Sleeping in Doolin

$$ Harbour View B&B offers six rooms in a fine modern house overlooking the coast a mile from the Doolin fiddles. Amy Lindner keeps the place immaculate (on main road halfway between Lisdoonvarna and Cliffs of Moher, next to Aran View Market and gas station, tel. 065/707-4154, www.harbourviewdoolin.com, clarebb@eircom.net).

$ The Lodge Doolin is a modern compound of four stone buildings with 21 bright, airy, good-value rooms (located halfway between Upper and Lower Villages, tel. 065/707-4888, mobile 087-223-9638, www.doolinlodge.com, info@doolinlodge.com). The lodge offers handy amenities (details listed earlier).

$$ Half Door B&B is the coziest place around, with six woody rooms and a pleasant sun porch. It's just a short walk from the best pubs in the Upper Village (cash only, family rooms, a keg's roll from McDermott's pub, tel. 065/707-5959, www.halfdoordoolin.com, ann@halfdoordoolin.com).

¢ Doolin Hostel, right in Doolin's Lower Village, caters creatively to the needs of backpackers in town for the music. Friendly Anthony and Dierdre are on top of the local scene (private rooms available, Lower Village, mobile 087-282-0587, www.doolinhostel.ie, anthony@doolinhostel.ie).

Eating in Doolin

The only gourmet option is **$$$ Cullinans,** facing the T-intersection as you come down the hill into the Upper Village (Easter-Sept Mon-Tue and Thu-Sat 18:00-21:00, closed Sept-Easter and Wed and Sun year-round, reservations smart in summer, tel. 065/707-4183, www.cullinansdoolin.com, info@cullinansdoolin.com).

The **$$ Ivy Cottage** in the Lower Village, just past the bridge, has a pleasant, leafy tea garden out front. They do a dish of the day as well as simple sandwiches, quiche, or chowder (daily 10:00-18:00). Next door, the **$ Sea Salt** chipper uses the same kitchen and does reasonable fish-and-chips to take away and enjoy with the coastal view of your choice (March-Oct daily 12:00-21:00).

Doolin has earned a reputation for consistently good pub grub. In the Lower Village, try **$$ Gus O'Connor's Pub,** and in the Upper Village, give **$$ McGann's** a spin. **Mac's Daybreak** is the town market (Mon-Sat 8:30-20:30, Sun 9:00-20:00, on R-478 above town next to the Harbour View B&B).

Doolin Connections

From Doolin by Bus to: Galway (5/day, 1.5 hours), **Ennis** (5/day, 1.5-2.5 hours). Buses depart from the recommended Doolin Hostel.

By Ferry to the Aran Islands: For the full rundown on ferries from Doolin, see page 341. In short, if you want to day-trip from Doolin, go with either **Doolin2Aran Ferries** (tel. 065/707-

5949, mobile 087-245-3239, www.doolin2aranferries.com) or **O'Brien Line** (tel. 065/707-5555, www.obrienline.com), both of which take you to the closest island, Inisheer (with time to explore), then back along the Cliffs of Moher. If you want to visit either or both of the farther islands—Inishmaan and Inishmore—plan on an overnight, due to the transit time involved.

Lisdoonvarna

Treated almost like an inland extension of Doolin, this town of 1,000 (4.3 miles/7 km from Doolin) is a bit bigger, with a few more amenities but no coastal charm. It was known for centuries for its spa, its matchmakers, and its traditional folk music festivals. Today, it's pretty sleepy, except for a few weeks in September, during its Matchmaking Festival (www.matchmakerireland.com), which partially inspired the 1997 film *The Matchmaker*. The nearest ATMs are in Lahinch or Ennistymon. Still, it's more of a town than Doolin and, apart from festival time, less touristy.

Sleeping in Lisdoonvarna: $ Ballinsheen House is the best value in town. It's perched on a hill with five tastefully decorated rooms and a pleasant, glassed-in breakfast terrace (parking, 5-minute walk north of town on N 67 Galway Road, tel. 065/707-4806, mobile 087-124-1872, www.ballinsheen.com, ballinsheenhouse@hotmail.com, Mary Gardiner).

Eating in Lisdoonvarna: The **$$ Roadside Tavern** is a favorite local hangout with filling pub grub, great atmosphere, and occasional traditional-music sessions (daily, tel. 065/707-4084, on N-67 in town tucked down behind the Spa Hotel in hard-to-miss bright red).

The Burren

Literally the "rocky place," the Burren is just that. This 10-square-mile limestone plateau, a ▲▲ sight, is so barren that a disappointed Cromwellian surveyor of the 1650s described it as "a savage land, yielding neither water enough to drown a man, nor a tree to hang him, nor soil enough to bury him." But he wasn't much of a botanist, because the Burren is in fact a unique ecosystem, with flora that has managed to adapt since the last Ice Age, 10,000 years ago. It's also rich in prehistoric and early Christian sites. This limestone land is  littered with hundreds of historic stone structures, including dozens of Iron Age stone forts. When the first human inhabitants of the Burren came about 6,000 years ago, they cut down its trees with shortsighted slash-and-burn methods, which accelerated erosion of the topsoil (already scoured to a thin layer by glaciers)—making those ancient people partially responsible for the stark landscape we see today.

❂SELF-GUIDED DRIVING TOUR

This self-guided drive from Kilfenora to Ballyvaughan offers the best quick swing through the historic Burren.

• Begin in the town of Kilfenora, eight kilometers (5 miles) southeast of Lisdoonvarna, at the T-intersection where R-476 meets R-481.

Kilfenora

This town's hardworking, community-run **Burren Centre** shows an informative 10-minute video explaining the geology and botany of the region, and then ushers you into its enlightening museum exhibits (€6, daily June-Aug 9:30-17:30, mid-March-May and Sept-Oct 10:00-17:00, closed Nov-mid-March, tel. 065/708-8030, www.theburrencentre.ie). You'll also see copies of a fine eighth-century golden collar and ninth-century silver brooch (originals in Dublin's National Museum).

The ruined **church** next door has a couple of 12th-century crosses, but there isn't much to see. Mass is still held in the church, which claims the pope as its bishop by papal dictate. As the smallest and poorest diocese in Ireland, Kilfenora was almost unable to function after the Great Potato Famine, so in 1866 Pope Pius IX supported the town as best he could—by personally declaring himself its bishop.

For lunch in Kilfenora, consider the cheap and cheery **Burren**

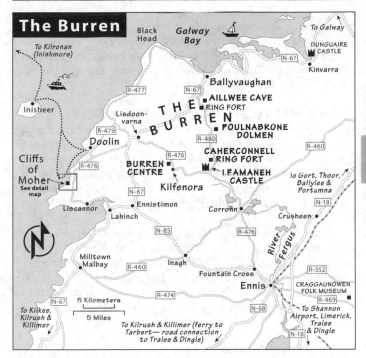

The Burren

Black Head · Galway Bay · To Galway

To Kilronan (Inishmore)

DUNGUAIRE CASTLE

N-67

Kinvarra

Inisheer

R-477 · N-67 · Ballyvaughan

AILLWEE CAVE
RING FORT

Lisdoon-varna

T H E · B U R R E N

POULNABRONE DOLMEN

R-479

R-480

Doolin

R-460

R-476 · CAHERCONNELL RING FORT

Cliffs of Moher
See detail map

R-478

BURREN CENTRE

LEAMANEH CASTLE

Kilfenora

To Gort, Thoor, Ballylee & Portumna

N-67

N-18

Liscannor · Ennistimon

Corrofin

Lahinch

Crusheen

N-85

R-476

Milltown Malbay

River Fergus

R-460 · Inagh

Fountain Cross

R-352

To Kilkee, Kilrush & Killimer

N-67

5 Kilometers

5 Miles

R-474

Ennis

CRAGGAUNOWEN FOLK MUSEUM

R-469

N-68

To Kilrush & Killimer (ferry to Tarbert— road connection to Tralee & Dingle)

To Shannon Airport, Limerick, Tralee & Dingle

N-18

Centre Tea Room (daily 9:30-17:30, located at far back of building) or the more atmospheric **Vaughan's Pub.** If you're spending the night in County Clare, make a real effort to join the locals at the fun set-dancing get-togethers run by the Vaughans in the **Barn Pub,** adjacent to their regular pub. This local dance scene is a memorable treat (€5, Sun at 21:30, may be more frequent in summer, call ahead to confirm schedule, tel. 065/708-8004).

• *To continue from Kilfenora into the heart of the Burren, head east out of town on R-476. After about five kilometers (3 miles), you'll come to the junction with northbound R-480. Take the sharp left turn onto R-480, and slow down to gaze up (on the left) at the ruins of...*

Leamaneh Castle

This ruined shell of a fortified house is closed to everyone except the female ghost that supposedly haunts it. From the outside, you can see how the 15th-century fortified tower house (the right quarter of the remaining ruin) was expanded 150 years later (the left three-quarters of the ruin). The castle evolved

from a refuge into a manor, and windows were widened to allow for better views as defense became less of a priority.

• *From the castle, continue north on R-480 (direction: Ballyvaughan). After about eight kilometers (5 miles), you'll hit the start of the real barren Burren. Keep an eye out for the next stop.*

Caherconnell (Cahercommaun) Ring Fort

One of many ring forts in the area, you can see the low stone profile of Caherconnell to the left on the crest of a hill just off the road. You can park in the gravel lot and walk up to the small visitors center and handy café for an informative 20-minute film followed by a quick wander through the small fort. The fort sometimes features a sheepherding demo with dogs (generally at 12:00 and 15:00—call to confirm).

Cost and Hours: €7, €9.60 includes sheepherding demo, daily July-Aug 10:00-18:00, Easter-June and Sept-Oct 10:30-17:30, closed Nov-Easter, tel. 065/708-9999, www.caherconnell.com.

• *The stretch from the ring fort north to Ballyvaughan offers the starkest scenery. Soon you'll see a 10-foot-high stone structure a hundred yards off the road to the right (east, toward an ugly gray metal barn). Pull over for a closer look.*

Poulnabrone Dolmen

While it looks like a stone table, this is a portal tomb. Two hundred years ago, locals called this a "druids' altar." Five thousand years ago, it was a grave chamber in a cairn of stacked stones. Amble over for a look. (It's crowded with tour buses at midday, but it's all yours early or late.)

Wander about for some quiet time with the wildflowers and try to think like a geologist. You're walking across a former seabed, dating from 250 million years ago when Ireland was at the equator (before continental drift nudged it north). Look for white smudges of fossils. Stones embedded in the belly of an advancing glacier ground the scratches you see in the rocks. The rounded boulders came south from Connemara, carried on a giant conveyor belt of ice, then left behind when the melting glaciers retreated north.

• *As you drive away from the dolmen (continuing north), look for the 30-foot-deep sinkhole beside the road on the right (a collapsed cave). From here, R-480 winds slowly downhill for about six kilometers (4 miles), eventually leaving the rocky landscape behind and entering a comparatively lush green valley. Watch for a broad left bend in the road*

Botany of the Burren in Brief

The Burren is a story of water, rock, geological force, and time. It supports the greatest diversity of plants in Ireland. Like nowhere else, Mediterranean and Arctic wildflowers bloom side by side in the Burren. It's an orgy of cross-pollination that attracts more insects than Doolin does music lovers—even beetles help out. Limestone, created from layers of coral, seashells, and mud, is the bedrock of the Burren. (The same formation resurfaces 10 miles or so out to sea to form the Aran Islands.)

Geologic forces in the earth's crust heaved up the land, and the glaciers swept it bare and shattered it like glass under their weight—dropping boulders as they receded. Rain, reacting naturally with the limestone to create a mild but determined acid, slowly drilled potholes into the surface. Rainwater cut through the limestone's weak zones, leaving crevices on the surface and one of Europe's most extensive systems of caves below. Algae grew in the puddles, dried into a powder, and combined with bug parts and rabbit turds (bunnies abound in the Burren) to create a very special soil. Plants and flowers fill the cracks in the limestone. Grasses and shrubs don't do well here, and wild goats eat any trees that try to grow, giving tender little blossoms a chance to enjoy the sun. Different blooms appear throughout the months, sharing space rather than competing. The flowers are best in June and July.

with a grove of trees beside the road on the left and park in the gravel pullout on the right, just opposite the grove. (It's not marked, but if you reach the Aillwee Cave right turn, you've gone 50 yards too far.) Get out of the car and carefully cross the busy road to find a...

Hidden Ring Fort

A grove of trees hides a gorgeous little secluded ring fort (free and unattended). Walk the rim of the circular earthen ring, stepping over roots, and notice the swampy moat beneath the outer edge. As Iron Age ring forts go, this one has a mystical vibe. Find the old stump in the center of the fort where old coins have been left undisturbed in the hopes of wishes coming true. A quiet 10 minutes here can be magic.

• *Just beyond, on the right, you'll find the turn up to...*

Aillwee Cave

As this is touted as "Ireland's premier show cave," I couldn't resist a look. While fairly touristy and not worth the time or money if you've seen a lot of caves, it's the easiest way to sample the massive system of caves that underlies the Burren. Your guide walks you 300 yards into the plain but impressive cave, giving a serious 40-minute geology lesson. During the Ice Age, underground rivers carved countless caves such as this one. Brown bears, which became extinct in Ireland a thousand years ago, found them great for hibernating. If you take the tour, you'll need a sweater: The cave is a constant 50°F.

Just below the cave (and on the same property) is the **Burren Birds of Prey Centre,** which houses owls, eagles, hawks, and falcons. During the demo talks, you'll see raptors in action and may be able to briefly hold one as the leather glove is passed around the crowd (bird demonstrations May-Aug at 12:00, 14:00, and 16:00, Sept-April at 12:00 and 15:00—but call for daily schedule).

Adjacent to the cave, the **Hawk Walk** gets visitors face-to-beak with a Harris hawk, "the world's only social raptor." After a brief training session, an instructor leads a small group on a 45-minute hike up a nearby mountain trail. Those paying the stiff €70 fee get to launch and call back the bird to perch on their arm (limited slots, must reserve).

Cost and Hours: Cave-€12, bird center-€10, €18 combo-ticket includes both sights but not Hawk Walk; open daily at 10:00, last tour at 18:30 July-Aug, otherwise 17:30, Dec-Feb call ahead for limited tours; clearly signposted just south of Ballyvaughan, tel. 065/707-7036, www.aillweecave.ie.

• *Continuing on, our final destination is...*

Kinvarra

This tiny town, between Ballyvaughan and Galway (30 minutes from each), is waiting for something to happen in its minuscule harbor. It faces Dunguaire Castle, a four-story tower house from 1520 that stands a few yards out in the bay.

The touristy but fun **Dunguaire Castle medieval banquet** is Kinvarra's most worthy attraction (€57, cheaper if you book online, mid-April-mid-Oct most evenings at 17:30 and sometimes at 20:30, closed mid-

Oct-mid-April, reservations required, tel. 061/360-788, castle tel. 091/637-108, www.shannonheritage.com). **Warning:** This company also operates banquets at two other castles in the region, so be sure that you make your reservation for the correct castle.

The evening is as intimate as a gathering of 55 tourists under one time-stained, barrel-vaulted ceiling can be. You get a decent four-course meal with wine (or mead if you ask sweetly), served amid an entertaining evening of Irish tales and folk songs. Remember that in medieval times, it was considered polite to flirt with wenches. It's a small and multitalented cast: one harpist and three singer/actors who serve the "lords and ladies" between tunes. The highlight is the 40-minute stage show, which features songs and poems by local writers, and comes with dessert.

You can visit the castle itself by day without taking in an evening banquet (€6, daily 10:00-16:30).

Sleeping in Kinvarra: $ Cois Cuain B&B is a small but stately house with a garden, overlooking the square and harbor of the most charming village setting you'll find. Mary Walsh rents three super-homey rooms (cash only, The Quay, tel. 091/637-119).

Irish Workhouse Centre

For those who want to see the Victorian "cure" for poverty, the Irish Workhouse Centre in Portumna is a memorable side-trip from Ennis or Kinvarra. This is one of the few remaining workhouses in Ireland. There were once 163; most were either knocked down or repurposed after Ireland's first step toward independence in 1922. Portumna's workhouse has been restored but not renovated; it stands in much the same condition it was when it was closed.

Cost and Hours: €7, March-Oct daily 9:30-17:00, closed Nov-Feb, St. Brigid's Road, Portumna, tel. 090/975-9200, http:// irishworkhousecentre.ie.

Getting There: The workhouse is about an hour east from Kinvarra or Ennis. As you enter Portumna, turn left at Bank of Ireland, continue on, and the Irish Workhouse Centre is on your right.

Tours: Helpful guides give 45-minute tours that add a human angle to the spartan buildings.

Visiting the Center: Workhouses were British institutions, set up by the government in the 1830s (unaware that Ireland's Great Potato Famine was less than a decade away) to provide vagrants with an alternative to starvation and death. However, as the government didn't want the "poorhouse" alternative to be too "tempting," punitive Poor Laws made them a gruesome alternative. In order to enter the poorhouse, you had to give up any assets you still had, and while you were allowed to enter with your family, you'd likely never see them again once you arrived. Men and women were housed separately; children were also separated by gender. Children over age three were expected to work. There were no common areas for mingling.

Imagine these grim surroundings during the Great Famine. Since their alternative was starvation, people flooded into these packed quarters—but since workhouses were often not funded properly, the inhabitants were also malnourished. Like cramped emigration "coffin ships," workhouses became transmission points for disease.

Law dictated that workhouses not compete with any local trades or businesses, and therefore they offered the dregs of labor, such as rock-breaking for men and corn-grinding for women. Unraveling old, worn rope and reweaving the salvageable strands into new rope was a task for anyone too weak to do heavy labor.

Life was bleak, food was scarce and of poor quality, and conditions were notoriously inhumane, especially for children. Ironically, it was cheaper for landlords to send paupers to North America than it was to keep them in poorhouses (workhouses were financed by a property tax). Another way to escape was to commit a crime: The food was better in prison, and the regimen was less strict.

GALWAY

Galway feels like a boomtown—rare in Western Ireland. Until the recession hit in 2008, it was the fastest growing city in Ireland. And it's still its most international city, as one out of every four residents was born outside of Ireland. With 76,000 people, Galway is the county's main city, a lively university town and the region's industrial and administrative center. As it's near the traditional regions of Connemara and the Aran Islands, it's also a gateway to these Gaelic cultural preserves.

While Galway has a long and interesting history, precious little from old Galway survives. What does remain has the interesting disadvantage of being built in the local limestone, which, even if medieval, looks like modern stone construction. The city's quincentennial celebration in 1984 awakened a spirit of preservation.

What Galway lacks in sights it makes up for in ambience. Spend an afternoon just wandering its medieval streets, with their delightful mix of colorful facades, labyrinthine pubs, weather-resistant street musicians, and steamy eateries. Galway also offers tourists plenty of traditional music, easy train connections to Dublin, and a convenient jumping-off point for a visit to the Aran Islands. After dark, blustery Galway heats up, with a fine theater and a pub scene that attracts even Dubliners. Visitors mix with old-timers and students as the traditional music goes round and round.

If you hear a strange language on the streets and wonder where those people are from, it's Irish, and so are they.

PLANNING YOUR TIME

Galway's sights are little more than pins on which to hang the old town. The joy of Galway is its street scene. You can see its sights

Galway's History

In 1234, the medieval fishing village of Galway went big time, when the Normans captured the territory from the O'Flaherty family. Making the town a base, the Normans invited in their Angle friends, built a wall (1270), and kicked out the Irish. Galway's Celtic name (Gaillimh) comes from an old Irish word, *gall*, which means "foreigner." Except for a small section in the Eyre Square Shopping Centre and a chunk at the Spanish Arch, that Norman wall is gone.

In the 14th century, 14 merchant families, or "tribes," controlled Galway's commercial traffic, including the lucrative wine trade with Spain and France. These English families constantly clashed with the local Irish. Although the wall was built to "keep out the O's and the Macs," it didn't always work. A common prayer at the time was, "From the fury of the O'Flahertys, good Lord deliver us."

Galway's support of the English king helped it prosper. But with the rise of Oliver Cromwell in the 1640s (see sidebar on page 174), Galway paid for that prosperity. After sieges by Cromwell's troops (in 1651) and those of Protestant King William of Orange (in 1691), Galway declined. It wasn't until the last half of the 20th century that it regained some of its importance and wealth.

in three hours, but without an evening in town, you've missed the best. Many spend three nights and two days: one for the town and another for a side-trip to the Burren (see previous chapter), the Aran Islands, or the Connemara region (see following chapters). Tour companies make day trips to all three regions cheap and easy.

Orientation to Galway

The center of Galway is Eyre (pronounced "air") Square. Within two blocks of the square, you'll find the TI, Aran boat offices, a tour pickup point, accommodations (from the best cheap hostel beds to fancy hotels), and the train station. The train and public bus station butt up against the Hotel Meyrick, a huge gray railroad hotel that overlooks and dominates Eyre Square. The lively old town lies between Eyre Square and the river. From Eyre Square, Williams Gate leads a pedestrian parade right through the old town (changing street names several times) to Wolfe Tone Bridge. Nearly everything you'll see and do is within a few minutes' walk of this spine.

TOURIST INFORMATION

The well-organized TI, located a block from the bus/train station, has regional as well as local information (Mon-Sat 9:00-17:00, closed Sun, Forster Street, tel. 091/537-700, www.

discoverireland.ie). Pick up the TI's free city guide with its simplified town map.

ARRIVAL IN GALWAY

Trains and most buses share the same station, virtually on Eyre Square (which has the nearest ATMs). The train station can store your bag (Mon-Fri 8:00-18:00, closed Sat-Sun). To get from the station to the TI, go left on Station Road as you exit the station (toward Eyre Square), and then turn right on Forster Street.

Don't confuse the public bus station (in same building as the train station) with the coach station (a block away, across the street from the TI), which handles only privately owned coaches. Citylink buses from Dublin and Dublin's airport, as well as regional day-tour buses, use the coach station.

Drivers staying overnight at a College Road B&B can park there for free (each has a small lot in front). For daytime parking, the most central and handiest parking garage is under the recommended Jurys Inn Galway in the town center (€2.20/hour, €20/24 hours, Mon-Sat 8:00-1:00 in the morning, Sun 9:00-18:00). Otherwise, you'll have to buy a pay-and-display ticket and put it on your dashboard (€2, 2-hour maximum, buy from machines on street).

HELPFUL HINTS

Exchange Rate: €1 = about $1.10

Country Calling Code: 353 (see page 530 for dialing instructions)

Crowd Control: Expect huge crowds—and much higher prices— during the Galway Arts Festival (mid-to-late-July, www. galwayartsfestival.com) and Galway Oyster Festival (late Sept, www.galwayoysterfest.com). The Galway Races are heaven for lovers of horse racing and hell for everyone else (summer races in late July-early Aug, fall races in mid-Sept and late Oct, www.galwayraces.com); prices double for food and lodging, and simple evening strolls feel like punt returns.

Markets: On Saturdays year-round and Sundays in summer, a fun market clusters around St. Nicholas' Church (all day, best 9:00-14:00).

Post Office: It squats on Eglinton Street (Mon-Sat 9:00-17:30, closed Sun).

Bookstore: Dubray Books is directly across the pedestrian drag from Lynch's Castle (Mon-Sat 9:00-18:00, Thu-Fri until 21:00, Sun 12:00-18:00, 4 Shop Street, tel. 091/569-070).

Laundry: Galway Dry Cleaners is close to the recommended B&Bs on College Road (€12 drop-off, Mon-Sat 9:30-17:30, closed Sun, on Bothar Ui Eithir, 2-minute walk uphill from TI, tel. 091/568-393).

Bike Rental: On Yer Bike rents bikes to tool around flat Galway

GALWAY

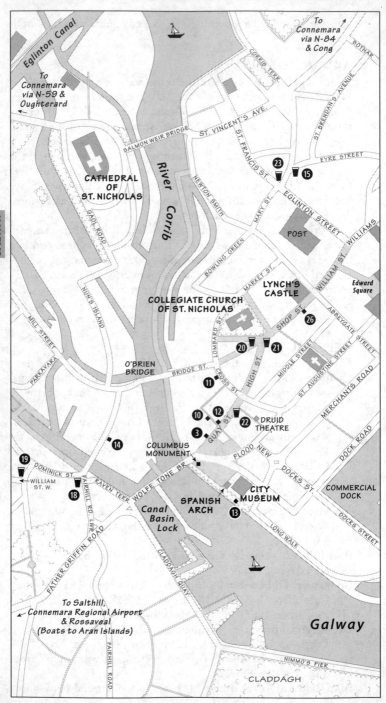

To Connemara via N-84 & Cong

BOTHAR

To Connemara via N-59 & Oughterard

Eglinton Canal

SALMON WEIR BRIDGE

ST. VINCENT'S AVE.

CORRIB TERR.

ST. FRANCIS ST.

ST. BRENDAN'S AVENUE

EYRE STREET

23

15

CATHEDRAL OF ST. NICHOLAS

River Corrib

NEWTON SMITH

MARY ST.

EGLINTON STREET

POST

WILLIAM ST.

WILLIAMS

GAOL ROAD

BOWLING GREEN

MARKET ST.

LYNCH'S CASTLE

Edward Square

NUN'S ISLAND

COLLEGIATE CHURCH OF ST. NICHOLAS

SHOP ST.

26

ABBEYGATE STREET

MILL STREET

PARKAVARA

LOMBARD ST.

20

21

HIGH ST.

MIDDLE STREET

ST. AUGUSTINE STREET

MERCHANT'S ROAD

O'BRIEN BRIDGE

BRIDGE ST.

CROSS ST.

11

10

12

3

QUAY ST.

22

DRUID THEATRE

DOCK ROAD

14

COLUMBUS MONUMENT

FLOOD NEW

DOCKS ST.

COMMERCIAL DOCK

19

DOMINICK ST.

WILLIAM ST. W.

18

FAIRHILL RD. LWR.

RAVEN TERR.

WOLFE TONE BR.

SPANISH ARCH

CITY MUSEUM

13

DOCKS STREET

FATHER GRIFFIN ROAD

Canal Basin Lock

CLADDAGH QUAY

LONG WALK

Galway

To Salthill, Connemara Regional Airport & Rossaveal (Boats to Aran Islands)

FAIRHILL ROAD

NIMMO'S PIER

CLADDAGH

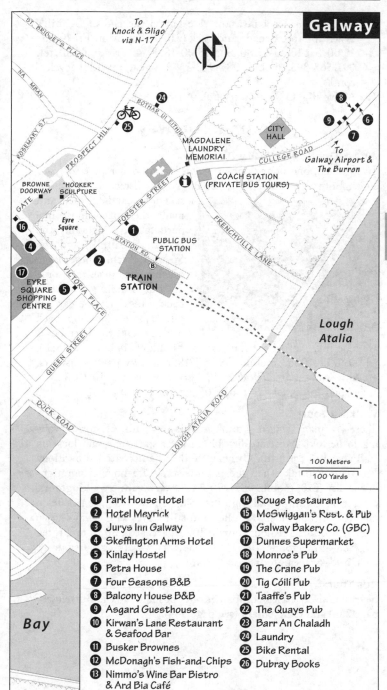

GALWAY

Galway

To Knock & Sligo via N-17

ST. BRIDGET'S PLACE

NA MBAN

ROSEMARY ST.

PROSPECT HILL

BÓTHAR UÍ LEITHIR

CITY HALL

COLLEGE ROAD

To Galway Airport & The Burren

MAGDALENE LAUNDRY MEMORIAL

COACH STATION (PRIVATE BUS TOURS)

BROWNE DOORWAY

"HOOKER" SCULPTURE

GATE

Eyre Square

FORSTER STREET

STATION RD

PUBLIC BUS STATION

FRENCHVILLE LANE

VICTORIA PLACE

TRAIN STATION

EYRE SQUARE SHOPPING CENTRE

QUEEN STREET

Lough Atalia

DOCK ROAD

LOUGH ATALIA ROAD

Bay

100 Meters
100 Yards

① Park House Hotel
② Hotel Meyrick
③ Jurys Inn Galway
④ Skeffington Arms Hotel
⑤ Kinlay Hostel
⑥ Petra House
⑦ Four Seasons B&B
⑧ Balcony House B&B
⑨ Asgard Guesthouse
⑩ Kirwan's Lane Restaurant & Seafood Bar
⑪ Busker Brownes
⑫ McDonagh's Fish-and-Chips
⑬ Nimmo's Wine Bar Bistro & Ard Bia Café
⑭ Rouge Restaurant
⑮ McSwiggan's Rest. & Pub
⑯ Galway Bakery Co. (GBC)
⑰ Dunnes Supermarket
⑱ Monroe's Pub
⑲ The Crane Pub
⑳ Tig Cóilí Pub
㉑ Taaffe's Pub
㉒ The Quays Pub
㉓ Barr An Chaladh
㉔ Laundry
㉕ Bike Rental
㉖ Dubray Books

town. Consider a pleasant ride out to the end of Salthill's beachfront promenade and back (€10-15/day, Mon-Fri 10:00-19:00, Sat 10:00-18:00, Sun 15:00-18:00, 42 Prospect Hill, tel. 091/563-393, mobile 087-942-5479, www.onyourbikecycles.com).

Taxi: Give **Big-O-Taxis** a try (tel. 091/585-858).

Tours in Galway

▲Hop-On, Hop-Off City Bus Tours

Two guided, one-hour double-decker bus tours compete for your euros. Both depart from the TI on Forster Street, have similar

schedules and prices, and make the dozen most important stops, including the cathedral, Salthill, and the Spanish Arch. These large coaches can't penetrate some of the winding medieval back streets, but you can get off, explore, and hop back on later. **Galway City** buses are blue (€8, April-Sept daily at 11:00, 12:30, 14:00, and 15:30, tel. 091/770-066, mobile 087-679-8525, www.galwaybustours.ie). **Lally's** buses are yellow (€12, April-Sept daily at 10:30, 12:00, 13:30, and 15:00, tel. 091/562-905, www.lallytours.com).

Walking Tours

There are many walking tours in this town full of stories waiting to be told. Most are flexible in their start time and location (call ahead to confirm). **Galway Walking Tours** are led by Fiona Brennan, who takes her guests on leisurely 1.5-hour explorations of the city (€10, mobile 087-290-3499, www.galwaywalkingtours.com, fiona@galwaywalkingtours.com). **Liam Silke** comes from one of Galway's oldest families and still serves as Galway's town crier as he leads 1.5-hour tours (€10, departs at 11:30 from TI, tel. 091/588-897, mobile 086-348-0958, www.walkingtoursgalway.com, info@walkingtoursgalway.com).

Bus Tours

Several Galway-based companies offer bus tours to the Burren (see page 284) and Connemara (see page 344).

Sights in Galway

MEDIEVAL GALWAY'S "LATIN QUARTER"

From the top of Eyre Square, Williams Gate—named for the old main gate of the Norman town wall that once stood here—is the spine of medieval Galway. While the road changes names several times (William, Shop, High, and Quay streets), it leads generally downhill to the River Corrib, straight past the following sights.

Lynch's Castle

Now the Allied Irish Bank, Galway's best late 15th-century fortified town-house was the home of the Lynch family—the most powerful of the town's 14 tribes—and the only one of their mansions to survive. More than 80 Lynch mayors ruled Galway in the 16th and 17th centuries.

Collegiate Church of St. Nicholas

This church, located a half-block off the main street on the right, is the finest medieval building in town (1320), and is dedicated to St. Nicholas of Myra, the patron saint of sailors. Columbus is said to have worshipped here in 1477, undoubtedly while contemplating a scary voyage. Its interior is littered with obscure town history (free entry but €3 suggested donation). Consider attending an evening concert of traditional Irish music in this atmospheric venue (see "Nightlife in Galway," later).

A wonderful **open-air market** surrounds the church most Saturdays year-round and also on Sundays in summer.

The Quays

This pub was once owned by "Humanity Dick," an 18th-century Member of Parliament who was the original animal-rights activist. His efforts led to the world's first conviction for cruelty to animals in 1822. It's worth a peek inside for its lively interior. The lane just before it leads to the...

Druid Theatre

This 100-seat venue offers top-notch contemporary Irish theater. Although the theater company is often away on tour, it's worth checking their schedule online or dropping by to see if anything's playing tonight (€20-30 tickets, Chapel Lane, tel. 091/568-660, www.druid.ie).

Directly across the alley from the theater door you'll find the **Hall of the Red Earl.** Wall diagrams and storyboards explain that these are the dusty foundations of Galway's oldest building, once

Galway Legends and Factoids

Because of the dearth of physical old stuff, the town milks its legends. Here are a few that you'll encounter repeatedly:

- In the 15th century, the mayor, one of the Lynch tribe, condemned his son to death for the murder of a Spaniard. When no one in town could be found to hang the popular boy, the dad—who loved justice more than he loved his son—did it himself.
- Columbus is said to have stopped in Galway in 1477. He may have been inspired by tales of the voyage of St. Brendan, the Irish monk who is thought by some (mostly Irish) to have beaten Columbus to the New World by almost a thousand years.
- On the main drag, you'll find a pub called The King's Head. It was originally given to the man who chopped off the head of King Charles I in 1649. For his safety, he settled in Galway—about as far from London as an Englishman could get back then.
- William Joyce, born in America, spent most of his childhood in Galway and later was seduced by fascist ideology in the 1930s. He moved to Germany and became "Lord Haw-Haw," infamous as the radio voice of Nazi propaganda during World War II. After the war, he was hanged in London for treason. His daughter had him buried in Galway.

the 13th-century hall of the Norman lord Richard DeBurgo (free, closed Sun).

Spanish Arch

Overlooking the River Corrib, this makes up the best remaining chunk of the old city wall. A reminder of Galway's former importance in trade, the Arch (c. 1584) is the place where Spanish ships would unload their cargo (primarily wine).

City Museum

Fragments of old Galway are kept in this modern museum, located just behind the Spanish Arch. Temporary exhibitions by local artists are on the upper two floors. Check out the intact Galway "hooker" fishing boat hanging from the ceiling. The ground floor houses the permanent exhibits: prehistoric and ancient Galway-related treasures such as medieval pottery, Iron Age ax heads, and Bronze Age thingamajigs.

Cost and Hours: Free, Tue-Sat 10:00-17:00, Sun 12:00-17:00, closed Sun Oct-March and Mon year-round, handy café with cheap lunches, tel. 091/532-460, www.galwaycitymuseum.ie.

River Corrib Sights

At the River Corrib, you'll find a riverside park that's perfect for a picnic (or get takeout from the recommended McDonagh's, the town's best chipper, across the street). Over the river (southeast of the bridge) is the modern housing project that replaced the original Claddagh in the 1930s. **Claddagh** (CLA-dah, like the "cla" in clatter) was a picturesque, Irish-speaking fishing village with a strong tradition of independence—and open sewers. This gaggle of thatched cottages functioned as an independent community with its own "king" until the early 1900s, when it was torn down for health reasons.

The old Claddagh village is gone, but the tradition of its popular ring (sold all over town) lives on. The Claddagh ring shows two hands holding a heart that wears a crown. The heart represents love, the crown is loyalty, and the hands are friendship. If the ring is worn with the tip of the heart pointing toward the wrist, it signifies that the wearer is married or otherwise taken. However, if the tip of the heart points toward the fingertip, it means the wearer is available.

Look at the **monument** (just before the bridge) given to Galway by the people of Genoa, Italy, to celebrate the 1477 visit here of Christopher Columbus—Cristoforo Colombo in Italian. (That acknowledgment, from an Italian town known for its stinginess, helps to substantiate the famous explorer's legendary visit.) From the middle of the bridge, look up the river. The green copper dome marks the city's Cathedral of St. Nicholas (described later). Down the river is a tiny swan-infested harbor with a few of Galway's famous square-rigged "hooker" fishing ships tied up and on display. Called "hookers" for their method of fishing with multiple hooks on a single line, these sturdy yet graceful boats were later used to transport turf from Connemara, until improved roads and electric heat made them obsolete. Beyond that, a huge park of reclaimed land is popular with the local kids for Irish football and hurling. From there, the promenade leads to the resort town of Salthill.

MORE SIGHTS IN GALWAY
▲Eyre Square

On a sunny day, grassy Eyre Square is a popular hangout. In the Middle Ages, it was a field just outside the town wall. The square is named for the mayor who gave the land to the city in 1710. While still called Eyre Square, it now contains John F. Kennedy Park—established in memory of the Irish-American president's visit in 1963 when he filled this space with adoring Irish for one of his speeches, a few months before he was assassinated. Though Kennedy is celebrated as America's first Irish-Catholic president, several US presidents were descended from Protestant Ulster stock (even

Barack Obama is part Irish, with roots in County Offaly). Take a look at the JFK bust near the kids' play area, which commemorates his visit.

Walk to the rust-colored "Hooker Sculpture," built in 1984 to celebrate the 500th anniversary of the incorporation of the city. The sails represent Galway's square-rigged fishing ships ("hookers") and the vessels that made Galway a trading center so long ago. The Browne Doorway, from a 1627 fortified townhouse, is a reminder of the 14 family tribes that once ruled the town (see Lynch's Castle, listed earlier, to get a feel for an intact townhouse). Each had a town castle—much like the towers that characterize the towns of Tuscany, with their feuding noble families. So little survives of medieval Galway that the town makes a huge deal of any remaining window or crest. Check out the 14 colorful flags lining the western edge of the square, each one with a different original Norman founding-tribe name.

The Eyre Square Shopping Centre—a busy, modern shopping mall (see the arcaded entry from the square)—contains a short stretch of the old town wall that includes two reconstructed towers (and an antique market).

▲Cathedral of St. Nicholas

Opened by American Cardinal Cushing in 1965, this is one of the

last great stone churches built in Europe. The interior is a treat and is worth a peek.

Cost and Hours: Free, open to visitors daily 8:30-18:30 as long as you don't interrupt Mass, church bulletins at doorway list upcoming Masses

and concerts, located across Salmon Weir Bridge on outskirts of town, tel. 091/563-577.

Visiting the Cathedral: Inside, you'll see mahogany pews set on green Connemara marble floors under a Canadian cedar ceiling. The acoustically correct cedar enhances the church's fine pipe organ. Two thousand worshippers sit on three sides facing the central altar. A Dublin woman carved the 14 larger-than-life Stations of the Cross. The carving above the chapel (left of entry) is from the old St. Nicholas church. Explore the modern stained glass. Find the Irish Holy Family—with Mary knitting and Jesus offering Joseph a cup of tea. The window depicting the Last Supper is particularly creative—find the 12 apostles.

Next, poke your head into the side chapel with a mosaic of

Magdalene Laundries Memorial

Recent documentaries and films such as *The Magdalene Sisters* and *Philomena* have highlighted the plight of unmarried, pregnant Irish women who were incarcerated and put to work doing laundry as virtual slaves. Viewing premarital pregnancy as one step short of prostitution, various Catholic orders operated these infamous "Magdalene laundries." (No such stigma applied to the men involved.) Across from the TI (at 47 Forster Street), a modest and easy-to-miss statue stands on the site of one such facility, operated by the Sisters of Mercy, which opened in 1824, with a capacity of 110 young women, and closed in 1984, with 18 inmates remaining. It's estimated that upwards of 10,000 women passed through the Magdalene laundry system. Magdalene survivors claim that they were held against their will, forced to work without pay, and physically abused...and their children were sold for adoption. The Irish government apologized in 2013 for turning a blind eye to the mistreatment of these "fallen women," who were imprisoned out of sight, often with the consent of their shamed families.

Christ's resurrection (if you're standing in the nave facing the main altar, it's on the left and closest to the front). Take a closer look at the profiled face in a circular frame, below and to the right of Christ—the one looking up while praying with clasped hands. It's JFK, nearly a saint in Irish eyes at the time this cathedral was built.

Salmon Weir Bridge

This bridge was the local "bridge of sighs." It led from the courthouse (opposite the church) to the prison (torn down to build the cathedral—unlikely in the US). Today, the bridge provides a fun view of the fishing action. Salmon run up this river most of the summer (look for them). Fishermen, who wear waders and carry walking sticks to withstand the strong current, book long in advance to get half-day appointments for a casting spot.

Canals multiplied in this city (once called the "Venice of Ireland") to power more water mills.

OUTER GALWAY
▲Salthill

This small resort town packs pubs, discos, a splashy water park, amusement centers, and a fairground up against a fine, mile-long beach promenade (Ireland's longest). Watch for local power walkers "kicking the wall" when they reach the western end of the promenade to emphasize that they've gone the entire distance.

At the **Atlantaquaria Aquarium,** which features native Irish aquatic life and some Amazonian species, kids can help feed the fish at 13:00 (fresh water), 15:00 (big fish), 16:00 (small fish), and 17:00 (naughty kids fed to piranhas). They can cuddle the crustaceans anytime (€12, Mon-Fri 10:00-17:00, Sat-Sun 10:00-18:00, touch tanks, The Promenade, tel. 091/585-100, www.nationalaquarium.ie).

For beach time, a relaxing sunset stroll, late-night traditional music, or later-night disco action, Salthill hops. For an accommodation recommendation in Salthill, see page 321.

Getting There: To get to Salthill, catch bus #401 from Eyre Square in front of the AIB bank, next to the Meyrick Hotel (3/hour, €2, runs 7:00-23:00).

Nightlife in Galway

▲TRADITIONAL IRISH MUSIC

Galway, like Dingle and Doolin, is a mecca for good Irish music (nightly 21:30-23:30). But unlike Dingle and Doolin, this is a university town (enrollment: 12,000), and many pubs are often overrun with noisy students. Still, your chances of landing a seat close to a churning band surrounded by new Irish friends are good any evening of the year.

Pubs

Touristy and student pubs are found and filled along the main drag down from Eyre Square to the Spanish Arch, and across Wolfe Tone Bridge (along William Street West and Dominick Street).

Across the Bridge: A good place to start is at **Monroe's,** with its vast, music-filled interior (check website for trad music schedule, Dominick Street, tel. 091/583-397, www.monroes.ie). Several other pubs within earshot frequently feature traditional music. **The Crane,** near Monroe's, has trad sessions nightly at 21:30 downstairs, a variety of other music upstairs, and Celtic Tales storytelling sessions on Thursdays from April to October (€10 for storytelling at 20:00, other sessions free, 2 Sea Road, tel. 091/587-419, www.thecranebar.com).

On the Main Drag: Pubs known for Irish music include **Tig Cóilí,** featuring Galway's best trad sessions (Mon-Sat at 18:00 and 22:00, Sun at 14:00 and 21:00, intersection of Main Guard Street

and High Street, tel. 091/561-294); **Taaffe's** (nightly music sessions at 17:30 and 21:30, Shop Street, across from St. Nicholas Church, tel. 091/564-066); and **The Quays** (trad music most nights at 21:30, sporadic schedule, young scene, Quay Street, tel. 091/568-347). A bit off the main drag, **Barr An Chaladh** is a scruffy little place offering nightly trad or ballad sessions and more locals (3 Daly's Place, tel. 091/895-762).

GALWAY

Performances

Instead of a pub, you can also attend a concert or performance.

Trad on the Prom: This fine, traditional, music-and-dance troupe was started by Galway-born performers, who returned home after years of touring with *Riverdance* and *The Chieftains*. Their show—so popular that it's lasted for more than a decade—is a great way to enjoy live step dancing and accomplished musicians in a fairly intimate venue (€30, mid-May-Sept only, shows at 21:00 Tue, Thu, and Sun—call to confirm, and best to reserve ahead online; in Galway Bay Hotel, 30-minute walk west of town along the Salthill promenade or short ride on bus #401 from Eyre Square; tel. 091/582-860, mobile 087-674-1877, www.tradontheprom.com).

Tunes in the Church: The Collegiate Church of St. Nicholas is a mellow, medieval venue hosting a rotating lineup of accomplished trad musicians. The 1.5-hour concerts are fun for early birds who don't want to stay up to catch the same great players in a local pub later that night (€15; June-July Mon-Fri at 20:00, daily in Aug; where High Street and Shop Street intersect, mobile 087-962-5425, www.tunesinthechurch.com).

Sleeping in Galway

There are three price tiers for most beds in Galway: off-season, high season (Easter-Oct), and charge-what-you-like festivals and race weekends (see "Crowd Control" on page 309).

HOTELS

For a fancy place, Park House Hotel offers the best value. For a budget hotel, go to Jurys Inn. For cheap beds, hit the hostel.

$$$$ Park House Hotel, a plush, business-class hotel, is ideally located a block from the train station and Eyre Square. Its 84

GALWAY

Sleep Code

Hotels are classified based on the average price of a typical en suite double room with breakfast in high season.

$$$$	**Splurge:** Most rooms over €170
$$$	**Pricier:** €130-170
$$	**Moderate:** €90-130
$	**Budget:** €50-90
¢	**Backpacker:** Under €50
RS%	**Rick Steves discount**

Unless otherwise noted, credit cards are accepted and free Wi-Fi is available. Comparison-shop by checking prices at several hotels (on each hotel's own website, on a booking site, or by email). For the best deal, *book directly with the hotel*. Ask for a discount if paying in cash; if the listing includes **RS%**, request a Rick Steves discount.

spacious rooms come with all the comforts you'd expect (expensive full Irish breakfast, elevator, pay parking, great restaurant, helpful staff, Forster Street, tel. 091/564-924, www.parkhousehotel.ie, reservations@parkhousehotel.ie).

$$$$ Hotel Meyrick, filled with palatial Old World elegance and 97 rooms, marks the end of the Dublin-Galway train line and the beginning of Galway. Since 1845, it has been Galway's landmark hotel...JFK stayed here in 1963 when it was the Great Southern (at the head of Eyre Square, tel. 091/564-041, www.hotelmeyrick.ie, reshm@hotelmeyrick.ie).

$$$ Jurys Inn Galway has 130 American-style rooms in a modern hotel, centrally located where the old town hits the river. The big, bright rooms have double beds and huge modern bathrooms (breakfast extra, elevator, lots of tour groups, pay parking, Quay Street, tel. 091/566-444, US tel. 800-423-6953, www.jurysinns.com, jurysinngalway@jurysinns.com).

$$$ Skeffington Arms Hotel feels more Irish than other hotels in town, but is furnished in a modern style. Centrally located on Eyre Square, it sits above a nightclub with noise from fun-loving stag/hen partygoers on weekends (family rooms, tel. 091/563-173, www.skeffington.ie, reception@skeffington.ie).

¢ Kinlay Hostel is a no-nonsense place just 100 yards from the train station, with 224 beds in bare, clean, and simple rooms, including 15 doubles/twins. Easygoing people of any age feel welcome here, but if you want a double, book well ahead—several months in advance for weekends (private rooms available, elevator, baggage storage, on Merchants Road just off Eyre Square, tel. 091/565-244, www.kinlaygalway.ie, info@kinlaygalway.ie).

B&BS

These B&Bs are homey, reasonably priced, and about a 10-minute walk from Eyre Square (from the train or bus stations, walk up Forster Street, which turns into College Road). The following places are lined up like battleships and all have free parking. They're quieter than the rowdy weekend scene at bigger hotels in the city center. Although there are other B&Bs on this road, my favorites are the ones where the owner lives on-site (and whose pride of ownership shows). All B&Bs include a full "Irish fry" breakfast.

$$ Petra House, a peaceful-feeling brick building, rents nine fresh rooms, including a family room. The owners, Joan and Frank Maher, keep everything lovingly maintained. Breakfasts are a highlight (family rooms, elegant sitting room, 29 College Road, tel. 091/566-580, 087/451-1711, www.petrahousegalway. net, petrahouse@eircom.net).

$$ Four Seasons B&B is well-kept, with seven inviting rooms hosted by Eddie and Helen Fitzgerald (family rooms, 23 College Road, tel. 091/564-078, www.fourseasonsgalway.com, info@fourseasonsgalway.com).

$$ Balcony House B&B rents eight pleasant rooms (family rooms, 27 College Road, tel. 091/563-438, www.aaabalconyhouse. com, info@aaabalconyhouse.com). Teresa Coyne provides treats in your room on arrival.

$$ Asgard Guesthouse offers eight restful rooms and an appealing glass-atrium breakfast room (family rooms, 21 College Road, tel. 091/566-855, www.galwaycityguesthouse.com, info@ galwaycityguesthouse.com, Mary O'Flynn).

NEAR GALWAY, IN SALTHILL

Salthill is Galway's equivalent of a beach town, with a fine sandy promenade for summer evening walks. (For more on Salthill, see page 318.)

$ Clarevilla B&B, a good, quiet choice 200 yards from the beach in a mellow residential area, has six serenely decorated, white rooms (cash only, closed Nov-March, 38 Threadneedle Road, tel. 091/522-520, clarevilla@yahoo.com, Christina Connolly). By car, it's a seven-minute drive from Galway. Follow the beach past Salthill, and take a right on Threadneedle Road just before the beach's high-diving board—it's on your left, 200 yards up, next to the Tennis Club.

Eating in Galway

This college town is filled with colorful, inexpensive eateries. People everywhere seem to be enjoying their food.

Restaurant Price Code

I've assigned each eatery a price category, based on the average cost of a typical main course. Drinks, desserts, and splurge items (steak and seafood) can raise the price considerably.

$$$$	**Splurge:** Most main courses over €25
$$$	**Pricier:** €20-25
$$	**Moderate:** €15-20
$	**Budget:** Under €15

In the Republic of Ireland, carryout fish-and-chips and other takeout food is **$**; a basic pub or sit-down eatery is **$$**; a gastropub or casual but more upscale restaurant is **$$$**; and a swanky splurge is **$$$$**.

AT THE BOTTOM OF THE OLD TOWN

Each of these places is within a few minutes' walk of Jurys Inn.

$$$ Kirwan's Lane Restaurant & Seafood Bar is considered Galway's best dining experience. Both the seafood bar downstairs and the restaurant up top are dressy places where reservations are required (both open Mon-Sat 12:30-14:30 & 18:00-22:00, Sun 17:00-21:00, on Kirwan's Lane a block from Jurys Inn, tel. 091/568-266, www.kirwanslane.com).

$$$ Busker Brownes, with three eateries in one sprawling block, is popular for its good, cheap food. Enter on Cross Street for the restaurant and walk to the back for better seating, or enter on Kirwan's Lane for the ground-floor pub; the third section is upstairs from the pub (daily 12:00-21:30, cleanse your palate with jazz sessions Sun at 13:00 and Mon at 21:30, Cross Street and Kirwan's Lane, tel. 091/563-377).

McDonagh's Fish-and-Chips is a favorite among residents. It has a fast, cheap, all-day **$ chipper** on one side and a sit-and-stay-awhile dinner-only **$$$ restaurant** on the other side. If you're determined to try Galway oysters, remember that they're in season from September through April only. At other times, you'll eat Pacific oysters—go figure (chipper open Mon-Sat 12:00-23:00, Sun 16:00-21:00; restaurant open Mon-Sat 17:00-22:00, closed Sun; 22 Quay Street, tel. 091/565-001).

$$$ Nimmo's Wine Bar Bistro and **$$ Ard Bia Café** peacefully coexist in an old stone warehouse behind the Spanish Arch. The upstairs is a mellow hangout with great cheese platters and wine. The candlelit ambience is great any night, even for a cup of coffee (open daily, café lunches 12:00-15:30, wine-bar dinners 18:00-21:30, Long Walk Street, tel. 091/561-114 or 091/539-897).

$$$ Rouge is a French splurge with leather couches and an extensive wine list (daily 18:00-23:00, reservations wise, 38

Lower Dominick Street, tel. 091/530-681, www.rougegalway. com).

NEAR EYRE SQUARE

$$$ McSwiggan's, with a downstairs pub and upstairs restaurant, is a maze of wooden stairways, brick walls, and hidden alcoves, serving hearty traditional Irish meals (daily 12:00-22:30, Eyre Street, tel. 091/568-917).

The **$$ Galway Bakery Company (GBC)** is a popular, basic place for a quick Irish meal (pricier restaurant upstairs, daily 12:00-21:00, 7 Williams Gate, near Eyre Square, tel. 091/563-087).

Supermarket: You can get to **Dunnes** through the Eyre Square Shopping Centre or around the corner at tiny Castle Street, off the pedestrian Williams Gate (Mon-Sat 9:00-19:00, Thu-Fri until 21:00, Sun 11:00-19:00, supermarket in basement). Lots of smaller grocery shops are scattered throughout town.

OUTSIDE GALWAY

If you have a car, consider a **Dunguaire Castle medieval banquet** in Kinvarra, a 30-minute drive south of Galway (for details, see page 304). You can fit in the banquet very efficiently when you're driving into Galway (B&Bs can accommodate late arrivals if you call ahead).

Galway Connections

From Galway by Train to: Dublin (8/day, 3 hours), **Limerick** (4/day, 2 hours), **Ennis** (5/day, 1.5 hours). For **Belfast, Tralee,** and **Rosslare,** you'll change in or near Dublin. Train info: Tel. 091/561-444, www.irishrail.ie.

By Bus to: Dublin (hourly, 3.5 hours; also see Citylink, below), **Kilkenny** (3/day, 5 hours), **Cork** (hourly, 4.5 hours), **Ennis** (hourly, 1.5 hours), **Shannon Airport** (hourly, 2 hours), **Cliffs of Moher** (8/day in summer, some with change in Ennis, 2 hours), **Doolin** (5/day, 1.5 hours), **Limerick** (hourly, 2 hours), **Dingle** (5/day, 6.5 hours), **Tralee** (8/day, 4.5 hours), **Westport** (5-7/day, 2-4 hours), **Rosslare** (2/day, 8 hours), **Belfast** (every 2 hours, 6 hours, change in Dublin), **Derry** (6/day, 5.5 hours). Bus info: Tel. 091/562-000, www.buseireann.ie.

Citylink runs cheap and fast bus service from the coach station near the TI to **Dublin** (arriving at Bachelor's Walk, a block from Tara Street DART station; hourly, 2.5 hours), **Dublin Airport** (hourly, 3 hours), and **Cork Airport** (6/day, 4 hours). Bus info: Tel. 091/564-164, www.citylink.ie.

By Car: For ideas on driving from Galway to Derry or Portrush in Northern Ireland, see "Between Galway and Derry" (on page 360), which describes sights in the Republic of Ireland. For sights on this route in Northern Ireland, see "Between Derry and Galway" (page 449 of the Derry and County Donegal chapter).

ARAN ISLANDS

Inishmore • Inisheer

Strewn like limestone chips hammered off the jagged west coast, the three Aran Islands—Inishmore, Inishmaan, and Inisheer—confront the wild Atlantic with stubborn grit. The largest, Inishmore (9 miles by 2 miles), is by far the most populated, interesting, and visited (try to spend a night here). Inisheer, the smallest (1.5 miles square), and best reached from Doolin, is worth considering for travelers with less time.

The landscape of all three islands ("Inish" is Irish for "island") is harsh. Steep, rugged cliffs fortify the southern flanks of each island. Windswept rocky fields, stitched together by stone walls, blanket the interiors. And the island's precious few sandy beaches hide in coves that dimple the northern shores. During the winter, severe gales sweep through; because of this, most of the settlements on the islands are found on the more sheltered northeastern side.

There's a stark beauty about the Aran Islands and the simple lives their inhabitants eke out of a mean sea and less than six inches of topsoil. Precious little of the land is productive. In the past, people made a precarious living here from fishing and farming. The scoured bedrock offered little in the way of soil, so it was created by the islanders—the result of centuries of layering seaweed with limestone sand and animal dung. Fields are small, divided by several thousand miles of "drystone" wall (made without mortar). Most of these are built in the Aran "gap" style, in which spaces between angled upright stones are filled with smaller stones. This allows a farmer who wants to move livestock to dismantle a short section of wall as a temporary gate, and then rebuild that section afterward. It also allows the harsh winter winds to blow through

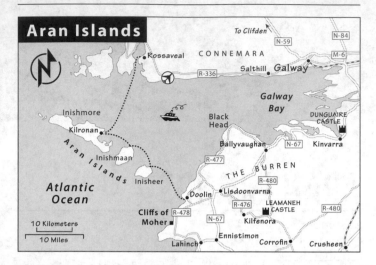

Aran Islands

To Clifden

CONNEMARA

Rossaveal

Salthill Galway

R-336

N-59

N-84

M-6

Inishmore

Kilronan

Aran Islands

Inishmaan

Inisheer

Galway
Bay

Black
Head

DUNGUAIRE
CASTLE

Ballyvaughan

N-67

Kinvarra

**Atlantic
Ocean**

R-477

THE BURREN

R-480

Doolin Lisdoonvarna

LEAMANEH
CASTLE

R-476

R-480

10 Kilometers

Cliffs of R-478
Moher

N-67

Kilfenora

10 Miles

Lahinch Ennistimon Corrofin Crusheen

without knocking down the wall. Nowadays, tourism boosts the islands' economy.

The islands are a Gaeltacht area. While the islanders speak Irish among themselves, they happily speak English for their visitors. Many islanders have direct, personal connections with close relatives in America. I once met an Aran minivan driver who served in the US Navy aboard a destroyer before coming back home to Inishmore. Five of his six children now have American passports.

Today, the 800 people of Inishmore (literally "the big island") greet as many as 2,000 visitors a day. The vast majority of these are day-trippers. They'll hop on a minivan at the dock for a 2.5-hour visit to Dun Aengus (the must-see Iron Age fort), grab a simple lunch, and then spend an hour or two browsing through the few shops or sitting at a picnic table outside a pub with a pint of Guinness.

The other islands, Inisheer and Inishmaan, are smaller, much less populated, and less touristy. While extremely quiet, they do have B&Bs, daily flights, and ferry service. For most, the big island is quiet enough. But Inisheer is a good alternative if your travel plans take you to Doolin, a 25-minute ferry ride away (and not Galway, which is closer to Rossaveal, the mainland port from where you sail to Inishmore).

Inishmore

The largest of the Aran Islands has a blockbuster sight: the striking Dun Aengus fort, set on a sheer cliff. Everyone arrives at Kilronan, the Aran Islands' biggest town, though it's just a village. Groups of backpackers wash ashore with the docking of each ferry. Minivans, bike shops, and a few men in pony carts sop up the tourists.

PLANNING YOUR TIME

Most travelers visit Inishmore (Inis Mór) as a day trip by boat from Galway. (Boats from Doolin are too slow and weather-dependent to allow enough time for a same-day round-trip to Inishmore.) Here's a good framework for a day trip: Leave Galway at 9:00 on the shuttle bus to Rossaveal, where you'll catch the 10:30 boat. You'll step off the boat in Kilronan at about 11:15. Arrange minivan transport or rent a bike, visit Dun Aengus, and grab a bite at one of the two simple cafés near the base of the Dun Aengus fort trail (or bring a picnic). Explore the island during low tide, and depart on the boat when high tides return between 16:00 and 18:00. You can squeeze an extra two or three hours out of your day trip by booking an early flight over and a late flight back from Connemara Regional Airport, near Rossaveal. For more details on these options, see "Aran Islands Connections" at the end of this chapter.

Staying Overnight: Travelers spending the night can savor the quiet time before and after the day-trip crowds. Here's how I'd suggest you spend your arrival day: Since most day-trippers make a beeline straight off the boat to Dun Aengus, head in the opposite direction to check out the subtle charms of the less-visited eastern end of the island. Buy a picnic at the Spar supermarket in Kilronan. Then walk to either the ruins of tiny St. Benen's Church (an easy 45-minute hike one way from Kilronan) or the rugged Black Fort ruins (a rocky 1-hour scramble one way from Kilronan). Save Dun Aengus for later in the afternoon, after the midday crowds have subsided (allow an hour at Dun Aengus, closes at 18:00 March-Oct, off-season at 16:00, last entry one hour before closing). Enjoy an evening in the pubs and take a no-rush midmorning boat trip or flight back to the mainland the next day.

Orientation to Inishmore

Your first stop on Inishmore is the town of Kilronan, huddling around the pier. There are about a dozen shops and B&Bs, about half as many restaurants, and a couple of **bike-rental huts** (regular bikes-about €10/day plus €10 deposit, electric bikes-€25/day plus €20 deposit).

ARAN ISLANDS

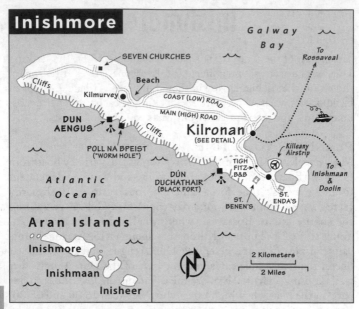

A few blocks inland up the high road, you'll find the best folk-music **pub** (Joe Watty's), a **post office** (Mon-Fri 9:00-13:00 & 14:00-17:30, Sat 9:00-13:00, closed Sun), and a tiny **bank** across from the roofless Anglican church ruins (open only on Wed 10:30-12:30 & 13:30-15:00, plus Thu June-Aug).

A friendly **café** with free Wi-Fi lurks behind the stony Aran Sweater Market building, across from the high cross (daily 10:00-20:00, shorter hours off-season; also has Irish lessons for tourists, a detailed map for hikers, and the *Man of Aran* film described later, under "Sights and Activities on Inishmore"). Public **WCs** are 100 yards beyond the TI (see below) on the harbor road.

The huge Spar **supermarket,** two blocks inland from the harbor, seems too big for the tiny community and has the island's only **ATM.** If you don't have plenty of cash on you, get some here—most B&Bs and quite a few other businesses don't accept credit cards.

TOURIST INFORMATION

Kilronan's TI is helpful (daily 10:00-17:00, July-Aug until 18:00, may close during lunch, shorter hours in winter, faces the harbor, tel. 099/61263). The free map given out by the TI or ferry operator is all the average day-tripper or leisure biker will need to navigate. But serious hikers who plan on scampering out to the island's craggy fringes will want to invest in the detailed black-and-white *Oileáin Árann* map and companion book by Tim Robinson (€16,

Currach and *Navogue* Boats

These are the traditional fishing boats of the west coast of Ireland—lightweight and easy to haul. In your coastal travels, you'll see a few actual *currach* or *navogue* boats—generally retired and stacked where visitors can touch them and ponder the simpler age when they were a key part of the economy. The *currach* (manned by three oarsmen) is native to the Aran Islands, while the *navogue* (four oarsmen) is native to the Dingle Peninsula. Few raw materials were needed to make the boats. Just cover a wooden frame with canvas (originally cowhide) and paint with tar—presto. A *currach*'s advantage was maneuverability on the sea and ease in getting into and out of the water (the seamanship of these skilled sailors is often underestimated). Its disadvantage was its fragility when hauling anything other than men or fish. When transporting sheep, farmers would lash each sheep's pointy little hooves together and place it carefully upside-down in the *currach*—so it wouldn't puncture the frail little craft's canvas skin.

sold at the café behind the Aran Sweater Market, and at some bookstores in Galway).

Events: Late June is when Inishmore shakes off its slumber and kicks up its heels. The **Patrún** is a three-day annual celebration during the last weekend in June (*currach* boat races, Galway "hooker" boat races, fun run). June 23 is **St. John's Eve Bonfire Night,** a Christian/pagan tradition held the night before St. John's Day, close to (but not on) the summer solstice. Each community stokes a raging fire around dusk, and dozens are visible not only on the island, but also on the distant shore of Connemara.

GETTING AROUND INISHMORE

Just about anything on wheels functions as a taxi here. A trip from Kilronan to Dun Aengus to the Seven Churches and back to Kilronan costs €10 per person in a shared minivan. These range in capacity from 8 to 20 passengers. Pony carts cost about €50 for two people (€80 for 4) for a trip to Dun Aengus and back.

Biking is great. Before heading out, check that your bike seat is correctly extended and stable enough so that you can comfortably extend both legs as you pedal. (The most frequent bike rental complaint is a seat that won't stay in place and slowly slips down...cramping your legs when you're far down the island.) Take it for a short test spin while you're still near the rental shop.

Novice bikers should be aware that the terrain is hilly and there are occasional headwinds and unpredictable showers (figure 30 minutes to ride from Kilronan to start of trailhead up to Dun Aengus). Cyclists should take the high road over and the low road back—fewer hills, scenic shoreline, and at low tide, a dozen seals basking in the sun. Keep a sharp lookout along the roads for handy, modern limestone signposts (with distances in kilometers) that point the way to important sights. They're in Irish, but you'll be clued in by the small metal depictions of the sights embedded within them.

Tours on Inishmore

▲Island Minivan Tours

Fewer than 100 vehicles roam the island, and most of them seem to be minivans. A line of vans (seating 8-18 passengers) awaits the

arrival of each ferry, offering €10 island tours. They're basically a shared taxi service that will take you to the various sights, drop you off, and return at an agreed time to take you to the next attraction.

Chat with a few drivers to find one who likes to talk. On my tour, I learned that 800 islanders live in 14 villages (actually just crossroads), with three elementary schools and three churches. Most islanders own a small detached field where they keep a couple of cows (sheep are too much trouble). When pressed for more information, my guide explained that there are 400 types of flowers and 19 types of bees on the island. Then he pointed to the 2,000-year-old ring fort on the hilltop and grinned, saying, "It's so popular with visitors that we plan to build another 2,000-year-old ring fort next year."

The tour, a convenient time-saver, zips you to the end of the island for a quick stroll in the desolate fields, gives you 15 minutes to wander through the historic but visually unimpressive Seven Churches, and then drops you off for two hours at Dun Aengus (30 minutes to hike up, 30 minutes at the fort, 20-minute hike back down, 40 minutes in café for lunch or shopping at drop-off point) before running you back to Kilronan. These sights can be linked together in various sequences, but the trailhead crossroads below Dun Aengus—with two cafés—makes the best lunch stop. Ask your driver to take you back along the smaller coastal road (scenic beaches and sunbathing seals at low tide).

Sights and Activities on Inishmore

IN KILRONAN
Man of Aran Film
This Oscar-winning 1934 movie (1.25 hours) is a documentary, partly staged, about traditional island life. It's basically a silent movie, with an all-local cast and the sounds of surf, seagull, and sailor (muttering in barely audible Irish) dubbed in. It's a strangely fascinating glimpse of the past and was groundbreaking in its time. The movie tries to re-create life in the early 1900s—when you couldn't rent bikes—and features *currach*s (canoe-like boats) in a storm, shark fishing with handheld harpoons, kids fishing off cliffs, and farmers cultivating the fields from bare rock. But make this film a rainy-day option: Don't waste time indoors when the real thing is right outside at your feet.

Cost and Hours: €5, 3 showings/day—usually on request, plays in café (upstairs) behind Aran Sweater Market—see page 328 for hours.

Irish Lessons: Gearóid (pronounced gair-OH-id), who runs the café, also teaches one-hour Irish lessons to tourists for €5. Learn how to say "please" and "thank you," order a beer, and more in this unusual language (don't worry, he writes everything down phonetically).

Music
Kilronan's pubs offer music sporadically on summer nights. Nothing is dependably scheduled, so ask at your B&B or look for posted notices on the front of the Spar supermarket or post office. **Joe Watty's Bar,** on the high road 100 yards past the post office, is worth the 10-minute walk from the dock. Its appealing front porch goes great with a pint, and Irish folk music warms the interior most nights. The more central **Joe Mac's Pub** (next to the hostel) and **The Bar** (next to the high cross at the base of the high road) are also possibilities.

BEYOND THE TOWN
▲▲▲Dun Aengus
(Dún Aonghasa)

This is the island's blockbuster sight. The stone fortress hangs spectacularly and precariously on the edge of a cliff 200 feet above the Atlantic. The crashing waves seem to say, "You've come to the end of the world." Gaze out to sea and consider this: Off this coast, Hy-Brasil—a phantom island cloaked in mist—was said to pop into view once every seven years. This mythical place appeared on maps as late as the mid-1800s.

Little is known about this 2,000-year-old Iron Age fort. Its concentric walls are 13 feet thick and 10 feet high. As an added defense, the fort is ringed with a commotion of spiky stones, sticking up like lances, called *chevaux-de-frise* (literally, "Frisian horses," named for the Frisian soldiers who used pikes to stop charging cavalry). Slowly, as the cliff erodes, hunks of the fort fall into the sea.

Dun Aengus doesn't get crowded until after 11:00. I enjoyed a half-hour completely alone at 10:00 in the height of tourist season; if you can, get there early or late. A small museum (housing the ticket office and controlling access to the trail) displays aerial views of the fort and tells the story of its inhabitants.

Cost and Hours: €5, daily March-Oct 9:00-18:00; Nov-Dec 9:30-16:00; Jan-Feb Wed-Sun 9:30-16:00, closed Mon-Tue; last entry one hour before closing, during June-Aug guides at the trailhead answer questions and can sometimes give free tours up at the fort if you call ahead, 5.5 miles from Kilronan, tel. 099/61008.

Warnings: Rangers advise visitors to wear sturdy walking shoes and watch kids closely; there's no fence between you and a crumbling 200-foot cliff overlooking the sea. Also, be very careful about unexpected gusts of wind and uncertain footing near the edge (uneven rocky ground that begs to be tripped on). The Irish don't believe in litigation, just natural selection.

Seven Churches (Na Seacht Teampaill)

Close to the western tip of the island, this gathering of ruined chapels, monastic houses, and fragments of a high cross dates from the 8th to 11th century. The island is dotted with reminders that Christianity was brought to the islands in the fifth century by St. Enda, who established a monastery here. Many great monks studied under Enda. Among these "Irish apostles" who started Ireland's "Age of Saints and Scholars" (A.D. 500-900) was Columba (Colmcille in Irish), the founder of a monastery on the island of Iona in Scotland—home of the Irish monks who produced the Book of Kells. Check out the ornate gravestones (best detail on sunny days) of the "seven Romans," located in the slightly elevated back corner of the graveyard, farthest from the road. These pilgrims came here from Rome in the ninth century, long after the fall of the Roman Empire.

Kilmurvey

The island's second-largest village sits below Dun Aengus. With a gaggle of homes, a B&B, a great sheltered swimming beach, and a pub, this is the place for peaceful solitude. This narrowest section of the island also has the best grazing land, a fact not lost on the local landlord who claimed it for himself.

The Worm Hole (Poll na bPeist)

Off the beaten path and accessible only by hiking, this site takes the "logic" out of geo-*logic*. It's a large, perfectly rectangular, 40-by-100-foot seawater-filled pool, cut by nature into the flat coastal bedrock. You'd swear that God used a cake knife to cut out this massive slab—just to mess with us. The Worm Hole was formed when the limestone fractured at right angles and a cave underneath (cut by wave and tidal action) collapsed just so. To add to the surreal scene, Red Bull Energy Drink has twice featured this site in its annual cliff-diving competition (search YouTube for thrilling video clips).

Boulder-hopping your way across the narrowest section of the island, you'll find the Worm Hole beneath the island's southern cliffs, one mile straight south of Kilmurvey's fine beach. It's signposted from the Main Road, but Tim Robinson's detailed map (see "Tourist Information," earlier) is handy for navigating here.

Ancient Sites near Killeany

The quiet eastern end of Inishmore offers ancient sites in evocative settings for overnight visitors with more time, or for those seeking rocky hikes devoid of crowds. First, get a good hiking map from the café behind the Aran Sweater Market. Then consider assembling a picnic, to fuel up either before or after you spend a couple of hours exploring these sights on foot. Ask the folks in town for directions (almost always a memorable experience in Ireland).

Closest to the road, amid the dunes one mile past the Tigh Fitz B&B and just south of the airport, is the eighth-century **St. Enda's Church** (Teaghlach Einne). Protected from wave erosion by a stubborn breakwater, it sits half-submerged in a sandy graveyard, surrounded by a sea of sawgrass and peppered with tombstones. St. Enda is said to be buried here, along with 125 other saints who flocked to Inishmore in the fifth century to learn from him.

St. Benen's Church (Teampall Bheanáin) perches high on a desolate ridge opposite the Tigh Fitz B&B. Walk up the stone-walled lane, passing a holy well and the stubby remains of a round tower. Then take another visual fix on the church's silhouette on the horizon, and zigzag up the stone terraces to the top. The 30-minute hike up from the B&B pays off with a great view. Dedicated to

Sleep Code

Hotels are classified based on the average price of a typical en suite double room with breakfast in high season.

$$$$	**Splurge:** Most rooms over €170
$$$	**Pricier:** €130-170
$$	**Moderate:** €90-130
$	**Budget:** €50-90
¢	**Backpacker:** Under €50
RS%	**Rick Steves discount**

Unless otherwise noted, credit cards are accepted and free Wi-Fi is available. Comparison-shop by checking prices at several hotels (on each hotel's own website, on a booking site, or by email). For the best deal, *book directly with the hotel.* Ask for a discount if paying in cash; if the listing includes **RS%,** request a Rick Steves discount.

St. Benen, a young disciple of St. Patrick himself, this tiny (12 foot by 6 foot) 10th-century oratory is aligned north-south (instead of the usual east-west) to protect the doorway from prevailing winds.

About a five-minute walk past the Tigh Fitz B&B (on your left as you head toward the airport), you'll notice an abandoned stone pier and an adjacent, modest medieval ruin. This was **Arkin Fort,** built by Cromwell's soldiers in 1652 using cut stones taken from the round tower and the monastic ruins that once stood below St. Benen's Church. The fort was used as a prison for outlawed priests before they were sent by English authorities to the West Indies to be sold into slavery.

Hidden on a remote, ragged headland an hour's walk from Kilronan to the south side of the island, you'll find the **Black Fort** (Dún Duchathair). After Dun Aengus, this is Inishmore's most dramatic fortification. A good map is essential to navigate here. Built on a promontory with cliffs on three sides, its defenders would have held out behind drystone ramparts, facing the island's interior attackers. Watch your step on the uneven ground, be ready to course-correct as you go, and chances are you'll have this windswept ruin all to yourself. Imagine the planning and cooperative effort that went into building these life-saving structures 2,000 years ago, before Gore-Tex and granola bars.

Sleeping on Inishmore

All of the following places are in Kilronan. Remember, this is a rustic island. Many rooms are plain, with simple plumbing. Luxury didn't make the leap from the mainland.

$$ The **Aran Islands (Ostan Aran) Hotel** is the only modern

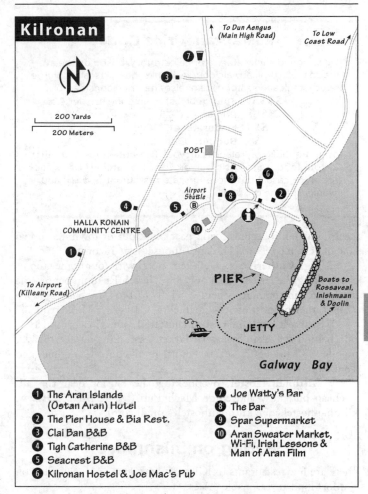

Kilronan

To Dun Aengus
(Main High Road)

To Low
Coast Road

N

200 Yards

200 Meters

POST

Airport
Shuttle

HALLA RONAIN
COMMUNITY CENTRE

To Airport
(Killeany Road)

PIER →

Boats to
Rossaveal,
Inishmaan
& Doolin

JETTY

Galway Bay

ARAN ISLANDS

1. The Aran Islands
   (Ostan Aran) Hotel
2. The Pier House & Bia Rest.
3. Clai Ban B&B
4. Tigh Catherine B&B
5. Seacrest B&B
6. Kilronan Hostel & Joe Mac's Pub
7. Joe Watty's Bar
8. The Bar
9. Spar Supermarket
10. Aran Sweater Market,
    Wi-Fi, Irish Lessons &
    Man of Aran Film

option on the island. Its 20 rooms (four with large harbor-facing porches) have the comforts you'd expect. Beware of loud weekend stag/hen parties drawn to their downstairs pub (tel. 099/61104, www.aranislandshotel.com, info@aranislandshotel.com, 10-minute walk east of the dock on the coast road heading toward Killeany).

$$ The Pier House stands solidly, 50 yards from the pier, offering 12 decent rooms, a good restaurant downstairs, and sea views from many of its rooms (tel. 099/61417, www.pierhousearan. com, pierhousearan@gmail.com).

$ Clai Ban, the only really cheery place in town, is run by friendly Marion and Bartley Hernon. Their six rooms and warm hospitality are worth the 10-minute uphill walk from the pier. The place is patrolled by their affectionate and pudgy Corgi, Guinness

Restaurant Price Code

I've assigned each eatery a price category, based on the average cost of a typical main course. Drinks, desserts, and splurge items (steak and seafood) can raise the price considerably.

$$$$ **Splurge:** Most main courses over €25
$$$ **Pricier:** €20-25
$$ **Moderate:** €15-20
$ **Budget:** Under €15

In the Republic of Ireland, carryout fish-and-chips and other takeout food is **$;** a basic pub or sit-down eatery is **$$;** a gastropub or casual but more upscale restaurant is **$$$;** and a swanky splurge is **$$$$.**

(cash only, family rooms, walk past bank out of town and down lane on left, tel. 099/61111, claibanhouse@gmail.com).

$ Tigh Catherine is a well-kept B&B with four homey rooms overlooking the harbor (cash only, on Church Road up behind the Halla Ronain community center, tel. 099/61464, mobile 087-980-9748, catherineandstiofain@gmail.com, Catherine Mulkerrin).

$ Seacrest B&B offers six uncluttered rooms in a central location behind the Aran Sweater Market (cash only, tel. 099/61292, mobile 087-161-6507, seacrestaran@gmail.com, Geraldine and Tom Faherty).

¢ Kilronan Hostel, overlooking the harbor near the TI, is cheap but noisy above Joe Mac's Pub (tel. 099/61255, www.kilronanhostel.com, kilronanhostel@gmail.com).

Eating on Inishmore

There are few restaurants in Kilronan and none are fancy. Plan on comfort food at reasonable prices.

I like the friendly vibe and tasty grub up the hill at **$$ Joe Watty's Bar.** Try the chicken goulash with a pint and stick around for the music (daily April-Oct 12:30-15:30 & 17:00-21:00, tel. 099/20892, pleasant front-porch seating).

The **Aran Islands Hotel** has a modern **$$ pub** serving simple soup-and-sandwich lunches and hot dinners (daily 12:00-21:00, tel. 099/61104).

The Pier House operates the dependable **$$$ Bia Restaurant** on the ground floor of its guesthouse (daily May-Sept 11:00-21:30, tel. 099/61811).

Otherwise, Kilronan's modest cafés dish up hearty soup, soda bread, sandwiches, and tea.

Supermarket: The **Spar** has all the groceries you'll need (Mon-Sat 9:00-18:00 except July-Aug until 19:00, Sun 10:00-17:00).

Inisheer

The roughly circular little island of Inisheer (Inis Oírr) has only a quarter of the land area and population of Inishmore—my island of choice. But Inisheer's close proximity to the mainland makes it an easy 25-minute boat journey from Doolin and a good option for those with limited time who aren't going north to Galway.

Inisheer offers a vivid glimpse of Aran Island culture and has an engaging smorgasbord of salty but modest sights. For some

reason, this quaint little island seems to attract as many German-speaking visitors as English-speaking ones.

Planning Your Time: Take an early boat from Doolin to maximize your time on Inisheer. For more details, see "Aran Islands Connections" at the end of this chapter.

Orientation to Inisheer

You'll dock on the north side of the island in its only settlement. Facing inland with your back to the pier, you'll be able to see nearly all of the island's landmarks (except for the *An Plassy* shipwreck and the lighthouse on the southern shore). Although a handful of pony carts and minivan drivers meet you at the pier, I'd rely on them only on a rainy day (€10, but prices are soft...negotiate).

For me, the joy of compact Inisheer is seeing it on a bike ride or a long breezy walk. The bike rental outfit is right at the base of the pier (€10/day, no deposit necessary "unless you look suspicious"). Any of the boat operators in Doolin can give you a free map of the island showing Inisheer's primitive road network. That's all you'll need to navigate.

There are three pubs on the island, one small grocery store, and no ATMs. All of the sights, with the exception of the lonely lighthouse on the southern coast, are concentrated on the northern half.

Inisheer lacks the dramatic (and much higher) coastal cliffs of Inishmore, but has its own unique photogenic charms. Fans of the 1990s British sitcom *Father Ted* may recognize parts of the island, which were featured in the show's intro depicting its fictional Craggy Island location.

ARAN ISLANDS

Inisheer

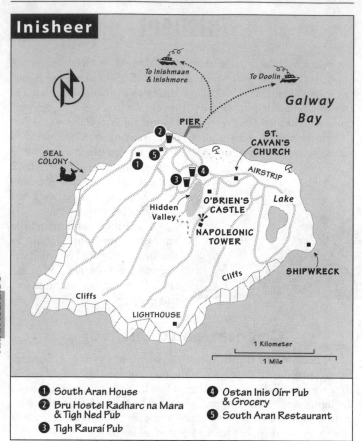

To Inishmaan & Inishmore

To Doolin

Galway Bay

PIER

ST. CAVAN'S CHURCH

AIRSTRIP

SEAL COLONY

① ②
⑤
③ ④

Hidden Valley

O'BRIEN'S CASTLE

Lake

NAPOLEONIC TOWER

SHIPWRECK

Cliffs

Cliffs

LIGHTHOUSE

1 Kilometer

1 Mile

ARAN ISLANDS

① South Aran House
② Bru Hostel Radharc na Mara & Tigh Ned Pub
③ Tigh Rauraí Pub

④ Ostan Inis Oírr Pub & Grocery
⑤ South Aran Restaurant

Sights on Inisheer

The following sights are free, open all the time, and marked on your free boat company map. See them in the order listed, from west to east, across the northern half of the island. If you bike rather than hike, be prepared to walk the bike up (or down) short, steep hills.

O'Brien's Castle
(Caislean Ui Bhriain)

The ruins of this castle dominate the hilltop and are visible from almost anywhere on the northern half of the island. It's a steep 20-minute walk from the pier up to the castle ruins. The small castle was built as a tower house refuge around 1400 by the O'Brien clan from nearby County Clare. It sits inside a low wall of a much older Iron Age ring fort. Cromwell's troops destroyed the castle in 1652, leaving the evocative ruins you see today.

If you've huffed your way up to O'Brien's Castle, then go another easy five minutes to the **Napoleonic Tower (An Tur Faire),** which was built in the early 1800s to watch for a feared French invasion that never took place. The views from this highest point on the island are worth it.

• *Consult your map and continue walking (south) on the paved road into the heart of the island. Take your first right turn, roughly 100 yards after the Napoleonic Tower, onto a rocky, grassy cow lane that zigzags downhill into a lush **hidden valley**, displaying the prettiest mosaic of ivy-tangled rock walls and small green fields I've seen anywhere on the Aran Islands. Unholster your camera and fire away.*

Once you've wound your way back down to the main north-shore road again, turn right and continue east with the airstrip on your left. On your right, you'll soon see a time-passed graveyard up atop a sandy hill. Hike the 50 yards up into the graveyard to find...

St. Cavan's Church (Teampall Chaomhain)

St. Cavan was the brother of St. Kevin, who founded the monastery at Glendalough in the Wicklow Mountains (see page 127). In the middle of the graveyard is a sunken sandpit holding the rugged, roofless remains of an 11th-century church. The shifting sand dunes almost buried it before sawgrass stabilized the hill. St. Cavan's reputed gravesite is protected by a tiny modern structure worth poking your head into for its candlelit atmosphere. Local folklore held that if you spent a night sleeping on the tomb lid, your particular illness would be cured.

• *Walk back down to the north-shore road and head out on the coast road (to the southeast) 30 minutes to the remote...*

Shipwreck of the *An Plassy*

This freighter was wrecked offshore on Finn's Rock in 1960. But islanders worked with the coastal patrol to help rescue the crew with no loss of life. A couple of weeks later the unmanned ship was washed high up onto the rocky shore, where it still sits today, a rusty but fairly intact ghost ship with a broken back. The fierce winter winds and record-breaking waves of 2013 shifted the wreck, further weakening it, and discussions are under way to remove it as it deteriorates. A local told me, "We

may have to go out some night with lanterns to bring in a new shipwreck." Beware of turning an ankle on the unstable footing of the rounded cobbles thrown up by the surf near the wreck.

• *With more time, consult your map and seek out the remaining intimate little church ruins and holy wells that the island has to offer. Or head back to town for a beverage while you await the return ferry.*

Sleeping on Inisheer

A scattering of B&Bs dots the northern half of the island. Here are two good options:

$ South Aran House is a quiet, well-run place with five spic-and-span, black-and-white rooms. Friendly Enda and Maria Conneely are generous with local tips and also run the nearby South Aran Restaurant, where you'll have breakfast (easy 10-minute walk west of pier on north-shore road, call ahead with your ferry arrival time so they can meet you with keys, tel. 099/75073, mobile 087-340-5687, www.southaran.com, info@southaran.com). Their small rental cottage sleeps two.

¢ Bru Hostel Radharc na Mara is a simple, economical, 40-bed option just 100 yards west of the pier, next to Tigh Ned Pub (includes continental breakfast, open mid-March-Oct, tel. 099/75024, radharcnamara@hotmail.com).

Eating on Inisheer

Inisheer's three main pubs offer decent pub grub (usually 12:30-20:30). **$$ Tigh Rauraí Pub** (House of Rory) is the epicenter of island social life (from the pier, head east to the edge of the beach and turn right—inland—up a narrow lane for 100 yards). Just below it, closer to the beach, is **$$ Ostan Inis Oírr Pub** (Hotel Inisheer) with a colorful collage of international flags draping the pub's ceiling. **$$$ Tigh Ned Pub** (House of Ned) is right next door to the hostel, near the pier on the north-shore road. Life could be worse than to sit outside at their appealing front tables on a summer evening, enjoying a pint in the salt air.

For a mellow evening meal, try the **$$ South Aran Restaurant,** a five-minute walk west of the pier on the north-shore road (daily 18:00-21:00, tel. 099/75073, mobile 087-340-5687).

Picnic lovers flock to the island's small **grocery,** Siopa XL, behind Ostan Inis Oírr Pub and below Tigh Rauraí Pub (Mon-Sat 9:00-17:00, Sun 10:00-15:00).

Aran Islands Connections

For an overview map of the region, see page 283.

BY FERRY
From Rossaveal (near Galway)

Island Ferries sails to Inishmore from the port of Rossaveal, 20 miles west of Galway. The company runs a shuttle bus from Galway to the Rossaveal dock (3/day April-Oct, 2/day Nov-March, bus ride and ferry crossing each takes 45 minutes; coming from Galway, allow 2 hours in transit one-way; €25 round-trip boat crossing plus €7 round-trip for shuttle bus, 10 percent discount if you book online, WCs on board). Catch shuttle buses from Galway on Queen Street, a block behind the Kinlay Hostel (check-in 1.5 hours before sailing); shuttles return to Galway immediately after each boat arrives. Ferry schedule for April-Oct: from Rossaveal at 10:30, 13:00, and 18:30; from Inishmore at 8:15, 12:00, 16:00, and 17:00 (plus 18:30 July-Aug). Island Ferries has two offices in Galway: on Forster Street across from the TI and at 19 Eyre Square (tel. 091/568-903, after-hours tel. 091/572-273, www.aranislandferries.com).

Beware: The boat you take out to the islands may not be the same as the one you come back on. And sometimes you'll board by walking up the gangplank of one boat and walking across its deck to another boat docked beside or behind it. Make sure to ask.

Drivers should go straight to the ferry landing in Rossaveal, passing several ticket agencies and pay parking lots. At the boat dock, you'll find a convenient €5/day lot and an office that sells tickets for Island Ferries (with better WCs than on the ferry). Check to see what's going when and for how much.

From Doolin

Boats from Doolin to the Aran Islands are often canceled or run late. Even a balmy day can be too windy (or the tide can be too low) to allow for a sailing from Doolin's crude little port. But a recently opened deeper-water pier should make sailing schedules more dependable.

While it's possible to travel from Doolin to Inishmore and back in one day, keep in mind that it's a longer trip to distant Inishmore than the other two Aran Islands (leaving far less time ashore to explore before you have to turn around and sail back to Doolin). Instead, consider an overnight stay on Inishmore, or opt for a day trip to nearby, though less spectacular, Inisheer.

Parking is free beside the Doolin pier, even overnight. If you have a car, Doolin is easy to reach; without one, it's better to get to Inishmore from Rossaveal (described earlier).

ARAN ISLANDS

The scene at the Doolin ferry dock is a confusing mosh pit of competition. Two ferry companies operate from three ticket huts with one thing in mind: snaring your business. They have similar schedules and might honor the other's return tickets (if you decide you want to return at a different time). Note that the wind and tides might cause cancellations, so confirm your departure (the larger boats sailing from Rossaveal are less weather-dependent). Prices can vary with the intensity of the competition. Although they may promise to get you to Inishmore in an hour, every one of my trips in the past few years has included brief stops at Inisheer and Inishmaan en route, making the actual crossing time more than 1.5 hours.

Doolin2Aran Ferries is run by friendly Donie Garrihy and his family (to Inishmore: €25 round-trip, 1.5 hours, generally departs Doolin at 10:00 and 13:00, departs Inishmore at 11:30 and 16:00; to Inisheer: €20 same-day round-trip, 30 minutes, departs Doolin at 10:00, 11:00, 13:00, and 17:30, departs Inisheer at 8:30, 12:15. They also offer a fun €30 triangular day trip that takes you from Doolin to Inisheer, drops you off on Inisheer for about four hours, then sails along the base of the Cliffs of Moher before docking back in Doolin (departs at 10:00 and 11:00, has you back in Doolin by 16:45, runs April-Oct, tel. 065/707-5949, mobile 087-245-3239, www.doolin2aranferries.com).

Doolin Ferry/O'Brien Line, run by Bill O'Brien, has been at it the longest, with similar schedules and occasionally cheaper prices. They also offer a cruise along the base of the Cliffs of Moher that includes a stop at Inisheer (tel. 065/707-5618, www.obrienline.com).

No matter which company you choose, it's smart to check online for discounts, and call a day or two ahead to confirm schedules and prices.

BY PLANE

Aer Arann Islands, a friendly and flexible little airline, flies daily from Connemara Regional Airport, stopping at all three islands (3/day, up to 11/day in peak season, €25 one-way (when boating back), €49 round-trip, groups of 4 or more pay €44 each, 10-minute flight, tel. 091/593-034, www.aerarannislands.ie, info@aerarannislands.ie). These eight-seat planes get booked up—reserve two or three days in advance with a credit card. Connemara Regional Airport is 20 slow miles west of Galway—allow 45 minutes for the drive,

plus 30 minutes to check in before the scheduled departure. A minibus shuttle—€3 one-way—runs from Victoria Hotel off Eyre Square in Galway an hour before each flight. Be sure to reserve a space on the shuttle bus at the same time you book your flight. The Kilronan airport on Inishmore is minuscule. A minibus shuttle (€3 one-way, €5 round-trip) travels the two miles between the airport and Kilronan (stop is behind the Aran Sweater Market).

From May through September, a sightseeing-only Aer Arann flight leaves from the same airport at 12:00 each day. You'll fly above all three Aran Islands with an extra swoop past the Cliffs of Moher (€60, 40 minutes, may not go if not enough people sign up).

CONNEMARA & COUNTY MAYO

If you have a car, consider spending a day exploring the wild western Irish fringe known as Connemara and straying into historic County Mayo. Gaze up at the peak of Croagh Patrick, the mountain from which St. Patrick supposedly banished the snakes from Ireland. Pass through the desolate Doo Lough Valley on a road stained with tragic famine history. Bounce on a springy peat bog, and drop in at a Westport pub owned by a member of the Chieftains (a well-known traditional Irish music group). This beautiful area also claims a couple of towns—Cong and Leenane—where classic Irish movies were filmed, as well as the photogenic Kylemore Abbey.

Connemara makes a satisfying day trip by car from Galway. Without a car, you can take a tour from Galway or at least get to Westport by bus. Public transportation in this region is patchy, and some areas are not served at all. Trains connect Galway and Westport to Dublin, but not to each other.

BUS TOURS OF CONNEMARA

Three Galway-based organizations—**Lally Tours, Healy Tours,** and **Galway Tour Company**—run all-day tours of nearby regions (€20-25). Tours of Connemara include the *Quiet Man* cottage, Kylemore Abbey, Clifden, and a "famine village." Galway Tour Company takes a slightly different route that includes Cong but omits the coast of Connemara. Tours go most days, heading out about 10:00 and returning at 17:30 (departing from the private coach station on Fairgreen Road in Galway—across from the TI, call to confirm exact itinerary: Lally Tours tel. 091/562-905, www.lallytours.com; Healy Tours tel. 091/770-066, mobile 087-259-

0160, www.healytours.ie; Galway Tour Company tel. 091/566-566, www.galwaytourcompany.com). All three companies also offer tours of the Burren and Cliffs of Moher, with discounts if you book two separate tours. Drivers take cash only; to pay with a credit card, book ahead.

Connemara and Mayo Driving Tour

This self-guided loop trip takes a full day and involves five hours of driving, not including stops (almost 200 miles/320 km, using Galway as your base). Start early, so your day will be less rushed. Those wanting to slow down and linger can sleep in Westport. These country roads, punctuated by blind curves and surprise bumps, are shared by trucks, tractors, cyclists, more tractors, and sheep. Drive sanely, and bring rain gear and your sense of humor. This is rural Ireland with all the trimmings.

Take along a good map (Ordnance Survey atlases are widely sold in Ireland). Before you start, study the loop connecting these points: Galway, Cong, Westport, Louisburgh, Leenane, Kylemore Abbey, Clifden, Roundstone, and back to Galway. Get on the road before 9:00 to ensure you'll have the time you need to do this region justice.

Route Summary: Take N-84 north out of Galway; the road becomes R-334 in Headford. At Cross, take R-346 into Cong and R-345 back out again. At Neale, go north, putting you back on R-334. Pick up N-84 again as it winds through Ballinrobe to Partry. Take R-330 from Partry to Westport. After lunch in Westport, go west on R-335 through Louisburgh and south through Doo Lough Valley all the way to Leenane. Meet N-59 in Leenane and take it to Kylemore Abbey, continuing to Letterfrack and Connemara National Park. Continue south to Clifden, where you'll turn off onto R-341. Hug the coast through Roundstone before finding the junction with N-59 near Recess. Follow N-59 back to Galway via Maam Cross and Oughterard.

LOOP TRIP FROM GALWAY

• *From Galway's Eyre Square, drive north out of town on Prospect Hill Road. Follow the signs at each roundabout in the direction of Castlebar onto N–84. You'll soon be out of Galway's suburbs and crossing miles of flat bogland laced with simple rock walls. At Headford, keep straight through town as the road changes names to R–334. At Cross, take R–346 to Cong. You'll pass the grand, gray gateway of Ashford Castle (on the left) as you approach the town.*

Cong

Plan to spend an hour in Cong (1.5 hours if you include the Ashford Castle grounds). Cross the small bridge and park in front of the abbey. Drop into the **TI** across from the abbey entrance for a map (Sun-Thu 9:15-17:30, closed Fri-Sat and Nov-Feb, tel. 094/954-6542). There are no banks or ATMs in Cong (the closest ATM is 10 miles away in Ballinrobe). Public WCs are 50 yards down the street.

Visiting Cong: Across from the WCs is the *Quiet Man* **cottage.** That's right, pilgrim, this town is where John Wayne and Maureen O'Hara made the famous John Ford film *The Quiet Man* in 1951. The gift shop is upstairs; downstairs are the cottage's modest historical exhibits and film props, only worth it for diehard fans of the Duke (€5, daily 10:00-16:00, closed Nov-mid-March, tel. 094/954-6089).

We're here for the ruins of **Cong Abbey** (free and always open). The abbey was built in the early 1100s, when Romanesque was going out of style and Gothic was coming in; you'll see the mixture of rounded Romanesque and pointy Gothic arch styles in the doorway. The famous Cross of Cong, which held a holy relic of what was supposedly a splinter of the True Cross, was hoisted aloft at the front of processions of Augustinian monks during High Masses in this church. This Irish art treasure is now on display in Dublin's National Museum. Rory O'Connor, the last Irish high king, died in this abbey in 1198. After O'Connor realized he could never outfight the superior Norman armies, he retreated to Cong and spent his last years here in monastic isolation.

Take a walk through the cloister and down the gravel path behind the abbey. The forested grounds are lush, and the stream water is incredibly clear. Cong's salmon hatchery contributes to western Ireland's reputation for great fishing. The monks fished for more than sinners. They built the modest **Monks' Fishing Hut,** just  over the footbridge, right on the bank so that the river flowed underneath. They lowered a net through the floor and attached a bell to the rope; whenever a fish was netted, the bell would ring.

To reach **Ashford Castle** from the abbey, face the Romanesque/Gothic main entrance and go left around the corner of the abbey, walking 15 minutes down the pleasant forested lane onto the grounds of the castle, which is hidden behind the trees. Garden lovers happily stroll the lakeside paradise once owned by the Guinness beer family. The castle evolved from the original, modest Norman keep into this sprawling Victorian complex that rents some of the finest rooms in all of Ireland. Casual gawkers are discouraged inside. Many scenes from *The Quiet Man* were filmed on the castle grounds. President Reagan stayed here in 1984, and actor Pierce Brosnan chose these gardens for his wedding reception in 2001. Bought for €50 million in 2008, the castle was resold for €20 million in 2013, a steep lesson in the burst bubble of Celtic Tiger property values. As you stroll the grounds, contemplate the fact that "tourism" (the notion of travel solely for enjoyment) didn't exist until the Victorian Age. Before that time, travel was a chore endured only by armies, refugees, traders, emigrants, and religious pilgrims.

Animal lovers, aviation engineers, and wannabe medieval hunters will thrill to the **Ireland School of Falconry,** hidden on the Ashford Castle grounds. You'll need to book ahead to visit the school, though you may get lucky and be able to see the birds if you are walking the grounds. Parking is available for falconers—ask for directions when you reserve. To walk there from the TI in Cong (30 minutes), head to the back side of the castle (with gardens and fountains). As you face the lake (with the castle behind you), turn right and follow *Falconry* signs 500 yards west, straight up the terraced sidewalk. Watch for the sign on the left leading you into the trees and up to the front gate (you may have to ring the buzzer).

Once inside the courtyard you'll be surrounded by pens housing falcons, owls, and hawks. After a brief Falcon and Owl 101 lesson, you're led on a "hawk walk" through the forest with an expert handler, sporting on his forearm a Harris hawk—a breed the school's brochure says is "renowned for its easygoing temperament and unusually sociable nature." The handler teaches you the surprising intricacies of falconry, and then you have an opportunity to launch and land a bird from your own arm...a unique opportunity you didn't realize you had on your bucket-list (great photo op, must reserve ahead, €80 for 1 participant, €65 each for 2, €55 each for 3, €50 each for 4-10 participants, no charge for spectators who don't launch and land the birds, tel. 094/954-6820, mobile 087-297-6092, www.falconry.ie, info@falconry.ie).

Eating in Cong: Fuel up with a cup of coffee and homemade dessert at the **$$ Hungry Monk Café** (Mon-Sat 10:00-17:00, closed Sun, shorter hours off-season, Wi-Fi, on Abbey Street across from public WCs and a few doors down from TI, tel. 094/954-5842). A solid pub-grub lunch can be had at the **$$ Crows Nest Pub** (daily 12:00-18:00, Main Street, tel. 094/954-6243).

• *Depart Cong over the same bridge on which you entered. As you head out, try to imagine the dry canal that once existed here. Cong (from*

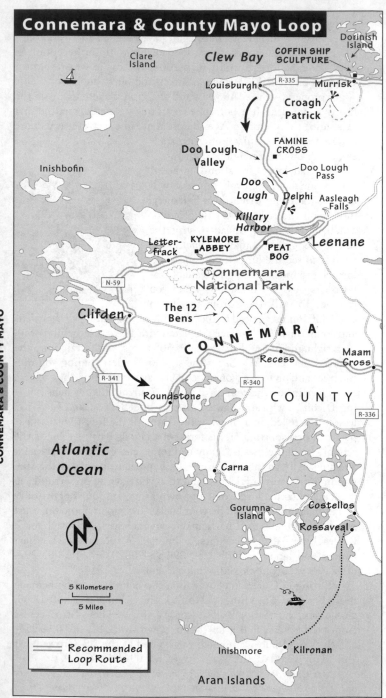

Connemara & County Mayo Loop

Dorinish Island

Clare Island

Clew Bay

COFFIN SHIP SCULPTURE

Louisburgh • R-335 • Murrisk

Croagh Patrick

Inishbofin

FAMINE CROSS

Doo Lough Valley

Doo Lough

Doo Lough Pass

Delphi

Aasleagh Falls

Killary Harbor

Letter-frack

KYLEMORE ABBEY

PEAT BOG

Leenane

Connemara National Park

N-59

The 12 Bens

Clifden •

C O N N E M A R A

Recess •

Maam Cross

R-341

Roundstone

R-340

C O U N T Y

R-336

Atlantic Ocean

Carna •

Gorumna Island

Costellos

Rossaveal

N

5 Kilometers

5 Miles

Inishmore

• Kilronan

Aran Islands

— Recommended Loop Route

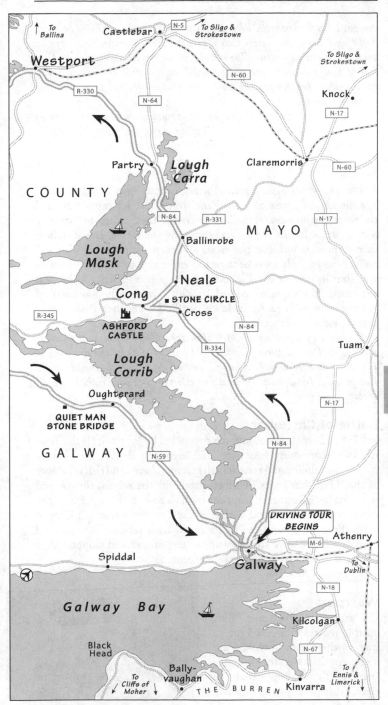

conga, *Irish for "isthmus"*) *lies between two large lakes. Built between 1848 and 1854, this canal was a Great Potato Famine work project that stoked only appetites. The canal, complete with locks, would have linked Lough Mask to the north with Lough Corrib to the south. But the limestone bedrock proved too porous, making the canal an idea that wouldn't hold water.*

Take R-345 out of Cong (left turn opposite the main stone gateway to the grounds of Ashford Castle). Heading north, you'll pass through the tiny hamlet of...

Neale

About 145 years ago, a retired army captain was hired to manage the nearby estate of Lord Erne. But the strict captain treated the tenants who worked the lands harshly. They united to ostracize him by deserting their jobs and shunning the estate. Local tradesmen stopped working at the estate and even the postman wouldn't deliver the mail. It soon became too expensive to supply the estate and ship in distant loyal laborers (with police escorts) to harvest the crops. The captain's name? Boycott. Eventually "boycotting" became a popular tactic in labor conflicts—another Irish export that took root in other lands.

• *At Neale, go north on R-334, then take N-84 from Ballinrobe to Partry. At Partry, turn left off N-84 onto R-330 in the direction of Westport (the easy-to-miss turnoff is just after you pass the thatch-roofed Village Inn). In the countryside a few kilometers to your right is the site of the...*

Battle of Castlebar

In 1798, a French invasion force supported by locals dealt the British an embarrassing loss here. The surprised British forces were routed, and their rapid retreat is slyly remembered in Irish rebel lore as the "Castlebar races." Unfortunately for the rebels, this proved to be the last glimmer of hope for Irish victory in that uprising. The redcoats reorganized and within weeks defeated the small force of 1,300 Frenchmen and the ill-equipped Irish rebels. The captured French soldiers were treated as prisoners of war and shipped back home, while the Irish rebels were executed.

• *Continue on R-330 to...*

Westport

On arrival in Westport, soak up the genteel vibe—lacking in many other Irish towns. Park along the Mall under the trees that line the shallow canal-like river. This is a planned town,

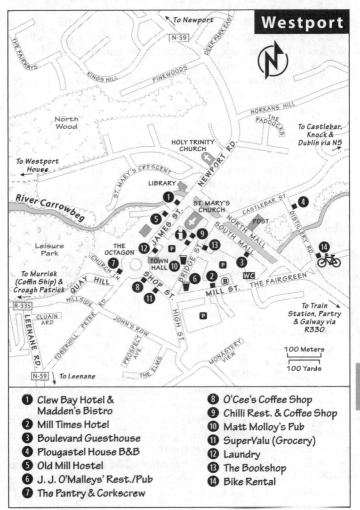

Westport

1. Clew Bay Hotel & Madden's Bistro
2. Mill Times Hotel
3. Boulevard Guesthouse
4. Plougastel House B&B
5. Old Mill Hostel
6. J. J. O'Malleys' Rest./Pub
7. The Pantry & Corkscrew
8. O'Cee's Coffee Shop
9. Chilli Rest. & Coffee Shop
10. Matt Molloy's Pub
11. SuperValu (Grocery)
12. Laundry
13. The Bookshop
14. Bike Rental

built in the Georgian style in the late 1700s to support the adjacent estate of Westport House (skip it for better manors at Mount Stewart House and Muckross House). The town once thrived on the linen industry created by local Irish handlooms. But after the Act of Union with Britain in 1801, Westport was unable to compete with the industrialized British linen makers and fell into decline. The town is still pretty and a good place for a relaxed lunch and some exploration on foot.

The **TI** is on Bridge Street (Mon-Fri 9:00-17:45, Sat 9:00-16:45 except July-Aug until 17:45, shorter hours Nov-Feb, closed Sun year-round, tel. 098/25711).

For a short visit, free **parking** is allowed on the street for two hours; for longer stays, park at your B&B or use the pay-and-display lots (€0.70/first hour, €0.30/hour after that, enforced Mon-Fri 8:30-19:00, Sat 10:00-18:00, free on Sun).

The **post office** is on the North Mall (Mon-Fri 9:00-17:30, Sat 9:00-13:00, closed Sun). **Laundry** can be dropped off early at Gills and picked up late the same day (€12/load, Mon-Fri 9:00-18:30, Sat 9:00-18:00, closed Sun, James Street, tel. 098/25819). For rainy-day browsing, check out **The Bookshop,** run by friendly Seamus (Mon-Sat 9:30-18:30, Sun 11:00-18:00, daily until 21:30 June-Aug, Bridge Street, tel. 098/26816). You gotta love one of the only shops in Ireland that stocks this guidebook.

Visiting Westport: As you stroll the South Mall in front of St. Mary's Church, you'll pass the bust of Westport-born **Major John MacBride,** one of the more colorful rebels of the 1916 Easter Uprising. He had previously fought with the Boers against the British, then wed beautiful stage actress Maude Gonne (much to the consternation of Maude's jealous suitor W. B. Yeats, who immortalized MacBride as a "drunken, vainglorious lout"). MacBride unexpectedly wandered into a band of rebels marching into position in Dublin at the start of the rebellion and joined them, and was among the 14 executed at Kilmainham Gaol after the failed rising.

For a scenic **hike or bike ride,** consider the 26-mile (42 km) route to Achill Island along the Great Western Greenway (www. greenway.ie). From 1895 to 1937, a narrow-gauge railway operated from Westport to Achill Island. By 2010, the rails had been replaced by a level, paved path, creating an ideal rural route dedicated to bikers and walkers (no vehicles, dogs, or horses allowed). You'll cross stone bridges, wind through forested sections as well as open bog stretches, and usually have the sea in sight as you hug the flatter coastline. For bike rentals, check out **Clew Bay Bike Hire and Outdoor Adventures;** if you want to bike only a section of the route, they can arrange a shuttle-bus pick-up for Newport, Mulranny, or Achill. They also offer more elaborate tours, such as ones that include fishing trips in the bay, as well as kayaking trips (€15/day for bikes, €40/day for electric bikes, daily 9:00-18:00, Distillery Road, tel. 098/24818 or 098/37675, www.clewbaybikehire.ie).

Sleeping in Westport: For those wanting extra time to explore, Westport is the best place along this route to spend a night. All of the following listings are centrally located. Prices vary quite a bit depending on the season (check for online deals at the two hotels).

$$ Clew Bay Hotel has 54 large, modern rooms decked out in cherrywood furniture (free use of adjacent pool and fitness center, James Street, tel. 098/28088, www.clewbayhotel.com, info@clewbayhotel.com).

$$ Mill Times Hotel has a fresh, woody feel, with 34 comfortable rooms and convenient, free underground parking (Mill Street, tel. 098/29200, www.milltimeshotel.ie, info@milltimeshotel.ie).

$ Boulevard Guesthouse is the best value in town. Located right on the leafy South Mall, it has six large, quiet, tasteful rooms and a cushy lounge with an interesting guest library under the stairs. Sadie and John Moran make you feel welcome (family rooms, cash only, discount with multiple-night stay, light continental breakfast, parking, South Mall, tel. 098/25138, mobile 087-284-4018, www. boulevard-guesthouse.com, boulevardguesthouse@gmail.com).

$ Plougastel House B&B, named after Westport's sister town in Brittany, has six inviting, smartly furnished earth-tone rooms with marble-floored bathrooms (cash only, Distillery Road, tel. 098/25198, www.plougastel-house.com, info@plougastel-house. com, Sandra Corcoran).

¢ Old Mill Hostel is a thick-walled stone structure that could stop a tank. Like many hostels, it's an inexpensive ramshackle bunkhouse for an international mix of youthful vagabonds (James Street, tel. 098/27045, www.oldmillhostel.com, info@ oldmillhostell.com).

Eating in Westport: Most of your best bets are clustered on Bridge Street. A good choice for dinner is **$$$ J. J. O'Malleys'** restaurant (daily 17:00-22:00, Bridge Street—upstairs, above their pub, tel. 098/27307). **$$$ The Pantry & Corkscrew** is a posh but friendly local favorite, serving creative Irish-Italian fusion in a woody, welcoming atmosphere (daily 17:00-22:00, Oct-mid-June closed Mon-Tue, reservations wise, The Octagon, tel. 098/26977, www.thepantryandcorkscrew.com). **$$ Madden's Bistro** is on the ground floor of the Clew Bay Hotel and offers contemporary casual dining (daily 12:30-21:00, James Street, tel. 098/28088).

For a quick and easy lunch, try **$ O'Cee's Coffee Shop** (cafeteria-style lunches, Mon-Sat 8:30-18:30, Sun 9:00-16:00, enter from Shop Street or inside SuperValu, tel. 098/27000) or **$ Chilli Restaurant & Coffee Shop** (daily 9:30-17.00, also Wed-Sun 18:00-21:00, Bridge Street, tel. 098/27007).

Irish music fans seek out **Matt Molloy's** pub (no food unless you're on an all-peanut diet, great sessions at 21:30, grab a seat by 20:30 or stand all night, Bridge Street, tel. 098/26655). Matt Molloy isn't just the owner of the pub—he's also a flutist for the Chieftains, the group credited with much of the worldwide resurgence of interest in Irish music over the past 50 years.

The **SuperValu** market has picnic fare (daily 8:00-22:00, Shop Street).

Westport Connections: To visit Westport without a car, you can take a **bus** to/from Galway (5-7/day, 2-4 hours), Derry (2-4/ day, 6 hours, change in Sligo), or Dublin (6-7/day, 4-6 hours). For details, see www.buseireann.ie. You can also reach Dublin by **train** (5/day, 3 hours, www.irishrail.ie).

• *Leave Westport heading west on R-335. After about eight kilometers (5 miles), as you're driving along scenic Clew Bay, you'll reach a wide spot in the road called Murrisk. Stop here. In the field on your right (opposite Campbell's Pub) is the...*

Coffin Ship

This bronze ship sculpture is one of the most powerful famine memorials that you'll see in Ireland. It's a "coffin ship," like those of the late 1840s that carried the sick and starving famine survivors across the ocean in hope of a new life. But many of the ships contracted to take the desperate emigrants were barely seaworthy, no longer fit for dependable commerce. The poor were weak from starvation and vulnerable to "famine fever," which they spread to others in the putrid, cramped holds of these ships. Many who lived through the six- to eight-week journey died shortly after reaching their new country. Pause a moment to look at the silent skeletons swirling around the ship's masts. Now contemplate the fact that

famine still exists in the world. And before judging the lack of effective relief intervention by the British government of that time, consider the rich world's ability to ignore similar suffering today.

• *Across the road from the coffin ship is...*

Croagh Patrick

This small mountain rises 2,500 feet above the bay. In the fifth century, St. Patrick is said to have fasted on its summit for the 40 days of Lent. It's from here that he supposedly rang his bell, driving all the snakes out of Ireland. The snakes never existed, of course, but they represent the pagan beliefs that Patrick's newly arrived Christianity replaced. Every year on the last Sunday of July, "Reek Sunday" (a "reek" is a mountain peak), as many as 30,000 pilgrims hike three hours up the rocky trail to the summit in honor of St. Patrick. The most penitent attempt the hike barefoot (and often come down on a stretcher). On that Sunday, Mass is celebrated throughout the day in a modest chapel on the top.

Hikers should allow three hours to reach the top and two hours to get back down (bring plenty of water, sunscreen, and rain gear). There is a primitive WC on the summit, 30 yards below the chapel. The trail is easy to follow, but the upper half of the mountain is a steep slope of loose, shifting scree that can bang or turn exposed ankles. Both times I've climbed this, I've been glad I wore boots.

A few years ago, valuable gold deposits were discovered within Croagh Patrick. Luckily, public sentiment has kept the sacred mountain free of any commercial mining activity.

• *Continue west on R-335.*

Stretched out beside you is **Clew Bay,** peppered with more than 300 humpbacked islands of glacial gravel dumped by retreating glaciers at the end of the last Ice Age. A notorious 16th-century local named Grace O'Malley (dubbed the "Pirate Queen") once ruled this bay, even earning the grudging respect of Queen Elizabeth I herself with her clever exploits. John Lennon later chose Dorinish Island to found a short-lived hippie commune. He bought it in 1967 for £1,700; after his death Yoko Ono sold it for £30,000 (which she donated to an Irish orphanage).

• *Passing through Louisburgh, you'll turn south to enter some of the most rugged and desolate country in Ireland.*

Doo Lough Valley

Signs of human habitation vanish from the bogland, and ghosts begin to appear beside the road. About 13 kilometers (8 miles) south of Louisburgh, stop at the simple gray-stone cross on the left. The lake ahead is Doo Lough (Irish for "Black Lake"). This is the site of one of the saddest famine tales.

In the early 1800s, County Mayo's rural folk depended almost exclusively on the potato for food and were the hardest hit when

the Great Potato Famine came in 1845. In the winter of 1849, about 600 starving Irish walked 12 miles from Louisburgh to Delphi Lodge, hoping to get food from their landlord, but they were turned away. On the walk back, almost 200 of them died along the side of this road. Today, the road still seems to echo with the despair of those hungry souls, and it inspires an annual walk that commemorates the tragedy. Archbishop Desmond Tutu made the walk in 1991, shortly before South Africa ended its apartheid system.

• *Continue south on R-335. You'll get a fine view of **Aasleagh Falls** on* *the left. In late May, the banks below the falls explode with lush, wild, purple rhododendron blossoms. Cross the bridge after the falls, and turn right onto N-59 toward Leenane. You'll drive along Killary Harbor, an Irish example of a fjord. This long, narrow body of water was carved by an advancing glacier.*

Leenane

This "town" (actually just a crossroads) is a good place for a break. The 1990 movie *The Field,* starring Limerick-born Richard Harris, was filmed here. Glance at the photos of the making of the movie on the wall of **Hamilton's Pub.** While you're there, find the old photo of the British dreadnought battleships that filled Killary Harbor when King Edward VII visited a century ago. Drop into the **Leenane Sheep and Wool Centre** (on the left as you enter town) to see interesting wool-spinning and weaving demonstrations (€5, daily 9:30-18:00, closed Nov-March; demos run 11:00-16:00, but with no set times—call ahead; cafe, tel. 095/42323, www.sheepandwoolcentre.com).

• *As you continue west on N-59, notice the rows of blue floats in Killary Harbor. They're there to mark mussel farms growing on hanging nets in the cold seawater. As you climb out of the fjord valley about 8 kilometers (5 miles) past Leenane, you'll pass (on the left) some areas that offer good, close looks at a turf cut in a peat bog.*

A Slog on the Bog

Walk a few yards onto the spongy green carpet. (Watch your step on wet days to avoid squishing into a couple of inches of water.) Find a dry spot and jump up and down to get a feel for it. Have your companion jump; you'll feel the vibrations 30 feet away.

These bogs once covered almost 20 percent of Ireland. As the climate got warmer at the end of the last Ice Age, plants began growing along the sides of the many shallow lakes and ponds. When the plants died in these waterlogged areas, there wasn't enough oxygen for them to fully decompose. Over the centuries, the moss built up, layer after dead layer, helping to slowly fill in the lakes. During World War I, this sphagnum moss was collected to use in bandages to soak up blood (it absorbs many times its weight in fluids).

It's this wet, oxygen-starved ecosystem that has preserved ancient artifacts so well, many of which can be seen in Dublin's National Museum. Even forgotten containers of butter, churned centuries ago and buried to keep cool, have been discovered. But most bizarre are the wrinkled bog mummies that are occasionally unearthed. These human remains (some of them close to 2,000 years old) are so incredibly intact that their eyelashes, hairstyles,

Ireland's Misunderstood Nomads

When you see a small cluster of trailers at the side of an Irish road, you're looking at a dying way of life. These are the Travellers, a nomadic throwback to the days when wandering craftsmen, musicians, and evicted unfortunates crowded rural Ireland. Often mislabeled as Gypsies, they have no ethnic ties to those Eastern European nomads, but rather have an Irish heritage going back centuries.

There were once many more Travellers, who lived in tents and used horse-drawn carts as they wandered the countryside in search of work. Before the famine, when Irish hospitality was a given, Travellers filled a niche in Irish society. They would do odd jobs, such as repairing furniture, sweeping chimneys, and selling horses. Skilled tinsmiths, they mended pots, pans, and stills for *poitín*—Irish moonshine. (Travellers used to be called "tinkers," but this label is now considered derogatory.) Settled-down farm folk, who rarely ventured more than 20 miles from home their entire lives, depended on the roaming Travellers for news and gossip from farther-flung regions. But post-famine rural depopulation and the gradual urbanization of the countryside forced this nomadic group to adapt to an almost sedentary existence on the fringes of towns.

Today, the 30,000 remaining Travellers are outsiders, usually treated with suspicion by other Irish. Locals often complain that petty thefts go up when Travellers set up camp in a nearby "halting site," and that they leave garbage behind when they depart. Although most visible in rural encampments, Travellers still frequent the outdoor horse market at Smithfield Village in Dublin on the first Sunday of each month. They are very religious and often camp near the pilgrimage town of Knock.

Travellers tend to keep to themselves, marry young, have large families, and speak their own Irish Gaelic-based language (called Shelta, Gammon, or Cant). Attempts to settle Travellers in government housing and integrate their children into schools have met with mixed success, as portrayed poignantly in the 1992 movie *Into the West*.

and the last meal in their stomachs can be identified. They were likely sacrificial offerings to the pagan gods of Celtic times.

Since these acidic bogs contain few nutrients, unique species of carnivorous plants have adapted to life here by trapping and digesting insects. The tiny pink sundew (less than an inch tall) has delicate spikes glistening with insect-attracting fluid. Find a mossy area and look closely at the variety of tiny plants. In summer, you'll see white tufts of bog cotton growing in marshy areas.

People have been cutting, drying, and burning peat as a fuel source for more than a thousand years. The cutting usually begins in April or May, when drier weather approaches. You'll probably see stacks of "turf" piled up to dry along recent cuts. Pick up a brick and fondle it. Dried peat is surprisingly light and stiff. In central Ireland, there are even industrial peat cuts that were begun after World War II to fuel power stations. But in the past few decades, bogs have been recognized as a rare habitat, and conservation efforts have been encouraged. These days, the sweet, nostalgic smell of burning peat is becoming increasingly rare.

• *Continue west on N-59. The road soon crosses a shallow lake, with a great view of Kylemore Abbey to the right. But don't stop here—you'll get a better photo from the parking lot, a few hundred yards ahead. Pull into the lot and enjoy the view (gate closes at 18:00).*

Kylemore Abbey

This Neo-Gothic country house was built by the wealthy English businessman Mitchell Henry in the 1860s, after he and his wife

had honeymooned in the area. Now they are both buried on the grounds. After World War I, refugee Benedictine nuns from Ypres, Belgium, took it over and ran it as an exclusive girls' boarding school—which peaked at 200 students—until it closed in 2010. In 2015 the Indiana-based University of Notre Dame signed a 30-year lease to use part of the facility for summer classes and student housing. The nuns still live upstairs, but you can visit the half-dozen open rooms downstairs that display the Henry family's cushy lifestyle (with a 15-minute audiovisual presentation).

For me, the best thing about the abbey is the view of it from the lakeshore. But garden enthusiasts will seek out the extensive walled Victorian gardens. From the abbey, the gardens are a one-mile, level walk or quick shuttle bus ride (runs every 15 minutes). Hourly tours of the abbey and gardens are so-so; it's best just to enjoy the setting.

Cost and Hours: Overpriced €13 combo-ticket for abbey and gardens, 10 percent discount if bought online, daily 9:00-18:00, July-Aug until 19:00, shorter hours off-season, WCs in gift shop next to parking lot, cafeteria swims with the chaos of multiple big-bus tour groups, tel. 095/52001, www.kylemoreabbeytourism.ie.

• *Heading west from the abbey, you'll drive less than 8 km (5 miles) to the town of Letterfrack. Pass through the town and go left off N–59 to reach...*

Connemara National Park

This park encompasses almost 5,000 acres of wild bog and moun-tain scenery. The visitors center displays worthwhile exhibits of local flora and fauna, which are well-explained in the 15-minute *Man and the Landscape* film that runs every half-hour (free; park open daily year-round; visitors center open daily 9:00-17:30, closed Nov-Feb, last entry 45 minutes before closing; tel. 095/41054, www.connemaranationalpark.ie). Nature lovers may want to re-verse the direction of my driving loop (and skimp on sightseeing time at other stops) in order to enjoy a two-hour walking tour with a park naturalist (July-Aug Wed and Fri at 11:00, departs from visitors center). Call ahead to confirm walking tour schedules, and bring rain gear and hiking shoes.

• *If you're running short on time, you could stay on N–59 the whole way back to Galway. But I prefer to turn south off N–59 in Clifden to enjoy a scenic coastal loop on R–341.*

Coastal Connemara

The essence of scenic Connemara—rocky yet seductive—is cap-tured in a neat little 24-mile (38 km) lumpy loop on R-341. The 12 Bens (peaks) of Connemara loom deeper inland. In the foreground, broad shelves of bare bedrock are netted with stone walls, which interlock through the landscape. The ocean slaps the hardscrabble shore. Fishermen cast into their favorite little lakes, and ponies trot in windswept fields. Abandoned, roofless stone cottages stand mute, keeping their stories to themselves. The only settlement on this loop to speak of is Roundstone, a perfect place to stop for a cup of coffee before turning home.

• *R-341 links back up with N-59 near Recess. At the junction with N-59, turn right, and follow Galway signs back through Recess, Maam Cross, and Oughterard. Our tour is over.*

Between Galway and Derry

Travelers continuing on to Northern Ireland (or County Donegal) should get an early start. Allow a day for the drive from Galway to Derry (or Portrush, one hour beyond Derry), with these interesting stops along the way. The town of Knock is right on N-17 as you head north out of Galway, while Strokestown is farther east in County Roscommon. Fill up your tank before crossing into Northern Ireland, since gas is a little cheaper here.

Town of Knock

In 1879, locals saw the Virgin Mary, St. Joseph, and St. John appear against the south gable of this tiny town's church. Word of miraculous healings turned the trickle of pilgrims into a flood and put Knock solidly on the pilgrimage map. Today, you can visit the shrine. At the edge of the site, a small but earnest folk museum shows religious knick-knacks, photos of a papal visit, and sturdy slices of traditional life (€4, daily 10:00-18:00, tel. 094/938-8100).

▲▲Strokestown Park National Famine Museum

The Great Potato Famine of 1845-1849 was the bleakest period in Irish history—so traumatic that its effects halved the Irish population over the next 50 years and sent desperate, hungry Irish peasants across the globe. It also crystallized Irish-nationalist hatred of British rule. The National Famine Museum fills a mansion on the former estate of the Mahon family in the market town of Strokestown, 60 miles (96.5 km) northeast of Galway.

Cost and Hours: You have several options: museum, house tour, six-acre Georgian walled gardens, or a combination of the three. One sight costs €9, two cost €12, and a combo-ticket for all three is €13.50. Open daily 10:30-17:30, Nov-mid-March until 16:00; "Big House" tours (45 minutes) go daily in high season at 12:00, 14:30, and 16:00; tel. 071/963-3013, www.strokestownpark. ie.

Eating: Drivers connecting Westport or Galway to either Dublin or Northern Ireland can stop here en route and grab lunch in the museum café.

Visiting the Museum: Thoughtful exhibits explain how three million Irish peasants survived on a surprisingly nutritious prefam-

Virgin Mary Shrines

During your time in Ireland, you'll frequently see pretty little roadside shrines and grottoes honoring the Virgin Mary. The  older ones were built in 1929 to celebrate 100 years of Catholic emancipation (the Roman Catholic Relief Act of 1829, spearheaded by Daniel O'Connell—see page 231). The majority were constructed in the "Marian Year" (devoted to Mary) of 1954. This was the 100th anniversary of Pope Pius IX's 1854 proclamation of the dogma of the Immaculate Conception (God kept the Virgin Mary "from the stain of original sin" from the moment she was conceived). A record number of devout Catholics flocked to the holy pilgrimage village of Knock to pray during the centenary, and many Irish girls born that year were named Marian.

A more recent, related event happened in 1985 on the other side of the country at a shrine devoted to the Virgin Mary, outside the tiny hamlet of Ballinspittle (4 miles southwest of Kinsale in County Cork). A number of locals claimed they had witnessed the statue of Mary moving spontaneously, and thousands of pilgrims flocked there that summer. Some pilgrims said they also witnessed the statue moving. Unlike the apparition of the Virgin Mary in Knock in 1879, the Catholic Church remained neutral on the Ballinspittle event, and interest in it eventually subsided.

ine diet of buttermilk and potatoes (12 pounds per day per average male laborer...potatoes are 80 percent water). When a fungus destroyed the potato crop, it sparked the Great Potato Famine, and as many as a million Irish people died of starvation.

Major Mahon, the ill-fated landlord here during the famine, found it cheaper to fill three "coffin ships" bound for America with his evicted, starving tenants than pay the taxes for their upkeep in the local workhouse. When almost half died at sea of "famine fever," he was assassinated.

The tours of the musty "Big House" provide insights into the gulf that divided the Protestant ascendancy and their Catholic house staff. Afterward, find the servants' tunnel—connecting the kitchen to the stable—built to avoid cluttering the Mahon family's views with unsightly common laborers.

NORTHERN IRELAND

NORTHERN IRELAND

The island of Ireland was once the longest-held colony of Great Britain. Unlike its Celtic cousins, Scotland and Wales, Ireland has always been distant from London—a distance due as much to its Catholicism as to the Irish Sea.

Four hundred years ago, Protestant settlers from England and Scotland were strategically "planted" in Catholic Ireland to help assimilate the island into the British economy. In 1620, the dominant English powerbase in London first felt entitled to call both islands—Ireland as well as Britain—the "British Isles" on maps (a geographic label that irritates Irish Nationalists to this day). These Protestant settlers established their own cultural toehold on the island, laying claim to the most fertile land. Might made right, and God was on their side. Meanwhile, the underdog Catholic Irish held strong to their Gaelic culture on their ever-diminishing, boggy, rocky farms.

Over the centuries, British rule hasn't been easy. By the beginning of the 20th century, the sparse Protestant population could no longer control the entire island. When Ireland won its independence in 1921 (after a bloody guerrilla war against British rule), 26 of the island's 32 counties became the Irish Free State, ruled from Dublin with dominion status in the British Commonwealth—similar to Canada's level of sovereignty. In 1949, these 26 counties left the Commonwealth and became the Republic of Ireland, severing all political ties with Britain. Meanwhile, the six remaining northeastern counties—the only ones with a Protestant majority who considered themselves British—chose not to join the Irish Free State and remained part of the UK.

But embedded within these six counties—now joined as the political entity called Northern Ireland—was a large, disaffected Irish (mostly Catholic) minority who felt they'd been sold down the river by the drawing of the new international border. Their political opponents were the "Unionists"—Protestant British eager to defend the union with Britain, who were primarily led by two groups: the long-established Orange Order, and the military muscle of the newly mobilized Ulster Volunteer Force (UVF). This was countered on the Irish Catholic side by the Irish Republican Army

(IRA), who wanted all 32 of Ireland's counties to be united in one Irish nation—their political goals were "Nationalist."

In World War II, the Republic stayed neutral while the North enthusiastically supported the Allied cause—winning a spot close to London's heart. Derry (a.k.a. Londonderry) became an essential Allied convoy port, while Belfast lost more than 800 civilians during four Luftwaffe bombing raids in 1941. After the war, the split between North and South seemed permanent, and Britain invested heavily in Northern Ireland to bring it solidly into the UK fold.

In the Republic of Ireland (the South), where 94 percent of the population was Catholic and only 6 percent Protestant, there was a clearly dominant majority. But in the North, at the time it was formed, Catholics were a sizable 35 percent of the population—enough to demand attention. To maintain the status quo, Protestants considered certain forms of anti-Catholic discrimination necessary. It was this discrimination that led to the Troubles, the conflict that filled headlines from the late 1960s to the late 1990s.

Four hundred years ago (during the Reformation), this was a fight over Protestant and Catholic religious differences. But over the last century, the conflict has been not about faith, but about politics: Will Northern Ireland stay part of the UK, or become

Northern Ireland Almanac

Official Name: Since Northern Ireland is not an independent state, there is no official country name. Some call it Ulster
(although historically that has
included three counties that
today lie on the Republic's side
of the border), while others
label it the Six Counties. Popu-
lation-wise, it's the smallest
country of the United Kingdom
(the other three are England,
Wales, and Scotland).

Population: Northern Ireland's
1.8 million people are about 45 percent Protestant (mostly Presbyterian and Anglican) and 40 percent Catholic. Another 5 percent profess different religions, and 10 percent claim no religious
ties. English is far and away the chief language, though Irish Gaelic is also spoken in staunchly Nationalist Catholic communities.

Despite the country's genetic homogeneity, the population
is highly segregated along political, religious, and cultural lines.
Roughly speaking, the eastern seaboard is more Unionist, Protestant, and of English-Scottish heritage, while the south and west
(bordering the Republic of Ireland) are Nationalist, Catholic, and
of Irish descent. Cities are often clearly divided between neighborhoods of one group or the other. Early in life, locals learn to
identify the highly symbolic (and highly charged) colors, jewelry,
music, names, accents, and vocabulary that distinguish the cultural groups.

Latitude and Longitude: 54°N and 5°W. It's as far north as parts
of the Alaskan panhandle.

Area: 5,400 square miles (about the size of Connecticut), con-
stituting a sixth of the island. Northern Ireland includes 6 of the
island's traditional 32 counties.

Geography: Northern Ireland is shaped roughly like a doughnut,
with the UK's largest lake in the middle (Lough Neagh, 150 square
miles and a prime eel fishery). The terrain comprises gently rolling
hills of green grass, rising to the 2,800-foot Slieve Donard. The
weather is temperate, cloudy, moist, windy, and hard to predict.

Biggest Cities: Belfast, the capital, has 300,000 residents. Half
a million people—nearly one in three Northern Irish—inhabit the

greater Belfast area. Derry (called Londonderry by Unionists) has 95,000 people.

Economy: Northern Ireland's economy is more closely tied to the UK than to the Republic of Ireland. Sectarian violence has held back growth, and the economy gets subsidies from the UK and the EU. Traditional agriculture (potatoes and grain) is fading fast, though modern techniques and abundant grassland make Northern Ireland a major producer of sheep, cows, and grass seed. Modern software and communications companies are replacing traditional manufacturing. Shipyards are rusty relics, and the linen industry is now threadbare; both are victims of cheaper labor available in Asia.

Currency: Northern Ireland uses not the euro, but the pound (£).

Exchange rate: £1 = about $1.50.

Government: Northern Ireland is not a self-governing nation, but is part of the UK, ruled from London by Queen Elizabeth II and Prime Minister Theresa May, and represented in Parliament by 18 elected Members of Parliament. For 50 years (1922-1972), Northern Ireland was granted a great deal of autonomy and self-governance, known as "Home Rule." The current National Assembly (108-seat Parliament)—after an ineffective decade of political logjams—has recently begun to show signs of rejuvenation.

Politics are dominated, of course, by the ongoing debate between Unionists (who want to preserve the union with the UK) and Nationalists (who want to join the Republic of Ireland). Two high-profile and controversial figures have been at opposite ends of this debate: the late firebrand Reverend Ian Paisley for the Unionists; and assassination-attack survivor Gerry Adams of Sinn Fein, the political arm of the IRA (who now serves in the Republic of Ireland's parliament). In a hopeful development in the spring of 2007, the two allowed themselves to be photographed together across a negotiation table (a moment both had once sworn would never happen) as London returned control of the government to Belfast.

Flag: The official flag of Northern Ireland is the Union flag of the UK. But you'll also see the green, white, and orange Irish tricolor (waved by Nationalists) and the Northern Irish flag (white with a red cross and a red hand at its center), which is used by Unionists (see "The Red Hand of Ulster" sidebar on page 396).

part of the Republic of Ireland? The indigenous Irish of Northern Ireland, who generally want to unite with Ireland, happen to be Catholic (like their cousins to the south). The descendants of the Scottish and English settlers, who generally want to remain part of Britain, happen to be Protestant (like their beloved monarch).

Partly inspired by Martin Luther King Jr. and the civil rights movement in America—beamed into Irish living rooms by the new magic of television news—in the 1960s, the Catholic minority in Northern Ireland began a nonviolent struggle to end discrimination, advocating for better jobs and housing. Extremists polarized issues, and demonstrations—also broadcast on TV news—became violent. Unionists were afraid that if the island became one nation, the relatively poor Republic of Ireland would drag down the comparatively affluent North, and that the high percentage of Catholics would spell repression for the Protestants. As Unionist Protestants and Nationalist Catholics clashed in 1969, the British Army entered the fray. Their role, initially a peacekeeping one, gradually evolved into acting as muscle for the Unionist government. In 1972, a tragic watershed year, more than 500 people died as combatants moved from petrol bombs to guns, and a new, more violent IRA emerged. In that 30-year (1968-1998) chapter of the struggle for an independent and united Ireland, more than 3,000 people were killed.

A 1985 agreement granted Dublin a consulting role in the Northern Ireland government. Unionists bucked this idea, and violence escalated. That same year, Belfast City Hall draped a huge, defiant banner under its dome, proclaiming, *Belfast Says No*.

In 1994, the banner came down. In the 1990s—with Ireland's membership in the EU, the growth of its economy, and the weakening of the Catholic Church's influence—the consequences of a united Ireland became slightly less threatening to the Unionists. Also in 1994, the IRA declared a cease-fire, and the Protestant Ulster Volunteer Force (UVF) followed suit.

The Nationalists wanted British troops out of Northern Ireland, while the Unionists demanded that the IRA turn in its arms. Optimists hailed the signing of a breakthrough peace plan in 1998, called the "Good Friday Accord" by Nationalists, or the "Belfast Agreement" by Unionists. This led to the release of political prisoners on both sides in 2000—a highly emotional event.

Recently, additional progress has taken place on both fronts. The IRA finally "verifiably put their arms beyond use" in 2005, and backed the political peace process. In 2009, most Loyalist paramilitary groups did the same. Meanwhile, British Army surveillance towers were dismantled in 2006, and the army formally ended its 38-year-long Operation Banner campaign in 2007.

A tiny splinter group of stubborn IRA diehards (calling themselves the "Real IRA") continues to smolder. Their efforts at publicity are roundly condemned not only by hard-line Unionists, but also by former IRA leaders like government minister Martin McGuinness and his Sinn Fein party, who now prefer to pursue their Nationalist goals through the democratic process.

In 2010, the peace process was jolted forward by a surprisingly forthright apology offered by then British Prime Minister David Cameron, who expressed regret for the British Army's offenses on Bloody Sunday (see sidebar on page 439). The apology was prompted by the Saville Report—the results of an investigation conducted by the UK government as part of the Good Friday Accord. It found that the 1972 shootings of Nationalist civil-rights marchers on Bloody Sunday by British soldiers was "unjustified" and the victims innocent (to the intense relief of the victims' families, who had fought since 1972 to clear their loved ones' names).

Major hurdles to a lasting peace persist, but downtown checkpoints and "bomb-damage clearance sales" have been gone for decades. In 2013, the G8 leaders of eight of the largest economies in the world (US President Barack Obama, Russia's President Vladimir Putin, and Germany's Chancellor Angela Merkel to name a few) chose serene, lake-splattered County Fermanagh to hold their annual summit.

Today, more tourists than ever are venturing north to Belfast and Derry, and cruise-ship crowds disembark in Belfast to board charter buses that fan out to visit the Giant's Causeway (see page 420) and Old Bushmills Distillery (see page 423).

SAFETY

A generation ago, Northern Ireland was a sadly contorted corner of the world. On my first visit, I remember thinking that even the name of this region sounded painful ("Ulster" sounded to me like a combination of "ulcer" and "blister").

Today tourists in Northern Ireland are no longer considered courageous (or reckless). When locals spot you with a map and a lost look on your face, they're likely to ask, "Wot yer lookin fer?" in their distinctive Northern accent. They're not suspicious of you, but rather trying to help you find your way. You're safer in Belfast than in many other UK cities—and far safer, statistically, than in most major US cities. You have to look for trouble to find it here. Just don't seek out spit-and-sawdust pubs in working-class neighborhoods and spew simplistic and naive opinions about sensitive local topics.

Tourists notice the tension mainly during the "marching season" (Easter-Aug, peaking in early July). July 12—"the Twelfth"—is traditionally the most confrontational day of the year in the North, when proud Protestant Unionist Orangemen march to cel-

Northern Ireland Terminology

Ulster (one of Ireland's four ancient provinces) consists of nine counties in the northern part of the island of Ireland. Six of these make up Northern Ireland (pronounced "Norn Iron" by locals), while three counties remain part of the Republic.

Unionists—and the more hardline, working-class **Loyalists**—want the North to remain in the UK. The **Ulster Unionist Party (UUP),** the political party representing moderate Unionist views, is currently led by Mike Nesbitt. (Nobel Peace Prize co-winner David Trimble led the UUP from 1995 to 2005.) The **Democratic Unionist Party (DUP),** led by First Minister Arlene Foster and supported by parliamentarian Jeffrey Donaldson, takes a harder stance in defense of Unionism. The **Ulster Volunteer Force (UVF),** the **Ulster Freedom Fighters (UFF),** and the **Ulster Defense Association (UDA)** are the Loyalist paramilitary organizations mentioned most frequently in newspapers and on spray-painted walls.

Nationalists—and the more hardline, working-class **Republicans**—want a united and independent Ireland ruled by Dublin. The **Social Democratic Labor Party (SDLP),** founded by Nobel Peace Prize co-winner John Hume and currently led by Colum Eastwood, is the moderate political party representing Nationalist views. **Sinn Fein** (shin fayn), led by Gerry Adams (working closely with Deputy First Minister Martin McGuinness), takes a harder stance in defense of Nationalism. The **Irish Republican Army (IRA)** is the Nationalist paramilitary organization (linked with Sinn Fein) mentioned most often in the press and in graffiti. The **Alliance Party,** led by David Ford, wants to bridge the gap between Unionists and Nationalists.

To gain more insight into the complexity of the **Troubles,** the 90-minute documentary *Voices from the Grave* provides an excellent overview (easy to find on YouTube). Also check out the University of Ulster's informative and evenhanded Conflict Archive at http://cain.ulst.ac.uk/index.html.

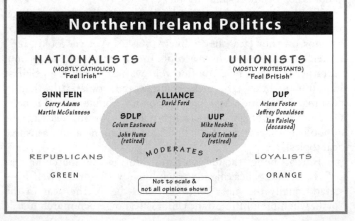

Northern Ireland Politics

NATIONALISTS
(MOSTLY CATHOLICS)
"Feel Irish"

UNIONISTS
(MOSTLY PROTESTANTS)
"Feel British"

SINN FEIN
Gerry Adams
Martin McGuinness

ALLIANCE
David Ford

DUP
Arlene Foster
Jeffrey Donaldson
Ian Paisley
(deceased)

SDLP
Colum Eastwood
John Hume
(retired)

UUP
Mike Nesbitt
David Trimble
(retired)

REPUBLICANS

MODERATES

LOYALISTS

GREEN

ORANGE

Not to scale &
not all opinions shown

ebrate their Britishness and their separate identity from the Republic of Ireland (often through staunchly Nationalist Catholic neighborhoods). Lie low if you stumble onto any big Orange parades.

NORTHERN IRELAND IS A DIFFERENT COUNTRY

The border is almost invisible. But when you leave the Republic of Ireland and enter Northern Ireland, you *are* crossing an international border (although you don't have to flash your passport). The 2016 British referendum vote to leave the EU may change the way this border crossing is handled in the future, but it's still too early to tell.

Gas is often a little cheaper in the Republic of Ireland than in Northern Ireland (so fill up before crossing the border). Meanwhile, groceries and dental procedures are cheaper in the North (put off that root canal until you hit Belfast). These price differences create a lively daily shopping trade for those living near the border.

You won't use euros here; Northern Ireland issues its own Ulster pound, which, like the Scottish pound, is interchangeable with the English pound (€1 = about £0.75; £1 = about $1.50). Some establishments near the border may take euros, but at a lousy exchange rate. So keep any euros for your return to the Republic, and get pounds from an ATM inside Northern Ireland instead. And if you're heading to Britain next, it's best to change your Ulster pounds into English ones (free at any bank in Northern Ireland, England, Wales, or Scotland).

BELFAST

Seventeenth-century Belfast was just a village. With the influx, or "plantation," of English and (more often) Scottish settlers, the character of the place changed. After the Scots and English were brought in—and the native Irish were subjugated—Belfast boomed, spurred by the success of the local linen, rope-making, and especially shipbuilding industries. The Industrial Revolution took root with a vengeance. While the rest of Ireland remained rural and agricultural, Belfast earned its nickname ("Old Smoke") during the time when many of the brick buildings that you'll see today were built. The year 1888 marked the birth of modern Belfast. After Queen Victoria granted city status to this boomtown of 300,000, its citizens built Belfast's centerpiece, City Hall.

Belfast is the birthplace of the *Titanic* (and many other ships that didn't sink). In 2012, to mark the 100th anniversary of the *Titanic* disaster, a modern new attraction was launched in Belfast's shipyard, telling the ill-fated ship's fascinating and tragic story. Nearby, two huge, mustard-colored cranes (built in the 1970s, and once the biggest in the world, nicknamed Samson and Goliath) rise like skyscrapers. They stand idle now, but serve as a reminder of this town's former shipbuilding might...strategic enough to be the target of four Luftwaffe bombing raids in World War II.

At the beginning of the 21st century, the peace process had begun to take root, and investments from south of the border—the Republic of Ireland—injected quiet optimism into the dejected shipyards where the *Titanic* was built. Though funding has declined, Belfast officials hope the historic Titanic Quarter will continue to attract development...and lots of tourists.

Despite the economic downturn, it feels like a new morning in

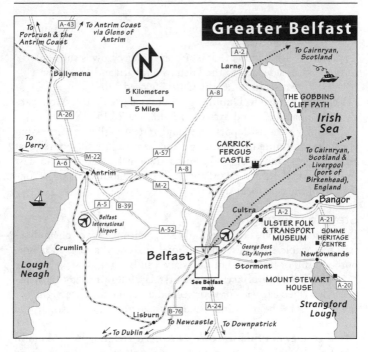

Belfast. It's hard to believe that the bright and bustling pedestrian center was once a subdued, traffic-free security zone. Now there's no hint of security checks, once a tiresome daily routine. These days, both Catholics and Protestants root for the Belfast Giants ice hockey team, one of many reasons to live together peacefully.

Still, it's a fragile peace and a tenuous hope. Mean-spirited murals, hateful bonfires built a month before they're actually burned, and pubs with security gates are reminders that the island is still split—and 900,000 Protestant Unionists in the North prefer it that way.

PLANNING YOUR TIME

Big Belfast is thin on sights. For most, one day of sightseeing is plenty. But I've also included advice for longer stays.

Day Trip from Dublin

Using the handy, two-hour Dublin-Belfast train (about €40 for "day return" tickets), you could make Belfast a day trip:

  7:35   Catch the early-morning train from Dublin's
         Connolly Station (arriving in Belfast's Central Station
         at 9:45)

 11:00   City Hall tour (12:00 on Sat-Sun), browse the

> > pedestrian zone, lunch, ride a shared black taxi up
> > Falls Road
> 15:00 Visit Titanic Belfast (after midday crowds subside)
> > or side-trip to the Ulster Folk Park and Transport
> > Museum in nearby Cultra (closed Mon)
> Evening Return to Dublin (last train departs Belfast Mon-Sat
> > at 20:05 and arrives in Dublin at 22:15)

Sunday's trains depart later and return earlier, compressing your already limited sightseeing time here to just six hours (first train departs Dublin at 10:30 and arrives in Belfast at 12:46; last train departs Belfast at 19:00 and pulls into Dublin at 21:05). Confirm train times at local stations.

Staying Overnight

Belfast makes a pleasant overnight stop, with plenty of cheap hostels, reasonable B&Bs, weekend hotel deals, and a relaxed neighborhood full of B&Bs 30 minutes away in Bangor.

Two Days in Belfast: On the first day, follow my day-trip itinerary described earlier. For your second day, take the City Sightseeing bus tour in the morning, then visit Carrickfergus Castle in the afternoon.

Two Days in Small-Town Northern Ireland: From Dublin (via Belfast), take the train to Portrush; allow two nights and a day to tour the Causeway Coast (castle, whiskey distilleries, Giant's Causeway, resort fun), then follow the Belfast-in-a-day plan described earlier. With a third day, add Derry.

Coming from Scotland or England: With cheap flights from Edinburgh or Glasgow (check www.skyscanner.com), as well as decent but slow ferry connections (from Cairnryan in Scotland or Liverpool in England; see "Belfast Connections," later), it's easy to begin your exploration of the Emerald Isle in Belfast, and then head south to Dublin and the Republic.

Orientation to Belfast

For the first-time visitor in town for a quick look, Belfast is pretty simple. There are four zones of interest: **northern** (Titanic Quarter—docklands with Odyssey entertainment complex and Titanic Belfast), **western** (working-class sectarian neighborhoods west of the A-12 freeway), **central** (Donegall Square, City Hall, pedestrian shopping, TI), and **southern** (Botanic Gardens, Queen's University, Ulster Museum).

The eastern part of Belfast is more affluent and residential, with little of interest to the average sightseer, except for Stormont (the seat of government in Northern Ireland).

The modern bookends of sightseeing interest are the Titanic

Belfast attraction (in the Titanic Quarter to the north) and the Lyric Theatre (near the university district to the south). Their contemporary angularities are hard to miss, as they contrast sharply with the red-brick uniformity of old Belfast. But the core of your city navigating will hinge on four more central landmarks (listed from north to south): Albert Clock Tower, City Hall, Shaftesbury Square, and Queen's University. Find them on your map, and use them to navigate as you stroll the town.

Belfast's "Golden Mile"—stretching from Hotel Europa to the university district—connects the central and southern zones with many of the best dinner and entertainment spots.

TOURIST INFORMATION

The modern TI (look for *Visit Belfast* sign) has a courteous staff and baggage storage (£3/bag for 4 hours, £4.50/bag for 8 hours; Mon-Sat 9:00-17:30, June-Sept until 19:00, Sun 11:00-16:00 year-round; a couple of doors down from the Linen Hall Library, just across Chichester Street, north of City Hall at 9 Donegall Square North, tel. 028/9024-6609, http://visitbelfast.com). City walking tours depart from the TI (see "Tours in Belfast," later). Be sure to pick up a free copy of *Visit Belfast*, which lists all the sightseeing and evening entertainment options.

ARRIVAL IN BELFAST

By Train: Arriving by train, you'll go directly to Belfast's Central Station (with ATMs and free city maps in the lobby). From the station, a free Centrelink bus loops to Donegall Square, with stops near Shaftesbury Square (recommended hostel), the bus station (some recommended hotels), and the TI (free with any train or bus ticket, 4/hour, none on Sun; during morning rush hour, bus runs only between station and Donegall Square). Allow about £5 for a taxi from Central Station to Donegall Square, or £8 to my accommodation listings south of the university.

Slower trains arc through the city, stopping at several downtown stations, including Central Station, Great Victoria Station (most central, near Donegall Square and most hotels), and Botanic Station (close to the university, Botanic Gardens, and some recommended lodgings). It's easy and cheap to connect stations by train (£1.50).

By Car: Driving in Belfast, although not as bad as in Dublin, is still a pain. Avoid it if possible. Street parking in the city center is geared for short shopping stops (use pay-and-display machines,

Belfast

To Belfast International Airport

CRUMLIN RD.

HILLVIEW RD.

NEW

CLIFTONPARK AVE.

ANTRIM RD.

CAMBRAI ST.

TENNENT ST.

AMBLESIDE ST.

SHANKILL ST.

AGNES ST.

CLIFTON ST.

WESTLINK

CLIFTON ST.

WOODVALE RD.

UNIONIST PROTESTANT MURALS

SHANKILL RD.

PETERS HILL

CARRICK HILL

SHANKILL

SHANKILL

LANARK WAY

PEACE WALL

CUPAR WAY

CUPAR ST.

CONWAY ST.

SHANKILL RD.

PETERS HILL

NORTH

SHANKILL ROAD TAXI QUEUE Ⓣ

FALLS ROAD TAXI GARAGE Ⓣ

SPRINGFIELD RD.

CLONARD GDNS.

CLONARD ST.

THE FALLS

NATIONALIST CATHOLIC MURALS

DIVIS ST.

DIVIS TOWER

DIVIS ST.

CASTLE ST.

KING ST.

QUEEN ST.

FALLS RD.

ALBERT ST.

LEESON ST.

COLLEGE SQ. N.

DURHAM

CROWN LIQUOR SALOON

IRIS ST.

CAVENDISH ST.

GROSVENOR RD.

A-12

GROSVENOR RD.

HOWARD ST.

OPERA

ROYAL HOSPITAL

EUROPA BUS STN.

GREAT VICTORIA STREET STATION

GREAT VICTORIA ST.

FALLS RD.

BROADWAY

To Sinn Fein HQ & Milltown Cemetery

WESTLINK (FREEWAY)

SANDY ROW

UNIONIST PROTESTANT MURALS

SANDY ROW

GOLDEN "MILE"

DUBLIN RD.

Shaftesbury Square

BOTANIC AVE.

DONEGALL RD.

DONEGALL RD.

City Hospital Station

CITY HOSPITAL

CLAREMONT ST.

CAMDEN ST.

UNIVERSITY SQ.

M-1

GLENMACHAN ST.

FRENCHPARK ST.

DONEGALL AVE.

FITZWILLIAM

ELMWOOD AVE.

UNIVERSITY RD.

QUEEN'S UNIVERSITY

To Dublin

TATES AVE.

A-1

COLLEGE GARDENS

MALONE RD.

BOUCHER RD.

TATES AVE.

NORTHBROOK ST.

LOWER WINDSOR AVE.

LISBURN RD.

WELLESLEY AVE.

WELLINGTON PARK

MALONE AVE.

EGLANTINE AVE.

Ⓑ #8 ULSTER MUSEUM

See South Belfast map

BELFAST

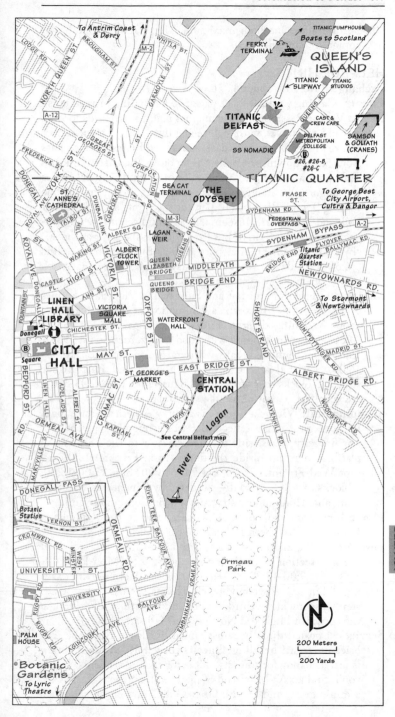

£0.30/15 minutes, one-hour maximum, Mon-Sat 9:00-18:00, free in evenings and on Sun).

HELPFUL HINTS

Exchange Rate: £1 = about $1.50

Country Calling Code: 44 (see page 530 for dialing instructions)

Belfast Visitor Pass: This pass combines iLink smartcards for free bus and rail travel, with sightseeing discounts, for one day or two or three consecutive days within the Belfast Visitor Pass Zone (all of downtown Belfast as far out as the Ulster Folk and Transport Museum in Cultra, but not as far as Carrickfergus or Bangor). The handy one-day pass saves money for anyone visiting Titanic Belfast (10 percent discount) and the Ulster Folk and Transport Museum (30 percent discount) while connecting them by train or bus (free with pass). Buy it at the TI, any train station, either airport, Europa Bus station, or online (£6.50 for 1-day pass, £11 for 2 days, £14.50 for 3 days, tel. 028/9066-6630, www.translink.co.uk).

Market: On Friday, Saturday, and Sunday, the Victorian confines of **St. George's Market** is a commotion of commerce and a people-watching delight. Friday is a variety market (6:00-14:00), Saturday blooms with food and garden items (9:00-15:00), and Sunday creaks with crafts and antiques (10:00-16:00). Located at the corner of Oxford and East Bridge streets, 5 blocks east of Donegall Square, tel. 028/9043-5704, www.belfastcity.gov.uk/markets.

Shopping Mall: Victoria Square is a glitzy American-style mall. Its huge glass dome reflects Belfast's economic rejuvenation. For fine city views, ride the free elevator to the observation platform high up inside the dome (Mon-Fri 9:30-18:00 except Wed-Fri until 21:00, Sat 9:00-18:00, Sun 13:00-18:00; 3 blocks east of City Hall—bordered by Chichester, Victoria, Ann, and Montgomery streets; www.victoriasquare.com).

Phone Tips: For details on making calls between the Republic of Ireland and Northern Ireland, see page 530.

Post Office: The main post office, with lots of fun postcards, is at the intersection of High and Bridge Streets (Mon-Fri 9:00-17:30, Sat 9:00-12:30, closed Sun, 3 long blocks north of Donegall Square). A second branch is located across from the Ulster Museum, and a third location lurks north of City Hall, at the corner of High and North Streets (all same hours).

Services: Located directly across University Road from the red-brick university building, **Queen's University Student Union** is just as handy for tourists as it is for college students. Inside you'll find an ATM (at end of main hall, on the right), WCs, a minimarket, and Wi-Fi. Grab a quick and cheap sandwich and coffee at **Clement's Coffee Shop** (long hours Mon-Sat, closed Sun).

Laundry: Globe Launderers is at 37 Botanic Avenue (£5 self-serve, £8 drop-off service, Mon-Fri 8:00-21:00, Sat 8:00-18:00, Sun 12:00-18:00, tel. 028/9024-3956). For the hotel neighborhood south of the university, the closest is **Whistle Cleaners** (£8 drop-off service, Mon-Fri 8:30-18:00, Sat 9:00-17:30, closed Sun, 160 Lisburn Road, at intersection with Eglantine Avenue, tel. 028/9038-1297). For locations, see the map on page 400.

Bike Rental: Belfast Bike Tours rents bikes only if reserved in advance (£15/day, daily but no set hours, off Wellington Park behind Wellington Park Hotel, mobile 078-1211-4235, www.belfastbiketours.com).

GETTING AROUND BELFAST

If you line up your sightseeing logically, you can do most of the town on foot. On wheels, you have several options. For most visitors, the Belfast Visitor Pass will save time and money. It combines iLink smartcards for local bus and train trips with sightseeing discounts (see "Helpful Hints," earlier).

By Train or Bus: Ask about iLink smartcards, which give individuals one day of unlimited train and bus travel. The Zone 1 card (£6.50) covers the city center and George Best Belfast City Airport. The handy Zone 2 card (£11) includes Cultra (Ulster Folk Park and Transport Museum), Bangor, and Carrickfergus Castle. The Zone 3 card (£14.50) is really only useful for reaching Belfast's distant international airport. Zone 4 (£17.50) gets you anywhere in Northern Ireland, including Portrush and Derry. For those lingering in the North, one-week cards offer even better deals. Buy your iLink card at any train station in the city.

If you're traveling from Belfast to only one destination—Carrickfergus Castle, Cultra, or Bangor—a "day return" ticket is cheaper than two one-way tickets.

Pink-and-white city buses go from Donegall Square East to Malone Road and my recommended accommodations (#8B or #8C, 3/hour, £2, all-day pass costs £3.90 Mon-Sat before 9:30—after 9:30 and on Sun it's £3.40). Sunday service is much less frequent.

For more information on iLink smartcards, trains, and buses in Belfast, contact Translink (tel. 028/9066-6630, www.translink.co.uk).

By Taxi: Taxis are reasonable and a good option. For general transport, as opposed to the taxi tours described later, try **Valu Cabs** (tel. 028/9080-9080). Rather than use their meters, many cabs charge a flat £5 rate for any ride up to two miles. It's £2 per mile after that. If you're going up Falls Road, ride a shared cab (explained later, under "Sights in Belfast").

Tours in Belfast

ON FOOT
▲General Walking Tours
Belfast Compass Tours introduces you to the city's 300-year history on a balanced two-hour stroll. Highlights include City Hall, St. George's Market, Albert Clock, and the opulent Merchant Hotel (£7, must book in advance, mobile 079-4425-6560 or 079-3440-7751, www.belfastcompasstours.com).

Cultural Neighborhood Walking Tours
Two walking tours offer opposite viewpoints on the Troubles and local culture. Listen and learn. Or, as an Irish friend once told me, "Never give unsolicited advice...wise men don't need it and fools won't heed it."

Coiste Irish Political Tours offers the Nationalist/Republican perspective on extended, two-hour walks along Falls Road. Led by former IRA prisoners, you'll visit murals, gardens of remembrance, peace walls, and community centers in this slowly rejuvenating section of gritty Belfast. Tours meet beside the Divis Tower (the 20-story apartment house at the east end of the Divis Road near the A-12 Westlink motorway overpass) and end at the Milltown Cemetery (£10; Tue, Thu, and Sat at 11:00, Sun at 14:00; tel. 028/9020-0770, www.coiste.ie, Seamus Kelley).

Sandy Row Walking Tours provides the Unionist/Loyalist point of view during its 1.5-hour walks that center on Sandy Row, Belfast's oldest residential neighborhood. Tours cover the city's industrial heritage, the Orange Order, both World Wars, and historic local churches. They depart from the King William Mural at the intersection of Sandy Row and Linfield Road (£7.50; daily at 10:00, 14:00, and 17:00; must book in advance, mobile 079-0925-4849, www.historicsandyrow.co.uk, info@historicsandyrow.co.uk).

ON WHEELS
Local Guide
Ken Harper has a vast knowledge of Belfast and does insightful tours from his taxi, focusing on both Catholic and Protestant neighborhoods, *Titanic*-related sights, and Belfast's favorite sons—author C. S. Lewis, musician Van Morrison, and soccer star/playboy George Best. He's also available for custom tours, which he calls "Pick Ken's Brain" (£30 minimum or £10/person, 1.25 hours, tel. 028/9074-2711, mobile 077-1175-7178, www.harpertaxitours.com, kenharper2004@hotmail.com).

▲Hop-On, Hop-Off Bus Tours

City Sightseeing offers the best quick introduction to the city's political and social history. Their open-top, double-decker buses link major sights and landmarks, including the Catholic and Protestant working-class neighborhoods, the Stormont Parliament building, Titanic Belfast, and City Hall, with commentary on political murals and places of interest. The route also has convenient stops near several lodging options listed later: Fisherwick Place (Jurys Inn), Shaftsbury Square (Benedicts Hotel and Belfast International City Hostel), and Malone Road (Malone Lodge and Wellington Park Hotel). Pay cash on bus or book online in advance (£12.50, 2/hour, fewer in winter, daily 10:00-16:00, tickets valid for 48 hours, 20 stops, 1.5-hour loop; departs from Castle Place on High Street, 2 blocks west of Albert Clock Tower; tel. 028/9032-1321, http://belfastcitysightseeing.com).

City Tours offers two routes with more than 20 stops each. The red route starts on High Street (near Albert Clock) and runs more frequently (9:45-16:45), veering westward to take in Falls and Shankill roads. The black route starts at Victoria Square and departs only at 12:00 and 15:00, heading eastward to reach Stormont (parliament) and a bigger slice of the Titanic Quarter (£10, ticket good for both routes for 72 hours, pay cash on bus or book in advance, tel. 028/9032-1912, www.citytoursbelfast.com).

Titanic Tours by Car

Former TV reporter and Rick Steves' Europe guide Susie Millar operates **Titanic Tours Belfast,** offering a three-hour car tour (yours or hers) that picks up and drops off at your hotel. This is by far Belfast's most intimate glimpse of the *Titanic*'s tragic history: Her great-grandfather was a crew member who perished on that fateful cruise. Ask Susie to tell you about her great-grandfather's departing two-penny promise (£30, book in advance, mobile 078-5271-6655, www.titanictours-belfast.co.uk, info@titanictours-belfast.co.uk). She is available for longer, customized itineraries when not on the road leading Rick's tours.

Sectarian Taxi Tours

See "Sectarian Neighborhoods in West Belfast," later, for details on Falls and Shankill roads.

Forty trained cabbies give one-hour **Falls Road** tours, presenting the Catholic perspective of Ireland's conflict (£30/1-3 people, £10/additional person, cheap for small groups, best views with 5 or fewer riders, at the intersection of Castle and King streets in Castle Junction Car Park, tel. 028/9031-5777 or mobile 078-9271-6660, www.taxitrax.com).

For the Protestant angle, ride a shared black cab through the **Shankill Road** area, departing from North Street near the inter-

BELFAST

section with Millfield Road. It's not well-marked, but watch where the cabs circle and pick up locals on the south side of the street (£30/1-2 people for one hour, £40/3-6 people, tel. 028/9032-8775).

Bike Tours

Belfast Bike Tours offers 2.5-hour rides in the countryside south of town. Departing from the front gate of Queen's University, you'll pedal along an old canal towpath to the Giant's Ring (ancient dolmen) and back on generally flat terrain (£15; April-Aug Mon, Wed, Fri-Sat at 10:30 and 14:00; Sept-March Sat 10:30 and 14:00; bikes, helmets, and bottle of water provided; must reserve ahead by phone or email, mobile 078-1211-4235, www.belfastbiketours. com, info@belfastbiketours.com).

Minibus Tours

McComb's Giant's Causeway Tour visits Carrickfergus Castle, the Giant's Causeway, Dunluce Castle (photo stop only), Carrick-a-Rede Rope Bridge, and Old Bushmills Distillery (£25, doesn't include distillery admission, daily depending on demand, book through and depart from the recommended Belfast International City Hostel, 9:00 pickup at hostel, 9:30 pickup at Europa Hotel—a block north of Central Station, back to Belfast by 19:00). Their *Game of Thrones* tour (see sidebar on page 424) visits many of the sites where the hit fantasy TV series was filmed (£35, 8:30 pickup at Belfast International City Hostel, 9:00 pickup at Opera House stage door on the corner of Glengall Street, back to Belfast by 19:00; separate £40 Winterfell tour runs Fridays at 10:00). They also have private guides (book in advance, tel. 028/9031-5333, www.mccombscoaches.com).

BY BOAT

Titanic Tours

The **Lagan Boat Company** shows you shipyards on this one-hour cruise, narrated by a member of the Belfast Titanic Society. The tour shows off the fruits of the city's £800 million investment in its harbor, including a weir built to control the tides and stabilize the depth of the harbor (it doubles as a free pedestrian bridge over the River Lagan). The heart of the tour is a lazy harbor cruise past rusty dry-dock gates, brought alive by the guide's proud commentary and passed-around historical photos (£10; April-Oct daily sailings at 12:30, 14:00, and 15:30; fewer off-season, tel. 028/9024-0124,

mobile 077-1891-0423, www.laganboatcompany.com). Tours depart from the Lagan Pedestrian Bridge and Weir on Donegall Quay. The quay is located just past the leaning Albert Clock Tower, a 10-minute walk from the TI.

Sights in Belfast

Most sights of interest are located in four areas: the Titanic Quarter to the north of the city center, the sectarian neighborhoods to the west of the city center, central Belfast, and south Belfast (clustered around Queen's University).

TITANIC QUARTER

Up until the mid-1990s, this district was a barren wasteland of cement slabs and rusting industrial relics. But during the Celtic Tiger boom years (which spilled over into the North), shrewd investors saw the real-estate potential and began building posh, high-rise condos.

The first landmark project to be completed was the Odyssey entertainment complex (in 2000). To draw more visitors and commemorate the proud shipbuilding industry of the Victorian and Edwardian Ages, another flagship attraction was needed. The 100th anniversary of the *Titanic* disaster in 2012 provided the perfect opportunity, and the result is a new attraction called Titanic Belfast.

The Odyssey

This huge millennium-project complex offers a food pavilion, bowling alley, and W5 science center with interactive, educational exhibits for youngsters. Where else can a kid play a harp with laser-light strings? The "W5" stands for "who, what, when, where, and why." There's also a 12-screen cinema, laser-tag gaming area, and an 8,000-seat arena where the Belfast Giants professional ice hockey team skates from September to March on Friday or Saturday nights (£15 game tickets, tel. 028/9073-9074, www.belfastgiants.com).

Cost and Hours: £8.50, kids-£6.50, Mon-Fri 10:00-17:00, Sat 10:00-18:00, Sun 12:00-18:00, last entry one hour before closing, 2 Queen's Quay, 10-minute walk north of Belfast's Central Station, tel. 028/9046-7790, www.w5online.co.uk.

▲▲▲Titanic Belfast

This £97 million attraction sits on the site of the original dry dock where the ship was built. High-tech displays tell the tale of the famous cruise liner, proudly heralded as the largest man-made moving object of its time. The sight has no actual artifacts from the underwater wreck (little has been brought up out of respect for the fact that it's a mass grave).

BELFAST

Belfast at a Glance

▲▲▲**Titanic Belfast** Excellent but crowded high-tech exhibit covering the famously infamous ship and local shipbuilding, housed in a stunning structure on the site of the original ship's construction. **Hours:** Daily April-Sept 9:00-18:00, June-Aug until 19:00; Oct-March 10:00-17:00. See page 383.

▲▲**Falls Road Taxi Tours** Local cabbies whisk visitors through West Belfast's once-contentious Falls Road neighborhood, offering personal perspectives on the slowly fading Troubles. See page 388.

▲▲**City Hall** Central Belfast's polished and majestic celebration of Victorian-era pride built with industrial wealth. **Hours:** Mon-Fri 8:30-17:00, Sat-Sun 10:00-16:00. See page 390.

▲**Ulster Museum** Mixed bag of local artifacts, natural history, and coverage of political events; a good rainy-day option near Queen's University. **Hours:** Tue-Sun 10:00-17:00, closed Mon. See page 393.

▲**Botanic Gardens** Belfast's best green space, featuring the Palm House loaded with delicate tropical vegetation. **Hours:** Daily 8:00 until dusk; Palm House open daily April-Sept 10:00-17:00, Oct-March until 16:00. See page 394.

Near Belfast

▲▲**Ulster Folk Park and Transport Museum** A glimpse into Northern Ireland's hard-working heritage, split between a charming re-creation of past rural life and large halls of innovative vehicular advances (8 miles east of Belfast). **Hours:** March-Sept Tue-Sun 10:00-17:00; Oct-Feb Tue-Fri 10:00-16:00, Sat-Sun 11:00-16:00; closed Mon year-round. See page 395.

▲**Carrickfergus Castle** Northern Ireland's first and most important fortified refuge for invading 12th-century Normans (14 miles northeast of Belfast). **Hours:** Daily April-Sept 10:00-17:00, Oct-March 10:00-16:00. See page 397.

▲**The Gobbins** Rugged, unique, wave-splashed hiking trail cut into coastal rock, accessible by guided tour (34 miles northeast of Belfast). **Hours:** Visitor center open daily 9:30-17:30, guided hikes approximately every hour in good weather. See page 397.

Near Bangor

▲**Mount Stewart House** Fine 18th-century manor house displaying ruling-class affluence, surrounded by lush and calming gardens (18 miles east of Belfast). **Hours:** Daily March-Oct 10:00-17:00, closed Nov-Feb. See page 406.

Cost and Hours: £17.50, includes entry to the SS *Nomadic;* daily April-Sept 9:00-18:00, June-Aug until 19:00; Oct-March 10:00-17:00; audioguide for infoholics-£3, located where the famous ship was built on Queen's Island, tel. 028/9076-6399, www. titanicbelfast.com. The £25 **White Star Premium Pass** covers the Titanic Belfast, Discovery Tour, and SS *Nomadic;* it's slightly more than paying separately but includes a souvenir photo and discounts to the restaurant and gift shop. For those interested in only a cursory look, the **Late Saver Premium Pass** is sold one hour before closing for a reasonable £7.50.

Crowd-Beating Tips: This attraction drew 800,000 visitors in its first year (double what was expected). Go early or late; big bus-tour crowds clog the exhibits from 10:00 to 14:00. Book ahead online to ensure the entry time you want.

Getting There: From Donegall Square, take bus #26 or #26B (both stop behind Belfast Metropolitan College, infrequent buses on Sun), or go by taxi (£6 ride). The Titanic Quarter train station is a 10-minute walk to the south of the Titanic Belfast.

Tours: The Discovery Tour explains the striking architecture of the Titanic Belfast building and the adjacent slipways where the great ship was built. You also get a peek inside nearby Harland and Wolff Drawing Offices, where plans for its construction were drawn up (£7, 45 minutes, call ahead for tour times).

Eating: The ground floor includes a sandwich café as well as a carvery-style restaurant. If these options are crowded, walk one block east, through the arch in the Drawing Offices building and across Queens Road to the battleship-gray **$$ Galley Café** for a sandwich, soup, or salad (daily 12:00-18:00).

Visiting the Sight: The spacey architecture of Titanic Belfast's new building is already a landmark on the city's skyline. Six stories tall, it's clad in more than 3,000 sun-reflecting aluminum panels. Its four corners represent the bows of the many ships that were built in these yards during the Golden Age of Belfast.

Inside, nine galleries take you from booming 1900s Belfast, through the construction and launch of the *Titanic,* and ultimately to a re-creation of its watery grave. A highlight is the Shipyard Ride, which takes you through a mock-up of the ship while it was being built. You'll learn how workers toughed out months of deafening and dangerous duty, working in five-man teams to hammer in red-hot rivets (they were paid by the rivet, and were frequently burned by chips flying off the metal). For ef-

Titanic Trio

Most of us already know the sad story of the famous *Titanic*, when the unthinkable happened to the unsinkable: Launched in Belfast in 1911, the *Titanic* was the largest and most celebrated luxury cruise liner of its time.

Locals thought themselves the best shipbuilders since Noah. The *Titanic*'s sudden demise in 1912 is the most famous sea disaster of the modern era. Only 716 of the 2,260 aboard were rescued; 70 percent of the first-class passengers, with first dibs on the few lifeboats, survived.

While everyone has heard of the *Titanic*, few people know that it was the middle sister of three unfortunate ships, each built in Belfast by the prestigious Harland and Wolff shipyards for the White Star Line.

In 1910, the **Olympic** was the first of the three similar vessels to be launched. It soon collided with the naval cruiser HMS *Hawke* and returned to Belfast to be repaired with parts taken from the still-under-construction **Titanic**. When World War I began, the *Olympic* served as a troop transport ship. During the war, it struck and sank a German submarine (the U-103). After the war, it returned to commercial service and later collided with the *Nantucket Lightship* (killing seven). The *Olympic*'s last voyage was in 1935, and it was demolished in 1937.

The last of the three to be built was the **Gigantic** in 1914. But after the *Titanic* sank, its name was changed (while still under construction) to **Britannic**...which was thought to be a luckier name. It was repainted white and converted to a hospital ship at the start of World War I. In 1915, it was serving in the Aegean Sea when it hit a mine—or was struck by a torpedo from a U-boat. Fortunately, it had more advanced safety features than its two older sisters—it had enough lifeboats for all onboard, and was designed to sink more slowly. The ship had no patients yet, as it was on its way to Greece to pick up wounded soldiers. Most of those onboard were saved (only 30 of the almost 1,100 crew and medical staff died). In 1976, French underwater explorer Jacques Cousteau found the wreck of the *Britannic* 400 feet down and brought up a few of its artifacts.

Amazingly, a single human thread ties all three ships together. A stewardess and nurse named Violet Jessop was aboard the *Olympic* when it collided with the HMS *Hawke*. She was also one of the lucky few to be rescued from the *Titanic*. And yes, incredibly, she was again among those rescued from the sinking *Britannic*. Talk about a buoyant personality...

ficiency, left- and right-handers were assigned specific hammering positions. Young boys had the hot and hazardous job of quickly catching the glowing rivets and placing them for the hammerers.

Other exhibits cover the wider story of the Harland and Wolff shipyards, including the construction of *Titanic's* lesser-known and also ill-fated sister ships: *Olympic* and *Britannic* (see sidebar). An upper-floor viewpoint employs innovative electronic windows to project an image of the huge, partially built *Titanic* in dry dock beside you, masking the reality of today's barren shipyard below. Another gallery surrounds you on three sides with animated screens that glide through multiple decks, giving you a realistic feel for the ship in all its full-steam-ahead glory.

The human story of its passengers—from promenade-deck aristocrats to heroic crew members to steerage-class rabble—is also here. The passenger manifest encompassed virtually every segment of society: In today's dollars, a first-class ticket would cost $70,000, while a third-class ticket would cost $650. Unbelievably, the families of dead crew members were charged for their missing uniforms. You'll see a broad cross-section of displays from the ship's short but opulent existence.

The big-screen "Titanic Beneath" theater shows the now-famous underwater footage of the wreck nearly 12,500 feet down on the ocean floor. Only 20 percent of the dead were ever recovered. Don't miss the see-through floor panels at the foot of the movie screen, which allow you to stand on top of the watery debris field as the virtual wreck slowly passes beneath your feet.

Outside, go to the northern corner of the building (diagonally across from the eight-foot-tall, rusted-iron *Titanic* sign at the main southern entry). Look down at the paving stones and get oriented: Gray tiles are land and white ones represent ocean. As you follow the metal strip marking the fateful route (many yards) across the Atlantic, you'll find the wreck's coordinates interrupting the uncompleted route. Then look up at the parallel rows of lampposts leading away from you for 300 yards (the length of the ship). This was the slipway for initial construction of the vessel. Visualize the *Titanic,* partially built and crawling with workmen, rising 175 feet into the air ahead of you. It filled most of the space between the long left and center rows of lampposts. Follow the lines in the paving stones along the left row of lights, which mirrors the ship's mammoth hull, including the (too few) lifeboats. At the far end, you'll come to the water's edge, where a curved railing simulates the stern (made famous by Kate Winslet and Leonardo DiCaprio's first and last meetings in the 1997 movie).

Nearby: The SS *Nomadic* tender ship, which once ferried passengers between the dock and the *Titanic,* is docked 50 yards south of Titanic Belfast and easily visible (£3 separately but included with Titanic Belfast ticket, same hours as Titanic Belfast).

Thompson Dry Dock and Pump-House

Those with an unsinkable interest in the *Titanic* may want to walk down into the massive footprint where it last rested on dry land, to get a feel for how colossal the vessel was. The pump house filled the dry dock with water—and emptied it—in record time. Personally, I'd skip the entry cost and just stand on tiptoes to take in the free view down into the dock from behind the fence.

Cost and Hours: £5, daily 10:30-16:00, www.titanicsdock. com.

Getting There: From the Titanic Belfast, it's a 15-minute walk north to the Dry Dock and Pump-House. En route, you'll pass the massive **Titanic Studios** building, where interiors of *Game of Thrones* and *City of Ember* were filmed.

SECTARIAN NEIGHBORHOODS IN WEST BELFAST

It will be a happy day when the sectarian neighborhoods of Belfast have nothing to be sectarian about. For a look at three of the original home bases of the Troubles, explore the working-class neighborhoods of Catholic Falls Road and Protestant Shankill Road (west of the Westlink motorway), or Protestant Sandy Row (south of the Westlink motorway).

Murals (found in working-class, sectarian areas) are a memorable part of any visit to Belfast. But with more peaceful times, the character of these murals is slowly changing. The Re-Imaging Communities Program has spent £3 million in government money to replace aggressive murals with positive ones. Paramilitary themes are gradually being covered over with images of pride in each neighborhood's culture. The *Titanic* was built primarily by proud Protestant Ulster stock and is often seen in their neighborhood murals—reflecting their industrious work ethic. Over in the Catholic neighborhoods, you'll see more murals depicting mythological heroes from the days before the English came.

You can get taxi tours of Falls Road or Shankill Road, but rarely are both combined without bias in one tour. Ken Harper is one of a new breed of Belfast taxi drivers who will give you an insightful private tour of both neighborhoods (see page 380 for details).

▲▲Falls Road (Catholic)

At the intersection of Castle and King streets, you'll find the Castle Junction Car Park. On the ground floor of this nine-story parking garage, a passenger terminal (entrance on King Street) connects travelers with old black cabs—and the only Irish-language signs in downtown Belfast. These shared black cabs efficiently shuttle residents from outlying neighborhoods up and down Falls Road and to the city center. This service originated more than 40 years ago at the beginning of the Troubles, when locals would hijack city buses and use them as barricades in the street fighting. When bus service was discontinued, local paramilitary groups established the shared taxi service. Although the buses are now running again, these cab rides are still a great value for their drivers' commentary.

Any cab goes up Falls Road, past Sinn Fein headquarters and lots of murals, to the Milltown Cemetery (£6, sit in front and

talk to the cabbie). Hop in and out. Easy-to-flag-down cabs run every minute or so in each direction on Falls Road. Or, take a one-hour tour from a trained black-taxi cabbie (see page 381).

The Sinn Fein office and bookstore are near the bottom of Falls Road. The **bookstore** is worth a look. Page through books featuring color photos of the political murals that decorated these buildings. Money raised here supports the families of deceased IRA members.

A sad, corrugated structure called the **peace wall** runs a block or so north of Falls Road (along Cupar Way), separating the Catholics from the Protestants in the Shankill Road area. The first cement wall was 20 feet high—it was later extended another 10 feet by a solid metal addition, and then another 15 feet with a metal screen. Seemingly high enough now to deter a projectile being lobbed over, this is one of

many such walls erected in Belfast during the Troubles. Meant to be temporary, these barriers stay up because of old fears among the communities on both sides. In 2013, the Northern Ireland Assembly announced its ambitious goal to remove all of these walls by 2023, but a lack of resources and weak community unity have resulted in little progress.

At the **Milltown Cemetery,** walk past all the Gaelic crosses down to the far right-hand corner (closest to the highway), where little green railings set apart the IRA Roll of Honor from the thousands of other graves. These martyrs are treated like fallen soldiers. Notice the memorial to Bobby Sands and nine other hunger strikers. They starved themselves to death in the nearby Maze Prison in 1981, protesting for political prisoner status as opposed to terrorist criminal treatment. Maze Prison closed in the fall of 2000.

Shankill Road and Sandy Row (Protestant)

A shared black cab brings you though the Shankill Road area (see "Tours in Belfast," earlier), but an easier and cheaper way to get

a dose of the Unionist side is to walk **Sandy Row.** From Hotel Europa, walk a block down Glengall Street, then turn left for a 10-minute walk along a working-class Protestant street. A stop in a Unionist memorabilia shop, a pub, or one of the many cheap eateries here may give you an opportunity to talk to a local. You'll see murals filled with Unionist symbolism. The mural of William of Orange's victory over the Catholic King James II (Battle of the Boyne, 1690) thrills Unionist hearts. You'll find it at the northern end of Sandy Row at the corner with Linfield Road.

CENTRAL BELFAST
▲▲City Hall

This grand structure's 173-foot-tall copper dome dominates the town center. Built between 1898 and 1906, with its statue of Queen Victoria scowling down Belfast's main drag and the Neoclassical dome looming behind her, the City Hall is a stirring sight. In the garden, you'll find memorials to the *Titanic* and the landing of the US Expeditionary Force in 1942—the first American troops to arrive in Europe en route to Germany.

Take the worthwhile and free 45-minute tour, which gives you a rundown on city government and an explanation of the decor that makes this an Ulster political hall of fame. Queen Victoria and King Edward VII look down on city council meetings. The 1613 original charter of Belfast granted by James I is on display. The Great Hall—bombed by the Germans in 1941—looks as great as it did the day it was made.

Cost and Hours: Free; building open Mon-Fri 8:30-17:00,

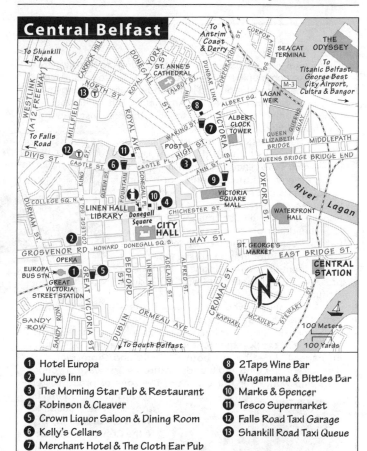

Central Belfast

1. Hotel Europa
2. Jurys Inn
3. The Morning Star Pub & Restaurant
4. Robinson & Cleaver
5. Crown Liquor Saloon & Dining Room
6. Kelly's Cellars
7. Merchant Hotel & The Cloth Ear Pub
8. 2 Taps Wine Bar
9. Wagamama & Bittles Bar
10. Marks & Spencer
11. Tesco Supermarket
12. Falls Road Taxi Garage
13. Shankill Road Taxi Queue

Sat-Sun 10:00-16:00; handy Bobbin coffee shop on ground floor, tel. 028/9032-0202, www.belfastcity.gov.uk/cityhall.

Tours: Free tours run Mon-Fri at 11:00, 14:00, and 15:00—entrance on north side of building behind Queen Victoria statue; Sat-Sun at 12:00, 14:00, and 15:00—entrance via south-facing back door only; call or check online to confirm schedule.

Visiting City Hall: If you can't manage a tour, at least step into the main lobby to admire the marble-swirl staircase and the view up into the dome. In 1912, at the center of the marble floor design beneath the dome, Sir Edward Carson signed the Ulster Covenant—to be followed by 470,000 other Unionists at dozens of desks surrounding City Hall that day. Some signed with their own blood. The Covenant stated Unionists would use "all means necessary" (including the might of the 100,000-strong UVF militia) to resist the Home Rule bill that had just passed in Parliament. The

1916

This pivotal year means vastly different things to Northern Ireland's two communities. When you say "1776" to most Americans, it means revolution and independence from tyranny (unless, perhaps, you're a Native American). But when you say "1916" to someone in Northern Ireland, the response depends on who's talking.

To Nationalists (who are usually Catholic), "1916" brings to mind the Easter Uprising—which took place in Dublin in April of that year and was the beginning of the end of 750 years of British rule for most of Ireland (see sidebar on page 54). Some Nationalist murals still use images of Dublin's rebel headquarters or martyred leaders like Patrick Pearse and James Connolly. To this community, 1916 emphasizes their proud Gaelic identity, their willingness to fight to preserve it, and their stubborn anti-British attitude.

To Unionists (who are usually Protestant), "1916" means the brutal WWI Battle of the Somme in France, which began that July. (For more on the Somme, visit the Somme Heritage Centre in Bangor, described on page 407.) Although both Catholic and Protestant soldiers died in this long and bloody battle, the first wave of young men who went over the top were the sons of proud Ulster Unionists. The Unionists hoped this sacrifice would prove their loyalty to the Crown—and assurance that the British would never let them be gobbled up by an Irish Nationalist state (a possible scenario just before the Great War's outbreak). You'll see Tommies heroically climbing out of their trenches in some of Belfast's Unionist murals. For the Unionists, 1916 is synonymous with devout, almost righteously divine, Britishness.

bill would have given the island of Ireland limited autonomy from Britain. These Protestant Unionists feared "Home Rule as Rome Rule," where they would have become the minority in an independent Catholic Ireland. World War I interrupted the implementation of Home Rule, and the partition of Ireland followed shortly after the war's end.

Linen Hall Library

Across the street from City Hall, the 200-year-old Linen Hall Library welcomes guests (notice the red hand above the front door facing Donegall Square North; for more on its meaning, see the sidebar on page 396). Described as "Ulster's attic," the library takes pride in being a neutral space where anyone trying to make sense of the sectarian conflict can view the Troubled Images, a historical collection of engrossing political posters. It has a fine hardbound ambience, a coffee shop, and a royal newspaper reading room.

Cost and Hours: Free; Mon-Fri 9:30-17:30, Sat until 16:00, closed Sun; 45-minute tours for £3.50 on Tue and Fri at 11:30, 17 Donegall Square North, tel. 028/9032-1707, www.linenhall.com.

Golden Mile

This is the overstated nickname of Belfast's liveliest dining and entertainment district, which stretches from the Opera House (Great Victoria Street) to the university (University Road).

The **Grand Opera House,** originally built in 1895, bombed and rebuilt in 1991, and bombed and rebuilt again in 1993, is extravagantly Victorian and *the* place to take in a concert, play, or opera (ticket office open Mon-Sat 10:00-17:30, closed Sun; ticket office to right of main front door on Great Victoria Street, tel. 028/9024-1919, www.goh.co.uk). The recommended **Hotel Europa,** next door, while considered to be the most-bombed hotel in the world, actually feels pretty casual (but is expensive to stay in).

Across the street is the museum-like **Crown Liquor Saloon.** Built in 1849, it's now a part of the National Trust. A wander through its mahogany, glass, and marble interior is a trip back into the days of Queen Victoria, although the privacy provided by the snugs—booths—allows for un-Victorian behavior (consider a lunch stop—see listing on page 400). Upstairs, the Crown Dining Room serves pub grub and is decorated with historic photos.

SOUTH BELFAST
▲Ulster Museum

While mediocre by European standards, this is Belfast's most venerable museum. It offers an earnest and occasionally thought-provoking look at a cross-section of local artifacts.

Cost and Hours: Free but £3 donation suggested; Tue-Sun 10:00-17:00, closed Mon; in Botanic Gardens on Stranmillis Road, south of downtown, tel. 028/9044-0000, www.nmni.com.

Visiting the Museum: The four-floor museum is free and pretty painless. Ride the elevator to the top floor and follow the spiraling exhibits downhill through various zones. The top floor is dedicated to rotating art exhibits, the next floor down covers local nature, and the one below that focuses on history. The ground floor covers the modern Troubles, and has a coffee shop and gift shop.

The Art Zone displays a beautifully crafted vase from Northern Ireland's Belleek factory, as well as fine crystal and china. In the Nature Zone, audiovisuals trace how the Ice Age affected the local landscape. Dinosaur skeletons lurk, stuffed wildlife plays possum, and geology rocks. Kids will enjoy the interactive Discover History room.

The delicately worded History Zone has an interesting British slant (such as the implication that most deaths in the Great Potato Famine of 1845-1849 were caused by typhus and fever epidemics—without mentioning the starvation that made peasants susceptible to these diseases in the first place). But the coverage of the modern-day Troubles is balanced and thought-provoking.

After a peek at a pretty good mummy, top things off with the *Girona* treasure. Soggy bits of gold, silver, leather, and wood were salvaged from the Spanish Armada's shipwrecked *Girona*, lost off the Antrim Coast north of Belfast in 1588.

▲Botanic Gardens

This is the backyard of Queen's University, and on a sunny day, you couldn't imagine a more relaxing park setting. On a cold day, step into the Tropical Ravine for a jungle of heat and humidity. Take a quick walk through the Palm House, reminiscent of the one in London's Kew Gardens, but smaller. The Ulster Museum is on the garden's grounds.

Cost and Hours: Free, gardens open daily 8:00 until dusk; Palm House open daily April-Sept 10:00-17:00, Oct-March until 16:00; tel. 028/9031-4762, www.belfastcity.gov.uk/parks.

Lyric Theatre

Rebuilt in 2011, this Belfast institution represents the cultural rejuvenation of the city. It's located beside the River Lagan (near Queen's University) in an architecturally innovative building partially funded by donations from famous actors such as Liam Neeson, Kenneth Branagh, and Meryl Streep. While there are no public tours, it's a good place to see quality local productions (tickets £15-25; box office open daily 10:00-17:00; 55 Ridgeway Street, tel. 028/9038-1081, www.lyrictheatre.co.uk).

NEAR BELFAST

▲▲Ulster Folk Park and Transport Museum

This sprawling 180-acre, two-museum complex straddles the road and rail line at Cultra, midway between Bangor and Belfast (8 miles east of town).

Cost and Hours: £9-Folk Park, £9-Transport Museum, £11 combo-ticket covers both, £29 for families; March-Sept Tue-Sun 10:00-17:00; Oct-Feb Tue-Fri 10:00-16:00, Sat-Sun 11:00-16:00; closed Mon year-round; check the schedule for the day's special events, tel. 028/9042-8428, www.nmni.com.

Getting There: From Belfast, you can reach Cultra by taxi (£15), bus #502 (2/hour, 30 minutes, from Laganside Bus Centre), or train (2/hour, 15 minutes, from any Belfast train station or from Bangor). Buses stop right in the park, but schedules are skimpy on Saturday and Sunday. Train service is more dependable (and more frequent on the weekend): Get off at the Cultra stop, which puts off between the two parks, a bit closer to the Transport Museum than to the Folk Park.

Planning Your Time: Allow three hours for your visit, and expect lots of walking. Most people will spend an hour in the Transport Museum and a couple of hours at the Folk Park. You'll arrive (by rail or car) between the two museums a bit closer to the Transport Museum. From here, you have a choice of going downhill to the Transport Museum or 200 panting yards uphill into the Folk Park. Assess your energy level and plan accordingly. Those with a car can drive between the museum and the folk park. Note that the Transport Museum is all indoors. The Folk Park involves more walking between buildings spread across the upper hillside.

Visiting the Museums: The **Transport Museum** consists of three buildings. Start at the bottom and trace the evolution of

transportation from 7,500 years ago—when people first decided to load an ox—to the first vertical take-off jet. In 1909, the Belfast-based Shorts Aviation Company partnered with the Wright brothers to manufacture the first commercially available aircraft. The middle building holds an intriguing section on the sinking of the Belfast-made *Titanic.* The top building covers the history of bikes, cars, and trains. The car section rumbles from the first car in Ireland (an 1898 Benz), through the "Cortina Culture" of the 1960s, to the local adventures of controversial automobile designer John DeLorean and a 1981 model of his sleek sports car.

The **Folk Park,** an open-air collection of 34 reconstructed

The Red Hand of Ulster

All over Belfast, you'll notice a curious symbol: a red hand facing you as if swearing a pledge or telling you to halt. You'll spot it, faded, above the Linen Hall Library door, in the wrought-iron fences of the Merchant Hotel, on old-fashioned clothes wringers (in the Ulster Folk Park and Transport Museum at Cultra), above the front door of a bank in Bangor, in the shape of a flowerbed at Mount Stewart House, in Loyalist paramilitary murals, on shield emblems in the gates of Republican memorials, and even on the flag of Northern Ireland (the white flag with the red cross of St. George). It's known as the Red Hand of Ulster—and it seems to pop up everywhere. It's one of the few emblems used by both communities in Northern Ireland.

Nationalists display a red-hand-on-a-yellow-shield as a symbol of the ancient province of Ulster. It was the official crest of the once-dominant O'Neill clan (who fought tooth and nail against English rule) and today signifies resistance to British rule in these communities.

But you'll more often see the red hand in Unionist areas. They see it as a potent symbol of the political entity of Northern Ireland. The Ulster Volunteer Force chose it for their symbol in 1913 and embedded it in the center of the Northern Irish flag upon partition of the island in 1921. You may see the red hand clenched as a fist in Loyalist murals. One Loyalist paramilitary group even named itself the Red Hand Commandos.

The origin of the red hand comes from a mythological tale of two rival clans that raced by boat to claim a far shore. The first clan leader to touch the shore would win it for his people. Everyone aboard both vessels strained mightily at their oars, near exhaustion as they approached the shore. Finally, in desperation, the chieftain leader of the slower boat whipped out his sword and lopped off his right hand...which he then flung onto the shore, thus winning the coveted land. Moral of the story? The fearless folk of Ulster will do *whatever it takes* to get the job done.

buildings from all over the nine counties of Ulster, showcases the region's traditional lifestyles. After wandering through the old-town site (church, print shop, schoolhouse, humble Belfast row house, silent movie theater, and so on), you'll head off into the country to nip into cottages, farmhouses, and mills. Some houses are warmed by a wonderful peat fire and a friendly attendant. Your visit can be dull or vibrant, depending upon whether attendants are available to chat. Drop a peat brick on the fire.

▲Carrickfergus Castle

Built during the Norman invasion of the late 1100s, this historic castle stands sentry on the shore of Belfast Lough. William of Or-

ange landed here in 1690, when he began his Irish campaign against deposed King James II. In 1778, the American privateer ship *Ranger* (the first ever to fly the Stars-and-Stripes), under the command of John Paul Jones, defeated the more heavily armed HMS *Drake* just offshore. These days the castle feels a bit sanitized and geared for kids, but it's an easy excursion if you're seeking a castle experience near the city.

Cost and Hours: £5; daily April-Sept 10:00-17:00, Oct-March until 16:00; tel. 028/9335-1273.

Getting There: It's a 20-minute train ride from Belfast (on the line to Larne). Turn left as you exit the train station and walk straight downhill for five minutes—all the way to the waterfront—passing under the arch of the old town wall en route. You'll find the castle on your right.

▲The Gobbins Cliff Path

Newly reopened in 2016, the Gobbins Cliff Path is an Edwardian adventure with birds, beautiful scenery, and occasional rogue waves. Located 20 miles northeast of Belfast via Carrickfergus, this complex path—a mix of tunnel bridges, railings, and steps carved, hammered, or fastened to the cliff—was first opened in 1902, designed to boost tourism. Once popular, it fell into disrepair during World War II and was closed for decades. The newly reinforced path (which, to spoil all the turn-of-the-century fun, now requires helmets and guides) takes two to three hours to hike, and is awkward and steep in places, but not terribly strenuous. You'll spot puffins, cormorants, and kittiwakes in nesting areas along the way.

Cost and Hours: £10, visitor center open daily 9:30-17:30, required guided hikes generally hourly (weather permitting), book in advance as tours can fill up, tel. 028/9337-2318, 68 Middle Road, Islandmagee, www.thegobbinscliffpath.com.

Getting There: By car, take A-2 from Belfast to Larne, turn right on B-90, and follow the signs to *Islandmagee* and *The Gobbins*. Without a car, take a train to Ballycarry (on the Larne line) and walk a mile to the center, or take a taxi (Ballycarry Cabs, tel. 028/9303-8131).

Sleeping in Belfast

Belfast is more of a business town than a tourist town, so business-class room rates are lower or soft on weekends (best prices booked from hotel websites).

IN CENTRAL BELFAST

To locate these hotels, see the map on page 391.

$$$$ Hotel Europa is Belfast's landmark hotel—fancy, comfortable, and central—with four stars and lower weekend rates. Modern yet elegant, this place is the choice of visiting diplomats (breakfast extra, Great Victoria Street, tel. 028/9027-1066, www.hastingshotels.com, res@eur.hastingshotels.com).

$$$ Jurys Inn, an American-style hotel that rents 190 identical modern rooms, is perfectly located two blocks from City Hall (breakfast extra, Fisherwick Place, tel. 028/9053-3500, www.jurysinns.com, jurysinnbelfast@jurysinns.com).

SOUTH OF QUEEN'S UNIVERSITY

Many of Belfast's best budget beds cluster in a comfortable, leafy neighborhood just south of Queen's University (near the Ulster Museum). The Botanic, Adelaide, and City Hospital train stations are nearby (I find Botanic the most convenient), and buses zip down Malone Road every 20 minutes. Any bus on Malone Road goes to Donegall Square East. Taxis take you downtown for about £6 (your host can call one).

$$$ Malone Lodge Hotel, by far the classiest listing in this neighborhood, provides slick, business-class comfort in 119 spacious rooms on a quiet street (elevator, restaurant, parking, 60 Eglantine Avenue, tel. 028/9038-8000, www.malonelodgehotel.com, info@malonelodgehotel.com).

$$$ Wellington Park Hotel is a dependable, if unimaginative, chain-style hotel with 75 rooms. It's predictable but in a good location (parking extra, 21 Malone Road, tel. 028/9038-1111, www.wellingtonparkhotel.com, info@wellingtonparkhotel.com).

$ Elms Village, a huge Queen's University dorm complex, rents 100 basic, institutional rooms (mostly singles, with a few doubles) to travelers during summer break (July and Aug only, coin-op laundry, self-serve kitchen; reception building is 50 yards down entry street, marked *Elms Village* on low brick wall, 78 Malone Road; tel. 028/9097-4525, www.stayatqueens.com, accommodation@qub.ac.uk).

Sleep Code

Hotels are classified based on the average price of a typical en suite double room with breakfast in high season.

$$$$	**Splurge:** Most rooms over £140
$$$	**Pricier:** £110-140
$$	**Moderate:** £80-110
$	**Budget:** £50-80
¢	**Backpacker:** Under £50
RS%	Rick Steves discount

Unless otherwise noted, credit cards are accepted and free Wi-Fi is available. Comparison-shop by checking prices at several hotels (on each hotel's own website, on a booking site, or by email). For the best deal, *book directly with the hotel*. Ask for a discount if paying in cash; if the listing includes **RS%**, request a Rick Steves discount.

BETWEEN QUEEN'S UNIVERSITY AND SHAFTESBURY SQUARE

$$ Benedicts Hotel has 32 rooms in a good location at the northern fringe of the Queen's University district. Its popular bar is a maze of polished wood and can be loud on weekend nights (elevator, 7 Bradbury Place, tel. 028/9059-1999, www.benedictshotel. co.uk, info@benedictshotel.co.uk).

$$ Ibis Belfast Queens Quarter, part of a major European hotel chain, has 56 practical rooms in a convenient location. It's a great deal if you're not looking for cozy character (breakfast extra, elevator, a block north of Queen's University at 75 University Street, tel. 028/9033-3366, www.ibisbelfast.com, h7288-re@accor.com).

Hostel: ¢ Belfast International City Hostel, big and creatively run, provides the best value among Belfast's hostels. It is located near Botanic Station, in the heart of the lively university district, and has 24-hour reception. Paul, the manager, is a veritable TI, with a passion for his work (private rooms available, 22 Donegall Road, tel. 028/9031-5435, www.hini.org.uk, info@hini.org.uk).

Eating in Belfast

DOWNTOWN

If it's pub grub you want, consider these drinking holes. For locations, see the map on page 391.

The Morning Star is woody and elegant (**$$$ restaurant** upstairs, daily 12:00-22:00; **$ afternoon buffet** Mon-Sat 12:00-16:00; down alley just off High Street at 17 Pottinger's Entry, alley entry is roughly opposite the post office, tel. 028/9023-5986).

$$ Robinson & Cleaver has a great central location, perfect

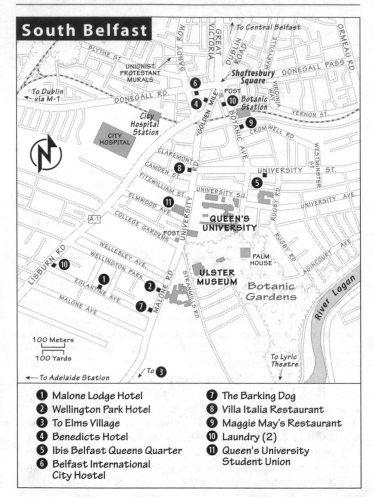

South Belfast

Map labels:
To Central Belfast
BLYTHE ST
UNIONIST PROTESTANT MURALS
To Dublin via M-1
DONEGALL RD.
SANDY ROW
VICTORIA
GREAT VICTORIA
DUBLIN ROAD
MARYVILLE
Shaftesbury Square
POST
DONEGALL PASS
ORMEAU RD.
City Hospital Station
CITY HOSPITAL
GOLDEN MILE
Botanic Station
BOTANIC AVE.
VIRGINIA
VERNON ST.
VIRGINIA WAY
CROMWELL RD.
CLAREMONT
CAMDEN ST.
FITZWILLIAM ST.
UNIVERSITY SQ
UNIVERSITY ST.
WESTMINSTER ST.
ELMWOOD AVE.
A-1
COLLEGE GARDENS
QUEEN'S UNIVERSITY
RUGBY RD.
UNIVERSITY AVE.
WELLESLEY AVE.
LISBURN RD.
WELLINGTON PARK
EGLANTINE AVE.
MALONE AVE.
MALONE RD.
POST
UNIVERSITY RD.
STRANMILLS RD.
ULSTER MUSEUM
PALM HOUSE
Botanic Gardens
AGINCOURT AVE.
River Lagan
100 Meters
100 Yards
To Adelaide Station
To ❸
To Lyric Theatre

Legend:
❶ Malone Lodge Hotel
❷ Wellington Park Hotel
❸ To Elms Village
❹ Benedicts Hotel
❺ Ibis Belfast Queens Quarter
❻ Belfast International City Hostel
❼ The Barking Dog
❽ Villa Italia Restaurant
❾ Maggie May's Restaurant
❿ Laundry (2)
⓫ Queen's University Student Union

for light lunches or tasty dinners. In good weather, their balcony has terrific views of City Hall (Mon-Sat 12:00-15:00, Wed-Sat also 17:00-21:30, closed Sun; Donegall Square North, a few doors east of the TI, tel. 028/9031-2666, www.robinsonandcleaver.com).

$$ Crown Liquor Saloon, a recommended stop along the Golden Mile, is small and antique. Its mesmerizing mishmash of mosaics and shareable snugs (booths—best to reserve) is topped with a smoky tin ceiling (food served Sun-Thu 11:30-19:00, Fri-Sat until 17:00, 46 Great Victoria Street, across from Hotel Europa, tel. 028/9024-3187, www.nicholsonspubs.co.uk). The **$$$**

Crown Dining Room upstairs offers dependable meals (daily 11:30-20:00, tel. 028/9024-3187, use entry on Amelia Street when the Crown Liquor Saloon is closed).

$$ Kelly's Cellars, once a rebel hangout (see plaque above door), still has a very gritty Irish feel. It's 300 years old and hard to find, but worth it. The pub grub is basic, but the atmosphere is delicious (Mon-Sat 11:30-24:30, Sun 13:00-23:30; live traditional music Tue-Fri and Sun at 21:30, Sat at 16:30; 32 Bank Street, 100 yards behind Tesco supermarket, access via alley on left side when facing Tesco, tel. 028/9024-6058).

Supermarkets: Marks & Spencer has a coffee shop serving skinny lattes and a supermarket in its basement (Mon-Sat 8:00-18:00, Thu until 21:00, Sun 13:00-18:00, WCs on second floor, Donegall Place, a block north of Donegall Square). **Tesco,** another supermarket, is a block north of Marks & Spencer and two blocks north of Donegall Square (open slightly later than Marks & Spencer, Royal Avenue and Bank Street). Picnic on the City Hall lawn.

ON WARING STREET, IN THE CATHEDRAL QUARTER

I like the cluster of culture surrounding the Cotton Court section of Waring Street. It's about a 10-minute walk northeast of the City Hall. For locations, see the map on page 391.

$$$$ Check out the lobby of **Merchant Hotel** (a grand former bank) for a glimpse of crushed-velvet Victorian splendor under an opulent dome, and consider indulging in Belfast's best afternoon tea splurge. Don't show up in shorts and sneakers (£22.50—Mon-Fri 12:00-16:30; £29.50—Sat-Sun, reserve ahead for seating at 12:30 or 15:00, 35 Waring Street, tel. 028/9023-4888, www.themerchanthotel.com).

$$$ 2Taps Wine Bar is a whiff of Mediterranean warmth in this cold brick city. Try a cheerful tapas or paella meal washed down with sangria (Tue-Sun 12:00-21:00, closed Mon, 42 Waring Street, tel. 028/9031-1414).

$$ The Cloth Ear is a friendly, modern, often-crowded bar serving better-than-average pub grub from the kitchen of the posh Merchant Hotel next door (daily 12:00-20:30, 33 Waring Street, tel. 028/9026-2719).

VICTORIA SQUARE AREA

Although Victoria Square is a big, glitzy mall, a couple of fun options are worth considering—one inside the mall (for food) and one next door (for drinks). For locations, see the map on page 391.

$ Wagamama, part of a British chain, is a Japanese noodle bar located on the first floor of the mall. Hearty portions of chicken

Restaurant Price Code

I've assigned each eatery a price category, based on the average cost of a typical main course. Drinks, desserts, and splurge items (steak and seafood) can raise the price considerably.

$$$$ **Splurge:** Most main courses over £16
$$$ **Pricier:** £12-16
$$ **Moderate:** £8-12
$ **Budget:** Under £8

In Northern Ireland, carryout fish-and-chips and other takeout food is **$**; a basic pub or sit-down eatery is **$$**; a gastropub or casual but more upscale restaurant is **$$$**; and a swanky splurge is **$$$$**.

ramen, *yakisoba,* and cumin beef salad are menu highlights (daily 12:00-21:00, Victoria Square, tel. 028/9023-6098).

Bittles Bar is a good place to stop for a pint. It's a tiny, wedge-shaped throwback to Victorian days, hidden in the shadows on the east side of the mall next to the ornate, yellow Victorian fountain. The minuscule, terraced interior is decorated with caricatures of literary and political figures (daily generally 12:00 until late, no food, 70 Upper Church Lane just off Victoria Street, mobile 077-9396-2329).

NEAR QUEEN'S UNIVERSITY

For locations, see the map on page 400.

$$$ The Barking Dog is closest to my cluster of accommodations south of the university. It's a hip grill serving tasty burgers, duck, scallops, and other filling fare. If the weather's fine, the outdoor tree-shaded front tables are ideal for people-watching (Mon-Sat 12:00-15:00 & 17:30-23:00, Sun 12:00-21:00, near corner of Eglantine Avenue at 33 Malone Road, tel. 028/9066-1885).

$$$ Villa Italia packs in crowds hungry for linguini and *bistecca.* With its checkered tablecloths and a wood-beamed ceiling draped with grape leaves, it's a little bit of Italy in Belfast (Mon-Sat 17:00-23:00, Sun 12:30-21:30, 3 long blocks south of Shaftesbury Square, at intersection with University Street, 39 University Road, tel. 028/9032-8356).

$$ Maggie May's serves hearty, simple, affordable meals (daily 8:00-22:00, one block south of Botanic Station at 50 Botanic Avenue, tel. 028/9032-2662).

Belfast Connections

BY TRAIN OR BUS

For updated schedules and prices for both trains and buses in Northern Ireland, check with Translink (tel. 028/9066-6630, www.translink.co.uk). Consider a Belfast Visitor Pass (see page 378) if you're visiting just Belfast. Those going beyond Belfast can make use of the Zone 4 iLink smartcard, good for all-day train and bus use in Northern Ireland (see page 379). Service is less frequent on Sundays.

From Belfast by Train to: Dublin (8/day Mon-Sat, 5/day Sun, 2 hours), **Derry** (7/day, 2.5 hours), **Larne** (hourly, 1 hour), **Portrush** (11/day, 5/day Sun, 2 hours, transfer in Coleraine), **Bangor** (2/hour, 30 minutes).

By Bus to: Portrush (12/day, 2 hours; scenic-coast route, 2.5 hours), **Derry** (hourly, 2 hours), **Dublin** (hourly, most via Dublin Airport, 3 hours), **Galway** (every 2 hours, 6 hours, change in Dublin), **Glasgow** (3/day, 6 hours), **Edinburgh** (3/day, 7 hours). The Europa Bus Centre is behind Hotel Europa (Ulsterbus tel. 028/9033-7003 for destinations in Scotland and England).

BY PLANE

Belfast has two airports. **George Best Belfast City Airport** (airport code: BHD, tel. 028/9093-9093, www.belfastcityairport.com) is a five-minute taxi ride from town (near the docks), while **Belfast International Airport** (airport code: BFS, tel. 028/9448-4848, www.belfastairport.com) is 18 miles west of town, connected by buses from the Europa Bus Centre behind the Europa Hotel.

If you're headed for Edinburgh or Glasgow, flying is generally better than taking the ferry, as it's a fairly cheap, short trip.

BY FERRY

To Scotland: You can sail between Belfast and **Cairnryan** on the Stena Line ferry. A Rail Link coach connects the Cairnryan port to Ayr, where you'll catch a train to Glasgow Central station (7/day, 2.5 hours by ferry plus 2.5 hours by bus and train, tel. 028/9074-7747, www.stenaline.co.uk). The P&O Ferry (toll tel. 087-1664-2121, www.poferries.com) goes from **Larne,** 20 miles north of Belfast, to **Cairnryan** (7/day, 2 hours), with bus or rail connections from there to Glasgow and Edinburgh. There are hourly trains between Belfast and Larne (1-hour trip, Larne TI tel. 028/2826-2495).

To England: You can sail from Belfast to **Liverpool** (generally 2/day, 8 hours, arrives in port of Birkenhead—10 minutes from Liverpool, tel. 028/9074-7747, www.stenaline.co.uk).

Bangor

To stay in a laid-back seaside hometown—with more comfort per pound—sleep 12 miles east of Belfast in Bangor (BANG-grr). With elegant old homes facing its spruced-up harbor and not even a hint of big-city Belfast, the city has appeal, and it's a handy alternative for travelers who find Belfast booked up by occasional conventions and conferences.

Formerly a Victorian resort and seaside escape from the big city nearby, Bangor now has a sleepy residential feeling. To visit two worthwhile sights near Bangor—the Somme Heritage Centre and Mount Stewart House—consider renting a car for the day (bus service to these sights is sporadic) at nearby George Best Belfast City Airport, a 15-minute train trip from Bangor. The harbor is a 10-minute walk from the train station.

GETTING THERE

Catch the train to Bangor from either Belfast's Central or Great Victoria Street stations; both are on the same line and cost the same (2/hour, 30 minutes, go to the end of the line—don't get off at Bangor West). Consider stopping en route at Cultra (Ulster Folk Park and Transport Museum; see page 395). The journey gives you a good, close-up look at the giant Belfast harbor cranes.

If day-tripping into Belfast from Bangor, get off at Central Station (free shuttle bus to town center, 4/hour, none on Sun; some trains may also stop at the more convenient Great Victoria Street Station), or stay on until Botanic Station for the Ulster Museum, the Golden Mile, and Sandy Row. Trains cost the same from Bangor to all three Belfast stations (Central Station, Great Victoria Station, and Botanic Station).

Orientation to Bangor

Tourist Information: Bangor's TI is in a stone tower house (from 1637) on the harborfront (Mon-Fri 9:15-17:00, Sat 10:00-17:00, Sun 13:00-17:00 except closed Sun Sept-April, 34 Quay Street, tel. 028/9127-0069, www.visitardsandnorthdown.com).

Helpful Hints: You'll find **Speediwash Launderette** at 96 Abbey Street, a couple of blocks south of the train station (Mon-Sat

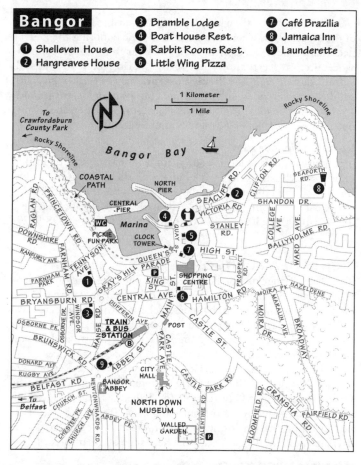

Bangor

1. Shelleven House
2. Hargreaves House
3. Bramble Lodge
4. Boat House Rest.
5. Rabbit Rooms Rest.
6. Little Wing Pizza
7. Café Brazilia
8. Jamaica Inn
9. Launderette

9:00-18:00, closed Sun, tel. 028/9127-0074). **Kare Cabs** provides local taxi service (tel. 028/9145-6777 or 028/9181-8001).

Sights in Bangor

Walks

For sightseeing, your time is better spent in Belfast. But if you have time to burn in Bangor, enjoy a walk next to the water on the **Coastal Path,** which leads west out of town from the marina. A pleasant three-mile walk along the water leads you to Crawfordsburn Country Park in the suburb of Helen's Bay. Hidden in the trees above Helen's Bay beach is Grey Point Fort, with its two WWI artillery bunkers guarding the shore (generally Sat-Sun 12:00-16:00, tel. 028/9185-3621). Allow 1.5 hours each way as you share the easy-to-follow and mostly paved trail with local joggers, dog walkers, and bikers.

BELFAST

For a shorter walk with views of the marina, head to the end of the **North Pier,** where you'll find a mosaic honoring the D-Day fleet that rendezvoused offshore in 1944, far from Nazi reconnaissance aircraft. Keep an eye out in the marina for Rose the seal. Little kids may enjoy the **Pickie Fun Park** next to the marina, with paddleboat swan rides, and miniature golf. **Bangor Castle** grounds are good for picnics, and include a peaceful walled garden (free, open Mon-Thu 10:00-17:00, Fri-Sun until 18:00).

North Down Museum

This museum covers local history, from monastic days to Viking raids to Victorian splendor. It's hidden on the grassy grounds behind the City Hall, uphill and opposite from the train station.

Cost and Hours: Free, July-Aug daily 10:00-16:30; Sept-June Tue-Sat 10:00-16:30, Sun 12:00-16:30, closed Mon, tel. 028/9127-1200.

SIGHTS NEAR BANGOR

The eastern fringe of Northern Ireland is populated mostly by people who consider themselves true-blue British citizens with a history of loyalty to the Crown that goes back more than 400 years. Two sights within reach by car from Bangor highlight this area's firm roots in British culture: the Somme Heritage Centre and Mount Stewart House. Call ahead to confirm sight opening hours.

Getting There: Bus service from Bangor is patchy (bus #6; check schedule with Bangor TI). I'd rent a car instead at nearby George Best Belfast City Airport (described on page 403), which is only 15 minutes by train from Bangor or 10 minutes from Belfast's Central Station. Because the airport is east of Belfast, your drive to these rural sights skips the headache of urban Belfast.

▲Mount Stewart House

No manor house in Ireland better illuminates the affluent lifestyle of the Protestant ascendancy than this lush estate. After the defeat of James II (the last Catholic king of England) at the Battle of the Boyne in 1690, the Protestant monarchy was in control—and the privileged status of landowners of the same faith was assured. In the 1700s, Ireland's many Catholic rebellions seemed finally to be squashed, so Anglican landlords felt safe flaunting their wealth in  manor houses surrounded by utterly perfect gardens. The Mount Stewart House in particular was designed to dazzle.

Cost and Hours: £8.50 for house and gardens; open daily March-Oct 10:00-17:00, closed Nov-Feb; 8 miles south of Bangor, just off A-20 beside Strangford Lough, tel. 028/4278-8387, www. nationaltrust.org.uk, enquiries@nationaltrust.org.uk.

Visiting the House: Hourly tours give you a glimpse of the cushy life led by the Marquess of Londonderry and his heirs over the past three centuries. The main entry hall is a stunner, with a black-and-white checkerboard tile floor, marble columns, classical statues, and pink walls supporting a balcony with a domed ceiling and a fine chandelier. In the dining room, you'll see the original seats occupied by the rears of European heads of state, brought back from the Congress of Vienna after Napoleon's 1815 defeat. A huge painting of Hambletonian, a prize-winning racehorse, hangs above the grand staircase, dwarfing a portrait of the Duke of Wellington in a hall nearby. The heroic duke (worried that his Irish birth would be seen as lower class by British blue bloods) once quipped in Parliament, "Just because one is born in a stable does not make him a horse." Irish emancipator Daniel O'Connell retorted, "Yes, but it could make you an ass."

Afterward, wander the expansive manicured **gardens.** The fantasy life of parasol-toting, upper-crust Victorian society seems to ooze from every viewpoint. Fanciful sculptures of extinct dodo birds and monkeys holding vases on their heads set off predictably classic Italian and Spanish sections. An Irish harp has been trimmed out of a hedge a few feet from a flowerbed shaped like the Red Hand of Ulster. Swans glide serenely among the lily pads on a small lake.

Somme Heritage Centre

World War I's trench warfare was a meat grinder. More British soldiers died in the last year of that war than in all of World War II. Northern Ireland's men were not spared—especially during the bloody Battle of the Somme in France, starting in July 1916 (see the "1916" sidebar on page 392). Among the Allied forces was the British Army's 36th Ulster Division, which drew heavily from this loyal heartland of Northern Ireland. The 36th Ulster Division suffered brutal losses at the Battle of the Somme—of the 760 men recruited from the Shankill Road area in Belfast, only 10 percent survived.

Exhibits portray the battle experience through a mix of military artifacts, photos, historical newsreels, and life-size figures posed in trench warfare re-creations. To access the majority of the exhibits, it's essential to take the one-hour guided tour (leaving hourly, on the hour). Visiting this place is a moving experience, but it can only hint at the horrific conditions endured by these soldiers.

Cost and Hours: £6.50; July-Aug Mon-Fri 10:00-16:00, Sat 11:00-16:00, closed Fri Sept-June and Sun year-round; hourly tours, 3 miles south of Bangor just off A-21 at 233 Bangor Road, tel. 028/9182-3202, www.irishsoldier.org. A coffee shop is located at the center.

Sleeping in Bangor

Visitors arriving in Bangor (by train) come down Main Street to reach the harbor marina. You'll find Hargreaves House to the right, along the waterfront east of the marina on Seacliff Road. The other two listings are to the left, just uphill and west of the marina.

$$ Shelleven House is an old-fashioned, well-kept, stately place with 13 prim rooms on the quiet corner of Princetown Road and Tennyson Avenue (RS%, parking, 61 Princetown Road, tel. 028/9127-1777, www.shellevenhouse.com, info@shellevenhouse. com, Sue and Paul Toner).

$ Hargreaves House, a homey Victorian waterfront refuge with three cozy rooms, is Bangor's best value (RS%—use code RS16, 15-minute walk from train station but worth it, 78 Seacliff Road, tel. 028/9146-4071, mobile 079-8058-5047, www. hargreaveshouse.com, info@hargreaveshouse.com, Pauline Mendez).

$ Bramble Lodge is closest to the train station (10-minute walk), offering three inviting and spotless rooms (1 Bryansburn Road, tel. 028/9145-7924, jacquihanna_bramblelodge@yahoo. co.uk, Jacquiline Hanna). Ask about their simple one-bedroom self-catering apartment around the corner.

Eating in Bangor

Be aware that most restaurants in town stop seating at about 20:30.

The **$$$$ Boat House** is a stout stone structure hiding the finest dining experience in Bangor. It's run by two Dutch brothers who specialize in some of the freshest fish dishes in Northern Ireland (Wed-Sat 12:30-14:30 & 17:30-21:30, Sun 12:30-20:00, closed Mon-Tue, reserve ahead, on Sea Cliff Road opposite the TI, tel. 028/9146-9253, www.theboathouseni.co.uk).

$$ The Rabbit Rooms serves hearty Irish food to local crowds (Mon-Thu 12:00-21:00, Fri-Sun until 21:30, near the harbor at 33 Quay Street, tel. 028/9146-7699).

$ Little Wing Pizza is a friendly joint serving tasty pizza, pasta, and salads. Grab your food to go and munch by the marina.

It's also one of the few places in town that serves food later at night (daily 11:00-22:00, 37 Main Street, tel. 028/9147-2777).

$ Café Brazilia, a popular locals' lunch hangout with a simple menu, is across from the stubby clock tower (Mon-Sat 8:00-16:30, Sun 10:00-16:30, 13 Bridge Street, tel. 028/9127-2763).

The **$$ Jamaica Inn** offers pleasant pub grub and a breezy waterfront porch (food served from about 12:00-21:00, 10-minute walk east of the TI, 188 Seacliff Road, tel. 028/9147-1610).

PORTRUSH &
THE ANTRIM COAST

The Antrim Coast—the north of Northern Ireland—is one of the most interesting and scenic coastlines in Ireland. Portrush, at the end of the train line, is an ideal base for exploring the highlights of the Antrim Coast. Within a few miles of the train terminal, you can visit evocative castle ruins, tour the world's oldest whiskey distillery, catch a thrill on a bouncy rope bridge, and hike along the famous Giant's Causeway.

PLANNING YOUR TIME

You need a full day to explore the Antrim Coast, so allow two nights in Portrush. An ideal day could lace together Dunluce Castle, Old Bushmills Distillery, and the Giant's Causeway, followed by nine holes on the Portrush pitch-and-putt course. In summer months, the long days this far north extend your sightseeing time (and most golf courses stay open until dusk).

GETTING AROUND THE ANTRIM COAST

By Car: A car is the best way to explore the charms of the Antrim Coast. Distances are short and parking is easy. If time allows, don't miss the slower-but-scenic coastal route from Portrush to Belfast via the Glens of Antrim.

By Bus: In peak season, an all-day bus pass helps you get around the region economically. The **Causeway Rambler** links Portrush to Old Bushmills Distillery, the Giant's Causeway, and the Carrick-a-Rede Rope Bridge hourly (£6.50/day, runs March-April every two hours, May-Sept hourly, fewer off-season, operates roughly 10:00-18:00). The bus journey from Portrush to Carrick-a-Rede (the easternmost point of interest on the route) takes 45 minutes. Pick up a Rambler bus schedule at the TI, and buy the ticket from the driver (in Portrush, the Rambler stops at Dunluce Avenue, next to public WC, a 2-minute walk from TI; operated by Translink, tel. 028/9066-6630, www.translink.co.uk).

By Bus Tour: If you're based in Belfast, you can visit most of the sights on the Antrim Coast with a **McComb's** tour (see page 382). Those based in Derry can get to the Giant's Causeway and Carrick-a-Rede Rope Bridge with **City Sightseeing** (see page 432).

By Taxi: Groups (up to four) can reasonably visit most sights by taxi (except the more distant Carrick-a-Rede and Rathlin Island sailings from Ballycastle). Rough one-way prices from Portrush: £6 (Dunluce Castle), £8 (Old Bushmills Distillery), £11 (Giant's Causeway). Try **Andy Brown's Taxi** (tel. 028/7082-2223), **Hugh's Taxi** (mobile 077-0298-6110), or **North West Taxi** (tel. 028/7082-4446).

Portrush

Homey Portrush used to be known as "the Brighton of the North." It first became a resort in the late 1800s, as railroads expanded to offer the new middle class a weekend by the shore. Victorian

society believed that swimming in salt water would cure many common ailments.

This is County Antrim, the Bible Belt of Northern Ireland. When a large supermarket chain decided to stay open on Sundays, a local reverend called for a boycott of the store for not honoring the Sabbath. And in 2012, when the Giant's Causeway Visitors Centre opened, local Creationists demanded their viewpoint (that, according to the Bible, the earth was only 6,000 years old) be represented beside modern geologic explanations of the age of the unique rock formations...carbon dating be damned.

While it's seen its best days, Portrush retains the atmosphere and architecture of a genteel seaside resort. Its peninsula is filled with lowbrow, family-oriented amusements, fun eateries, and B&Bs. Summertime fun-seekers promenade along the tiny harbor and tumble down to the sandy beaches, which extend in sweeping white crescents on either side.

Superficially, Portrush has the appearance of any small British seaside resort, but its history and large population of young people (students from nearby University of Ulster at Coleraine) give the town a little more personality. Along with the usual arcade amusements, there are nightclubs, restaurants, summer theater productions (July-Aug) in the town hall, and convivial pubs that attract customers all the way from Belfast.

Orientation to Portrush

Portrush's pleasant and easily walkable town center features sea views in every direction. On one side are the harbor and most of the restaurants, and on the other are Victorian townhouses and vast, salty vistas. The tip of the peninsula is filled with tennis courts, lawn-bowling greens, putting greens, and a park.

The town is busy with students during the school year. July and August are beach-resort boom time. June and September are laid-back and lazy. There's a brief but intense spike in visitors in mid-May for a huge annual motorcycle race (see "Helpful Hints," later). Families pack Portrush on Saturdays, and revelers from Belfast crowd its hotels on Saturday nights.

TOURIST INFORMATION

The TI is located underneath the very central, red-brick Town Hall (July-Aug Mon-Sat 9:00-18:00, Sun 11:00-18:00; April-June and Sept Mon-Fri 9:30-17:00, Sat-Sun 12:00-17:00; closed Oct-March; Kerr Street, tel. 028/7082-3333). Get the Collins Northern Ireland Visitors Map (£5), the free *Visitor Attractions* brochure, and, if needed, a free Belfast map.

ARRIVAL IN PORTRUSH

The train tracks stop at the base of the tiny peninsula that Portrush fills (no baggage storage at station). Most of my listed B&Bs are within a 10-minute walk of the train station. The bus stop is two blocks from the train station.

HELPFUL HINTS

Exchange Rate: £1 = about $1.50

Country Calling Code: 44 (see page 530 for dialing instructions)

Crowds: Over a four-day weekend in mid-May, thousands of die-hard motorcycle fans converge on Portrush, Port Stewart, and Coleraine to watch the **Northwest 200 Race.** Fearless racers scorch the roads at 200 miles per hour on the longest straightaway in motorsports. Accommodations fill up a year ahead, and traffic is the pits (dates and details at www.northwest200.org).

Laundry: Causeway Laundry charges £10/load for full service (Mon-Tue and Thu-Fri 9:00-16:30, Sat 9:00-13:00, closed Wed and Sun, 68 Causeway Street, tel. 028/7082-2060).

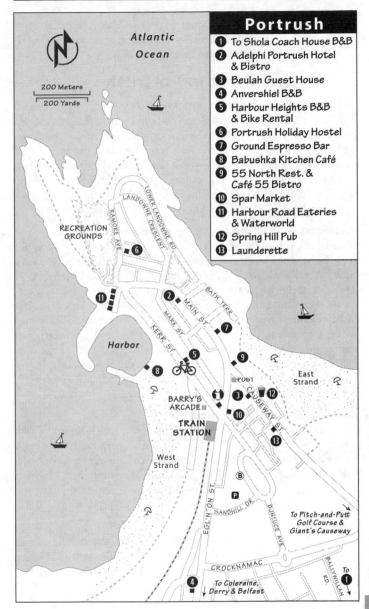

Portrush

1. To Shola Coach House B&B
2. Adelphi Portrush Hotel & Bistro
3. Beulah Guest House
4. Anvershiel B&B
5. Harbour Heights B&B & Bike Rental
6. Portrush Holiday Hostel
7. Ground Espresso Bar
8. Babushka Kitchen Café
9. 55 North Rest. & Café 55 Bistro
10. Spar Market
11. Harbour Road Eateries & Waterworld
12. Spring Hill Pub
13. Launderette

Atlantic Ocean

200 Meters
200 Yards

RECREATION GROUNDS

LOWER LANDOWNE RD.

LANDOWNE CRESCENT

RAMORE AVE.

BATH TERR.

MAIN ST.

MARK ST.

KERR ST.

Harbor

POST

East Strand

BARRY'S ARCADE

TRAIN STATION

CAUSEWAY ST.

West Strand

B

P

EGLINTON ST.

SANDHILL DR.

DUNLUCE AVE.

To Pitch-and-Putt Golf Course & Giant's Causeway

CROCKNAMAC

BALLYWILLAN RD.

To 1

To Coleraine, Derry & Belfast

Bike Rental: The recommended **Harbour Heights B&B** rents sturdy new mountain bikes for £12/day, a great way to experience the gorgeous Antrim Coast.

Sights in Portrush

Barry's Old Time Amusement Arcade

This fun arcade is a chance to see Northern Ireland at play. Located just below the train station on the harbor, it's filled with "candy floss" (cotton candy) stands and little kids learning the art of one-armed bandits, 10p at a time. Get £1 worth of 10p coins from the machine and go wild, or brave the tiny roller coaster and bumper cars (July-mid-Sept daily 12:30-22:30, shorter hours May-June, closed mid-Sept-April; tel. 028/7082-2340, www.barrysamusements.com).

Pitch-and-Putt at the Royal Portrush Golf Club

Irish courses, like those in Scotland, are highly sought after for their lush greens in glorious settings. Serious golfers can get a tee time at the Royal Portrush, which hosted the British Open in 1951 and is set to host it again in 2019 (green fees Mon-Fri-£160, Sat-Sun-£180). Those on a budget can play the adjacent, slightly shorter Valley Course (green fees Mon-Fri-£42.50, Sat-Sun-£55). Meanwhile, rookies can get a wee dose of this wonderful golf setting at the neighboring Skerries 9 Hole Links pitch-and-putt range. You get two clubs and balls for £8 (daily June-Aug 8:30-19:00, shorter hours off-season, 10-minute walk from station, tel. 028/7082-2311, www.royalportrushgolfclub.com).

Portrush Recreation Grounds

For some easygoing exercise right in town, this well-organized park offers lawn-bowling greens (£5/hour with gear), putting greens, tennis courts, and a great kids' play park. You can rent tennis shoes, balls, and rackets, all for £10/hour (mid-May-mid-Sept Mon-Sat 10:00-dusk, Sun 13:00-19:00, closed mid-Sept-mid-May, tel. 028/7082-4441).

Waterworld

For more fun, consider Waterworld, with pools, waterslides, and bowling (£5; open daily June-Aug, generally 10:00-18:00 but hours vary, closed Sept-May; wedged between Harbour Bistro and Ramore Wine Bar, tel. 028/7082-2001).

Sleeping in Portrush

Portrush has a range of hotels, from depressing to ritzy. Some B&Bs can be well-worn. August and Saturday nights can be tight (and loud) with young party groups. Otherwise, it's a "you take half a loaf when you can get it" town. Rates vary with the view

Sleep Code

Hotels are classified based on the average price of a typical en suite double room with breakfast in high season.

$$$$	**Splurge:** Most rooms over £140
$$$	**Pricier:** £110-140
$$	**Moderate:** £80-110
$	**Budget:** £50-80
¢	**Backpacker:** Under £50
RS%	Rick Steves discount

Unless otherwise noted, credit cards are accepted and free Wi-Fi is available. Comparison-shop by checking prices at several hotels (on each hotel's own website, on a booking site, or by email). For the best deal, *book directly with the hotel*. Ask for a discount if paying in cash; if the listing includes **RS%**, request a Rick Steves discount.

and season—probe for softness. Many listings face the sea, though sea views are worth paying for only if you get a bay window. Ask for a big room (some doubles can be very small; twins are bigger). Lounges are invariably grand and have bay-window views. Most places listed have lots of stairs. All but Shola Coach House are perfectly central and within a few minutes' walk of the train station. Parking is easy.

$$$ Shola Coach House is a memorable treat that exceeds other B&B experiences in Northern Ireland. About 1.5 miles south of town, it's easiest for drivers (otherwise it's a 30-minute uphill walk or £4 taxi ride). The secluded, 165-year-old, renovated stone structure once housed the coaches and horses for a local landlord. The decor of the four rooms is tasteful, the garden patio is delightful, and Sharon and David Schindler keep it spotless (parking, no kids under 16, Gateside Road at top of Ballywillan Road, tel. 028/7082-5925, mobile 075-6542-7738, www.sholabandb.com, sholabandb@gmail.com).

$$ Adelphi Portrush is a breath of fresh air, with 28 tastefully furnished modern rooms, friendly staff, and a hearty bistro downstairs (family rooms, 67 Main Street, tel. 028/7082 5544, www.adelphiportrush.com, stay@adelphiportrush.com).

$ Beulah Guest House is a traditional, good-value place. It's centrally located and run by cheerful Helen and Charlene McLaughlin, with 11 prim rooms (cheaper rooms with shared bath, parking at rear, 16 Causeway Street, tel. 028/7082-2413, www.beulahguesthouse.com, stay@beulahguesthouse.com).

$ Anvershiel B&B, with six rooms, is a 10-minute walk south of the train station (cash only, family rooms, parking, 16 Coleraine Road, tel. 028/7082-3861, www.anvershiel.com, enquiries@ anvershiel.com, Alan and Janice Thompson).

$ Harbour Heights B&B rents nine retro-homey rooms, each named after a different town in County Antrim. It has an inviting guest lounge, supervised by two tabby cats, overlooking the harbor. Friendly South African hosts Sam and Tim Swart—a photographer—manage the place with a light hand (family rooms, bike rentals, 17 Kerr Street, tel. 028/7082-2765, mobile 078-9586-6534, www.harbourheightsportrush.com, info@harbourheightsportrush. com).

Hostel: ¢ Portrush Holiday Hostel offers clean, well-organized, economical lodging for bottom-feeding vagabonds (private rooms available, tel. 028/7082-1288 or mobile 078/5037-7367, 24 Princess Street, www.portrushholidayhostel.com, info@ portrushholidayhostel.com).

Eating in Portrush

Being both a get-away-from-Belfast and close-to-a-university (at Coleraine) beach town, Portrush has more than enough chips joints. Eglinton Street is lined with cheap and cheery eateries.

LUNCH SPOTS

$ Ground Espresso Bar makes fresh sandwiches and *panini*, soup, and great coffee (daily July-Aug 9:00-22:00, Sept-June 9:00-17:00, 52 Main Street, tel. 028/7082-5979).

$ Babushka Kitchen Café serves fresh sandwiches and creative desserts with an unbeatable view (daily 9:15-17:00, on the pier at West Strand Promenade, mobile 077-8750-2012).

$$ Café 55 Bistro serves basic sandwiches with a great patio view (May-Sept Mon-Fri 9:00-17:00, Sat-Sun 9:00-21:30, shorter hours off-season, 1 Causeway Street, beneath fancier 55 North restaurant run by same owners—listed below, tel. 028/7082-2811).

The **Spar Market** has what you'll need for your Antrim Coast picnic (daily 7:00-20:00, June-Aug until 23:00, across from Barry's Arcade on Main Street, tel. 028/7082-5447).

FINE DINING

$$$ 55 North (named for the local latitude) has the best sea views in town, with windows on three sides. The filling pasta-and-fish plates are a joy (daily 12:30-14:00 & 17:00-21:00 except closed Mon Sept-June, 1 Causeway Street, tel. 028/7082-2811).

$$ Adelphi Bistro is a good bet for its relaxed, family-friendly atmosphere and hearty meals (daily 12:00-15:00 & 17:00-21:00, 67 Main Street, tel. 028/7082-5544).

HARBOUR ROAD EATERIES

The following four restaurants, located within 50 yards of each other (all under the same ownership and overlooking the harbor on Harbour Road), offer some of the best food values in town.

$$ Ramore Wine Bar—salty, modern, and much-loved—bursts with happy eaters. They have the most inviting menu that I've seen in Ireland, featuring huge meals ranging from steaks to vegetarian food. Share a piece of the decadent banoffee (banana toffee) pie with a friend (daily 12:15-14:15 & 17:00-21:30, tel. 028/7082-4313).

Downstairs, sharing the building with Ramore Wine Bar, is the energetic **$$ Coast Pizzeria,** with great Italian dishes. Come early for a table, or sit at the bar (Mon-Sat 17:00-21:30, Sun 15:00-21:30; Sept-June closed Mon-Tue, tel. 028/7082-3311).

The **$$$ Harbour Bistro** offers a more subdued, darker bistro ambience than the previous two eateries, with meals for a few pounds more (Mon-Sat 17:00-21:30, Sun 12:30-15:00 & 17:00-21:30, tel. 028/7082-2430).

Meanwhile, the **$$ Mermaid Kitchen & Bar** is all about fresh fish dishes with a Spanish twist and great harbor views. Those sitting at the bar get a bird's-eye view of the fun banter and precision teamwork of the kitchen staff (Wed-Sat 17:30-22:00, Sun 13:00-22:00, closed Mon-Tue, tel. 028/7082-6969).

PUBS

The **Harbour Bar** (next to the Harbour Bistro) has an old-fashioned pub downstairs and a plush, overstuffed, dark lounge upstairs. Or try the **Spring Hill Pub** (17 Causeway Street, tel. 028/7082-3361), with a friendly vibe and occasional music session nights.

Portrush Connections

Consider a £17.50 Zone 4 iLink smartcard, good for all-day train and bus use in Northern Ireland year-round (£16.50 top-up for each additional day; for more on iLink cards, see page 379). Translink has useful updated schedules and prices for both trains and buses in Northern Ireland (tel. 028/9066-6630, www.translink.co.uk).

From Portrush by Train to: Coleraine (hourly, 12 minutes, sparse on Sun morning), **Belfast** (11/day, 5/day Sun, 2 hours, transfer in Coleraine), **Dublin** (7/day, 2/day Sun, 5 hours, transfer in Coleraine or Belfast).

By Bus to: Belfast (12/day, 2 hours; scenic coastal route, 2.5 hours), **Dublin** (4/day, 5.5 hours).

Antrim Coast

The craggy 20-mile stretch of the Antrim Coast extending eastward from Portrush to Ballycastle rates second only to the tip of the Dingle Peninsula as the prettiest chunk of coastal Ireland. From your base in Portrush, you have a varied grab bag of sightseeing choices: the Giant's Causeway, Old Bushmills Distillery, Dunluce Castle, Carrick-a-Rede Rope Bridge, and Rathlin Island.

It's easy to weave these sights together by car, but connections are patchy by public transportation. Bus service is viable only in summer, and taxi fares are reasonable only for the sights closest to Portrush (Dunluce Castle, Old Bushmills Distillery, and the Giant's Causeway). For more on your transportation options, see "Getting Around the Antrim Coast," earlier.

PLANNING YOUR TIME

With a car, you can visit the Giant's Causeway, Old Bushmills Distillery, Carrick-a-Rede Rope Bridge, and Dunluce Castle in one busy day. Call ahead to reserve the Old Bushmills Distillery tour, and get an early start. Arrive at the Giant's Causeway by 9:00, when crowds are sparse. Park your car in the visitors center lot (opens at 9:00; parking is included with your entry fee). Early birds will find that the trails are free and always open. Spend an hour and a half scrambling over Ireland's most unique geology.

The Scottish Connection

The Romans called the Irish the "Scoti" (meaning pirates).

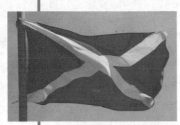

When the Scoti crossed the narrow Irish Sea and invaded the land of the Picts 1,500 years ago, that region became known as Scoti-land. Ireland and Scotland were never conquered by the Romans, and they retained similar clannish Celtic traits. Both share the same Gaelic branch of the linguistic tree.

On clear summer days from Carrick-a-Rede, the island of Mull in Scotland—only 17 miles away—is visible. Much closer on the horizon is the boomerang-shaped Rathlin Island, part of Northern Ireland. Rathlin is where Scottish leader Robert the Bruce (a compatriot of William "Braveheart" Wallace) retreated in 1307 after defeat at the hands of the English. Legend has it that he hid in a cave on the island, where he observed a spider patiently rebuilding its web each time a breeze knocked it down. Inspired by the spider's perseverance, Robert gathered his Scottish forces once more and finally defeated the English at the decisive battle of Bannockburn.

Flush with confidence from his victory, Robert the Bruce decided to open a second front against the English...in Ireland. In 1315, he sent his brother Edward over to enlist their Celtic Irish cousins in an effort to thwart the English. After securing Ireland, Edward hoped to move on and enlist the Welsh, thus cornering England with their pan-Celtic nation. But Edward's timing was bad—Ireland was in the midst of famine. His Scottish troops had to live off the land and began to take food and supplies from the starving Irish. He might also have been trying to destroy Ireland's crops to keep them from being used as a colonial "breadbasket" to feed English troops. The Scots quickly wore out their welcome, and Edward the Bruce was eventually killed in battle near Dundalk in 1318.

This was the first time in history that Ireland was used as a pawn by England's enemies. Spain and France saw Ireland as the English Achilles' heel, and both countries later attempted invasions of the island. The English Tudor and Stuart royalty countered these threats in the 16th and 17th centuries by starting the "plantation" of loyal subjects in Ireland. The only successful long-term settlement by the English was here in Northern Ireland, which remains part of the United Kingdom today.

It's interesting to imagine how things might be different today if Ireland and Scotland had been permanently welded together as a nation 700 years ago. You'll notice the strong Scottish influence in this part of Ireland when you ask a local a question and he answers, "Aye, a wee bit." The Irish joke that the Scots are just Irish people who couldn't swim home.

Then catch a late-morning tour of the Old Bushmills Distillery. Grab a cheap lunch in the hospitality room afterward. A 20-minute drive east brings you to Carrick-a-Rede, where you can enjoy a scenic cliff-top trail hike all the way to the lofty rope bridge (one hour round-trip, 1.5 hours if you cross the rope bridge and explore the sea stack). Hop in your car and double back west all the way to dramatically cliff-perched Dunluce Castle for a late-afternoon tour. From here, you're only a five-minute drive from Portrush.

Those with extra time, a car, and a hankering to seek out dramatic coastal cliff scenery may want to spend a half-day boating out to Rathlin Island, Northern Ireland's only inhabited island.

Sights on the Antrim Coast

▲▲Giant's Causeway

This five-mile-long stretch of coastline, a World Heritage Site, is famous for its bizarre basalt columns. The shore is covered with largely hexagonal pillars that stick up at various heights. It's as if the earth were offering God a choice of 37,000 six-sided cigarettes.

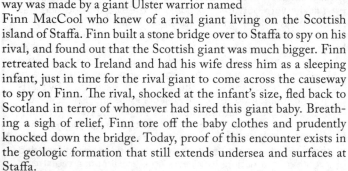

Geologists claim the Giant's Causeway was formed by volcanic eruptions more than 60 million years ago. As the surface of the lava flow quickly cooled, it contracted and crystallized into columns (resembling the caked mud at the bottom of a dried-up lakebed, but with deeper cracks). As the rock later settled and eroded, the columns broke off into the many stair-like steps that now honeycomb the Antrim Coast.

Of course, in actuality, the Giant's Causeway was made by a giant Ulster warrior named Finn MacCool who knew of a rival giant living on the Scottish island of Staffa. Finn built a stone bridge over to Staffa to spy on his rival, and found out that the Scottish giant was much bigger. Finn retreated back to Ireland and had his wife dress him as a sleeping infant, just in time for the rival giant to come across the causeway to spy on Finn. The rival, shocked at the infant's size, fled back to Scotland in terror of whomever had sired this giant baby. Breathing a sigh of relief, Finn tore off the baby clothes and prudently knocked down the bridge. Today, proof of this encounter exists in the geologic formation that still extends undersea and surfaces at Staffa.

Cost and Hours: The visitors center costs £9 (includes parking and a great audioguide) and is open daily 9:00-19:00. The causeway is free and always open, and hiking trails are open from dawn to dusk. Tel. 028/2073-1855, www.nationaltrust.org.uk/giantscauseway. A gift shop and café are in the visitors center.

Visiting the Causeway: For cute variations on the Finn story, as well as details on the ridiculous theories of modern geologists, start in the **Giant's Causeway Visitors Centre.** It's filled with interactive exhibits giving a worthwhile history of the Giant's Causeway, with a regional overview. On the far wall opposite the entrance, check out the interesting three-minute film showing the evolution of the causeway from molten lava to the geometric, geologic wonderland of today. The large 3-D model of the causeway offers a bird's-eye view of the region. Some of the exhibits are geared to kids who get a kick out of all things giant-related.

The causeway itself is the highlight of the entire coast. The audioguide (included with the visitors center ticket) highlights 15 stops along the causeway, each with a photo of the formation being described; all stops are shown on the map you'll receive with your ticket.

From the visitors center, you have several options for visiting the causeway:

By Minibus: A minibus (4/hour from 9:00, £1 each way) zips tired tourists a half-mile from the visitors center down a paved road and along the tidal zone to the causeway. This standard route (the blue dashed line on your map) offers the easiest access and follows the stops on your audioguide. Some choose to walk down this route to the causeway, and then take the shuttle back up.

By Foot: For a more varied dose of causeway views, consider the cliff-top trail (red dashed line on your map). Take the easy-to-follow trail uphill from the visitors center 10 minutes and catch your breath at Weir's Snout, the great fence-protected precipice viewpoint. It's only 15 level minutes farther to reach the Shepherd's Steps. Then grab the banister on the steep (and slippery on wet days) stairs that zigzag down the switchbacks toward the water. At the T-junction, go 100 yards right, to the towering rock pipes of "the Organ." (You can walk another 500 yards east around the headland, but the trail dead-ends there.) Now retrace your steps west on the trail (don't go up the steps again), continuing down to the tidal zone, where the "Giant's Boot" (6 feet tall, on the right) provides some photo fun. Another 100 yards farther is the dramatic point where the causeway meets the sea. Just beyond that, at the asphalt turnaround, is the bus stop where you can catch a shuttle bus back to the visitors center.

Explore the uneven, wave-splashed rock terraces, watching your every easy-to-trip step. Look for "wishing coins"—rusted and bent—that have been jammed into the cracks of rock just behind the turnaround (where the trail passes through a notch in the 20-foot-high rock wall). With time and energy, you can skip the

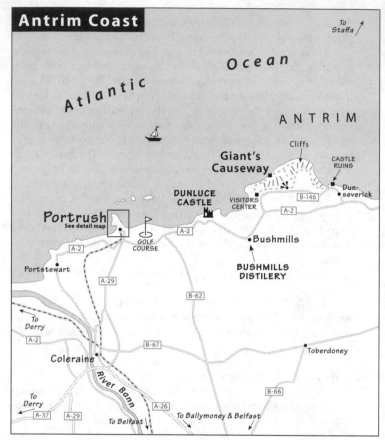

bus and walk back up to the visitors center, listening to the audioguide at the highlighted stops.

The Full Monty: Hardy hikers can spend a couple of hours exploring the trail that runs along a five-mile section of the Causeway Coast (yellow dashed line on your map). However, occasional rock falls and slides can close this route (ask first at Portrush TI, or call ahead to visitors center). A £1 hiking guide, sold at the TI, points out the highlights named by 18th-century guides (Camel's Back, Giant's Eye, and so on).

A good plan is to take the Causeway Rambler bus or a taxi from Portrush to the meager ruins of Dunseverick Castle (east of Giant's Causeway on B-146). Get off there and hike west, following the cliff-hugging contours of Benbane Head back to the visitors center. Then travel back to Portrush by taxi or Rambler bus (check bus schedules ahead of time at Portrush TI or at www.translink.co.uk).

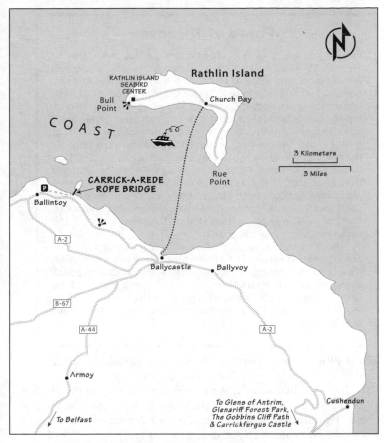

▲▲Old Bushmills Distillery

Bushmills claims to be the world's oldest distillery. Though King James I (of Bible fame) only granted Bushmills its license to distill "Aqua Vitae" in 1608, whiskey has been made here since the 13th century. Distillery tours waft you through the process, making it clear that Irish whiskey is triple distilled—and therefore smoother than Scotch whisky (distilled merely twice and minus the "e").

Cost and Hours: £7.50; April-Oct tours on the half-hour Mon-Sat from 9:30, Sun from 12:00, last tour at 16:00; Nov-March tours Mon-Sat 10:00-16:00, Sun from 12:00 with less-rigid and less-frequent tour schedule, last tour at 15:30. To find Bushmills, look for the *distillery* sign a quarter-mile from Bushmills town center. Tel. 028/2073-3218, www.bushmills.com.

Visiting the Distillery: The 45-minute tour starts with the mash pit, which is filled with a porridge that eventually becomes whiskey. (The leftovers of that porridge are fed to the county's par-

Fame of Thrones

Even if you don't give a bloody Stark about the *Game of Thrones* TV saga, you'll notice references to it as you travel around Northern Ireland. Much of the series is filmed here, both on location and in the Titanic Quarter studio in Belfast. Other scenes are shot in Croatia, Spain, Morocco, and Iceland, but the cast is subjected most often to Irish weather. An average visit to the Antrim Coast is a traipse through the set: Dragonstone, the Stormlands, and the Iron Islands were brought to life along the same route that travelers use to see Dunluce Castle and Carrick-a-Rede Rope Bridge. For those who are truly interested in the approach of a very long winter, there are several options: both McCombs (www.mccombscoaches.com) and Game of Thrones Tours (www.gameofthronestours.com) run £40 day tours from Belfast to various spots in the seven kingdoms (see page 382).

With a car, use the map at www.discovernorthernireland.com/GameofThrones to find filming locations. Without leaving County Antrim, you can visit Ballintoy Harbour (Stormlands), Larrybane (Iron Islands), Murlough Bay (Storm's End), and the Dark Hedges (King's Road) with no more than an hour's driving time. Just avoid any re-enactments, as the nearest major hospital that treats dragon burns is in Belfast.

ticularly happy cows.) You'll see thousands of oak casks—the kind used for Spanish sherry—filled with aging whiskey.

The finale, of course, is the opportunity for a sip in the 1608 Bar—the former malt barn. Visitors get a single glass of their choice. Hot-drink enthusiasts might enjoy a cinnamon-and-cloves hot toddy. Teetotalers can just order tea, totally.

To see the distillery at its lively best, visit when the 100 workers are staffing the machinery—Monday morning through Friday noon (weekend tours see a still still). Stick close to the guide to hear the commentary in this loud environment. Tours are limited to 30 people and book up. In summer, call ahead to put in your name and get a tour time. After the tour, you can get a decent lunch in the tasting room.

▲▲Carrick-a-Rede Rope Bridge

For 200 years, fishermen hung a narrow, 90-foot-high bridge (planks strung between wires) across a 65-foot-wide chasm between the mainland and a tiny island. Today, the bridge (while not the original version) gives access to the sea stack where salmon nets were set (until 2002) during summer months to catch the fish turning and hugging the coast's corner. (The complicated system is described at the gateway.) A pleasant, 30-minute, one-mile walk from the parking lot takes you to the rope bridge. Cross over to the island for fine views and great seabird-watching, especially during nesting season.

Cost and Hours: £5.90 trail and bridge fee, pay at hut beside parking lot; daily 9:30-18:00, June-Aug until 19:00; Nov-Feb until 14:45; tel. 028/2076-9839, www.nationaltrust.org.uk. A coffee shop and WCs are near the parking lot.

Nearby: If you have a car and a picnic lunch, don't miss the terrific coastal **viewpoint** rest area one mile steeply uphill and east of Carrick-a-Rede (on B-15 to Ballycastle). This grassy area offers one of the best picnic views in Northern Ireland (picnic tables but no WCs). Feast on bird's-eye views of the rope bridge, nearby Rathlin Island, and the not-so-distant Island of Mull in Scotland.

▲Dunluce Castle

These romantic ruins, perched dramatically on the edge of a rocky headland, are a testimony to this region's turbulent past. During the Middle Ages, the castle resisted several sieges. But on a stormy night in 1639, dinner was interrupted as half of the kitchen fell into the sea, taking the servants with it (Ireland's first fast food?). That was the last straw for the lady of the castle. The

countess of Antrim packed up and moved inland, and the castle "began its slow submission to the forces of nature."

Cost and Hours: £5, includes audioguide; daily April-Sept 10:00-17:30, Oct-March 10:00-16:00, tel. 028/2073-1938.

Visiting the Castle: While it's one of the largest castles in Northern Ireland and is beautifully situated, there's precious little left to see among Dunluce's broken walls.

Before entering, catch the great seven-minute film about the history of the castle (across from the ticket desk). The ruins themselves are dotted with anchored plaques that show interesting artists' renditions of how the place would have looked 400 years ago. The six-stop audioguide fleshes out the story.

The 16th-century expansion of the castle was financed by treasure salvaged from a shipwreck. In 1588, the Spanish Armada's *Girona*—overloaded with sailors and the valuables of three abandoned sister ships—sank on her way home after the aborted mission against England. More than 1,300 drowned, and only five survivors washed ashore. The shipwreck was more fully excavated in 1967, and a bounty of golden odds and silver ends wound up in Belfast's Ulster Museum. (The Tower Museum in Derry has a similar collection of Armada artifacts from a different shipwreck farther west.)

Rathlin Island

The only inhabited island off the coast of Northern Ireland, Rathlin is a quiet haven for hikers, birdwatchers, and seal spotters. Less than seven miles from end to end, this "L"-shaped island is reachable by ferry from the town of Ballycastle.

Getting There: The Rathlin Island ferry departs from Ballycastle, just east of Carrick-a-Rede. It does 10 crossings per day in summer. Six are fast 25-minute trips on passenger boats, and four are slower 45-minute trips on car ferries (£12 round-trip per passenger on either type of boat, reserve ahead, tel. 028/2076-9299, www.rathlinballycastleferry.com).

Travelers with rental cars will have no problem reaching Ballycastle. A taxi from Portrush to Ballycastle runs £25 one-way. Bus service from Portrush to Ballycastle is spotty (check with the TI in Portrush, or contact Translink—tel. 028/9066-6630, www.translink.co.uk).

Visiting Rathlin Island: Rathlin's population of 75 islanders clusters around the ferry dock at Church Bay. Here you'll find the **Rathlin Boathouse Visitor Centre,** which operates as the island's TI (April-Sept daily 10:00-12:30 & 13:00-17:00, on the bay 100 yards east of the ferry dock, mobile 077-0886-9605).

In summer, the Puffin shuttle bus (£5 round-trip) meets arriving ferries and drives visitors to the **Rathlin Island Seabird Centre** at the west end of the island. Here a lighthouse extends down the cliff with its beacon at the bottom. It's upside-down because the coast guard wants the light visible only from a certain distance out to sea. The bird observation terrace at the center (next to the lighthouse) overlooks one of the most dramatic coastal views in Ireland—a sheer drop of more than 300 feet to craggy sea stacks just offshore that are draped in thousands of sea birds. Bring your most powerful zoom lens for photos.

For such a snoozy island, Rathlin has seen its fair share of history. Flint ax heads were quarried here in Neolithic times. The island was one of the first in Ireland to be raided by Vikings, in 795. Robert the Bruce hid out from English pursuers on Rathlin in the early 1300s (see "The Scottish Connection" sidebar, earlier). In the late 1500s, local warlord Sorely Boy MacDonnell stashed his extended family on Rathlin and waited on the mainland at Dunluce Castle to face his English enemies...only to watch in horror as they headed for the island instead to massacre his loved ones. And in 1917, a WWI U-boat sank the British cruiser HMS *Drake* in Church Bay. The wreck is now a popular scuba-dive destination.

▲Antrim Mountains and Glens

Not particularly high (never more than 1,500 feet), the Antrim Mountains are cut by a series of large glens running northeast to the sea. Glenariff, with its waterfalls—especially the Mare's Tail—is the most beautiful of the nine glens (described next). Travelers going by car can take a pleasant drive from Portrush to Belfast, sticking to the (more scenic but less direct) A-2 road that stays near the coast and takes in parts of all of the Glens of Antrim.

▲Glenariff Forest Park

Glenariff Forest Park offers scenic picnic spots and hiking trails as well as a cozy tea shop. The parking lot alone has a lovely view down the glen to the sea. You'll find more spectacular scenery on the two-mile waterfall trail along the river gorge, while an easygoing half-mile stroll on the viewpoint trail via the ornamental gardens also provides lovely views.

Cost and Hours: £5 parking fee, daily 10:00-dusk, trail map available at café onsite, tel. 028/7034-0870, www.nidirect.gov.uk.

Getting There: The entry is off A-43 (via A-26; eight miles south of Cushendall, follow signs).

Nearby: Continue along the A-2 scenic coastal route and take a short jog up to Cushendall, where there's a nice beach for a picnic, or just head south on A-2 toward the Gobbins Cliff Path (see page 397) and the castle at Carrickfergus (see page 397).

DERRY & COUNTY DONEGAL

The town of Derry (to Nationalists) or Londonderry (to Unionists) is the mecca of Ulster Unionism. When Ireland was being divvied up, the River Foyle was the logical border between the North and the Republic. But, for sentimental and economic reasons, the North kept Derry, which is otherwise on the Republic's side of the river. Consequently, this predominantly Catholic-Nationalist city has been much contested throughout the Troubles.

Even its name is disputed. While most of its population and its city council call it "Derry," some maps, road signs, and all UK train schedules use "Londonderry," the name on its 1662 royal charter and the one favored by Unionists. I once asked a Northern Ireland rail employee for a ticket to "Derry"; he replied that there was no such place, but he would sell me one to "Londonderry." I'll call it Derry in this book since that's what the majority of the city's inhabitants do.

Still, the conflict is only one dimension of Derry; this pivotal city has a more diverse history and a prettier setting than Belfast. Derry was a vibrant city back when Belfast was just a mudflat. With roughly a third of Belfast's population (95,000), Derry feels more welcoming and manageable to visitors.

County Donegal, to the west of Derry, is about as far-flung as Ireland gets. A forgotten economic backwater (part of the Republic but riding piggyback on the North), it lacks blockbuster museums or sights. But a visit here is more about the journey, and adventurous drivers—a car is a must—will be rewarded with a time-capsule peek into old Irish ways and starkly beautiful scenery.

PLANNING YOUR TIME

Travelers heading north from Westport or Galway should get an early start. Donegal town makes a good lunch stop, with lots of options surrounding its triangular town square. Try the comfy café above Magee's tweed shop (Mon-Sat 10:00-18:00, Sun 14:00-18:00), and take half an hour to visit the small but historic O'Donnell clan's castle just around the corner. And then it's on to Derry, where you can spend a couple of hours seeing the essentials: Visit the Tower Museum and catch some views from the town wall before continuing on to Portrush for the night.

With more time, spend a night in Derry, so you can see the powerful Bogside murals and take a walking tour around the town walls—you'll appreciate this underrated city. With two nights in Derry, consider crossing the border into the Republic for a scenic driving loop through part of remote County Donegal.

Derry

No city in Ireland connects the kaleidoscope of historical dots more colorfully than Derry. From a leafy monastic hamlet to a Viking-pillaged port, from a cannonball-battered siege survivor to an Industrial Revolution sweatshop, from an essential WWII naval base to a wrenching flashpoint of sectarian Troubles...Derry has seen it all.

But the past decade has brought some refreshing changes. Manned British Army surveillance towers were taken down in 2006, and most British troops finally departed in mid-2007, after 38 years in Northern Ireland. In June 2011, a new, curvy pedestrian bridge across the River Foyle was completed. Locals dubbed it the Peace Bridge because it links the predominantly Protestant Waterside (east bank) with the predominantly Catholic Cityside (west bank). Today, you can feel comfortable wandering the streets and enjoying this "legend-Derry" Irish city.

Orientation to Derry

The River Foyle flows north, slicing Derry into eastern and western chunks. The old town walls and almost all worthwhile sights are on the west side. (The tiny train station and Ebrington Square—at the end of the Peace Bridge—are the main reasons to spend time on the east side.) Waterloo Place and the adjacent Guildhall Square, just outside the north corner of the old city walls, are the pedestrian hubs of city activity. The Strand Road area extending north from Waterloo Place makes a comfortable home base, with the major-

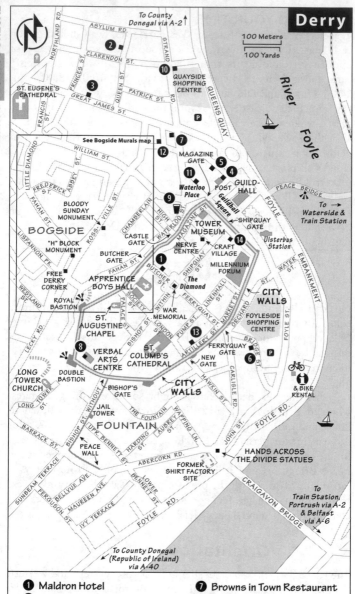

Derry

100 Meters
100 Yards

To County Donegal via A-2

River Foyle

To Waterside & Train Station

To Train Station, Portrush via A-2 & Belfast via A-6

To County Donegal (Republic of Ireland) via A-40

❶ Maldron Hotel
❷ Merchant's House
❸ Saddler's House
❹ Custom House Restaurant & Wine Bar
❺ Exchange Restaurant & Wine Bar
❻ Fitzroy's Restaurant
❼ Browns in Town Restaurant
❽ Bloom's Cafe
❾ Peadar O'Donnell's Pub
❿ Tesco Supermarket
⓫ SuperValu Supermarket
⓬ Laundry
⓭ Playhouse Theatre
⓮ Bogside Artists' Office

ity of lodging and restaurant suggestions within a block or two on either side. The Diamond and its War Memorial statue mark the heart of the old city within the walls.

TOURIST INFORMATION

The TI sits on the riverfront and offers a room-finding service, rents bikes (£5/2 hours, £8/4 hours, £12/8 hours), and books bus and walking tours (July-Sept Mon-Fri 9:00-17:30, Sat until 18:00, Sun 10:00-17:00; Oct-June Mon-Fri 9:00-17:30, Sat-Sun 10:00-17:00; 44 Foyle Street, tel. 028/7126-7284, www.visitderry.com).

ARRIVAL IN DERRY

By Train: Next to the river on the east side of town, Derry's little end-of-the-line train station (no storage lockers) has service to Portrush, Belfast, and Dublin. Each arriving train is greeted by free shuttle buses to Ulsterbus Station (on the west side of town, a couple of minutes' walk south of Guildhall Square on Foyle Street; luggage storage at parcel office around corner in same building, variable fee based on bag size, Mon-Fri 9:30-17:30—beware of lunch closure, closed Sat-Sun). Otherwise, it's a £5 taxi ride to Guildhall Square. The same free shuttle service leaves Ulsterbus Station 15 minutes before each departing train. Unfortunately, there's not yet a footpath from the train station to the pedestrian Peace Bridge.

    By Bus: All intercity buses stop at the Ulsterbus Station, on Foyle Street close to Guildhall Square.

    By Car: Derry is compact enough to see on foot; drivers stopping for a few hours can park at the Foyleside parking garage across from the TI (£1/hour, £3/4 hours, Mon-Sat 8:00-19:00 or later, Sun 12:00-19:00, tel. 028/7137-7575). Drivers staying overnight can ask about parking at their B&B, or try the Quayside parking garage behind the Travelodge (£0.80/hour, £3/4 hours, £8 additional for overnight, daily 7:30-21:00, closes earlier on weekends).

HELPFUL HINTS

Exchange Rate: £1 = about $1.50

Country Calling Code: 44 (see page 530 for dialing instructions)

Money: Danske Bank is on Guildhall Square (Mon-Sat 9:30-16:30, closed Sun), and the **Bank of Ireland** is on Strand Road (Mon-Fri 9:30-16:30, closed Sat-Sun).

Post Office: The main post office is just off Waterloo Place (Mon-Fri 9:00-17:30, Sat 9:00-12:30, closed Sun, Custom House Street).

Bookstore: Foyle Books is a dusty little pleasure for random browsing (Mon-Sat 11:00-17:00, closed Sun, 12 Magazine Street at entrance to Craft Village, tel. 028/7137-2530).

Laundry: Smooth Operators can do a load of laundry for about £9 (drop off in morning to pick up later that day, Mon-Sat 8:30-17:30, closed Sun, 8 Sackville Street, tel. 028/7136-0529).

Taxi: Try **City Cabs** (tel. 028/7126-4466), **The Taxi Company** (tel. 028/7126-2626), or **Foyle Taxis** (tel. 028/7127-9999).

Car Rental: Enterprise is handy (70 Clooney Road, tel. 028/7186-1699, www.enterprise.co.uk). Another option is **Desmond Motors** (173 Strand Road, tel. 028/7136-7136, www.desmondmotors.co.uk).

Tours in Derry

Walking Tours

McCrossan's City Tours leads insightful hour-long walking tours, giving a rounded view of the city's history. Tours depart from 11 Carlisle Road, just below Ferryquay Gate (£4; daily at 10:00, 12:00, 14:00, and 16:00—but call to confirm; tel. 028/7127-1996, mobile 077-1293-7997, www.derrycitytours.com, derrycitytours@aol.com). They also offer private tours (one-hour city tour-£25, four-hour Giant's Causeway or County Donegal tour-£100).

Bogside History Tours offers walks led by Bogside residents who lost loved ones in the tragic events of Bloody Sunday (£6, March-Oct daily at 11:00 and 13:00, also at 15:00 in June-Aug, depart from in front of the Guildhall, mobile 077-3145-0088 or 078-0056-7165, www.bogside-history-tours.com, paul@bogsidehistorytours.com). Tour guides also offer various taxi tours (£25/hour, call or email for options).

Hop-On, Hop-Off Bus Tour

City Sightseeing's double-decker buses are a good option for a general overview of Derry. The one-hour loop covers both sides of the river (seven stops overall), including the Guildhall, the old city walls, political wall murals, cathedrals, and former shirt factories. Your ticket is good for 24 hours (£12.50, pay driver, bus departs April-Sept daily on the hour 10:00-16:00 from in front of TI and Guildhall Square, tel. 028/7137-0067, www.citysightseeingderry.com).

City Sightseeing also offers trips from Derry to the Giant's Causeway, Dunluce Castle, Old Bushmills Distillery, and Carrick-a-Rede Rope Bridge in County Antrim (£25, price does not include Bushmills entry, runs daily May-Sept, depart TI at 10:00, return by 17:00, minimum 10 people). In addition, they offer tours to Glenveagh National Park in County Donegal (depart TI at 9:00, return by 15:00, minimum 10 people). You can book any of their tours online or by phone.

Walks in Derry

Though calm today, Derry is stamped by years of tumultuous conflict. These two self-guided walks (each taking less than an hour) will increase your understanding of the town's history. My Walk the Walls, starting on the old city walls and ending at the Anglican Cathedral, focuses on Derry's early days. My Bogside Murals Walk guides you to the city's compelling murals, which document the time of the Troubles. These tours, each worth ▲▲, can be done separately or linked, depending on your time.

WALK THE WALLS

Squatting determinedly in the city center, the old city walls of Derry (built 1613-1618 and still intact, except for wider gates to handle modern vehicles) hold an almost mythic place in Irish history.

It was here in 1688 that a group of brave apprentice boys, many of whom had been shipped to Derry as orphans after the great fire of London in 1666, made their stand. They slammed the city gates shut in the face of the approaching Catholic forces of deposed King James II. With this act, the boys galvanized the city's indecisive Protestant defenders inside the walls.

Months of negotiations and a grinding 105-day siege followed, during which a third of the 20,000 refugees and defenders crammed into the city perished. The siege was finally broken in 1689, when supply ships broke through a boom stretched across the River Foyle. The sacrifice and defiant survival of the city turned the tide in favor of newly crowned Protestant King William of Orange, who arrived in Ireland soon after and defeated James at the pivotal Battle of the Boyne.

To fully appreciate the walls, take a walk on top of them (free and open from dawn to dusk). Almost 20 feet high and at least as thick, the walls form a mile-long oval loop that you can cover in less than an hour. But the most interesting section is the half-circuit facing the Bogside, starting at Magazine Gate (stairs face the Tower Museum Derry inside the walls) and finishing at Bishop's Gate.

• *Enter the walls at Magazine Gate and find the stairs opposite the Tower Museum. Once atop the walls, head left.*

Walk the wall as it heads uphill, snaking along the earth's contours like a mini Great Wall of China. In the row of buildings

Derry's History

Once an island in the River Foyle, Derry (from *doire,* Irish for "oak grove") was chosen by St. Colmcille (St. Columba in English) circa A.D. 546 for a monastic settlement. He later banished himself to the island of Iona in Scotland out of remorse for sparking a bloody battle over the rights to a holy manuscript that he had secretly copied.

A thousand years later, the English defeated the last Ulster-based Gaelic chieftains in the battle of Kinsale (1601). With victory at hand, the English took advantage of the power vacuum. They began the "plantation" of Ulster with loyal Protestant subjects imported from Scotland and England. The native Irish were displaced to less desirable rocky or boggy lands, sowing the seeds of resentment that fueled the modern-day Troubles.

A dozen wealthy London guilds (grocers, haberdashers, tailors, and others) took on Derry as an investment and changed its name to "Londonderry." They built the last great walled city in Ireland to protect their investment from the surrounding—and hostile—Irish locals. The walls proved their worth in 1688-1689, when the town's Protestant defenders, loyal to King William of Orange, withstood a prolonged siege by the forces of Catholic King James II. "No surrender" is still a passionate rallying cry among Ulster Unionists determined to remain part of the United Kingdom.

The town became a major port of emigration to the New World in the early 1800s. Then, when the Industrial Revolution provided a steam-powered sewing factory, the city developed a thriving shirt-making industry. The factories here employed

on the left (just before crossing over Castle Gate), you'll see an arch entry into the **Craft Village,** an alley lined with a cluster of cute shops and cafés that showcase the economic rejuvenation of Derry (Mon-Sat 9:30-17:30, closed Sun).

• *After crossing over Butcher Gate, stop in front of the grand building with the four columns to view the...*

First Derry Presbyterian Church: This impressive-looking building is the second church to occupy this site. The first was built by Queen Mary in the 1690s to thank the Presbyterian community for standing by their Anglican brethren during the dark days of the famous siege. That church was later torn down to make room for this stately Neoclassical, red-sandstone church finished in 1780. Over the next 200 years, time took its toll on the structure, which

mostly Catholic women who had honed their skills in rural County Donegal. Although Belfast grew larger and wealthier, Unionists tightened their grip on "Londonderry" and the walls that they regarded with almost holy reverence. In 1921, they insisted that the city be included in Northern Ireland when the province was partitioned from the new Irish Free State (later to become the Republic of Ireland). A bit of gerrymandering (with three lightly populated Unionist districts outvoting two densely populated Nationalist districts) ensured that the Protestant minority maintained control of the city, despite its Catholic majority.

Derry was a key escort base for US convoys headed for Britain during World War II, and 60 surviving German U-boats were instructed to surrender here at the end of the war. After the war, poor Catholics—unable to find housing—took over the abandoned military barracks, with multiple families living in each dwelling. Only homeowners were allowed to vote, and the Unionist minority, which controlled city government, was not eager to build more housing that would tip the voting balance away from them. Over the years, sectarian pressures gradually built—until they reached the boiling point. The ugly events of Bloody Sunday on January 30, 1972, brought worldwide attention to the Troubles (for more details, see "Bloody Sunday" sidebar on page 439).

Today, life has stabilized in Derry, and the population has increased by 25 percent in the last 30 years. The modern Foyleside Shopping Centre, bankrolled by investors from Boston, opened in 1995. The 1998 Good Friday Peace Accord has provided significant progress toward peace, and the British Army withdrew 90 percent of its troops in mid-2007. With a population that is 70 percent Catholic, the city has agreed to alternate Nationalist and Unionist mayors. There is a feeling of cautious optimism as Derry—the epicenter of bombs and bloody conflicts in the 1960s and 1970s—now boasts a history museum that airs all viewpoints.

was eventually closed due to dry rot and Republican firebombings. But in 2011, the renovated church reopened to a chorus of cross-community approval (yet one more sign of the slow reconciliation taking place in Derry). The **Blue Coat School** exhibit behind the church highlights the important role of Presbyterians in local history (free but donation expected, closed Sat-Tue in summer and all of Oct-April, tel. 028/7126-1550).

• *Just up the block is the...*

Apprentice Boys Memorial Hall: Built in 1873, this houses the private lodge and meeting rooms of an all-male Protestant organization. The group is dedicated to the memory of the original 13 apprentice boys who saved the day during the 1688 siege. Each year, on the Saturday closest to the August 12 anniversary date, the modern-day Apprentice Boys Society celebrates the end of the siege with a controversial march atop the walls. These walls are considered sacred ground for devout Unionists, who claim that many who died during the famous siege were buried within the battered walls because of lack of space. Surprisingly, the modern society that honors these heroic boys named their organization the Apprentice Boys of *Derry* (the detested Nationalist name for the city) not Londonderry (the beloved Unionist name). The newly built **Siege Museum** stands behind the hall, giving a narrow-focus Unionist view of the siege (£3, Mon-Sat 10:00-16:30, closed Sun, tel. 028/7126-1219).

Next, you'll pass a large, square pedestal on the right atop Royal Bastion. It once supported a column in honor of Governor George Walker, the commander of the defenders during the famous siege. In 1972, the IRA blew up the column, which had 105 steps to the top (one for each day of the siege).

• *Opposite the empty pedestal is the small Anglican...*

St. Augustine Chapel: Set in a pretty graveyard, this Anglican chapel is where some believe the original sixth-century monastery of St. Colmcille (St. Columba in English) stood. The quaint grounds are open to visitors (Mon-Sat 10:30-16:30, closed Sun except for worship). In Victorian times, this stretch of the walls was a fashionable promenade walk.

As you walk, you'll pass a long wall (on the left)—all that's left of a former **British Army base,** which stood here until 2006. Two 50-foot towers used to loom out of it, bristling with cameras and listening devices. Soldiers built them here for a bird's-eye view of the once-turbulent Catholic Bogside district below. The towers' dismantlement—as well as the removal of most of the British Army from Northern Ireland—is another positive sign in cautiously optimistic Derry. The walls of this former army base now contain a parking lot.

Stop at the **Double Bastion** fortified platform that occupies this corner of the city walls. The old cannon is nicknamed "Roaring Meg" for the fury of its firing during the siege.

From here, you can see across the Bogside to the not-so-faraway hills of County Donegal in the Republic. Derry was once an island, but as the River Foyle gradually changed its course, the area you see below the wall began to drain. Over time, and especially after the Great Potato Famine (1845-1849), Catholic peasants from rural Donegal began to move into Derry to find work during the Industrial Revolution. They settled on this least desirable land...on the soggy bog side of the city.

Directly below and to the right are **Free Derry Corner** and **Rossville Street,** where the tragic events of Bloody Sunday took place in 1972 (see page 439). Down on the left is the 18th-century **Long Tower** Catholic church, named after the monk-built round tower that once stood in the area (see page 447).

• *Head to the grand brick building behind you. This is the...*

Verbal Arts Centre: A former Presbyterian school, this center promotes the development of local literary arts in the form of poetry, drama, writing, and storytelling. You can drop in for a cup of coffee in Bloom's Cafe and see what performances might be on during your visit (Mon-Fri 9:00-17:30, Sat 12:00-14:00, closed Sun, tel. 028/7126-6946, www.verbalartscentre.co.uk).

• *Go left another 50 yards around the corner to reach...*

Bishop's Gate: From here, look up Bishop Street Within (inside the walls). This was the site of another British Army surveillance tower. Placed just inside the town walls, it overlooked the

neighborhood until 2006. Now look in the other direction to see Bishop Street Without (outside the walls). You'll spot a modern wall topped by a high mesh fence, running along the left side of Bishop Street Without.

This is a so-called **"peace wall,"** built to ensure the security of the Protestant enclave living behind it in Derry's Fountain neighborhood. When the Troubles reignited 45 years ago, 20,000 Protestants lived on this side of the river. Sadly, this small housing development of 1,000 people is all that remains of that proud community today. The rest have chosen to move across the river to the mostly Protestant Waterside district. The stone tower halfway down the "peace wall" is all that remains of the old jail that briefly held doomed rebel Wolfe Tone after the 1798 revolt against the British.

• *From Bishop's Gate, those short on time can descend from the walls and walk 15 minutes directly back through the heart of the old city, along Bishop Street Within and Shipquay Street to Guildhall Square. With more time, consider visiting St. Columb's Cathedral, the Long Tower Church, and the murals of the Bogside.*

BOGSIDE MURALS WALK

The Catholic Bogside area was the tinderbox of the modern Troubles in Northern Ireland. Bloody Sunday, a terrible confrontation during a march that occurred more than 40 years ago, sparked a sectarian inferno, and the ashes have not yet fully cooled. Today, the murals of the Bogside give visitors an accessible glimpse of this community's passionate perception of those events.

Getting There: The events are memorialized in 12 murals painted on the ends of residential flats along a 300-yard stretch of

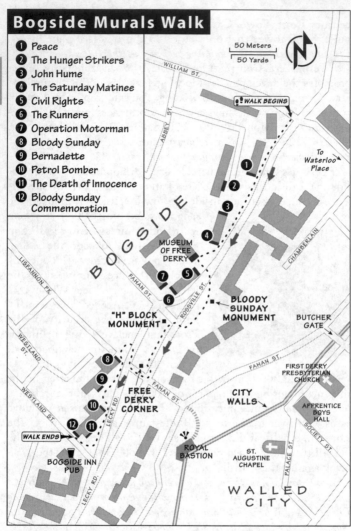

Bogside Murals Walk

1 Peace
2 The Hunger Strikers
3 John Hume
4 The Saturday Matinee
5 Civil Rights
6 The Runners
7 Operation Motorman
8 Bloody Sunday
9 Bernadette
10 Petrol Bomber
11 The Death of Innocence
12 Bloody Sunday Commemoration

Rossville Street and Lecky Road, where the march took place. You can reach them from Waterloo Place via William Street, from the old city walls at Butcher Gate via the long set of stairs extending below Fahan Street on the grassy hillside, or by the stairs leading down from the Long Tower Church. These days, this neighborhood is gritty but quiet and safe.

The Artists: Two brothers, Tom and William Kelly, and their childhood friend Kevin Hasson are known as the Bogside Artists. They grew up in the Bogside and witnessed the tragic events that took place there, which led them to begin painting the murals in

Bloody Sunday

Inspired by civil rights marches in America in the mid-1960s, and the Prague Spring uprising and Paris student strikes of 1968, civil rights groups began to protest in Northern Ireland around this time. Initially, their goals were to gain better housing, secure fair voting rights, and end employment discrimination for Catholics in the North. Tensions mounted, and clashes with the predominantly Protestant Royal Ulster Constabulary police force became frequent. Eventually, the British Army was called in to keep the peace.

On January 30, 1972, about 10,000 people protesting internment without trial held an illegal march sponsored by the Northern Ireland Civil Rights Association. British Army barricades kept them from the center of Derry, so they marched through the Bogside neighborhood.

That afternoon, some youths rioted on the fringe of the march. An elite parachute regiment had orders to move in and make arrests in the Rossville Street area. Shooting broke out, and after 25 minutes, 13 marchers were dead and 13 were wounded (one of the wounded later died). The soldiers claimed they came under attack from gunfire and nail-bombs. The marchers said the army shot indiscriminately at unarmed civilians.

The clash, called "Bloody Sunday," uncorked pent-up frustration as moderate Nationalists morphed into staunch Republicans overnight and released a flood of fresh IRA volunteers. An investigation at the time exonerated the soldiers, but the relatives of the victims called it a whitewash and insisted on their innocence.

In 1998, then-British Prime Minister Tony Blair promised a new inquiry, which became the longest and most expensive in British legal history. In 2010, a 12-year investigation—the Saville Report—determined that the Bloody Sunday civil rights protesters were innocent and called the deaths of 14 protesters unjustified.

In a dramatic 2010 speech in the House of Commons, British Prime Minister David Cameron apologized to the people of Derry. "What happened on Bloody Sunday was both unjustified and unjustifiable. It was wrong," he declared. Cheers rang out in Derry's Guildhall Square, where thousands had gathered to watch the speech on a video screen. After 38 years of struggle, Northern Ireland's bloodiest wound started healing.

1994. One of the brothers, Tom, gained a reputation as a "heritage mural" painter, specializing in scenes of life in the old days. In a surprising and hopeful development, Tom was later invited into Derry's Protestant Fountain neighborhood to work with a youth club there on three proud heritage murals that were painted over paramilitary graffiti. For more about this unique trio, visit their website—www.bogsideartists.com—or drop by their office right next to the Tower Museum.

The Murals: Start out at the corner of Rossville and William streets.

The Bogside murals face different directions (and some are partially hidden by buildings), so they're not all visible from a single viewpoint. Plan on walking three long blocks along Rossville Street (which becomes Lecky Road) to see them all. Residents are used to visitors and don't mind if you photograph the murals.

From William Street, walk south along the right side of Rossville Street toward Free Derry Corner. The murals will all be on your right.

The first mural you'll walk past is the colorful ❶ *Peace,* showing the silhouette of a dove in flight (left side of mural) and an oak leaf (right side of mural), both created from a single ribbon. A peace campaign asked Derry city schoolchildren to write suggestions for positive peacetime images; their words inspired this artwork. The dove is a traditional symbol of peace, and the oak leaf is a traditional symbol of Derry—recognized by both communities. The dove flies from the sad blue of the past toward the warm yellow of the future.

❷ *The Hunger Strikers,* repainted during the summer of 2015, features participants of the 1981 Maze Prison hunger strike, as well as their mothers, wives, and sisters, who sacrificed and supported them in their fatal decision (10 strikers died). The prison was closed after the release of all prisoners (both Unionist and Nationalist) in 2000.

Smaller and easy to miss (above a ramp with banisters) is ❸ *John Hume.* It's actually a collection of four faces (clockwise

from upper left): Nationalist leader John Hume, Martin Luther King Jr., Nelson Mandela, and Mother Teresa. The Brooklyn Bridge in the middle symbolizes the long-term bridges of understanding that the work of these four Nobel Peace Prize-winning activists created. Born in the Bogside, Hume still maintains a home here.

Now look for ❹ *The Saturday Matinee,* which depicts an outgunned but undaunted local youth behind a screen shield. He holds a stone, ready to throw, while a British armored vehicle approaches (echoing the famous Tiananmen Square photo of the lone Chinese man facing the tank). Why *Saturday Matinee?* It's because the weekend was the best time for locals to "have a go at" the army; people were off work and youths were out of school.

Nearby is ❺ *Civil Rights,* showing a marching Derry crowd carrying an anti-sectarian banner. It dates from the days when Martin Luther King Jr.'s successful nonviolent marches were being seen worldwide on TV, creating a dramatic, global ripple effect. Civil rights marches, inspired by King and using the same methods to combat a similar set of grievances, gave this long-suffering community a powerful new voice.

In the building behind this mural, you'll find the intense **Museum of Free Derry** (£4, open Mon-Fri 9:30-16:30 year-round, also open April-Sept Sat-Sun 13:00-16:00, 55 Glenfada Park, tel. 028/7136-0880, www.museumoffreederry.org). Photos, shirts with bullet holes, and a 45-minute video documentary convey the experiences of the people of the Bogside during the worst of the Troubles. The museum's outdoor walls are decorated by copies of two famous paintings that depict massacres—the *Third of May 1808* by Francisco Goya and *Guernica* by Pablo Picasso. These reproductions draw stark parallels to the local events that occurred here.

Cross over to the other side of Rossville Street to see the **Bloody Sunday Monument.** This small, fenced-off stone obelisk lists the names of those who died that

day, most within 50 yards of this spot. Take a look at the map pedestal by the monument, which shows how a rubble barricade was erected to block the street. A 10-story housing project called Rossville Flats stood here in those days. After peaceful protests failed (with Bloody Sunday being the watershed event), Nationalist youths became more aggressive. British troops were wary of being hit by Molotov cocktails thrown from the rooftop of the housing project.

Cross back again, this time over to the grassy median strip that runs down the middle of Rossville Street. At this end stands a granite letter *H* inscribed with the names of the 10 IRA hunger strikers who died (and how many days they starved) in the H-block of Maze Prison in 1981 (see *"The Hunger Strikers,"* earlier in the walk).

From here, as you look across at the corner of Fahan Street, you get a good view of two murals. In ❻ *The Runners* (right), three

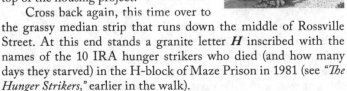

rioting youths flee tear gas from canisters used by the British Army to disperse hostile crowds. More than 1,000 canisters were used during the Battle of the Bogside; "nonlethal" rubber bullets killed 17 people over the course of the Troubles. Meanwhile, in ❼ *Operation Motorman* (left), a soldier wields a sledgehammer to break through a house door, depicting the massive push by the British Army to open up the Bogside's barricaded "no-go" areas that the IRA had controlled for three years (1969-1972).

Walk down to the other end of the median strip where the white wall of **Free Derry Corner** announces "You are now entering Free Derry" (imitating a similar-

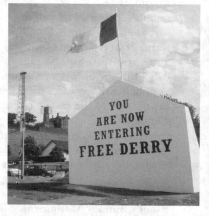

ly defiant slogan of the time in once-isolated West Berlin). This was the gabled end of a string of houses that stood here more than 40 years ago. During the Troubles, it became a traditional meeting place for speakers to address crowds.

Cross back to the right side of the street (now Lecky Road) to see ❽ *Bloody Sunday*, in which a small group of men carry a body from that ill-fated march. It's based on a famous photo of Father Edward Daly that was taken that day. Hunched over, he waves a white handkerchief to request safe passage in order to evacuate a mortally wounded protester. The bloodstained civil rights banner was inserted under the soldier's feet for extra emphasis. After Bloody Sunday, the previously marginal IRA suddenly found itself swamped with bitterly determined young recruits.

Near it is a mural called ❾ *Bernadette.* The woman with the megaphone is Bernadette Devlin McAliskey, an outspoken civil rights leader, who at age 21 became the youngest elected member of British Parliament. Behind her kneels a female supporter, banging a trash-can lid against the street in a traditional expression of protest in Nationalist neighborhoods. Trash-can lids were also used to warn neighbors of the approach of British patrols.

❿ *Petrol Bomber,* showing a teen wearing an army-surplus gas mask, captures the Battle of the Bogside, when locals barricaded their community, effectively shutting out British rule. Though the main figure's face is obscured by the mask, his body clearly communicates the resolve of an oppressed people. In the background, the long-gone Rossville Flats housing project still looms, with an Irish tricolor flag flying from its top.

In ⓫ *The Death of Innocence,* a young girl stands in front of

Political Murals

The dramatic and emotional murals you'll encounter in Northern Ireland will likely be one of

your trip's most enduring travel memories. During the 19th century, Protestant neighborhoods hung flags and streamers each July to commemorate the victory of King William of Orange at the Battle of the Boyne in 1690. Modern murals evolved from these colorful annual displays. With the advent of industrial paints, temporary seasonal displays became permanent territorial statements.

Unionist murals were created during the extended Home Rule political debate that eventually led to the partitioning of the island in 1921 and the creation of Northern Ireland. Murals that expressed opposing views in Nationalist Catholic neighborhoods were outlawed. The ban remained until the eruption of the modern Troubles, when staunchly Nationalist Catholic communities isolated themselves behind barricades, eluding state control and gaining freedom to express their pent-up passions. In Derry, this form of symbolic, cultural, and ideological resistance first appeared in 1969 with the simple "You are now entering Free Derry" message that you'll still see painted on the surviving gable wall at Free Derry Corner.

Found mostly in working-class neighborhoods of Belfast and Derry, today's political murals have become a dynamic form of popular culture. They blur the line between art and propaganda, giving visitors a striking glimpse of each community's history, identity, and values.

bomb wreckage. She is Annette McGavigan, a 14-year-old who

was killed on this corner by crossfire in 1971. She was the 100th fatality of the Troubles, which eventually took more than 3,000 lives (and she was also a cousin of one of the artists). The broken gun beside her points to the ground, signifying that it's no longer being wielded. The large butterfly above her shoulder symbolizes the hope for peace. For years, the artists left the butterfly an empty silhouette until they felt confident that the peace process had succeeded. They finally filled in the butterfly with optimistic colors in the summer of 2006.

Finally, around the corner, you'll see a circle of male faces. This mural, painted in 1997 to observe the 25th anniversary of the tragedy, is called ⑫ *Bloody Sunday Commemoration* and shows the 14 victims. They are surrounded by a ring of 14 oak leaves—the symbol of Derry. When relatives of the dead learned that the three Bogside Artists were beginning to paint this mural, many came forward to loan the artists precious photos of their loved ones, so they could be more accurately depicted.

Across the street, drop into the **Bogside Inn** for a beverage and check out the black-and-white photos of events in the area during the Troubles. This pub has been here through it all, and lives on to tell the tale.

While these murals preserve the struggles of the late 20th century, today sectarian violence has given way to negotiations and a settlement that seems to be working. The British apology for the Bloody Sunday shootings was a huge step forward. Nationalist leader John Hume (who shared the 1998 Nobel Peace Prize with Unionist leader David Trimble) once borrowed a quote from Gandhi to explain his nonviolent approach to the peace process: "An eye for an eye leaves everyone blind."

Sights in Derry

▲▲Tower Museum Derry

Occupying a modern reconstruction of a fortified medieval tower house that belonged to the local O'Doherty clan, this well-organized museum provides an excellent introduction to the city. Combining modern audiovisual displays with historical artifacts, the exhibits tell the story of the city from a skillfully unbiased viewpoint, sorting out some of the tangled historical roots of Northern Ireland's Troubles.

Cost and Hours: £4, includes audioguide for Armada exhibits, daily 10:00-17:30, last entry one hour before closing, Union Hall Place, tel. 028/7137-2411, www.derrycity.gov.uk/museums/tower-museum.

Visiting the Museum: The museum is divided into two sections: the Story of Derry (on the ground floor) and the Spanish Armada (on the four floors of the tower).

Start with the **Story of Derry,** which explains the city's monastic origins 1,500 years ago. The exhibit moves through pivotal events, such as the 1688-1689 siege, as well as unexpected blips, like Amelia Earhart's emergency landing. Don't miss the thought-provoking 15-minute film in the small theater—it offers an even-handed local perspective on the tragic events of the modern sectarian conflict, giving you a better handle on what makes this unique city tick. Scan the displays of paramilitary paraphernalia in the hallway lined with colored curbstones—red, white, and blue Union Jack colors for Unionists; and the green, white, and orange Irish tricolor for Nationalists.

The tower section holds the **Spanish Armada** exhibits, filled with items taken from the wreck of *La Trinidad Valencera*. The ship sank off the coast of Donegal in 1588 in fierce storms nicknamed the "Protestant Winds." A third of the Armada's ships were lost in storms off the coasts of Ireland and Scotland. Survivors who made it ashore were hunted and killed by English soldiers. But a small number made it to Dunluce Castle (see page 425), where the sympathetic lord, who was no friend of the English, smuggled them to Scotland and eventual freedom in France.

Guildhall

This Neo-Gothic building, complete with clock tower, is the ceremonial seat of city government. It first opened in 1890 on reclaimed lands that were once the mudflats of the River Foyle. Destroyed by fire and rebuilt in 1913, it was massively damaged by IRA bombs in 1972. In an ironic twist, Gerry Doherty, one of those convicted of the bombings, was elected as a member of the Derry City Council a dozen years later. In November 1995, US President Bill Clinton spoke to thousands who packed into Guildhall Square.

Cost and Hours: Free, daily 10:00-17:30, tel. 028/7137-6510, www.derrycity.gov.uk/guildhall.

Visiting the Hall: Inside the hall are the Council Chamber, party offices, and an assembly hall featuring stained-glass windows showing scenes from Derry history. Take an informational pamphlet from the front window and explore, if civic and cultural events are not taking place inside. Rotating exhibits fill a ground-floor hall just to the right of the front reception desk. The Ulster Plantation exhibition is worth a visit.

On the back terrace, facing the river, you'll find locals lunching at the pleasant Guild Café (daily 9:30-17:00). And across the street is the modest but heartfelt Peace Park, with hopeful, nonsectarian children's quotes on tiles that line the path.

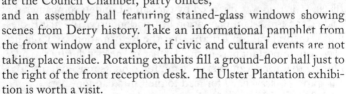

Peace Bridge Stroll

A stroll across the architecturally fetching Peace Bridge rewards you with great views as you look back west over the river toward the city center. The €14 million pedestrian Peace Bridge opened in 2011, linking neighborhoods long divided by the river (Catholic Nationalists on the west bank and Protestant Unionists on the east bank). On the far side from the old city walls, the former Ebrington Barracks British Army base (1841-2003) sits on prime real estate and surrounds a huge square that was once the military parade ground. This area will eventually be developed with a hotel, restaurant, and museum complex. The site has already become an outdoor concert venue and gathering place for the whole community.

Hands Across the Divide

Designed by local teacher Maurice Harron, this powerful metal sculpture of two figures extending their hands to each other was inspired by the growing hope for peace and reconciliation in Northern Ireland (located in a roundabout at the west end of Craigavon Bridge).

The Tillie and Henderson's shirt factory (opened in 1857 and burned down in 2003) once stood on the banks of the river beside the bridge, looming over the figures. In its heyday, Derry's shirt industry employed more than 15,000 workers (90 percent of whom were women) in sweathouses typical of the human toll of the Industrial Revolution. Karl Marx mentioned this factory in *Das Kapital* as an example of women's transition from domestic to industrial work lives.

St. Columb's Cathedral

Marked by the tall spire inside the walls, this Anglican cathedral was built from 1628 to 1633 in a style called "Planter's Gothic." Its construction was financed by the same London companies that backed the Protestant plantation of Londonderry. The first Protestant cathedral built in Britain after the Reformation, St. Columb's played an important part in the defense of the city during the siege. During that time, cannons were mounted on its roof, and the original spire was scavenged for lead to melt into cannon shot.

Cost and Hours: £2 donation, Mon-Sat 9:00-17:00, closed Sun, tel. 028/7126-7313, www.stcolumbscathedral.org.

Visiting the Cathedral: Before you enter, walk over to the "Heroes' Mound" at the end of the churchyard closest to the town wall. Underneath this grassy dome is a mass grave of some of those who died during the 1689 siege.

In the cathedral entryway, you'll find a hollow cannonball

that was lobbed into the city—it contained the besiegers' surrender terms. Inside, along the nave, hangs a musty collection of battle flags and Union Jacks that once inspired troops during the siege, the Crimean War, and World War II. The American flag hangs among them, from the time when the first GIs to enter the European theater in World War II were based in Northern Ireland. Check out the small chapter-house museum in the back of the church to see the huge original locks of the gates of Derry and more relics of the siege.

Long Tower Church

Built below the walls on the hillside above the Bogside, this modest-looking church is worth a visit for its stunning high altar. The name comes from a stone monastic round tower that stood here for centuries but was dismantled and used for building materials in the 1600s.

Cost and Hours: Free, generally open Mon-Sat 8:30-20:30, Sun 7:30-18:00—depending on available staff and church functions, tel. 028/7126-2301, www.longtowerchurch.org.

Visiting the Church: Long Tower Church, the oldest Catholic church in Derry, was finished in 1786, during a time of enlightened relations between the city's two religious communities. Protestant Bishop Hervey gave a generous-for-the-time £200 donation and had the four Corinthian columns shipped in from Naples to frame the Neo-Renaissance altar.

Outside, walk behind the church and face the Bogside to find a simple shrine hidden beneath a hawthorn tree. It marks the spot where outlawed Masses were secretly held before this church was built, during the infamous Penal Law period of the early 1700s. Through the Penal Laws, the English attempted to weaken Catholicism's influence by banishing priests and forbidding Catholics from buying land, attending school, voting, and holding office.

Nearby: The adjacent **St. Columba Heritage Centre** fleshes out the life of Derry's patron saint and founding father (free, Mon-Fri 9:30-16:30, Sat-Sun 13:00-16:00, closed Mon Oct-April, tel. 028/7136-8491, www.stcolumbaheritage.org).

Nightlife in Derry

The **Millennium Forum** is a modern venue that reflects the city's revived investment in local culture, concerts, and plays (box office open Mon-Sat 9:30-17:00, inside city walls on Newmarket Street near Ferryquay Gate, tel. 028/7126-4455, www.millenniumforum. co.uk, boxoffice@millenniumforum.co.uk).

The **Nerve Centre** shows a wide variety of art-house films and live concerts (inside city walls at 7 Magazine Street, near Butcher Gate, tel. 028/7126-0562, www.nervecentre.org).

The **Playhouse Theatre** is an intimate venue for plays (£9-20 tickets, inside the walls on Artillery Street, between New Gate and Ferryquay Gate, tel. 028/7126-8027, www.derryplayhouse.co.uk).

To get away from tourists and mingle with Derry residents, try **Peadar O'Donnell's** pub on Waterloo Street for Derry's best nightly traditional music sessions (often start late, at 23:00; 53 Waterloo Street, tel. 028/7137-2318).

Sleeping in Derry

($$$$ = Splurge, $$$ = Pricier, $$ = Moderate, $ = Budget)

$$$ Maldron Hotel is actually inside Derry's historic walls. It features 93 modern and immaculate rooms, a classy bistro restaurant, and 20 private basement parking spaces (Butcher Street, tel. 028/7137-1000, www.maldronhotelderry.com, info.derry@ maldronhotels.com).

$ Merchant's House, on a quiet street a 10-minute stroll from Waterloo Place, is a fine Georgian townhouse with a grand, colorful drawing room and nine rooms sporting marble fireplaces and ornate plasterwork (family rooms, 16 Queen Street, tel. 028/7126-9691, www.thesaddlershouse.com, saddlershouse@ btinternet.com). Joan and Peter Pyne also run the recommended Saddler's House, and offer appealing self-catering townhouse rentals inside the walls (great for families or anyone needing extra space).

$ Saddler's House, run by the owners of Merchant's House, is a charming Victorian townhouse with seven rooms located a couple of blocks closer to the old town walls (36 Great James Street, tel. 028/7126-9691, www.thesaddlershouse.com, saddlershouse@ btinternet.com).

Eating in Derry

$$$ Custom House Restaurant & Wine Bar is the classiest place in town, serving great meals and fine wines in a posh, calm space. It faces the river a block from the Guildhall (Wed-Sat 12:00-21:30, Sun 14:00-21:00, closed Mon-Tue, Queens Quay, tel. 028/7137-3366).

The hip, trendy **$$$ Exchange Restaurant and Wine Bar** offers lunches and quality dinners with flair, in a central location near the river behind Waterloo Place (Mon-Sat 12:00-14:30 & 17:30-22:00, Sun 16:00-21:00, Queen's Quay, tel. 028/7127-3990).

Busy **$$$ Fitzroy's,** tucked below Ferryquay Gate and stacked with locals, serves good lunches and dinners (Mon-Sat 12:00-22:00, Sun 13:00-20:00, 2 Bridge Street, tel. 028/7126-6211).

$$ Browns in Town is a casual, friendly lunch or dinner option near my recommended lodgings (Mon-Sat 12:00-15:00 & 17:30-21:00, Sun 17:00-20:30, 21 Strand Road, tel. 028/7136-2889).

$$ Bloom's Cafe, a cheap and cheery basic lunch option, hides inside the Verbal Arts Centre atop the walls near Double Bastion (Mon-Sat 9:00-15:00, closed Sun, tel. 028/7127-2517).

Supermarkets: Tesco has everything for picnics and road munchies (Mon-Sat 8:00-21:00, Sun 13:00-18:00, corner of Strand Road and Clarendon Street). **SuperValu** meets the same needs (Mon-Sat 8:30-19:00, Sun 12:30-17:30, Waterloo Place).

Derry Connections

From Derry, it's an hour's drive to Portrush. If you're using public transportation, consider spending £17.50 for a Zone 4 iLink smartcard (£16.50 top-up for each additional day), good for all-day train and bus use in Northern Ireland (see page 379). Translink has useful updated schedules and prices for both trains and buses in Northern Ireland (tel. 028/9066-6630, www.translink.co.uk). Keep in mind that some bus and train schedules, road signs, and maps may say "Londonderry" or "L'Derry" instead of "Derry."

From Derry by Train to: Portrush (8/day, 1.5 hours, change in Coleraine), **Belfast** (8/day, 2.5 hours), **Dublin** (6/day, 5.5 hours, change in Belfast).

By Bus to: Galway (6/day, 5.5 hours), **Portrush** (5/day, 1.5 hours, change in Coleraine), **Belfast** (hourly, 2 hours), **Dublin** (12/day, 4 hours).

Between Derry and Galway

If you're driving into Northern Ireland from Galway, Westport, or Strokestown and don't have time to explore Donegal, consider these two interesting stops in the interior.

Belleek Pottery Visitors Centre

Just over the Northern Ireland border (30 miles/48 km northeast of Sligo) is the cute town of Belleek, famous for its pottery. The Belleek Parian China factory welcomes visitors with a small gallery and museum, a 20-minute video, a cheery cafeteria, and fascinating 30-minute guided tours of its working factory.

Crazed shoppers who forget to fill out a VAT refund form will find their finances looking Belleek.

Cost and Hours: Free; Mon-Fri 9:00-17:30, Sat 10:00-17:30, Sun 14:00-17:30; longer hours in July-Sept, shorter hours in Oct-Feb and possibly closed Sat or Sun; £4 tours (Sat tours June-Sept only, none on Sun)—call to confirm tour schedule and reserve a spot, tel. 028/6865-8501, www.belleekpottery.ie, customerenquires@belleek.ie.

▲Ulster American Folk Park

North of Omagh (5 miles/8 km on A-5), this combination museum and folk park commemorates the many Irish who left their homeland during the hard times of the 18th century. Exhibits show life before emigration, on the boat, and in America. You'll gain insight into the origins of the tough Scots-Irish stock—think Davy Crockett (his people were from Derry) and Andrew Jackson (Carrickfergus roots)—who later shaped America's westward migration. You'll also find good coverage of the *Titanic* tragedy, and its effect on the Ulster folk who built the ship and the loved ones it left behind.

Cost and Hours: £9; March-Sept Tue-Sun 10:00-17:00; Oct-Feb Tue-Fri 10:00-16:00, Sat-Sun 11:00-16:00; closed Mon year-round; cafeteria, 2 Mellon Road, tel. 028/8224-3292, www.nmni.com.

Nearby: The adjacent **Mellon Centre for Migration Studies** is handy for genealogy searches (Tue-Fri 10:30-16:30, Sat until 16:00, closed Sun-Mon, tel. 028/8225-6315, www.qub.ac.uk/cms).

County Donegal

Donegal is the most remote (and perhaps the most ruggedly beautiful) county in Ireland. It's not on the way to anywhere, and it wears its isolation well. With more native Irish speakers than in any other county, the old ways are better preserved here. The northernmost part of Ireland, Donegal remains connected to the Republic by a slim, five-mile-wide umbilical cord of land on its southern coast. It's also Ireland's second-biggest county, with a wide-open "big sky" interior and a shattered-glass, 200-mile, jagged coastline of islands and inlets.

This is the home turf of St. Colmcille (St. Columba in English; means "dove of the church" in Irish), who was born here in 521. In the hierarchy of revered Irish saints, he's second only to St. Patrick. A proud Gaelic culture held out in Donegal to the bitter end, when the O'Donnells and the O'Dohertys, the two most famous local clans, were finally defeated by the English in the early 1600s. After their defeat, the region became known as Dun na nGall ("the fort of the foreigner"), which was eventually anglicized to Donegal.

As the English moved in, four Donegal-dwelling friars (certain that Gaelic ways would be lost forever) painstakingly wrote down Irish history from Noah's Ark to their present. This labor of love became known as the Annals of the Four Masters, and without it, much of our knowledge of early Irish history and myth would have been lost. An obelisk stands in their honor in the main square of Donegal town.

The hardy people of County Donegal have come out on the short end of the modern technology stick. They were famous for their quality tweed weaving, a cottage industry that has gradually given way to modern industrial production in far-off cities. A small but energetic Irish fishing fleet still churns offshore—in the wake of larger EU factory ships scooping traditionally Irish waters (see sidebar on page 459).

But culturally, the county shines. The traditional Irish musicians of Donegal play a driving style of music with a distinctively fast and forceful rhythm. Meanwhile, Enya (local Gweedore gal made good) has crafted languid, ethereal tunes that glide from mood to mood. Both *Dancing at Lughnasa* and *The Secret of Roan Inish* were filmed in County Donegal. Today, emigration has taken its toll, and the region relies on a trickle of tourism spilling over from Northern Ireland.

County Donegal Driving Tour

Here's my choice for a scenic mix of Donegal highlands and coastal views, organized as a self-guided daylong circuit for drivers based across the border in Derry. If you're coming north from Galway or Westport, you could incorporate parts of this drive into your itinerary. Remember, you are leaving the UK for the Republic of Ireland. Once you cross into the Republic, all currency is in euros, not pounds.

Route Summary: The total drive is about 240 km (150 miles). Drive west out of Derry (direction: Letterkenny) on Buncrana Road, which becomes A-2 (and then N-13 across the border in the Republic). Follow the signs into Letterkenny, and take R-250 out the other (west) end of town. Veer right (north) onto R-251, and stay on it through Church Hill, all the way across the highlands, until you link up with N-56 approaching Bunbeg. After a couple of kilometers on N-56, take R-258 from Gweedore; it's another six kilometers (four miles) into Bunbeg. Depart Bunbeg going north on R-257, around Bloody Foreland, and rejoin N-56 near Gortahork. Take N-56 through Dunfanaghy (possible additional Horn Head miniloop option here) and then south, back into Letterkenny. Retrace your route from Letterkenny via N-13 and A-2 back into Derry.

Driving Tips: An early start is essential, and an Ordnance Survey atlas is helpful. It's cheapest to top off your gas tank in Letterkenny. Consider bringing along a picnic lunch to enjoy from a scenic roadside pullout along the Bloody Foreland R-257 road, or out on the Horn Head loop. Bring your camera and remember—not all who wander are lost.

The sights along this route are well-marked. Don't underestimate the time it takes to get around here, as the narrow roads are full of curves and bumps. Dogs, bred to herd sheep, dart from side lanes to practice their bluffing techniques. If you average 65 kilometers per hour (about 40 mph) over the course of the day, you've got a very good suspension system. Folks wanting to linger at more than a couple of sights will need to slow down and consider an overnight stop in Dunfanaghy.

DONEGAL LOOP TRIP FROM DERRY

• *Leave Derry on A-2, which becomes N-13 near the town of Bridge End. You'll see a sign for the* Grianan Aileach Ring Fort *posted on N-13, not far from the junction with R-239. Turn up the steep hill at the modern church with the round roof, and follow signs three kilometers (2 miles) to find...*

▲Grianan Aileach Ring Fort

This dramatic, ancient ring fort perches on an 800-foot hill just inside the Republic, a stone's throw from Derry. It's an Iron Age fortification, built about the time of Christ, and was once the royal stronghold of the O'Neill clan, which dominated Ulster for centuries. Its stout dry-stone walls (no mortar) are 12 feet thick and 18 feet high, creating an interior sanctuary 80 feet in diameter (entry is free and unattended).

Once inside, you can scramble up the stairs, which are built into the walls, to enjoy panoramic views in all directions. Murtagh O'Brien, King of Desmond (roughly, today's Limerick, Clare, and Tipperary counties), destroyed the fort in 1101...the same power-play year in which he gave the Rock of Cashel to the Church. Legend says he had each of his soldiers carry away one stone, attempting to make it tougher for the O'Neill clan to find the raw materials to rebuild. What you see today is mostly a reconstruction from the 1870s.

• *Return to N-13 and head to and through Letterkenny, continuing out the other (west) end of town on R-250. Eight kilometers (5 miles) west of Letterkenny on this road, you'll reach the...*

Newmills Corn and Flax Mills

Come here for a glimpse of the 200-year-old Industrial Revolution, shown high-tech Ulster style. Linen, which comes from flax, was king in this region. The 15-minute film does a nifty job of explaining the process, showing how the common flax plant ends up as cloth. Working in a mill sounds like a mellow job, but conditions were noisy, unhealthy, and exhausting. Veteran mill workers often braved respira-  tory disease, deafness, lost fingers, and extreme fire danger. For their trouble, they usually got to keep about 10 percent of what they milled.

The corn mill is still in working condition but requires a skilled miller to operate it. This mill ground oats—"corn" means oats in Ireland. (What we call corn, they call maize.) The huge waterwheel, powered by the River Swilly, made five revolutions per minute and generated eight horsepower.

The entire operation could be handled by one miller, who knew every cog, lever, and flume in the joint. Call ahead to see when working mill demonstrations are scheduled; otherwise, tours last 20 minutes and are available on request.

Cost and Hours: Free, mid-May-mid-Sept daily 10:00-18:00, closed off-season, last entry 45 minutes before closing, Churchill Road, Letterkenny, tel. 074/912-5115.

• *Continue on R-250, staying right at Driminaught as the road becomes R-251. Watch for Glenveagh Castle and National Park signs, and park in the visitors center lot.*

▲▲Glenveagh Castle and National Park

One of Ireland's six national parks, Glenveagh's jewel is pristine Lough Veagh (Loch Ghleann Bheatha in Irish). The lake is three miles long, occupying a U-shaped valley scoured out of the Derryveagh Mountains by powerful glaciers during the last Ice Age.

In the 1850s, this scenic area attracted the wealthy land speculator John George Adair, who bought the valley in 1857. Right away, Adair clashed with local tenants, whom he accused of stealing his sheep. After his managing agent was found murdered, he evicted all 244 of his bitter tenants to great controversy, and set about creating a hunting estate in grand Victorian style.

His pride and joy was his country mansion, Glenveagh Castle,

County Donegal Loop Trip

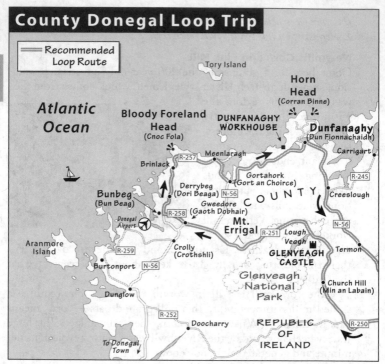

Recommended Loop Route

Atlantic Ocean

Tory Island

Horn Head (Corran Binne)

Bloody Foreland Head (Cnoc Fola)

DUNFANAGHY WORKHOUSE

Dunfanaghy (Dún Fionnachaidh)

Carrigart

R-257   Meenlaragh

Brinlack

Gortahork (Gort an Choirce)

R-245

Derrybeg (Dorí Beaga)   N-56

COUNTY

Creeslough

Bunbeg (Bun Beag)

Gweedore (Gaoth Dobhair)

R-258

N-56

Donegal Airport

Mt. Errigal   R-251   Lough Veagh

Termon

Aranmore Island

R-259

Crolly (Crothshli)

GLENVEAGH CASTLE

Burtonport   N-56

Glenveagh National Park

Church Hill (Min an Labain)

Dunglow

R-252   Doocharry

REPUBLIC OF IRELAND

R-250

To Donegal Town

finished in 1873 on the shore of Lough Veagh. After his death, his widow added to the castle and introduced rhododendrons and rare red deer to the estate. After her death, Harvard art professor Kingsley Porter bought the estate and promptly disappeared on the Donegal coast. (He's thought to have drowned.) The last owner was Philadelphia millionaire Henry McIlhenny, who filled the mansion with fine art and furniture while perfecting the lush surrounding gardens. He donated the castle to the Irish nation in 1981.

Cost and Hours: Park entry-free, guided castle tour-€7, garden tour-€5 (advance reservation required), daily March-Oct 9:00-18:00, Nov-Feb 9:00-17:00, tel. 074/913-7090, www.glenveaghnationalpark.ie, glenveaghbookings@ahg.gov.ie. Without a car, you can reach Glenveagh Castle and National Park by bus tour from Derry (see "Tours in Derry," earlier).

Visiting the Castle and National Park: The **Glenveagh National Park Visitors Centre** explains the region's natural history. Hiking trails in the park are scenic and tempting, but beware of the tiny midges that seem to want to nest in your nostrils.

The **castle** is accessible only by a 30-minute hike or a 10-minute shuttle-bus ride (€3 round-trip, 4/hour, depart from visitors center, last shuttle 1.25 hours before closing). Take the 45-minute castle tour, letting your Jane Austen and Agatha Christie fantasies

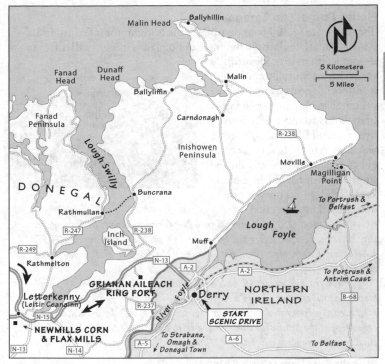

go wild. Antlers abound on walls, in chandeliers, and in paintings by Victorian hunting artists. A table crafted from rare bog oak (from ancient trees hundreds of years old, found buried in the muck) stands at attention in one room, while Venetian glass chandeliers illuminate a bathroom. A round pink bedroom at the top of a tower is decorated in Oriental style, with inlaid mother-of-pearl furnishings. The library, which displays paintings by George Russell, has the castle's best lake views.

Afterward, stroll through the gardens and enjoy the lovely setting. A lakeside swimming pool had boilers underneath it to keep it heated. It's no wonder that Greta Garbo was an occasional guest, coming to visit whenever she "vanted" to be alone.

• *Leave the national park and follow R-251 west, watching for the Mount Errigal trailhead. It's southeast of the mountain, and starts at the small parking lot beside R-251 on the mountain's lower slope (easy to spot, with a low surrounding stone wall in the middle of open bog land).*

Mount Errigal (An Earagail)

The mountain (2,400 feet) dominates the horizon for miles around. Rising from the relatively flat interior bog land, it looks taller from a distance than it is. Beautifully cone-shaped (but not a volcano), it offers a hearty, nontechnical climb with panoramic views (four hours round-trip, covering five miles). Hikers should get a weather report before setting out (frequent mists squat on the summit). Ask the TI in Letterkenny or Donegal town for more detailed hiking directions.

• *Continue on R-251 as it merges into N-56 headed west; at Gweedore, stay west on R-258. After six kilometers (4 miles), you'll reach R-257, where you'll turn right and pass through the hamlet of Bunbeg (Bun Beag).*

The eight kilometers (5 miles) of road heading north—as Bunbeg blends into Derrybeg (Dori Beaga) and a bit beyond—are some of the most densely populated sections of this loop tour. Modern holiday cottages pepper the landscape in what the Irish have come to call "Bungalow Bliss" (or "Bungalow Blight" to nature lovers). Next you'll come to the...

Bloody Foreland (Cnoc Fola)

Named for the shade of red that heather turns at sunset, this scenic headland is laced with rock walls and forgotten cottage ruins. Pull off at one of the lofty roadside viewpoints and savor a picnic lunch and rugged coastal views.

• *Continue on R-257, meeting N-56 near Gortahork. Stay on N-56 to the Dunfanaghy Workhouse, about a kilometer south of Dunfanaghy town.*

Dunfanaghy Workhouse

Opened in 1845, this structure was part of an extensive workhouse compound (separating families by gender and age)—a dreaded last resort for the utterly destitute of coastal Donegal. There were once many identical compounds built across Ireland, a rigid Victorian solution to the spiraling problem of Ireland's rapidly multiplying poor. Authorities at the time thought that poverty stemmed from laziness and should be punished. So, to motivate those lodging at the workhouse to pull themselves up by their bootstraps, conditions were made hard. But the system was unable to cope with the starving, homeless multitudes who were victims of the famine.

The harsh workhouse experience is told through the true-life narrative of Wee Hannah Herrity, a wandering orphan and former resident of this workhouse. During the famine, more than 4,000

Donegal or Bust

Part of western County Donegal is in the Gaeltacht, where locals speak the Irish Gaelic language. In the spring of 2005, a controversial law was passed that erased all English place names from local road signs in Gaeltacht areas. Signs now have only the Irish-language equivalent, an attempt to protect the region from the further (and inevitable) encroachment of the English language.

Here's a cheat sheet to help you decipher the signs as you drive the Donegal loop (parts of which are in the Gaeltacht). There's also a complete translation of all Irish place names in the recommended *Complete Road Atlas of Ireland* by Ordnance Survey (€10-13), in the Gazetteer section in the back.

Irish	English
Leitir Ceanainn *(LET-ir CAN-ning)*	Letterkenny
Min an Labain *(MEEN on law-BAWN)*	Churchill
Loch Ghleann *(LOCKH thown)*	Lough (Lake)
Bheatha *(eh-VEH-heh)*	Veagh
An Earagail *(on AIR-i-gul)*	Mt. Errigal
Gaoth Dobhair *(GWEE door)*	Gweedore
Crothshli *(CROTH-lee)*	Crolly
Bun Beag *(bun bee-OWG)*	Bunbeg
Dori Beaga *(DOR-uh bee-OWG-uh)*	Derrybeg
Cnoc Fola *(NOK FAW-luh)*	Bloody Foreland
Gort an Choirce *(gurt on HER-kuh)*	Gortahork
Dun Fionnachaidh *(doon on-AH-keh)*	Dunfanaghy
Corran Binne *(COR-on DIN-eh)*	Horn Head

young orphan workhouse girls from across Ireland were shipped to Australia as indentured servants in an attempt to offset the mostly male former convict population there. But Hannah's fate was different. She survived the famine by taking meager refuge here, dying at age 90 in 1926. With the audioguide, you'll visit three upstairs rooms where stiff papier-mâché figures relate the powerful episodes in her life.

Cost and Hours: €4.50, includes audioguide; May-Sept daily 9:30-17:30, Oct-April until 16:30, call to confirm winter hours, good bookstore, coffee shop and helpful TI desk— pick up map for Horn Head loop here, tel. 074/913-6540, www.dunfanaghyworkhouse.ie.

• *Now continue into the town of...*

Dunfanaghy (Dun Fionnachaidh)

This planned town, founded by the English in the early 1600s for local markets and fairs, has a prim and proper appearance. In

Dunfanaghy (dun-FAN-ah-hee), you can grab a pub lunch or some picnic fixings from the town market. Enjoy them from a scenic viewpoint on the nearby Horn Head loop drive (described later).

The modest town square, mostly a parking lot, marks the center of Dunfanaghy. The post office is at the southern end of the village (closed Sun). Groceries are sold in the **Centra Market** (daily 7:30-21:00) on the main road opposite the town square.

Sleeping in Dunfanaghy: $$$ The Mill Restaurant and Accommodation is a diamond in the Donegal rough. Susan Alcorn nurtures seven wonderful rooms with classy decor, while her husband Derek is the chef in their fine restaurant downstairs (one mile out of town past the Dunfanaghy Workhouse on the right, parking, tel. 074/913-6985, www.themillrestaurant.com, info@themillrestaurant.com).

$$$ Arnold's Hotel is a comfortable, old-fashioned place that's been in the Arnold family since 1922. In the center of town, it has 30 cozy rooms that are well-kept by a helpful staff (family rooms, parking, tel. 074/913-6208, www.arnoldshotel.com, enquiries@arnoldshotel.com).

$$ The Whins B&B has five inviting rooms with tasteful furnishings, which range from exotic African accents to a sturdy four-poster bed (cash only, parking, 10-minute walk north of town, tel. 074/913-6481, mobile 087-707-3985, www.thewhins.com, barbara@thewhins.com, John & Barbara Scholz).

Eating in Dunfanaghy: $$$$ The Mill Restaurant and Accommodation is gourmet all the way, specializing in memorable lamb or lobster dinners. It's worth booking days ahead (July-Aug Tue-Sun 19:00-21:00, closed Mon, Sept-June variable hours and closed days, tel. 074/913-6985, www.themillrestaurant.com). **$ Muck & Muffin** is a simple sandwich café, great for quick, cheap lunches. It's above the pottery shop in the stone warehouse on the town square (daily 9:30-17:00, until 18:00 in summer, tel. 074/913-6780). **$ The Great Wall** is a hole-in-the-wall Chinese takeaway place (daily 16:30-23:00, tel. 074/910-0111, next door to Centra Market). A few doors down, **$$ The Oyster Bar** does pub grub and live music on Friday and Saturday nights.

• *From Dunfanaghy, you can head back to Derry via Letterkenny. If you have time, consider a detour to Horn Head.*

Irish Fishermen Feel the Squeeze

The biggest fishing port in Ireland is Killybegs, about 30 kilometers (19 miles) west of Donegal town. But today, fishing is a sadly withering lifestyle. When Ireland joined the EU in 1973, Irish farmers and infrastructure benefited most from generous subsidies that helped transform the country a generation later into the "Celtic Tiger." But as the country reaped over €35 billion from the EU in its first 25 years of membership, the Irish fishing industry suffered. With the Mediterranean overfished, other EU nations set sail for rich Irish waters that were newly opened to them. Some estimate that 40 percent of the fish caught each year in Europe—valued at €175 billion—come from Irish territorial seas. Huge factory ships from Spain are far more efficient at hauling in a catch than the 1,500 remaining Irish boats (most of which are under 40 feet long). Irish fishermen lament that for every €1 accepted in EU subsidies, €5 have gone out in foreign nets. And the irony is that much of the fish sold in Irish grocery stores and restaurants is now imported from other EU nations...who caught the fish off the Irish coast.

Horn Head Loop (Corran Binne)

If you have extra time, take an hour to embark on a lost-world plateau drive. This heaving headland with few trees has memorable

coastal views that have made it popular with hikers in recent years.

Consult your map and get off N-56, following the *Horn Head* signs all the way around the eastern lobe of the peninsula. There are fewer than eight kilometers (5 miles) of narrow, single-lane road out here, with very little traffic. But be alert and willing to pull over at wide spots to cooperate with other cars.

This stone-studded peninsula was once an island. Then, shortly after the last Ice Age ended, ocean currents deposited a sandy spit in the calm water behind the island. A hundred years ago, locals harvested its stabilizing dune grass, using it for roof thatching and sending it abroad to Flanders, where soldiers used it to create beds for horses during World War I. With the grass gone, the sandy spit was free to migrate again. It promptly silted up the harbor, created a true peninsula, and ruined Dunfanaghy as a port town.

A short spur road leads to the summit of the headland, where you can park your car and walk another 50 yards up to the abandoned WWII lookout shelter. The views from here are dramatic, looking west toward Tory Island and south to Mount Errigal. Some may choose to hike an additional 20 minutes across the heather, to the ruins of the distant signal tower (not a castle, but instead a lookout for a feared Napoleonic invasion), clearly visible near the cliffs. New hiking trails are being created on the peninsula. But from here, it's still easy to bushwhack your way through (in sturdy footwear) to the rewarding cliff views at the base of the old signal tower. Navigate back to your car, using the lookout shelter on the summit as a landmark.

IRELAND: PAST & PRESENT

Ireland is rich with history, culture, and language. And the country continues to transform and grow today, learning from its experience with the Celtic Tiger economy (a bittersweet memory), making progress toward peace, and reexamining some of its long-held social customs.

Irish History

PREHISTORY

Ireland became an island when rising seas covered the last land bridge (7000 B.C.), a separation from Britain that the Irish would fight to maintain for the next 9,000 years. Snakes were too slow to migrate before the seas cut Ireland off, despite later legends about St. Patrick banishing them. By 6000 B.C., Stone Age hunter-fishers had settled on the east coast, followed by Neolithic farmers (from the island of Britain). These early inhabitants left behind impressive but mysterious funeral mounds (passage graves) and large Stonehenge-type stone circles.

THE CELTS (500 B.C.-A.D. 450)

Perhaps more an invasion of ideas than of armies, the Celtic culture from Central Europe (particularly that of the most influential tribe, called the **Gaels**) settled in Ireland, where it would dominate for a thousand years. A warrior people with more than a hundred petty kings, they feuded constantly with rival clans and gathered in ring forts for protection. There were more than 300 *tuatha* (kingdoms) in Ireland, each with its own *rí* (king), who would've happily chopped the legs off anyone who called him "petty." The island was nominally ruled by a single *Ard Rí* (high king) at the **Hill of Tara** (north of Dublin), though there was no centralized nation.

What's a Celt?

The Irish are a Celtic people. The Celts, who came from Central Europe, began migrating west in about 1500 B.C. Over time, many settled in the British Isles and in western France. When the Angles and Saxons came later, grabbing the best land in the British Isles (which became Angle-land...or England), the Celts survived in Brittany, Cornwall, Wales, Scotland, and Ireland. Today, this "Celtic Crescent" still nearly encircles England. The word "Celtic" (pronounced with a hard *C*) comes from the Greek "Keltoi," meaning barbarian.

From about 700 B.C. on, various Celtic tribes mixed, mingled, and fought in Ireland. The last and most powerful of the Celtic tribes to enter the fray were the Gaels, who probably came to Ireland from Scotland. The Irish and Scottish language, Gaelic, is named for them.

Celtic society revolved around warrior kings, who gathered groups of families into regional kingdoms. These small kingdoms combined to make the five large provincial kingdoms of ancient Ireland (whose names survive on maps today): Leinster, Munster, Connacht, Ulster, and the Middle Kingdom (now County Meath).

For defensive purposes, these early Irish peoples lived in small thatched huts built on man-made islands or on high ground surrounded by ditches and a stone or earthen wall. A strictly observed hierarchy governed Celtic societies: the king on top, followed by poets, druids (priests), legal men, skilled craftsmen, freemen, and slaves. Rarely did a high king rule the entire island. Loyalty to one's clan came first, and alliances between clans were often temporary, lasting only until a more advantageous alliance could be struck with a rival clan. This fluid system of alliances ebbing and flowing across the Celtic-warrior cultural landscape meant that the Celts would never unite as a single nation. It also meant that an invading army could not destroy one main capital or kill one king to bring the entire island to its knees. Celtic culture was a multiheaded monster...tough to slay.

Unlike the Celtic tribes living in Western Europe and England, the Celts in Ireland were never conquered by the Romans. This gives Ireland a cultural continuity and uniqueness rare in Europe. Their culture—which evolved apart from Europe—remained strong and independent for centuries. Then, in the 12th century, English dominance led to suppression of the Gaelic language and Celtic traditions. But with Irish independence—won only in the 20th century—Irish ways are no longer threatened. The most traditional areas (generally along the west coast, such as the Dingle Peninsula) are protected as a Gaeltacht. The Gaeltacht (literally, places where the Irish Gaelic language is spoken) is a kind of national park for the traditional culture. If much of Ireland's charm can be credited to its Celtic roots, that charm is most vivid in the Gaeltacht.

Druid priests conducted pagan, solar-calendar rituals among the megalithic stones erected by earlier inhabitants. The Celtic people peppered the countryside with thousands of Iron Age monuments. While most of the sights are little more than rock piles that take a vigorous imagination to reconstruct (ring forts, wedge tombs, standing stones, and so on), just standing next to a megalith that predates the pharaohs is stirring.

The Celtic world lives on today in the Gaelic language and in legends of Celtic warriors such as **Finn MacCool,** who led a merry band of heroes in battle and in play. Tourists marvel at large ritual stones decorated with ogham (rhymes with "poem") script, the peculiar Celtic-Latin alphabet that used lines as letters. The **Tara Brooch** and elaborately inscribed, jewel-encrusted daggers in Dublin's National Museum attest to the sophistication of this warrior society.

In 55 B.C., the Romans conquered the Celts in England, but Ireland and Scotland remained independent, their history forever skewed in a different direction—Gaelic, not Latin. The Romans called Ireland **Hibernia,** meaning Land of Winter; it was apparently too cold and bleak to merit an attempt at colonization. The biggest nonevent in Irish history is that the Romans never invaded. While the mix of Celtic and Roman is part of what makes the French French and the English English, the Irish are purely Celtic. Hurling, the wild Irish national pastime, goes back more than 2,000 years to Celtic days, when it was played almost as a substitute for warfare. Perhaps best described as something like airborne hockey with no injury time-outs, hurling is as central to the Irish culture as cricket is to the English, or *boules* to the French.

THE AGE OF SAINTS AND SCHOLARS
(A.D. 450-800)

When Ancient Rome fell and took the Continent—and most of the achievements of Roman culture—with it, Gaelic Ireland was

unaffected. There was no Dark Age here, and the island was a beacon of culture for the rest of Europe. Ireland (population c. 750,000) was still a land of many feuding kings, but the culture was stable.

Christianity and Latin culture arrived first as a trickle from trading contacts with Christian Gaul (France), then more emphatically in A.D. 432 with **St. Patrick,** who persuasively converted the sun-and-nature-worshipping Celts. (Perhaps St. Patrick had an easy time converting the locals because they had so little sun to worship.) Patrick (c. 389-461), a Latin-speaking Christian from Roman Britain, was kidnapped as a teenager and carried off into slavery for six years in Ireland. He escaped back to Britain, then traveled to Gaul to study for a life in the clergy. Inspired by a dream, he eventually returned to Ireland, determined to convert the pagan, often hostile, Celtic inhabitants. Legends say he drove Ireland's snakes (symbolic of pagan beliefs) into the sea and explained the Holy Trinity with a shamrock—three leaves on one stem.

Later monks (such as **St. Columba,** 521-597) continued Christianizing the island, and foreign monks flocked to isolated Ireland. They withdrew to scattered, isolated monasteries, living in stone igloo beehive huts, translating and illustrating (illuminating) manuscripts. Perhaps the greatest works of art from all of Dark Age Europe are these manuscripts, particularly the ninth-century **Book of Kells,** which you'll see at Dublin's Trinity College Library. Irish monks—heads shaved crosswise across the top of the skull from ear to ear, like the former druids—were known throughout Europe as ascetic scholars.

St. Columbanus (c. 600; different from St. Columba) was one of several traveling missionary monks who helped to bring Christianity back to Western Europe, which had reverted to paganism and barbarism after the fall of the Roman Empire. The monks established monastic centers of learning that produced great Christian teachers and community builders. One of the monks, **St. Brendan,** may have sailed to America.

By 800, **Charlemagne** was importing Irish monks to help run his Frankish kingdom. Meanwhile, Ireland remained a relatively cohesive society based on monastic settlements rather than cities. Impressive round towers from those settlements still dot the Irish landscape—silent reminders of this exalted age.

VIKING INVASION AND DEFEAT (800-1100)

In 795, Viking pirates from Norway invaded, first testing isolated island monasteries, then boldly sailing up Irish rivers into the interior. The many raids immediately wreaked havoc on the monasteries and continued to shake Irish civilization for two chaotic centuries. The Vikings raped, pillaged, and burned Christian churches, making off with prized monastic booty such as gold chalices, silver candlestick holders, and the jeweled book covers of sacred illuminated manuscripts. Monks stood guard from their round towers to spy approaching marauders, ring the warning bells, and protect the citizens. In 841, a conquering Viking band decided to winter in Ireland, eventually building the island's first permanent walled cities, Dublin and Waterford. Viking raiders slowly evolved into Viking traders. They were the first to introduce urban life and commerce to Ireland.

Finally, **High King Brian Ború** led a Gaelic revival, briefly controlling the entire island in the late 900s. His rule ended at the Battle of Clontarf (1014), near Dublin. Though he defeated a mercenary Viking army, which had allied with rebellious clans, Ború and most of his sons died in the battle, and his unified kingdom quickly fell apart. Over the centuries, Viking settlers married Gaelic gals and slowly blended in.

PAST & PRESENT

ANGLO-NORMAN ARRIVAL (1100-1500)

The Normans were Ireland's next aggressive guests. In 1169, a small army of well-armed and fearless soldiers of fortune invaded Ireland under the pretense of helping a deposed

Irish king regain his lands. With the blessing of the only English pope in history (Adrian IV and his papal bull), a Welsh conquistador named **Strongbow** (c. 1130-1176) took Dublin and Waterford, married the local king's daughter, then succeeded his father-in-law as king of Leinster. This was the spearhead of a century-long invasion by the so-called Anglo-Normans—the French-speaking rulers of England, descended from William the Conqueror and his troops, who had invaded and conquered England a hundred years earlier at the Battle of Hastings (1066).

King Henry II of England soon followed (1171) to remind Strongbow who was boss, proclaiming the entire island under English (Anglo-Norman) rule. By 1250, the Anglo-Normans occupied two-thirds of the island, controlling the best land while clustered in walled cities surrounded by hostile Gaels. These invaders, who were big-time administrators, ushered in a new age in which society (government, cities, and religious organizations) was organized on a grander scale. They imposed feudalism and scoffed at the old Gaelic clan system that they intended to replace. Riding on the coattails of the Normans, monastic orders (Franciscans, Augustinians, Benedictines, and Cistercians) came over from the Continent and eclipsed Ireland's individual monastic settlements, once the foundation of Irish society, back in the Age of Saints and Scholars.

Normans lived in tightly packed settlements surrounded by their superior fortifications. But when the **Black Death** came in 1348, it spread more rapidly and fatally in these tight Norman quarters than it did in rural, far-flung Gaelic clan settlements. The

Stone Circles: The Riddle of the Rocks

Ireland is home to more than 200 evocative stone circles. These jaggedly sparse boulder rings are rudimentary in comparison to Britain's more famous Stonehenge. But their misty, mossy settings provide curious travelers with an intimate and accessible glimpse of the mysterious people who lived in Ireland before the arrival of the Celts.

Bronze Age Ireland (2000-600 B.C.) was populated by farming folk who had mastered the craft of smelting heated tin and copper together to produce bronze, which was used to produce more durable tools and weapons. Late in the Bronze Age, many of these primitive, clannish communities also put considerable time and effort into gathering huge rocks and arranging them into ceremonial circles for use in rituals with long-forgotten meanings. Scholars believe that these circles may have been used as solar observatories, to calculate solstices and equinoxes as they planned life-sustaining seasonal crop-planting cycles. Archaeologists have discovered a few ancient remains in the center of some circles, but their primary use seems to have been ceremonial rather than as burial sites. And without any written records, we can only make educated guesses as to their exact purpose.

In the Middle Ages, superstitious people believed that the stones had been arranged by an earlier race of giants. Later, some thought that at least one circle was made up of petrified partiers

plague, along with Normans intermarrying with Gaels, eventually diluted Norman identity and shrank English control.

England, preoccupied with the Hundred Years' War with France and its own internal Wars of the Roses, "ruled" through deputized locals such as the earls of Kildare. Many Irish landowners actually resided in England, a pattern of absentee-landlordism that would persist for centuries. England's laws were fully enforced only in a 50-mile foothold around Dublin (**the Pale**—from the Norman-French word for a defensive ditch). A couple of centuries after invading, the Anglo-Normans saw their area of control shrink to only the Pale (perhaps 20 percent of the island)—with the rest of the island "beyond the Pale."

Even as their power eroded, the English kings considered Ireland theirs. To keep their small islands of English culture undiluted by Irish heathen ways, they passed the **Statutes of Kilkenny** (1366). These laws prohibited the settlers from going native and

who had dared to dance on the Sabbath. A nearby standing stone was supposed to be the frozen figure of the piper who had been playing the dance tunes.

Irish stone circles are concentrated in two main regional clusters consisting of more than a hundred circles each: central Ulster, in the North (radiocarbon-dated 1500-700 B.C.); and County Cork and County Kerry, in the south (radiocarbon-dated 1000-700 B.C.). The remaining dozen circles are scattered across central Ireland. Some circles have only recently been rediscovered, having been buried over the centuries by rapidly accumulating bog growth.

Dedicated travelers seeking stone circles will find them marked in the Ordnance Survey atlas and signposted along rural Irish roads. Ask a local farmer for directions—and savor the experience (wear shoes impervious to grass dew and sheep doo).

Here are my five favorite Irish stone circles, all within a druid's dance of other destinations mentioned in this book:

Kenmare is in County Kerry, on the western fringe of Kenmare town. It's the most easily accessible of the circles listed here.

Drombeg is in County Cork, 35 miles (56 km) southwest of Kinsale, up a narrow winding lane just south of the R-597 coastal road.

Glebe is in County Mayo, two miles (3 km) east of Cong and 100 yards south of the R-345 road to Neale (across a minefield of sheep droppings).

Beltany is in County Donegal, 10 miles (16 km) southeast of Letterkenny, straight south of Raphoe.

Beaghmore is in County Tyrone, 20 miles (32 km) east of Omagh, north off A-505 (Cookstown Road).

being seduced by Gaelic ways...or people. Intermarriage between Irish locals and English settlers, adoption of Irish dress, and the speaking of the Irish Gaelic language were all outlawed. In practice, the statutes were rarely enforced.

THE END OF GAELIC RULE (1500s)

As European powers raced west to establish profitable colonies in North and South America, Ireland's location on the western edge of Europe took on more strategic importance. England's naval power grew to threaten Spain's monopoly on New World riches. Meanwhile, Spain viewed Ireland as England's vulnerable back door—the best place to attack. (Think of how the USSR used Cuba to threaten the US in the early 1960s.) Martin Luther's **Reformation** split the Christian churches into Catholic and Protestant, making Catholic Ireland an even hotter potato for newly Protestant England to handle. Catholic Spain and, later, France would use

Typical Castle Architecture

Castles were fortified residences for medieval nobles. In Ireland, they were introduced by Norman (evolving into English) warlords in the late 1100s. Castles come in all shapes and sizes, but knowing a few general terms will help you understand them.

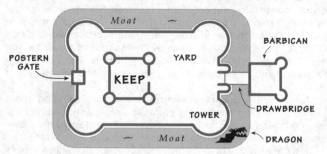

Barbican: A fortified gatehouse, sometimes a stand-alone building located outside the main walls.

Crenellation: A gap-toothed pattern of stones atop the parapet.

Drawbridge: A bridge that could be raised or lowered, using counterweights or a chain-and-winch.

Great Hall: The largest room in the castle, serving as throne room, conference center, and dining hall.

Hoardings (or Gallery or Brattice): Wooden huts built onto the upper parts of the stone walls. They served as watch towers, living quarters, and fighting platforms.

Keep (or Donjon): A high, strong stone tower in the center of the complex; the lord's home and refuge of last resort.

Loopholes (or Embrasures): Narrow wall slits through which soldiers could shoot arrows.

Machicolation: A stone ledge jutting out from the wall, with holes through which soldiers could drop rocks or boiling oil onto wall-scaling enemies below.

Moat: A ditch encircling the wall, sometimes filled with water.

Parapet: Outer railing of the wall walk.

Portcullis: An iron grille that could be lowered across the entrance.

Postern Gate: A small, unfortified side or rear entrance. In wartime, it became a "sally-port" used to launch surprise attacks, or as an escape route.

Towers: Square or round structures with crenellated tops or conical roofs serving as lookouts, chapels, living quarters, or the dungeon.

Turret: A small lookout tower rising from the top of the wall.

Wall Walk (or Allure): A pathway atop the wall where guards could patrol and where soldiers stood to fire at the enemy.

Yard (or Bailey): An open courtyard inside the castle walls.

Typical Church Architecture

The oldest stone churches that survive in Ireland were designed and built by religious orders (Cistercians, Benedictines, Franciscans, and Dominicans) that came to Ireland from the Continent in the mid-1100s, and were supported by the Norman invaders who soon followed. Even if you wouldn't know your apse from a hole in the ground, learning a few simple terms will enrich your experience.

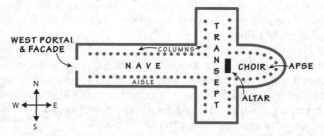

Aisles: The long, generally low-ceilinged arcades that flank the nave.

Altar: The raised area with a ceremonial table (often adorned with candles or a crucifix), where the priest prepares and serves the bread and wine for Communion.

Apse: The space beyond the altar, often bordered with small chapels.

Barrel Vault: A continuous round-arched ceiling that resembles an extended upside-down U.

Choir: A cozy area, often screened off, located within the church nave and near the high altar where services are sung in a more intimate setting.

Cloister: Covered hallways bordering a square or rectangular open-air courtyard, traditionally where monks and nuns got fresh air.

Facade: The front exterior of the church's main (west) entrance, generally highly decorated.

Groin Vault: An arched ceiling formed where two equal barrel vaults meet at right angles. Less common usage: term for a medieval jock strap.

Narthex: The area (portico or foyer) between the main entry and the nave.

Nave: The long, central section of the church (running west to east, from the entrance to the altar) where the congregation sits or stands through the service.

Transept: In a traditional cross-shaped floor plan, the transept is one of the two parts forming the "arms" of the cross. The transepts run north-south, perpendicularly crossing the east-west nave.

West Portal: The main entry to the church (on the west end, opposite the main altar).

their shared Catholicism with Ireland as divine justification for alliances against heretical England.

In 1534, angered by **Henry VIII** and his break with Catholicism (and taking advantage of England's Reformation chaos), the **Earls of Kildare** (father, then son) led a rebellion. Henry crushed the revolt, executed the earls, and confiscated their land. Henry's daughter, **Queen Elizabeth I,** gave the land to colonists ("planters"), mainly English Protestants. The next four centuries would see a series of rebellions by Catholic, Gaelic-speaking Irish farmers fighting to free themselves from rule by Protestant, English-speaking landowners.

Hugh O'Neill (1540-1616), a Gaelic chieftain educated in Queen Elizabeth's court, was angered by planters and English abuses. He soon led a Gaelic revolt, in 1595. The rebels were supported by the Spanish, who were fellow Catholics and England's archrival on the high seas. At the Battle of Yellow Ford (1598), guerrilla tactics brought about an initial Irish victory.

But the **Battle of Kinsale** (1601) ended the revolt. The exhausted Irish, who had marched the length of Ireland in winter, arrived to help Spanish troops, who were pinned down inside the town. Though the Irish were skilled at guerrilla warfare on their own turf, they were no match for the English on open and unfamiliar ground, and were quickly crushed before they could join the Spanish. The Spanish soon surrendered, and O'Neill knelt before the conquering general, ceding half a million acres to England. Then he and other proud, Gaelic, Ulster-based nobles unexpectedly abandoned their remaining land and sailed to the Continent (the Flight of the Earls, 1607). They searched for further support on the Continent, but died before they could enlist additional armies to bring back to Ireland. Their flight signaled the end of Gaelic Irish rule.

ENGLISH COLONIZATION AND IRISH REBELLIONS (1600s)

King James I took advantage of the Gaelic power vacuum and sent 25,000 Protestant English and Scottish planters into the confiscated land (1610-1641), making Ulster (in the northeast) the most English area of the island. The Irish responded with two major rebellions.

In 1642, while England was embroiled in a civil war between a divine-right monarch (who answered only to God) and a power-hungry Parliament, Irish rebels capitalized on the instability. Tensions were already high, as tenant farmers had recently taken up pitchforks against their English landlords, slaughtering 4,000 in the **Massacre of the Planters** (1641). The landless, Irish-speaking rebels hadn't attacked the middle tier of Irish society—the English-speaking, but still Irish, landed gentry (descendants of the first Anglo-Norman invaders, they were called, rather confusingly, "Old English"). Like the peasant rebels, the "Old English" were Catholic, and they wanted more autonomy for Ireland. Both groups feared the rise of Protestant power in England, and together they formed a pro-Royalist confederation in opposition to the new Protestant Parliament of **Oliver Cromwell.** (This meant, oddly enough, that the Irish now found themselves on the side of the English monarchy.)

Once Cromwell had pulled off his coup d'état and executed King Charles I, he invaded Ireland with 12,000 men (1649-1650). Out to obliterate the last Royalist forces and to exact retaliation for the Massacre of the Planters, and armed with Puritanical, anti-Catholic religious zeal, he conquered the country—brutally. Thousands were slaughtered, priests were tortured, villages were pillaged, and rebels were sold into slavery. Cromwell confiscated 11 million acres of land from Catholic Irish landowners to give to English Protestants. Cromwell's scorched-earth invasion was so harsh that it became known as the "curse of Cromwell"—and it still raises hackles in Ireland (for more on Cromwell, see the sidebar on page 176).

In 1688-1689, rebels again took advantage of England's political chaos. They rallied around Catholic **King James II,** who had been deposed by the English Parliament in the "Glorious Revolution" of 1688 and then had fled to France. He wound up in Ireland, where he formed an army to retake the crown. In the **Siege of Londonderry,** James' Catholic army surrounded the city, the last loyal Protestant power base. But some local apprentice boys locked them out, and after months of negotiations and a 105-day siege, James went away empty-handed.

The showdown came at the massive **Battle of the Boyne** (1690), north of Dublin. Catholic James II and his 25,000 men were defeated by the 36,000 troops of Protestant **King William III** of Orange. From this point on, the color orange became a symbol in Ireland for pro-English, pro-Protestant forces.

As the 17th century came to a close, Protestant England had successfully put down every rebellion. To counter Irish feistiness, the ruling English out-and-out attacked the indigenous Gaelic culture through legislation called the **Penal Laws.** Catholics couldn't vote, hold office, buy land, join the army, play the harp, or even own a horse worth more than £5. Catholic education was banned and priests were outlawed. But the Penal Laws were difficult to enforce, and many Catholics were taught at hidden outdoor "hedge schools," and worshipped in private or at secluded "Mass rocks" in the countryside.

PROTESTANT RULE (1700s)

During the 18th century, urban Ireland thrived economically, and even culturally, under the English. Dublin in the 1700s (pop. 50,000) was Britain's second city, one of Europe's wealthiest and most sophisticated. It's still decorated in Georgian (Neoclassical) style, named for the English kings of the time (consecutive kings George I, II, III, and IV, who ruled for more than a century).

But beyond the Pale surrounding Dublin, rebellion continued to brew. Over time, greed on the top and dissent on the bottom led to more repressive colonial policies. The Enlightenment provided ideas of freedom, and the Revolutionary Age emboldened the Irish masses. Irish nationalists were inspired by budding democratic revolutions in America (1776) and France (1789). The Irish say, "The Tree of Liberty sprouted in America, blossomed in France, and dropped seeds in Ireland." Increasingly, the issue of Irish independence was less a religious question than a political one, as poor, disenfranchised colonists demanded a political voice.

In Dublin, **Jonathan Swift** (1667-1745), the dean of St. Patrick's Cathedral, published his satirical *Gulliver's Travels* with veiled references to English colonialism. He anonymously wrote pamphlets advising, "Burn all that's British, except its coal."

The **Irish Parliament** was an exclusive club, and only Protestant male landowners could be elected to a seat (1 percent of the population qualified). In 1782, led by **Henry Grattan** (1746-1820), the Parliament negotiated limited autonomy from England (while remaining loyal to the king) and fairer treatment of the Catholics. England, chastened by the American Revolution (and soon preoccupied with the French Revolution), tolerated a more-or-less independent Irish Parliament for two decades.

Then, in 1798, came the bloodiest Irish Rebellion. Inspired by the American and French revolutionary successes and buoyed by an "if they can do it, so can we" attitude, a band of Irish idealists rose up and rebelled. The **United Irishmen** (whose goals included introducing the term "Irishman" for all Irish, rather than labeling people as either Protestant or Catholic) revolted against Britain, led by **Wolfe Tone** (1763-1798), a Protestant Dublin lawyer. Tone, trained in the French Revolution, had gained French aid for the Irish cause (though a French naval invasion in 1796 already had failed after a freakish "Protestant wind" blew the ships away from Ireland's shores). The Rebellion was marked by bitter fighting—30,000 died

over six weeks—before British troops crushed the revolt.

England tried to solve the Irish problem politically by forcing Ireland into a "Union" with England as part of a "United Kingdom" (**Act of Union,** 1801). The 500-year-old Irish Parliament was dissolved, with its members becoming part of England's Parliament in London. Catholics were not allowed in Parliament. From then on, "Unionists" have been those who oppose Irish independence, wanting to preserve the country's union with England.

PAST & PRESENT

VOTES, VIOLENCE, AND THE FAMINE (1800s)

Irish politicians lobbied in the British Parliament for Catholic rights, reform of absentee-landlordism, and for **Home Rule**— i.e., the return of an Irish Parliament and more self-government. Meanwhile, secret societies of revolutionaries pursued justice through violence.

Daniel O'Connell (1775-1847), known as The Liberator, campaigned for Catholic equality and for the repeal of the Act of Union (to gain autonomy). Having personally witnessed the violence of the French Revolution in 1789 and the 1798 United Irishman Rebellion, O'Connell chose peaceful, legal means to achieve his ends. He was a charismatic speaker, drawing half a million people to one of his "monster meeting" demonstrations at the Hill of Tara (1843). But any hope of an Irish revival was soon snuffed out by the biggest catastrophe in Irish history: the Great Potato Famine.

The **Great Potato Famine** (1845-1849) was caused by a fungus *(Phytophthora infestans)* that destroyed Ireland's main food crop.

Legions of people starved to death or died of related diseases (estimates range between 500,000 and 1.1 million). Another one to two million emigrated—most to America and others to Canada and Australia.

The poorest were hardest hit. They depended on potatoes because other crops— grown by tenant farmers on their landlords' land—went to pay the rent and were destined for export.

Britain—then the richest nation on earth, with an empire stretching around the globe— could seemingly do nothing to help its starving citizens. A toxic combination of laissez-faire economic policies, racial bigotry, and religious self-righteousness conspired to blind the English to the plight of the Irish. While the British tend to blame the Famine on overpopulation among the undisciplined and backward Irish (Ireland's population had doubled in the 45 years leading up to this period), some Irish believe it was a calculated attempt to take advantage of a natural disaster to starve down the local population through lack of effective relief. While the potato crop failed, there was more than enough food, in the form of other crops and cattle, to feed the starving, but it was exported off the island instead. For this reason, many do not refer to this period as "the Famine" (implying a lack of food) but rather as "An Gorta Mór" (The Great Hunger...imposed by British colonial policies). Over the course of five long years, Ireland was ruined. To this day, Irish weather reports include mention of potential potato-blight conditions.

The island's population was suddenly cut by almost a third (from 8.4 million to 6 million). Many of their best and brightest had fled, and the island's economy—and spirit—took generations to recover. The Irish language, spoken by the majority of the population before the Famine, became a badge of ignorance and was considered useless to those hoping to emigrate.

By 1900, emigration had further cut the island's population to just over 4 million (half of what it had been just before the Famine). Before the Famine, land was subdivided—each son got a piece of the family estate (so individual plots shrunk with each generation). Afterwards, the oldest son got the estate, and the younger siblings—with fewer options for making a living in Ireland (primarily joining the priesthood)—emigrated to Britain, Australia, Canada, or the US. Meanwhile, women could make more money than men abroad by working as domestic servants, thus more quickly saving up enough to bring their siblings over. As a result, women often beat men to new homes in foreign lands.

The tradition of an "American Wake" was a sad farewell by family and friends who gathered the night before an emigrant boarded the ship (likely never to be seen by them again, but at least heard from by letter). Because of the huge emigration to the US (today there are 50 million Irish Americans), US influence increased. (During the negotiations between Northern Ireland and the Irish Republic, US involvement in the talks was welcomed and considered essential by nearly all parties.)

Occasional violence demonstrated the fury of Irish nationalism, with the tragedy of the Famine inflaming the movement. In 1848, the **Young Irelander** armed uprising was easily squelched. In 1858, the **Irish Republican Brotherhood** was formed (the forerunner of the IRA). Also called the **Fenians,** they launched a campaign for independence by planting terrorist bombs. Irish Americans sent money to help finance these revolutionaries. Uprising after uprising made it clear that Ireland was ready to close this 800-year chapter of invasions and colonialism.

Home Rule Party leader **Charles Stuart Parnell** (1846-1891), an Irishman educated in England, made "the Irish problem" the focus of London's Parliament. Parnell lobbied for independence and for the rights of poor tenant farmers living under absentee landlords, pioneering the first boycott tactics. Then, in 1890, at the peak of his power and about to achieve Home Rule for Ireland, he was drummed out of politics by a scandal involving his mistress, scuttling the Home Rule issue for another 20 years (for more on Parnell, see page 43).

Culturally, the old Gaelic, rural Ireland was being crushed under the Industrial Revolution and the political control wielded by Protestant England. The **Gaelic Athletic Association** was founded in 1884 to resurrect pride in ancient Irish sports such as hurling (see sidebar on page 79). Soon after, in 1893, writers and educators formed the **Gaelic League** to preserve the traditional language, music, and poetry. Building on the tradition of old Celtic bards, Ireland turned out a series of influential writers: **W. B. Yeats, Oscar Wilde, George Bernard Shaw,** and **James Joyce** (see "Irish Literature," later).

EASTER UPRISING, WAR OF INDEPENDENCE, PARTITION, AND CIVIL WAR (1900-1950)

As the century turned, Ireland prepared for the inevitable showdown with Britain.

The **Sinn Fein** party (meaning "Ourselves") lobbied politically for independence. The **Irish Volunteers** were more Catholic and more militant. Also on the scene was the **Irish Citizens Army,** with a socialist agenda to protect labor unions and clean up Dublin's hideous tenements, where 15 percent of children died before the age of one.

Of course, many Irish were Protestant and pro-British. The **Ulster Volunteers** (Unionists, and mostly Orangemen) feared that Home Rule would result in a Catholic-dominated state that would oppress the Protestant minority.

Meanwhile, Britain was preoccupied with World War I, where it was "fighting to protect the rights of small nations" (except Ireland's), and so it delayed granting Irish independence. The increasingly militant Irish rebels, believing that England's misfortune was Ireland's opportunity, decided to rise up and take independence while the time was ripe.

On Easter Monday, April 24, 1916, 1,500 Irish Volunteers, united with members of the Irish Citizens Army, marched on Dublin, occupied the General Post Office (and six other key buildings across town), and raised a green, white, and orange flag. The teacher and poet **Patrick Pearse** stood in front of the post office and proclaimed Ireland an independent republic.

British troops struck back—in a week of street fighting and intense shelling, some 300 died. By Saturday, the greatly outnumbered rebels had been killed or arrested. The small-scale uprising—which failed to go national and was never popular even in Dublin—was apparently over.

However, the British government over-reacted by swiftly executing the 16 ringleaders, including Pearse. Ireland was outraged, no longer seeing the rebels as troublemakers but as martyrs. From this point on, Ireland was resolved to win its independence at all costs. A poem by W. B. Yeats, "Easter, 1916," captured the struggle with his words: "All changed, changed utterly: A terrible beauty is born."

In the 1918 elections, the Sinn Fein party won big, but the new members of Parliament refused to go to London, instead forming their own independent Irish Parliament in Dublin. Then Irish rebels began ambushing policemen—seen as the eyes and ears of British control—sparking two years of confrontations called the **War of Independence.** The fledgling Irish Republican Army faced 40,000 British troops, including the notorious Black and Tans (named for the color of their clothes: black for police and tan for army-surplus uniforms). A thousand people died in this war of street fighting, sniper fire, jailhouse beatings, terrorist bombs, and reprisals (for a more detailed timeline of the war and events leading up to it, see the sidebar on page 54).

Finally, Britain, tired of extended war after the slaughterhouse of World War I, agreed to Irish independence. But Ireland itself was a divided nation—the southern three-quarters of the island was mostly Catholic, Gaelic, rural, and for Home Rule; the northern quarter was Protestant, English, industrial, and Unionist. The solution? In 1920, in the **Government of Ireland Act,** the British Parliament partitioned the island into two independent, self-governing countries within the British Commonwealth: **Northern Ireland** and the **Irish Free State.** While the northern six counties (the only ones without a Catholic majority) chose to stay with Britain as Northern Ireland, the remaining counties became the Irish Free State. (For a review of the ongoing issues between the North and the Republic, see the Northern Ireland chapter.)

Ireland's various political factions wrestled with this compromise solution, and the island plunged into a yearlong **Civil War** (1922-1923). The hard-line IRA opposed the partition, unwilling to accept a divided island, an oath of loyalty to the Crown, or the remaining British navy bases on Irish soil. They waged a street war on the armies of the Irish Free State, whose leaders supported the political settlement as a stepping stone toward future independence. Dublin and the southeast were ravaged in a year of bitter fighting before the Irish Free State, led by the charismatic young Nationalist **Michael Collins,** emerged victorious. The IRA went underground, moving its fight north and trying for the rest of the century to topple the government of Northern Ireland.

Out of the ashes of the Civil War came the two parties that still dominate Ireland's politics today. **Fine Gael** spawned from those who approved the treaty and the creation of the Irish Free State. **Fianna Fáil** was founded by **Eamon de Valera,** the figurehead of the antitreaty side. Interestingly, Fianna Fáil, which developed from the losing side of the Civil War, has been in power 70 percent of the time since its inception.

In 1937, the Irish Free State severed more ties with the British Commonwealth, writing up a new national constitution and taking an old name—**Éire** (pronounced AIR-uh). This new constitution reflected de Valera's conservative views, giving the Catholic Church "special status" and decreeing that a woman's place was in the home. Ireland called World War II "The Emergency" and remained neutral. In 1949, the separation from Britain was completed, as the Irish Free State left the Commonwealth and officially became the **Republic of Ireland**.

CELTIC TIGER IN THE SOUTH, TROUBLES IN THE NORTH (1950-2000)

In the 1950s, Ireland hemorrhaged its best and brightest as emigration soared. But beginning in the 1960s, the Republic of Ireland—formerly a poor, rural region—began its transformation into a modern, economic nation. The dropping of trade-strangling tariffs lured foreign investors. In 1973, membership in the European Union opened new Continental markets to Irish trade. No longer would Britain be the dominant trade partner. At the same time, reforms to Ireland's antiquated education system created a new generation of young people prepared for more than life on the farm.

The big social changes in the Republic were reflected in the 1990 election of Mary Robinson (a feminist lawyer who was outspoken on issues of divorce, contraception, and abortion) as the first female president of a once ultraconservative Ireland. Her much-respected seven-year tenure was followed by the equally graceful presidency of Mary McAleese (1997-2011). Born in the North,

McAleese is another example of the shrinking divide between the two political states that occupy the island.

Through the late 1990s, the Republic's booming, globalized economy grew a whopping 40 percent, and Dublin's property values tripled (between 1995 and 2007), earning the Republic's economy the nickname "The Celtic Tiger." (Like elsewhere, the global recession hit hard here in 2008—the property bubble burst, sending home values plummeting and driving up unemployment.)

Meanwhile, as the Republic moved toward prosperity, Northern Ireland—with a slight Protestant majority and a large, disaffected Catholic minority—was plagued by the **Troubles.** In 1967, the Northern Ireland Civil Rights Movement, inspired by the African American rights movement in the US, organized marches and demonstrations demanding equal treatment for Catholics (better housing, job opportunities, and voting rights). But they didn't have a Martin Luther King or a Bishop Desmond Tutu to advocate for them from a position of moral authority. Protestant **Unionist Orangemen** countered by continuing their marches through Catholic neighborhoods, flaunting their politically dominant position in the name of tradition, and thus provoking riots. In 1969, Britain sent troops to help Northern Ireland keep the peace and met resistance from the IRA, which saw them as an occupying army supporting the Protestant pro-British majority.

From the 1970s to the 1990s, the North was a low-level battlefield, with the IRA using terrorist tactics to achieve their political ends. The Troubles, which claimed some 3,000 lives, continued with bombings, marches, hunger strikes, rock-throwing, and riots (notably Derry's **Bloody Sunday** in 1972—see sidebar on page 439). These were interrupted by periods of cease-fires, broken cease-fires, and a string of failed peace agreements.

Then came the watershed 1998 settlement known as the **Good Friday Peace Accord** (to pro-Irish Nationalists) or the **Belfast Agreement** (to pro-British Unionists).

GLOBAL NATIONS (2000 AND BEYOND)

After years of negotiation, in 2005 the IRA formally announced an end to its armed campaign, promising to pursue peaceful, democratic means to achieve its goals. In 2006, I was stunned to learn that the British Army surveillance towers in Derry—disturbing fixtures since my very first visit—had been torn down. In the spring of 2007, the unthinkable happened when **Gerry Adams,** leader of the ultra-Nationalist Sinn Fein party, sat down across a table from **Reverend Ian Paisley,** head of the ultra-Unionist DUP party. It was their first face-to-face meeting. Also in 2007, London returned control of Northern Ireland to the popularly elected Northern Ireland Assembly. Perhaps most important of all, after almost 40 years, the British Army withdrew 90 percent of its forces from Northern Ireland that summer. In 2010, the long-awaited Saville Report—the result of a 12-year investigation by the British government—found that the Bloody Sunday shootings were unjustified, and the victims legally innocent.

Now it's up to Northern Ireland to keep the peace. The 1998 **peace accord** gives Northern Ireland the freedom to leave the UK if ever the majority of the population approves a referendum to do so. At the same time, the Republic of Ireland withdrew its constitutional claim to the entire island of Ireland. Northern Ireland now has limited autonomy from London, with its own democratically elected, power-sharing government. It will be up to this body to untie this stubborn Gordian knot.

Great Britain is also trying to mend its relationship with the Republic. In 2011, Queen Elizabeth II became the first British monarch to visit the Republic of Ireland since it broke away in 1921 (she has been to the North numerous times). The Queen took the gutsy step of visiting Dublin's Croke Park stadium, where British Black and Tan troops massacred 14 people at a 1921 Gaelic football match (see sidebar on page 79). She also visited Dublin's Garden of Remembrance, a quiet urban plot devoted to the 1916 Easter Uprising. In 2012, she took it a step further by shaking hands with ex-IRA leader and current Deputy First Minister of Northern Ireland, Martin McGuinness. These acts of reconciliation, though controversial and dramatic, were another step toward building an amicable relationship between the two countries.

In 2016, the unexpected British referendum vote to depart the European Union (the so-called **"Brexit"**) reshuffled the political cards in the region. Northern Ireland had voted to remain in the EU, as did Scotland. With the possibility of Scotland leaving the UK on the horizon, the Unionist community in Northern Ireland (which holds both their Britishness and Scottish ancestry dear) has become split on the question of whether or not to remain part of the United Kingdom or instead prioritize membership in the European Union.

Today, both Northern Ireland and the Republic of Ireland have reason to be optimistic about the future. In spite of the recent recession, their economic growth through the 1990s and 2000s was impressive, and political and cultural problems have diminished. The formerly isolated island is welcoming tourists with open arms and reaching out to the rest of the globe. In 1999, the number of tourists visiting Ireland topped the six million mark, exceeding for the first time the native population of the island. And visitors returning to Ireland are amazed at the country's transformation.

During its **Celtic Tiger economic boom,** the Irish imported labor and surpassed the English in per-capita income—both for the first time ever. Starting in 1980, when Apple set up its European headquarters here, streams of multinational and US corporations opened offices in Ireland. Ireland has one of the youngest populations in Europe. And those young Irish, beneficiaries of one of Europe's best education systems, provide these corporations with a highly skilled workforce. Ireland's big pharmaceutical and software industries (although usually foreign-owned) are well-established—this little country is second only to the US in the exportation of software. The island's close business ties to its American partners mean its economy is highly reactive to US market fluctuations. The Irish say, "When America sneezes, we get pneumonia."

By 2003, the rising economic tide had lifted Ireland to float beside Finland as one of the two most expensive countries in the European Union. But by 2011 that tide had receded: The global recession has been a cold shower on Ireland's long period of economic good times, and the Irish economy fell further, by percentage, than any other EU country during this period.

This century's rapid growth and then decline has caused other problems. Urban sprawl, big-city traffic snarls, water and air pollution, and the homogenizing effects of globalization have left their mark. Per-capita consumption of alcohol has tripled since 1970. Health organizations lament that, ounce for ounce, liquor has become cheaper than milk, juice, or mineral water.

In 2008, the irrationally exuberant Irish **housing bubble** burst, wiping out retirement nest eggs and littering the Irish landscape with empty "ghost estates" (built on spec during the boom, these housing developments remain mostly unsold and are slowly deteriorating). The average value of Irish homes dropped 45 percent between 2007 and 2011. The final stage of this humbling financial buzzkill came in the fall of 2010, when the EU bailed out Ireland's teetering banks (an event wedged painfully between similar bailouts of Greece and Portugal). To Ireland's credit, they fulfilled their banking obligations and bounced back from the bailout faster than the other troubled European economies.

Today's Irish parents (who remember 20 percent unemployment in the early 1980s) worry how their young adult children, who may have grown up surrounded by affluence, will adjust to the new economic realities. Still, the Celtic Tiger economy, although tamed by the recession, taught the formerly downtrodden Irish that their

Irish Brogue with a Polish Accent

Walking down the street in an Irish city these days, you might overhear an unfamiliar language. It's Polish, and it is to Ireland

what Spanish is to the US: the language needed to communicate with a huge immigrant population. Polish food sections are popping up in grocery stores, and English-Polish menus appearing in some restaurants. Ask that chambermaid or waiter with the unusual accent where they're from; the likely response is Warsaw or Kraków.

When 10 mostly Eastern European nations joined the EU in 2004, Ireland's booming economy at that time needed a cheap labor force to fill the growing number of minimum-wage jobs. Hardworking, ambitious young Poles headed west to the land of opportunity. Ireland was their first choice because of its Catholicism, stronger economy, and opportunity to learn English (the international language of business). From 2006 to 2011, the number of Polish residents in the Republic of Ireland increased by 93.7 percent, beating out UK nationals as the largest group of non-Irish nationals living in Ireland. And Polish has replaced Irish Gaelic as Ireland's second most-spoken language.

PAST & PRESENT

luck can change for the better. The Irish—skilled and business-savvy—are rapidly recovering. It can't come soon enough.

Meanwhile, the challenges of **immigration** (new arrivals into Ireland) have replaced problems associated with the generations of emigration (young people leaving Ireland). Until a few years ago, Ireland had the most liberal citizenship laws in the European Union, granting Irish citizenship to anyone born on Irish soil (even if neither parent had an Irish passport). This led to a flood of pregnant immigrant women arriving from Eastern Europe and Africa to give birth in Ireland so their children would gain EU citizenship. Families with a child born in an EU country faced fewer border restrictions, increasing their chances of moving into one of the EU nations. In 2004, the Irish people closed that legal loophole in a referendum vote.

Marking 2016 as the **hundredth anniversary of the Easter Uprising,** Ireland looks back in amazement at the highs and lows of its turbulent first hundred years of modern nationhood. No longer an agricultural backwater in the shadow of British colonial domination, the country has forged a unique identity and proved it can compete successfully in the ever-accelerating 21st century. In the past decade, the Irish enjoyed views from their lofty Celtic

Tiger peak (with the hottest economy in the EU) and then suffered the helpless freefall of the merciless global recession. But now the roller coaster has bottomed out and "green shoots" are sprouting once again.

While the Irish are embracing the new economies and industries of the 21st century, some still see their island as an oasis of morality and **traditional values** when it comes to sex and marriage. But a seismic shift began when homosexuality was decriminalized in 1993. In 2015, the doors were blown off the closet when the Republic of Ireland became the first country to legalize same-sex marriage by a referendum (62 percent were in favor).

The Catholic Church continues to exert some influence on Irish society. But the popular demands of the youngest population in Europe will likely push the Irish government to make some changes on contentious issues like birth control (which is employed here at rates lower than in any other EU nation), abortion (which is illegal here but becoming an increasingly contentious issue), and divorce (which requires that strict conditions be met).

Irish Art

Megalithic tombs, ancient gold- and metalwork, illuminated manuscripts, high crosses carved in stone, paintings of rural Ireland, and provocative political murals—Ireland comes with some fascinating art. To best appreciate this art in your travels, kick off your tour in Ireland's two top museums, both in Dublin: the **National Museum of Ireland** and the **National Gallery.** Each provides a good context to help you enjoy Irish art and architecture—from ancient to modern and both rural and urban. Here's a quick survey.

Megalithic Period: During the Stone Age, 5,000 years ago, farmers living in the **Valley of the Boyne,** north of Dublin, built a "cemetery" of approximately 40 **burial mounds.** The most famous of these mound tombs is the passage tomb at Newgrange (part of Brú na Bóinne). About 250 feet across, 40 feet high, and composed of 200,000 tons of loose stone, Newgrange was constructed so that the light from the winter solstice sunrise (Dec 21) would pass through the eastern entrance to the tomb, travel down a 60-foot passage, and illuminate the inner burial chamber (not bad engineering for Stone Age architects). The effect is now re-created daily, so visitors can experience this ancient ritual of renewal and rebirth any time of year (see the Near Dublin chapter).

Some of Europe's best examples of megalithic (big rock) art are also at Newgrange. Carved on the tomb's stones are zigzags, chevrons, parallel arcs, and concentric spirals. Scholars think these designs symbolize a belief in the eternal cycle of life and the continuation of the life force, or that they pay homage to the elements in nature on which these ancient peoples depended for their existence.

Exploring these burial mounds (only Newgrange and Knowth are open to the public), you begin to understand the reverence that

these ancient people had for nature, and the need they felt to bury their dead in these great mound tombs, returning their kin to the womb of Mother Earth.

Bronze Age: As ancient Irish cultures developed from 2000 B.C., so did their metalworking skills. Gold and bronze were used to create **tools, jewelry,** and **religious objects.** (The National Museum: Archaeology and History in Dublin houses the most dazzling of these works.) Gold neck rings worn by both men and women, cufflink-like dress fasteners, bracelets, and lock rings (to hold hair in place) are just a few of the personal adornments fashioned by the ancient Irish.

Most of these objects were deliberately buried, often in bogs, as votive offerings to their gods or to prevent warring tribes from stealing them. Like the earlier megaliths, they're decorated with geometric and organic motifs.

Iron Age: The Celts, a warrior society from Central Europe, arrived in Ireland perhaps as early as the seventh century B.C. With their metalworking skills and superior iron weaponry, they soon overwhelmed the native population. And, though the Celts may have been fierce warriors, they wreaked havoc with a flair for the aesthetic. **Shields, swords,** and **scabbards** were embellished with delicate patterns, often enhanced with vivid colors. The dynamic energy of these decorations must have reflected the ferocious power of the Celts.

The Age of Saints and Scholars: Christianity grew in Ireland from St. Patrick's first efforts in the fifth century A.D. In the sixth and seventh centuries, its many great saints (such as St. Columba) established monastic settlements throughout Ireland, Britain, and the Continent, where learning, literature, and the arts flourished. During this Golden Age of Irish civilization, monks, along with metalworkers and stonemasons, created imaginative designs and distinctive stylistic motifs for **manuscripts, metal objects,** and **crosses.**

Monks wrote out and richly decorated manuscripts of the Gospels. These manuscripts—which preserved the written word in Latin, Greek, and Irish—eventually had more power than the oral tales of the ancient pagan heroes.

The most beautiful and imaginative of these illuminated manuscripts is the **Book of Kells** (c. A.D. 800), on display in the Old Library at Trinity College in Dublin. Crafted by Irish monks at a monastery on the Scottish island of Iona, the book was brought to Ireland for safekeeping from rampaging Vikings. The skins of 150 calves were used to make the vellum, which is painted with rich pigments from plants and minerals. The entire manuscript is colorfully decorated with flat, stylized human or angelic forms and intricate, interlacing animal and knot patterns. Full-page illustrations depict the life of Christ, and many pages are given over to highly complex yet symmetrical designs that resemble an Eastern carpet. Many consider this book the finest piece of art from Europe's Dark Ages.

The most renowned metalwork of this period is the **Ardagh Chalice,** made sometime in the eighth century. Now on display at the National Museum in Dublin, the silver and bronze gilt chalice is as impressive as the Book of Kells. Ribbons of gold wrap around the chalice stem, while intricate knot patterns ring the cup. A magnificent gold ring and a large glass stone on the chalice bottom reflect the desire to please God. (He would see this side of the chalice when the priest drank during the Mass.)

The monks used Irish high crosses to celebrate the triumph of Christianity and to provide a means of educating the illiterate masses through simple stone carvings. The **Cross of Murdock** (Muiredach's Cross, A.D. 923) is 18 feet tall, towering over the remains of the monastic settlement at Monasterboice. It is but one of many monumental crosses that you'll come across throughout Ireland. Typically, stone carvers depicted Bible sto-

ries and surrounded these with the same intricate patterns seen in the Book of Kells and the Ardagh Chalice.

Early Irish art focused on organic, geometric, and linear designs. Unlike Mediterranean art, Irish art of this early period was not preoccupied with a naturalistic representation of people, animals, or the landscape. Instead, it reflects Irish society's rituals and the elements and rhythms of nature.

The Suppression of Native Irish Art: After invading Ireland in 1169, the English suppressed Celtic Irish culture. English traditions in architecture, painting, and literature replaced native styles until the late 19th century, when revivals in Irish language, folklore, music, and art began to surface.

Painters in the late 19th and early 20th centuries went to the west of Ireland, which was less affected by English dominance and influence, in search of traditional Irish subject matter. **Jack B. Yeats** (1871-1957, brother of the poet W. B. Yeats), Belfast-born painter **Paul Henry** (1876-1958), and **Sean Keating** (1889-1977) were among those who looked to the west for inspiration. The National Gallery in Dublin holds many of these artists' greatest works, with an entire gallery dedicated to Jack Yeats. Many of his early paintings illustrate scenes of his beloved Sligo. His later paintings are more expressionistic in style and patriotic in subject matter.

Henry's paintings depict the rugged beauty of the Connemara region and its people, with scenes of rustic cottages, mountains, and boglands. Keating, the most political of the three painters, featured stirring scenes from Ireland's struggle against the English for independence.

Contemporary Irish art is often linked to the social, political, and environmental issues that face Ireland today. Themes include

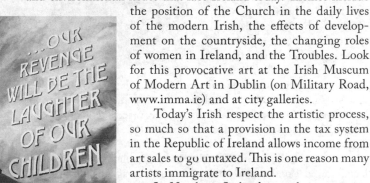

the position of the Church in the daily lives of the modern Irish, the effects of development on the countryside, the changing roles of women in Ireland, and the Troubles. Look for this provocative art at the Irish Muscum of Modern Art in Dublin (on Military Road, www.imma.ie) and at city galleries.

Today's Irish respect the artistic process, so much so that a provision in the tax system in the Republic of Ireland allows income from art sales to go untaxed. This is one reason many artists immigrate to Ireland.

In Northern Ireland, murals in sectarian neighborhoods (such as the Shankill and Falls Roads in Belfast and the Bogside in Derry) are stirring public testaments to the martyrs and heroes of the Troubles.

If you want to learn more about Irish history, consider *Europe 101: History and Art for the Traveler,* written by Rick Steves and Gene Openshaw (available at www.ricksteves.com).

Irish Literature

Since the Book of Kells, Ireland's greatest contributions to the world of art have been through words. As there was no Irish Gaelic written language, the inhabitants of Ireland were illiterate until Christianity came in the fourth century. Far from ignorant, Celtic society maintained a complex set of laws and historical records and legends...verbally. The druid priests and bards who passed down this rich oral tradition from generation to generation were the most respected members of the clan, next to the king. After Christianity transformed Ireland into a refuge of literacy (while the rest of Europe crumbled into the Dark Ages), Charlemagne's imported Irish monks invented "minuscule," which became the basis of the lower-case letters we use in our alphabet today. The cultural importance placed on the word (spoken, and for the past 1,500 years, written) is today reflected in the rich output of modern Irish writers.

Three hundred years ago, Dublin native **Jonathan Swift** created his masterpiece, *Gulliver's Travels*, as an acidic satire of British colonialism. It pokes fun at religious hard-liners and the pompous bureaucrats in London who shaped England's misguided Irish policies, and ironically has survived as a children's classic.

William Butler Yeats, also born and raised in Dublin, dedicated his early writings in the 1880s to the "Celtic Twilight" rebirth of pride in mythic Irish heroes and heroines. His early poems and plays are filled with fairies and idyllic rural innocence, while his later poems reflect Ireland's painful transition to independence. Yeats' Nobel Prize for literature (1923) was eventually matched by three later, Nobel-winning Irish authors: **George Bernard Shaw** (1925), **Samuel Beckett** (1969), and **Seamus Heaney** (1995).

Oscar Wilde, born in Dublin and a graduate of Trinity College, wowed London with his quick wit, outrageous clothes, and

flamboyant personality. Wilde wrote the darkly fascinating novel *The Picture of Dorian Gray* (1890) and skewered upper-class Victorian society in witty comedic plays (such as *The Importance of Being Earnest,* 1895), with characters who speak very elegantly about the trivial concerns of the idle rich. He was the toast of London in the 1890s—before the scandal of his homosexuality turned Victorian society against him. Meanwhile, **Bram Stoker** was conjuring up a Gothic thriller called *Dracula* (1897).

Most inventive of all, perhaps, was **James Joyce,** who broke new ground and captured literary lightning in a bottle when he focused on Dublin's seedier side in a modern, stream-of-consciousness style. His famous novel *Ulysses,* set on a single day (June 16, 1904), follows Dubliners on an odyssey through the city's pubs, hospitals, libraries, churches, and brothels.

The **Abbey Theatre** (championed by W. B. Yeats) was the world's first national theater, built to house plays intended to give a voice to Ireland's flowering playwrights. When **J. M. Synge** staged *The Playboy of the Western World* there in 1907, his unflattering comic portrayal of Irish peasant life (and mention of women's underwear) caused riots. Twenty years later, **Sean O'Casey** provoked more riots at the Abbey when his *Plough and the Stars* production depicted the 1916 Uprising in a way that was at odds with the audience's cherished views of their heroes.

In recent decades, the bittersweet Irish literary parade has been inhabited by tragically volcanic characters like **Brendan Behan,** who exclaimed, "I'm not a writer with a drinking problem...I'm a drinker with a writing problem." Bleak poverty experienced in childhood was the catalyst for **Frank McCourt**'s memorable *Angela's Ashes*. Among the most celebrated of today's Irish writers is **Roddy Doyle,** whose feel for working-class Dublin resonates in his novels of contemporary life (such as *The Commitments*) as well as in historical slices of life (such as *A Star Called Henry*). **Seamus Heaney,** a poet who has won the Nobel and Pulitzer prizes, published a new translation in 1999 of the Old English epic *Beowulf*—wedding the old with the new.

Irish Language

The Irish have a rich oral tradition that goes back to their ancient fireside storytelling days. Part of the fun of traveling here is getting an ear for the way locals express themselves.

Irish Gaelic is one of four surviving Celtic languages, along with Scottish Gaelic, Welsh, and Breton (spoken in parts of French Brittany). A couple of centuries ago, there were seven surviving Celtic languages. But Cornish (spoken in Cornwall) is on life support, and two others—Manx (from the Isle of Man) and Gallaic (spoken in Northern Spain)—have died out. Some proud Irish choose to call their native tongue "Irish" instead of "Gaelic" to ensure that there is no confusion with what is spoken in parts of Scotland.

I ʒcuiṁne aʒus in onóir
na nʒael, sa ċeantair seo,
a ʒlaċ páirt san éirí amaċ i '98
ar san saoirse na h-éireann
ar óeis láṁ óé ʒo raib siaö.

Only 165 years ago, the majority of the Irish population spoke Irish Gaelic. But most of the speakers were of the poor laborer class that either died or emigrated during the Famine. After the Famine, Irish Gaelic was seen as a badge of backwardness. Parents and teachers understood that English was the language that would serve children best when they emigrated to better lives in the US, Canada, Australia, or England. Children in schools wore a tally stick around their necks, and a notch was cut by teachers each time a child was caught speaking Irish. At the end of the day, the child received a whack for each notch in the stick. It wasn't until the resurgence of cultural pride, brought on by the Gaelic League in 1884, that an attempt was made to promote use of the language again.

Gaeltacht Regions

AREAS SHOWN IN GREY
ARE PART OF THE GAELTACHT

These days, less than 5 percent of the Irish population is fluent in their native tongue. However, it's taken seriously enough that all national laws passed must first be written in Irish, then translated into English. Irish Gaelic can be heard most often in the western counties of Kerry, Galway, Mayo, and Donegal. Each of these counties has a slightly different dialect. You'll know you're entering an Irish Gaelic-speaking area when you see a sign saying *Gaeltacht* (GAIL-takt).

Irish Gaelic doesn't use the letters *j, k, q, x,* or *z.* And there's no "th" sound—which you can hear today when an Irish person says something like "turdy-tree" (33, mostly in the Dublin accent). There is also no equivalent of the simple words "yes" or "no." Instead, answers are given in the affirmative or negative rephrasing of the question. For example, a question like "Did you mail the letter today?" would be answered with "I did," rather than a simple "yes." Or "It's a nice day today, isn't it?" would be answered with "It is," or "'Tis."

IRISH PUB AND MUSIC WORDS

The Irish love to socialize. Pubs are like public living rooms, where friends gather in a corner to play tunes and anyone is a welcome guest. Here are some useful pub and music words:

Irish	English
poitín (po-CHEEN)	moonshine, homemade liquor
craic (crack)	fun atmosphere, good conversation
bodhrán (BO-run)	traditional drum
uilleann (ILL-in)	elbow (*uilleann* pipes are elbow bagpipes)
trad (trad)	traditional Irish music
ceilidh (KAY-lee)	Irish dance gathering
fleadh (flah)	music festival
Slainte! (SLAWN-chuh)	Cheers! (To your health!)
Táim súgach! (taw im SOO-gakh)	I'm tipsy!
lei thras (LEH-hrass)	toilets
mná (min-AW)	women's room
fír (fear)	men's room

IRISH POLITICS

Politics is a popular topic of conversation in Ireland. Whether you pick up a local newspaper or turn on your car radio, you're likely to encounter these Irish political terms in the media:

Irish	English
Taoiseach (TEE-shock)	Prime minister of Irish Republic
Seanad (SHAN-ud)	Irish Senate
Dáil (DOY-ill)	Irish House of Representatives
Teachta Dála (TD) (TALK-tah DOLL-ah)	Member of Irish Parliament
Is féidir linn. (ess FAY-dur lin)	Yes we can.
Fine Gael (FEE-nuh GWAIL)	Political party "Clan of the Gaels"
Fine Fáil (FEE-nuh FOIL)	Political party "Soldiers of Destiny"
Sinn Féin (shin-FAIN)	Political party "We Ourselves"

PAST & PRESENT

IRISH PLACE NAMES

Here are a few words that appear in Irish place names. You'll see these on road signs or at tourist sights.

Irish	English
alt (ahlt)	cliff
an lár (ahn lar)	city center
ard (ard)	high, height, hillock
baile (BALL-yah)	town, town land
beag (beg)	little
bearna (bar-na)	gap
boireann (burr-en)	large rock, rocky area
bóthar (boh-er)	road
bun (bun)	end, bottom
caiseal (CASH-el)	circular stone fort
caisleán (cash-LAWN)	castle
cathair (CAHT-her)	circular stone fort, city
cill (kill)	church
cloch (clockh)	stone
doire (dih-ruh)	oak
droichead (DROCKH-ed)	bridge
drumlin (DRUM-lin)	small hill
dún (doon)	fort
fionn (fi-UN)	white, fair-haired person
gaeltacht (GAIL-takt)	Irish language district
gall (gaul)	foreigner
garda (gar-dah)	police officer
gort (gort)	field
inis (in-ish)	island
mileac (MIL-yach)	low marshy ground
mór (mor)	large
muc (muck)	pig
oifig an phoist (UFF-ig un fusht)	post office
poll (poll)	hole, cave
rath (rath)	ancient earthen fort
ros (ross)	wood or headland
sí (shee)	fairy mound, bewitching
slí (slee)	route, way
sliabh (sleeve)	mountain
sráid (shrayd)	street
teach (chockh)	house
trá (traw)	beach, strand

IRISH PLEASANTRIES

When you reach the more remote western fringe of Ireland, you're likely to hear folks speaking Irish. Although locals in these areas can readily converse with you in English, it's fascinating to hear their ancient Celtic language spoken. Here are some basic Irish phrases:

Irish	English
Fáilte. (FAHLT-chuh or FAHLT-uh)	Welcome.
Conas tá tú? (CONN-us A-ta too)	How are you?
Go raibh maith agat. (guh rov mah UG-ut)	Thank you.
Slán. (slawn)	Bye.

IRISH NAMES

Here are some of the most common Celtic first names you'll encounter in your travels. Amaze your new Irish friends by pronouncing them correctly, or at least not mangling them.

Irish	English
Aoife (EE-fuh)	Ava
Áine (ON-yuh)	Anna
Eammon (A-mun)	Edmond
Liam (LEE-um)	William
Mairéad (mahr-AID)	Margaret
Michael (ME-hall)	Michael
Niall (NILE)	Neil
Pádraig (POD-rig)	Patrick
Peadar (PAD-er)	Peter
Roisín (ROW-sheen)	Rosaleen
Seamus (SHAME-us)	James
Sean (SHAWN)	John
Sinéad (shin-AID)	Jane
Siobhán (shiv-AWN)	Joan

Irish-Yankee Vocabulary

If some of these words seem more British than Irish, those are ones you're likely to hear more often in Northern Ireland (part of the UK).

advert: advertisement
anticlockwise: counterclockwise
aubergine: eggplant
banger: sausage
bang on: correct
banjaxed: messed up
bank holiday: government holiday
bar: except
beer mat: coaster
bespoke: custom
billion: a thousand of our billions (a trillion)
biro: ballpoint pen
biscuit: cookie
Black Mariah: police van
black pudding: sausage made from pig's blood
black stuff: Guinness
blather: rambling, empty talk
bloody: damn (from medieval blasphemy: "Christ's blood")
blow off: fart
boffin: nerd
bog: slang for toilet
bolshy: argumentative
bonnet: car hood
boot: car trunk
braces: suspenders
bridle way: path for walkers, bikers, and horse riders
brilliant: cool
bum: bottom or "backside"
busker: street musician
cacks: trousers, underpants
candy floss: cotton candy
caravan: trailer
car boot sale: temporary flea market, often for charity
car park: parking lot
carry on: nonsense
casualty: emergency room
cat's eyes: road reflectors
ceilidh: dance, party
champ: mashed potatoes and onions
chemist: pharmacist
chicory: endive

chippy: fish-and-chips shop
chips: French fries
chock-a-block: jam-packed
chuffed: pleased
cider: alcoholic apple cider
clearway: road where you can't stop
coach: long-distance bus
concession: discounted admission
cos: romaine lettuce
cotton buds: cotton swabs
courgette: zucchini
craic (pronounced "crack"): fun, good conversation
crèche (pronounced "creesh"): preschool
crisps: potato chips
Croker: Croke Park (GAA Dublin sports stadium)
crusties: New Age hippies
culchie: hick, country yokel
cuppa: cup of tea
CV: résumé (curriculum vitae)
Da: father
deadly: really good
dear: expensive
digestives: round graham crackers
dinner: lunch or dinner
diversion: detour
dodgy: iffy, risky
dole: welfare
done and dusted: completed
donkey's years: until the cows come home, forever
draughts (pronounced "drafts"): checkers
draw: marijuana
dual carriageway: divided highway (four lanes)
Dubs: people from Dublin
Dutch courage: alcohol-induced bravery
eejit: moron
Emergency, The: World War II
en suite: bathroom attached to room
face flannel: washcloth
fair play (to you): well done, good job
fanny: vagina
fiddler's fart: worthless thing
first floor: second floor (one floor above ground)
fiver: five-euro note
flat: apartment
fluthered: drunk
flutter: a bet

football: Gaelic football
fortnight: two weeks
full monty: the whole shebang, everything
GAA: Gaelic Athletic Association
gallery: balcony
gammon: ham
gangway: aisle
gaol: jail (same pronunciation)
Garda: police
gargle: to have an alcoholic drink
gasman: the life of the party
give way: yield
giving out: chewing out, yelling at
glen: valley
gob: mouth
gobsmacked: astounded
grand: good, well ("How are you?" "I'm grand, thanks")
guards: police *(Garda)*
gurrier: hooligan
half eight: 8:30 (not 7:30)
hen night: bachelorette party
holiday: vacation
homely: likable or cozy
hooley: party or informal shindig
hoover: vacuum cleaner
hurling: Irish field hockey
iced lolly: popsicle
interval: intermission
ironmonger: hardware store
jacket potato: baked potato
jacks: toilet
jars: drinks (alcohol)
jelly: Jell-O
jumble: sale, rummage sale
jumper: sweater
just a tick: just a second
kipper: smoked herring
knackered: exhausted
knickers: ladies' panties
knocked: torn down (buildings)
knocking shop: brothel
knock up: wake up or visit
ladybird: ladybug
lash: a try ("give it a lash")
left luggage: baggage check
let: rent

lift: elevator
listed: protected historic building
lorry: truck
Ma, Mam, Mammy: mother
mac: mackintosh (trench) coat
mangetout: snow peas
mate: buddy (boy or girl)
mean: stingy
mental: crazy
minced meat: hamburger
minerals: soft drinks
mobile (MOH-bile): cellphone
mod cons: modern conveniences (not convicts in bell-bottoms)
naff: dorky, tacky
nappy: diaper
natter: talk and talk
"Norn Iron": Northern Ireland
nought: zero
noughties: the decade from 2000-2009
noughts & crosses: tic-tac-toe
OAP: old-age pensioner (qualified for senior discounts)
off-license: liquor store
Oirish: exaggerated Irish accent
on offer: for sale
paddywhackery: exaggerated Irish accent
paralytic: passed-out drunk
pasty (PASS-tee): crusted savory (usually meat) pie
pavement: sidewalk
pear-shaped: messed up, gone wrong
petrol: gas
pissed (rude), paralytic, bevvied, wellied, popped up, ratted, pissed as a newt: drunk
pitch: playing field
plaster: Band-Aid
publican: pub manager
pull: to attract romantic attention
punter: partygoer, customer
put a sock in it: shut up
quay (pronounced "key"): waterside street, ship offloading area
queue: line
queue up: line up
quick smart: immediately
quid: pound (money in Northern Ireland, worth about $1.50)
ramps: speed bumps
randy: horny
rat run: shortcut

redundant, made: laid off
return ticket: round-trip
ride: have sex with
ring up: call (telephone)
ROI: Republic of Ireland
roundabout: traffic circle
RTE: Irish Republic's broadcast network
rubber: eraser
runners: tennis shoes
sanitary towel: sanitary pad
sat-nav: satellite navigation technology
sausage roll: sausage wrapped in a flaky pastry (like a pig in a blanket)
scarlet: embarrassed
Scotch egg: hard-boiled egg wrapped in sausage meat
self-catering: apartment with kitchen
sellotape: Scotch tape
serviette: napkin
session: musical evening
shag: have sex with
shag all: hardly any
shebeen: illegal drinking hole
single ticket: one-way ticket
skint: broke, poor
skip: dumpster
slag: to ridicule, tease
smalls: underwear
snogging: kissing, making out
solicitor: lawyer
sort out: figure out, organize
spanner: wrench
spend a penny: urinate
splash out: splurge
stag night: bachelor party
starkers: buck naked
starters: appetizers
stick: criticism
stone: 14 pounds (weight)
strand: beach
stroppy: bad-tempered
subway: underground pedestrian passageway
sultanas: golden raisins
surgical spirit: rubbing alcohol
swede: rutabaga
take the mickey: tease
tatty: worn out or tacky
taxi rank: taxi stand

tenner: 10-euro note
theatre: live stage
tick: a check mark
tight as a Scotsman (derogatory): cheapskate
tights: panty hose
Tipp: County Tipperary
tipper lorry: dump truck
tin: can
to let: for rent
top up: refill a drink or your mobile-phone credit
torch: flashlight
towpath: path along a river
trad: traditional music
Travellers: itinerants, once known as Tinkers
turf accountant: bookie
twee: corny, too cute
twitcher: bird-watcher
verge: grassy edge of road
victualler: butcher
wain: small child
way out: exit
wee (v.): urinate
wee (n.): tiny (in the North)
Wellingtons, wellies: rubber boots
whacked: exhausted
whinge (rhymes with hinge): whine
witter on: gab and gab
woolies: warm clothes
your man: that guy, this guy
zebra crossing: crosswalk
zed: the letter Z

PRACTICALITIES

Tourist Information....................498
Travel Tips..........................499
Money 500
Sightseeing..........................506
Sleeping.............................510
Eating...............................523
Traditional Irish Music................528
Staying Connected....................529
Transportation.......................535
Resources from Rick Steves............551

This chapter covers the practical skills of European travel: how to get tourist information, pay for things, sightsee efficiently, find good-value accommodations, eat affordably but well, use technology wisely, and get between destinations smoothly. To study ahead and round out your knowledge and skills, I've included information on traditional Irish music and a "Resources from Rick Steves" section.

Tourist Information

TOURIST OFFICES

Ireland's national tourist office has a confusing array of names. It's called **Tourism Ireland** (in the US), **Fáilte Ireland** (in Ireland), and **Discover Ireland** (in cyberspace). It offers a wealth of information on both the Republic of Ireland and Northern Ireland. Before your trip, scan their website (www.discoverireland.ie) and download brochures and maps. You can ask questions and request that information be mailed to you (such as the free vacation planning packet, regional and city maps, walking routes, and festival schedules).

In **Ireland,** your best first stop in every town is generally the tourist information office—abbreviated **TI** in this book. Fáilte Ireland TIs are information dispensaries with trained staff that don't sell anything or take commissions (beware of ad agencies masquerading as TIs, especially in Dublin). I make a point to swing by the local TI to confirm sightseeing plans, pick up a city map, and get information on public transit (including bus and train schedules), walking tours, special events, and nightlife. Prepare a list of questions and a proposed plan to double-check. Many TIs have information on the entire country or at least the region, so try to pick up maps and printed information for destinations you'll be visiting later in your trip.

In **Dublin,** try to get everything you'll need for all of Ireland in one stop at the TI (see page 25). The general nationwide tourist-information phone number for travelers calling from within Ireland is 1-850-230-330 (office open Mon-Sat 9:00-17:00, closed Sun).

Travel Tips

Emergency and Medical Help: In Ireland, dial 999 for police or a medical emergency. If you get sick, do as the locals do and go to a pharmacist for advice. Or ask at your hotel for help—they'll know the nearest medical and emergency services.

Theft or Loss: To replace a passport, you'll need to go in person to an embassy (see page 555). If your credit and debit cards disappear, cancel and replace them (see "Damage Control for Lost Cards" on page 504). File a police report, either on the spot or within a day or two; you'll need it to submit an insurance claim for lost or stolen rail passes or travel gear, and it can help with replacing your passport or credit and debit cards. For more information, see www.ricksteves.com/help.

Time Zones: Ireland, which is one hour earlier than most of continental Europe, is five/eight hours ahead of the East/West coasts of the US. The exceptions are the beginning and end of Daylight Saving Time: Ireland and Europe "spring forward" the last Sunday in March (two weeks after most of North America) and "fall back" the last Sunday in October (one week before North America). For a handy online time converter, see www.timeanddate.com/worldclock.

Business Hours: In Ireland, most stores are open Monday through Saturday from roughly 10:00 to 17:30, with a late night on Wednesday or Thursday (until 19:00 or 20:00), depending on the neighborhood. Saturdays are virtually weekdays, with earlier

PRACTICALITIES

closing hours and no rush hour (though transportation connections can be less frequent than on weekdays). Sundays have the same pros and cons as they do for travelers in the US: special events, limited hours, banks and many shops closed, limited public transportation, no rush hours, street markets lively with shoppers. Friday and Saturday evenings are rowdy; Sunday evenings are quiet.

Watt's Up? Europe's electrical system is 220 volts, instead of North America's 110 volts. Most newer electronics (such as laptops, battery chargers, and hair dryers) convert automatically, so you won't need a converter, but you will need an adapter plug with three square prongs, sold inexpensively at travel stores in the US. Avoid bringing older appliances that don't automatically convert voltage; instead, buy a cheap replacement in Europe. Low-cost hair dryers and other small appliances are sold at Dunnes and Tesco stores in bigger cities; ask your hotelier for the closest branch.

Discounts: Discounts for sights (called "concessions" in Ireland) are generally not listed in this book. However, many Irish sights offer discounts for youths (up to age 18), students (with proper identification cards, www.isic.org), families, seniors (loosely defined as retirees or those willing to call themselves seniors), and groups of 10 or more. Always ask. Some discounts are available only for citizens of the European Union (EU).

Laundry: If you're not planning to wash your clothes in your hotel sink, it's a good idea to plan ahead for laundry. Basic wash-and-wear clothes have nothing to fear from an Irish launderette (but don't tempt fate with your favorite silk kimono—it might come back leprechaun-size). At most launderettes in Ireland, you drop off your load first thing in the morning and pick it up late that afternoon (washed, dried, and kind-of folded). Figure €12-15 per load. This works well for travelers—the savings from doing it yourself are not worth the lost sightseeing time. Note that late-morning drop-off may delay delivery until the next day, and most places are closed on Sunday; a Monday morning pick-up time may cramp your plans. Confirm closing time when you drop off, and set an alarm to remind you to pick up.

Money

This section offers advice on how to pay for purchases on your trip (including getting cash from ATMs and paying with plastic), dealing with lost or stolen cards, VAT (sales tax) refunds, and tipping.

WHAT TO BRING

Bring both a credit card and a debit card. You'll use the debit card at cash machines (ATMs) to withdraw local currency for most purchases, and the credit card to pay for larger items. Some travelers carry a third card, in case one gets demagnetized or eaten by a temperamental machine.

For an emergency stash, bring $100-200 in hard cash ($100 bills are suspect by Irish who've been burned by counterfeiters). Although banks in some countries don't exchange dollars, in a pinch you can always find exchange desks at major train stations and airports—convenient but with crummy rates.

CASH

Although credit cards are widely accepted in Europe, day-to-day spending is generally more cash-based. I find cash is the easiest—and sometimes only—way to pay for cheap food, bus fare, taxis, and local guides. Some vendors will charge you extra for using a credit card, some won't accept foreign credit cards, and some won't take any credit cards at all. Having cash on hand can help you avoid a stressful predicament if you find yourself in a place that won't accept your card.

Throughout Europe, ATMs are the easiest and smartest way for travelers to get cash. They work just like they do at home. To withdraw money from an ATM, you'll need a debit card (ideally with a Visa or MasterCard logo), plus a PIN code (numeric and four digits). For increased security, shield the keypad when entering your PIN code, and don't use an ATM if anything on the front of the machine looks loose or damaged (a sign that someone may have attached a "skimming" device to capture account information). Try to withdraw large sums of money to reduce the number of per-transaction bank fees you'll pay.

When possible, use ATMs located outside banks—a thief is less likely to target a cash machine near surveillance cameras, and if your card is munched by a machine during banking hours, you can go inside for help. Stay away from "independent" ATMs such as Travelex, Euronet, YourCash, Cardpoint, and Cashzone, which charge huge commissions, have terrible exchange rates, and may try to trick users with "dynamic currency conversion" (described later). Although you can use a credit card to withdraw cash at an ATM, this comes with high bank fees and only makes sense in an emergency.

While traveling, if you want to access your accounts online, be sure to use a secure connection (see page 534).

Even in mist-kissed Ireland, pickpockets target tourists, especially in Dublin. To safeguard your cash, wear a money belt—a pouch with a strap that you buckle around your waist like a belt—or a neck wallet. Either way, the key is to wear it out of sight, under your clothes. Keep your cash, credit cards, and passport secure in your money belt or neck wallet, and carry only a day's spending money in your front pocket or wallet.

CREDIT AND DEBIT CARDS

For purchases, Visa and MasterCard are more commonly accepted than American Express. Just like at home, credit and debit cards work easily at larger hotels, restaurants, and shops. I typically use my debit card to withdraw cash to pay for daily purchases. I use my credit card sparingly: to book and pay for hotel rooms, to buy advance tickets for events or sights, to cover major expenses (such as car rentals or plane tickets), and to pay for things online or near the end of my trip (to avoid another visit to the ATM). While you could instead use a debit card for these purchases, a credit card offers a greater degree of fraud protection.

Ask Your Credit- or Debit-Card Company: Before your trip, contact the company that issued your debit or credit cards.

Confirm that your **card will work overseas,** and alert them that you'll be using it in Europe; otherwise, they may deny transactions if they perceive unusual spending patterns.

Ask for the specifics on transaction **fees.** When you use your credit or debit card—either for purchases or ATM withdrawals—you'll typically be charged additional "international transaction" fees of up to 3 percent (1 percent is normal). If your fees seem high, consider getting a different card just for your trip: Capital One (www.capitalone.com) and most credit unions have low-to-no international fees.

Verify your daily ATM **withdrawal limit,** and if necessary, ask your bank to adjust it. I prefer a high limit that allows me to take out more cash at each ATM stop and save on bank fees; some travelers prefer to set a lower limit in case their card is stolen. Note that foreign banks also set maximum withdrawal amounts for their ATMs.

Get your bank's emergency **phone number** in the US (but not its 800 number, which isn't accessible from overseas) to call collect if you have a problem.

Ask for your credit card's **PIN** in case you need to make an emergency cash withdrawal or encounter payment machines using the chip-and-PIN system; the bank won't tell you your PIN over the phone, so allow time for it to be mailed to you.

Chip-and-PIN Credit Cards: Europeans use chip-and-PIN credit cards (embedded with an electronic security chip and requir-

Exchange Rates

I've priced things throughout this book in the local currencies. The Republic of Ireland uses the euro currency. Northern Ireland, which is part of the United Kingdom, has retained its tra-

ditional currency, the British pound sterling. Border towns in the North might take euros, but at a lousy exchange rate. (Check www. oanda.com for the latest exchange rates.)

1 euro (€1) = about $1.10
1 British pound (£1) = about $1.50

Republic of Ireland: To convert prices in euros to dollars, add about 10 percent: €20 = about $22, €50 = about $55. Just like the dollar, one euro (€) is broken down into 100 cents. You'll find coins ranging from €0.01 to €2, and bills ranging from €5 to €200 (bills over €50 are rarely used; €500 bills are being phased out).

Northern Ireland: To convert prices in pounds to dollars, add 50 percent: £20 = about $30, £50 = about $75. The British pound (£), also called a "quid," is broken into 100 pence (p). Pence means "cents." You'll find coins ranging from 1p to £2 and bills from £5 to £50. Fake pound coins are easy to spot (real coins have an inscription on their outside rims; the edges of fakes resemble tree bark).

Northern Ireland issues its own currency, which is worth the same as an English pound. If you're traveling on to Great Britain, note that English and Northern Ireland's Ulster pounds are technically interchangeable in both regions, although Ulster pounds are "undesirable" in Britain. Banks in either region will convert your Ulster pounds into English pounds at no charge. Don't worry about the coins, which are accepted throughout Great Britain and Northern Ireland.

PRACTICALITIES

ing a four-digit PIN). Most of the chip cards now being offered by major US banks are not true chip-and-PIN cards, but instead are chip-and-signature cards, for which your signature verifies your identity. These cards work in Europe for live transactions and at most payment machines, but won't work for offline transactions such as at unattended gas pumps.

Older American cards with just a magnetic stripe also may not work at unattended payment machines, such as those at train and subway stations, toll plazas, parking garages, bike-rental kiosks, and gas pumps. If you have problems with either type of American card, try entering your card's PIN, look for a machine that takes cash, or find a clerk who can process the transaction manually.

If you're concerned, ask if your bank offers a true chip-and-PIN card. Andrews Federal Credit Union (www.andrewsfcu.org) and the State Department Federal Credit Union (www.sdfcu.org) offer these cards and are open to all US residents.

No matter what kind of card you have, it pays to carry euros and/or pounds; remember, you can always use an ATM to withdraw cash with your magnetic-stripe debit card.

Dynamic Currency Conversion: If merchants or hoteliers offer to convert your purchase price into dollars (called dynamic currency conversion, or DCC), refuse this "service." You'll pay extra for the expensive convenience of seeing your charge in dollars. Some ATMs and retailers try to confuse customers by presenting DCC in misleading terms. If an ATM offers to "lock in" or "guarantee" your conversion rate, choose "proceed without conversion." Other prompts might state, "You can be charged in dollars: Press YES for dollars, NO for euros." Always choose the local currency.

Damage Control for Lost Cards

If you lose your credit or debit card, you can stop people from using your card by reporting the loss immediately to the respective global customer-assistance centers. Call these 24-hour US numbers collect: Visa (tel. 303/967-1096), MasterCard (tel. 636/722-7111), and American Express (tel. 336/393-1111). In the Republic of Ireland, to make a collect call to the US, dial 1-800-550-000. In Northern Ireland, dial 0-800-89-0011. Press zero or stay on the line for an operator. European toll-free numbers (listed by country) can be found at the websites for Visa and MasterCard.

If you are the secondary cardholder, you'll need to provide the primary cardholder's identification-verification details (such as birth date, mother's maiden name, or Social Security Number). You can generally receive a temporary card within two or three business days in Europe (see www.ricksteves.com/help for more).

If you report your loss within two days, you typically won't be responsible for any unauthorized transactions on your account, although many banks charge a liability fee of $50.

TIPPING

Tipping in Ireland isn't as automatic and generous as it is in the US. For special service, tips are appreciated, but not expected. As in the US, the proper amount depends on your resources, tipping philosophy, and the circumstances, but some general guidelines apply.

Restaurants: At a pub or restaurant with waitstaff, check the menu or your bill to see if the service is included; if not, tip about 10 percent. At pubs where you order food at the counter, a tip is not expected but is appreciated. Do not tip bartenders pouring drinks in Ireland.

Taxis: For a typical ride, round up your fare a bit (for instance, if the fare is €9, give €10). If the cabbie hauls your bags and zips you to the airport to help you catch your flight, you might want to toss in a little more. But if you feel like you're being driven in circles or otherwise ripped off, skip the tip.

Services: In general, if someone in the tourism or service industry does a super job for you, a small tip of a euro or two is appropriate...but not required. If you're not sure whether (or how much) to tip, ask a local for advice.

GETTING A VAT REFUND

Wrapped into the purchase price of your Irish souvenirs is a Value-Added Tax (VAT); it's 23 percent in the Republic and 20 percent in Northern Ireland. You're entitled to get most of that tax back if you purchase more than €30/£30 (about $33/$40) worth of goods at a store that participates in the VAT-refund scheme. Typically, you must ring up the minimum at a single retailer—you can't add up your purchases from various shops to reach the required amount.

Getting your refund is straightforward and, if you buy a substantial amount of souvenirs, well worth the hassle. If you're lucky, the merchant will subtract the tax when you make your purchase. (This is more likely to occur if the store ships the goods to your home.) Otherwise, you'll need to:

Get the paperwork. Have the merchant completely fill out the necessary refund document, called a "Tax-Free Shopping Cheque." You'll have to present your passport. Get the paperwork done before you leave the store to ensure you'll have everything you need (including your original sales receipt).

Get your stamp at the border or airport. Process your VAT document at your last stop in the European Union (such as at the airport) with the customs agent who deals with VAT refunds. Arrive an additional hour before you need to check in for your flight to allow time to find the local customs office—and to stand in line. It's best to keep your purchases in your carry-on. If they're too large or dangerous to carry on (such as knives), pack them in your checked bags and alert the check-in agent. You'll be sent (with your tagged bag) to a customs desk outside security; someone will examine your bag, stamp your paperwork, and put your bag on the belt. You're not supposed to use your purchased goods before you leave. If you show up at customs wearing your new Irish sweater, officials might look the other way—or deny you a refund.

Collect your refund. You'll need to return your stamped document to the retailer or its representative. Many merchants work with a service, such as Global Blue or Premier Tax Free, that have offices at major airports, ports, or border crossings (either before or after security, probably strategically located near a duty-free shop). These services, which extract a 4 percent fee, can refund your money immediately in cash or credit your card (within two billing cycles). Other refund services may require you to mail the documents from home, or more quickly, from your point of departure (using an envelope you've prepared in advance or one that's been provided by the merchant). You'll then have to wait—it can take months.

CUSTOMS FOR AMERICAN SHOPPERS

You are allowed to take home $800 worth of items per person duty-free, once every 31 days. You can take home many processed and packaged foods: vacuum-packed cheeses, dried herbs, jams, baked goods, candy, chocolate, oil, vinegar, mustard, and honey. Fresh fruits and vegetables and most meats are not allowed, with exceptions for some canned items. As for alcohol, you can bring in one liter duty-free (it can be packed securely in your checked luggage, along with any other liquid-containing items).

To bring alcohol (or liquid-packed foods) in your carry-on bag on your flight home, buy it at a duty-free shop at the airport. You'll increase your odds of getting it onto a connecting flight if it's packaged in a "STEB"—a secure, tamper-evident bag. But stay away from liquids in opaque, ceramic, or metallic containers, which usually cannot be successfully screened (STEB or no STEB).

For details on allowable goods, customs rules, and duty rates, visit http://help.cbp.gov.

Sightseeing

Sightseeing can be hard work. Use these tips to make your visits to Ireland's finest sights meaningful, fun, efficient, and painless.

MAPS AND NAVIGATION TOOLS

A good map is essential for efficient navigation while sightseeing. The maps in this book are concise and simple, designed to help you locate recommended destinations, sights, and local TIs, where you can pick up more in-depth maps. Maps with even more detail are sold at newsstands and bookstores.

Train travelers do fine with a simple rail map (available as part of the free Intercity Timetable found at Irish train stations) and city maps from the TI offices. (You can get free maps of Dublin and Ireland from Tourism Ireland before you go; see "Tourist Offices" at the beginning of this chapter.)

You can also use a mapping app on your mobile device. Be aware that pulling up maps or looking up turn-by-turn walking directions on the fly requires an Internet connection: To use this feature, it's smart to get an international data plan (see page 532) or only connect using Wi-Fi. With Google Maps or Apple Maps, it's possible to download a map while online, then go offline and navigate without incurring data-roaming charges, though you can't search for an address or get real-time walking directions. A handful of other apps—including City Maps 2Go, OffMaps, and Navfree—also allow you to use maps offline.

PLAN AHEAD

Set up an itinerary that allows you to fit in all your must-see sights. For a one-stop look at opening hours, see the "At a Glance" side-bars for Dublin, Dingle, and Belfast. Most sights keep stable hours, but you can easily confirm the latest by checking with the TI or visiting museum websites.

Don't put off visiting a must-see sight—you never know when a place will close unexpectedly for a holiday, strike, or restoration. Many museums are closed or have reduced hours at least a few days a year, especially on holidays such as Christmas, New Year's, and Labor Day (first Monday in May). A list of holidays is on page 556; check online for possible museum closures during your trip. In summer, some sights may stay open late; in the off-season, hours may be shorter.

Going at the right time helps avoid crowds. This book offers tips on the best times to see specific sights. Try visiting popular sights very early or very late. Make that first sight of the day the one that is the most physically or mentally demanding, while you've still got wind in your sails. Evening visits are usually peaceful, with fewer crowds.

Study up. To get the most out of the self-guided walks and sight descriptions in this book, read them before you visit.

AT SIGHTS

Here's what you can typically expect:

Entering: Be warned that you may not be allowed to enter if you arrive less than 30 to 60 minutes before closing time. And guards start ushering people out well before the actual closing time, so don't save the best for last.

Many sights have a security check, where you must open your bag or send it through a metal detector. Allow extra time for these lines in your planning. Some sights require you to check daypacks and coats. (If you'd rather not check your daypack, try carrying it tucked under your arm like a purse as you enter.)

Photography: If the museum's photo policy isn't clearly post-ed, ask a guard. Generally, taking photos without a flash or tripod is allowed. Some sights ban photos altogether; others ban selfie sticks.

Temporary Exhibits: Museums may show special exhibits in addition to their permanent collection. Some exhibits are included in the entry price, while others come at an extra cost (which you may have to pay even if you don't want to see the exhibit).

Expect Changes: Artwork can be on tour, on loan, out sick, or shifted at the whim of the curator. Pick up a floor plan as you enter, and ask museum staff if you can't find a particular item.

Audioguides and Apps: Many sights rent audioguides, which generally offer dry-but-useful recorded descriptions (sometimes included with admission). If you bring your own earbuds, you can enjoy better sound and avoid holding the device to your ear. To save money, bring a Y-jack and share one audioguide with your travel partner. Museums and sights often offer free apps that you can download to your mobile device (check their websites).

Services: Important sights may have a reasonably priced on-site café or cafeteria (handy places to rejuvenate during a long visit). The WCs at sights are free and generally clean.

Before Leaving: At the gift shop, scan the postcard rack or thumb through a guidebook to be sure that you haven't overlooked something that you'd like to see.

Every sight or museum offers more than what is covered in this book. Use the information in this book as an introduction—not the final word.

SIGHTSEEING PASSES

Ireland offers two passes (each covering a different set of sights) that can save you money. The first is smart for anyone, and the second works best for two people traveling together. Twosomes who love to sightsee should get both passes.

Heritage Card: This pass gets you into 97 historical monuments, gardens, and parks maintained by the OPW (Office of Public Works) in the Republic of Ireland. It will pay off if you plan on visiting half a dozen or more included sights over the course of your trip (€25, seniors age 60 and older-€20, students-€10, families-€60, covers entry to all Heritage sights for one year, comes with handy map and list of sights' hours and prices, purchase

at the first Heritage sight you visit, cash only, tel. 01/647-6592, www.heritageireland.ie, heritagecard@opw.ie). People traveling by car are most likely to get their money's worth out of the card.

Without the Heritage Card, your costs will add up fast, and

you'll waste time in line (the card moves you through ticket lines more quickly). An energetic sightseer with three weeks in Ireland will probably pay to see nearly all 20 of the following sights (covered in this book):

- Dublin Castle-€7
- Kilmainham Gaol-€9 (Dublin)
- Brú na Bóinne (Knowth and Newgrange tombs and Visitors Centre-€12—Valley of the Boyne)
- Battle of the Boyne-€5
- Hill of Tara-€5 (Valley of the Boyne)
- Old Mellifont Abbey-€5 (Valley of the Boyne)
- Trim Castle-€5 (Valley of the Boyne)
- Glendalough Visitors Centre-€5 (Wicklow Mountains)
- Kilkenny Castle-€8
- Rock of Cashel-€8
- Reginald's Tower-€5 (Waterford)
- Charles Fort-€5 (Kinsale)
- Desmond Castle-€5 (Kinsale)
- Muckross House-€9 (near Killarney)
- Derrynane House-€5 (Ring of Kerry)
- Garnish Island Gardens-€5 (near Kenmare)
- Great Blasket Centre-€5 (near Dingle)
- Ennis Friary-€5 (Ennis)
- Dun Aengus-€5 (Inishmore, Aran Islands)
- Glenveagh Castle and National Park-€7 (Donegal)

Together these sights total €125; a pass saves you €100 (about $110) per person over paying individual entrance fees. Note that scheduled tours given by OPW guides at any of these sites are included in the price of admission—regardless of whether you have the Heritage Card. The card covers no sights in Northern Ireland.

Heritage Island Visitor Attraction Guide: Ambitious travelers covering more ground should seriously consider this €8 essential attractions guide and discount book, which is best bought online (allow 2 weeks for free delivery to North America). It does not overlap with the above Heritage Card sights and gives a variety of discounts (usually 2-for-1 discounts, but occasionally 10-20 percent off) at 88 sights in both the Republic of Ireland and Northern Ireland. This is a great no-brainer deal for two people traveling together—you just need to buy one, so you'll save the cost of the guide after only a couple of stops. (Solo travelers might have to go

PRACTICALITIES

to half a dozen sights before the discounts recoup the initial €8.) At some sites that already have free admission, you may get 10 percent off purchases at their shop or café. Study the full list of sights first (tel. 01/775-3870, www.heritageisland.com). A Heritage Ireland map available for free at Fáilte Ireland TIs offers some discounts at the same sights.

Discounted sights mentioned in this guidebook include:
- Trinity College Library (Book of Kells, Dublin)
- St. Patrick's Cathedral (Dublin)
- Dublin City Hall
- Dublinia
- Guinness Storehouse (Dublin)
- *Jeanie Johnston* Famine Ship (Dublin)
- Irish National Stud (Kildare)
- Gardens of Powerscourt (Enniskerry)
- Avondale House (Wicklow Mountains)
- *Dunbrody* Famine Ship (New Ross)
- Waterford Crystal Visitor Centre
- Blarney Castle (County Cork)
- Burren Centre (Kilfenora)
- Aillwee Cave (Burren)
- Atlantic Edge exhibit (Cliffs of Moher)
- Clare Museum (Ennis)
- Kylemore Abbey (Letterfrack)
- Strokestown Park National Famine Museum (Strokestown)
- Mount Stewart House (near Bangor)
- Titanic Belfast (Belfast)
- Ulster Museum (Belfast)
- Ulster Folk Park and Transport Museum (Cultra)
- Tower Museum (Derry)
- Belleek Pottery Visitors Centre (Belleek)
- Ulster American Folk Park (Omagh)

Sleeping

I favor hotels and restaurants that are handy to your sightseeing activities. Rather than list hotels scattered throughout a city, I choose hotels in my favorite neighborhoods. My recommendations run the gamut, from dorm beds to fancy rooms with all the comforts. Outside of Dublin you can expect to find good doubles for $100-150, including tax and a cooked breakfast.

A major feature of the Sleeping sections of this book is my extensive and opinionated listing of good-value rooms. I like places that are clean, central, relatively quiet at night, reasonably priced, friendly, small enough to have a hands-on owner or manager and stable staff, and run with a respect for Irish traditions. I'm more

PRACTICALITIES

impressed by a convenient location and a fun-loving philosophy than flat-screen TVs and a fancy gym. Most places I recommend fall short of perfection. But if I can find a place with most of these features, it's a keeper.

Book your accommodations well in advance, especially if you want to stay at one of my top listings or if you'll be traveling during busy times. Also reserve in advance for Dublin for any weekend, for Galway during its many peak-season events, and for Dingle throughout July and August. See page 556 for a list of major holidays and festivals throughout Ireland; for tips on making reservations, see page 516.

Some people make reservations as they travel, calling hotels and B&Bs a few days to a week before their arrival. If you anticipate crowds (weekends are worst), on the day you want to check in, call hotels at about 9:00 or 10:00, when the receptionist knows who'll be checking out and which rooms will be available. Some apps—such as HotelTonight.com—specialize in last-minute rooms, often at business-class hotels in big cities.

The Republic of Ireland and Northern Ireland have banned smoking in the workplace (pubs, offices, taxicabs, etc.), but some hotels still have a floor or two of rooms where guests are allowed to smoke. If you don't want a room that a smoker might have occupied before you, let the hotelier know when you make your reservation. All of my recommended B&Bs prohibit smoking. Even in places that allow smoking in the sleeping rooms, breakfast rooms are nearly always smoke-free.

RATES AND DEALS

I've categorized my recommended accommodations based on price, indicated with a dollar-sign rating (see sidebar). The price ranges suggest an estimated cost for a one-night stay in a double room with a private toilet and shower in high season, include a hearty breakfast, and assume you're booking directly with the hotel (not through a booking site, which extracts a commission and logically closes the door on special deals). Room prices can fluctuate significantly with demand and amenities (size, views, room class, and so on), but these relative price categories remain constant.

Room rates are especially volatile at larger hotels that use "dynamic pricing" to predict demand. Rates can skyrocket during festivals and conventions, while business hotels can have deep discounts on weekends when demand plummets. For this reason, of the many hotels I recommend, it's difficult to say which will be the best value on a given day—until you do your homework.

Once your dates are set, check the specific price for your preferred stay at several hotels. You can do this either by comparing prices online on the hotels' own websites, or by emailing several hotels directly and asking for their best rate. Even if you start your search on a booking site such as TripAdvisor or Booking.com, you'll usually find the lowest rates through a hotel's own website. Be aware that if you are using any booking site to secure a room, you will not get the Rick Steves discount when you arrive, as the B&B or hotel has already taken a commission hit from the site you booked on.

Many hotels offer a discount to those who pay cash or stay longer than three nights. To cut costs further, try asking for a cheaper room (for example, with a shared bathroom or no window) or offer to skip breakfast.

Additionally, some accommodations offer a special discount for Rick Steves readers, indicated in this guidebook by the abbreviation "RS%." Discounts vary: Ask for details when you book. Generally, to qualify you must book direct (that is, not through a booking site), mention this book when you reserve, show the book upon arrival, and sometimes pay cash or stay a certain number of nights. In some cases, you may need to enter a discount code (which I've provided in the listing) in the booking form on the hotel's website. Rick Steves discounts apply to readers with ebooks as well as printed books. Understandably, discounts do not apply to promotional rates.

When establishing prices, confirm if the charge is per person or per room (if a price is too good to be true, it's probably per person). Because many places in Ireland charge per person, small groups often pay the same for a single and a double as they would for a triple. In this book, however, room prices are listed per room, not per person.

LODGING VOUCHERS

Many US travel agents sell vouchers for lodging in Ireland. In essence, you're paying ahead of time for your lodging, with the assurance that you'll be staying in B&Bs and guesthouses that live up to certain standards. I don't recommend buying these, since your choices will be limited to only the places in Ireland that accept vouchers. Sure, there are hundreds in the program to choose from. But in this guidebook, I list any place that offers a good value—a useful location, nice hosts, and a comfortable and clean room—regardless of what club they do or don't belong to. Lots of great B&Bs choose not to participate in the voucher program because they have to pay to be part of it, slicing into their already thin profit. And many Irish B&B owners lament the long wait between the date a traveler stays with them and the date the voucher company reimburses them. In short, skip it. The voucher program is just an expensive middleman between you and the innkeeper.

TYPES OF ACCOMMODATIONS

Ireland has a rating system for hotels and B&Bs. These stars and shamrocks are supposed to imply quality, but I find that they mean only that the place sporting symbols is paying dues to the tourist board. These rating systems often have little to do with value: One of my favorite Irish B&Bs (also loved by readers) will never be tourist-board approved because it has no dedicated breakfast room (a strict requirement in the eyes of the board). Instead, guests sit around a large kitchen table and enjoy a lively chat with the friendly hosts as they cook breakfast 10 feet away.

Hotels

Many of my recommended hotels have three floors of rooms and steep stairs; expect good exercise. Elevators are rare except in some hotels, and they're often very small—pack light. If you're concerned about stairs, call and ask about ground-floor rooms or pay for a hotel with a lift (elevator).

Know the terminology: "Twin" means two single beds, and "double" means one double bed. If you'll take either one, let them know, or you might be needlessly turned away. An "en suite" room has a bathroom (toilet and shower/tub) inside the room; a room with a "private bathroom" can mean that the bathroom is all yours, but it's across the hall; and a "standard" room has access to a bathroom down the hall that's shared with other rooms. Figuring there's little difference between "en suite" and "private" rooms, some places charge the same for both. If you want your own bathroom inside the room, request "en suite."

If money's tight, ask for a standard room. You'll almost always have a sink in your room, and as more rooms go "en suite," the hallway bathroom is shared with fewer standard rooms.

Most hotels offer family deals, which means that parents with young children can easily get a room with an extra child's bed or a discount for a larger room. Call to negotiate the price. Teenagers are generally charged as adults. Kids under five sleep almost free.

Note that to be called a "hotel," a place technically must have certain amenities, including a 24-hour reception (though this rule is loosely applied). TVs are standard in rooms.

If you're arriving in the morning, your room probably won't be ready. Drop your bag safely at the hotel and dive right into sightseeing.

Hoteliers can be a good source of advice. Most know their city well, and can assist you with everything from public transit and airport connections to finding a good restaurant, the nearest launderette, or a late-night pharmacy.

Even at the best places, mechanical breakdowns occur: Sinks leak, hot water turns cold, toilets may gurgle or smell, the Wi-Fi goes out, or the air-conditioning dies when you need it most. Report your concerns clearly and calmly at the front desk. For more complicated problems, don't expect instant results.

If you suspect night noise will be a problem (if, for instance, your room is over a rowdy pub), ask for a quieter room in the back or on an upper floor. Pubs are plentiful and packed with revelers on weekend nights. (James Joyce once said it would be a good puzzle to try to walk across Dublin without passing a pub.)

To guard against theft in your room, keep valuables out of sight. Some rooms come with a safe, and other hotels have safes at the front desk. I've never bothered using one.

While it's customary to pay for your room upon departure, it can be a good idea to settle your bill the day before, when you're not in a hurry and while the manager's in. That way you'll have time to discuss and address any points of contention.

Above all, keep a positive attitude. Remember, you're on vacation. If your hotel or B&B is a disappointment, spend more time out enjoying the place you came to see.

Small Hotels and B&Bs

Compared to hotels, bed-and-breakfast places give you double the cultural intimacy for half the price. While you may lose some of the conveniences of a hotel—such as lounges, in-room phones, frequent bedsheet changes, and being able to pay with a credit card—I happily make the trade-off for the lower rates and personal touches. If you have a reasonable but limited budget, skip hotels and go the B&B way. In 2017, you'll generally pay €45-65 (about $50-72) per person for a double room in a B&B in Ireland. Prices include a big cooked breakfast. The amount of coziness, teddies, tea, and biscuits tossed in varies tremendously.

B&Bs range from large guesthouses with 10-15 rooms to small homes renting out a couple of spare bedrooms, but typically

have six rooms or fewer. A "town-house" or "house" is like a big B&B or a small family-run hotel—with fewer amenities but more character than a hotel. The philosophy of the management determines the character of a place more than its size and facilities offered. Avoid places run as a business by absentee owners (their hired hands often don't provide the level of service that pride of ownership brings). My top listings are run by people who enjoy welcoming the world to their breakfast table.

PRACTICALITIES

Book direct. If you buy the lodging vouchers sold by many US travel agents, you'll only be taking money from the innkeeper and putting it in the pocket of a middleman. If you have a local TI book a room for you or use a website like Booking.com, the B&B will pay a 10-15 percent commission. But if you book direct, the B&B gets it all, and you'll have a better chance of getting a discount. I have negotiated special discounts with this book (often for payment in cash, and always for booking direct).

Small hotels and B&Bs come with their own etiquette and quirks. Keep in mind that B&B owners are subject to the whims of their guests—if you're getting up early, so are they; and if you check in late, they'll wait up for you. It's polite to call ahead to confirm your reservation the day before and give them a rough estimate of your arrival time. This allows your hosts to plan their day and run errands before or after you arrive...and also allows them to give you specific directions for driving or walking to their place. If you are arriving past the agreed time, please call and let them know.

A few tips: B&B proprietors are selective as to whom they invite in for the night. At some B&Bs, children are not welcome. Risky-looking people (two or more single men are often assumed to be troublemakers) find many places suddenly full. If you'll be staying for more than one night, you are a "desirable." In popular weekend-getaway spots, you're unlikely to find a place to take you

for Saturday night only. If my listings are full, ask for guidance.

Making Hotel Reservations

Reserve your rooms several weeks or even months in advance—or as soon as you've pinned down your travel dates. Note that some national holidays merit your making reservations far in advance (see page 556).

Requesting a Reservation: It's easiest to book your room through the hotel's website. (For the best rates, always use the hotel's official site and not a booking agency's site.) If there's no reservation form, or for complicated requests, send an email (see facing page for a sample request).

The hotelier wants to know:

- the size of your party and type of rooms you need
- your arrival and departure dates, written European-style—day followed by month and year (for example, 18/06/17 or 18 June 2017); include the total number of nights
- special requests (such as en suite bathroom vs. down the hall, cheapest room, twin beds vs. double bed, quiet room)
- applicable discounts (such as a Rick Steves reader discount, cash discount, or promotional rate).

If you don't get a response to your email, it usually means the hotel is already fully booked...but it could be that an overly aggressive email spam filter blocked the hotel's correspondence. If you don't get an email response from an Irish hotel or B&B, don't assume they are ignoring you. Many innkeepers have shown me emails they sent to travelers—who later complained that they never got a response. To avoid this problem, include an alternate email address (for example, if you're using a Comcast address, also include a Gmail address). Phone the hotel or B&B directly if you haven't heard back within a week.

Confirming a Reservation: Most places will request a credit-card number to hold your room. If they don't have a secure online reservation form—look for the *https*—you can email it (I do), but

(Mentioning this book can help.) Owners usually work together and can call up an ally to land you a bed.

B&Bs serve a hearty "Irish fry" breakfast (for more about B&B breakfasts, see "Eating," later in this chapter). You'll quickly figure out which parts of the "fry" you do and don't like. B&B owners prefer to know this up front, rather than serve you the whole shebang and have to throw out uneaten food. Because your B&B owner is also the cook, there's usually a quite limited time span when breakfast is served (typically about an hour, starting at about 8:00—make sure you know the exact time before you turn in for the night). It's an unwritten rule that guests shouldn't show up at the very end of the breakfast period and expect a full cooked breakfast. If you do arrive at the last minute (or if you need to leave before breakfast is served), most B&B hosts are happy to let you

From:	rick@ricksteves.com
Sent:	Today
To:	info@hotelcentral.com
Subject:	Reservation request for 19-22 July

Dear Hotel Central,

I would like to reserve a room for 2 people for 3 nights, arriving 19 July and departing 22 July. If possible, I would like a quiet room with a double bed and private bathroom inside the room.

Please let me know if you have a room available and the price.

Thank you!
Rick Steves

it's safer to share that confidential info via a phone call or fax.

Canceling a Reservation: If you must cancel, it's courteous—and smart—to do so with as much notice as possible, especially for smaller family-run places. Cancellation policies can be strict; read the fine print or ask about these before you book. Many discount deals require prepayment, with no refunds for cancellations.

Reconfirming a Reservation: Always call or email to reconfirm your room reservation a few days in advance. For B&Bs or very small hotels, I call again on my day of arrival to tell my host what time I expect to get there (especially important if arriving late—after 17:00).

Phoning: For tips on calling hotels overseas, see page 530.

help yourself to cereal, fruit or juice, and coffee; ask politely if it's possible.

Some B&Bs stock rooms with an electric kettle, along with cups, tea bags, and coffee packets (if you prefer decaf, buy a jar at a grocery, and dump the contents into a baggie for easy packing).

B&Bs are not hotels. Think of your host as a friendly acquaintance who's invited you to stay in her home, rather than someone you're paying to wait on you. Americans often assume they'll get new towels each day. The Irish don't. Hang them up to dry and reuse. And pack a washcloth (many Irish B&Bs don't provide them).

Electrical outlets sometimes have switches that turn the current on or off; if your electrical appliance isn't working, flip the switch at the outlet. When you unplug your appliance, don't forget your adapter—most B&Bs have boxes of various adapters and converters that guests have left behind (which is handy if you left yours at the last place).

Most B&Bs come with thin walls and doors. This can make for a noisy night, especially with people walking down the hall to use the bathroom. If you're a light sleeper, bring earplugs. And please be quiet in the halls and in your rooms (gently shut your door, talk softly, and keep the TV volume low)...those of us getting up early will thank you for it.

Virtually all rooms have sinks. You'll likely encounter unusual bathroom fixtures. The "pump toilet" has a flushing handle that doesn't kick in unless you push it just right: too hard or too soft, and it won't go. (Be decisive but not ruthless.) There's also the "dial-a-shower," an electronic box under the showerhead where you'll turn a dial to select the heat of the water, and (sometimes with a separate dial or button) turn on or shut off the flow of water. If you can't find the switch to turn on the shower, it may be just outside the bathroom.

Your B&B bedroom might not include a phone. Some B&B owners will allow you to use their phone, but understandably they don't want to pay for long-distance charges. If you must use their phone, use an international calling card (see page 533) and keep the call short (5-10 minutes max). If you plan to stay in B&Bs and make frequent calls, consider bringing a mobile phone or buying one in Ireland (see page 533). At a B&B, some rooms might have better Wi-Fi reception than others; usually the ground-floor lobby or breakfast room is your best bet.

A few B&B owners are also pet owners. And, while pets are rarely allowed into guest rooms, and B&B proprietors are typically very tidy, those with pet allergies might be bothered. I've tried to list which B&Bs have pets, but if you're allergic, ask about pets when you reserve.

You'll likely need to pay cash for your room. Think ahead so you have enough cash to pay up when you check out.

Big, Cheap, Modern Hotels

Hotel chains—popular with budget tour groups—offer predictably comfortable, no-frills accommodations at reasonable prices. These hotels are popping up in big cities in Ireland. They can be located near the train station, in the city center, on major arterials, and outside the city center. What you lose in charm, you gain in savings.

I can't stress this enough: Check online for the cheapest deals. But be sure to go through the hotel's website rather than an online middleman.

Chain hotels are ideal for families, offering simple, clean, and modern rooms for up to four people (two adults/two children) for

€110-165, depending on the location. Note that couples often pay the same price for a room as do families (up to four). Most rooms have a double bed, single bed, five-foot trundle bed, private shower, WC, TV, and Wi-Fi. Hotels usually have an attached restaurant, good security, an elevator, and a 24-hour staffed reception desk. Of course, they're as cozy as a Motel 6, but many travelers love them. You can book online (be sure to check their websites for deals) or over the phone with a credit card, then pay when you check in. When you check out, just drop off the key, Lee.

The biggies are **Jurys Inn** (call their hotels directly or book online at www.jurysinns.com), **Comfort/Quality Inns** (Republic of Ireland tel. 1-800-500-600, Northern Ireland tel. 0800-444-444, US tel. 877-424-6423, www.choicehotels.com), and **Travelodge** (also has freeway locations for tired drivers, reservation center in Britain tel. 08700-850-950, www.travelodge.co.uk).

Short-Term Rentals

Travelers wanting to slow down and base themselves in one place for extended periods can rent a cottage or an apartment (sometimes called a "flat" in Ireland). Renting an apartment, house, or villa can be a fun and cost-effective way to go local, especially if you plan to settle in one location for four nights or longer. This type of lodging varies greatly, but almost always includes a kitchen and living room. The owners discourage short stays and some require a minimum one-week rental, plus a deposit.

I focus on short-term-stay sleeping recommendations in this book (B&Bs, guesthouses, and hotels), rather than self-catering options. But if a B&B I've listed also offers a worthwhile self-catering option, I'll mention it.

A variety of organizations specialize in this longer-term alternative. Your most reliable source for places that live up to certain standards is Tourism Ireland (www.discoverireland.com). Websites such as www.airbnb.com, www.roomorama.com, and www.vrbo.com also let you browse properties and correspond directly with European property owners or managers. If combing through listings and contacting homeowners sounds like too much effort, consider going through a rental agency such as www.interhomeusa.com or www.rentavilla.com. If you want a place to sleep that's free, Couchsurfing.com is a vagabond's alternative to Airbnb. It lists millions of outgoing members, who host fellow "surfers" in their homes.

Hostels

Ireland has hundreds of hostels of all shapes and sizes. Choose yours selectively; hostels can be historic castles or depressing tenements, serene and comfy or overrun by noisy school groups.

Irish Castle Lodging

The stone castles that dot the Irish landscape are some of the most famous and evocative in the world. Built in the 11th to the 15th centuries, they were the fortified homes of chieftains and Anglo-Norman settlers, designed for defense. Modern-day visitors can get an intimate feel for medieval Irish life by spending the night in one of these fortresses of yore.

These are not the modern, boxy hotels with cheesy crenellated rooflines that call themselves "castles," but the real thing (or in some instances a heavily modified version). The true-to-history castle lodgings are rustic, isolated tower houses, while the modified ones amount to fancy mansion splurges.

Be honest with yourself about how much cushiness you need and don't be swept away with frilly Camelot film-set expectations.

RUSTIC

For an authentic experience, search out a real tower-house castle built by native Gaelic lords in the 1400s. Usually four to six stories high, these age-old fortifications sleep 8 to 12 and are rented to small groups (3 night minimum stay). A visiting cook may prepare meals, but all have self-catering kitchens so you can whip up some medieval fare of your own.

Authenticity comes with surprises, such as the occasional spider, drafty window sill, or flake of medieval dust sprinkling down from original wicker-imprinted ceilings. Canopy beds protect you as you sleep...just like the lord and lady 600 years ago.

You'll carry your bags up tight stone stairways and may have to share a bathroom. Wi-Fi can't handle the three-foot-thick walls, so unplug for a few days. However, floor heating and electrical lighting takes the edge off of "roughing it."

These remote castles don't come with fancy landscaping—your windows will likely overlook bogs or grazing land. Get clear directions and be sure to arrive in daylight. Prices vary wildly depending on number of nights and time of year. Figure €1,000 for two nights and up to €3,000 for a week (give or take a crown jewel). Split that cost by 10 friends and you've got the recipe for a unique, good-value evening à la the 15th century. Turn off the lights, light the candles, stoke up the fireplace, and uncork the wine—a convivial night in a castle can be truly magical.

Three well worth considering can be found on www.historiccastlesofireland.com.

Ballyportry Castle (10 miles north of Ennis in County Clare) was built by a branch of the O'Brien family in the 15th century.

Turin Castle (9 miles east of Cong in County Mayo) was built by the locally powerful De Burgo family in the 13th century.

Ballybur Castle (5 miles south of Kilkenny town in County Kilkenny) was built in the 16th century as the seat of the Comerford clan.

FANCY

Despite their castle-like exteriors, these fancy versions are now

castles in name only. In reality, they are plush, pampered estates with spas and adjacent golf courses. They have all the comforts you could ever expect, and then some.

The current structure may indeed include a smaller fortified castle that once stood alone hundreds of years ago. But then wealthy Romantic-age Anglo-Irish aristocrats built luxurious additions and surrounded them with lush gardens and gurgling fountains. Real fortified castles would never have had the ground-floor bay windows you see on these palaces today.

These dolled-up dream-houses are not really a good value for your money unless you're looking for a fanciful indulgence to celebrate an anniversary or honeymoon. In summer months, don't expect basic room prices below €400 per night. The upside? A chance to live like a privileged character in a Victorian novel for a day or two.

A couple to consider:

Dromoland Castle (www.dromoland.ie, 8 miles south of Ennis or 9 miles north of Shannon Airport) once secretly hosted Beatles John and George as they attempted to hide out during the height of "Beatlemania."

Ashford Castle (www.ashfordcastle.com, 28 miles north of Galway near the town of Cong) has hosted Ron and Nancy Reagan, John Wayne, Maureen O'Hara, and former 007 Pierce Brosnan (for his wedding).

The Good and Bad of Online Reviews

User-generated review sites and apps such as Yelp, Booking. com, and TripAdvisor are changing the travel industry. These sites can give you a consensus of opinions about everything from hotels and restaurants to sights and nightlife. If you scan reviews of a hotel and see several complaints about noise or a rotten location, it tells you something important that you'd never learn from the hotel's own website.

Review sites are only as good as the judgment of their reviewers. While these sites work to weed out bogus users, my hunch is that a significant percentage of user reviews are posted by friends or enemies of the business being reviewed. Ignore high and low grades. Focus on the median.

As a guidebook writer, my sense is that there is a big difference between this uncurated information and a guidebook. A user-generated review is based on the experience of one person, who likely stayed at one hotel and ate at a few restaurants, and doesn't have much of a basis for comparison. A guidebook is the work of a trained researcher who visited many alternatives to assess their relative value. I recently checked out some top-rated user-reviewed hotel and restaurant listings in various towns; when stacked up against their competitors, some were gems, while just as many were duds. Both types of information have their place, and in many ways, they're complementary. If something is well-reviewed in a guidebook, and also gets good ratings on one of these sites, it's likely a winner.

A hostel provides cheap beds in dorms where you sleep alongside strangers for about €25 per night. Travelers of any age are welcome if they don't mind dorm-style accommodations and meeting other travelers. Most hostels offer kitchen facilities, guest computers, Wi-Fi, and a self-service laundry. Hostels almost always provide bedding, but the towel's up to you (though you can usually rent one for a small fee). Family and private rooms are often available.

Independent hostels tend to be easygoing, colorful, and informal (no membership required, www.hostelworld.com). You may pay slightly less by booking direct with the hostel. Ireland's Independent Holiday Hostels (www.hostels-ireland.com) is a network of independent hostels, requiring no membership and welcoming all ages. All IHH hostels are approved by Tourism Ireland.

Official hostels are part of Hostelling International (HI) and share an online booking site (www.hihostels.com). HI hostels typically require that you be a member or pay extra per night.

Eating

Denis Leary once quipped, "Irish food isn't cuisine...it's penance." For years, Irish food was just something you ate to survive rather than to savor. In this country, long known as the "land of potatoes," the diet reflected the economic circumstances. But times have changed. A study in 2010 found that the average Irishman was eating half as many spuds as he had a decade before. You'll find

modern-day Irish cuisine delicious and varied, from vegetables, meat, and dairy products to fresh- and salt-water fish. Try the local specialties wherever you happen to be eating.

The traditional breakfast, the "Irish Fry" (known in the North as the "Ulster Fry"), is a hearty way to start the day—with juice, tea or coffee, cereal, eggs, bacon, sausage, a grilled tomato, sautéed mushrooms, and optional black pudding (made from pigs' blood). Toast is served with butter and marmalade. Home-baked Irish soda bread can be an ambrosial eye-opener for those of us raised on Wonder bread. This meal tides many travelers over until dinner. But there's nothing un-Irish about skipping the "fry"—few locals actually start their day with this heavy traditional breakfast. You can simply skip the heavier fare and enjoy the cereal, juice, toast, and tea (surprisingly, the Irish drink more tea per capita than the British).

When restaurant-hunting, choose a spot filled with locals, not tourists. Venturing even a block or two off the main drag leads to higher-quality food for less than half the price of the tourist-oriented places. Locals eat better at lower-rent locales.

Picnicking saves time and money. Try boxes of orange juice (pure, by the liter), fresh bread (especially Irish soda bread), tasty Cashel blue cheese, meat, a tube of mustard, local-eatin' apples, bananas, small tomatoes, a small tub of yogurt (it's drinkable), rice crackers, trail mix or nuts, plain digestive biscuits (the chocolate-covered ones melt), and any local specialties. At open-air markets and supermarkets, you can get produce in small quantities. Supermarkets often have good deli sections, packaged sandwiches, and sometimes salad bars. Hang on to the half-liter mineral-water bottles (sold everywhere for about €1.50). Buy juice in cheap liter boxes, then drink some and store the extra in your water bottle. I often munch a relaxed "meal on wheels" in a car, train, or bus to save 30 precious minutes for sightseeing.

Tipping: At a sit-down place with table service, tip about 10 percent—unless the service charge is already listed on the bill. If you order at a counter, there's no need to tip.

PRACTICALITIES

Restaurant Price Code

I've assigned each eatery a price category, based on the average cost of a typical main course. Drinks, desserts, and splurge items (steak and seafood) can raise the price considerably.

$$$$ **Splurge:** Most main courses over €25/£16
$$$ **Pricier:** €20-25/£12-16
$$ **Moderate:** €15-20/£8-12
$ **Budget:** Under €15/£8

In the Republic of Ireland, carryout fish-and-chips and other takeout food is **$**; a basic pub or sit-down eatery is **$$**; a gastropub or casual but more upscale restaurant is **$$$**; and a swanky splurge is **$$$$**.

RESTAURANT PRICING

I've categorized my recommended eateries based on price, indicated with a dollar-sign rating (see sidebar). The price ranges suggest the average price of a typical main course—but not necessarily a complete meal. Obviously, expensive items (like steak, seafood), fine wine, appetizers, and dessert can significantly increase your final bill.

The dollar-sign categories also indicate the overall personality and "feel" of a place:

$ Budget eateries include street food, takeaway, order-at-the-counter shops, basic cafeterias, bakeries selling sandwiches, and so on.

$$ Moderate eateries are typically nice (but not fancy) sit-down restaurants, ideal for a straightforward, fill-the-tank meal. Most of my listings fall in this category—great for getting a good taste of the local cuisine on a budget.

$$$ Pricier eateries are a notch up, with more attention paid to the setting, presentation, and cuisine. These are ideal for a memorable meal that's still relatively casual and doesn't break the bank. This category often includes affordable "destination" or "foodie" restaurants.

$$$$ Splurge eateries are dress-up-for-a-special-occasion-swanky—Michelin star-type restaurants, typically with an elegant setting, polished service, pricey and intricate cuisine, and an expansive (and expensive) wine list.

I haven't categorized places where you might assemble a picnic, snack, or graze: supermarkets, delis, ice cream-stands, cafés or bars specializing in drinks, chocolate shops, and so on. At classier restaurants, look for "early-bird specials," which allow you to eat well and affordably, but early (about 17:30-19:00).

PUB GRUB AND BEER

If beer is not your cup of tea, don't wine about it. Pubs are a basic part of the Irish social scene, and whether you're a teetotaler or a beer-guzzler, they should be a part of your travel here. Whether in rural villages or busy Dublin, a pub (short for "public house") is an extended living room where, if you don't mind the stickiness, you can feel the pulse of Ireland.

Smart travelers use pubs to eat, drink, get out of the rain, watch the latest sporting event, and make new friends. Unfortunately, many city pubs have been afflicted with an excess of brass, ferns, and video games. Today the most traditional atmospheric pubs are in Ireland's countryside and smaller towns.

Pub grub gets better every year—it's Ireland's best eating value. But don't expect high cuisine; this is, after all, comfort food. For about $15-20, you'll get a basic hot lunch or dinner in friendly surroundings. Pubs that are attached to restaurants, advertise their food, and are crowded with locals are more likely to have fresh food and a chef than sell lousy microwaved snacks.

Pub menus consist of a hearty assortment of traditional dishes, such as Irish stew (mutton with mashed potatoes, onions, carrots, and herbs), soups and chowders, coddle (bacon, pork sausages, potatoes, and onions stewed in layers), fish-and-chips, collar and cabbage (boiled bacon coated in bread crumbs and brown sugar, then baked and served with cabbage), boxty (potato pancake filled with fish, meat, or vegetables), and champ (potato mashed with milk and onions). Irish soda bread nicely rounds out a meal. In coastal areas, seafood is available, such as mackerel, mussels, and Atlantic salmon. There's seldom table service in Irish pubs. Order drinks and meals at the bar. Pay as you order, and only tip (by rounding up to avoid excess coinage) if you like the service. Don't expect every pub to offer grub. Some only have peanuts and potato chips.

I recommend certain pubs to eat in, and your B&B host is usually up-to-date on the best neighborhood pub grub. Ask for advice (but adjust for nepotism and cronyism, which run rampant).

When you say "a beer, please" in an Irish pub, you'll get a pint of Guinness (the tall blonde in a black dress). If you want a small beer, ask for a glass, which is a half-pint. Never rush your bartender when he's pouring a Guinness. It's an almost-sacred two-step process that requires time for the beer to settle.

The Irish take great pride in their beer. At pubs, long hand pulls are used to draw the traditional, rich-flavored "real ales" up from the cellar. These are the connoisseur's

"My Goodness, My Guinness!"

Every year on March 17, bars around the US serve pint after pint of green beer. But if you go to Ireland on Saint Patrick's Day, the beer is never green. It's black—or actually "dark ruby," according to the Guinness Brewery.

In 1759, Arthur Guinness signed an astounding 9,000-year lease on a dilapidated Dublin brewery. The rent: £45 a year. Competition was fierce among Dublin brewers, and friends of the 34-year-old entrepreneur thought his idea was ridiculous. He began pumping out two varieties of beer—an ale, and a darker "stout porter," so named because it was popular among porters in London. Against big odds, his dark beer thrived. By 1868, Guinness had the largest brewery in the world.

Today, Guinness remains one of the world's largest beer producers, with breweries in 50 countries. Around the world, 10 million pints of Guinness stout are consumed each day (with a few extra on St. Patrick's Day).

Over the years, a clever ad campaign has helped fuel the beer's success. In the 1930s, the brewery was known for its animal cartoons that featured simple but catchy slogans such as, "Guinness is good for you," "My goodness, my Guinness!" and "Have a Guinness when you're tired." Whether or not it's a good idea to drink alcohol when you're fighting fatigue, the slogan certainly helped sell beer.

Guinness stout is known for its dark color and creamy white head. The color and slightly burnt flavor come from roasting the barley before the beer is brewed. The beer is carbonated with nitrous oxide in addition to the usual carbon dioxide, producing the thick white foam on top. Traditionally, Guinness is served at a slightly warmer temperature than most ales and lagers.

Because of the high carbonation, pouring a Guinness takes skill, and ordering one takes patience. To tap a perfect pint, Guinness instructs bartenders to use a "two-part pour." The glass should be tilted at a 45-degree angle and filled to three-quarters capacity. Then you must wait for the surge of bubbles beneath the foam to settle before the glass is filled to the brim. The overall process takes about two minutes.

Several years ago, a Dublin company worked on developing a process to cut down the pouring-and-settling time without disrupting the beer's quality...but Guinness aficionados weren't impressed. A bartender at one of Dublin's oldest pubs told CNN, "Our customers will certainly not go for that. Guinness is a traditional drink and I don't think people will sacrifice that for a little extra speed and efficiency."

PRACTICALITIES

favorites: They're fermented naturally, vary from sweet to bitter, and often have a hoppy or nutty flavor. Experiment with obscure local microbrews (a small but growing presence on the Irish beer scene). Short hand pulls at the bar mean colder, fizzier, mass-produced, and less interesting keg beers. Stout is dark and more bitter, like Guinness. If you think you don't like Guinness, try it in Ireland. It doesn't travel well and is better in its homeland. Murphy's is a very good Guinness-like stout, but a bit smoother and milder. For a cold, refreshing, basic, American-style beer, ask for a lager, such as Harp. Ale drinkers swear by Smithwick's (I know I do). Caffrey's is a satisfying cross between stout and ale. Try the draft cider (sweet or dry)...carefully. Teetotalers can order a soft drink.

Pubs are generally open daily from 11:00 to 23:30 and Sunday from noon to 22:30. Children are served food and soft drinks in pubs (sometimes in a courtyard or the restaurant section). You'll often see signs behind the bar asking that children vacate the premises by 20:00. You must be 18 to order a beer, and the Gardí (police) are cracking down hard on pubs that don't enforce this law.

You're a guest on your first night; after that, you're a regular. A wise Irishman once said, "It never rains in a pub." The relaxed, informal atmosphere feels like a refuge from daily cares. Women traveling alone need not worry—you'll become part of the pub family in no time.

Craic (pronounced "crack"), Irish for "fun" or "a good laugh," is the sport that accompanies drinking in a pub. People are there to talk. To encourage conversation, stand or sit at the bar, not at a table.

In 2004, the Irish government passed a law making all pubs in the Republic smoke-free. Smokers now take their pints outside, turning alleys into covered smoking patios. An incredulous Irishman responded to the law by saying, "What will they do next? Ban drinking in pubs? We'll never get to heaven if we don't die."

It's a tradition to buy your table a round, and then for each person to reciprocate. If an Irishman buys you a drink, thank him by saying, "*Go raibh maith agat*" (guh rov mah UG-ut). Offer him a toast in Irish—"*Slainte*" (SLAWN-chuh), the equivalent of "cheers." A good excuse for a conversation is to ask to be taught a few words of Irish Gaelic.

Traditional Irish Music

Traditional music is alive and popular in pubs throughout Ireland. "Sessions" (musical evenings) may be planned and advertised or impromptu. Traditionally, musicians just congregate and play for the love of it. There will generally be a fiddle, a flute or tin whistle, a guitar, a *bodhrán* (goatskin drum), and maybe an accordion or mandolin. Things usually get going at about 21:30 (but note that Irish punctuality is unpredictable). Last call for drinks is at about 23:30.

The music often comes in sets of three songs. The wind and string instruments embellish melody lines with lots of tight ornamentation. Whoever happens to be leading determines the next song only as the current tune is about to be finished. If he wants to pass on the decision, it's done with eye contact and a nod. A *ceilidh* (KAY-lee) is an evening of music and dance...an Irish hoedown.

Percussion generally stays in the background. The *bodhrán* (BO-run) is played with a small, two-headed club. The performer's hand stretches the skin to change the tone and pitch. You'll sometimes be lucky enough to hear a set of bones crisply played. These are two cow ribs (boiled and dried) that are rattled in one hand like spoons or castanets, substituting for the sound of dancing shoes in olden days.

Watch closely if a piper is playing. The Irish version of bagpipes, the *uilleann* (ILL-in) pipes are played by inflating the airbag (under the left elbow) with a bellows (under the right elbow) rather than with a mouthpiece like the Scottish Highland bagpipes. *Uilleann* is Irish Gaelic for "elbow," and the sound is more melodic, with a wider range than the Highland pipes. The piper fingers his chanter like a flute to create individual notes. When he taps the chanter on his thigh, it closes the end and raises the note one octave. He uses the heel of his right hand to play chords on one of three regulator pipes. It takes amazing coordination to play this instrument well, and the sound can be haunting.

Occasionally, the fast-paced music will stop and one person will sing a lament. Called *sean nos* (Irish Gaelic for "old style"), this slightly nasal vocal style may be a remnant of the ancient storytelling tradition of the bards whose influence died out when Gaelic culture waned 400 years ago. This is the one time when the entire pub will stop to listen as sad lyrics fill the room. Stories—often of love lost, emigration to a faraway land, or a heroic rebel death struggling against English rule—are always heartfelt. Spend a lament studying the faces in the crowd.

A session can be magical or lifeless. If the chemistry is right, it's one of the great Irish experiences. The music churns intensely while members of the group casually enjoy exploring each other's musical styles. The drummer dodges the fiddler's playful bow. Sipping their pints, they skillfully maintain a faint but steady buzz. The floor on the musicians' platform is stomped paint-free, and barmaids scurry artfully through the commotion, gathering towers of empty, cream-crusted glasses. Make yourself right at home, "playing the boot" (tapping your foot) under the table in time with the music. Talk to your neighbor. Locals often have an almost evangelical interest in explaining the music.

Staying Connected

One of the most common questions I hear from travelers is, "How can I stay connected in Europe?" The short answer is: more easily and cheaply than you might think. For a very practical one-hour lecture covering tech issues for travelers, see www.ricksteves.com/travel-talks.

The simplest solution is to bring your own device—mobile phone, tablet, or laptop—and use it just as you would at home (following the tips below, such as connecting to free Wi-Fi whenever possible). Another option is to buy a European SIM card for your mobile phone—either your US phone or one you buy in Europe. Or you can travel without a mobile device and use European landlines and computers to connect. Each of these options is described below.

Because dialing instructions vary between in the Republic and Northern Ireland, carefully read "How to Dial," on the next page. You'll find even more details about staying connected at www.ricksteves.com/phoning.

USING YOUR OWN MOBILE DEVICE IN EUROPE

Without an international plan, typical rates from major service providers (AT&T, Verizon, etc.) for using your device abroad are about $1.70/minute for voice calls, 50 cents to send text messages, 5 cents to receive them, and $10 to download one megabyte of data. At these rates, costs can add up quickly. Here are some budget tips and options.

Use free Wi-Fi whenever possible. Unless you have an unlimited-data plan, you're best off saving most of your online tasks for Wi-Fi. You can access the Internet, send texts, and make voice calls over Wi-Fi.

Many cafés (including Starbucks and McDonald's) have free hotspots for customers; look for signs offering it and ask for the Wi-Fi password when you buy something. You'll also often find

How to Dial

International Calls

Whether phoning from a US landline or mobile phone, or from a number in another European country, here's how to make an international call. I've used recommended hotels in Dublin (tel. 01/679-6500) and in Belfast (tel. 028/9027-1066) as examples.

Initial Zero: Drop the initial zero from international phone numbers—except when calling Italy.

Mobile Tip: If using a mobile phone, the "+" sign can replace the international access code (for a "+" sign, press and hold "0").

US/Canada to Europe

Dial 011 (US/Canada international access code), country code (353 for the Republic of Ireland, 44 for Northern Ireland), and phone number.

▸ To call the Dublin hotel from home, dial 011-353-1-679-6500.
▸ To call the Belfast hotel, dial 011-44-28-9027-1066.

Country to Country Within Europe

Dial 00 (Europe international access code), country code, and phone number.

▸ To call the Dublin hotel, whether from Northern Ireland or elsewhere in Europe, dial 00-353-1-679-6500.
▸ To call the Belfast hotel from the Republic of Ireland or elsewhere in Europe, dial 00-44-28-9027-1066.

Europe to the US/Canada

Dial 00, country code (1 for US/Canada), and phone number.

▸ To call from Europe to my office in Edmonds, Washington, dial 00-1-425-771-8303.

Domestic Calls

To call within the Republic of Ireland or within Northern Ireland (from one Irish landline or mobile phone to another), simply dial the phone number, including the initial 0 if there is one.

▸ To call the Dublin hotel from Wexford, dial 01/679-6500.
▸ To call the Belfast hotel from Derry, dial 028/9027-1066.

More Dialing Tips

Republic of Ireland to Northern Ireland: To avoid international rates when calling from any Republic of Ireland phone number to a landline in Northern Ireland (prefix 028), you can dial 048, then the local number (skipping the access code, country code, and Northern Ireland's area code).

▸ To call the Belfast hotel from a Dublin landline, dial 048-9027-1066.

Dialing from Northern Ireland to Republic of Ireland
From a Northern Ireland phone number, dial 00-353, then the area code without its initial 0, and then the local number.
▶ To call the Dublin hotel from a Belfast number, dial 00-353-1-679-6500.

Irish Phone Numbers: Phone numbers in both the Republic and Northern Ireland can vary in length. I keep things simple by always dialing the full number (including the area code or prefix). Mobile phone numbers in the Republic start with 083, 085, 086, 087, and 089. Mobile phone numbers in Northern Ireland (and the rest of the UK) start with 07. Note that calls to a European mobile phone are more expensive than calls to a landline.

Toll and Toll-Free Calls: In the Republic, numbers starting with 1-800 are toll-free, but numbers starting with 15, 1850, or 0818 are toll numbers. In Northern Ireland, numbers starting with 080 are toll-free, but those beginning with 084, 087, or 03 are inexpensive toll numbers. Numbers beginning with 09 are pricey toll lines. International rates apply to US toll-free numbers dialed from Ireland—they're not free.

More Phoning Help: See www.howtocallabroad.com.

European Country Codes			
Austria	43	Italy	39
Belgium	32	Latvia	371
Bosnia-Herzegovina	387	Montenegro	382
Croatia	385	Morocco	212
Czech Republic	420	Netherlands	31
Denmark	45	Norway	47
Estonia	372	Poland	48
Finland	358	Portugal	351
France	33	Russia	7
Germany	49	Slovakia	421
Gibraltar	350	Slovenia	386
Great Britain	44	Spain	34
Greece	30	Sweden	46
Hungary	36	Switzerland	41
Ireland & N. Ireland	353 / 44	Turkey	90

Wi-Fi at TIs, city squares, major museums, public-transit hubs, and airports, and aboard trains and buses.

Sign up for an international plan. Most providers offer a global calling plan that cuts the per-minute cost of phone calls and texts, and a flat-fee data plan. Your normal plan may already include international coverage (T-Mobile's does).

Before your trip, call your provider or check online to confirm that your phone will work in Europe, and research your provider's international rates. Activate the plan a day or two before you leave, then remember to cancel it when your trip's over.

Minimize the use of your cellular network. When you can't find Wi-Fi, you can use your cellular network to connect to the Internet, text, or make voice calls. When you're done, avoid further charges by manually switching off "data roaming" or "cellular data" (in your device's Settings menu; for help, ask your service provider or Google it). Another way to make sure you're not accidentally using data roaming is to put your device in "airplane" or "flight" mode (which also disables phone calls and texts), and then turn on Wi-Fi as needed.

Don't use your cellular network for bandwidth-gobbling tasks, such as Skyping, downloading apps, and watching YouTube: Save these for when you're on Wi-Fi. Using a navigation app such as Google Maps over a cellular network can take lots of data, so do this sparingly or use it offline.

Limit automatic updates. By default, your device constantly checks for a data connection and updates apps. It's smart to disable these features so your apps will only update when you're on Wi-Fi, and to change your device's email settings from "auto-retrieve" to "manual" (or from "push" to "fetch").

It's also a good idea to keep track of your data usage. On your device's menu, look for "cellular data usage" or "mobile data" and reset the counter at the start of your trip.

Use Skype or other calling/messaging apps for cheaper calls and texts. Certain apps let you make voice or video calls or send texts over the Internet for free or cheap. If you're bringing a tablet or laptop, you can also use them for voice calls and texts. All you have to do is log on to a Wi-Fi network, then contact any of your friends or family members who are also online and signed into the same service. You can make voice and video calls using Skype, Viber, FaceTime, and Google+ Hangouts. If the connection is bad, try making an audio-only call. WhatsApp only offers voice calls.

You can also make voice calls from your device to telephones worldwide for just a few cents per minute using Skype, Viber, or Hangouts if you buy credit first.

To text for free over Wi-Fi, try apps like Google+ Hangouts,

WhatsApp, Viber, Facebook Messenger, and iMessage. Make sure you're on Wi-Fi to avoid data charges.

USING A EUROPEAN SIM CARD IN A MOBILE PHONE

This option works well for those who want to make a lot of voice calls at cheap local rates, and those who need faster connection speeds than their US carrier provides. Either buy a basic cell phone in Europe (as little as $40 from mobile-phone shops anywhere), or bring an "unlocked" US phone (check with your carrier about unlocking it). With an unlocked phone, you can replace the original SIM card (the microchip that stores info about the phone) with one that will work with a European provider.

In Europe, buy a European SIM card. Inserted into your phone, this card gives you a European phone number—and European rates. SIM cards are sold at mobile-phone shops, department-store electronics counters, newsstands, and vending machines. Costing about $5-10, they usually include about that much prepaid calling credit, with no contract and no commitment. A SIM card that also includes data costs (including roaming) will cost $20-40 more for one month of data within the country you bought it. This can be faster than data roaming through your home provider. To get the best rates, buy a new SIM card whenever you arrive in a new country.

I like to buy SIM cards at a mobile-phone shop where there's a clerk to help explain the options and brands. Certain brands—including Lebara and Lycamobile, both of which operate in multiple European countries—are reliable and economical. Ask the clerk to help you insert your SIM card, set it up, and show you how to use it. In some countries you'll be required to register the SIM card with your passport as an antiterrorism measure (which may mean you can't use the phone for the first hour or two).

Find out how to check your credit balance. When you run out of credit, you can top it up at newsstands, tobacco shops, mobile-phone stores, or many other businesses (look for your SIM card's logo in the window), or online.

UNTETHERED TRAVEL: PUBLIC PHONES AND COMPUTERS

It's possible to travel in Europe without a mobile device. You can check email or browse websites using public computers and Internet cafés, and make calls from your hotel room and/or public phones.

Phones in your **hotel room** generally have a fee for placing local and "toll-free" calls, as well as long-distance or international calls—ask for the rates before you dial. Since you're never charged for receiving calls, it's better to have someone from the US call you in your room.

Tips on Internet Security

Using the Internet while traveling brings added security risks, whether you're getting online with your own device or at a public terminal using a shared network. Here are some tips for securing your data:

First, make sure that your device is running the latest version of its operating system and security software, and that your apps are up-to-date. Next, ensure that your device is password- or passcode-protected so thieves can't access it if your device is stolen. For extra security, set passwords on apps that access key info (such as email or Facebook).

On the road, use only legitimate Wi-Fi hotspots. Ask the hotel or café staff for the specific name of their Wi-Fi network, and make sure you log on to that exact one. Hackers sometimes create a bogus hotspot with a similar or vague name (such as "Hotel Europa Free Wi-Fi"). The best Wi-Fi networks require a password. If you're not actively using a hotspot, turn off your device's Wi-Fi connection so it's not visible to others.

Be especially cautious when accessing financial information online. Experts say it's best to use a banking app rather than sign in to your bank's website via a browser (the app is less likely to get hacked). Refrain from logging in to any personal finance sites on a public computer. Even if you're using your own mobile device at a password-protected hotspot, there's a remote chance that a hacker who's logged on to the same network could see what you're doing.

Never share your credit-card number (or any other sensitive information) online unless you know that the site is secure. A secure site displays a little padlock icon, and the URL begins with *https* (instead of the usual *http*).

If these fees are low, hotel phones can be used inexpensively for calls made with cheap international phone cards (sold at many newsstands, street kiosks, tobacco shops, and train stations). You'll either get a prepaid card with a toll-free number and a scratch-to-reveal PIN code, or a code printed on a receipt. Some cards work in both the Republic of Ireland and the UK—confirm before buying a card by checking for both a 1800 access number (used in the Republic of Ireland) and an 0800 access number (for the UK—don't use the 0845, 0870, or 0871 numbers, which cost about 10p per minute).

Phones are rare in **B&Bs,** but if your room has one, the advice above applies. If there's no phone in your B&B room, and you have an important, brief call to make, politely ask your hosts if you can use their personal phone. Ideally use a cheap international phone card with a toll-free access number, or offer to pay your host for the call.

You'll see **public pay phones** in a few post offices and train stations. In the Republic, Telecom Éireann phone cards are sold for €5, €10, or €20 at newsstands, TIs, and post offices. To use the card, take the phone off the hook, insert the card, wait for a dial tone, and dial away. Unlike in the Republic, pay phones in Northern Ireland (and the rest of Britain) don't use dedicated, insertable phone cards; instead, you'll pay with a major credit card (which you insert into the phone—minimum charge for a credit-card call is £1.20) or coins (have a bunch handy; minimum fee is £0.60). These phones are expensive, but they clearly show how your money supply's doing. Only unused coins will be returned, so put in biggies with caution. Avoid using an international phone card at a Northern Ireland pay phone— a surcharge for their use effectively eliminates any savings.

Public computers are easy to find. Many hotels have one in their lobby for guests to use; otherwise you can find them at Internet cafés and public libraries (ask your hotelier or the TI for the nearest location). If typing on a European keyboard, use the "Alt Gr" key to the right of the space bar to insert the extra symbol that appears on some keys. If you can't locate a special character (such as @), simply copy it from a Web page and paste it into your email message.

MAIL

You can mail one package per day to yourself worth up to $200 duty-free from Europe to the US (mark it "personal purchases"). If you're sending a gift to someone, mark it "unsolicited gift." For details, visit www.cbp.gov, select "Travel," and search for "Know Before You Go."

The Irish postal service works fine, but for quick transatlantic delivery (in either direction), consider services such as DHL (www.dhl.com). Get stamps at the neighborhood post office, newsstands within fancy hotels, and some minimarts and card shops. Don't use stamps from the Republic of Ireland on postcards mailed in Northern Ireland (part of the UK), and vice versa.

Transportation

To see all of Ireland, especially the sights with far-flung rural charm, I prefer the freedom of a rental car. Connemara, the Ring of Kerry, the Antrim Coast, County Donegal, County Wexford, and the Valley of the Boyne are really only worth it if you have wheels.

Cars are best for three or more traveling together (especially families with small kids), those packing heavy, and those scouring the countryside. Trains and buses are best for solo travelers, blitz tourists, city-to-city travelers, and those who don't want to drive in Ireland.

Ireland has a good train-and-bus system, though departures are not as frequent as the European norm. Most rail lines spoke

PRACTICALITIES

Ireland Public Transportation

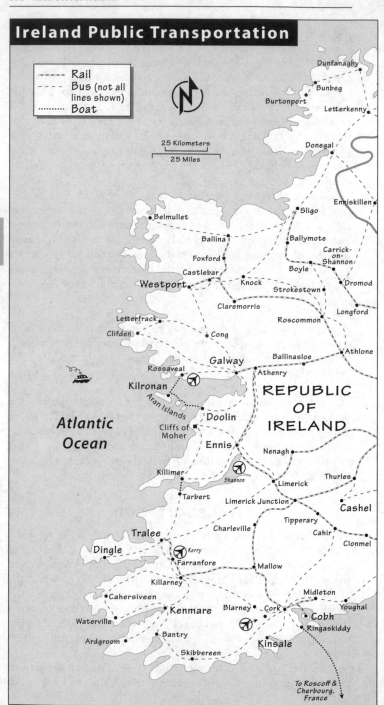

Rail ----
Bus (not all lines shown) ----
Boat ....

N

25 Kilometers
25 Miles

Dunfanaghy
Bunbeg
Burtonport
Letterkenny
Donegal
Enniskillen
Belmullet
Sligo
Ballina
Ballymote
Foxford
Carrick-on-Shannon
Castlebar
Boyle
Westport
Knock
Strokestown
Dromod
Claremorris
Roscommon
Longford
Letterfrack
Cong
Clifden
Athlone
Galway
Ballinasloe
Rossaveal
Athenry

REPUBLIC OF IRELAND

Kilronan
Aran Islands
Doolin
Cliffs of Moher
Ennis
Nenagh
Atlantic Ocean
Killimer
Shannon
Limerick
Thurles
Tarbert
Limerick Junction
Cashel
Charleville
Tipperary
Cahir
Tralee
Clonmel
Dingle
Kerry
Farranfore
Mallow
Killarney
Cahersiveen
Midleton
Blarney
Cork
Youghal
Kenmare
Waterville
Cobh
Bantry
Ringaskiddy
Ardgroom
Kinsale
Skibbereen

To Roscoff & Cherbourg, France

Rail Passes

Prices listed are for 2016 and are subject to change. For the latest prices, details, and train schedules (and easy online ordering), see www.ricksteves.com/rail.

IRELAND PASS

	1st Class Adult	2nd Class Adult	1st Class Saver	2nd Class Saver	1st Class Youth	2nd Class Youth
3 days in 1 month	$221	$178	$193	$152	$178	$146
4 days in 1 month	$265	$213	$231	$182	$213	$174
5 days in 1 month	$306	$246	$266	$210	$246	$201
8 days in 1 month	$412	$331	$359	$282	$331	$270

Covers trains (not buses) in the Republic and Northern Ireland. Stena Line ferries to Britain and Irish Ferries to France are discounted 30% during the validity of the pass. Saver prices are per person based on two or more traveling together. Youth passes are for travelers under 26 only. Up to two kids aged 4-11 travel free with each adult. Additional kids pay youth rate. Under 4 travel free without a ticket. Prices subject to change.

DEALS ONCE YOU GET TO IRELAND:

These local specials are sold at major train stations in Ireland. €1 = about $1.10 US.

Pass Name	Version	Area	Duration	Price
Irish Explorer	Rail only	Republic only	5 out of 15 days	€160

Open Road Pass

This pass covers buses in the Republic of Ireland; see www. buseireann.ie.

Duration	Price	Duration	Price
3 out of 6 days	€60	10 out of 20 days	€175
4 out of 8 days	€77	11 out of 22 days	€192
5 out of 10 days	€93	12 out of 24 days	€209
6 out of 12 days	€110	13 out of 26 days	€225
7 out of 14 days	€126	14 out of 28 days	€242
8 out of 16 days	€143	15 out of 30 days	€258
9 out of 18 days	€159		

Map key:

Approximate point-to-point one-way second-class fares in US dollars by rail (solid line), bus (dashed line), and ferry (dotted line). First class trains cost 50 percent more. Add up fares for your itinerary to see whether a rail and/or bus pass will save you money.

PRACTICALITIES

outward from Dublin, so you'll need to mix in bus transportation to bridge the gaps. Buses pick you up when the trains let you down.

Given the choice of either a bus or a train between the same two towns, I prefer trains, which are sometimes faster and are not subject to the vehicle traffic that can delay buses (although bus travel can be more direct). The best overall source of schedules for public transportation in the Republic of Ireland as well as Northern Ireland—including rail, cross-country and city buses, and Dublin's LUAS transit—is the Tourism Ireland domestic website: www. discoverireland.ie (select "Getting Around" near the bottom of the home page).

I've included a sample itinerary for drivers (with tips and tweaks for those using public transportation) to help you explore Ireland smoothly; you'll find it on page 8.

Trains

To research Irish rail connections online, you need to access two sites. For the Republic of Ireland, use www.irishrail.ie. For Northern Ireland, use www.translink.co.uk. For train schedules on the rest of the European continent, check www.bahn.com (Germany's excellent Europe-wide timetable).

It really pays to buy your train tickets online ahead of time. Fifty-percent online discounts are not unheard of, but online fares fluctuate widely and unpredictably. Online and off, fares are often higher for peak travel on Fridays and Sundays. Remember that the quoted price will be in euros or British pounds. Booking ahead online can also help you avoid long ticket lines in Dublin and elsewhere at busy times. Alternatively, you can book by phone with your credit card or in person at the Iarnrod Éireann Travel Centre in Dublin (Mon-Fri 9:00-17:00, closed Sat-Sun, 35 Lower Abbey Street, tel. 01/703-4070).

It's easy to purchase Irish rail passes in Ireland at major stations (Dublin info tel. 01/836 6222; see chart). But most tourists don't travel enough in Ireland to make a rail or bus pass pay off. Chances are that you'll save money by buying point-to-point tickets as you go. For more information about rail passes, visit the Trains & Rail Passes section of my website at www.ricksteves.com/rail.

Be aware that very few Irish train stations have storage lockers.

Buses

If you opt for public transportation, you'll probably spend more time on Irish buses than Irish trains. But be aware: Public transportation (especially cross-country Irish buses) will likely put your travels into slow motion.

For example, driving across County Kerry from Kenmare to Dingle takes two hours. If you go by bus, the same trip takes four hours—twice as long. The trip by bus requires two transfers (in Killarney and Tralee, each involving a wait for the next bus), and the buses often take a rural milk-run route, making multiple stops along the way. Not every Irish coach trip will involve this kind of delay. They're sometimes more direct than trains; for example, the bus from Dublin to Derry takes four hours with few stops, while the train takes six and requires a change. But in general buses tend to be slower than trains (by about a third), so if you opt to go by coach, be realistic about your itinerary and study the schedules ahead of time. The Bus Éireann Expressway Bus Timetable comes in handy (free, available at some bus stations or online at www.buseireann.ie, bus info toll tel. 1850-836-611).

Buses are much cheaper than trains. Round-trip bus tickets usually cost less than two one-way fares. For example, Tralee to Dingle is €14 one-way and €19 round-trip, and Kinsale to Cork is €9 one-way and €13 round-trip when purchased the day before. The Irish distinguish between "buses" (for in-city travel with lots of stops) and "coaches" (long-distance cross-country runs).

You may need to do some trips partly by train. For instance, if you're going from Dublin to Dingle without a car, you'll need to take a train to Tralee and catch a bus from there. Similarly, to go from Dublin to Kinsale without a car, take a train to Cork and then a bus; and from Dublin to Doolin, take a train to Galway or Ennis and then a bus.

If you're traveling up and down Ireland's west coast, buses are best (or a combination of buses and trains); relying on rail only here is too time-consuming. Note that some rural coach stops are by "request only." This means the coach will drive right on by unless you flag it down by extending your arm straight out, with your palm open.

Bus stations are normally at or near train stations. On some Irish buses, sporting events are piped throughout the bus; have earplugs handy if you prefer a quieter ride.

Some companies offer **backpacker's bus circuits.** These hop-on, hop-off bus circuits take mostly youth hostelers around the country cheaply and easily, with the assumption that they'll be sleeping in hostels along the way. For example, Paddy Wagon cuts Ireland in half and offers three- to six-day "tours" of each half (north and south) that can be combined into one whole tour connecting Dublin, Cork, Killarney, Dingle, Galway, Westport, Donegal, Derry, and Belfast (May-Oct, 5 Beresford Palace, Dublin, tel. 01/823-0822, toll-free from UK tel. 0800-783-4191, www.paddywagontours.com). They also offer day tours to the Giant's Causeway, Belfast, Cliffs of Moher, Glendalough, or Kilkenny.

Students can use their ISIC (student card, www.isic.org) to

get discounts on cross-country coaches (up to 50 percent). Children 5-15 pay half-price on trains, and wee ones under age 5 go free.

RENTING A CAR

Travelers from North America are understandably hesitant when they consider driving in Ireland, where you must drive on the left side of the road. The Irish government statistics say that 10 percent of all car accidents on Irish soil involve a foreign tourist. But careful drivers—with the patient support of an alert navigator—usually get the hang of it by the end of the first day.

Rental companies require you to be at least 21 years old and to have held your license for two years. Drivers under 25 may incur a young-driver surcharge. In the Republic of Ireland, you generally can't rent a car if you're 75 or older (unless you have a note from your doctor), and you'll usually pay extra if you're 70-74. Some companies in Northern Ireland won't rent to anyone over 69. (Note that you can't lease a car in Ireland; you can only rent.)

Research car rentals before you go. It's cheaper to arrange most car rentals from the US. Consider several companies to compare rates. Most of the major US rental agencies (including Avis, Budget, Enterprise, Hertz, and Thrifty) have offices throughout Ireland. Also consider the two major Europe-based agencies, Europcar and Sixt. It can be cheaper to use a consolidator, such as Auto Europe/Kemwel (www.autoeurope.com—or the often cheaper www.autoeurope.eu) or Europe by Car (www.europebycar.com), which compares rates at several companies to get you the best deal—but because you're working with a middleman, it's especially important to ask in advance about add-on fees and restrictions.

Always read the fine print carefully for add-on charges—such as one-way drop-off fees, airport surcharges, or mandatory insurance policies—that aren't included in the "total price." You may need to query rental agents pointedly to find out your actual cost.

For the best deal, rent by the week with unlimited mileage. To save money on fuel, ask for a diesel car. In midsummer expect to pay at least $300 per week (more for an automatic), not including fuel and minimum insurance, for a basic compact-size car (like a Ford Escort 1.3-liter). With full insurance, the price of the same car goes up about $180 per week ($575 for an automatic). Smaller economy-size cars cost about $75 less per week, but they don't feel as smooth on the motorways or as safe on small roads. Minibuses are a great, budget way to go for larger groups (five to nine people). A larger vehicle has more room for luggage, but can be more difficult to park.

Almost all rentals are manual by default, so if you need an automatic, you must request one in advance. Beware that an automatic transmission costs more and is usually more available in larger

PRACTICALITIES

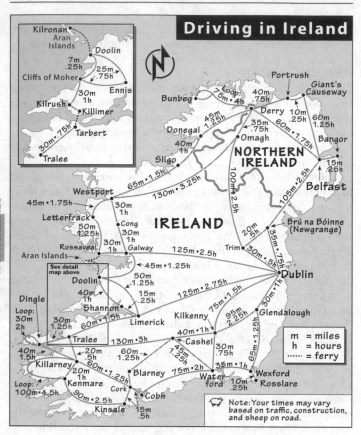

Driving in Ireland

models (which are not as maneuverable on narrow, winding roads). Weigh these considerations against the fact that in Ireland you'll be sitting on the right side of the car and shifting with your left hand... while driving on the left side of the road. The floor pedals are in the same locations as in the US, and the gears are still found in the same basic "H" pattern as at home (i.e., first gear, second, etc.).

Picking Up Your Car: Big companies have offices in most cities; ask whether they can pick you up at your hotel. Small local rental companies can be cheaper but aren't as flexible. Some companies, such as Auto Europe (www.autoeurope.com) or Dan Dooley (www.dan-dooley.ie), will do longer-term rentals at a slight discount.

Compare pickup costs (downtown can be less expensive than the airport—but isn't recommended in congested urban Dublin), and explore drop-off options. Always check the hours of the location you choose: Many rental offices close from midday Saturday until Monday morning and, in smaller towns, at lunchtime.

The Wild Atlantic Way

This Irish tourism marketing initiative offers drivers "the world's longest defined touring route." Stretching 1,550 miles (2,500 km) from Kinsale in the south to Derry in the North, the Wild Atlantic Way snakes along the inlets and outcrops of Ireland's west coast, passing through nine counties and bagging some of the best coastal views along the way. This is the scenic, long-way-around route for travelers not in a hurry. You'll frequently see signs with a large blue "WW" meant to symbolize waves, which tells you that you're driving on a section of the route (www.wildatlanticway.com).

When selecting a location, don't trust the agency's description of "downtown" or "city center." In some cases, a "downtown" branch can be on the outskirts of the city—a long, costly taxi ride from the center. Before choosing, plug the addresses into a mapping website. You may find that the "train station" location is handier. But returning a car at a big city train station or downtown agency can be tricky; get precise details on the car drop-off location and hours and allow ample time to find it.

When you pick up the rental car, check it thoroughly and make sure any damage is noted on your rental agreement. Rental agencies in Europe are very strict when it comes to charging for even minor damage, so be sure to mark everything. Before driving off, find out how your car's gearshift, lights, turn signals, wipers, radio, and fuel cap function, and know what kind of fuel the car takes (diesel vs. unleaded). When you return the car, make sure the agent verifies its condition with you. Some drivers take pictures of the returned vehicle as proof of its condition.

If your trip covers both Ireland and Great Britain (Scotland, England, and Wales), you're better off with two separate car rentals, rather than paying for your car to ride the ferry between the two islands. On an all-Ireland trip, you can drive your rental car from the Republic of Ireland into Northern Ireland, but be aware of drop-off charges (as much as $150-200) if you return it in the North. You'll pay a smaller drop-off charge (as much as $50-100) for picking up the car at one place and dropping it off at another within the same country (even picking up in downtown Dublin and dropping off at Dublin Airport). If you pick up the car in a smaller city, you'll more likely survive your first day on the Irish roads. If

PRACTICALITIES

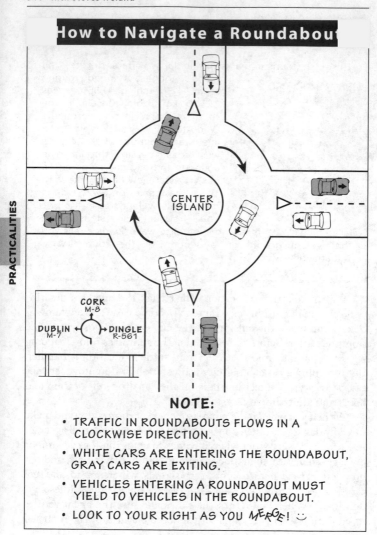

How to Navigate a Roundabout

CENTER ISLAND

CORK
M-8

DUBLIN   DINGLE
M-7   R-561

NOTE:

- TRAFFIC IN ROUNDABOUTS FLOWS IN A CLOCKWISE DIRECTION.
- WHITE CARS ARE ENTERING THE ROUNDABOUT, GRAY CARS ARE EXITING.
- VEHICLES ENTERING A ROUNDABOUT MUST YIELD TO VEHICLES IN THE ROUNDABOUT.
- LOOK TO YOUR RIGHT AS YOU MERGE! ☺

you drop the car off early or keep it longer, you'll be credited or charged at a fair, prorated price.

Navigation Options

If you'll be navigating using your phone or a GPS unit from home, remember to bring a car charger and device mount.

Your Mobile Device: The mapping app on your mobile phone works fine for navigation in Europe, but for real-time turn-by-turn directions and traffic updates, you'll generally need access to a cellular network. A helpful exception is Google Maps, which provides turn-by-turn driving directions and recalibrates even when it's offline.

To use Google Maps offline, you must have a Google account and download your map while you have a data connection. Later—even when offline—you can call up that map, enter your destination, and get directions. View maps in standard view (not satellite view) to limit data demands.

GPS Devices: If you prefer the convenience of a dedicated GPS unit, consider renting one with your car ($10-30/day). These units offer real-time turn-by-turn directions and traffic without the data requirements of an app. Note that the unit may only come loaded with maps for its home country; if you need additional maps, ask. Also make sure your device's language is set to English before you drive off.

A less-expensive option is to bring a GPS device from home. Be aware that you'll need to buy and download European maps before your trip.

Maps and Atlases: Even when navigating primarily with a mobile app or GPS, I always make it a point to have a paper map. The free maps you get from your car-rental company usually don't have enough detail. It's smart to get a road atlas that covers all of Ireland. Ordnance Survey atlases are best (€10 in TIs, gas stations, and bookstores). Drivers, hikers, and cyclists may want more detailed maps for Dingle, Connemara, Donegal, Wexford, the Antrim Coast, the Ring of Kerry, and the Valley of the Boyne (easy to buy locally at TIs).

Car Insurance Options

When you rent a car, you're liable for a very high deductible, sometimes equal to the entire value of the car. Limit your financial risk with one of these two options: Buy Collision Damage Waiver **(CDW)** coverage with a low or zero deductible from the car-rental company, or get coverage through your credit card (more complicated, and few credit cards now offer free coverage in Ireland).

Basic CDW includes a very high deductible (typically $1,000-1,500). Though each rental company has its own variation, basic CDW costs $10-30 a day (figure roughly 30 percent extra) and reduces your liability, but does not eliminate it. When you reserve or pick up the car, you'll be offered the chance to "buy down" the basic deductible to zero (for an additional $10-30/day; this is sometimes called "super CDW" or "zero-deductible coverage").

If you opt for **credit-card coverage** (and your credit card is one of the few accepted for this type of coverage in Ireland), there's a catch. You'll technically have to decline all coverage offered by the car-rental company, which means they can place a hold on your card (which can be up to the full value of the car). In case of dam-

PRACTICALITIES

Tips on Driving

Driving gives you access to the most rural sights and is my favorite mode of transportation in Ireland. Here's what I've learned in the school of hard brakes and adrenaline rushes:

- *The Complete Road Atlas of Ireland* by Ordnance Survey (€10, handy ring-binder style, 1:210,000 scale) is the best Irish road map, and includes translations of Irish place names on the last pages. It covers every road your car can wedge onto. Flipping to the next page of an atlas is easier to manage in a cramped front seat than wrestling with a large, ungainly folding map. Buy the atlas at the first bookstore or gas station you come to.

- Study your map before taking off. Get a sense of the areas you'll be visiting, as road numbers are inconsistent.

- Road signs can be confusing, too little, and too late. There are three main kinds of signs: (1) Those with white lettering on a green background are found on major routes and give distances in kilometers. (2) Signs with black lettering on a white background are older and trickier: Distances shown with a "km" following the numbers are in kilometers, while distances with nothing following the numbers are in miles (and are slowly being phased out). (3) Brown signs with white lettering alert drivers to sights, lodging, and tourist offices.

- Figure out your lights, wipers, and radio before you're on the road. Nervous Nellie navigators will thank you.

- Adjust your side-view mirrors and get in the habit of using them. Narrow roads with lush vegetation are an Irish fact of life. Get comfortable with the sound of vegetation whisking the side of your car.

- Drive with your lights on to make your vehicle more visible.

- Get used to shifting with your left hand. Find reverse...before you need it. (I love the smell of burnt clutch in the morning.)

- The most common mistake is getting a late start, which causes you to rush, which makes you miss turns, which causes you stress, which decreases your enjoyment, which makes your trip feel less like a vacation.

- Car travel in Ireland isn't fast (although more motorways are being built). Plan your itinerary estimating an average speed of 40 mph (1 km per minute). Give your itinerary a reality check by finding distances and driving times between towns on the driving map (see the chart in this chapter) or online (www.google.com/maps or www.viamichelin.com).

- The shortest distance between any two points is usually the motorway (highway). Miss a motorway exit and you can lose 30 minutes.

- Avoid driving in big cities if possible; use ring roads to skirt the congestion. Dublin is clogged with traffic—you'll find sightseeing easier on foot, by bus (particularly the hop-on, hop-off tours), or by taxi. Spare yourself the traffic stress and parking expense (€3/hour) of trying to drive in Dublin.

- When it comes to narrow rural roads, adjust your perceptions of personal space. It's not "my side of the road" or "your side of the road." It's just "the road"—and it's shared as a cooperative adventure. Locals are usually courteous, pulling over against a hedgerow and blinking their headlights for you to pass while they wait. Return the favor when you are closer to a wide spot in the road than they are. Pull over frequently—to let faster drivers pass and to check the map.

- Watch the road ahead and expect a slow tractor, a flock of sheep, a one-lane bridge, and a baby stroller to lurk around the next turn. Honk when approaching blind corners to alert approaching drivers.

- On narrow rural roads, buses always have the right of way, so you'll need to back up to give way.

- Tune in to RTE Radio 1, the national radio station (89 FM), for long drives. Its interviews and music are an education in Irish culture (for more on RTE, see page 20). The same goes for BBC Ulster (94.5 FM) in Northern Ireland.

- Make your road trip fun. Establish a cardboard-box pantry of munchies. Keep a rack of liter boxes of juice in the trunk. Buy some window-cleaner and a roll of paper towels for cleaner sightseeing. A bottle of sparkling mineral water makes a dandy windshield cleaner in a pinch.

- Don't drink and drive. The Gardí (police) set up random checkpoints. If you've had more than one pint, you're legally drunk in Ireland.

- If you're driving between the Republic and Northern Ireland, keep these basic differences in mind: In the Republic, the speed limit is in kilometers per hour, unleaded costs about €1.30 per liter ($5.50 per gallon), and the roads can be bumpy, narrow, and winding. In Northern Ireland, the speed limit is in miles per hour, unleaded costs about £1.20 per liter ($5.20 per gallon), and roads are better maintained.

- Diesel fuel pumps (which are usually green in the US) are black in Ireland. Mixing them up while fueling is a sure way to ruin your day. Insurance doesn't cover this mistake.

- Travelers who want to use designated disabled parking spaces in Ireland can bring their Disabled Persons Parking Card from the US (even though the Irish have a different card that they set on their dashboard). For more information, call the Irish Wheelchair Association at tel. 045/893-094 (from the US, dial 011-353-45-893-094).

age, it can be time-consuming to resolve the charges with your credit-card company. Before you decide on this option, quiz your credit-card company about how it works.

For more on car-rental insurance, see www.ricksteves.com/cdw.

DRIVING

Ireland's new motorways have vastly improved the cross-country driving experience and now link most major cities (Dublin, Belfast, Cork, Waterford, Limerick, and Galway). But the best intimate sites still require you to drive on narrow country lanes.

Note that your US credit and debit cards are unlikely to work at self-service gas pumps and automated parking garages, which use chip-and-PIN credit cards. Even a US card with a chip may not work, since most are chip-and-signature cards, but if you know your PIN, try it anyway. Luckily, the vast majority of Irish gas stations have a live attendant inside who can process your gas purchase (as long as it's not too late at night). The easiest solution is carrying sufficient cash in euros (pounds in the North).

An Irish Automobile Association membership comes with most rentals (www. theaa.ie). Understand its towing and emergency road-service benefits.

Road Rules: Driving in Ireland is basically wonderful—once you remember to stay on the left and after you've mastered the roundabouts. Don't let a roundabout spook you. After all, you routinely merge into much faster traffic with cars slipping into your blind spot on American highways back home. The traffic in a roundabout has the right-of-way; entering traffic yields (look to your right as you merge). It helps to remember that the driver is always in the center of the road.

STOP AND LEARN THESE ROAD SIGNS

Speed Limit (km/hr) · Yield · No Passing · End of No Passing Zone

Danger · Intersection · Roundabout Ahead · Expressway

No Through Road · No Entry · Restrictions No Longer Apply · No Stopping

Parking · No Parking · Road Narrows · Peace

Be warned: Every year I get a few emails from traveling readers advising me that, for them, trying to drive in Ireland was a nerve-wracking and regrettable mistake. If you want to get a little slack on the roads, try to time your car rental to begin on a Sunday morning when you can acclimate to driving at a mellower pace.

Ferry Information

INTERNATIONAL FERRY CONNECTIONS

Ireland has good ferry connections with Britain and France. Check the websites listed per route below for specifics on price, frequency, and length of journey.

Republic of Ireland

Irish Port	To...	Web Site
Dublin	Liverpool (England)	www.poirishsea.com and www.poferries.com
Dublin	Holyhead (Wales)	www.irishferries.com and www.stenaline.com
Rosslare	Fishguard (Wales)	www.stenaline.com
Rosslare	Pembroke (Wales)	www.irishferries.com
Rosslare	Cherbourg (France)	www.irishferries.com and www.stenaline.com
Rosslare	Roscoff (France)	www.irishferries.com
Ringaskiddy (near Cork)	Roscoff (France)	www.brittanyferries.ie

Northern Ireland

Belfast	Liverpool (England)	www.stenaline.com
Belfast	Cairnryan (Scotland)	www.stenaline.com
Larne (near Belfast)	Troon (Scotland)	www.poirishsea.com
Larne	Cairnryan (Scotland)	www.poirishsea.com

Be aware of typical European road rules; for example, you may not use a mobile phone while driving (unless you have a hands-free headset), and headlights must be on in poor day lighting. In Ireland, you're not allowed to turn left on a red light unless a sign or signal specifically authorizes it, and on motorways it's illegal to pass drivers on the left. Seat belts are mandatory for all, and kids under 12 or under 1.5 meters tall (about 4 feet, 9 inches) must ride in a child-safety seat.

Ask your car-rental company about these rules, or check the US State Department website (www.travel.state.gov, search for your country in the "Learn about your destination" box, then click on "Travel and Transportation").

Speed Limits: Speed limits are 50 kilometers per hour (roughly 30 miles per hour) in towns, 80 kph (approximately 50 mph) on rural roads (such as R-257, R-600, etc.), 100 kph (about 60 mph) on national roads (N-8, N-30, etc.), and 120 kph (roughly 75 mph) on motorways (M-1, M-50, etc.). Note that road-surveillance cameras strictly enforce speed limits. Any driver (including foreigners renting cars) photographed speeding will get a nasty bill in the mail. (Cameras—you'll see the foreboding gray boxes—flash on your rear license plate in order not to invade the privacy of anyone sharing the front seat with someone they shouldn't be with.)

Tolls: The M-50 ring road surrounding Dublin carries a €3.40 toll, paid electronically with an eFlow pass. Get details from your rental-car company at Dublin Airport (see page 29; more details at www.eflow.ie). Many rental car companies will charge you automatically, so if you pay the toll, you're paying twice. Be sure to ask. Other Irish motorways, linking smaller cities farther from Dublin, may carry tolls ranging from €1.40 to €2.90 which must be paid as you pass through (easiest with cash).

Parking: Parking is confusing. One yellow line marked on the pavement means no parking Monday through Saturday during business hours. Double yellow lines mean no parking at any time. Broken yellow lines mean short stops are OK, but you should always look for explicit signs or ask a passerby.

Even in small towns, rather than fight it, I just pull into the most central parking lot I can find. As for street parking, signs along the street will state whether pay-and-display or parking disk laws are in effect for that area. The modern pay-and-display machines are solar-powered and placed regularly along the street (about six feet tall, look for blue circle with white letter *P*). I keep some extra coins in the ashtray for these machines (no change given for large coins). The use of parking disks is less common these days, but if you need disks, they're sold at nearby shops. You buy one disk for each hour you want to stay. Scratch off the time you arrived on the disk and put it on your dashboard.

FLIGHTS

The best comparison search engine for both international and intra-European flights is www.kayak.com. For inexpensive flights within Europe, try www.skyscanner.com.

Flying to Europe: Start looking for international flights at least four to six months before your trip, especially for peak-season travel. Depending on your itinerary, it can be efficient to fly into one city and out of another. If your flight requires a connection in Europe, see our hints on navigating Europe's top hub airports at www.ricksteves.com/hub-airports.

Flying Within Europe: If you're considering a train ride that's more than five hours long, a flight may save you both time and money. When comparing your options, factor in the time it takes to get to the airport and how early you'll need to arrive to check in.

Well-known cheapo airlines include easyJet (www.easyjet.com), Aer

Lingus (www.aerlingus.com), Flybe (www.flybe.com), and Ryanair (www.ryanair.com). For flights within Ireland, try Aer Arann, a regional subsidiary of Aer Lingus.

But be aware of the potential drawbacks of flying with a discount airline: nonrefundable and nonchangeable tickets, minimal or nonexistent customer service, pricey and time-consuming treks to secondary airports, and stingy baggage allowances with steep overage fees. If you're traveling with lots of luggage, a cheap flight can quickly become a bad deal. To avoid unpleasant surprises, read the small print before you book. These days you can also fly within Europe on major airlines affordably—and without all the aggressive restrictions—for around $100 a flight.

Flying to the US and Canada: Because security is extra tight for flights to the US, be sure to give yourself plenty of time at the airport. It's also important to charge your electronic devices before you board because security checks may require you to turn them on (see www.tsa.gov for the latest rules).

Ireland's Airports: All direct flights from the US land in either Dublin, Shannon, or Belfast. Cork has become a handy arrival point as well (via connecting flights from London). If you're offered a choice and have no interest in sightseeing in busy, congested Dublin, you'll find Shannon Airport to be a far less stressful entry or exit point into or out of Ireland. Drivers will especially appreciate getting used to the "other side of the road" around rural Shannon, as compared to urban Dublin. Be aware that smaller regional airports may have fewer car-rental offices.

Resources from Rick Steves

Begin your trip at www.ricksteves.com: My mobile-friendly **website** is *the* place to explore Europe. You'll find thousands of fun articles, videos, photos, and radio interviews organized by country; a wealth of money-saving tips for planning your dream trip; monthly travel news dispatches; a collection of more than 30 hours of practical travel talks; my travel blog; my latest guidebook updates (www.ricksteves.com/update); and my free Rick Steves Audio Europe app. You can also follow me on Facebook and Twitter.

Our **Travel Forum** is an immense, yet well-groomed collection of message boards, where our travel-savvy community answers questions and shares their personal travel experiences—and our well-traveled staff chimes in when they can be helpful (www.ricksteves.com/forums).

Our **online Travel Store** offers travel bags and accessories that I've designed specifically to help you travel smarter and lighter. These include my popular bags (rolling carry-on and backpack versions, which I helped design...and live out of four months a year), money belts, totes, toiletries kits, adapters, other accessories, and a wide selection of guidebooks and planning maps.

Choosing the right **rail pass** for your trip—amid hundreds of options—can drive you nutty. Our website will help you find the perfect fit for your itinerary and your budget: We offer easy, one-stop shopping for rail passes, seat reservations, and point-to-point tickets.

Tours: Want to travel with greater efficiency and less stress? We organize tours with more than three dozen itineraries and more than 900 departures reaching the best destinations in this book... and beyond. We offer 8- and 14-day Ireland tours, as well as multiple tours in nearby England, Wales, and Scotland. You'll enjoy great guides, a fun bunch of travel partners (with small groups of 24 to 28 travelers), and plenty of room to spread out in a big, comfy bus when touring between towns. You'll find European adventures to fit every vacation length. For all the details and to get our Tour Catalog, visit www.ricksteves.com or call us at 425/608-4217.

Books: *Rick Steves Ireland 2017* is one of many books in my series on European travel, which includes country guidebooks (such as *Rick Steves Great Britain*, covering nearby Wales, Scotland, and England), city guidebooks (London, Rome, Florence, Paris, etc.), Snapshot guidebooks (excerpted chapters from my country guides), Pocket guidebooks (full-color little books on big cities), "Best of" guidebooks (condensed country guides in a full-color, easy-to-scan format, including Ireland), and my budget-travel skills handbook, *Rick Steves Europe Through the Back Door*. Most of my titles are available as ebooks. My phrase books—for French, Italian, German, Spanish, and Portuguese—are practical and budget-oriented.

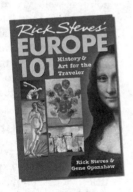

My other books include *Europe 101* (a crash course on art and history designed for travelers); *Mediterranean Cruise Ports* and *Northern European Cruise Ports* (how to make the most of your time in port); and *Travel as a Political Act* (a travelogue sprinkled with tips for bringing home a global perspective). A more complete list of my titles appears near the end of this book.

TV Shows: My public television series, *Rick Steves' Europe*, covers Europe from top to bottom with over 100 half-hour episodes. To watch full episodes online for free, see www.ricksteves.com/tv.

Travel Talks on Video: You can raise your travel I.Q. with video versions of our popular classes (including talks on travel skills, packing smart, cruising, tech for travelers, European art for travelers, travel as a political act, and individual talks covering most European countries). See www.ricksteves.com/travel-talks.

Audio: My weekly public radio show, *Travel with Rick Steves*, features interviews with travel experts from around the world. A complete archive of 10 years of programs (over 400 in all) is available in the radio section of www.ricksteves.com/radio. Most of this audio content is available for free through my Rick Steves Audio Europe app (see page 10).

APPENDIX

Useful Contacts 555
Holidays and Festivals 556
Recommended Books and Films........ 557
Conversions and Climate................ 561
Packing Checklist 563

Useful Contacts

Note that calls beginning with 1800 are free throughout Ireland, but 1850 calls cost the same as local calls.

Emergency Needs
Emergency (Police and Ambulance)
In the Republic of Ireland and Northern Ireland: Tel. 999

US Embassies and Consulates
In the Republic of Ireland: 42 Elgin Road, Dublin, Mon-Fri 8:30-17:00, closed Sat-Sun, tel. 01/630-6200, http://dublin.usembassy.gov
In Northern Ireland: Danesfort House, 223 Stranmillis Road, Belfast, Mon-Fri 8:30-17:00, closed Sat-Sun, tel. 028/9038-6104, after-hours emergency mobile 012-5350-1106, http://belfast.usconsulate.gov

Canadian Embassies
In the Republic of Ireland: 7 Wilton Terrace, Dublin, Mon-Fri 9:00-13:00 & 14:00-16:30; consular and passport services Mon-Fri 9:00-12:00, closed Sat-Sun; tel. 01/234-4000, www.canada.ie
In Northern Ireland: Honorary Consul in Belfast, tel. 028/9754-2405. This office does not offer passport services; instead contact the Canadian High Commission in London (www.unitedkingdom.gc.ca).

Directory Assistance

In the Republic of Ireland

Operator Assistance: Tel. 10 for Ireland, tel. 114 to call outside Ireland

Directory Assistance Within Ireland: Tel. 11811

International Info: Tel. 11818

In Northern Ireland

Operator Assistance: Tel. 100 for Britain, tel. 155 to call outside Britain

Directory Assistance Within Britain: Tel. 192 (£1.50)

International Info: Tel. 153 (£1.50)

Holidays and Festivals

This list includes selected festivals in major cities, plus national holidays observed throughout Ireland in 2017. Many sights and banks close on national holidays—keep this in mind when planning your itinerary. Before planning a trip around a festival, verify its dates by checking the festival's website or the TI site (www.discoverireland.com).

Jan 1	New Year's Day (banks closed)
Jan 25-29	Temple Bar Trad, Dublin (Irish music and culture festival, http://templebartrad.com)
March 16-19	St. Patrick's Day celebration throughout Ireland (parades, drunkenness, 4-day festival in Dublin, www.stpatricksday.ie)
April 14	Good Friday (banks closed)
April 16-17	Easter Sunday and Monday
Late April	International Pan Celtic Festival
May 1	Labor Day; Early May Bank Holiday, Ireland and UK (banks closed)
May 22-30	Fleadh Nua, Ennis (traditional music and dance festival, www.fleadhnua.com)
May 29	Spring Bank Holiday, UK (banks closed)
June 5	June Holiday, Ireland (banks closed)
Mid-June	Bloomsday, Dublin (James Joyce festival, www.jamesjoyce.ie)
Late June	Patrún Festival, Kilronan (*currach* boat races)
Late June	St. John's Eve Bonfire Night (Kilronan)
July 12	Battle of the Boyne anniversary, Northern Ireland (Protestant marches, protests)

Mid- to late July	Galway Arts Festival
Late July–early Aug	Galway Races (horse races, www.galwayraces.com)
Aug 7	August Bank Holiday, Ireland (banks closed)
Early Aug	Dingle Races (horse races, www.dingleraces.ie)
Early-mid-Aug	Dingle Regatta (boat races)
Early-mid-Aug	Puck Fair, Killorglin, Kerry ("Ireland's Oldest Fair" and drink-fest, www.puckfair.ie)
Early-mid-Aug	Féile an Phobail, West Belfast (Irish cultural festival, www.feilebelfast.com)
Aug 14-22	Fleadh Cheoil, Ennis (traditional music festival, www.fleadhcheoil.ie)
Aug 28	Late Summer Bank Holiday, UK only (banks closed)
Late Aug	Rose of Tralee International Festival, Tralee (http://roseoftralee.ie)
Late Aug–Early Sept	Blessing of the Boats, Dingle (maritime festival)
Mid-Sept	Galway Races (www.galwayraces.com)
Late Sept	Galway Oyster Festival (4 days, www.galwayoysterfest.com)
Late Sept–Early Oct	Dingle Food Festival (www.dinglefood.com)
Oct 30	October Bank Holiday, Ireland (banks closed)
Late Oct	Galway Races (www.galwayraces.com)
Dec 25	Christmas holiday, Ireland and UK
Dec 26	St. Stephen's Day, Ireland (religious festival); Boxing Day, UK
Dec 31	New Year's Eve

APPENDIX

Recommended Books and Films

To learn more about Ireland past and present, check out a few of these books or films:

Nonfiction

Angela's Ashes (Frank McCourt, 1996). This evocative memoir documents an Irish family's struggles during the Great Depression.

Are You Somebody? The Accidental Memoir of a Dublin Woman (Nuala O'Faolain, 1996). A woman steps out of the traditional shoes she was always told to fill.

The Back of Beyond: A Search for the Soul of Ireland (James Charles Roy, 2002). Roy, an authority on Irish history, leads a group of Americans on an unconventional tour through the byways of Ireland.

How the Irish Saved Civilization (Thomas Cahill, 1995). Cahill explains how the "island of saints and scholars" changed the course of world history.

Immortal Irishman (Tim Egan, 2016). This well-written biography spans three continents to describe the incredible, passionate, and short life of Thomas Francis Meagher.

Ireland: A Concise History (Máire and Conor Cruise O'Brien, 1972). This is a riveting account of Irish history from pre-Christian Ireland to the Northern Irish civil rights movement.

O Come Ye Back to Ireland (Niall Williams and Christine Breen, 1987). Two New Yorkers adjust to life in a tiny Irish village after leaving their careers for a simpler life.

Round Ireland with a Fridge (Tony Hawks, 1997). For a humorous jaunt through the countryside, read Hawks' account of his attempt to hitchhike around Ireland with a fridge.

A Short History of Ireland (Richard Killeen, 1994). Killeen's well-illustrated book is among the most accessible introductions to Irish history.

To School Through the Fields (Alice Taylor, 1988). In one of the best-selling Irish memoirs of all time, Taylor fondly remembers growing up in a rural Irish town.

Fiction

The Barrytown Trilogy (Roddy Doyle, 1992). This trilogy includes Doyle's first three novels—*The Commitments, The Snapper,* and *The Van*—each capturing the day-to-day lives of working-class Dubliners.

The Bódhran Makers (John B. Keane, 1986). Keane documents the struggles of hard-living farmers in 1950s Ireland.

Circle of Friends (Maeve Binchy, 1990). One of Binchy's many soapy novels, *Circle of Friends* tells the story of a group of friends starting college in Dublin.

Dublin Saga (Edward Rutherfurd, 2004). Rutherfurd's historical saga traces the lives of rich and poor families through key events in Irish history, from A.D. 430 to the fight for independence.

Dubliners (James Joyce, 1914). Joyce's classic short-story collection describes Irish life in the 1900s, told through the experiences of 15 ordinary Dubliners.

Finbar's Hotel and *Ladies' Night at Finbar's Hotel* (Dermot Bolger, 1997/1999). These novels, about a collection of guests at a Dublin hotel, were collaboratively written, with each chapter penned by a different modern Irish author.

Ireland (Frank Delaney, 2004). Delaney's historical epic follows Ronan O'Mara on his journey to find a beloved Irish story-teller.

The Last Prince of Ireland (Morgan Llywelyn, 1992). An Irishman and his clan are determined to hold onto their homeland following the 1601 Battle of Kinsale, in which the Gaelic nobility were defeated by English invaders.

Long Lankin (John Banville, 1970). This collection of short stories by the Man Booker Prize-winning Irish author explores themes of alienation, jealousy, and love lost.

A Star Called Henry (Roddy Doyle, 1999). Doyle's political thriller, set in Ireland during the 1916 Easter Rising, is narrated by the young Henry Smart, a soldier in the Irish Citizen Army.

Trinity (Leon Uris, 1976). Uris dramatizes the sectarian struggles in the decades just prior to modern Irish independence.

Film and TV

Cal (1984). This complicated love story centers on a widow who must cope when her lover is hunted by the Irish Republican Army.

The Commitments (1991). Working-class Dubliners form a soul band in this adaption of Roddy Doyle's popular novel. Other film adaptions of Doyle's books include *The Snapper* (1993) and *The Van* (1996).

Dancing at Lughnasa (1998). This drama following five unmarried sisters in 1930s rural Ireland is based on a play that first opened in Dublin and then on Broadway.

Evelyn (2002). Single dad Pierce Brosnan must fight the Irish courts to keep his kids after being abandoned by his wife.

Far and Away (1992). Tom Cruise and Nicole Kidman star as penniless Irish immigrants seeking their fortune in late 19th century America.

The Field (1990). A farmer fights to keep his land in 1930s Ireland.

Fifty Dead Men Walking (2008). Director Kari Skogland's crime thriller features an IRA informer navigating a brutal world during the Troubles.

In the Name of the Father (1993). Daniel Day-Lewis plays wrongly accused IRA bomber Gerry Conlon in this biopic.

Into the West (1992). Two boys hide their beloved horse in urban Dublin before fleeing cross-country with it in this film written by Jim Sheridan, director of *My Left Foot*.

Leap Year (2009). In this movie set in Dingle (but filmed on the island of Inishmore), Amy Adams plays a woman who travels to Dublin to propose to her boyfriend.

The Magdalene Sisters (2003). Director Peter Mullan tells the story of three unwed Irish mothers struggling to survive an abusive 1960s nunnery.

Man of Aran (1934). Directed by Robert J. Flaherty, this haunting, near-silent documentary about life on the Aran Islands in the early 20th century is a classic.

Michael Collins (1996). Director Neil Jordan's biopic stars Liam Neeson as the famous Irish patriot and revolutionary who was killed in the Irish Civil War.

My Left Foot (1989). Daniel Day-Lewis plays an Irishman with cerebral palsy who learns to write and paint with his left foot.

Odd Man Out (1947). This British film noir, about the early IRA, is set in Northern Ireland with a great scene filmed in Belfast's Crown Bar.

Omagh (2004). "Best Drama" winner of the 2005 British Academy of Film and Television awards, *Omagh* recounts the deadly 1998 IRA bombing that killed 29 people in Northern Ireland.

Once (2006). An Irish street musician joins a Czech classical musician to compose heartfelt melodies in a sensitive tale set in gritty modern Dublin.

Philomena (2013). This poignant but clear-eyed story centers on an Irish woman's search for the son she had to give up.

The Quiet Man (1952). John Wayne plays a disgraced boxer who returns to the Irish village where he was born.

Ryan's Daughter (1970). David Lean's epic WWI love story documents an affair between a married Irish woman and a British officer.

The Secret of Roan Inish (1995). This whimsical and sensitive film explores the Irish and Orcadian folklores of selkies—seals that can shed their skins to become human.

71 (2015). In this true story, a solitary British Army soldier flees on foot through hostile IRA-controlled territory at the height of the Troubles in 1971.

Some Mother's Son (1996). Helen Mirren stars in this movie about families of IRA hunger strikers.

Titanic Town (1998). A brave mother tries to protect her family while living on the bleak front lines of sectarian Belfast during the Troubles.

Veronica Guerin (2003). Cate Blanchett stars as Veronica, an Irish journalist who exposes Dublin's drug lords—and pays the price.

Waking Ned Devine (1998). A deceased villager wins the lottery in this funnier-than-it-sounds comedy that showcases beautiful island landscapes and the wit of the Irish people.

The Wind That Shakes the Barley (2006). Two brothers fight in the Irish Republican Army during the country's struggle for independence from Britain.

Conversions and Climate

NUMBERS AND STUMBLERS

- In Europe, dates appear as day/month/year, so Christmas 2017 is 25/12/17.
- What Americans call the second floor of a building is the first floor in Europe.
- On escalators and moving sidewalks, Europeans keep the left "lane" open for passing. Keep to the right.

METRIC CONVERSIONS

Both the Republic of Ireland and Northern Ireland use the metric system for everything but driving measurements. Weight and volume are typically calculated in metric: A kilogram is 2.2 pounds, and a liter is about a quart. The weight of a person is measured by "stone" (one stone equals 14 pounds). Temperatures are generally given in both Celsius and Fahrenheit.

On the road, the Republic of Ireland is still converting from miles to kilometers, and you'll likely see signs in both (especially in rural destinations). Northern Ireland uses miles and posts speed limits in miles per hour.

1 foot = 0.3 meter	1 square yard = 0.8 square meter
1 yard = 0.9 meter	1 square mile = 2.6 square kilometers
1 mile = 1.6 kilometers	1 ounce = 28 grams
1 centimeter = 0.4 inch	1 quart = 0.95 liter
1 meter = 39.4 inches	1 kilogram = 2.2 pounds
1 kilometer - 0.62 mile	32°F - 0°C

CLOTHING SIZES

When shopping for clothing, use these US-to-Ireland comparisons as general guidelines (but note that no conversion is perfect).

Women: For clothing, add 4 (US women's size 10 = UK size 14). For shoes, subtract 2½ (US size 8 = UK size 5½)

Men: For clothing, US and UK sizes are the same. For shoes, subtract about ½ (US size 9 = UK size 8½)

IRELAND'S CLIMATE

First line, average daily high; second line, average daily low; third line, average days without rain. For more detailed weather statistics for destinations in this book (as well as the rest of the world), check www.wunderground.com.

J	F	M	A	M	J	J	A	S	O	N	D
Dublin											
46°	47°	51°	55°	60°	65°	67°	67°	63°	57°	51°	47°
34°	35°	37°	39°	43°	48°	52°	51°	48°	43°	39°	37°
18	18	21	19	21	19	18	19	18	20	18	17

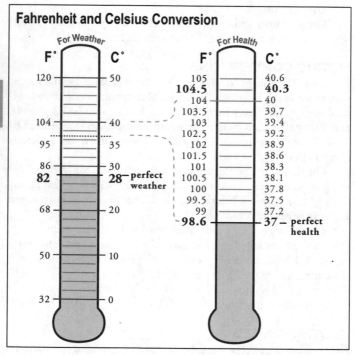

Fahrenheit and Celsius Conversion

Ireland uses both Celsius and Fahrenheit to take its temperature. For a rough conversion from Celsius to Fahrenheit, double the number and add 30. For weather, remember that 28°C is 82°F—perfect. For health, 37°C is just right. At a launderette, 30°C is cold, 40°C is warm (usually the default setting), 60°C is hot, and 95°C is boiling. The room temperature for your air-conditioner should be about 20°C.

Packing Checklist

Whether you're traveling for five days or five weeks, you won't need more than this. Pack light to enjoy the sweet freedom of true mobility.

Clothing

- ❑ 5 shirts: long- & short-sleeve
- ❑ 2 pairs pants (or skirts/capris)
- ❑ 1 pair shorts
- ❑ 5 pairs underwear & socks
- ❑ 1 pair walking shoes
- ❑ Sweater or warm layer
- ❑ Rainproof jacket with hood
- ❑ Tie, scarf, belt, and/or hat
- ❑ Swimsuit
- ❑ Sleepwear/loungewear

Money

- ❑ Debit card(s)
- ❑ Credit card(s)
- ❑ Hard cash ($100-200 in US dollars)
- ❑ Money belt

Documents

- ❑ Passport
- ❑ Tickets & confirmations: flights, hotels, trains, rail pass, car rental, sight entries
- ❑ Driver's license
- ❑ Student ID, hostel card, etc.
- ❑ Photocopies of important documents
- ❑ Insurance details
- ❑ Guidebooks & maps
- ❑ Notepad & pen
- ❑ Journal

Toiletries Kit

- ❑ Basics: soap, shampoo, toothbrush, toothpaste, floss, deodorant, sunscreen, brush/comb, etc.
- ❑ Medicines & vitamins
- ❑ First-aid kit
- ❑ Glasses/contacts/sunglasses

- ❑ Sewing kit
- ❑ Packet of tissues (for WC)
- ❑ Earplugs

Electronics

- ❑ Mobile phone
- ❑ Camera & related gear
- ❑ Tablet/ebook reader/media player
- ❑ Laptop & flash drive
- ❑ Headphones
- ❑ Chargers & batteries
- ❑ Smartphone car charger & mount (or GPS device)
- ❑ Plug adapters

Miscellaneous

- ❑ Daypack
- ❑ Sealable plastic baggies
- ❑ Laundry supplies: soap, laundry bag, clothesline, spot remover
- ❑ Small umbrella
- ❑ Travel alarm/watch

Optional Extras

- ❑ Second pair of shoes (flip-flops, sandals, tennis shoes, boots)
- ❑ Travel hairdryer
- ❑ Picnic supplies
- ❑ Water bottle
- ❑ Fold-up tote bag
- ❑ Small flashlight
- ❑ Mini binoculars
- ❑ Small towel or washcloth
- ❑ Inflatable pillow/neck rest
- ❑ Tiny lock
- ❑ Address list (to mail postcards)
- ❑ Extra passport photos

INDEX

A

Abbey Theatre (Dublin): 41, 67, 81, 487

Abbeys and monasteries: Cong Abbey, 346; Ennis Friary, 289; Hore Abbey, 152; Jerpoint Abbey, 145–146; Kells Priory, 146–147; Kylemore Abbey, 358–359; Monasterboice, 117–118; Old Mellifont Abbey, 116–117; Reasc Monastery, 274; St. Mary's Abbey (Howth), 105

Accommodations. *See* Sleeping *and specific destinations*

Act of Union: 473

Adams, Gerry: 479

Afternoon tea: 89–90

Aillwee Cave: 303–304

Air travel: airfare, 7–8; Aran Islands, 342–343; general information, 550–551

Aircoach: 29, 100

Airlines: 96, 342–343

Airlink: 28–29

Airports: 551; Belfast International Airport, 403; Connemara Regional Airport, 342–343; Cork Airport, 200, 323; Dublin Airport, 28–29, 323; George Best Belfast City Airport, 403; Kerry Airport, 241, 280; Shannon Airport, 288, 293, 323; tourist information, 25

Amphibious vehicle tours: 38

An Plassy shipwreck: 339–340

Ancient Stone Circle (Kenmare): 209

Anglo-Irish Treaty: 55

Antrim Coast: general information, 410, 418–420; Portrush, 411–418; sightseeing, 420–427; transportation, 410–411

Antrim Mountains and glens: 427

Apprentice Boys Memorial Hall (Derry): 435–436

Apps: 10, 13, 20, 508, 544–545

Aran Islands: general information, 325–326; Inisheer, 337–343; Inishmore, 327–336; transportation, 341–343

Archaeological sites: Ancient Stone Circle (Kenmare), 209; Arkin Fort (Killeany), 334; Black Fort (Killeany), 334; Caherconnell ring fort, 302; Cahergal ring fort, 234; Dun Aengus (Inishmore), 331–332; Dunluce Castle, 425–426; fairy fort, 276; Gallarus Oratory, 275; Glendalough, 127–131; Grianan Aileach ring fort, 452; hidden ring fort, 303; Hill of Tara, 50–51, 116; Knowth (Brú na Bóinne), 113; Leacanabuaile ring fort, 234; Newgrange (Brú na Bóinne), 112–113; O'Brien's Castle (Inisheer), 338–339; Poulnabrone Dolmen, 302; ring forts of Kerry, 226–227, 234; Rock of Cashel, 147–154; ruined church of Kilmalkedar, 276; Seven Churches (Inishmore), 332; Spanish Arch (Galway), 314; St. Benen's Church (Killeany), 333–334; St. Enda's Church (Killeany), 333; stone circles, 466–467

Architecture: castles, 468; churches, 469

Ardagh Chalice: 484

Ardmore: 200–201

Arkin Fort (Killeany): 334

Art: 482–484; suppression of native Irish art, 484–485. *See also specific museums*

Ashford Castle: 346–347

Atlantaquaria Aquarium (Salthill): 318

ATMs: 501–502; Belfast, 378; County Clare, 283; Inishmore, 328. *See also* Money

Audio Europe: 10, 553

Audioguides: 508

Avondale House: 131

B

B&Bs: 514–518, 534. *See also* Sleeping

Back Door travel philosophy: 14

Bacon, Francis: 71–72

Baggage: packing checklist, 563

Ballyferriter: 274

Bangor: eating, 408–409; general

information, 404–405; sightseeing, 405–408; sleeping, 408
Bangor Castle: 406
Banks: Derry, 431; Dingle, 242; Inishmore, 328; Kenmare, 206; Kinsale, 180. *See also* ATMs; Money
Barry's Old Time Amusement Arcade (Portrush): 414
Battle of Castlebar: 350
Battle of Kinsale: 470
Battle of the Boyne: 114–115, 471
Beal na Blath: 203
Beara Peninsula: 212–213
Beckett, Samuel: 486
Beehive huts: 271
Beer: 526; Guinness Storehouse (Dublin), 75–77; Smithwick's Experience Kilkenny, 140–141
Behan, Brendan: 487
Belfast: eating, 399–402; general information, 372–373, 374–375, 378–379; at a glance, 384; itinerary, 373–374; sightseeing, 383–397; sleeping, 398–399; tourist information, 375; tours, 380–383; transportation, 375–378, 379–380, 403; Visitor Pass, 378
Belfast Agreement: 478
Belfast International Airport: 403
Belfast Titanic Society: 382–383
Belleek Pottery Visitors Centre: 449–450
Belt Shrine: 52
Bike rental: Belfast, 379; Dingle, 242; Dublin, 31; Galway, 309–312; Inishmore, 327; Kenmare, 208; Kilkenny, 137; Kinsale, 181; Portrush, 414; Westport, 352
Bike tours: Belfast, 382; Dingle Peninsula loop trip, 267–276; Dublin, 37; Kilkenny, 137–138
Biking: Dingle (town), 251; Inishmore, 329–330; Westport, 352
Bishop's Gate (Derry): 437
Bishop's Palace (Waterford): 165–166
Black Death: 465–466
Black Fort (Killeany): 334
Blarney Stone and Castle: 202–203
Blasket Islands: 277–278
Blennerville Windmill (Tralee): 279
Bloody Foreland: 456
Bloody Sunday: 439, 478
Bloody Sunday Monument: 441
Boats and cruises: Belfast, 382–383;

Cliffs of Moher, 296; *currach* boats, 329; Dingle, 243–244; Doolin, 297; Kenmare, 211; Kinsale, 182; *navogue* boats, 329; Valentia Island, 234. *See also* Ferries
Bog Bodies (Dublin): 51–52
Bogs: 356–358
Bogside murals (Derry): 437–444
Book of Kells: 45–49, 464, 484
Books, recommended: 557–559
Bookstores: Belfast, 389; Derry, 431; Dingle, 242; Dublin, 30; Ennis, 288; Kenmare, 208; Kilkenny, 137; Kinsale, 181; Waterford, 160; Westport, 352
Botanic Gardens (Belfast): 394
Boyne Valley. *See* Valley of the Boyne
Brazen Head (Dublin): 82
Brexit: 479
Brian Ború: 465
Britannic: 386
Broighter Hoard: 52
Brú na Bóinne: 110–113
Brú na Bóinne Visitors Center and Museum: 111–112
Bunratty Castle and Folk Park: 283
Burren, the: botany, 303; general information, 300; self-guided driving tour, 300–305; tours, 284–285
Burren Birds of Prey Centre: 304
Burren Centre: 300–301
Bus tours: Antrim Coast, 411; Belfast, 381, 382; the Burren, 284–285; Connemara, 344–345; Derry, 432; Dingle, 243; Dublin, 37–38; Ennis, 288; Galway, 312
Busáras Central Bus Station (Dublin): 27
Buses: Aircoach, 29; Airlink, 28–29; Antrim Coast, 410–411; Belfast, 379, 403; County Clare, 283; Derry, 431, 449; Dingle, 241; Dingle (town), 266; Doolin, 299; Dublin, 27, 31, 95–96; Dun Laoghaire, 99–100; Ennis, 288, 293; Galway, 309, 323; general information, 539–541; Kenmare, 216; Kilkenny, 144; Killarney, 217–218; Portrush, 418; Tralee, 280; Westport, 353–354
Business hours: 499–500

C

Cabs. *See* Taxis

INDEX

Caherconnell ring fort: 302

Cahergal ring fort: 234

Car rental: Derry, 432; driving tips, 546–547; Dublin, 31; general information, 541–544; insurance, 545–548

Car travel: Antrim Coast, 410; Belfast, 375–378; Brú na Bóinne, 111; the Burren, 300–305; Cobh, 195–196, 199–200; Connemara and Mayo driving tour, 345–359; County Clare, 282–283; County Donegal, 451–460; Derry, 431; Dingle, 241; Dingle Peninsula loop trip, 267–276; driving tips, 546–547; in Dublin, 29–30; Dun Laoghaire, 100; Ennis, 288; Galway, 309, 324; Kenmare, 208; map, 542; Military Road over Sally Gap, 127; navigation options, 544–545; parking, 550; Ring of Kerry, 223–228; road rules, 548–549; Rock of Cashel, 148; roundabouts, 544; speed limits, 549–550; three-week itinerary, 8–9; toll roads, 29–30; tolls, 550; Tralee, 280–281; Trim, 119; Wicklow Mountains, 125; Wild Atlantic Way, 543

Carnegie Arts Center (Kenmare): 208

Carrick-a-Rede rope bridge: 424–425

Carrickfergus Castle: 397

Cash. See ATMs; Money

Cashel (town): 155–156

Cashel, Rock of. See Rock of Cashel

Castles: architecture, 468; Ashford Castle, 346–347; Bangor Castle, 406; Blarney Castle, 202–203; Bunratty Castle and Folk Park, 283; Carrickfergus Castle, 397; Desmond Castle, 186–187; Dublin Castle, 59–60; Dunguaire Castle, 304–305; Dunluce Castle, 425–426; Glenveagh Castle and National Park, 453–455; Kilkenny Castle, 138; Leamaneh Castle, 301–302; lodging at, 520–521; Minard Castle, 252–253; O'Brien's Castle (Inisheer), 338–339; Trim Castle, 120–121

Cathedral of St. Nicholas (Galway): 316–317

Cathedral of the Holy Trinity (Waterford): 166

Cell phones: 13, 529–533

Celtic Tiger economic boom: 480

Celts: 461–463

Chalice of Ardagh: 52

Charlemagne: 464

Charles Fort (Kinsale): 183–186

Chester Beatty Library (Dublin): 60–63

Chorister's Hall Medieval Museum (Waterford): 165

Christ Church Cathedral (Dublin): 63–64

Christ Church Cathedral (Waterford): 166–167

Churches and cathedrals: architecture, 469; Cathedral of St. Nicholas (Galway), 316–317; Cathedral of the Holy Trinity (Waterford), 166; Christ Church Cathedral (Dublin), 63–64; Christ Church Cathedral (Waterford), 166–167; Collegiate Church of St. Nicholas (Galway), 313, 319; Cormac's Chapel (Rock of Cashel), 150–151; First Derry Presbyterian Church (Derry), 434–435; Holy Cross Church (Kenmare), 209–211; Long Tower Catholic church (Derry), 437, 447; Saints Peter and Paul Cathedral (Trim), 122; St. Augustine Chapel (Derry), 436; St. Canice's Cathedral (Kilkenny), 140; St. Cavan's Church (Inisheer), 339; St. Columb's Cathedral (Derry), 446–447; St. Kieran's Church (Glendalough), 130–131; St. Mary's Pro-Cathedral (Dublin), 42; St. Patrick's Cathedral (Dublin), 64–65

Cinema. See Films

City Hall (Belfast): 390–392

City Museum (Galway): 314

Claddagh: 315

Claddagh Records (Dublin): 66

Clare, County: 282–299

Clare Museum (Ennis): 289

Cliffs of Moher: 294–296, 297

Climate: 562

Clogher Head: 273–274

Cobblestone Pub (Dublin): 73

Cobh: 178; eating, 198–199; general information, 194–196; sightseeing, 196–197; sleeping, 197–198; tours, 196; transportation, 199–200

Coffin Ship famine memorial: 354

Cois na hAbhna (Ennis): 291
Collegiate Church of St. Nicholas (Galway): 313, 319
Collins, Michael: 54, 203, 477
Cong: 345–350
Cong Abbey: 346
Connemara: bus tours, 344–345; coast, 359; driving tour, 345–359
Connemara National Park: 359
Connemara Regional Airport: 342–343
Connolly, James: 54
Connolly Station (Dublin): 26–27
Consulates: 555
Cork, County: 178
Cork Airport: 200, 323
Cormac's Chapel (Rock of Cashel): 150–151
Corrib River: 315
Costs: airfare, 7–8; Dublin, 30; entertainment, 10; room and board, 9–10; shopping, 10; sightseeing, 10; transportation, 8–9
Country houses: Avondale House, 131; Derrynane House, 228–230; Gardens of Powerscourt, 126–127; Mount Stewart House, 406–407; Rothe House (Kilkenny), 138–140
County Clare: 282–299
County Cork: 178
County Donegal: 428–429, 450–460
County Kilkenny: 135–156
County Mayo: 344–361
County Wexford: 156–158, 169–177
Craggaunowen (Ennis): 289–290
Crean, Tom: 253, 254–255
Credit cards: 12, 502–504. *See also* Money
Croagh Patrick: 354–355
Croke Park Stadium (Dublin): 78–80
Cromwell, Oliver: 171, 174–175, 210, 471
Crooke: 171–172
Cross of Murdock: 484
Crown Liquor Saloon (Belfast): 393
Cruises. *See* Boats and cruises
Currach boats: 329
Curragh Racecourse: 133

D
DART trains: 31, 103
Day trips to Northern Ireland: 373–374
De Valera, Eamon: 54, 477

Debit cards: 12, 502–504. *See also* Money
Derry: eating, 448–449; general information, 428–432; history, 434–435, 439; nightlife, 447–448; self-guided walks, 433–444; sightseeing, 444–447; sleeping, 448; tours, 432; transportation, 431, 449
Derrynane House: 228–230
Desmond Castle: 186–187
Dingle (town): activities, 250–252; eating, 262–266; general information, 239–243, 244; at a glance, 246; history, 248; nightlife, 255–258; self-guided walk, 245–248; shopping, 253–255; sightseeing, 249–253; sleeping, 258–262; tours, 243–244; transportation, 266
Dingle Hillwalking Club: 242–243
Dingle Peninsula: general information, 238–239; loop trip, 267–276; vs. Ring of Kerry, 229
Dining. *See* Eating *and specific destinations*
Discounts: 500; Belfast Visitor Pass, 378; Dublin Pass, 25; Freedom Pass, 32; Heritage Card, 508–509; Heritage Island Visitor Attraction Guide, 509–510; Leap Card/Leap Visitor Card, 32; railpasses, 538; Rambler Pass, 32
Discover Ireland. *See* Tourist information
Distilleries. *See* Whiskey
Donegal, County: 428–429, 450–460
Doo Lough Valley: 355
Doolin: 296–299, 341–342
Doyle, Roddy: 487
Druid Theatre (Galway): 313–314
Dublin: bike tours, 37; Dublin Pass, 25; eating, 89–95; entertainment, 81–82; general information, 22–23, 24–25, 30–31; at a glance, 34–35; itinerary, 23–24; literary life, 70; maps, 25; O'Connell Street stroll, 39–44; pub crawls, 33–36; shopping, 80–81; sightseeing, 44–80; sleeping, 82–89; student tours, 38; tourist information, 25, 499; transit cards, 32; transportation, 25–30, 31–32, 95–97; walking tours, 33, 36–37
Dublin Airport: 28–29, 96, 323
Dublin Bay: 97–107

Dublin Castle: 59–60
Dublin City Hall: 63
Dublin Writers Museum: 66–68
Dublinia: 64
Dun Aengus (Inishmore): 331–332
Dun Laoghaire: eating, 102; general information, 98–99, 100; sightseeing, 101; sleeping, 101–102; transportation, 99–100
Dunbeg Fort: 270–271
Dunbrody Famine Ship (County Wexford): 173–175
Dunfanaghy: 457–458
Dunfanaghy Workhouse: 456–457
Dunguaire Castle: 304–305
Dunluce Castle: 425–426

E

Earls of Kildare: 470
East Pier (Howth): 105–106
Easter Uprising: 54, 481
Eating: Ardmore, 201; Bangor, 408–409; Belfast, 399–402; Cashel, 156; Cobh, 198–199; Cong, 347; costs, 9–10, 524; Derry, 448–449; Dingle (town), 262–266; Doolin, 298; Dublin, 89–95; Dun Laoghaire, 102; Dunfanaghy, 458; Ennis, 292; Galway, 321–323; general information, 523; Howth, 106–107; Inisheer, 340; Inishmore, 336; Kenmare, 215–216; Kilkenny, 143–144; Kinsale, 192–193; Lisdoonvarna, 299; Portmagee, 232; Portrush, 416–417; pub grub and beer, 525–527; tipping, 504–505, 523; Trim, 123–124; Waterford, 168–169; Westport, 353. *See also* Pubs
Éire: 477
Electricity: 500
Elizabeth I (Queen): 470
Embassies: 555
Emergencies: 499, 555
Ennis: eating, 292; general information, 285–288; nightlife, 291; sightseeing, 289–290; sleeping, 291–292; transportation, 293
Ennis Friary: 289
Entertainment: costs, 10; Dublin, 81–82; Kilkenny, 141–142
Exchange rates: 503
Eyre Square (Galway): 315–316

F

Fahrenheit and Celsius conversion: 562
Fáilte Ireland. *See* Tourist information
Fairy fort: 276
Falls Road (Belfast): 388–390
Famine. *See* Great Potato Famine
Father Matthew: 42
Fenians: 474
Ferries: Aran Islands, 341–342; Belfast, 403; Dingle, 244; Doolin, 299; Dublin, 29, 96–97; general information, 549. *See also* Boats and cruises
Festivals: 30, 288, 329, 556–557
Fianna Fáil: 477
The Field (film): 356
Films: 258, 331, 346, 559–561
Fine Gael: 477
First Derry Presbyterian Church (Derry): 434–435
Fishing: 459
Folk music. *See* Music
Food. *See* Eating
Football. *See* Gaelic football
Four Courts (Dublin): 39
Free Derry Corner: 436, 442
Freedom Pass: 32
Fungie (Dingle): 249–250

G

Gaelic Athletic Association: 475
Gaelic Athletic Association Museum (Dublin): 78
Gaelic football: 78–80
Gaelic language: 265, 457, 487–488; Irish pleasantries, 491; Irish-Yankee vocabulary, 492–497; lessons, 331; names, 491; place names, 490; political words, 489; pub and music words, 489
Gaelic League: 475
Gallarus Oratory: 275
Galway: eating, 321–323; general information, 307–312; history, 308; legends and factoids, 314; nightlife, 318–319; sightseeing, 313–318; sleeping, 319–321; tours, 312; transportation, 323–324
Game of Thrones (TV show): 424
Gardens: Botanic Gardens (Belfast), 394; Garden of Remembrance (Dublin), 43–44; Gardens of Powerscourt, 126–127; Japanese

Gardens (Kildare), 134; Muckross House and Farms, 218–220; St. Fiachra's Garden (Kildare), 134
Garnish Island: 212
Genealogy: 197, 198–199, 450
General Post Office (Dublin): 41–42
George Best Belfast City Airport: 403
Giant's Causeway: 420–422
Gigantic: 386
Glasnevin Cemetery and Museum (Dublin): 80
Glenariff Forest Park: 427
Glendalough: 125, 127–131
Glenveagh Castle and National Park: 453–455
Glór Irish Music Centre (Ennis): 291
Gobbins Cliff Path (Belfast): 397
Gogarty's Pub (Dublin): 82
Golden Mile (Belfast): 393
Golfing: 211, 252, 414
Good Friday Peace Accord: 478, 479
Government of Ireland Act: 476
GPO Witness History Exhibit (Dublin): 42, 72
Grafton Street (Dublin): 58, 80, 90–91
Grand Opera House (Belfast): 393
Grattan, Henry: 472
Gray, John: 41
Great Blasket Centre: 278
Great Potato Famine: 74, 473–475; Coffin Ship famine memorial, 354; Strokestown Park National Famine Museum, 360–361
Gresham Hotel (Dublin): 42–43
Grianan Aileach ring fort: 452
Griffith, Arthur: 55
Guides: Belfast, 380; Dublin, 37; reserving ahead, 13. *See also* Tours
Guildhall (Derry): 445
Guinness beer: 526
Guinness Storehouse (Dublin): 75–77
Guinness World Records: 76, 77

H
Ha' Penny Bridge (Dublin): 39, 66
Hall-Walker, William: 132
Hands Across the Divide: 446
Harry Clark Windows of Díseart (Dingle): 249
Hawk Walk: 304
Healy Pass: 212–213
Heaney, Seamus: 486, 487

Henry, Paul: 485
Henry II (King): 465
Henry Street (Dublin): 80
Henry VIII (King): 470
Heritage Card: 508–509
Heritage Centre (Kenmare): 208–209
Heritage Island Visitor Attraction Guide: 509–510
Heuston Station (Dublin): 25–27
Hibernia: 463
Hiking: Cliffs of Moher, 297; Croagh Patrick, 354–355; Dingle, 242–243, 251; Giant's Causeway, 421–422; Howth, 106; Kenmare, 211; Westport, 352
Hill of Tara: 50–51, 116, 461
History: 54–55, 74, 233; Bloody Sunday, 439; Derry, 434–435; Dingle (town), 248; Galway, 308; Ireland, 461–482; Kenmare, 210; Kinsale, 188–189; Northern Ireland, 392; Waterford, 161
Holidays: 556–557
Holy Cross Church (Kenmare): 209–211
Holy Well of St. Bridget: 296
Hook Head Lighthouse: 171–172
Hore Abbey: 152
Horn Head: 459–460
Horse Museum (Kildare): 134
Horse racing: 133
Horseback riding: 211, 251–252
Horses: 132–134
Hospital of St. John the Baptist (Trim): 122
Hostels: 519–522. *See also* Sleeping
Hotel Europa (Belfast): 393
Hotels: 513–514, 518–519. *See also* Sleeping
Howth: eating, 106–107; general information, 103, 104–105; sightseeing, 105–106; sleeping, 106
Hugh Lane Gallery (Dublin): 70–72
Hurling: 78–80, 140
Hurling Museum (Kilkenny): 140

I
Immigration: 481
Inch Strand: 253
Inisheer: 325; eating, 340; general information, 337; sightseeing, 338–340; sleeping, 340
Inishmore: 325; eating, 336; general information, 327–329; sightseeing,

331–334; sleeping, 334–336; tours, 330–331; transportation, 329–330

Insurance: 545–548

Internet: public computers, 535; security, 534

IRA. *See* Irish Republican Army

Ireland. *See* Republic of Ireland

Ireland School of Falconry: 347

Irish Citizens Army: 475

Irish Civil War: 55

Irish Ferries: 29, 97. *See also* Ferries

Irish Film Institute (Dublin): 66

Irish genealogy. *See* Genealogy

Irish Handmade Glass Company (Waterford): 160

Irish langauge. *See* Gaelic language

Irish music. *See* Music

Irish National Heritage Park (County Wexford): 176

Irish National Stud: 132–134

Irish Parliament: 472

Irish Republican Army: 55

Irish Republican Brotherhood: 474

Irish Volunteers: 475

Irish War of Independence: 55

Irish whiskey. *See* Whiskey

Irish Workhouse Centre (Portumna): 305–306

Itineraries: Dublin, 23–24; in Northern Ireland, 373–374; sightseeing priorities, 11; three-week trip by car, 8–9; when to go, 11–12

Iveragh Peninsula. *See* Ring of Kerry

J

James Fort (Kinsale): 186

James I (King): 470

James II (King): 471

James Joyce Cultural Centre (Dublin): 68–70

James Joyce Tower and Museum (Dun Laoghaire): 101

Japanese Gardens (Kildare): 134

Jeanie Johnston Tall Ship and Famine Museum (Dublin): 72–73

Jerpoint Abbey: 145–146

JFK. *See* Kennedy, John F.

Joyce, James: 486; James Joyce Cultural Centre (Dublin), 68–70; James Joyce Tower and Museum (Dun Laoghaire), 101

K

Keating, Sean: 485

Kells Priory: 146–147

Kenmare: eating, 215–216; general information, 205–208; history, 210; nightlife, 211; sightseeing, 208–211; sleeping, 211–215; transportation, 216

Kenmare Lace and Design Centre: 209

Kennedy, John F.: 172–173, 175

Kennedy Homestead (County Wexford): 172–173

Kerry, Ring of. *See* Ring of Kerry

Kerry Airport: 241, 280

Kerry County Museum (Tralee): 279

Key to this book: 3

Kilfenora: 300–301

Kilkenny: eating, 143–144; general information, 135–137; nightlife, 141–142; sightseeing, 138–141; sleeping, 142–143; tours, 137–138; transportation, 136–137, 144

Kilkenny, Statutes of: 466–467

Kilkenny Castle: 138

Kilkenny Design Centre: 138

Killarney: 217–218

Killarney National Park: 220

Kilmainham Gaol (Dublin): 75

Kilmurvey: 332–333

Kinsale: eating, 192–193; general information, 178–181; history, 188–189; nightlife, 187–190; sightseeing, 182–187; sleeping, 190–191; tours, 181–182; transportation, 194

Kinsale Regional Museum (Kinsale): 187

Kinvarra: 304–305

Kissane Sheep Farm: 221

Knock (town): 360

Knowth (Brú na Bóinne): 113

Kylemore Abbey: 358–359

L

Lace: 210; Kenmare Lace and Design Centre, 209

Language. *See* Gaelic language

Larkin, James: 41

Laundry: 500; Bangor, 404–405; Belfast, 379; Derry, 431–432; Dingle, 242; Dublin, 30–31; Dun Laoghaire, 100; Ennis, 288; Galway, 309; Kenmare, 206–208; Kilkenny, 137; Kinsale, 181; Portrush, 412; Trim, 119; Waterford,

160; Westport, 352
Leacanabuaile ring fort: 234
Leamaneh Castle: 301–302
Leap Card/Leap Visitor Card: 32
Leenane: 356
Leenane Sheep and Wool Centre: 356
Liberty Hall (Dublin): 39–41
Libraries: Chester Beatty Library (Dublin), 60–63; National Library (Dublin), 57
Linen Hall Library (Belfast): 393
Lisdoonvarna: 299
Literature: 485–487
Little Museum of Dublin: 59
Local guides. *See* Guides
Lodging. *See* Sleeping *and specific destinations*
Londonderry. *See* Derry
Long Tower Catholic church (Derry): 437, 447
LUAS light rail: 32
Luggage: packing checklist, 563
Lusitania: 187, 197
Lynch's Castle (Galway): 313
Lyric Theatre (Belfast): 394

M
MacBride, John: 352
MacCool, Finn: 463
Macroom: 204
Magdalene Laundries Memorial (Galway): 317
Mail: 535. *See also* Post offices
Man of Aran (film): 331
Marcie Regan's Pub (Trim): 122
Markets: Belfast, 378; Dingle, 242; Dublin, 42, 73, 81; Ennis, 288; Galway, 309; Inishmore, 328; Kilkenny, 137; Kinsale, 180. *See also* Shopping
Massacre of the Planters: 470–471
Mayo, County: 344–361
McCourt, Frank: 487
Meagher, Thomas Francis: 164
Medical help: 499
Meet a Dubliner: 30, 59
Meeting House Square (Dublin): 66
Megalithic art. *See* Archaeological sites
Mellon Centre for Migration Studies: 450
Merrion Square (Dublin): 57–58
Metalworking: 51, 52–53

Metric conversions: 561
Military Road over Sally Gap: 127
Millennium Bridge (Dublin): 39
Millennium Walk (Dublin): 81
Milltown Cemetery (Belfast): 389–390
Milltown House (Dingle Peninsula): 267
Minard Castle: 252–253
Mobile phones and devices: 13, 529–535. *See also* Telephones
Moher. *See* Cliffs of Moher
Monasterboice: 117–118
Monasteries. *See* Abbeys and monasteries
Money: ATMs, 501–502; cash, 501–502; customs and duty, 506; debit and credit cards, 12, 502–504; dynamic currency conversion, 504; exchange rate, 503; getting a VAT refund, 505–506; in Northern Ireland, 371; tipping, 504–505; what to bring, 501
Moore Street Market (Dublin): 42
Mount Errigal: 456
Mount Stewart House: 406–407
Muckross House and Farms: 218–220
Murals: 437–444
Museum of Free Derry: 441
Museum of Treasures Complex (Waterford): 163–166
Museum of Vintage Radio (Howth): 105
Museums: Brú na Bóinne Visitors Center and Museum, 111–112; City Museum (Galway), 314; Clare Museum (Ennis), 289; Craggaunowen (Ennis), 289–290; Dublin Writers Museum, 66–68; Glasnevin Cemetery and Museum (Dublin), 80; Horse Museum (Kildare), 134; Hugh Lane Gallery (Dublin), 70–72; James Joyce Tower and Museum (Dun Laoghaire), 101; *Jeanie Johnston* Tall Ship and Famine Museum (Dublin), 72–73; Kerry County Museum (Tralee), 279; Kinsale Regional Museum (Kinsale), 187; Little Museum of Dublin, 59; Museum of Free Derry, 441; Museum of Treasures Complex (Waterford), 163–166; Museum of Vintage Radio (Howth), 105;

National Gallery (Dublin), 56–57; National Leprechaun Museum (Dublin), 72; National Maritime Museum of Ireland (Dun Laoghaire), 101; National Museum, Archaeology (Dublin), 49–56; National Museum, Natural History (Dublin), 57; National Transport Museum (Howth), 105; North Down Museum (Bangor), 406; Queenstown Story (Cobh), 197; Siege Museum (Derry), 436; Strokestown Park National Famine Museum, 360–361; Titanic Experience (Cobh), 196–197; Tower Museum Derry, 444–445; Transport Museum (Belfast), 395–396; Ulster Museum (Belfast), 393–394; Valentia Heritage Museum, 234

Music: Dingle (town), 255–257; Doolin, 297; Dublin, 81; Dun Laoghaire, 101; Ennis, 291; Galway, 318–319; Inishmore, 331; Kenmare, 211; Kilkenny, 141–142; Kinsale, 190; traditional Irish music, 528–529

N

Napoleonic Tower (Inisheer): 339
Nassau Street (Dublin): 80
National 1798 Centre (County Wexford): 176–177
National Concert Hall (Dublin): 81
National Gallery (Dublin): 56–57
National Leprechaun Museum (Dublin): 72
National Library (Dublin): 57
National Maritime Museum of Ireland (Dun Laoghaire): 101
National Museum: Archaeology (Dublin): 49–56
National Museum: Decorative Arts and History (Dublin): 77–78
National Museum: Natural History (Dublin): 57
National Transport Museum (Howth): 105
Navogue boats: 329
Neale: 350
New Ross: 173–175
Newgrange (Brú na Bóinne): 112–113
Newmills Corn and Flax Mills: 453
Newtown: 122

Nightlife: Derry, 447–448; Dingle (town), 255–258; Ennis, 291; Galway, 318–319; Kenmare, 211; Kilkenny, 141–142; Kinsale, 187–190
North Down Museum (Bangor): 406
North Pier (Bangor): 406
Northern Ireland: almanac, 366–367; general information, 364–369, 371; history, 392; politics, 370; safety, 369–371. *See also specific destinations*
Number Twenty-Nine Georgian House (Dublin): 58
Numbers: 561

O

O'Brien, William Smith: 41
O'Brien's Castle (Inisheer): 338–339
O'Casey, Sean: 487
Oceanworld (Dingle): 250
O'Connell, Daniel: 41, 231, 473
O'Connell Bridge (Dublin): 39–41
O'Connell Street stroll (Dublin): 39–44
Odyssey, the (Belfast): 383
Old Bushmills Distillery: 423–424
Old Jameson Distillery (Dublin): 73
Old Mellifont Abbey: 116–117
Old Midleton Distillery: 201–202
Olympic: 386
O'Neill, Hugh: 470
O'Shea's Merchant Pub (Dublin): 82

P

Packing checklist: 563
Paisley, Ian: 479
Palace Bar (Dublin): 82
Parking. *See* Car travel
Parnell, Charles Stewart: 43, 475
Passes: Belfast Visitor Pass, 378; Dublin Pass, 25; Freedom Pass, 32; Leap Card/Leap Visitor Card, 32; railpasses, 538; Rambler Pass, 32
Passports: 12
Pavilion Theatre (Dun Laoghaire): 101
Peace Bridge (Derry): 446
Peace wall (Belfast): 389
Peace wall (Derry): 437
Pearse, Patrick: 54, 476
Penal Laws: 471–472
Pickie Fun Park (Bangor): 406
Pickpockets: 30

Pitch-and-Putt at the Royal Portrush Golf Club: 414
Plain of Tipperary: 152
Plane travel. *See* Air travel
Planning: costs, 7–10; overview, 4–6; time in Dublin, 23–24; when to go, 11–12
Porterhouse (Dublin): 82
Portmagee: 230–232
Portrush: eating, 416–417; general information, 411–414; sightseeing, 414; sleeping, 414–416; transportation, 418
Portrush Recreation Grounds: 414
Post offices: 535; Belfast, 378; Cobh, 196; Derry, 431; Dingle, 242; Dun Laoghaire, 100; Ennis, 288; Galway, 309; General Post Office (Dublin), 41–42; Howth, 105; Inishmore, 328; Kenmare, 206; Kilkenny, 137; Kinsale, 181; Trim, 119; Waterford, 160; Westport, 352
Potato famine. *See* Great Potato Famine
Poulnabrone Dolmen: 302
Prehistoric sites. *See* Archaeological sites
Pub crawls: Dingle (town), 256–257; Dublin, 33–36
Pubs: Derry, 448; Dingle (town), 246, 247, 253, 255–257; Doolin, 297; Dublin, 33–36, 73, 82; Ennis, 291; Galway, 313, 318–319; Inishmore, 328; Kilkenny, 141–142; Leenane, 356; pub grub and beer, 525–527; Trim, 122. *See also* Eating *and specific destinations*
Puicin Wedge Tomb: 253

Q
Queen's University Student Union (Belfast): 378–379
Queenstown Story (Cobh): 197
The Quiet Man (film): 346

R
Radio: 20
Raidió Teilifís Éireann. *See* RTE
Rail travel. *See* Train travel
Railpasses: 538
Rambler Pass: 32
Rathlin Boathouse Visitor Centre: 426

Rathlin Island: 426–427
Rathlin Island Seabird Centre: 426
Reasc Monastery: 274
Red Hand of Ulster: 396
Reginald's Tower (Waterford): 163–165
Republic of Ireland: 477; almanac, 18; overview, 16–21. *See also specific destinations*
Restaurants. *See* Eating *and specific destinations*
Rick Steves resources: 10, 551–553
Ring forts. *See* Archaeological sites
Ring of Kerry: 205, 215, 217–218, 221–223; vs. Dingle Peninsula, 229; driving tour, 223–228; sightseeing, 228–234
River Corrib: 315
Rock of Cashel: 135; general information, 147–149; self-guided tour, 149–154
Room and board: 9–10. *See also* Eating; Sleeping; *and specific destinations*
Ros Tapestry (County Wexford): 175
Rossaveal: 341
Rossville Street (Derry): 436
Rothe House (Kilkenny): 138–140
RTE: 20

S
Saints Peter and Paul Cathedral (Trim): 122
Sally Gap: 127
Salmon Weir Bridge (Galway): 317
Salthill: 318
Sandy Row (Belfast): 390
Scotland: 419
Seasons: 11–12
Self-guided walks: Bangor, 405–406; Derry, 433–444; Dingle (town), 245–248, 250–251; O'Connell Street stroll (Dublin), 39–44; Rock of Cashel, 149–154. *See also* Walking tours
Seven Churches (Inishmore): 332
Shankill Road (Belfast): 390
Shannon Airport: 288, 293, 323
Shaw, George Bernard: 486
Shopping: Belfast, 378; clothing sizes, 561; costs, 10; customs and duty, 506; Dingle (town), 253–255; Dublin, 80–81; getting a VAT refund, 505–506; Waterford, 160.

See also Markets

Short-term rentals: 519. *See also* Sleeping

Siege Museum (Derry): 436

Siege of Londonderry: 471

Sightseeing: Antrim Coast, 420–427; Bangor, 405–408; Belfast, 383–397; booking online, 12–13; Cobh, 196–197; costs, 10; County Wexford, 171–177; Derry, 444–447; Dingle (town), 249–253; Dublin, 44–80; Dun Laoghaire, 101; Ennis, 289–290; Galway, 313–318; Howth, 105–106; Inisheer, 338–340; Inishmore, 331–334; Kenmare, 208–211; Kilkenny, 138–141; Kinsale, 182–187; maps and navigation tools, 506–507; passes, 508–510; planning ahead, 507; Portrush, 414; priorities, 11; Ring of Kerry, 228–234; at the sites, 507–508; Tralee, 279; Trim, 120–122; Waterford, 162–167; Wicklow Mountains, 126–131

Silver Paten: 52

Sinn Fein party: 54, 475

Skellig Experience Centre: 232–234

Skellig Michael: 235–237, 269

Skype: 532–533

Slea Head (Dingle Peninsula): 271–272

Sleeping: Ardmore, 201; Bangor, 408; Belfast, 398–399; Cashel, 155–156; Cobh, 197–198; costs, 9–10; Derry, 448; Dingle (town), 258–262; Doolin, 298; Dublin, 82–89; Dun Laoghaire, 101–102; Dunfanaghy, 458; Ennis, 291–292; Galway, 319–321; general information, 510–511; Howth, 106; Inisheer, 340; Inishmore, 334–336; Kenmare, 211–215; Kilkenny, 142–143; Kinsale, 190–191; Lisdoonvarna, 299; lodging vouchers, 513; online reviews, 522; Portmagee, 231–232; Portrush, 414–416; rates and deals, 512; reservations, 12, 516–517; Trim, 122–123; types of accommodations, 513–522; Waterford, 167–168; Westport, 352–353

Smartphones. *See* Cell phones; Telephones

Smithfield Village (Dublin): 73

Smithwick's Experience Kilkenny: 140–141

Sneem: 228

Somme Heritage Centre (Bangor): 407–408

Spanish Arch (Galway): 314

Sports and recreation: biking, 251; boating, 211; Gaelic Athletic Association Museum (Dublin), 78; Gaelic football, 78–80; golfing, 211, 252, 414; hiking, 106, 211, 242–243, 251, 297, 421–422; horseback riding, 211, 251–252; hurling, 78–80, 140; swimming, 101

SS *Nomadic*: 387–388

St. Augustine Chapel (Derry): 436

St. Brendan the Navigator: 290, 464

St. Canice's Cathedral (Kilkenny): 140

St. Cavan's Church (Inisheer): 339

St. Columba: 464

St. Columba Heritage Centre (Derry): 447

St. Columbanus: 464

St. Columb's Cathedral (Derry): 446–447

St. Fiachra's Garden (Kildare): 134

St. Kevin's bed (Glendalough): 131

St. Kevin's Cross (Glendalough): 130

St. Kieran's Church (Glendalough): 130–131

St. Mary's Abbey (Howth): 105

St. Mary's Pro-Cathedral (Dublin): 42

St. Patrick: 463–464

St. Patrick's Cathedral (Dublin): 64–65

St. Patrick's Cross (Rock of Cashel): 149–150

St. Stephen's Green (Dublin): 58–59

Staigue Fort: 228

Statutes of Kilkenny: 466–467

Stena Line: 29

Stoker, Bram: 486

Stone circles: 466–467. *See also* Archaeological sites

Strokestown Park National Famine Museum: 360–361

Strongbow: 465

Student tours: 38

Swift, Jonathan: 67, 472, 486

Swimming: 101

Synge, J.M.: 487

T

Tara, Hill of: 50–51

Tara Brooch: 52–53, 463

Taxis: Antrim Coast, 411; Belfast, 379–380, 381–382; Derry, 432; Dingle, 242; Dublin, 29, 32; Dun Laoghaire, 100; Ennis, 288; Galway, 312; Howth, 103; Kenmare, 208; Kinsale, 181; tipping, 505; Trim, 119; Waterford, 160

Telephones: cell (mobile) phones, 13; country calling code, 30, 137, 160, 180, 206, 241, 288, 309, 378, 412, 431; country calling codes, 531; dialing, 530–531; directory assistance, 556; hotel room phones, 533–534; public pay phones, 534–535; SIM cards, 533; useful telephone numbers, 555–556

Television: 20

Temple Bar (Dublin): 65–66, 80–81, 95

Temple Bar Square (Dublin): 65–66

Theater: Belfast, 394; Derry, 448; Dublin, 81; Dun Laoghaire, 101; Galway, 313–314; Kilkenny, 141–142; Waterford, 160

Theft: 30, 499, 504

Thompson Dry Dock and Pump-House (Belfast): 388

Time zones: 499

Tipperary: 135, 152

Tipping: 504–505

TIs. *See* Tourist information

Titanic: 386; in Belfast, 382–383; in Cobh, 196–197

Titanic Belfast: 383–388

Titanic Experience (Cobh): 196–197

Tone, Wolfe: 472

Torc Waterfall: 220

Tour guides. *See* Guides

Tourism Ireland. *See* Tourist information

Tourist information: Bangor, 404; Belfast, 375; Cobh, 195; Derry, 431; Dingle, 240–241; Dublin, 25; Ennis, 285; Galway, 308–309; general information, 498–499; Howth, 104; Inishmore, 328–329; Kenmare, 206; Kilkenny, 136; Kinsale, 180; Portrush, 412; Trim, 119; Waterford, 160; Westport, 351

Tours: Belfast, 380–383; the Burren, 284–285; Cobh, 196; Derry, 432;

Dingle, 243–244; Galway, 312; Inishmore, 330–331; Kenmare, 208; Kilkenny, 137–138; Kinsale, 181–182; from Rick Steves, 552; Rock of Cashel, 147–148; Trim, 119; Valley of the Boyne, 109–110; Wicklow Mountains, 125–126

Tower Museum Derry: 444–445

Train travel: Belfast, 375, 379, 403; Cobh, 200; County Clare, 283; DART, 31, 103; Derry, 431, 449; Dublin, 25–27, 95; Ennis, 288, 293; Galway, 309, 323; general information, 539; Kilkenny, 144; Killarney, 218; LUAS light rail, 32; Portrush, 418; railpasses, 538; Tralee, 280

Tralee: 278–281

Transportation: Antrim Coast, 410–411; Aran Islands, 341–343; Belfast, 375–378, 379–380, 403; Cashel, 156; Cobh, 199–200; costs, 8–9; Derry, 431, 449; Dingle, 241; Dingle (town), 266; Doolin, 299; in Dublin, 25–30; Dublin, 31–32, 95–97; Dun Laoghaire, 99–100; Ennis, 288; Galway, 309, 323–324; general information, 535–539; Howth, 103; Inishmore, 329–330; Kenmare, 216; Kilkenny, 136–137, 144; Killarney, 217–218; Kinsale, 180, 194; Portrush, 418; public transportation map, 536–537; Ring of Kerry, 222; Tralee, 280–281; Trim, 124; Waterford, 169; Westport, 353–354; Wicklow Mountains, 125–126. *See also* Air travel; Boats and cruises; Buses; Car travel; Ferries; Passes; Taxis; Train travel

Travel agencies: 242

Travellers: 357

Trim: eating, 123–124; general information, 118–119; sightseeing, 120–122; sleeping, 122–123; tours, 119; transportation, 124

Trim Castle: 120–121

Trinity College (Dublin): 44–49

Trinity Old Library (Dublin): 45–49

Troubles, the: 370, 478

Tully Walk (Kildare): 134

U

Ulster American Folk Park: 450

Ulster Folk Park and Transport Museum (Belfast): 395–396
Ulster Museum (Belfast): 393–394
Ulster Volunteers: 475
Unionist Orangemen: 478
United Irishmen: 472

V
Valentia Heritage Museum: 234
Valentia Island: 232
Valley of the Boyne: Battle of the Boyne site, 114–115; Brú na Bóinne, 110–113; general information, 108; planning, 109; tours, 109–110; Trim, 118–124
VAT refunds: 505–506
Ventry: 269
Verbal Arts Centre (Derry): 437
Views: Dun Laoghaire, 100; Killarney National Park, 220
Vikings: 53–55, 464–465
Vinegar Hill: 177
Virgin Mary shrines: 361

W
Walking tours: Belfast, 380; the Burren, 284; Cobh, 196; Derry, 432; Dublin, 33, 36–37; Ennis, 288; Galway, 312; Kilkenny, 137; Kinsale, 181–182; Trim, 119; Waterford, 160. *See also* Self-guided walks

War of Independence: 476
Waterford: eating, 168–169; general information, 156–160; history, 161; sightseeing, 162–167; sleeping, 167–168; transportation, 169
Waterford Crystal Visitor Centre: 162–163
Waterloo Bridge (Monet): 70–71
Waterworld (Portrush): 414
Weather: 562
Websites: RTE, 20; www.ricksteves.com, 551–552
West Pier (Howth): 105–106
Westport: 350–354
Wexford, County: 156–158, 169–177
Whiskey: Dingle Distillery, 268; Old Bushmills Distillery, 423–424; Old Jameson Distillery (Dublin), 73; Old Midleton Distillery, 201–202
Wicklow Mountains: 125–131
Wi-Fi: 529–533
Wild Atlantic Way: 543
Wilde, Oscar: 486
William III (King): 471
Worm Hole (Inishmore): 333

Y
Yeats, Jack B.: 485
Yeats, W.B.: 67, 486
Young Irelander: 474

MAP INDEX

Color Maps
Ireland: IV–V
Dublin: VI–VII
Dingle & "Ring of Kerry"
    Peninsulas: VIII–IX

Introduction
Map Legend: 2
Top Destinations in Ireland: 4
Ireland's Best Three-Week Trip by
    Car: 9

Republic of Ireland
Republic of Ireland: 17

Dublin
Dublin: 26–27
Greater Dublin: 28
O'Connell Street Stroll: 40
South Dublin: 46–47
National Museum: Archaeology: 50
North Dublin: 68–69
Dublin Accommodations: 84–85
SE Dublin Hotels: 87
Dublin Restaurants: 92–93
Dun Laoghaire: 98–99
Howth: 104

Near Dublin
Valley of the Boyne: 109
Trim: 121
South of Dublin: 126
Glendalough: 128

Kilkenny & the Rock of Cashel
Kilkenny & Cashel: 136
Kilkenny: 139
Rock of Cashel: 148

Waterford & County Wexford
Waterford: 159
County Wexford: 170

Kinsale & Cobh
Kinsale & Cobh: 179
Kinsale: 184–185
Cobh: 195

Kenmare & the Ring of Kerry
Kenmare: 207
Beara Peninsula: 213
Ring of Kerry Loop Trip: 224–225

Dingle Peninsula
Dingle Area: 239
Dingle Peninsula: 240–241
Dingle Accommodations &
    Services: 260–261
Dingle Restaurants & Pubs: 263
Dingle Peninsula Loop Trip: 268
Gallarus Oratory Area: 275

County Clare & the Burren
County Clare & the Burren: 283
Ennis: 286–287
Cliffs of Moher: 295
The Burren: 301

Galway
Galway: 310–311

Aran Islands
Aran Islands: 326
Inishmore: 328
Kilronan: 335
Inisheer: 338

Connemara & County Mayo
Connemara & County Mayo Loop:
    348–349
Westport; : 351

Northern Ireland
Northern Ireland: 365

Belfast
Greater Belfast: 373
Belfast: 376–377
Central Belfast: 391
South Belfast: 400
Bangor: 405

Portrush & the Antrim Coast
Portrush: 413
Antrim Coast: 422–423

Derry & County Donegal
Derry: 430
Bogside Murals Walk: 438
County Donegal Loop Trip:
    454–455

Ireland: Past & Present
Typical Castle Architecture: 468
Typical Church Architecture: 469
Gaeltacht Regions: 488

Practicalities
Ireland Public Transportation:
    536–537
Driving in Ireland: 542
How to Navigate a Roundabout: 544

Start your trip at

Our website enhances this book and turns

Explore Europe

At rcksteves.com you can browse through thousands of articles, videos, photos and radio interviews, plus find a wealth of money-saving travel tips for planning your dream trip. And with our mobile-friendly website, you can easily access all this great travel information anywhere you go.

TV Shows

Preview the places you'll visit by watching entire half-hour episodes of Rick Steves' Europe (choose from all 100 shows) on-demand, for free.

your travel dreams into affordable reality

Radio Interviews

Enjoy ready access to Rick's vast library of radio interviews covering travel

tips and cultural insights that relate specifically to your Europe travel plans.

Travel Forums

Learn, ask, share! Our online community of savvy travelers is a great resource

for first-time travelers to Europe, as well as seasoned pros. You'll find forums on each country, plus travel tips and restaurant/hotel reviews. You can even ask one of our well-traveled staff to chime in with an opinion.

Travel News

Subscribe to our free Travel News e-newsletter, and get monthly updates from Rick on what's happening in Europe.

Audio Europe™

Pack Light and Right

Gear up for your next adventure at ricksteves.com

Light Luggage

Pack light and right with Rick Steves' affordable, custom-designed rolling carry-on bags, backpacks, day packs and shoulder bags.

Accessories

From packing cubes to moneybelts and beyond, Rick has personally selected the travel goodies that will help your trip go smoother.

Shop at ricksteves.com

Experience maximum Europe

Save time and energy

This guidebook is your independent-travel toolkit. But for all it delivers, it's still up to you to devote the time and energy it takes to manage the preparation and logistics that are essential for a happy trip. If that's a hassle, there's a solution.

Rick Steves Tours

A Rick Steves tour takes you to Europe's most interesting places with great

with minimum stress

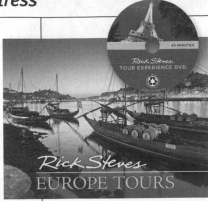

guides and small groups of 28 or less. We follow Rick's favorite itineraries, ride in comfy buses, stay in family-run hotels, and bring you intimately close to the Europe you've traveled so far to see. Most importantly, we take away the logistical headaches so you can focus on the fun.

customers—along with us on 40 different itineraries, from Ireland to Italy to Istanbul. Is a Rick Steves tour the right fit for your travel dreams? Find out at ricksteves.com, where you can also get Rick's latest tour catalog and free Tour Experience DVD.

Join the fun

This year we'll take 18,000 free-spirited travelers— nearly half of them repeat

Europe is best experienced with happy travel partners. We hope you can join us.

See our itineraries at ricksteves.com

Rick Steves

BEST OF GUIDES

Best of France
Best of Germany
Best of Ireland
Best of Italy
Best of Spain

EUROPE GUIDES

Best of Europe
Eastern Europe
Europe Through the Back Door
Mediterranean Cruise Ports
Northern European Cruise Ports

COUNTRY GUIDES

Croatia & Slovenia
England
France
Germany
Great Britain
Ireland
Italy
Portugal
Scandinavia
Scotland
Spain
Switzerland

CITY & REGIONAL GUIDES

Amsterdam & the Netherlands
Belgium: Bruges, Brussels, Antwerp & Ghent
Barcelona
Budapest
Florence & Tuscany
Greece: Athens & the Peloponnese
Istanbul
London
Paris
Prague & the Czech Republic
Provence & the French Riviera
Rome
Venice
Vienna, Salzburg & Tirol

SNAPSHOT GUIDES

Basque Country: Spain & France
Berlin
Copenhagen & the Best of Denmark
Dublin
Dubrovnik
Edinburgh
Hill Towns of Central Italy
Italy's Cinque Terre
Krakow, Warsaw & Gdansk
Lisbon

Nearly all Rick Steves guides are available as ebooks. Check with your favorite bookseller.

Rick Steves guidebooks are published by Avalon Travel, an imprint of Perseus Books, a Hachette Book Group company.

Maximize your travel skills with a good guidebook.

Credits

CONTRIBUTOR

Gene Openshaw

Gene has co-authored a dozen Rick Steves books and contributes to many others. For this book, he wrote material on Europe's art, history, and contemporary culture. When not traveling, Gene enjoys composing music, recovering from his 1973 trip to Europe with Rick, and living everyday life with his daughter.

RESEARCHER

To help update this book, Rick and Pat relied on...

Darbi Macy

Darbi has spent nine years working in Scotland and Ireland researching guidebooks, guiding tours, and searching for the perfect piece of banoffee pie.

ACKNOWLEDGMENTS

Thanks to Rozanne Stringer for her writing on the Celts, the Celtic Tiger, St. Brendan, and Irish art. Thanks also to Dave Fox of Globejotting.com for his writing on Guinness beer.

Avalon Travel
An imprint of Perseus Books
A Hachette Book Group company
1700 Fourth Street
Berkeley, CA 94710

Text © 2016 by Rick Steves.
Maps © 2016 by Rick Steves' Europe, Inc.
Printed in Canada by Friesens.
First printing January 2017.

ISBN 978-1-63121-441-7
ISSN 1538-1587
For the latest on Rick's lectures, guidebooks, tours, public radio show, and public
television series, contact Rick Steves' Europe, 130 Fourth Avenue North, Edmonds,
WA 98020, tel. 425/771-8303, www.ricksteves.com, rick@ricksteves.com.

Rick Steves' Europe

Managing Editor: Jennifer Madison Davis
Special Publications Manager: Risa Laib
Editors: Glenn Eriksen, Tom Griffin, Katherine Gustafson, Suzanne Kotz,
    Cathy Lu, Carrie Shepherd
Editorial & Production Assistant: Jessica Shaw
Editorial Intern: Lester Tobias
Contributor: Gene Openshaw
Researcher: Darbi Macy
Graphic Content Director: Sandra Hundacker
Maps & Graphics: David C. Hoerlein, Lauren Mills, Mary Rostad

Avalon Travel

Senior Editor and Series Manager: Madhu Prasher
Editor: Jamie Andrade
Associate Editor: Sierra Machado
Copy Editor: Patrick Collins
Proofreader: Janet Walden
Indexer: Claire Splan
Production & Typesetting: Sarah Wildfang, Jane Musser
Cover Design: Kimberly Glyder Design
Maps & Graphics: Kat Bennett, Mike Morgenfeld

Photo Credits

Front Cover: Giants' Causeway © Stephen Emerson / Alamy Stock Photo
Title Page: Irish musicians © Dominic Arizona Bonuccelli
Front Matter Color: p. x, Dingle Peninsula © Dominic Arizona Bonuccelli; p. xxiv,
    Skellig Michael © Dominic Arizona Bonuccelli
Additional Photography: Dominic Arizona Bonuccelli, David C. Hoerlein,
    Pat O'Connor, Rick Steves, Wikimedia Commons (PD-Art/PD-US). Photos
    are used by permission and are the property of the original copyright owners.

More for your trip!
Maximize the experience with Rick Steves as your guide

Guidebooks